Human
Capital
Formation
and
Manpower
Development

Human Capital Formation

THE FREE PRESS, NEW YORK
COLLIER-MACMILLAN LIMITED, LONDON

EDITED BY RONALD A. WYKSTRA
Department of Economics
Colorado State University

and

Manpower

Development

The Free Press
A Division of The Macmillan Company
866 Third Avenue, New York, New York 10022

Collier-Macmillan Canada Ltd., Toronto, Ontario

Library of Congress Catalog Card Number: 71-150377

printing number
1 2 3 4 5 6 7 8 9 10

Contents

Part Six
Manpower and Educational Planning   423

Preface

The passage of the Employment Act of 1946 marked this nation's formal concern for attaining the goal of full employment, an attempt furthered in the decade of the 1960s by the emergence of still another concern: human resource quality. The formation of human capital and strategies for manpower development have increasingly captured the attention of public policymakers, the business community, and scholars in once-distinct disciplines such as education and economics.

Several recent events here and in other nations help to explain the new emphasis. Private affluence and a rising concern for social goods such as education and health; concern for urban strife, riots, and rural blight; and the meager subsistence of poor and otherwise disadvantaged persons all are a part of the manpower problem in developed nations. Strategies for economic development invariably emphasize human resource development through investment in health, education, mobility, and the alteration of social customs in lesser developed countries. Student unrest and riots throughout the world reflect increasing concerns for the quality of life and human resource development. The absolute magnitude of problems such as these is only intensified by relative comparisons. Educational expenditures in the United States, for example, increased from $9 billion to approximately $70 billion between 1940 and 1970. Social tension and needs in areas such as remedial education, crime prevention, and public health are similarly growing in relative importance. Solutions to these problems demand, in part, that greater attention be devoted to the economics of human resources. Although it is impossible to treat fully the many dimensions to human resources, economic analysis of manpower and human capital formation can add much to our understanding of the role of human resources in contemporary society.

The purpose of this collection of essays is to describe the study of human resources from the perspective of economic analysis. That all of the selections are of post-1960 vintage suggests that economists' attention to this subject matter has a comparatively recent history; yet, there is much in the literature of the past that identifies manpower problems still with us. Research in human capital economics continues to multiply prodigiously—a fact clearly revealed by the excellent bibliographies furnished by several contributors to this volume.

The selections are arranged in six parts. Parts I and II introduce the subject and relate human capital to the economic growth process. Part III presents several outstanding articles on economic efficiency in allocating human capital investments. Parts IV and V concentrate on empirical studies of investment returns in areas such as education, health, and mobility, and they also consider the economics of poverty, discrimination, and manpower retraining. Some economic development and manpower planning aspects of human capital are then discussed in Part VI.

I am indebted to numerous persons, including E. K. Smith, R. G. Walsh, and R. D. Peterson, colleagues of mine at Colorado State University. T. W. Schultz, professor of economics at the University of Chicago, and C. R. McConnell, professor of economics at the University of Nebraska also were kind enough to offer numerous suggestions. Miss Kay Kilburn patiently assisted in the many details such a volume requires. Finally, editor and reader alike are indebted to the authors of these articles for the contributions they have made to the subject of this volume.

R. A. W.

Introduction

The last four decades have witnessed remarkable changes in the social and economic life of mankind—changes which must be reflected in contemporary subjects taught in universities if current economic problems and policies are to be relevant to students in the 1970s. This volume examines one of the many new subjects we face in contemporary times: the economics of human resources.

The Changing Scope of Human Resource Economics

During the 1930s and 1940s economists' interest in human factors of production was rekindled in part because of socioeconomic problems and policies associated with the depression and war experienced in that era. Moreover, this was a period in the history of economic ideas when it was fashionable to study market imperfections—particularly trade unionism—and forcefully question the neoclassical view of economic theory, including the dominance of the marginal productivity doctrine concerning factor market pricing and resource allocation.

The general outcome of these changes was the emergence of a new emphasis on labor policy, sometimes loosely termed "labor economics." Speaking in very general terms, three identifiable areas of emphasis emerged:[1]

1. The role of institutions and laws associated with collective bargaining by workers.
2. Amelioration of socially undesirable working conditions leading to certain kinds of economic insecurity and deprivation.
3. Study of the causes of unemployment and early formulation of policies, most of which remained in the world of theory rather than reality until the 1960s.

During the 1930s collective bargaining emerged as a socially and legally sanctioned process usually denied workingmen's associations during the prior two centuries. Hazardous working conditions, excessive hours, low wages, child labor, and economic insecurity due to age and unemployment bent to the new will of a concerned society. Economic thought on the subject of unemployment and economic instability were so forcefully

Notes to this Introduction are on pages xxiv–xxvi.

shaken by the Keynesian revolution that the new and perhaps dominant dimension of macroeconomics was added to the subject matter. For the most part, however, the attention of labor economists was narrowly restricted to labor unions, collective bargaining, and social welfare issues such as unemployment compensation and economic security for the aged. These interests became imbedded in public policy and academia along with a newfound fascination with macroeconomic problems. The Employment Act of 1946 declared the policy of this nation to be promotion of "maximum employment, production, and purchasing power"—thus paving the way for the manpower and human capital emphasis with us today.

Revolutions of all types tend to mature; this is the predicament of the subject matter of labor economics today. Only a small proportion of the contemporary American labor force are labor union members in the conventional view.[2] Furthermore, the human resource problems of what promises to be some 100 million workers and 230 million persons in the American economy at the close of the decade of the 1970s extend far beyond the once dominant concerns of labor economists weaned in the tradition of unionism.

What is the new emphasis? Unfortunately, the question is easier to answer by simply saying what it is not—a common dilemma in newly emerged areas of inquiry. The new order is not confined solely, as we have said, to the institution of unions, collective bargaining, and government programs some three decades old, such as unemployment compensation or child labor legislation. Horizons have broadened beyond these matters which nevertheless remain a part of human resource and manpower economics today. Valuable though history may be, concern for the more encompassing manpower problems must transcend conventional thinking and relate to human resource issues of the 1970s and beyond.

Since the mid-1950s economists, sociologists, educators, and psychologists increasingly have devoted attention to a broad range of human resource problems. The new order is, then, very much interdisciplinary. Furthermore, it is problem-policy oriented and, as such, the tool kit of economics can be utilized and adopted to the analysis of human resources. The new order embodies so many economic interests that it is neither possible nor wise to pretend to cover the subject here—a task that is not ours to accomplish in any event. Review of the *Manpower Report of the President* or the *Economic Report of the President* (both of which are post-WWII creations) gives some perspective to the subject of human resources and manpower. Some of the problem areas revealed are persistent unemployment, subemployment, future job opportunities, productivity and economic growth, the incidence of poverty, disadvantaged workers, the quality of work, job displacement, discrimination, and manpower planning and forecasting. This new recognition of age-old problems demands a new perspective and

contemporary policies. Thus, manpower retraining, education and health
investments, income maintenance, urban renewal, work incentives, on-the-
job training, and a host of other programs and policies characterize the
contemporary scene.

WHY HUMAN CAPITAL?

Even so meager a description as provided above correctly suggests that
it is impossible to characterize *fully* all facets of the new order. Nevertheless,
it is possible to narrow our search down to that which has attracted the
predominant attention of economists. In doing this we find that one of the
major areas of economic inquiry concerning manpower economics is the
formation of human "capital"—a process of further developing the productive capacity of human resources through investment. We do not delude
ourselves by assuming that human capital economics constitutes the subject
matter of manpower economics in its entirety, a myth quickly dispelled
once one recognizes the interdisciplinary character of the topic. There are
three general reasons for the proposed orientation, however.

First, it is quite apparent that the formation of human capital is important
to several traditional concerns of economists such as the efficiency of resource
allocation, economic growth and stability, and distributional equity of
factor income.[3] The development of manpower through investment in
human capital certainly relates to economic efficiency as the time-enhanced
organizational skills of management and labor suggest. Many factors
contribute to economic growth in a quantitative *and qualitative* sense—and
it is the latter which may be influenced most directly by human capital
formation. Moreover, the distribution of income is connected in an obvious
way to the value of human factors of production and thus connected to the
quality as well as the quantity of resources supplied in a market economy.

A second explanation for the human capital orientation toward man-
power economics is that most of the western world has viewed much of the
formation of human capital as being the proper province of the public
sector. Education, health, and welfare have been generally regarded as
social goods properly supplied by the public instead of the private sector.
Little is known about the efficient allocation of resources to these areas,
because much of contemporary human capital formation occurs outside
the market economy. The analytical tools of economics have required some
adaptation to the extra-market environment. Although much remains to be
done in this regard, progress has been made in economic studies of allocative
efficiency in the extra-market environment for public goods such as education and health. The education and health industries alone represent
direct expenditure areas which now absorb more than $100 billion annually,
most of which represents public sector outlays. Unless rising affluence and

consumption desires are blunted by military holocaust, these industries promise to be of increasing relative importance in decades to come.

Finally, the human capital orientation toward more encompassing manpower problems is partially explained by the goodness or poorness of fit (depending upon one's view of progress to date) between the tools of economic analysis and the character of the problems posed and the policies proposed. If the multibillion dollar education industry functions outside of the price-directed market system, imperfect though the latter may be, what can be said about the efficiency of resource allocation in education? How does one evaluate the worth of such expenditures? To whom is such a "good" distributed and upon what terms of financial sacrifice? How does education relate to future economic growth? These questions, as we said before, have not been asked forcefully enough by economists primarily interested in the market economy where the private sector reigns supreme. Economists may well be able to contribute to solving the manpower questions of the 1970s by adopting a human capital formation perspective. Even though this vantage point does not represent the complete manpower scope, it certainly represents one important dimension. Less charitable views also prevail, suggesting that the human capital emphasis is at best an untested allegation and at worst blatant error. In view of progress to date, this is an issue which can best be judged by reading the original articles presented in the selections that follow.

DEVELOPMENT OF THE HUMAN CAPITAL CONCEPT

The word *capital* generally refers to the reproductive power of natural and manmade producer goods. Typically, capital resources are factors of production which must themselves be produced at some cost and are subject to changing value with use or disuse. The treatment of human beings as a capital component that is an integral input in the economic development process is by no means a novel idea, as is demonstrated in the literature of the early classical economists.[4] Nevertheless, the discipline of economics failed to incorporate fully the human capital component into the stream of economic thought. This has been rectified in recent years as economists have reappraised three diverse but related economic problems: the causes of economic growth; economic efficiency for public sector expenditures not regimented by the conventional price mechanism; and the nature of economic development and manpower planning.

Early interest in the human capital concept was motivated by a desire to draw public attention to the value of conservation of life and the need to develop systems of compensation for injury or death. The development of more equitable tax systems, the effects of education on the distribution of earnings, and attempts to delineate the costs of war also motivated classical economists. Finally, interest in human capital was sparked by its implications for understanding the sources of wealth and the power of nations, the role of government, socioeconomic control, and class stratification.[5] Those few classical economists who argued that human beings should be viewed in a capital context defended the proposition by noting that (a) there were costs associated with the development and formation of human resources (largely education), (b) the output of skilled human resources added incrementally to the national product, and (c) expenditures on human resources which increased national product also increased national wealth.

Human capital formation is affected by investment in formal education, improved health, on-the-job training, manpower rehabilitation, and improved mobility. Factors unrelated to investment expenditures (*e.g.*, labor force participation or age-sex changes in manpower supply) also affect the formation of human capital. In this sense human capital may represent a most significant explanation of our inability to identify the sources of economic growth and development. Human capital formation is also important because of the magnitude of expenditures on formal education and health as we noted earlier. In slightly more than a decade, for example, direct expenditures on formal education in the United States nearly tripled.[6] The educational system is a sizable industry by most standards. Consequently, investment in formal education constitutes one focal point in the study of economic development and the formation of human capital.[7] Formal education, however, is not the only concern of human capital economics. Manpower mobility, the economics of poverty, investments in health and manpower retraining, the "costs" of discrimination, and planning for future manpower and educational needs also concern the contributors to this volume. An array of topics such as these necessarily involves a variety of approaches deserving of brief introduction.

Alternative Approaches to Human Capital Analysis

The approaches used in analyzing human capital formation vary, depending on whether one's interests are more directly related to problems associated with economic growth and development, allocative efficiency of investment in human capital, or manpower and educational planning.[8]

HUMAN CAPITAL STOCKS AND ECONOMIC GROWTH

Estimates of the value of the stock of human capital at different points in time constitute one approach to manpower and economic growth analysis. The major methodological contribution in the area of estimating the educational stock of human capital remains that of Theodore W. Schultz who has developed such data for the United States.[9] Mushkin and Weisbrod have developed cost-based estimates for health and welfare expenditures for the United States, and development economists are applying similar techniques to studies of less developed nations.[10]

Other authors obtain the present value of future earnings to estimate human capital stocks. Derivation of the present value (Bv) of a human capital asset is a function of the summed incremental lifetime earnings and other benefits (B) associated with different levels of human capital formation $(e.g.,$ education), discounted by some interest rate (r) applied to the productive life (t) of the asset as follows:

$$Bv = \sum_{i=1}^{n} \frac{Bt}{(1+r)^t}$$

The production cost approach presents difficulties that require careful consideration, including the extent to which the costs of education constitute investment in contrast to consumption expenditures, and the appropriateness of including foregone earnings as a cost component. The discounted earnings approach raises numerous unresolved problems, including changes in future mortality, the validity of earnings and other readily measured economic variables as a surrogate for benefits, the implied assumption that earnings reflect marginal productivity, the proper rate of discount, and the treatment of human capital appreciation or depreciation—to name but a few. Although both human capital stock approaches are subject to qualification, identification of the relative importance of human capital represents a long-needed addition to the conventional view of capital-output relationships in the theory of economic growth and development. At the same time, numerous noneconomic and qualitative variables are not easily incorporated, and inferences drawn from such analyses must remain cognizant of the inherent limitations of the methodology.

Knowing something about human capital stocks allows one to delineate the form and magnitude of quantitative relationships between inputs (labor and capital), outputs (national income), and whatever unexplained growth in output might remain. This unexplained difference, or residual, is typically labeled productivity or technological change. In some instances the character of the production function has been postulated,[11] whereas in other studies the growth rates of inputs and outputs are measured and compared to estimate the residual.[12]

Estimation of a growth residual or specification of alternative production functions is a useful but frustrating exercise. Factor substitution as well as the complementary interplay of technology and physical factors of production remain difficult to identify or are assumed away in many studies. The residual nature of the unexplained growth component is challenging because of its relative size, and it also is mysterious because of the heterogeneity of the unspecified growth components it masks. More than one-half of the 2.9 per cent growth rate of the American economy from 1909 to 1957 is unexplained after accounting for the observed growth in physical capital stocks and the quantity of labor inputs. The omnipresent existence of so large a growth residual has forcefully reminded all concerned that economic growth entails much more than the accumulation of saving, investment in physical capital, or even the formation of human capital, for that matter.[13] In recognition of situations similar to this in a variety of countries at various stages of development, students of development economics have been forced to extend their research inquiry considerably. The subject matter of human capital represents one of the time-worn assumptions or "givens" that simply had to be released if we were ever to begin to fully understand economic growth and development.

INVESTMENT RETURNS

Analysis of costs, benefits, or returns to investment in human capital is a widely used method of studying human capital formation.[14] The central purpose of benefit-cost analysis is to determine the relative efficiency of alternative expenditure programs. Interest in this approach is, in part, a product of the muted role played by the price system in the allocation of resources in the public sector, including expenditures on education as well as other forms of human capital investment. The discounted ratio of benefits to costs over the lifetime of the asset is one way of reflecting the extent to which investment alternatives are preferable. Rate-of-return studies are similar to benefit-cost analysis in that the present value of lifetime returns is equated to cost outlays to derive a percentage return on investment. The internal rate of return is that rate of discount which just equates the present value of prospective returns and costs. Although the analytical difficulties posed by this approach are extensively discussed by the articles presented in Part Three, it can be noted here that the need to measure social benefits and costs, as distinct from those which are private, constitutes a serious analytical bottleneck. This raises a host of issues such as (a) the extent to which earnings reflect marginal productivity in contrast to market imperfections, (b) nonmonetary returns, including consumption returns, (c) benefits that possess external or spillover qualities, and (d) the selection of an appropriate discount rate (in benefit-cost analysis) or comparative rates of return (if internal rates of return are derived). These difficulties suggest that interpretive care is required, even though this approach generates valuable empirical information. If nothing else, investment return analysis has made a major contribution by redirecting the attention of economists to long unresolved issues in the fields of manpower and economic development (*e.g.*, externalities or multiple public policy objective functions). In addition, this approach may help planning efforts focus more sharply on rationalizing alternative patterns of resource allocation within the public sector.

EDUCATION AND MANPOWER PLANS

Correlation techniques may be used in an attempt to identify the relationship between health or educational expenditures and a nation's output, or growth in the stock of human capital and technological change. Intertemporal correlation may be used in an attempt to relate growth in human capital or educational expenditures to stages of economic development. Although analyses of these types can be useful, data availability and comparability often plague such efforts. Unknown causation between output and expenditure levels and problems of multicollinearity are the two more frequent limitations to this approach. This approach sharply identifies the problem of association among independent variables such as ability and education. Positive correlation between economic growth in income and educational expenditures, for example, supports two alternative hypotheses: (a) education promotes economic development and growth in income; or (b) additional educational expenditures are a consequence of rising levels of income and a more advanced state of development. Multicollinearity between health and wealth, or ability and education, produces a bias of an uncertain magnitude, making it difficult to attribute all or a portion of improved rates of development to increased education alone. Although these relationships cannot be easily disentangled using existing information and techniques, the correlation approach reveals useful information about economic development and human capital formation relations.[15] Regional, international, and development economists utilize spatial correlation techniques when the rather difficult topics of manpower planning and development of education systems arise.[16] Less developed nations, for example, may be able to approximate educational levels required at given stages of development and levels of output through comparative studies. Spatial comparisons may also be useful in understanding labor mobility, the approximate relationship between stages of manpower and economic development, and future development needs and prospects. Understanding future development needs and prospects is all the more acute because of the lengthy lead-time period required in the production of a unit of human capital. The greatest obstacle to this approach, particularly at the international level, is incomparability of data. Much care is also required in such comparisons because "other things" are seldom, if ever, equal.

Analysis of manpower demand characteristics and the supply of trained manpower as an output of the education industry constitutes a complementary manpower planning approach. Many authorities have argued for better analyses of manpower requirements on the basis of skill-level characteristics and have placed less emphasis on rate-of-return studies and manpower planning by aggregative occupation profiles. Studies of the United States, Great Britain, UNESCO, and the OECD are numerous, but nevertheless limited because they tend to emphasize demand and supply conditions for particular skill levels of manpower, especially teachers, engineers, and high-level manpower. Translation of human capital requirements into educational planning and manpower development is a vital but difficult link in economic development.[17] Among the obvious problems are: (a) the uncertain extent of human capital substitution, (b) the skill-level impact of a changing technology, (c) the specificity or generality of training required, (d) difficulties associated with the accuracy of long-run projections of manpower supply, (e) the production lag in human capital formation, and (f) issues related to educational goals, means, and structure. The planning need is particularly acute in less developed countries because development policy cannot avoid economic planning and the creation of an education industry. Furthermore, the limited resources constraining the developing world make it all the more imperative that development policy avoid clichés and standards of an old world which may or may not apply to human capital requirements in the future.

Plan of the Book*

This, then, is a broad overview of the dimensions to our topic. A more definitive description of the economics of human capital formation and manpower development is furnished by the contributors whose articles on the subject are arranged as follows.

Part One The initial selections in this section establish the framework for human capital formation from the viewpoint of economic history, problems, theory, and policy. Human capital, as a concept, is not without its own history. B. F. Kiker, the author of the first selection, anchors this idea firmly by resurrecting views expressed by economists of the past, noting their failures as well as accomplishments. But what is the contemporary nature of building a strong human resource base? The Council of Economic Advisers **2** sketches several dimensions of this problem, emphasizing education, manpower policy, health, and equal opportunity. Finally, Ingvar Svennilson **3** introduces some of the ignored or unidentified factors in the growth of contemporary economies, many of which relate to human capital formation.

Part Two The notion that there are interdependencies between the economic growth of a society and its stock of human capital, suggested in Part One by Svennilson **3**, is more firmly established by the five articles in this section, even though the exact nature of these interdependencies

---

* Most of the readings introduced in preliminary sections of this kind will be identified only by the name(s) of the author(s), and the essay number assigned in this book. The reader should take note of the styles of abbreviation: See, for instance, "Ingvar Svennilson **3**" and "Svennilson **3**."

remains uncertain. Each author presents worthy information on the subject of human capital and the methodology of analyzing economic growth. The pioneering efforts of Theodore W. Schultz, presented in the fourth selection, establishes our base of knowledge concerning the stock of human capital in the United States throughout the greater part of the twentieth century. Edward F. Denison's work 5 for the Committee on Economic Development has contributed much to our understanding of growth ingredients in contemporary times. Interest in economic growth, emerging as it has out of Keynesian macroeconomic theory, constitutes a subject matter which only recently has been linked with the human capital concept thrust forth by Schultz in his presidential address to the American Economic Association in 1961. Robert M. Solow 6 explains the "embodiment" notion of unknown growth factors in his discussion of technological change and the residual of ignorance. Richard R. Nelson and Edmund S. Phelps 7 introduce similar ideas and go even further into the subject of interdependence between technology and education in the economic growth process. Finally, Earl R. Brubaker 8 further explores the embodiment idea in his study of Soviet growth. This study illustrates one possible interpretation of the relative role of human capital and reveals as well how little we know about the "unexplained" sources of growth.

  Part Three   Economists have been interested in using resources efficiently because of the scarcity of resources and potential opportunity uses. Microeconomics explains the nature of allocative efficiency in the private sector. When public sector investments are contemplated, much of the conventional price-directed market allocating device is avoided. Benefit-cost analysis in a variety of forms represents one technique for bridging the gap between market and extramarket decisions about resource allocation. The purpose and nature of benefit-cost analysis is introduced in Part Three. Roland N. McKean 9 launches this discussion by describing the power and political dimensions to public sector decision making. Robert Dorfman 10 and Arthur Maass 11 both explain and evaluate the role of benefit-cost as a tool of economic analysis. Finally, Otto Eckstein 12 evaluates the "proper" interest rate to use for discounting purposes, a major issue in using these techniques. Part Three also clearly reveals that economists are in disagreement about the use of benefit-cost techniques for human capital analyses. Several of the problems encountered in using the techniques are identified in selection 13 written by Tei-wei Hu, Jacob J. Kaufman, Maw Lin Lee, and Ernst W. Stromsdorfer. Jack Wiseman 14 illuminates several of the problems encountered in applying benefit-cost techniques to human capital investments. T. Balogh and P. P. Streeten 15 express similar concerns, particularly in work related to developing nations. Finally, Neil W. Chamberlain 16 examines the entire human capital orientation in relation to the broad range of manpower problems, expressing the fear that a narrowed econometric search for determinate solutions may distort the subject altogether.

Part Four   The first four selections in Part Four describe some of the relationships between investment in education and returns from these investments. Herman P. Miller **17** analyzes income by education level over time using 1950 and 1960 census data. The internal rate of return on investments in schooling is estimated by Giora Hanoch **18** who also explains several analytical problems encountered in empirical studies. Orley Ashenfelter and Joseph D. Mooney **19** concentrate upon returns to graduate training. A variety of less easily dealt with benefits from investments in education are explained by Burton A. Weisbrod **20** in an article ‌representative of a positive attempt to deal with some of the criticisms presented earlier. Human capital formation is not an exclusive function of ‌investments in education as the last three selections of Part Four on health and mobility suggest. Herbert E. Klarman's **21** general review of benefit-cost analysis in health economics suggests that health is an important dimension to manpower development. Selma J. Mushkin and Burton A. Weisbrod **22** examine the formation of human capital through investments in health using techniques similar to those described earlier by Schultz. Mobility or the transfer of human capital represents still another dimension of human capital, the topic of Mary Jean Bowman and Robert G. Myers **23**.

Part Five   Poverty, discrimination, and manpower retraining represent environmental manpower issues encompassing the disadvantaged. Poverty and the economics of discrimination are treated in the first three selections of Part Five. The President's Council of Economic Advisers **24** discusses the magnitude and policy implications of poverty in America. John P. Formby **25** appraises the extent of discrimination against nonwhites, holding the quantity of educational capital constant; and Walter Fogel **26** discusses the effect of low educational attainment on incomes for ethnic minority groups. Benefit-cost studies of programs to retrain disadvantaged workers are presented in the last three selections of Part Five. Gerald G. Somers and Ernst W. Stromsdorfer **27** evaluate the economics of retraining under certain manpower programs once in progress, and Worth Bateman **28** reports on a similar study applied to rehabilitation of public assistance recipients. The sequel to these studies is summarized by David O. Sewell's **29** evaluation of benefit-cost techniques applied to training the disadvantaged.

Part Six   As is true of previous topics covered in this volume, a vast quantity of literature exists on the subject of manpower planning, human capital and economic development, and educational planning. Much of the progress in planning has emerged out of the long-standing international concerns in this area and past efforts of agencies such as the Organization for Economic Cooperation and Development (OECD) and the United

Nations Educational, Scientific, and Cultural Organization (UNESCO). Although we can only touch upon the subject here, Mary Jean Bowman **30** sets a delicate balance between relevant planning for economic development and liturgical approaches to planning, thereby identifying some of the pitfalls that can emerge in this area. Gottfried Bombach **31** discusses manpower forecasting in developed nations, and Anthony Bottomley **32** examines manpower planning and optimal educational investment conditions for developing nations. The final selection by Mark Blaug **33** is concerned with educational planning in relationship to manpower needs—a subject worthy of a volume in its own right.[18]

Conclusion

Human capital formation is the central theme of the selections described above. It turns out, however, that our inquiry touches many related problems in the area of human resource economics including economic growth and development; the efficiency of public sector investments; educational formation of human capital; manpower development through investments in health, mobility, and manpower training; the manpower problems of poverty, discrimination, and retraining; and the development of manpower and educational policies.

Notes

1 This should not be interpreted as meaning these directions were unrecognized previously. Nothing could be further from the truth, as is witnessed by the array of economic literature on these subjects extending back several decades.

2 Membership in American labor unions has remained virtually unchanged for the last fifteen years at 18 million (or fewer) workers and has declined in relative terms to approximately one-fifth of the American work force today.

3 I am indebted to Burton A. Weisbrod for making available to me "Benefits of Manpower Programs: Theoretical and Methodological Issues," an unpublished paper presented at the North American Conference on Cost-Benefit Analysis of Manpower Policies presented at Madison, Wisconsin, May 1969 (to be published in a Conference volume).

4 One of the more valuable collections of material demonstrating the increasing

significance of human capital to economic development is M. J. Bowman, M. Debeauvais, V. Komarov, and J. Vaizey, eds., *Readings in the Economics of Education* (Paris: United Nations Educational, Scientific and Cultural Organization, 1968). For additional information on the concept of human capital see M. Debeauvais, "The Concept of Human Capital," *International Social Science Journal* 14 (1962): 660–76; W. J. Miller, "The Economics of Education in English Classical Economics," *Southern Economic Journal* 32 (1966): 294–309; John Vaizey, *The Economics of Education* (London: Faber & Faber, 1962), chapter 2; E. A. J. Johnson, "The Place of Learning, Science, Vocational Training and 'Art' in Pre-Smithian Economic Thought," *Journal of Economic History* 24 (1964): 129–44.

5 B. F. Kiker, "The Historical Roots of the Concept of Human Capital," *Journal of Political Economy* 74 (1966): 481; and Miller, "Economics of Education," p. 308.

Also see J. S. Nicholson, "The Living Capital of the United Kingdom," *Economic Journal* 1 (1891): 95–107; S. J. Strumlin, "The Economic Significance of National Education," *Planovoe Khoziaistvo* 9–10 (1924); and J. R. Walsh, "Capital Concept Applied to Man," *Quarterly Journal of Economics* 49 (1935): 255–85.

6 Richard F. Young, "Educational Expenditures in the United States," *Monthly Review*, Federal Reserve Bank of Kansas City (September–October 1967): 5.

7 See T. W. Schultz, "Capital Formation by Education," *Journal of Political Economy* 68 (1960): 580, for additional comments on measurement of human capital stocks.

8 Methodological alternatives are also discussed in W. G. Bowen, "Assessing the Economic Contributions of Education: An Appraisal of Alternative Approaches," *Economic Aspects of Higher Education* (Paris: Organisation for Economic Co-Operation and Development, 1964), pp. 177–201; and Debeauvais, "Concept of Human Capital," pp. 660–76.

9 T. W. Schultz, *The Economic Value of Education* (New York: Columbia University Press, 1963). A review of the problems and alternative approaches used to estimate the stock of human capital are carefully described in a paper by Mary Jean Bowman, "Human Capital: Concepts and Measures," *Economics of Higher Education*, United States Department of Health, Education, and Welfare (Washington, D.C.: U.S. Government Printing Office, 1962), pp. 62–92.

10 Health and medical care investments in human capital in the United States are estimated by S. J. Mushkin and B. A. Weisbrod, "Investment in Health: Lifetime Health Expenditures on the 1960 Work Force," *Kyklos* 16 (1963): 583–99. Two early efforts using the discounting approach can be found in Nicholson, "Living Capital of United Kingdom," and Walsh, "Capital Concept." Estimates have been made more recently by B. A. Weisbrod, "The Valuation of Human Capital," *Journal of Political Economy* 77 (1969): 425–36.

11 Odd Aukrust clearly postulated the significance of the "human factor" and its strong implications for the then conventional approach to theories of economic growth that placed heavy reliance on physical capital formation in his "Investment and Economic Growth," *Productivity*

Measurement Review 16 (1959): 35–50. Also see R. M. Solow, "Technical Change and the Aggregate Production Function," *Review of Economics and Statistics* 39 (1957): 312–20; and Z. Griliches, "Research Expenditures, Education, and the Aggregate Agricultural Production Function," *American Economic Review* 54 (1964): 425–36 in addition to those selections presented in Part Two of this volume.

12 If aLg and bKg represent the relative growth rate contributions of labor and capital inputs in a quantitative context, and Yg denotes the rate of growth in output, then the residual (R) is:

$$R = Yg - (aLg + bKg)$$

13 See John Kendrick, *Productivity Trends in the United States* (Princeton: Princeton University Press, 1961), Appendix A; E. F. Denison, *The Sources of Economic Growth in the United States and Alternatives Before Us* (New York: Committee for Economic Development, 1962), p. 30; R. M. Solow, "Technical Progress, Capital Formation, and Economic Growth," *American Economic Review* 52 (1962): 76–86; and Kenneth J. Arrow, "The Economic Importance of Learning by Doing," *Review of Economic Studies* 29 (1962): 155–74.

14 Gary S. Becker, "Investment in Human Capital: A Theoretical Analysis," *Journal of Political Economy*, Supplement, 70 (1962): 9–50. Selected empirical studies include W. L. Hansen, "Total and Private Rates of Return to Investment in Schooling," *Journal of Political Economy* 71 (1963): 128–40; H. S. Houthakker, "Education and Income," *Review of Economics and Statistics* 41 (1969): 24–28; G. S. Becker, "Underinvestment in College Education?" *American Economic Review* 50 (1960): 346–54; B. A. Weisbrod, "Education and Investment in Human Capital," *Journal of Political Economy*, Supplement, 70 (1962): 106–23; and L. F. Renshaw, "Estimating the Returns to Education," *Review of Economics and Statistics* 42 (1960): 318–24.

15 Among studies using this approach, see F. Harbison and C. Myers, *Education, Manpower and Economic Growth* (New York: McGraw-Hill Co., 1964); and D. C. McClelland, "Does Education Accelerate Economic Growth?" *Economic Development and Cultural Change* 14 (1966): 257–78.

16 Spatial comparisons include B. A. Weisbrod, *External Benefits of Public Educa-*

tion, Industrial Relations Section (Princeton: Princeton University Press, 1964); R. Fein, "Education Patterns in Southern Migration," *Southern Economic Journal* 32 (1965): 106–28; and Harbison and Myers, *Education, Manpower and Economic Growth.* The latter is a classical study at the international level. On manpower forecasting see H. S. Parnes, ed., *Planning Education for Economic and Social Development* (Paris: Organisation for Economic Co-Operation and Development, 1964); and R. S. Eckaus, "Economic Criteria for Education and Training," *Review of Economics and Statistics* 44 (1964): 181–90.

17 Koichi Emi, "Economic Development and Educational Investment in the Meiji Era," in Bowman, Debeauvais, Komarov, and Vaizey, *Readings,* pp. 94–108; R. C. Blitz, "Maintenance Costs and Economic Development," *Journal of Political Economy* 67 (1959): 560–70; and M. Blaug, "Approaches to Educational Planning," *Economic Journal* 77 (1967): 262–87.

18 It goes without saying that many worthy contributions are not directly represented by this collection because of space limitations. The extensive bibliographies furnished by the authors of several of the papers in this collection will lead the interested reader to even further contributions in those areas of his chosen interests.

The Nature of
Human Resource
Economics

The authors of the selections reprinted in Part One review the methodological character and importance of human capital formation, thus laying a foundation for the human resource and economic growth, efficiency, and equity issues which characterize this volume. B. F. Kiker's historical summary **1** of the human capital concept introduces the reader to the actuarial principles used in benefit-cost analysis of human resources and reviews the historical treatment of this subject as well. The Council of Economic Advisers **2** generally reveals in the 1966 report to the president the ways that human resources can be strengthened through public policy. Ingvar Svennilson **3** explains that what economists do not know about economic growth may well be a greater quantum than the known.

1

The Historical Roots
of the Concept of Human Capital

The surge of interest in human capital since the mid-1950s could lead to the erroneous conclusion that the subject is new in economics. Professor B. F. Kiker of the University of South Carolina dispels this myth by carefully reviewing the concept and role of human capital formation in the history of economic

B. F. KIKER

thought. Like their predecessors, contemporary economists concentrate on a variety of forms of investment in human resources leading to a recognizable concept of the capital value of man as a productive agent.

I n recent years, economists have devoted a great deal of effort to developing and quantifying the concept of "human capital" and to applying it, through the concept of investment in the formation of human capital, to such activities as education, whether academic study or on-the-job training, migration, and medical care.[1] The concept of human capital, however, is by no means new. The object of this paper is to review some of the past literature, in order primarily to determine which authors treated human beings as capital, their motives for doing so, and their procedures for valuing man as capital. Although this essay is not exhaustive, it will be shown, in essence, that the concept of human capital was somewhat prominent in economic thinking until Marshall discarded the notion as "unrealistic."

Reprinted from B. F. Kiker, "The Historical Roots of the Concept of Human Capital," *Journal of Political Economy* 74 (October 1966), pp. 481–99, with the permission of the author and publisher. Copyright 1966 by The University of Chicago.

[1] See, for example: Schultz (1959, 1961a, 1961b, 1962); Weisbrod (1961); Machlup (1962); Mushkin (1962); Becker (1964).

Economists who considered human beings or their skills as capital include such well-known names in the history of economic thought as Petty, Smith, Say, Senior, List, von Thünen, Roscher, Bagehot, Ernst Engel, Sidgwick, Walras, and Fisher. Basically, two methods have been used to estimate the value of human beings: the cost-of-production and the capitalized-earnings procedures. The former procedure consists of estimating the real costs (usually net of maintenance) incurred in "producing" a human being; the latter consists of estimating the present value of an individual's future income stream (either net or gross of maintenance). Several motives for treating human beings as capital and valuing them in money terms have been found: (1) to demonstrate the power of a nation; (2) to determine the economic effects of education, health investment, and migration; (3) to propose tax schemes believed to be more equitable than existing ones; (4) to determine the total cost of war; (5) to awaken the public to the need for life and health conservation and the significance of the economic life of an individual to his family and country; and (6) to aid courts and compensation boards in making fair decisions in cases dealing with compensation for personal injury and death.

I

Statisticians and actuaries have developed relatively scientific procedures for estimating the money (or capital) values of either a human being as such or the population of a nation. Their methods, which are essentially a cost-of-production approach or some form of a capitalized-earnings approach, are examined in this section, as are variations in the approaches.

One of the first attempts to estimate the money value of a human being was made around 1691 by Sir William Petty. Labor to him was the "father of wealth." It must therefore be included in any estimate of national wealth. This led Petty to place a money value on laborers. Petty's interest in the monetary evaluation of human beings developed out of his interest in public finance (Hull, 1899, I, 589–95). Soon, however, he used the notion of human capital in attempts to demonstrate the power of England (Hull, 1899, I, 505–13; II, 192), the economic effects of migration (Hull, 1899, I, 192), the money value of human life destroyed in war (Hull, 1899, I, 152), and the monetary loss to a nation resulting from deaths (Hull, 1899, I, 108–10). Petty estimated the value of the stock of human capital by capitalizing the wage bill to perpetuity, at the market interest rate; the wage bill he determined by deducting property income from national income (Hull, 1899, I, 108).[2]

---

[2] Petty's evaluation of human beings in money terms was bitterly satirized by Dean Swift in his "A Modest Proposal for Preventing the Children of Poor People from Being a Burden to Their Parents or the Country."

Petty's method makes no allowance for the cost of maintenance of workers before capitalization.[3] In spite of this limitation, his procedure gives a close approximation for determining the capital value of a nation. It is wholly inadequate, however, when used for purposes where human-capital values by age, sex, and economic status are needed, as in several of the cases mentioned above.

The first truly scientific procedure and the one followed today by many economists and others for finding the capital or money value of a human being was devised in 1853 by William Farr. Like Petty's, Farr's interest in the evaluation of human capital developed out of his interest in public finance. He advocated the substitution for the existing English income tax system of a property tax that would include property consisting of the capitalized value of earning capacity. His procedure for estimating the latter was to calculate the present value of an individual's net future earnings (future earnings minus personal living expenses), allowance being made for deaths in accordance with a life table (Farr, 1853). Farr's work suggests a way in which "human capital" can be a misleading analogy. He suggested that since human beings are productive they should be regarded and taxed as capital. Since this would oblige people to pay tax on wealth that they do not have in hand, it could lead to absurd results.[4] Farr's method was almost identical with the method utilized some eighty years later by Louis Dublin and Alfred Lotka (1930). Their procedure is discussed below.

Ernst Engel, writing around 1883, preferred a cost-of-production procedure for estimating the monetary value of human beings. Although he discussed Petty's approach and modified it somewhat to allow for the limited number of years a man is employed, he felt that the yield value of certain human beings (for example, a Goethe, Newton or Benjamin Franklin) could not be determined. Since, however, their rearing was a cost to their parents, it might be estimated and taken as a measure of their monetary value to society. This monetary value at age x may be determined from a formula:

$$C_x = c_0\{1 + x + k[x(x+1)/2]\}$$

where C_x is the total cost of producing a human being (neglecting interest,

[3] Perhaps, however, no great error is committed if maintenance costs are not considered when this approach is taken. Almost three hundred years later Mushkin and Weisbrod (1963, p. 595) assert: "Maintenance of physical capital prolongs its life, and thereby reduces annual depreciation. The result is that the reported stock of physical capital net of depreciation is larger than it would be if maintenance expenditures were lower. If depreciation were reduced by the exact amount of maintenance expenditures this would be equivalent to counting the maintenance as investment. Thus the treatment of maintenance of human and non-human capital may be reasonably consistent after all."

[4] Imagine a tax structure in which Elizabeth Taylor's tax bill at age sixteen is the same function of her capitalized expected earnings as a landlord's tax bill is of his capitalized expected earnings.

depreciation, and maintenance) through age x, c_0 denotes costs incurred up to the point of birth, and k is the annual percentage increase in cost. The constant, c_0, was empirically found by Engel to be 100, 200, and 300 marks for the lower, middle, and upper German social classes, respectively. He observed k to be 0.1. This formula applies, however, only when $x \leq 26$. After age twenty-six the individual was assumed by Engel to be "fully produced" (Engel, 1883, pp. 15–20, 58–78; Sencini, 1908, pp. 481–86).[5]

There is, however, no simple and necessary relationship between the cost of producing an item and its economic value. This is especially true for human beings, whose cost of production is not undertaken primarily with a view to economic gain. Although I see very little use for the cost-of-production procedure in evaluating human beings as such, a modification of Engel's approach is useful in determining the components, such as education and health-service capital, of a human-capital value. This is so, simply because it is less difficult to estimate the direct (and opportunity, if appropriate) cost incurred in forming a particular component of human-capital value than to attribute future earning differentials to specific items such as education and health services.

Theodor Wittstein in 1867 defined human beings as capital goods and employed a variation of both Farr's capitalized-earnings and Engel's cost-of-production approaches to value human capital. Wittstein's interest in the concept of human capital arose from a desire to determine a guide to be used as a basis for claims for compensation from loss of life. Since he assumed that an individual's lifetime earnings are equal to his lifetime maintenance cost plus education, the approaches yield the same estimates —which inevitably come out to be zero at birth. His procedure may be summarized in the following formulas:

$$C_{(n)} = aR_{(0)} \frac{L_{(0)}}{L_{(n)}} r^n - aR_{(n)}$$

$$C_{(n)} = XR_{(N)} \frac{L_{(N)}}{L_{(n)}} p^{N-n} - aR_{(n)}$$

where a is annual consumption expenditures including education for an average German male in a particular occupation, $r = (1+i)$, where i is the market interest rate; $p = 1/r$; $L_{(n)}$ is the number of men living at age n in a life table; $R_{(n)}$ is the value at age n of a 1-thaler annuity (for a given r and

[5] A French economist of the early eighteenth century, Richard Cantillon, discussed the cost of rearing a child (both free and slave) to working age. He estimated this cost to be equal to twice the value of the land needed to sustain an adult male. This formula applied to both slaves and freemen, since "free peasants . . . will probably maintain them[selves] upon a better foot than slaves according to the custom of the place he lives in" and will require, therefore, more land (Cantillon, 1959, p. 35).

purchased at birth); X is the value of the future output of an average man in a particular occupation; N is the age at which this man enters the labor force (Wittstein, 1867).

Wittstein (1867, p. 50) assumed for simplicity that a and X are constant over the life of an individual. He asserted, moreover, that the former equation (which is based on past values) for valuing a human being in money terms should be used when $N>n$ but that when $N<n$ the latter equation (which is based upon expected values) could be utilized more easily (Wittstein, 1867, p. 53). Although Wittstein's analysis is interesting, his basic postulate that lifetime earnings and lifetime maintenance cost are equal is unjustified. Moreover, any combination of the capitalized-earnings and cost-of-production methods is dangerous, owing to the possibility of duplication of values.

Dublin and Lotka were in the life-insurance business. They considered that calculations of human values could be useful in ascertaining how much life insurance a man should carry. Such calculations might also be useful in estimating the economic costs of preventable disease and premature death (Dublin and Lotka, 1930, Preface). The result of their calculations was a formula:

$$V_0 = \sum_{x=0}^{\infty} v^x P_x (y_x E_x - c_x)$$

where V_0 is the value of the individual at birth; $v^x = (1+i)^{-x}$ is the present value of \$1.00 due x years later; P_x is the probability at birth of an individual living to age x; y_x is yearly earnings per individual from age x to $x+1$; E_x is the proportion of individuals employed from age x to $x+1$ (Farr had assumed full employment); c_x is the cost of living for an individual from age x to $x+1$. To find the money value of an individual at a particular age, a, the formula may be modified (Dublin and Lotka, 1930, p. 167) to

$$V_a = \frac{P_0}{P_a} \left[\sum_{x=a}^{\infty} v^{x-a} P_x (y_x E_x - c_x) \right]$$

This method of capitalizing an individual's earnings, minus his consumption or maintenance, gives a useful estimate for some purposes. It estimates, for example, the economic value of the man to his family—which was Dublin and Lotka's purpose. If the wage earner is killed, his family is impoverished by the amount of his contribution to them—which, presumably, is his income less his maintenance. There is considerable question, however, as to the validity of such an approach when the value of a human being to himself or in society is sought. To make estimates for these purposes, the capitalized-gross-earnings procedure (including living expenses) should be used.

The cost of producing (rearing) an individual, C, up to age a, according to Dublin and Lotka, is

$$C_a = \frac{1}{P_a}\left[\sum_{x=0}^{a-1} v^{x-a} P_x (c_x - y_x E_x)\right]$$

which may be simplified to

$$C_a = V_a - \frac{1}{P_a v^a} V_0$$

Hence, the cost of producing an individual up to age a is equal to the difference between his value at age a and his value at birth, multiplied by $(1+i)^a/P_a$ (Dublin and Lotka, 1930, p. 168). This is, of course, a sophisticated version of Engel's approach.

Dublin, somewhat earlier, had estimated the capital value of the population of the United States in 1922 to be *five* times the stock of material wealth. The basis of this estimate is unknown and the estimate itself not entirely plausible, though it has been often quoted. His estimate of the size of this stock led him to advocate a more liberal expenditure policy for maintaining it (Dublin, 1928).

The works of Farr and Dublin and Lotka should be starting points for anyone interested in estimating either human-capital values or their components. Dublin and Lotka's discussion of the capitalized-earnings approach (either net or gross of living expenses) is clear, concise, and one of the best expositions available. Although there are obvious conceptual difficulties associated with this approach, it gives the most accurate results if the data necessary for measurement are available.

Allowances for depreciation are not taken into account when the cost-of-production approach to determine human-capital value is utilized. The capitalized-earnings approach, however, implicitly includes depreciation. Since a young man, *ceteris paribus*, is expected to be productive over a longer period than an older cohort, his capital value would be greater.

Maintenance costs were neglected by Petty and Engel. They were, however, considered to be equal to personal living expenses by Farr, Wittstein, and Dublin and Lotka. This was a dubious procedure then, particularly at the date Dublin and Lotka published, and would be wrong in developed countries today. Maintenance costs have been neglected by present-day economists who have advocated the human-capital concept. Some of these costs, however, are incurred during the investment period; a portion of them are continuous throughout the life of the human capital.[6]

---

[6] For other work similar to that discussed in this section see: Lüdtge (1873a, 1873b), Lindheim (1909), and Meyer (1930–32).

II

From time to time throughout the history of economic thought, economists have included human beings, or their acquired abilities and skills, as
a component of capital. Although some of them attempted to estimate the
value of this capital—on both the microeconomic and the macroeconomic
levels—and to employ these estimates for a specific purpose (for example,
to estimate the total economic losses resulting from war), others have
merely included human beings, or their acquired abilities and skills, in
their definition of capital and recognized the importance of investment in
human beings as a means of increasing their productivity. The latter group,
generally, neither attempted an evaluation of human capital nor employed
the concept for any specific purpose.[7] Most of these economists held that
human beings should be included in the concept of capital for three reasons:
(1) the cost of rearing and educating human beings is a real cost; (2) the
product of their labor adds to the national wealth; (3) an expenditure on a
human being that increases this product will, *ceteris paribus*, increase national
wealth.

Although he did not specifically define the term "capital," Adam Smith
included in his category of fixed capital the skills and useful abilities of
human beings. The skill of a man, he said, may be regarded as a machine
that has a genuine cost and returns a profit (Smith, 1937, pp. 101, 259–66).
Jean Baptiste Say (1821, pp. 92–94) asserted likewise that since skills and
abilities are acquired at a cost and tend to increase worker productivity
they should be regarded as capital. This was also the contention of John
Stuart Mill (1909, p. 47), William Roscher (1878, p. 151), Walter Bagehot
(1953, pp. 55–56), and, at the microeconomic level, Henry Sidgwick (1901,
pp. 132–34). According to W. Stark, Jeremy Bentham's most interesting
passage, from the point of view of economic theory, was one in which he
stated that "labour is distinguished into mere physical exertion and the
skill or mental power displayed in the exercise of the bodily act" (Stark,
1952, p. 53).

To Friedrich List, skills and acquired abilities of human beings, which
are largely an inheritance from the past and the result of past labor and self-
restraint, were the most important components of a nation's stock of capital.
He asserted that, in both production and distribution, the contribution of
this human capital to output must be considered (List, 1928, pp. 108–18).

These economists, who basically define capital as "produced means of
production," do not explicitly include the human beings as capital. J. S.
Mill (1909, p. 47) asserted: "The human being himself I do not class as

---

[7] There are, however, a few exceptions: List used the notion in demonstrating the
importance of protectionism, and von Thünen advocated utilizing the notion as an aid in
dealing out social justice. Marshall, moreover, offered some estimates of human-capital values.

wealth. He is the purpose for which wealth exists. But his acquired capacities, which exist only as a means, and have been called into existence by labor, fall rightly, as it seems to me, within that designation." Their reason for not explicitly including the man himself may be found in their interest in distribution and production. Sidgwick (1901, p. 134) pointed out: "We have to consider it [conventional capital] as a joint factor with labour in production, by the aid of which the labourers . . . are enabled to produce more than they would otherwise do; and in order to keep this view of it clear, we have to maintain the distinction between capital and labourers."

In contrast, J. R. McCulloch clearly defined the human being as such as capital: "Instead of understanding by capital all that portion of the produce of industry extrinsic to man, which may be made applicable to his support, and to the facilitating of production, there does not seem to be any good reason why man himself should not, and very many why he should be considered as forming a part of the national capital" (McCulloch, 1870, p. 66; see pp. 57, 67). He said, moreover, that there is a close analogy between conventional and human capital. An investment in a human being should yield a rate of return consistent with other investments, plus a normal rate of return determined by the market interest rate, during the probable lifetime of the individual (McCulloch, 1870, p. 66).

Nassau Senior suggested that human beings can usefully be treated as capital. In most of his discussion of the topic he referred to skills and acquired abilities and not to man himself (Senior, 1939, pp. 68–69, 204–6). On occasion, however, he treated the human being himself as capital with a maintenance cost—incurred with the expectation of obtaining a future yield (Senior, 1939, pp. 68–69). He asserted that there is little difference between talking about the value of a slave and about the value of a free man. The principal difference is that the free man sells himself for a certain period of time and only to a certain extent, whereas the slave is sold for his lifetime (Senior, 1939, p. 10).

Several current writers, dealing with investment in education, maintain that this investment is undertaken primarily for future return. It is interesting to compare this view to that of Senior (1939, pp. 205–6), who considered the higher education of a gentleman's son: "Neither the labour which the boy undergoes, nor the expense borne by his father, is incurred principally in order to obtain future profit. The boy works under the stimulus of immediate punishment. It never occurs to the father that . . . he is engaging in a speculation which is likely to be unprofitable. To witness a son's daily improvement is, with all well-disposed men . . . one of the sources of immediate gratification. The expense incurred for that purpose is as much repaid by immediate enjoyment as that which is incurred to obtain the most transitory pleasures. It is true that a further object may also be obtained but the immediate motive is ample."

Hence, not all education is undertaken with a view to future yields. It is, however, capital, and it is the "quantity and diffusion of this capital" that determine the wealth of a nation. Senior (1939, pp. 134–35) asserted, moreover, that the value of the stock of England's human capital exceeded the value of the stock of all Great Britain's "material capital."

Henry D. Macleod considered productive human beings as fixed capital. In his view, however, if they are not productive they do not enter economic analysis (Macleod, 1881, pp. 134, 205–6, 213). This view contrasted sharply with that of Léon Walras, who included all human beings in the concept of capital. And the value, or price, of these human beings, Walras (1954, pp. 40, 214–16, 271) said, is determined like that of any other capital good. He, moreover, was aware of the inner reluctance of economists to treat human beings as capital. He argued, however, that in pure theory "it is proper to abstract completely from considerations of justice and practical expediency" and to regard human beings "exclusively from the point of view of value in exchange" (Walras, 1954, p. 216).

Johann H. von Thünen also recognized this reluctance to evaluate human beings. But from this reluctance, he said, "stems lack of clarity and confusion of concepts on one of the most important points of political economy" (von Thünen, 1875, p. 5). "Moreover, it may be proved that freedom and dignity of man may be successfully preserved, even if he is subject to the laws of capital" (von Thünen, 1875, p. 5). Von Thünen asserted that many social injustices might be eliminated if expenditures that increase labor productivity were treated within the human-capital analytical framework. The capital value of these expenditures, moreover, should be included as a component of the aggregate capital stock (von Thünen, 1875, pp. 1–10). While many present-day writers attribute the absence of the notion of human capital from the mainstream of economic thought to sentimentalism (Schultz, 1959, p. 110), it is interesting to note that here (and in a number of other cases in the past) the presence of the idea was due to sentimentalism.

Although Alfred Marshall admitted that an estimate of the capital value of a man might be useful and discussed clearly the capitalized-net-earnings approach to human-capital evaluation (consumption being deducted from earnings before capitalizing), he disregarded the notion as "unrealistic," since human beings are not marketable (Marshall, 1959, pp. 469–70, 705–6).

Human beings are included in Irving Fisher's definition of capital. Capital, he asserted, is a "useful appropriated material object," and since human beings have these characteristics, consistency required that they be included in the concept of capital (Fisher, 1897, pp. 201–2; 1927, pp. 5, 51–52, 68; 1965, pp. 12–13). Moreover, the skill of an individual is not capital in addition to the individual himself. It is, Fisher (1927, p. 9) said, the skilled individual who should be placed in the category of capital.

This brings up the interesting question: Are the value of skills and useful abilities and the value of an individual possessing them the same? Edward Denison (1964, p. 91) suggests that to speak of technological progress embodied in physical capital is simply to refer to changes in the quality of capital goods. An analogy may be made regarding human beings. Skills and acquired abilities are embodied in the human being and presumably increase his quality as a producing unit. Since these skills and abilities acquired by an individual are inalienable, it is questionable whether one should speak of them alone as capital; it is, if this view is taken, the skilled individual who is the capital. It has been suggested, however, that the answer to the question posed above depends upon the definition of value. If value is defined as "net benefit" to society where the excess of total output over total consumption determines net benefit, the addition of a skill or useful ability would increase output, whereas the addition of an individual increases not only output but also consumption. The value of a skill and a useful ability and the value of an individual, both measured by the amount of net benefit added, in this case might certainly be different (Dublin and Lotka, 1930, p. 4). Whether we call skills and acquired abilities only, or the acquirer of them, capital is relatively unimportant. The distinction, however, between skills and acquired abilities and the person is in any event important, for example, for purposes of taxation.

T. W. Schultz (1961b, p. 3) has pointed out that, "among the few [economists] who have looked upon human beings as capital, there are three distinguished names ... Adam Smith ... von Thünen ... and Irving Fisher." Schultz (1959, p. 110) has asserted also that "the mainstream of modern economics has bypassed undertaking any systematic analysis of human wealth." It would be interesting to know the time period denoted by Schultz's use of the word "modern." Presumably, he means "current." If, however, another definition of "modern" were adopted (it has been said that modern economics began with Sir William Petty), his comment would be questionable.

III

As suggested above, the concept of human capital has been used to demonstrate the magnitude and economic importance of the stock of human resources. Estimates of the value of a nation's human wealth were thought to give some insight into the economic power of a nation.

While attempting to estimate the stock of human, or "living," capital in the United Kingdom in 1891, J. Shield Nicholson (1891) capitalized the portion of national income that he assumed to be derived from "living" capital.[8] To do so he attempted to find the capital value of such things as the wage bill, the earnings of management, the earnings of capitalists, the earnings of salaried government officials, and "domesticated humanity" (that is, the people of a nation "as 'things in themselves,' or rather superior domestic animals reared for their affectionate disposition and intellectual and moral activities") (Nicholson, 1896, pp. 112–14). He, unfortunately, included the latter category because it has a cost of maintenance, and he estimated its value by assuming that, since people spend 10 per cent of their income on their own maintenance and 10 per cent on rent, it is proper to value an individual as "a thing in itself" as equal in value to the house he occupies (Nicholson, 1896, p. 109). There is, of course, no simple relationship between the cost of production (or maintenance) of a good and its monetary value. Any attempt, moreover, to estimate in money terms the sentimental value of a human being "appears to be trifling with a serious subject."[9]

Nicholson capitalized the wage bill to determine the capital value of the "wage earner," and he added this to the other values he estimated, including the value of "domesticated humanity." Since the cost of production of wage earners appears in the estimate of the value of "domesticated humanity" and also in the estimate of the capitalized value of their earnings, there is a duplication of values, which seems to be historically characteristic of combinations of the cost-of-production and capitalized-earnings approaches. He concluded by asserting that the value of the stock of "living" capital of the United Kingdom was about *five* times the value of the stock of conventional capital (Nicholson, 1896, p. 114).

In his attempt to estimate the value of the stock of capital in France around 1900, Alfred de Foville asserted that any procedure for estimating the value of the stock of human capital by capitalizing the earnings before deducting consumption expenditures is incorrect. It is the error in this procedure, he averred, that has led writers to assert that the value of the stock of human capital is greater than the value of the stock of conventional capital. By deducting consumption expenditures (maintenance) from earnings and then applying Petty's method, he estimated the value of the stock of human capital in France. For some purposes, this approach is an improvement over Petty's, and it improves the analogy between the valuations of the aggregate stocks of human and conventional capital. He cautioned, however, that the whole notion of human capital is dubious.

---

[8] This article appears as chapter v in Nicholson (1896). The central idea of these works (that is, recognizing human beings as capital and estimating their money value) is found also in Nicholson (1892).

[9] This phrase was borrowed from Longfield (1931, pp. 201–2). He, however, was referring to estimating the cost of producing common laborers.

How can the capital value of a Goethe, a Newton, or a Jeanne d'Arc be determined? he asked (De Foville, 1905).[10]

A French actuary, A. Barriol, in 1908 utilized Farr's capitalized-earnings procedure, although he did not deduct maintenance from earnings, to determine the "social value" of a man in France. He defined "social value" as the amount of his earnings that an individual restores to society. Since he implicitly assumed that lifetime consumption equals lifetime earnings, the "social value" of an individual depends upon his total earnings. He attempted to estimate this value by age groups by assuming certain earnings scales and capitalizing them, allowance being made for deaths in accordance with a mortality table (Barriol, 1910).

He used these values to attempt to estimate the total and per capita value of the stock of human capital in several countries. The French values were multiplied by the population in the various age groups of the particular country. These values were then summed and divided by the total population figure to obtain a weighted per capita average value of a citizen of the country in question. Since the countries he considered had different levels of economic development and therefore different levels of wages, he applied a coefficient of increase or reduction to his estimates to compensate for the difference. He recognized, moreover, that the values obtained were too high, since he had assumed the female to earn as much as the male. He adjusted for this by multiplying his estimates by a "reduction coefficient." Although his estimates of the capital (or social) value of a human being were not definitive, he concluded that they might offer some insight into the economic power of nations (Barriol, 1911).

Barriol's procedure for adjusting his figures is interesting but the results obviously dubious. His adjusted estimates, as will be pointed out subsequently, were used as a basis for computation by other writers.

Human capital, according to S. S. Huebner (1914), should receive the same scientific treatment that is given to conventional capital. This can be done, he said, by "capitalizing human life values with bonds to give them perpetuity as a working force and fluidity as a source of credit, of subjecting them to the principles of depreciation, and of using the sinking-fund method to assure realization of the contemplated object whenever man has a future business or family obligation to fulfill that involves the hazard of uncertainty of the duration of the working life" (Huebner, 1914, pp. 18–19). This scientific treatment of human values is justified, he said, because of their importance in economic affairs.

In general equilibrium theory, with short-term contracts postulated,

---

[10] This, of course, is the same question asked by Engel. Engel's answer was that, although their cost of production could be estimated, it was impossible to determine their capitalized yield to society.

entrepreneurs have little incentive to invest in the work force. Today, however, with long-run growth widely recognized as a dominant factor in business planning, Huebner's comment is particularly relevant. Entrepreneurs are becoming increasingly cognizant of the importance of investments that become an integral part of man, and such awareness is leading to deliberate investment in human beings (see Becker, 1962). Hence, a symmetrical treatment of the work force and conventional capital may be necessary.

Huebner (1914, pp. 18–19) estimated the value of the stock of human capital in the United States around 1914—capitalized at the market interest rate and allowing for deaths in accordance with a mortality table—to be *six* to *eight* times the value of the stock of the nation's conventional capital.

Edward A. Woods and Clarence B. Metzger employed five procedures to obtain five different estimates of the stock of human capital in the United States in 1920. They did this to show the very large monetary value and importance of the nation's population and "to awaken a sluggish public . . . by appealing to its material interest" to the needs of conserving human life (Woods and Metzger, 1927, p. 32).

Woods and Metzger's (1927, p. 101) first estimate of the value of the 1920 stock of human capital was based upon governmental suggestions of life insurance for workers. Their second method of valuing the stock of human capital was to base its value upon the value of property, that is, to approximate the former by applying a multiplier to the latter (Woods and Metzger, 1927, pp. 104–5). They applied several multipliers but concluded that "the multiple *five* seems to be the most accurate one to express life values to the national wealth" (Woods and Metzger, 1927, p. 106). Neither of these procedures, however, is scientifically valid.

Their third estimate employed the capitalized-national-income and the capitalized-wage-bill approaches. In the former case they capitalized the 1920 national income (Woods and Metzger, 1927, p. 108). This estimate made the unrealistic assumption that all national income is the product of labor. In the latter case, following Petty, they capitalized the wage bill to obtain an estimate of the value of the human-capital stock (Woods and Metzger, 1927, pp. 110–11). The difficulty here is the separation of returns to conventional capital from those to labor. Moreover, they assumed that labor earnings were constant through time. Neither approach considers depreciation or maintenance. Both procedures imply that the "value of American society" goes on indefinitely (Woods and Metzger, 1927, p. 111).

The fourth estimate employed the familiar Farr-type capitalized-earnings approach. They estimated both gross and net values for the value of the 1920 stock of human capital. Unlike Farr, however, they assumed constant earnings and consumption expenditures in all age groups (Woods and Metzger, 1927, pp. 114–39).

Woods and Metzger realized that symmetry of treatment as between human and conventional capital is achieved only if depreciation, maintenance, and obsolescence are considered. Maintenance is accounted for when consumption expenditures are deducted from earnings and depreciation and obsolescence are allowed for by the manner in which average earnings are estimated: "This factor [depreciation and obsolescence] is taken into consideration in the make-up of the 'average yearly wage' for workers, which included the lower wages of old workers along with the higher ones of the more efficient producers. The former naturally receive less salary and wages than workers in the prime of life, health, and efficiency but the wages of the latter are diluted in the 'average' by the lower wages of the former group plus those of the very young, untrained workers" (Woods and Metzger, 1927, p. 122).

To make their fifth estimate of the value of the stock of human capital, Woods and Metzger (1927, p. 142) applied the per capita human-capital estimates of some Americans who had previously valued human beings to the 1920 population data. Several of these estimates, however, were limited to adult male values at specific ages for workers or were otherwise limited in scope.

They concluded that the monetary value of the population is a country's greatest asset, and that it is "important that public-spirited citizens and students of social welfare strongly support those movements conducive to the conservation of human life and the enjoyment of as perfect health as possible, so that the lives of productive individuals might be further lengthened and thereby add to the wealth of society" (Woods and Metzger, 1927, p. 162). This conclusion contrasts sharply with that of one present-day economist, who argues that the point has now been reached in developed countries where further increases in health expenditures will be "health-producing but not wealth-producing" and therefore, in an economic sense, unproductive (Lees, 1962). Although I view the latter argument as doubtful, definitive judgment cannot be reached until the quality of our information on this subject has improved. As will be pointed out below, many writers of the early twentieth century held Wood and Metzger's view.

IV

Economists and statisticians have utilized the human-capital concept to estimate the total economic losses to combatants resulting from war. The presumption is that a man's capitalized-earnings stream is capital and that his death or disability reduces the stock of wealth.

In attempting to estimate the total cost to the combatants of the Franco-German War, Sir Robert Giffen used what was essentially Petty's method of valuing in money terms the lives destroyed in the war. He emphasized, however, that his estimates were crude and imperfect and that the loss of human life was not amenable to monetary evaluation. Hence, he omitted it from his estimate of the total cost of the war (Giffen, 1880, pp. 29–31, 76).

Several writers utilized Barriol's estimates of the capital value of a man in an attempt to estimate the money value of human life destroyed as the result of World War I (Guyot, 1914; Crammond, 1915; Bogart, 1919, pp. 274–77). Man is capital, Yves Guyot (1914, pp. 1193–98) said, and society should be interested in loss of life not only for humanitarian but also for economic reasons. Although Ernest Bogart (1919, p. 274) asserted that an estimate of the monetary value of human lives destroyed in war is "a procedure of doubtful statistical propriety," he felt that only a monetary value could convey to the mind the enormous economic importance of these human lives destroyed.

These writers erred, however, in taking Barriol's adjusted estimates of the capital value of an average individual in the population to apply to the casualties of male combatants mainly of military age, particularly when the original unadjusted values were available. Bogart recognized the error. He said, however, that "it is evident from the fact that the estimates are low that the figures err on the side of underestimation rather than exaggeration, and that no grave error will be committed in using them" (Bogart, 1919, p. 275).

William S. Rossiter questioned the significance of including the capital value of life destroyed in estimates of the economic costs of war. The only case in which an estimate of human capital destroyed by war would have any significance, he said, would be that in which the value of the total stock of a nation's human capital had been computed and included in national wealth estimates. Then the loss resulting from war might be meaningfully compared with this estimate. With this in mind, he used Barriol's estimates to estimate the value of human life within the active male age group in the population of the nations at war in World War I (Rossiter, 1919).

Harold Boag (1916, p. 7) in 1916 considered the question of whether it is "correct to include in any estimates of the cost of war the diminution of capital due to loss of human life." He concluded that it is correct since there is a close analogy between "material and personal" capital (Boag, 1916, p. 9). Boag, moreover, enunciated several important points pertinent to human-capital evaluation: the method of evaluation should depend upon the purpose for which the estimates are to be used; care should be taken to avoid counting an item as both human and conventional capital; and the interdependence of the values of conventional and human capital should be kept in mind (Boag, 1916, p. 10).

Boag (1916, pp. 16–17) pointed out that the capitalized-earnings approach to human-capital evaluation is preferable since it attempts to value material things, while the cost-of-production approach may include expenditures on the individual apart from those that increase his earning power. And the "gross" concept is preferred when valuing monetary losses resulting from war: "In calculations of material loss, the loss of income is usually compared with the total national income and not with the national savings and, therefore, it is often better to arrive at a capitalized value of the diminution of gross income instead of the surplus income" (Boag, 1916, p. 14). Although Senior had previously suggested it, Boag was the first to point out explicitly one of the difficulties associated with the cost-of-production approach to human-capital evaluation: "It is impossible to determine how much of the cost of education, maintenance, etc., is strictly necessary to produce an income-earner, as distinct from those capacities for 'love, joy and admiration,' which may not be incidental to the production of material wealth" (Boag, 1916, p. 17). It has been suggested recently that the inseparability of consumption and investment makes the entire analysis of human (education) capital dubious (Shaffer, 1961, p. 1027). T. W. Schultz (1961c, p. 1035) correctly points out, however, that, although a wholly satisfactory empirical method for dealing with the consumption-investment dichotomy has not been found, the economic logic for allocating (education) expenditures between consumption and investment is clear.

J. M. Clark, in a discussion of the costs of World War I to the American people, included the monetary value of human life destroyed in the war and set forth a modified Farr-type capitalized-net-earnings procedure for computing the capital values. In order to determine the loss in human capital to dependents resulting from the war, Clark constructed an "imaginary army" which represented the characteristics (age and number of dependents) of the actual losses. He then multiplied human-capital values by age by the estimated corresponding numbers of losses so as to obtain the total value of human capital destroyed in the war (Clark, 1931).

V

The human-capital analytical framework has been employed in the past for some of the same purposes for which it is currently being used, namely, to demonstrate the economic profitability of human migration, health investment, premature-death prevention, and education.

An interesting discussion occurred around the end of the nineteenth century regarding the monetary value of immigration to the United States. There was general agreement that immigration was economically profitable to the United States and that the subject fitted properly within the human-capital analytical framework. There was, however, some question as to the degree of profitability and the procedure for calculating an immigrant's monetary value.

Friedrich Kapp utilized Engel's cost-of-production procedure which, it will be recalled, neglects depreciation and maintenance, to estimate the capital value of an immigrant arriving in the United States. He concluded that if the immigration trend continued the country would gain almost a million dollars a day in the value of its human capital (Kapp, 1870). Charles L. Brace criticized both Kapp's procedure for valuing immigrants and his estimates of their value.[11] He argued correctly that the capital value of an object is not determined solely by its cost of production but also by the demand for it. Hence, he said, each immigrant is worth to the country the capitalized difference between his contribution to output and his maintenance: "Each laborer's average cost to his employer is, say $20 per month and 'keep,' or about $400 per annum. It is believed that an ordinary profit on common labor upon a farm is from 15 to $18\frac{3}{4}$ per cent. This would leave the gain to the country from $60 to $75 annually. This, at seven per cent interest, would represent the capital value . . . about $1,000 or $1,100 for an average male laborer" (Kapp, 1870, p. 149).

Richard Mayo-Smith, in 1895, followed Brace in criticizing Kapp's procedure for the monetary evaluation of immigrants. An immigrant who has ability and finds an opportunity to use it, Mayo-Smith said, has a monetary value to the country which he enters whatever the cost of his production. He furthermore considered the cost of rearing a child as a consumption expenditure. Although Mayo-Smith explicitly excluded human beings from the concept of capital—on the basis of the ownership criterion for defining capital—he clearly enunciated Farr's capitalized-net-earnings approach as the means for estimating their "economic" value. There is, however, a fallacy in this procedure, Mayo-Smith asserted, because the capitalized value of an immigrant's future earnings depends on his having an opportunity to earn them. Hence, he must secure employment upon his arrival. He must, moreover, secure it without displacing another worker. Otherwise, the stock of human wealth in the receiving country will not have increased (Mayo-Smith, 1901).[12]

In an article written in 1904, Miles M. Dawson proposed the use of actuarial principles for human-capital evaluation. He asserted correctly that the methods used by courts for determining compensation to others for the pecuniary injuries resulting from a death where another party is liable are unscientific. Actuarial science, utilizing the capitalized-net-earnings approach

[11] The relevant part of Brace's criticism, which appeared in an article in the New York *Tribune*, is quoted by Kapp (1870, pp. 147–49).

[12] Similar discussions regarding the monetary, or capital, value of immigrants to other countries are now taking place. See, for example, Abraham-Frois (1964).

to human-capital evaluation, he said, furnishes the means of computing the monetary value of life destroyed—given the age, net earnings, and general health of the decedent (Dawson, 1904). Although the human-capital concept is now being used on a small scale for such purposes, the concept should be exceedingly useful and likely to be more widely utilized.

Several works appeared in the first quarter of the twentieth century in which the authors utilized the human-capital analytical framework to attempt to ascertain monetary losses resulting from preventable illness and death (Fisher, 1908; Forsyth, 1914–15; Crum, 1919; Fisk, 1921). Their hypothesis was that illness and death involved a loss in human wealth and that a saving could be effected by preventing or postponing some of the preventable illnesses and deaths that occurred. To determine this saving, Irving Fisher suggested that Farr's capitalized-net-earnings approach be used to estimate the value of human beings. He estimated the money value of an average American by adjusting Farr's estimates to correct for the higher average earnings in the United States. He then used the age distribution of deaths and the "percentages of preventability" to estimate the average capital value of lives sacrificed by preventable deaths in 1907. The value of an average American multiplied by the 1907 U.S. population, Fisher said, gives a minimum estimate of the value of the stock of human capital existing in that year. This value, he asserted, greatly exceeded all other wealth (Fisher, 1908, pp. 739–41). There is, however, a serious error in Fisher's analysis. By substituting only average earnings of an American for average earnings of an Englishman in Farr's computations, Fisher implicitly assumed that maintenance costs were constant over time and equal in the two countries.[13]

Theoretically, since investments in health services increase the labor supply by reducing mortality, disability, and debility, it is necessary to assume that the existing population is below the optimum size (defined by a zero rate of return on the existing stock of conventional capital). Neither this assumption nor the assumption of full employment (when unaccounted for in the statistical procedure) was explicitly made by most past writers. General acceptance of the stationary-state notion and Say's Law accounts for this.

Turning now to education, J. R. Walsh (1935, p. 255) in 1935 pointed out: "Since the days of Sir William Petty, many economists have included man in the category of fixed capital, because like capital man costs an expense and serves to repay that expense with a profit. Their conclusions, however, have been carried on chiefly in general terms, reference being made to *all* men as capital, and to *all* kinds of expenses in rearing and training as their cost." Walsh then took up the subject now being treated

[13] For a historical discussion of the relationship between public health and the economic value of a man, see Sand (1952, esp. pp. 583–87).

by T. W. Schultz, Gary Becker, and others, of the economic importance of higher education. Walsh was particularly interested in whether expenditures incurred by persons for professional careers were a capital investment made in a profit-seeking, equalizing market, and in response to the same motives that lead to investments in conventional capital. He asserted that they were. To test his hypothesis he examined the earnings of men at various levels of education. Their present value was estimated, using the capitalized-gross-earnings approach, at the average age at which their education ended. The costs of the various levels of education were then estimated, and a comparison was made of these costs and capital values to determine if they were equal (Walsh, 1935, pp. 255–69).

Walsh found that the value of a general college education exceeded the cost of its acquisition. Hence, his hypothesis of a competitive equalizing market in education was rejected. When he calculated the capital values and costs of professional training, however, he found that cost exceeded value in the cases of M.A., Ph.D., and M.D. degree holders. The reason for this, Walsh said, was that only monetary returns were considered and individuals with these degrees receive special satisfactions and advantages such as travel, vacations, and service to man. A consideration of these factors would equate the value estimate to its cost. Value exceeded cost in the cases of engineers, B.B.A. degree holders, and lawyers. The reason for this, Walsh said, was because of a short-run excess demand for their services. More people would be trained in the occupations over time, and value would become equated to cost. Hence, he said, there is no evidence that the ordinary adjustment which is characteristic of a competitive market is prevented from taking place (Walsh, 1935, pp. 269–84).

Walsh's optimistic conclusion about the competitiveness of the market for education was, however, arrived at by questionable ad hoc arguments. In actual fact, he found that value of education differed from cost of training in every professional-training case he studied. When training costs exceeded the increment to capital value resulting from the training, he assumed a long-run market equilibrium and explained the disparity by bringing in additional value attributable to non-monetary remuneration; but when value exceeded cost he abandoned the assumption of long-run market equilibrium, and he explained the disparity by a short-run disequilibrium which he arbitrarily assumed would be eliminated by a long-run adjustment.

Walsh's work is open to two other criticisms. First, his inclusion of all the costs of room, board, and personal expenses in his estimates of the average cost of various levels of education (Walsh, 1935, pp. 267–69) is clearly wrong, because an individual would have to incur these costs whether he attended college or not. Second, he overlooked the possibility that earnings differentials may result from factors other than the level of education.

It should be pointed out that Walsh's work is quite similar to that currently being done on the economics of education. He applied the human-capital analytical framework to the topic and asked many of the questions being posed today.

VI

In summary, treating human beings within the capital analytical framework is by no means new. Many past economists, and non-economists, have considered human beings or their skills as capital. Although several motives for treating human beings as capital and valuing them in money terms are to be found in this literature, most of the well-known names in the history of economic thought neither attempted an evaluation of human capital nor employed the concept for any specific purpose. They did, however, include humans or their skills in their definition of capital and recognized the importance of investment in human beings as a factor increasing their productivity. Although some economists included man himself as capital, most of them included only human skill. The former view was taken by economists such as Walras and Fisher, whose theoretical approach did not necessitate their classifying the factors of production into the traditional trio of land, labor, and capital. The latter view, held particularly by the English Classical school, was adopted by economists interested in the distribution of income and the theory of production. Whether or not we define skills and/or the acquirer of them as capital is relatively unimportant. The distinction between skills and the person is important however. Economists, legislators, and private institutions when faced with concrete policy questions have fairly consistently recognized both that skills require prior effort and continuous maintenance and that to deny this analogy between humans and conventional capital in practice (for example, in tax laws and philanthropy) means a misuse of resources.

Since the human-capital concept was not fully explored by these economists, they did not calculate rates of return on investments in human beings. Recognition of the difficulty of resolving the investment-consumption dichotomy may have accounted for this failure.

Basically, two methods were used to estimate the value of human beings: the cost-of-production and the capitalized-earnings procedures. The former method is the less useful, since there is no simple and necessary relationship between the cost of producing an item and its economic value. The inseparability of consumption and investment and the difficulty of treating depreciation and maintenance make any cost-of-production value dubious. Economists engaged in research in this area will find little of value in past works in which this approach was adopted.

Farr's capitalized-earnings approach was the first truly scientific procedure and is the one followed today by the majority of economists for evaluating human beings. His work, and that of Dublin and Lotka, should be starting points for anyone interested in determining either human-capital values or their components. Use of this approach avoids the depreciation difficulty. Since a young man, *ceteris paribus*, is expected to be productive over a longer period than an older one, his capital value would be greater. Although maintenance costs were neglected by those who used the cost-of-production approach, they were considered by Farr and Dublin and Lotka to be equal to personal living expenses.

Current writers are employing the human-capital concept for many of the same purposes for which it was used in the past, namely, to demonstrate the economic profitability of human migration, health investment, premature-death prevention, and education. Since many of them fail to cite predecessors, it is hoped that this essay will be helpful as a reference source. The human-capital concept was also used by past writers to demonstrate the power of a nation, propose new tax schemes, determine the total cost of war, emphasize the economic significance of human life, and aid courts in making decisions in cases dealing with compensation for personal injury and death. These uses may suggest interesting additional problems to contemporary economists.

References

Abraham-Frois, G. "Capital humain et migrations internationales," *Rev. d'écon. polit.*, LXXIV (March–April, 1964), 526–54.

Bagehot, Walter. *Economic Studies*. Stanford, Calif.: Academic Reprints, 1953.

Barriol, A. "La valeur sociale d'un individu," *Rev. écon. internat.* (December, 1910), pp. 552–55.

———. "Complément à la note sur la valeur sociale d'un individu," *ibid.* (May, 1911), pp. 356–61.

Becker, Gary S. "Investment in Human Capital: A Theoretical Analysis," *J.P.E.*, LXX, Suppl. (October, 1962), 9–49.

———. *Human Capital: A Theoretical and Empirical Analysis, with Special Reference to Education*. New York: National Bureau of Economic Research, 1964.

Boag, Harold. "Human Capital and the Cost of War," *Royal Statis. Soc.* (January, 1916), pp. 7–17.

Bogart, Ernest L. *Direct and Indirect Costs of the Great World War*. New York: Oxford Univ. Press, 1919.

Cantillon, Richard, *Essai sur la nature du commerce en général*. Translated by Henry Higgs. London: Frank Cass Co., 1959.

Clark, John M. *The Costs of World War to the American People*. New Haven, Conn.: Yale Univ. Press, 1931.

Crammond, Edgar. "The Cost of War," *J. Royal Statis. Soc.*, LXXVIII (May, 1915), 361–99.

Crum, Frederick S. "Public Accidents and Their Cost," *Proc. Nat. Safety Council* (8th Annual Safety Congress, 1919), pp. 1061–82.

Dawson, Miles H. "Valuation, in Actions for Damages for Negligence, of Human Life, Destroyed or Impaired," *Proc. Internat. Congress Actuaries*, I (1904), 929–39.

Denison, Edward F. "The Unimportance of the Embodied Question," *A.E.R.*, LIV (March, 1964), 90–93.

Dublin, Louis I. *Health and Wealth, a Survey of the Economics of World Health*. New York: Harper & Bros., 1928.

Dublin, Louis I., and Lotka, Alfred. *The Money Value of Man*. New York: Ronald Press Co., 1930.

Engel, Ernst. *Der Werth des Menschen.* Berlin: Verlag von Leonhard Simion, 1883.

Farr, William. "Equitable Taxation of Property," *J. Royal Statis. Soc.,* XVI (March, 1853), 1–45.

Fisher, Irving. "Senses of 'Capital,'" *Econ. J.,* VII (June, 1897), 199–213.

———. "Cost of Tuberculosis in the United States and Its Reduction." Read before the International Congress on Tuberculosis, Washington, 1908.

———. *The Nature of Capital and Income.* London: Macmillan & Co., 1927.

———. *The Theory of Interest.* New York: Augustus M. Kelley, 1965.

Fisk, Eugene L. "Health of Industrial Workers," *Waste in Industry.* Washington: Federated American Engineering Societies, 1921.

Forsyth, C. H. "Vital and Monetary Losses in the United States Due to Preventable Deaths," *American Statis. Assoc. Publication,* XIV (1914–15), 758–89.

Foville, A. de. "Ce que c'est la richesse d'un peuple," *Bull. Institut Internat. Statis.,* XIV (1905), 62–74.

Giffen, Robert. *Essays in Finance.* 1st ser. London: G. Bell & Sons, 1880.

Guyot, Yves M. "The Waste of War and the Trade of Tomorrow," *Nineteenth Century and After,* LXXVI (December, 1914), 1193–1206.

Huebner, S. S. "The Human Value in Business Compared with the Property Value," *Proc. Thirty-fifth Ann. Convention Nat. Assoc. Life Underwriters* (July, 1914), pp. 17–41.

Hull, Charles R. (ed.). *The Economic Writings of Sir William Petty.* 2 vols. Cambridge: Cambridge Univ. Press, 1899.

Kapp, Friedrich. *Immigration and the Commissioners of Emigration of the State of New York.* New York: E. Steigen & Co., 1870.

Lees, D. S. "An Economist Considers Other Alternatives," *Financing Medical Care* ed. Helmut Shoeck. Caldwell, Idaho: Caxton Printers Ltd., 1962.

Lindheim, A. *Saluti Senectutis.* Leipzig und Wien: F. Deuticke, 1909.

List, Friedrich. *The National System of Political Economy.* Translated by Sampson S. Lloyd. New York: Longmans, Green & Co., 1928.

Longfield, Mountiford. *Lectures on Political Economy.* London: The London School of Economics and Political Science, 1931.

Lüdtge, R. "Über den Geldwert des Menschen," *Deutsche Versicherungszeitung,* No. 56 (1873). (*a*)

———. "Über den Versicherungswert des Menschen," *Deutsche Versicherungszeitung,* No. 62 (1873). (*b*)

McCulloch, J. R. *The Principles of Political Economy.* Alex. Murray & Son, 1870.

Machlup, Fritz. *The Production and Distribution of Knowledge in the United States.* Princeton, N.J.: Princeton Univ. Press, 1962.

Macleod, Henry D. *The Elements of Economics.* Vol. II. New York: D. Appleton & Co., 1881.

Marshall, Alfred. *Principles of Economics.* New York: Macmillan Co., 1959.

Mayo-Smith, Richard. *Emigration and Immigration.* New York: Charles Scribner's Sons, 1901.

Meyer, Ida. "Der Geldwert des Menschenlebens und seine Benziehungen zur Versicherung," *Veroffentlichungen Deutschen Vereins Versicherungs-Wissenschaft,* XLVII (September, 1930–May, 1932), 1–75.

Mill, John Stuart. *Principles of Political Economy.* New York: Longmans, Green & Co., 1909.

Mushkin, Selma J. (ed.). *Economics of Higher Education.* Washington: Government Printing Office, 1962.

Mushkin, Selma J., and Weisbrod, Burton A. "Investment in Health—Lifetime Health Expenditures on the 1960 Work Force," *Kyklos,* XVI (1963), 583–98.

Nicholson, J. Shield. "The Living Capital of the United Kingdom," *Econ. J.,* I (March, 1891), 95–107.

———. "Capital and Labour: Their Relative Strength," *ibid.,* II (September, 1892), 478–90.

———. *Strikes and Social Problems.* London: Macmillan & Co., 1896.

Roscher, Wilhelm G. F. *Principles of Political Economy.* Translated by John J. Lalor. Chicago: Callaghan & Co., 1878.

Rossiter, William S. "The Statistical Side of the Economic Costs of War," *A.E.R.,* VI (March, 1919), 94–117.

Sand, René. *The Advance to Social Medicine.* London: Staples Press, 1952.

Say, Jean Baptiste. *A Treatise on Political Economy.* Vol. I. Translated by C. R. Prinsep. Boston: Wells & Lilly, 1821.

Schultz, T. W. "Investment in Man: An Economist's View," *Social Service Rev.,* XXXIII (June, 1959), 109–17.

———. "Education and Economic Growth," in H. G. Richey (ed.), *Social*

Forces Influencing American Education. Chicago: Univ. of Chicago Press, 1961. (*a*)

———. "Investment in Human Capital," *A.E.R.*, LI (March, 1961), 1–17. (*b*)

———. "Investment in Human Capital: Reply," *ibid.*, LI (December, 1961), pp. 1035–59. (*c*)

——— (ed.). "Investment in Human Beings," *J.P.E.*, Vol. LXX, Suppl. (October, 1962).

Sencini, Guido. "Il metodo ordinario di calcodo del costo di produzione dell'umo," *Giornale degli Econ.*, XXXVI (1908), 481–96.

Senior, Nassau William. *An Outline of the Science of Political Economy.* New York: Farrar & Rinehart, 1939.

Sidgwick, Henry. *The Principles of Political Economy.* London: Macmillan & Co., 1901.

Smith, Adam. *The Wealth of Nations.* New York: Modern Library, 1937.

Stark, W. (ed.). *Jeremy Bentham's Economic Writing.* London: George Allen & Unwin, 1952.

Thünen, Johann Heinrich von. *Der isolierte Staat.* Vol. II, Part II. Translated by Bert F. Hoselitz. Chicago: Comparative Education Center, Univ. of Chicago; originally published 1875.

Walras, Léon. *Elements of Pure Economics.* Translated by William Jaffé. Homewood, Ill.: Richard D. Irwin, Inc., 1954.

Walsh, John R. "Capital Concept Applied to Man," *Q.J.E.*, XLIX (February, 1935), 255–85.

Weisbrod, Burton A. *Economics of Public Health.* Philadelphia: Univ. of Pennsylvania Press, 1961.

Wittstein, Theodor. *Mathematische Statistik und deren Anwendung auf National-Ökonomie und Versicherung-wissenschaft.* Hanover: Hahn'sche Hofbuchlandlung, 1867.

Woods, Edward A., and Metzger, Clarence B. *America's Human Wealth: Money Value of Human Life.* New York: F. S. Crofts & Co., 1927.

2

Strengthening Human Resources

In its report to the president, the Council of Economic Advisers tentatively reviews the state of the economy and contemporary problems and policies. "Strengthening Human Resources" covers a wide array of human resource problems and establishes a rationale for many official programs with us today in the areas of education, health,

COUNCIL OF
ECONOMIC ADVISERS

poverty, manpower training, and equal opportunity. This excerpt was written at a time during which Gardner Ackley was Chairman of the Council and when Arthur Okun and Otto Eckstein also served as Council members.

The 89th Congress, in its first session, enacted a body of domestic legislation unparalleled in 3 decades. The content and purpose of the Great Society programs are not purely economic. Yet, their consequences for the economy are so profound that they must be viewed as an integral part of economic policy. . . .

The common goal of the programs discussed here is to strengthen our human resources: to improve the education, health, and productivity of our working force, and to break down barriers which have prevented some citizens from the full development and use of their abilities and training.

Since these programs were undertaken, the burdens on our national resources have expanded. Even our wealthy Nation cannot realize all its goals at once. The programs begun in 1965 have already invested an additional $1.5 billion in our human resources. The investment will rise further in 1966, but at a slower rate than initially planned. Over time, economic growth and lessened defense demands should again permit resumption of

Reprinted from Council of Economic Advisers, "Strengthening Human Resources," *Annual Report of the Council of Economic Advisers* (January 1966), pp. 94–110.

a more rapid investment in human resources. The objectives and the instruments for such investment were importantly expanded in 1965; the foundation has been laid for great progress in the years ahead.

Education

"Education will not cure all the problems of society, but without it no cure for any problem is possible. It is high among my own concerns, central to the purposes of this Administration, and at the core of our hopes for a Great Society." With these remarks to the White House Conference on Education last July, President Johnson again affirmed education's high priority.

Even when viewed in the narrow perspective of economic benefit alone, the direct returns to individuals and society from investment in education have been shown by recent studies to be high, and to compare favorably with the returns available from other forms of investment. Although much of the economic return from education accrues to individuals in the form of higher productivity and earnings, education also enhances the well-being and supports the economic growth of the community that provides it. Recognition of the economic and social benefits of a literate and efficient population and an informed electorate was responsible for the adoption many years ago, and the subsequent extension and improvement, of free, compulsory education by State and local governments.

More recently, the Federal Government's interest and responsibility in the field of education have greatly expanded. In the late 1950's, a keener awareness of the critical role of science and technology in determining the Nation's economic and military strength as well as its esteem in the world prompted the Federal Government to undertake massive new support for scientific and technical education.

In the last two years, Federal support for primary and secondary education has also greatly expanded. Two closely related premises underlie the decision that exclusive reliance on State and local support for primary and secondary education is no longer adequate from the standpoint of the national interest. The first is the recognition that every community suffers from inadequate education in other parts of the country. The second is the recognition that education must be a key element in the attack on poverty to which the Nation is now committed.

The resources devoted to schooling and the resultant quality of education vary widely among areas of the United States. In 1964–65, the mean current expenditure per pupil in average daily attendance in public elementary and secondary schools was $484; it ranged from $273 in Mississippi to $790 in New York. Even the high average expenditure in New York did not provide a satisfactory education for many young people in that State.

States with low personal incomes often spend relatively more on education than their wealthier neighbors. Mississippi, with the lowest absolute expenditure per pupil in average daily attendance, devoted 4.4 percent of personal income to education last year, compared with the national average of 3.8 percent. New Mexico spent 5.8 percent—the highest proportion of any State—yet its per pupil expenditure still fell short of the national average.

When nearly 6.5 million people move across State lines every year and far larger numbers move within States, it is obvious that no community is immune to the effects of substandard education in other localities. Studies have shown that areas that are losing population—particularly their young people—spend less per student on education than those which are growing. The communities gaining population—typically our larger cities—are crowded with migrants who are often inadequately prepared to assume their social responsibilities or to qualify for urban jobs.

Moreover, the Nation has accepted the fundamental objective of eradicating poverty wherever it is found. Whether or not they migrate elsewhere, inadequately educated children of poor parents are handicapped in escaping the poverty in which they were reared. Education is the most powerful tool we have for raising the productivity and motivation of the children of poor families, and for breaking the cycle of poverty and dependency.

The tax base in communities with many poor families is often too weak to finance good schools. Even communities with more ample resources have frequently not provided schools which would encourage and assist children of the poor to make their own way out of poverty. Federal assistance clearly is required if every school district is to provide an education that is adequate for an economy of growing interdependence and for a society that is determined to eradicate poverty.

BUILDING THE LADDER OF EDUCATIONAL OPPORTUNITY

Programs adopted in 1965 will open new educational opportunities for millions of children and youths. These new programs will aid many disadvantaged children to get off to an equal start with others; assure them school facilities comparable with those of others; and remove some of the financial blocks which might prematurely halt their progress toward higher education. For persons no longer in school, the new measures will provide useful skills and training, or help to update skills outmoded by rapid technological change, thus making them more productive and preparing them for better jobs.

Much of the direct return from these new measures will accrue to the disadvantaged in the form of increased incomes which will help to lift them—and their children—out of poverty. Indirectly, all Americans will benefit through greater economic growth and reduced social tensions.

Project Head Start   Each year close to a million children from poor families begin their formal schooling. Most of these children suffer from extreme cultural and social deprivation. They have lacked the chance to build a vocabulary and to develop the other tools of learning. When they begin school, they are in a world that they do not understand.

In the summer of 1965, project Head Start—under the auspices of the Community Action Program of the Office of Economic Opportunity—was inaugurated to help these youngsters. To encourage widespread community involvement, parents and volunteers also participated in the program, which reached 560,000 preschool children at 13,400 Head Start Centers in 2,500 urban and rural communities. The summer program will be continued, and plans are being developed to extend Head Start on a year-round basis for 100,000 children in 1966.

Last summer, thousands of children had books for their own use for the first time; children whose diets typically consist of starches received fresh fruits and vegetables; many whose world had been confined to crowded slums began to explore their communities and visited zoos or museums.

Project Head Start is also concerned with a child's health. In examinations conducted as part of the program in Boston, volunteer doctors discovered that 71 percent of the children had one or more problems—pediatric, dental, or emotional—which required referral for further diagnosis and treatment. Without the Head Start program, many serious defects would have remained undetected and uncorrected for many years—perhaps to become uncorrectable.

This program will give millions of children a better chance to succeed in school. Unfortunately, however, many of these deprived youngsters will enter schools which—rather than being the best—are among the weakest in the country.

Elementary and Secondary Education   After years of controversy over Federal aid to education, the Elementary and Secondary Education Act of 1965 brought the Federal Government into a creative partnership with States and communities to improve the quality of all schools, and particularly those serving disadvantaged children. The Act authorizes more than $1 billion annually in grants to school districts with heavy concentrations of children from low-income families. Each district is eligible for a Federal payment of up to one-half the average State expenditure per child multiplied by the number of its poor school-age children. These grants will finance special programs to meet the needs of 5 million educationally deprived children from low-income families—10 percent of the 50 million school-age children.

The Act also provides funds for books, maps, and other educational materials which many schools currently lack. More than two-thirds of public elementary schools, serving almost 10 million children, have no library.

Supplementary educational centers will be established throughout the country to bring more of the cultural resources of an area into the educational process. Regional laboratories connected with major universities will seek better ways of teaching, and will seek to promote the transfer of new knowledge to the classroom. Funds are also provided to improve the operations of State educational agencies, thus strengthening their capacity for planning and decision-making.

Higher Education Although setbacks to the educational progress of the disadvantaged occur most frequently prior to the completion of high school, many talented students from poor families are unable to attend college for financial reasons. The Higher Education Act of 1965 established a broad program to make higher education available to all who may benefit from it. Its most important innovation is a program of educational opportunity grants of up to $1,000 for 115,000 high school graduates from low-income families. In addition, a guaranteed-loan program and an expanded Work-Study program will aid more than 700,000 students.

The Act will also help institutions of higher education to become more responsive to the current problems. It will encourage them to undertake community service programs, including extension, continuing education, and research programs designed to assist in the solution of community problems. It also sets up a new grant program to upgrade the academic quality of small developing colleges and establishes fellowships to encourage qualified persons to teach at these institutions.

The legislation authorizes the creation of a National Teachers Corps to augment the supply of qualified instructors in poor areas. Although the Congress did not appropriate funds to establish the Teacher Corps in 1965, the Administration continues to give this program high priority.

Most programs of direct financial aid to students have been directed toward the college-bound graduate and have failed to provide for many youths who wish to obtain training in business, trade, and technical schools. This omission will be corrected by the establishment of a vocational student loan insurance program which, when fully funded, will help as many as 100,000 students a year.

Out-of-School Programs The 1965 legislation also strengthened several programs which provide job training and work experience as well as basic education. These programs are designed to equip workers with the skills and productivity required to raise their potential earnings.

The Neighborhood Youth Corps program encourages persons aged 16–21 to stay in or return to school by providing full-time and part-time work experience and training. It provides counseling and basic literacy training, and it places young men and women in newly created positions to do work that would normally not be done in hospitals, settlement houses, schools, libraries, and other community agencies. Almost 1,500 projects have been approved in communities throughout the Nation for the employment of 350,000 young men and women in 1966.

The Job Corps provides education and work experience in rural conservation centers and in urban training centers where enrollees live, work, and learn. About 300,000 young people have expressed interest in joining this program. It is expected that about 30,000 will be enrolled by June 1966.

The Work Experience Program is designed to demonstrate the benefits of helping heads of families with dependent children to prepare for productive employment by providing them with work experience and job training along with basic literacy instruction. In 1965, the program aided 66,000 participants with 198,000 dependents.

The Adult Basic Education program is aimed at the 7.3 million Americans age 25 and over who have less than 5 years of education. It provides basic education when a lack of schooling stands in the way of successful training or employment. In fiscal 1965, about 38,000 adults in 15 States were enrolled. By June 1966, the program is expected to reach 229,000 adults in all the States and the territories.

Active Manpower Policies

Manpower policies have three principal objectives: to fit the unskilled for better jobs, to augment the supply of scarce skills, and to improve the efficiency of labor markets. These policies not only help individuals to achieve their full capabilities, but also add to the national productive potential. They are a continuation of the educational opportunity programs and should serve to keep the quality of the labor force advancing in pace with the demands created by technological progress.

TRAINING PROGRAMS

The Manpower Development and Training Act (MDTA) programs provide training and basic literacy instruction for unemployed (and some underemployed) persons who have had previous work experience, in order to up-grade their job skills. Between passage of the law in 1962 and the end of 1965, enrollment had reached a cumulative total of 370,000, with 315,000 in institutional training and 55,000 in on-the-job training. About 30 percent have been trained for skilled occupations and another 30 percent for clerical, sales, and service jobs.

Amendments to the MDTA in 1965 have made it possible to extend the scope and to increase the effectiveness of these training projects. The maximum period during which training allowances can be paid has been extended from 72 to 104 weeks, making it possible to train persons for more highly skilled work. Eligibility for training allowances has been broadened;

and the previous limitation on the number of youths who can benefit has been liberalized.

It is appropriate that MDTA training programs have been strengthened during a period of rapidly rising employment and increasing demand for labor. Workers who are now being trained can count on finding jobs quickly and benefiting immediately from the training they receive. And the upgrading of skills for thousands of the unemployed will help to provide a more flexible and mobile labor force, thus contributing to the stability of costs and prices in our expanding economy.

IMPROVING THE EFFICIENCY OF THE LABOR MARKET

Expansion of the economy is facilitated when labor markets operate efficiently. The Federal-State Employment Service is the principal agency of our manpower policy designed to help to match people with available jobs.

Most jobs are filled by direct hiring "at the gate" and through informal contacts with relatives and friends; many others are filled with the assistance of advertisements, unions, private agencies, college placement officers, and other means. But through its more than 2,000 local offices, the Employment Service maintains an active placement service for all workers desiring assistance.

A major task of the Employment Service has been to provide job counseling and placement service to those in the labor force (including new workers, the handicapped, and nonwhites) who require special assistance to enable them to compete in the job market. The Service also provides a flow of information about changing manpower requirements in local labor markets. This information is useful in planning occupational training under the MDTA; in reorientation of our vocational education programs; and in helping individuals to make rational vocational choices, and guiding them to areas of favourable employment opportunities.

A Special Task Force appointed by the Secretary of Labor has studied the operation of the Employment Service and recommended ways to make it achieve its goals more effectively.

RAISING LABOR PRODUCTIVITY

By 1985, the labor force will total about 110 million workers. On the assumption that present programs will be continued on the scale now projected, about one-tenth of these workers will be more productive because they have benefited from an MDTA or other out-of-school training program. Nearly one-half will be better educated as a result of one or more of the newly enacted programs. And these benefits will be concentrated among those individuals now least likely to climb the ladder of educational opportunity.

America has always invested heavily in education and training, and our economic achievements show that it has paid off handsomely. But the investment was not made sufficiently in all Americans, and perhaps as many as a third enter the work force ill-equipped to assume a fully productive role. The programs that have been begun will extend a more adequate investment in education and training to that third of our people.

Health

America is a healthy nation, and Americans take justifiable pride in the quantity and quality of available medical services. Yet, such significant indicators of U.S. health as life expectancy, infant mortality, and the incidence of heart disease must cause concern when compared with rates prevailing abroad or when our recent progress is measured against that of other nations.

After declining steadily and dramatically throughout the first half of this century, the U.S. death rate has remained close to 9.4 per 1,000 of the

Table 1—Health indicators, selected years 1940–64

Indicator	1940	1950	1960	1964
Life expectancy[a]		Years		
At birth	63.6	68.1	69.7	70.2
White	64.9	69.0	70.6	71.0
Nonwhite	53.9[b]	60.7	63.6	64.1
At age 45	26.9	28.5	29.4	29.7
White	27.3	28.9	29.7	30.1
Nonwhite	22.8[b]	24.8	26.2	26.6
Infant mortality rate		Deaths per 1,000 live births		
Total	47.0	29.2	26.0	24.8
White	43.2	26.8	22.9	21.6
Nonwhite	73.8	44.5	43.2	41.1
Maternal mortality rate		Deaths per 10,000 live births		
Total	37.6	8.3	3.7	3.3
White	32.0	6.1	2.6	2.2
Nonwhite	77.4	22.2	9.8	9.0
Death rates		Deaths per 1,000 population		
All causes	10.8	9.6	9.5	9.4
Diseases of cardiovascular system	4.1	4.9	5.2	5.1
Cancer	1.2	1.4	1.5	1.5
Influenza and pneumonia	.7	.3	.4	.3
Accidents	.7	.6	.5	.5
All other	4.1	2.4	1.9	2.0

[a] Life expectancy figures in first two columns are for 1939–41 and 1949–51, respectively.
[b] Negroes only.

Source: Department of Health, Education, and Welfare.

population since 1955. By contrast, in a number of other industrial countries, death rates have fallen sharply during the past decade, and life expectancy at birth exceeds that in the United States by a significant margin—as much as 5 years among males. Infant mortality has declined little since 1955 and remains close to 25 per 1,000 live births, whereas it is substantially lower and falling more rapidly in many other developed countries. Changes since 1940 in selected health indicators are shown in Table 1.

Between 1910 and 1940, the death rate from influenza and pneumonia was reduced by 55 percent, and since 1940 it has been halved again. Maternal mortality has been cut by nearly 95 percent over the past half century and by 60 percent during the last 15 years. Since 1940, however, death rates from heart disease and cancer have each increased by one-fourth; the U.S. rate for heart disease is among the highest in the world. Mortality rates among males in the productive age bracket of 40 to 54 years are substantially and consistently higher in the United States than in other industrial countries and almost twice the rate in Sweden.

Foodborne diseases are being increasingly recognized as a leading cause of acute sickness in this country and probably account for more illness than all other environmental elements combined. Salmonellosis—the most serious such disease—now is much more widespread than it was 15 years ago because of inadequate controls in new methods of food production and processing. Further, almost one-third of the U.S. population is drinking water which is not assured of meeting minimal standards.

COST OF ILLNESS

The total cost to society of illness and premature death cannot be accurately measured, if for no other reason than our inability to quantify the value of human life or the cost of suffering, pain, and grief. It is impossible to say, on the basis of economic criteria alone, how much should be spent on health care, research and facilities. Nevertheless, at close to full employment of our resources—particularly of scientific and technical manpower—a decision to spend more for health implies spending less elsewhere. The issue facing the Nation is not whether better health is desirable, but how best to allocate resources within the health area and between health and all other competing uses.

Outlays for health are important in building and maintaining a productive labor force as well as in improving the lives of people and the quality of our society. The productivity of American workers could not have reached its present height if, in the past, there had not been investment in medical knowledge, in disease prevention, and in treatment and rehabilitation. Yet the potential return from further health investment remains large.

The annual expenditure on all health and medical care services in this country increased from $13 billion in 1950 and $27 billion in 1960 to approximately $40 billion last year. Such expenditures now amount to 5.9 percent of the gross national product (GNP). Private spending for personal health care—more than $26 billion last year—accounts for about 6.1 percent of personal consumption expenditures.

In 1963, disease and mortality during the year cost society the potential product of 4.6 million man-years of work. Direct public and private expenditures for personal health care associated with illnesses in that year amounted to about $22.5 billion, whereas the indirect costs from output lost totaled almost $24 billion. These figures make no allowance for the much larger losses in that year that were due to deaths occurring in earlier years or the present value of economic losses in future years resulting from current illness or death. Recent estimates of the direct and indirect costs associated with certain specific illnesses in 1963 are summarized in Table 2.

Table 2—Economic costs of illness, 1963[a]

Diagnostic category	Total costs	Direct expenditures[b]	INDIRECT COSTS[c]	
			Mortality[d]	Morbidity
Economic cost of illness: Total	46,303	22,530	2,731	21,042
Mental, psychoneurotic, and personality disorders	7,036	2,402	10	4,624
Diseases of circulatory system	6,413	2,267	1,226	2,920
Diseases of digestive system	5,502	4,158	123	1,220
Diseases of respiratory system	4,887	1,581	139	3,166
Injuries	3,755	1,703	242	1,811
Diseases of nervous system and sense organs	3,242	1,416	300	1,526
Neoplasms	2,614	1,279	484	851
Other	12,855	7,723	207	4,925

[a] In millions of dollars.
[b] Includes only hospital and nursing home care and services of physicians, dentists, nurses, and other health professionals associated with 19 major diagnostic categories; excludes drugs, medical research and facilities construction, training expenditures, and other nonpersonal health services.
[c] Equivalent to the value of lost output.
[d] Losses in 1963 due to deaths throughout that year; no allowance made for present discounted value of future losses.

Source: Department of Health, Education, and Welfare.

PUBLIC POLICY AND LEGISLATIVE ACCOMPLISHMENTS

The rapid growth of demand for medical services is a consequence of a multitude of factors, some of which are strongly influenced by public policy. Rising incomes, better education, urbanization, expanding insurance coverage, the changing age structure of the population, and the increased availability and effectiveness of health services are all raising demand. Supply has not kept pace with the expansion of demand, and at present the supply of most health services falls short of the Nation's needs as determined by reference to medical standards of adequacy. Deliberate public and private action—including new and more efficient forms of organization—are required to increase the supply and accessibility of these services. But to improve the health of our population, it is not enough to graduate more doctors or build more clinics. Programs are also required to translate medical needs into effective demand for health services. At the same time, there must be greater coordination between demand-creating policy measures and those aimed at improving the supply and distribution of medical services and facilities.

Average figures conceal large differences in the incidence of illness and the availability of medical services within the United States. The distribution of doctors, for example, continues to vary widely from region to region and between urban and rural communities. Some differences in the distribution of facilities and the utilization of health services are consistent with an efficient allocation of resources and varying personal consumption patterns. However, existing disparities in both the supply and effective demand seriously affect the relative availability and accessibility of health care throughout the country and among different income groups. Thus, high morbidity and mortality rates resulting from causes that have been successfully controlled in other groups still exist for nonwhites and the poor. Mortality rates among nonwhite infants more than 1 month old are almost three times as high as those for white infants. Poverty and its attendant circumstances are a major source of increased health hazards and, despite a popular desire to believe otherwise, low income is often a serious barrier to obtaining medical care. The 1960–62 National Health Survey found that the number of physician visits a year for children from families with annual incomes below $2,000 was only 40 percent of the number of children from high-income families.

The Administration's basic health goal, as stated by the President, is "to assure the availability of and accessibility to the best health care for all Americans, regardless of age or geography or economic status." To meet this goal, four types of effort are necessary: (1) expanding medical knowledge through increased basic research in the life sciences; (2) faster dissemination of new information and techniques to health practitioners, health policy-makers, and the public; (3) more and better organized health facilities and manpower, including research laboratories and medical schools, general hospitals and nursing homes, highly trained specialists and nursing aides; and (4) improved financing of medical services.

The first session of the 89th Congress passed a dozen major bills in the health field, designed to strengthen and improve health services in all four ways.

Medical Research Total medical and health-related research expenditures in 1965 amounted to almost $1.9 billion—nearly 9 percent of the Nation's outlay for all research and development. Expenditure on medical research was more than ten times that in 1950, representing an annual increase of almost 18 percent. Federal support rose from 45 percent to 64 percent of the total, but the Government's role in the direct conduct of such research declined slightly—from 22 percent to 17 percent. Public investment in health research is channeled mainly through the National Institutes of Health (NIH) whose budget for research, research facilities, and training has grown from less than $100 million 10 years ago to over $1 billion today. NIH support now accounts for two-fifths of all medical research expenditures in the United States.

Dissemination of Medical Knowledge   Our knowledge of life processes and of new methods of preventing and treating disease has rapidly moved ahead of our ability to apply this knowledge widely to the health needs of the Nation. Shortening the interval between the discovery and general application of medical advances is perhaps the single most important way to improve the productivity of the medical care industry.

Today, one cancer patient in three is being saved, but wider use of existing knowledge and techniques could save half the victims of this disease. More extensive use of new detection and diagnostic procedures and improved means of reaching and treating patients could reduce deaths from cervical cancer by 25 percent by 1970 and by 80 percent a decade from now. Instrumentation now in existence or being perfected could forestall many of the 400,000 strokes which occur each year.

To help close such gaps between knowledge and application, the Congress took a number of important steps in 1965. The Heart Disease, Cancer, and Stroke Amendments authorize support for a network of regional medical complexes. (The three diseases noted in the title of the Amendments account for 70 percent of all deaths in the United States.) The grants will assist hospitals, universities, and other institutions to establish cooperative programs for research, training, and demonstration. Such programs will bring new scientific advances more quickly to America's practicing physicians and their patients.

Medical Facilities and Manpower   A country's health standards change as income grows, knowledge accumulates, and concepts of adequacy evolve. Our current requirements for medical facilities and manpower reflect not only changes in the size and composition of the population and shifting patterns of disease and disability, but also a growing consensus that access to high-quality services is a right of all citizens.

Since passage of the Hill-Burton legislation in 1946, more than $7.7 billion, including a Federal share of $2.4 billion, has been invested through this program to provide additional hospital and nursing-home capacity of more than 340,000 beds. New general-hospital capacity is now being made available nationally at the rate of about 30,000 beds a year. Nevertheless, it is estimated that about one-third of the general-hospital capacity in the country is obsolete; a majority of the obsolete facilities are in metropolitan areas where two-thirds of the Nation's population live. Facilities containing 260,000 beds are in need of immediate modernization or replacement and those containing another 130,000 beds will require modernization before 1975. In dollar terms, current modernization needs of general hospitals have been estimated at more than $6 billion, compared with new general-hospital requirements of less than $1 billion. New financing techniques must be found to facilitate the modernization of hospitals, particularly in the large urban areas where deficiencies are now largest and where existing Federal programs have their smallest impact.

There are also large and rising needs for medical manpower. Part of this need is being met through organizational changes that raise the productivity of doctors, dentists, and nurses. For example, the development of group practice arrangements, the use of more elaborate (and more expensive) hospital and office equipment, reductions in travel time, and the employment of paramedical personnel to perform routine or less complicated procedures have made it possible for doctors to render more and better service to larger numbers of patients than ever before.

The ratio of physicians to the population of the United States has been approximately constant since before World War II. The proportion actually engaged in clinical practice—as opposed to teaching and research—has declined markedly, however. Despite measures to economize on the use of physicians' time, a substantial decline in their availability would impose strains on the cost and quality of medical services. To maintain the existing ratio of doctors to population, it would be necessary for admissions to medical schools to increase approximately 50 percent during the next decade. The Health Professions Educational Assistance Act of 1963 authorized a program of grants and loans in support of medical schools and students. In 1965, for the first time, Congress established a scholarship program for needy students in the health field, and added a four-year grant program for the improvement of teaching programs in the health professions.

Too frequently, today, the administration and organization of public health services are badly fragmented. Measures to stimulate better coordination of Federal, State, and local efforts in planning for and providing these services and the gradual replacement of prevailing categorical programs with comprehensive community health services would be desirable.

Financing Medical Care Private health insurance has made a major contribution to the better financing of health costs. The proportion of Americans with some form of private health insurance has risen from 9 percent in 1940 to 80 percent today. But gross benefits from such insurance covered only 25 percent of total expenditures for personal health needs in 1965. Furthermore, those most in need of assistance in meeting medical payments are frequently unable to buy insurance. Only about one-third of persons in families with annual incomes under $2,000, and about one-half of all elderly persons, were covered by any type of private hospital insurance in 1963. Yet these groups spend a particularly large fraction of their low incomes for health. In 1961, average medical expenses amounted to 10 percent for families with annual incomes between $1,000 and $2,000, compared with 4 percent for families with incomes between $10,000 and $15,000.

Among the most important actions of the 89th Congress was the provision of health insurance for the aged under Social Security. Medicare will protect families against the economic risk of major medical expenses in old age. Benefits for 17 million Social Security beneficiaries, plus benefits from general revenues for almost 2 million additional elderly persons not covered by Social Security, will amount to about $3.5 billion in 1967 and will cover at least 40 percent of the total medical costs of the aged. The basic program consists of hospital insurance, extended care, and home health services for the aged, financed through a separate trust fund supported by employee and employer payroll taxes. A voluntary, supplementary program covers physicians' fees and other services and is financed through monthly premiums (currently $3) by individuals over 65, which are matched equally by a general revenue contribution.

The legislation also greatly improved the quality and expanded the coverage of State medical assistance programs. The Kerr-Mills program for the aged was expanded to cover a total of about 8 million needy persons, including, for the first time, the blind, the disabled, and dependent children.

The 1965 Child Health amendments will make more health services available to expectant mothers, infants, and children, including crippled and retarded children. The progressive extension of crippled children's and child health services to youngsters throughout each State is required by 1975. Previously, these programs were aimed primarily at rural areas, but in the future they will provide equal assistance for low-income families in urban centers. Family planning services will also be strengthened.

Equality of Opportunity

Not all groups of Americans share equally in their country's prosperity. In 1964, the average income of nonwhite families was only 56 percent of the average income of white families. This and similar figures provide telling indicators of the task that the Nation still faces in assuring equality of opportunity and achievement for all its citizens (Table 3). They also indicate an incredible waste of our human resources.

Three important and distinct types of discrimination help to explain the difference between white and nonwhite incomes.

Discrimination results in lower wages for Negroes (who comprise 90 percent of the nonwhite group) even when they are doing the same kind of work as whites. Available data show that Negroes receive less income in every industry, in every occupation, and at every level of education.

Table 3—Selected measures of discrimination and inequality of opportunity, 1965

Selected measure	White	Nonwhite
Income[a]		
Median income of families	$6,858	$3,839
Percent of households in poverty[b]	17.1	43.1
Percent of families with incomes of $10,000 or more	24.1	8.3
Education		
Median years of school completed, males 25 years of age and over	12.0	9.0
Percent completed high school, persons 20–24 years of age	76.3	50.2
Male	75.6	51.3
Female	77.0	49.4
Percent college graduates, persons 25 years of age and over	9.9	5.5
Labor force participation rate (percent of noninstitutional population)[c]		
Male	78.6	76.0
Female	37.0	46.1
Employment (percent of total civilian employment)[c]		
White-collar occupations	47.5	19.5
Craftsmen-foremen occupations	13.5	6.7
Unemployment rate (percent of civilian labor force)[c]		
Adult males	2.9	6.0
Adult females	4.0	7.4
Teenagers	12.2	25.3

[a] Data relate to 1964.
[b] Households are defined here as the total of families and unrelated individuals.
[c] Relates to persons 14 years of age and over.

Sources: Department of Commerce, Department of Health, Education, and Welfare, and Department of Labor.

Discrimination also excludes many Negroes from higher-paying jobs that would fully utilize their talents or training. Negroes are frequently forced to hold jobs that whites with the same experience and training would not ordinarily hold; and Negroes suffer from higher unemployment rates within all skill categories.

Finally, part of the income difference is explained by past discrimination which has lowered the potential productivity of Negroes by providing less investment in human resources for them than for their white contemporaries. This type of discrimination is manifested by lower expenditures for schools and health facilities in Negro neighborhoods.

Low family incomes are a product of these factors; but low incomes would tend to perpetuate these factors even if discrimination were eliminated. Low incomes for poor whites also result in lesser educational achievement, poorer health, fewer skills, and consequently higher unemployment. To promote real equality, Negroes must break through the barrier of discrimination; but this will not be sufficient. They must also break out of the cycle of poverty.

PROSPERITY: A CONDITION FOR NEGRO PROGRESS

A combination of social and economic change is necessary to correct the disparities between Negroes and whites. But prosperity is also an essential requirement because it creates and opens up jobs for the disadvantaged. This has been effectively demonstrated by postwar experience.

During the period of slow economic growth in the middle and late 1950's, the absolute gap between Negro and white incomes and employment widened. In 1952, the median income of nonwhite families was 57 percent of the median income of white families, and the unemployment rate for nonwhites was 4.6 percent, compared with a rate of 2.4 percent for whites. By 1958, the median income of nonwhite families had fallen to 51 percent of that of white families, and the unemployment rate of nonwhites had risen to 12.6 percent, compared with 6.0 percent for whites.

In 1964, a high-growth year, the median income of white families increased 4.7 percent over 1963, and that of nonwhites, 10.8 percent; the income gap narrowed in both percentage and absolute terms as income of nonwhites rose by $374 and that of whites by $310. As a result, the median income of nonwhites rose from 53 percent of the median income of whites in 1963 to 56 percent in 1964. The gains in median incomes were representative of increases throughout the income scale. In 1964, the proportion of nonwhite families with incomes of more than $10,000 rose from 5.7 percent to 8.3 percent, but it was still far below the figure of 24.1 percent for white families. The proportion with less than $3,000 dropped from 43.1 percent to 37.3 percent. Final data for 1965 will not be available for several months, but preliminary indications suggest that incomes of Negroes again rose substantially.

The progress of the last two years confirms a crucial lesson. A prosperous economy and the labor demand that it generates are potent forces for eliminating discriminations and income differentials even though they cannot create equality. Improved Negro purchasing power will not fully overcome the effects of discrimination, but it will have a beneficial influence.

CIVIL RIGHTS LAWS AND ECONOMIC DISCRIMINATION

The 1964 Civil Rights Act contains several important provisions that alter those conditions which make discrimination possible. Its Title VII directly outlaws discrimination in hiring, firing, conditions of work, apprenticeship, or training. The Equal Employment Opportunity Commission was established to carry out these provisions. The Commission began operation in

July 1965 and in its first 100 days processed more than 1,300 complaints. Hiring attitudes will not change abruptly, but the Civil Rights Act makes an important, direct attack on this basic barrier to full equality.

Negroes are also at a disadvantage in the housing market. Many Negroes live in substandard housing because their incomes are low; but others are forced to do so by direct discrimination. While 57 percent of nonwhite households with annual incomes of less than $4,000 live in substandard housing, only 27 percent of whites at these same income levels live in such housing. Among households with more than $4,000 a year, 6 percent of the white families live in substandard housing, compared with 20 percent for nonwhite families. Discrimination in housing forces Negroes to pay higher rents and in many places to attend inferior schools. The President has announced that he will ask for legislation to prevent discrimination in private sales or rental of housing.

To help Negroes achieve equality of educational opportunity, the Civil Rights Act authorizes the Attorney General to file suit for the desegregation of public schools and colleges upon receipt of written complaints from parents unable to bring their own actions. After 10 years of slow progress following the Supreme Court decision outlawing segregated schools, the pace of integration has now accelerated; but segregated housing continues to retard this process. In addition to eliminating segregation, the Government is trying to improve the quality of Negro education by its new programs for primary and secondary education, Project Head Start, and other anti-poverty programs. Also, Title VI of the Civil Rights Act assures that access to schools, hospitals, and other federally aided facilities will not be denied to anyone on the basis of his race.

ECONOMIC COST OF DISCRIMINATION

Although economic losses are not the major reason for eliminating discrimination, they serve to emphasize its economic cost to all Americans. When there is a surplus of labor of all types and skills, eliminating discrimination results mainly in a redistribution of income. The economic cost of discrimination becomes most evident when there is near full employment of the white labor force.

If economic and social policies could be specifically designed to lower Negro unemployment to the current unemployment level of whites, the resulting gain in GNP would be $5 billion. Part of this gain would be in wages of the new Negro employees, and part would accrue as other forms of income. A further gain would result if all Negroes were able to obtain jobs which would better utilize their abilities and training.

National output can be further expanded by improving the average level of productivity of each individual. Education and training are two of the most important means to this end. If the average productivity of the Negro and white labor force were equalized at the white level, total production would expand by $22 billion. If both unemployment rates and productivity levels were equalized, the total output of the economy would rise by about $27 billion—4 percent of GNP. This is a measure of the annual economic loss as a result of discrimination. Of course, to achieve this increase in output, some resources would have to be devoted to investment in the human capital of America's Negro citizens. But this would be an investment yielding important economic as well as social returns for the entire Nation. . . .

3

Education, Research and Other Unidentified Factors in Growth

Economic growth is a complex process that involves much more than physical capital formation alone. Ingvar Svennilson describes how education, human skills, innovative knowledge, and human resource mobility are factors in the economic growth of nations and the welfare of a citizenry. If these are growth ingredients, as suggested by

INGVAR SVENNILSON

Professor Svennilson of the Institute for International Economic Studies (Stockholm), then economic development and planning must take cognizance of such factors, even in the "market" economies where planning is a less relied upon procedure.

I Trends in Theory and Their Relation to Economic Policy

The assumption *ceteris paribus* is, indeed, a necessary prerequisite for any theory that aims at explaining certain specific characteristics of an economic system. Without this assumption the theoretical tools cannot be sharpened. Without it, economics deteriorates to a descriptive or institutional science incapable of explaining economic development.

The *ceteris* has, however, to be chosen according to the type of economic phenomenon we want to explain. The main body of economic theory has

Reprinted from Ingvar Svennilson, "Education, Research and Other Unidentified Factors in Growth," *The Economics of Education*, Proceedings of the International Economic Association (New York: St. Martin's Press, 1966), pp. 71–85, with permission of the author and publisher.

been designed to explain short-term variations. Interest has, then, been concentrated on variations in quantities such as demand for, and supply of, factors and products, and their relation to income and prices. In the short term, the social and technological framework within which such variations take place can as a first approximation be assumed to be unchanged; as a consequence, the quantity-price-income relations can be assumed to be stable. A next step in the analysis will be to let quantity-price-income relations shift, regarding these shifts as the result of *exogenous* factors which are kept outside the theoretical model.

However, it has often turned out that the *ceteris paribus* cannot be maintained without abstracting from obvious causal relationships between the variables of the theoretical models and shifts in their inter-relations. The *ceteris paribus* has, then, to be reduced in scope. A classical example is the development of Keynesian theory. In his *General Theory* Keynes did not take into account the fact that investment, as a result of capital accumulation, leads to a shift of supply functions. This fact was taken as a starting-point for the extension of the Keynesian theory along the Harrod-Domar line. A more general expression of such a development of economic theory is that functions expressing economic relationships are found *not to be reversible*. As a result of a movement along such a function, the conditions contained in the *ceteris paribus* assumption change in such a way that we will not turn back to the point from which we started. Once this fact has been recognized, we have evidently embarked on a theory of processes over time, perhaps resulting in growth, where a number of exogenous conditions are integrated into the analysis. Even such dynamic theories have, however, their *ceteris paribus*.

There is, on the other hand, also a long tradition of analysis that has broken away from the classical delimitation of economic variables and has taken as a starting-point for the analysis processes within the *ceteris paribus* field. This tradition is marked by such names as Adam Smith, Malthus, Marx, Veblen, Max Weber and Schumpeter. They have formulated theories of social and institutional transformation as an integrated part of processes of economic development. Along this line, research has developed based on historical and sociological methods. It has dealt with problems of the social and institutional conditions for invention and innovation, entrepreneurship and market domination, supply of labor, education, consumption and savings, flows of capital, etc. This type of research has been stimulated by the new interest in speeding up of the transition from under-development to more developed conditions in the poor parts of the world. It has become evident that in these countries a condition for development has been a policy concerned with broad changes of the social and institutional framework within which economic policy in a narrower sense may be evolved.

This diversity of trends in research and doctrine poses problems both for theory and for policy in the field of growth.

For social science there arises a problem of integration versus disintegration of theory. It has to be accepted that various aspects of a process of growth have to be studied with different methodological instruments. Some can be attacked by developing the tools of economic analysis in the traditional sense, leaving a wide field of other factors as a *terra incognita*. Other aspects of a process of growth have to be studied by using sociological, psychological or political science methods. At the same time, the results of these various types of research must be related to each other. The need for integration of the various social sciences is today stronger than ever before. This integration has to be reflected in the organization of social science studies at our universities. The isolation of economics, tending toward econometrics, from other social sciences that often exists has as far as possible to be broken, even if for obvious reasons a certain degree of specialization must remain.

From the point of view of economics, an integration will mean that "other factors" will have to be given a place as inter-related variables in economic models. The integration may even have to go deeper. The very concepts of economic analysis, which reflect the institutional conditions of a given society at a given time, must be adjusted to changing social conditions. As an example, it may be mentioned that a study of under-developed countries may lead to new conceptual ideas of employment and under-employment. As another example, labor input may have to be broken up into various new elements.

Such an integration and an adjustment of economic theory to new research about exogenous factors is strongly needed from a policy point of view. The formulation of economic theory may be regarded as expressing a bias as regards essentials in a process of growth. In any case, it may intentionally or unintentionally convey false ideas about the relevant parameters of action for development policy. Economists have to confess that their formulation of growth theory has not always been adequate for solving the policy problems of under-developed countries. Methods of national accounting have been uncritically applied. Economists may also be partly responsible for the fact that the shift of emphasis in development policy from the volume of investment toward various types of social and institutional change has come about so late. A growth policy that is well balanced must be supported by economics that are conceptually adjusted to the actual social and institutional conditions and that have as far as possible integrated factors which have traditionally been regarded as exogenous.

A central notion in any theory of growth must evidently be *productivity*. I shall in the following pages concentrate attention on the problem of how various social phenomena might be related to productivity trends. The traditional theory of production relates output to the input of capital and labor, assuming a given supply of land and a given state of—or exogenously determined change in—technical knowledge. It assumes that at a given input of capital and labor, the most productive methods of production known are applied. On this basis, econometric studies of past historical growth have been made, separating the contribution of labor, capital and technical change. The results of such studies have formed the basis for forecasts and planning.

Modern development of economics is to a large extent oriented toward penetrating behind the façade of this rather simple theory. The efforts are concerned with the forces behind technical change and in this process the highly aggregated concepts of "capital" and "labor" tend to be dissolved. The field of study is so rich that I shall only try in a very general way to indicate some of the aspects that seem to be of special importance.

II Education

One of the trends in modern society is the expansion of formal education as an institution separated from the production process itself. Education in this form may, to a varying extent, serve several purposes, all of which from a general development point of view may be highly important. Education may be regarded as an *investment* in a productive agent. There are, however, also *consumption* aspects of education: it makes a direct contribution to the standard of living and creates a lasting consumption asset. The consumption effect and the production effect of education may be regarded as *complementary* from the point of view of the social values that form the basis for our conception of growth in a wide sense. The increased production of goods and services, made possible through the productive effects of education, may in the future assume a greater value, according to prevalent scales of preferences, to the extent that it will be combined with a better education of the population as consumers. The relative weight attributed to the consumption and the production effect of education may be expected to vary betweeen poorer and richer countries and will be reflected in the content of education. Starving countries would be expected to spend relatively more on education for production, while countries approaching affluence, at the same time increasing leisure time, would be expected to spend more on education for consumption.

This character of a *joint production* with varying emphasis on "wool" and "meat" (to draw a parallel with the classical textbook case) makes it questionable whether any close correlation can be found between the aggregate amount of education—measured by the investment cost or the number of student-years embodied in the labor force—and the growth of production. In studying the productive effects of education we evidently must choose a more differentiated approach. We have to distinguish between systems of education, methods of education, curricula and levels. There are also inventions and innovations in the field of education, which may increase the efficiency of the investment in education, including the cost of spending more years in the classroom.

The economics of education is emerging as a science in its own right, corresponding to the study of other types of production. It is still in an early experimental stage. There are problems of measurement which are unsolved, and knowledge about the production function is still rudimentary. It would, therefore, be premature to try to integrate the education industry into aggregated economic growth models, even if it is evident how in principle this could be done.

A general outline of the economic problems of education can be indicated in terms well known from the theory of real capital investment. The *gestation period* for the individual finished product of education is long. It can be varied within wide limits, and one main problem, from the point of view of growth, is how far to prolong education with regard to its marginal effect on production. As in the case of land, the fertility of the human raw material is widely scattered. As regards the enrollment rates in higher education the law of declining marginal return will, therefore, sooner or later appear on the stage. As a result of imperfections in the social selection system, students are, however, not enrolled in an order corresponding to that of land in the textbooks. A democratization of the selection process may postpone the advent of declining marginal return.

The length of education, as well as the choice of the types of education, has to be economically adjusted to the pattern of future production of the country concerned, whether under-developed or highly developed. The choice is complicated by the fact that labor with different types and levels of education is in a position of *complementarity from a production point of view*. Too many lawyers in an otherwise under-developed environment will yield a low, or even negative, marginal return. The number of university engineers must be balanced against the number of lower level technicians. The marginal return of increasing the engineer density of the population may decline beyond a certain point, at least if we extend the concept of growth beyond what is included in national accounts as production. We should not presume that, under all circumstances, the marginal return of higher education in art, humanities and social sciences is necessarily lower than that of education in science and technology.

The difficulty of making an adequate investment decision in the field of education is immensely increased by the fact that this is a very *long-term investment* which affects production several decades ahead. There are uncertainties not only about rates and directions of growth and about technological trends that determine the demand for, and the productivity of, labor with various types and levels of education. Even if we disregard uncertainty, we cannot take the future economic development for granted and adjust education to it. Education will evidently have an effect on the overall rate of growth. In this respect, there is a parallel with decisions about the rate of real capital investment. Decisions about investment in education must be related to prevailing preferences as regards the time-flow of production and consumption. This relation is complicated by the fact that the possibilities of replacing special types of education by other factors of production are often strictly limited. A condition of perfect, or almost perfect, complementarity often exists which creates *bottleneck* problems as regards various types of educated skills, specialized workers, teachers, doctors, architects, chemists, mathematicians, etc. In so far as growth must be balanced between sectors of the economy, the balance of education as regards specialization and levels will, therefore, determine the future growth that is made possible. There will be no chemical industry, if chemical engineers are not available. Supply will to a large extent determine future effective demand.

In one important respect, the human character of educational capital, as distinct from that of real capital, creates a special problem for analysis and policy. By educating students, we may create people better able to invent and innovate in the field of technology, political life, organization and culture. This will affect the trend of technology and production in a way that is unique, when compared with investment in other factors. In econometric studies, various shares of overall growth have been imputed to the volume of capital and labor, leaving an unexplained technological trend as a residual factor. In some studies, the rise in the average level of education of labor has been added as another factor that explains a (comparatively small) share of overall growth. This analysis, however, overlooks the fact that technological trends may largely be explained by qualities in the population that are related to education. This effect will not be brought out by a correlation analysis based on broad aggregates; it is closely linked to comparatively small groups within the population engaged in the pursuit of research, invention and innovation. Even if the results within this field are largely of a stochastic nature—the view of a great son of Vienna, Joseph Schumpeter—their systematic relation to education in society of today cannot be overlooked.

There are good reasons to stick to the traditional pattern of economic thinking and regard education as *another factor* in economic growth. Policy should be balanced as regards allocation of resources between investment in education and real capital. They can to some extent be substituted for each other and thus compete for available resources. We must also take into account that they are, to some degree, complementary from a production point of view. Increased education will increase the marginal productivity of real capital, and vice versa. The bottleneck position of some types of education, especially of higher education, and its far-reaching effects on the social and technical transformation of society, give it, however, a special place in analysis, policy and planning directed towards growth.

In this connection we have to take into account that economic growth is inseparably dependent on a transformation of society as regards technology, sectoral structure, location of industry and population, social services including education and the general cultural, social and political environment of the population. This complex transformation must be systematically prepared and planned, and plans have to be transferred from drawing boards, offices and committees into operation. The capacity to perform this transformation within a limited period of time and to do it in an effective way depends on the supply of various types of highly educated professionals. The demand for such people is, thus, only partly related to the *level* of development that is reached at any point of time but partly also to the *rate of growth* that is desired. A rate of growth of 6 per cent a year will demand a larger number of administrators, educationalists, scientists, engineers and architects, than a rate of growth of, say, 3 per cent a year. Countries which try to accelerate their growth often find this sector—and not the rate of real capital investment—to be *the* bottleneck. New plans for industry, public services including education, urban and rural development, are too slow to develop. To the economist, this phenomenon can be described in terms of the familiar *acceleration principle*.

From these considerations follows the conclusion—self-evident but often overlooked—that the evolution of education cannot be determined as a demand derived from an independent forecast of production. Educational policy and planning should be regarded as an integral part of development planning, the scope and direction being determined by the rate of growth, the kind of growth and the kind of society in general that we want to see in the future.

These are long-term considerations. In the *medium-long-term* other problems arise, which call for a *strategy* for the more near future. The root of these problems is the length of the gestation period for the formation of educational capital. A prolongation of studies not only delays the entry of students into industry. Higher education is to a large extent the education of teachers, or even of teachers for teachers. An expansion of the educational system makes it necessary to divert an increased number of graduates from research and employment in industry to teaching. This *feed-back* may, over a number of years, seriously reduce the output from the educational system, especially on its narrow peak—the doctoral level. On the other hand, the supply of people to research and industry will grow faster in the long run. A problem, then, arises of the *timing* of economic expansion. The growth in the next decade has to be weighed against more long-term growth. The choice will partly depend on the teacher/student (the capital/output) ratio of the educational system at various levels—thus, on its internal efficiency. It would be an important task for economists to explore the logistics of such processes over time as a basis for growth policy.

III Knowledge, Skill and Innovation

Formal education should be regarded as one link of an integrated system of *generating and transferring knowledge*. Other links are *research* institutions and the *production system (industry)* itself. A many-faced system of *documentation* functions as an intermediary:

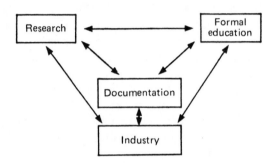

In modern society, this is a highly diversified and complicated system. On its efficiency depends the progress of technical knowledge and its application. One of the main innovations in modern society is that the functioning of this system is not regarded in a *laissez-aller* fashion. It is an object for policy. We may invest in its various parts so as to speed up the rate of economic growth.

The efficiency of this system can be formulated in terms of the relation between input of resources and output in the form of production of goods and services. One would not, however, expect easily to arrive at a measurement of the yield of various types of investment in this field. This, for several reasons. First, the process within each sector is of a complicated cumulative nature. Second, there are complicated circular chains of interaction between the various sectors of the system—research, education and industry. Third, it is not only in the sector of formal education that the gestation period may be long; the effects on production may also be scattered over a long period. Fourth, the relation between input and output is stochastic, especially in the case of research and industrial innovation. Research in this field has, in any case, to begin with partial studies of the behaviour of the system. A vast literature on such problems has grown up in late years.

I shall here restrict myself to a few observations, which seem to be relevant from a policy point of view.

THE FUNCTIONAL INTEGRATION OF THE SYSTEM

In reality, research, education and industry are not entirely organized as separate institutions with different specialized functions; they merge into each other. Higher education is, or should be, integrated with research. Research may be conducted within industrial units. The distinction between basic and applied research is tending to disappear as industrial production becomes more scientific. On the other hand, the development of processes and products cannot be sharply distinguished from research. Formal education is combined with training in production. Education may take place in built-in units within industry, and production itself may be regarded as a learning process, which may be speeded up by systematic education.

Innovations in the organization of this system may accelerate economic growth. Research may become better integrated with industrial activities, education with research and industry with education.

INNOVATIONS AND THE LEARNING PROCESS

Innovations may be defined as shifts in the production function, resulting in increased productivity. A well-known description of the process of innovation has been the following. The inventor and the scientist create inventions that accumulate into a pool of technical knowledge. The entrepreneur-innovator creates a new combination of such technical elements, profitably adjusted to the current market conditions. In such a process there may be considerable time-lags, perhaps of several decades, between an invention and its application. In the end, the industrial innovator adds to technical knowledge, which is usually assumed to be available to anybody. It will sooner or later be imitated by other enterprises.

This description of a process of invention and innovation must be modified in various respects in order to arrive at a more realistic interpretation of its characteristics.

First, it overlooks the tendency toward *integration of research and industry*. Those engaged in research and development work, whether inside or outside industry, may today be regarded as partners in innovating activities. Innovations are often not spontaneous but planned, with the expectation that research will provide the necessary inventions. In this way, the time-lags in the invention-innovation process may be reduced to zero, and as a result technological progress may accelerate.

Second, the earlier treatment of innovations naturally tended to emphasize the rôle of the big, striking innovations that historically dominated cycles of growth. The diversification of industrial technology in highly developed industrial systems makes it less likely that any single innovation will dominate an overall process growth. Various studies also have shown that innovations in the form of the gradual improvement of earlier innovations play an important rôle. It would also be misleading to reserve the term "innovation" for the activities of top management and research. Labor all along the line may improve methods of operation or the quality of products. On all levels, a *learning process* may develop that gradually increases efficiency. In some special cases, it has been possible to study the course of such learning processes. The improvement in efficiency, which takes place in this way, may only partly be described as the result of increased technical knowledge, in part it takes the form of growing skill acquired by repeated experience and training. An important aspect of the efficiency problem is how to speed up this learning process. It can be achieved through systematic organizational studies such as motion studies. It also depends on systems of incentives for all participants in industrial operations, and not only on profit incentives.

It is an open question how much weight in overall growth should be attributed to large discontinuous innovations and how much to the broad and more continuous stream of small innovations. The latter type of innovation may very well carry greater weight.

Third, the linking of research to industrial innovations and the broad stream of innovation poses special problems for the *transfer of technology* between various parts of the economic system. Technical knowledge and skill become, to a large extent, invested in the individual industrial unit and in its labor force. It forms what may be labelled its *know-how*. The transfer of this know-how to other units may be restricted in various ways. First, only part of this know-how can be documented as knowledge. Some of this knowledge may be freely available; other parts may be subject to patent and licensing, while other parts may, at least transitionally, be kept secret and only slowly leak out. Many details of knowledge as well as the skill acquired can only be transferred by instruction and training, the transfer will, then, depend on such conditions as the willingness of firms to receive apprentices and on the movement of personnel to other firms.

Other types of institutions may serve as intermediaries, transferring know-how from one producing unit to another. Professional societies, independent research institutes or educational institutions may serve this purpose. Firms delivering machinery may advise their customers how to use it, drawing on experiences from various enterprises. A growing importance as a transfer medium may be attributed to independent consulting firms who serve various clients.

The transfer of knowledge and skill is thus a very complicated process. If restrictions to transfer were reduced, innovations would be more easily spread, and the progress of technological standards would be accelerated. The problem is evidently one of economic organization. Restrictions to transfer form an element in the game of a competitive system; a delay in transfer will increase the profit of the progressive firm and will stimulate its efforts to keep abreast of competitors. This stimulus to innovation must, however, be balanced against losses due to slow transfer.

These transfer problems also have an international aspect. Owing to various forms of national integration, technical knowledge and skill may more easily be disseminated within a country than across national frontiers. It is part of the external economics of national industries that they may reach different levels of knowledge and skill in different countries. These conditions form the background of the difficulties encountered in technical assistance from more developed to less developed countries. Other difficulties are the lack of education in the receiving countries and the lack of experience in adjusting technology to the conditions of less developed countries. One conclusion that can be drawn from an analysis of the nature of the transfer problem is that an effective international technical assistance has to take into account the knowledge and skill that has been accumulated within industrial units. The knowledge-skill that exists in the producing units is spread among their employees who complement each other in team activities. Individual experts are, therefore, much less effective than teams representing an integrated enterprise. The team method is used when industrial firms establish subsidiaries in other markets. The team can transfer the knowledge-skill of the mother firm to the new unit by planning, organization, information, demonstration and training. The success of such operations indicates a method for technical assistance that, with advantage, could be used also in cases when the technical assistance is divorced from investment and ownership.

It has been said that "ideas know no frontiers." To the extent that this applies to technology, the need for organizing an international market would be no greater than in the case of the winds that blow across seas and continents. This picture does, however, only to a limited extent correspond to reality. The process of transfer is complicated, and the market structure is far from perfect. One of the main problems in the field of growth is to improve international marketing of knowledge and skill in order to reduce the disadvantages of less developed countries.

IV   Mobility of Resources

The case of knowledge and skill is just one example of the general rule that growth can be accelerated by increasing the mobility of factors of production.

Capital equipment is to a high degree fixed as regards location and technical design. The mobility of capital is, therefore, mainly dependent on replacement. The durability of capital equipment is mainly responsible for the rigidity of a production system that has once been established, partly so for sound economic reasons. There are, however, imperfections in the replacement process that reduce the rate of growth and that may be overcome by a more adequate economic policy. One may mention the fiscal rules for depreciation allowances which may affect the replacement policy of firms. Probably more important, however, is a public policy that aims at reducing features in the market restricting competition within national and international markets. Actually, the most important effect of a policy aiming at reducing monopolistic elements and Government protection of trade or producers may not be that it reduces profits but that it reduces the cost of production by speeding up the transformation process.

The inertia in the transformation process is, however, also linked to the restricted *mobility of labor*, locally and occupationally. Obsolete capital and industries may be kept running for a long period because immobile labor has to accept lower wages than those of other industries. Such obstacles to transformation may partly be overcome by minimum wage laws or by inter-industry solidarity in the wage-bargaining of centralized trade-union systems. But the effect of such policies may only be that low-wage employment is exchanged for unemployment in depressed areas or industries.

One of the main innovations of economic policy after the Keynesian revolution is the initiation of a new labor-market policy aiming towards increasing mobility of labor between occupations and geographical areas. The new policy requires that society be prepared to cover the cost of re-education and re-training, the loss of income during this period and the cost of travel and resettlement of families. Labor mobility was earlier largely regarded as an exogenous factor outside the influence of economic policy. The new labor-market policy (as it now is formulated for example in Sweden) is based on the estimate that from the point of view of society as a whole it is profitable in terms of growth to invest a considerable part of the GNP in transfer of labor between areas and occupations. The short-term gains corresponding to differentials in productivity may be large; even larger gains may accrue in the long run as a result of a more rapid development of growth industries.

This new deal in labor-market policy links up with the Keynesian full-employment policy in another important respect that is relevant from the point of view of growth. The employment policy may stop short of full employment because bottlenecks are reached in some industries before other industries have become fully employed. Inflationary tendencies, partly emanating from the wage level, may, if the general level of employment is raised further, appear in the bottleneck industries and spread to the entire economic system. The new labor market policy may help to remove this obstacle to full employment, break the bottlenecks by increasing mobility of labor and, thus, establish a more even front of full employment in all industries. The short-term gain may amount to only a small per cent of the GNP. But, again, forces of growth may be released in industries which, otherwise, would tend towards technological stagnation because of a low level of employment. The out-flow of labor from these industries would force them to modernize their structure, including their capital structure.

V Planning

A common denominator for the factors of growth that have been discussed above is that their growth effects may extend over a long future period and that policy, consequently, must be adjusted to the *long-term development* of the economy. Immediate action in the field of education, research, innovation and allocation of capital and labor must be oriented so as to agree with the long-term transformation and growth of the economy. Mobility of factors is not enough ; equally important is in which *direction* they move. A good adjustment in these respects will diminish the risk of mistakes in investment, smooth the path of transformation and, consequently, make a contribution to the rate of growth. A development of the *technique* of long-term forecasting and planning thus forms an important element of growth policy.

In highly centralized economies of the Soviet type, forecasting may be identified with planning by the central Government. Even in such cases, however, there is a considerable scope for independent decisions of individual citizens, and uncertainties exist about new technology and developments abroad. Long-term plans may, therefore, serve as targets, but the possibility of future revisions of the plans must reasonably be anticipated at the outset.

In decentralized *market economies* the element of uncertainty is for several reasons more predominant. The development of industry and the innovating activities are ultimately dependent on private decisions. As a rule foreign trade has a bigger share, and its development depends on economic trends abroad. In *mixed economies*, Government provides the infra-structure for private activities. These are also influenced—although in a way that is difficult to forecast—by Government policy in the field of public finance, central banking, labor market and foreign trade. Any projection of future trends must, therefore, be based on a combination of Government plans for action and forecasts of private reactions to this policy. Uncertainties speak for *flexibility* in planning. Plans must be subject to *rolling adjustment*, as new experience is gained, and plans for the near future may be envisaged as a first step in a more long-term *policy strategy*, including alternative lines for action corresponding to alternatives of development in the market.

At the same time, there is also in a mixed economy a need to indicate some *broad targets* for long-term growth. These may, even if provisional, serve as a guide for the planning by various private and public units within sectors of the economy. There are advantages in a decentralization of planning activities which also have been recognized in the Soviet system. A combination of full-employment policies with national planning and forecasting will, in the first place, *induce* firms and sectors, private and public, to take a longer view. A national system of planning and forecasting may also provide information to each unit within an economy about plans and trends in its other parts. It may, finally, become an instrument for coordinating sector plans by giving them a direction consistent with overall targets and trends.

One of the main innovations in the field of growth policy after the last world war has been the development of long-term planning activities in the market economies of countries such as France, Japan and Sweden. This innovation is being spread to other countries of a similar type. An expression of this tendency is the recent OECD declaration that member countries should aim, as a collective target, at a 50 per cent increase of their production in the 1960 decade. To the extent that this target generally is followed by action, a firmer basis has been created for planning and expansion in each country separately. This development opens fascinating perspectives for a more general coordination of planning activities in various parts of the world.

Part Two

Human Capital and

Economic Growth

Growth in output (Q) of contemporary economies is most simply specified as a function of growth in the stocks of factor inputs, usually represented as labor (L) and capital (K), plus an unknown residual or error term (R):

$$Q = f(L, K, R).$$

Unfortunately, economists have had partial success in empirically explaining Q, largely because the interdependent factor input variables (L and K) usually fail to account for even as much as $.5Q$, depending upon the nation and time period one studies. The unknown R, then, represents a "residual of ignorance"—sometimes given the perhaps more palatable but still unsatisfactory label of "productivity or technological change."

Each of the authors of the five selections contained in this section is interested in leaving less of the explanation of Q to the residual—a feat tackled empirically by Theodore W. Schultz **4** and Edward F. Denison **5** and examined in a theoretical context by Robert M. Solow **6**, Richard R. Nelson and Edmund S. Phelps **7**, and Earl R. Brubaker **8**. Although their analytical tactics and assumptions vary somewhat, there is a theme common to their affair with the unknown. Input quality such as advances in knowledge and education (human capital formation) is felt to be buried in R. Among the more important problems encountered in analyses such as these are the unknown character of factor interdependencies and substitution, the impact of sociological and cultural forces on the growth process, the interaction of technology with human and physical capital, the quantitative changes in explanatory variables, and the appropriate weights to assign to individually identified inputs.

Rise in the Capital Stock Represented by Education in the United States, 1900–1957

A major source of investment in human capital consists of direct and indirect education costs. Theodore W. Schultz, Professor of Economics at the University of Chicago, argues that the stock of human capital formed by investment in education must be dealt with in a measurable way because of its significance to economic growth. Measurement of the stock of education embodied in the population and labor force can be approximated by estimating the real-cost of a year of schooling that

THEODORE W. SCHULTZ

includes income foregone as well as direct educational costs. Based upon Schultz's real-cost measure, the stock of education embodied in the labor force increased twice as fast from 1900 to 1957 as did the stock of physical capital. Schultz concludes this paper, which is a summary of his extensive work in the area, by noting several limitations to his analysis.

Investment in human capital is a distinctive and important feature of the economy.[1] People invest in themselves, and these investments have become large, and knowledge about the human capital that is thus formed is

Reprinted from Theodore W. Schultz, "Rise in the Capital Stock Represented by Education in the United States, 1900–57," in Selma J. Mushkin, ed., *Economics of Higher Education* (Washington, D.C.: United States Government Printing Office, 1962), pp. 93–101, with the permission of the author. Based on Professor Schultz's essay, "Education and Economic Growth," in the National Society for the Study of Education 60th Yearbook.

[1] Theodore W. Schultz, Investment in Human Capital. *American Economic Review*, 51: 1–17, March 1961.

fundamental to an understanding of economic growth. A major source of
this human capital is education.

To look upon education as an activity that develops human capital is
not to disparage its cultural purposes,[2] but among its other contributions are
knowledge and skills that are useful in economic endeavor. Economic
progress is greatly dependent upon these contributions. Surely the most
universal limiting factor in achieving economic growth is ignorance. For
attaining an optimum rate of such growth, investment in skills and knowledge is essential.[3]

Education has various measurable dimensions, which differ depending
upon the purpose of the measurement. School attendance is one such;
others are the years of schooling completed and the number of students
finishing elementary school, high school, and college. The real cost of
entering into education is still another way of measuring education.[4] It is
indeed meaningful to treat education as something that is measurable.

Economists make much of the distinction between *flows* and *stocks*.
Investment is a flow; plants and equipment are stocks. Land is a stock; the
productive service that it renders is a flow, and so is rent. The size, composition, and capabilities of the labor force represent a stock; the work that is
done in an hour or a week is, on the other hand, a flow, and so are wages
and salaries. Inputs, whether they are the results of the efforts of man or the
contributions made by material things, are all flow concepts. The natural
endowment (land); reproducible physical capital (plant, equipment, and
inventories); and the labor force (workers) are all stock concepts.

The connections between additions to the stock of capital as a store of
wealth and the corresponding additions to output capacity are very
intricate.[5] Things that differ only with respect to durability may represent
different stocks of value, although their annual output capacity is the same.
Consider two engineers who are equally capable and who do the same
amount of engineering work during a particular year. Their respective
contributions as engineers during that year are the same, although the two
may be very different when viewed as a stock of engineering capabilities
because one of them may be a young man just starting his career and with a
long productive life ahead of him, and the other an old man doing his last

[2] It is necessary to underscore this point because of the widespread apprehensions that
arise whenever economic analysis is brought to bear on education. I have gone to much
trouble to take account of these apprehensions, as may be seen in my "Investment in Man:
an Economist's View," *Social Service Review*, 33: 109–117, June 1959; and also in more
recent papers referred to herein.

[3] Branko Horvat. The Optimum Rate of Investment. *Economic Journal*, London, 68: 747–
767, December 1958.

[4] Theodore W. Schultz. Capital Formation by Education. *Journal of Political Economy*,
68: 571–583, December 1960.

[5] Trygve Haavelmo. *A Study in the Theory of Investment*. University of Chicago Press,
1960. p. 12–17.

year of work before he retires. In gauging the value of the stock of engineering capabilities, the age of engineers is therefore important.

Education is more durable than most forms of nonhuman reproducible capital. A high-school education, for example, will serve the person during the rest of his life, and of this period 40 years or more are likely to be spent in productive work. Most nonhuman capital has a much shorter productive life than this. Education can be augmented because it is durable, and the fact that it has a relatively long life means that a given gross investment adds more to the stock than the same gross investment typically adds to the stock of nonhuman capital.

In the United States young people entering the labor force have on the average more education than older workers. When the young people who enter the labor force have more education than the old people who are retiring, the value of the stock of education in the labor force rises, even with no change in the number of workers. Such has been the case in the United States for a long time. Though younger workers back in 1900 had only a little more schooling than older ones, this difference has become much larger, much to the advantage of those in the younger age groups. The stock of education accordingly becomes more valuable in two ways: (1) The level of education of the population rises, and (2) a larger share of the total education is embodied in the younger workers than formerly.

Why Estimate the Stock of Education?

Estimates of the stock of education may seem remote and academic to persons who are concerned about expenditures for classrooms and for teachers' salaries. There are, however, issues that can be settled only through knowledge about the stock of education; What are our scientific and engineering capacities and at what rates are these increasing? We are constantly devising better methods for measurement of inventories, plants, equipment, natural resources, and other forms of capital because such measurements are necessary in gauging changes in them. Similarly, there is a growing awareness that knowledge is required about changes in the stock of human capabilities.[6]

Comparisons of skills and knowledge in different countries are based as a rule on crude guesses concerning the respective stocks of education. To illustrate, in the United States the number of persons with a high school or a college education has been rising in relation to the number of persons in the labor force. This kind of advance in education has also been taking place in some other countries. Yet the differences among countries in the

---

[6] There is already a substantial body of literature treating human resources, talents, and skills, and the demand for and supply of scientific and other personnel.

rates of this advance are impressive. Countries in Western Europe have lagged in this respect compared to the United States, whereas Japan and more recently the Soviet Union, both starting from much lower levels several decades ago, have been moving ahead at a higher rate than has the United States. Moreover, it is altogether possible for the level of education of the labor force to decline, as it appears to have done in recent years in East Germany mainly as a consequence of the large outmigration of doctors, teachers, lawyers, and skilled technicians. Israel's unique pattern of immigration is also instructive. There came to Israel a large number of highly educated people. But there were not enough secondary schools for preparing young people for college and university instruction to maintain the high level of education which the immigration of talent had established. Thus, until enough secondary schools and college and university facilities were established, there was a prospect that the level of education of the labor force would decline.

International and other comparisons aside, the economist is turning to human capital to see whether changes in the stock of such capital will account for the otherwise large unexplained increases in output. As things stand, increases in nonhuman capital and in man-hours combined appear to account for only a small fraction of the increases in national income.[7]

Three Measures of the Stock of Education

The alternative measures that follow are at this stage only clues to what we are seeking. This is necessarily only a progress report. First we examine the concept of a *year of schooling completed* as a unit of measurement. National statistics based on this concept are readily available and they are widely used. Next we present an *equivalent year of schooling completed*, based on 1940, when the average period of school attendance was 152 days. A third measure will then be developed, based on the *real cost of a year of schooling*.

YEARS OF SCHOOLING COMPLETED

Although "years of schooling completed" is a convenient unit of measurement, it is like counting the acres of land in farms without taking any account of the differences in land; an acre of low-productive semidesert land and an acre of highly productive irrigated land are simply added together. Likewise, we can aggregate the education of a population by counting the number of years of schooling completed as one might count acres, houses, or tractors.

---

[7] "Education and Economic Growth," op. cit., pp. 49–50.

Table 1 presents the results of such a count for education. It shows that the years of schooling completed per person rose by about two-fifths between 1900 and 1957. It follows, of course, that the total number of years of schooling completed rose relative both to the population and to the labor force. If each year of schooling completed were the same in amount and value, the inference would be that the stock of education in the labor force, measured in this way, increased somewhat more than $3\frac{1}{2}$ times (from an index of 100 to 359) between 1900 and 1957.

Table 1—Years of schooling completed by the population 14 years and older and by the labor force 18–64 years of age [a]

		POPULATION			LABOR FORCE	
Year and Index 1957	Number (millions)	Years of schooling completed per person	Total years of schooling completed (millions)	Number (millions)	Years of schooling completed per person	Total years of schooling completed (millions)
1900	51.2	7.64	391	28.1	7.70	216
1910	64.3	7.86	505	35.8	7.91	283
1920	74.5	8.05	600	41.4	8.12	336
1930	89.0	8.32	741	48.7	8.41	410
1940	101.1	8.85	895	52.8	9.02	476
1950	112.4	9.95	1,118	60.1	10.10	607
1957	117.1	10.70	1,253	70.8	10.96	776
Index 1957 (1900 = 100)	229	140	320	252	142	359

[a] United States, 1900–57.

EQUIVALENT YEARS OF SCHOOLING COMPLETED

As a standard, a "year of schooling completed" is much too elastic, for the school year is now 60 percent longer than it was six decades ago. In 1900 the average daily attendance of enrolled pupils aged 5–15 was only 99 days, whereas in 1957 it had reached 159 days. Moreover, the labor force of 1900 consisted mostly of workers who had been in school when the average attendance was even less than 99 days; for example, most workers who then were 35–45 years of age were presumably in school in 1870 when the average attendance was only 78 days (this leaves aside the schooling of immigrants).

I have adopted a procedure developed by Clarence D. Long[8] to adjust the figures on school years completed for these changes in length of school

[8] Set forth in his study, *The Labor Force Under Changing Income and Employment*, National Bureau of Economic Research. Princeton, N.J., Princeton University Press, 1958 (see especially app. F). Professor Long has kindly made available to me his basic worksheets, which provide the adjustment factors on which my estimates of "equivalent years of school" are based.

attendance. It gives me comparable figures for years of schooling completed, which I have based on the 1940 experience of an average of 152 days of school attendance.

This simple adjustment for changes in school attendance alters the picture considerably. As is shown in Table 2, the rise in equivalent years of schooling completed, adjusted for differences in the length of the school years, is much larger than that shown by the unadjusted figures on which Table 1 is based. For the labor force, whereas years of schooling completed rose by about two-fifths between 1900 and 1957, the equivalent years of schooling completed became $2\frac{1}{2}$ times as high in that period (rising from an index of 100 to 252). During these same years, 1900–57, the total number of years of schooling completed by persons in the labor force, on a 1940 equivalent basis, rose $6\frac{1}{3}$ times (from an index of 100 to 638).

Table 2—Equivalent 1940 years of schooling completed by the population 14 years and older and by the labor force 18–64 years of age [a]

Year and Index 1957	POPULATION			LABOR FORCE		
	Number (millions)	Equivalent 1940 years of schooling completed per person	Total equivalent 1940 years of schooling completed (millions)	Number (millions)	Equivalent 1940 years of schooling completed per person	Total equivalent 1940 years of schooling completed (millions)
1900	51.2	4.13	212	28.1	4.14	116
1910	64.3	4.65	299	35.8	4.65	167
1920	74.5	5.21	388	41.4	5.25	217
1930	89.0	6.01	535	48.7	6.01	293
1940	101.1	7.07	715	52.8	7.24	382
1950	112.4	8.46	951	60.1	8.65	520
1957	117.1	10.02	1,173	70.8	10.45	740
Index 1957 (1900 = 100)	229	243	553	252	252	638

[a] United States, 1900–57.

COST AS A MEASURE OF SCHOOLING

The two concepts presented above treat a year of elementary school the same as a year of either high school or college, although they differ greatly in value. A year of high school costs 5 times as much as a year of elementary school, and a year of college almost 12 times as much. I propose to use the following 1956 price tags for a year of schooling:[9] Elementary school, $280; high school, $1,420; and college, $3,300.

[9] For the underlying estimates, see "Capital Formation by Education," op. cit., and "Education and Economic Growth," op. cit., p. 64. The reader should bear in mind that these estimates of costs include *income forgone* by mature students and that this component in the real costs of education is large both for high-school and for college and university education.

Table 3 shows that in 1957 the members of the labor force had completed on the average 7.52 elementary-school years, 2.44 high school years, and

Table 3—Cost of education per member of the labor force 18–64 years of age, in 1957, according to years of schooling completed [a]

Type of schooling	Years of schooling per member, 1957	Cost of schooling per year in 1956 prices	TOTAL COST PER MEMBER [b] Amount	Percent
Elementary school	7.52	$280	$2,106	28
High school	2.44	1,420	3,458	45
College and university	0.64	3,300	2,099	27
Total	10.60	723 [c]	7,663	100

[a] Based on table 138 of the *Statistical Abstract of the United States 1959* (U.S. Department of Commerce, Bureau of the Census), which gives the percentage distribution by years of schooling completed for the labor force 18 to 64 years òld, 1957. The elementary-school subtotal is $(4 \times 5.6) + (7 \times 26.2) + (8 \times 68.3) \div 100 = 7.522$; the high-school subtotal is $(2.5 \times 19.8) + (4 \times 48.5) \div 100 = 2.435$; and the college subtotal is $(2 \times 8.8) + (5 \times 9.2) \div 100 = 0.636$. Col. 5 is based on these unrounded numbers. It should be noted that the total years of schooling completed per member (10.60) is slightly larger than the total (10.45) 1940 equivalent years of schooling completed, shown in table 2 for the labor force, because of a small difference in the data and procedure used.

[b] Each amount is the product of the corresponding items in cols. 2 and 3.

[c] Average cost per member per year, obtained by dividing $7,663 by 10.60.

0.64 college and university year. At 1956 prices, the cost of an average year of this composition was $723.

Two estimates were made for 1900, which are, in substance, a lower and an upper estimate of schooling and costs. In the lower estimate, high-school

Table 4—Cost of education per member of the labor force in 1900, according to years of schooling completed [a]

Type of schooling	YEARS OF SCHOOLING PER MEMBER Lower estimate	Upper estimate	Cost of schooling per year	TOTAL COST PER MEMBER [b] Amount (upper estimate)	Percent
Elementary school	3.75	3.437	$280	$962	43
High school	.31	.556	1,420	790	35
College and university	.08	.147	3,300	485	22
Total	4.14	4.140	540 [c]	2,237	100

[a] These estimates are computed from a study of the high-school enrollment and graduates, and also of college enrollment and graduates from 1900 back to 1850. High-school enrollment represented about 0.636 of 1 percent of the population, and high-school graduates, 0.351 of 1 percent. For college and university students, the 2 comparable estimates were 0.270 and 0.135 of 1 percent. Distributing all of these among the labor force of 1900, we have for elementary school $(83.5 \times 2.53) + (16.5 \times 8) \div 100 = 3.437$; high school $(2 \times 5.16) + (4 \times 11.33) \div 100 = 0.556$; college, $(2 \times 2.46) + (4 \times 2.46) \div 100 = 0.147$. The average cost per year of schooling becomes $423 instead of $540 if the lower estimate of years of schooling per labor force member is used (col. 2) both at 1956 prices.

[b] Each amount is the product of the corresponding item in cols. 3 and 4.

[c] Average cost of schooling per member per year, obtained by dividing $2,237 by 4.14.

and college education is allocated within the labor force roughly as it was distributed in the population among the comparable age groups; in the higher estimate, all of this education was allocated to the labor force. Table 4 gives the years of schooling per member of the labor force for both estimates and then the costs for the upper one. At 1956 prices the costs of an average year of schooling of these two compositions comes to $540 for the upper estimate and to $423 for the lower one.

The results of these preliminary steps in using costs to measure the stock of education are shown in Table 5. It should be observed that Table 5 is

Table 5—Stock of education measured by costs and stock of reproducible nonhuman wealth [a]

Year	Cost of an equivalent year of schooling (1956 prices in dollars)	Cost of educational stock, population 14 years and older (in billions)	Cost of educational stock, labor force members 14 years and older (in billions)	Stock of reproducible nonhuman wealth (in billions)	Percentage col. 4 is of col. 5
(1)	(2)	(3)	(4)	(5)	(6)
1900	$540	$114	$63	$282	22
1910	563	168	94	403	23
1920	586	227	127	526	24
1930	614	328	180	735	24
1940	650	465	248	756	33
1950	690	656	359	969	37
1957	723	848	535	1,270	42
Index 1957 (1900 = 100)	134	744	849	450	191

[a] The procedure for deriving the estimates of the cost of an equivalent 1940 year of schooling shown for 1900 appears in table 4, and for 1957 in table 3. A similar procedure was used for 1940. Estimates for the rest of the year were obtained by extrapolation. Table is for United States, 1900–57.

In col. 3 each item is obtained by multiplying the corresponding item in col. 4 of table 2 by that in col. 2 of table 5. In col. 4 each item is obtained by multiplying the corresponding item in col. 7 of table 2 by that in col. 2 of table 5.

Cols. 3 and 4 are based on 1956 prices. Col. 5 is derived from the work of Raymond W. Goldsmith, who kindly made available his estimates of U.S. (national) reproducible wealth at 1947–49 prices, which I then adjusted to 1956 prices.

based on the upper estimate of costs for 1900. The cost of the educational stock of the labor force, thus defined, in 1957 was 8½ times the 1900 level (from an index of 100 to 849). If the lower estimate figure for 1900 is used, that is, $423 instead of $540, the stock of education in the labor force rose virtually 11 times between 1900 and 1957. The stock of nonhuman reproducible wealth (Raymond W. Goldsmith's estimates)[10] rose only 4½ times, as shown in column 5 of Table 5.

[10] Personal communication.

Concluding Observations

1. A comparison of the several measures presented shows how much they differ. The estimates that follow are restricted to the education of members of the labor force.

Measure of educational stock	Increase between 1900 and 1957 Index 1957 (1900 = 100)
I. Years of schooling completed (Table 1)	359
II. Equivalent 1940 years of schooling completed (Table 2)	638
III. Cost of schooling:	
(a) Upper estimate cost in 1900 (Table 5)	849
(b) Lower estimate cost in 1900 (Table 4), also related text	1,092
Stock of reproducible nonhuman wealth cost (Table 5)	450

2. The measure, "year of schooling completed," understates greatly the increase in the stock of education that has been realized over the decades if for no other reason than that the average daily attendance of enrolled pupils rose 60 percent between 1900 and 1957.

3. "Equivalent years of schooling completed" also understates the increase in the stock of education because it does not distinguish among years of elementary, high-school, and college and university schooling; each year regardless of the level is treated the same. From an investment point of view, a year of elementary schooling costs much less than a year of high school or of college, and the latter two have been increasing much more rapidly, as the following estimates show.

Table 6—Years of schooling completed per member of the labor force

Type of schooling	1900 (upper estimate)	1957	Increase between 1900 and 1957 Index 1957 (1900=100)
Elementary school	3.437	7.52	219
High school	.556	2.44	439
College and university	.147	.64	435
Total	4.140	10.60	256

4. Our third measure based on costs of schooling is a preliminary estimate of "stock of output capacity" represented by education. It does not

distinguish between the younger and the older workers in the labor force in measuring their education; for example, a year of high school is given the same weight whether the worker is 25 or 60 years of age. There is also the implicit assumption that a year of schooling of a given level (elementary school or high school or college) acquired recently or many years ago are comparable once an adjustment has been made for differences in length of school attendance. Nor is there any allowance for obsolescence of education. Surely some instruction is better now than it was several decades ago, and also, some education is subject to obsolescence.

5. The equivalent years of schooling completed per member of the labor force have risen more for those in the younger than in the older age groups, as the following estimates make clear.

Table 7—Years of schooling completed by members of the labor force, by age group, 1900 and 1957

	NUMBER OF YEARS OF SCHOOLING		Increase between 1900 and 1957, Index 1957
Age group	1900	1957	(1900 = 100)
14–19	4.2	11.0	262
20–24	4.6	12.8	278
25–44	4.2	12.2	290
45–64	3.8	7.8	205
65 and over	3.3	5.6	170

6. Despite the greater increase in education of workers in the younger groups relative to those in the older groups, the average productive life of the entire stock of this education may not have changed appreciably. Assuming a productive life up to the 68th year of life and the same rate of deaths and disabilities for each age group, a crude estimate indicates that the average productive life of all of the education in the labor force was slightly more than 30 years in 1900 and about the same in 1957. The reason for this result seems to be the fact that young people now enter the labor force at a somewhat older age than they did in former years, mainly because they continue their schooling for more years.

7. If the above statement about the average productive life of education of the labor force proves to be approximately correct, our estimate that the stock of education in the labor force increased 8½ times between 1900 and 1957, as compared with the increase in the stock of reproducible nonhuman wealth of 4½ times takes on added significance. As I have attempted to show elsewhere, investments in education may explain a large part of the otherwise unexplained economic growth of the United States.[11]

[11] "Education and Economic Growth," op. cit., pp. 78–82.

5

The Sources
of Past and Future Growth

In the following selection Edward F. Denison, currently with the Brookings Institution, summarizes his detailed study of the sources of American economic growth, which was developed under the auspices of the Committee for Economic Development. Considerable importance is attached to quantitative and qualitative growth in human capital as a growth ingredient as the author's remarks demonstrate.

EDWARD F. DENISON

Growth projections for the 1960 to 1980 period are presented after capital and labor inputs were disaggregated into reasonably identifiable components. The author's tentative projections are based upon his historical study of changes in these growth components throughout the first half of this century.

In this chapter the allocation of past economic growth among its sources is completed and a similar allocation of the projected future growth rate under high-employment conditions is derived. This chapter is wholly concerned with the sources of growth in the real national income or product as it is actually measured. In some respects this differs appreciably from the growth of a "truer" measure of national income or product.

Derivation of the Tables

Table 1 gives the growth rates of ... various factor inputs ... and provides ... projected rates computed from the 1960 high-employment

Reprinted from Edward F. Denison, *The Sources of Economic Growth in The United States and the Alternatives Before Us*, Supplementary Paper No. 13 (New York: Committee for Economic Development), pp. 264–74, with the permission of the author and publisher.

estimate to the 1980 high-employment projection. . . . The adjustment to eliminate the increase in inputs that is not reflected in the measured national product is introduced on a summary basis. This lowers the growth rate of total inputs and raises that of output per unit of input.

Table 1—Growth rates for real national income and underlying series [a]

	TOTAL			PER PERSON EMPLOYED		
	1909–29	1929–57	1960–80[b]	1909–29	1929–57	1960–80[b]
Real national income	2.82	2.93	3.33	1.22	1.60	1.62
Increase in total inputs, adjusted	2.24	1.99	2.16	.65	.67	.47
Adjustment	−.09	−.11	−.11	−.09	−.11	−.11
Increase in total inputs, unadjusted	2.33	2.10	2.27	.74	.78	.58
Labor, adjusted for quality change	2.30	2.16	2.29	.71	.84	.60
Employment and hours	1.62	1.08	1.27	—	—	—
Employment	1.58	1.31	1.68	—	—	—
Quality of a man-year's work due to shorter hours	.03	−.23	−.41	.03	−.23	−.41
Annual hours	−.34	−.73	−.53	−.34	−.73	−.53
Quality of a man-hour's work due to shorter hours	.38	.50	.12	.38	.50	.12
Education	.56	.93	.89	.56	.93	.89
Increased experience and better utilization of women workers	.10	.15	.12	.10	.15	.12
Changes in age-sex composition of labor force	.01	−.01	−.01	.01	−.01	−.01
Land	.00	.00	.00	−1.58	−1.32	−1.65
Capital	3.16	1.88	2.50	1.55	.56	.81
Nonfarm residential structures	3.49	1.46	NA[c]	1.87	.13	NA
Other structures and equipment	2.93	1.85	NA	1.33	.52	NA
Inventories	3.31	1.90	NA	1.70	.58	NA
U.S.-owned assets abroad	4.20	1.97	NA	2.58	.64	NA
Foreign assets in U.S. (an offset)	−1.85	1.37	NA	−3.46	.06	NA
Increase in output per unit of input, adjusted	.56	.92	1.14	.56	.92	1.14

[a] Per cent per annum.
[b] Growth rates based on high-employment projection.
[c] NA—not available.

Table 1 refers to the growth rates of the various factor inputs shown. From 1929 to 1957, for example, total labor input grew at an annual rate of

2.16 per cent, education raised the average quality of labor 0.93 per cent a year, and capital input increased 1.88 per cent a year. Similarly, the amount of total capital input per person employed increased .56 per cent a year and the quantity of inventories per person employed .58 per cent, while the quantity of land per person employed declined 1.32 per cent a year.

Table 2 allocates the growth rate of total real national income among the sources of growth, and Table 3 does the same for real national income per person employed. The portions of these tables referring to inputs are based on empirical analysis of past periods, and constructed in similar fashion for the future period. However, the overstatement of the contribution of inputs to the *measured* growth rate resulting from the conventions used to measure real output in general government, households and institutions, and construction has been eliminated. This was done by reducing the contributions ascribed to the increase in labor input deriving from the improvement in the quality of an hour's work resulting from shorter hours, education, and experience and utilization of women workers, and to the increased quantity of capital per man.[1] The portions of Tables 2 and 3 that refer to output per unit of input assemble estimates provided in Part III. Since the percentage allocation of the growth rate for 1909–29 depends upon whether the total growth rate is based upon the Commerce or the Kendrick-Kuznets series, results of using each are given.

The Sources of Growth of Total National Income

I shall discuss first the sources of growth of total national income (Table 2) and then of national income per person employed. My results depend, of course, upon assumptions introduced at various points in this study. I shall not repeat them here except to state again that the most important concern the relationship of hours of output, the fraction of income differentials *associated with* differences in education that is *due to* differences in education, and the size of economies of scale. I may also note that I do not show in the tables entries for the many possible sources of growth that I

---

[1] The allocation of the adjustment among these four sources in each period was made proportional to the contribution of each to the growth rate of output per person employed, except that capital was given only half its weight in the calculation since it does not enter into measured input in much of the industrial area to which the adjustment refers. The estimated adjustment in 1909–29 was put at .09 percentage points as compared with .11 in the 1929–57 period because the increase in output per person employed due to these sources was smaller.

It may be noted that this adjustment eliminates the slight positive figure for the contribution of shorter hours to growth in the 1909–29 period, reflecting the fact that the output estimates in certain sectors *assume* output declined with shorter hours.

Table 2—Allocation of growth rate of total real national income among the sources of growth

	PERCENTAGE POINTS IN GROWTH RATE			PER CENT OF GROWTH RATE			
	1909–29a (Commerce)	1929–57	1960–80b	1909–29a (Commerce)	1909–29a (Kendrick-Kuznets)	1929–57	1960–80b
Real National Income	2.82	2.93	3.33	100	100	100	100
Increase in total inputs	2.26	2.00	2.19	80	71	68	66
Labor, adjusted for quality change	1.53	1.57	1.70	54	48	54	51
Employment and hours	1.11	.80	.98	39	35	27	29
Employment	1.11	1.00	1.33	39	35	34	40
Effect of shorter hours on quality of a man-year's work	.00	–.20	–.35	0	0	–7	–11
Annual hours	–.23	–.53	–.42	–8	–7	–18	–13
Effect of shorter hours on quality of a man-hour's work	.23	.33	.07	8	7	11	2
Education	.35	.67	.64	12	11	23	19
Increased experience and better utilization of women workers	.06	.11	.09	2	2	4	3
Changes in age-sex composition of labor force	.01	–.01	–.01	0	0	0	0
Land	.00	.00	.00	0	0	0	0
Capital	.73	.43	.49	26	23	15	15
Nonfarm residential structures	.13	.05	NA	5	4	2	NA
Other structures and equipment	.41	.28	NA	15	13	10	NA
Inventories	.16	.08	NA	6	5	3	NA
U.S.-owned assets abroad	.02	.02	NA	1	1	1	NA
Foreign assets in U.S.	.01	.00	NA	0	0	0	NA
Increase in output per unit of input	.56	.93	1.14	20	29	32	34
Restrictions against optimum use of resources	NA	–.07	.00	NA	NA	–2	0
Reduced waste of labor in agriculture	NA	.02	.02	NA	NA	1	1
Industry shift from agriculture	NA	.05	.01	NA	NA	2	0
Advance of knowledge	NA	.58	.75	NA	NA	20	23
Change in lag in application of knowledge	NA	.01	.03	NA	NA	0	1
Economies of scale—independent growth of local markets	NA	.07	.05	NA	NA	2	2
Economies of scale—growth of national market	.28	.27	.28	10	10	9	8

a "Commerce" and "Kendrick-Kuznets" headings refer only to the growth rate of total product. Contributions in percentage points under the Kendrick-Kuznets heading would be identical with those shown under the Commerce heading except for "real national income," 3.17; "output per unit of input," .91, and "economies of scale—growth of national market," .32.

b Growth rate based on high-employment projection.

NA: Not available.

Note: Contributions in percentage points are adjusted so that the sum of appropriate details equals totals. Per cents of the growth rate have not been so adjusted.

Table 3—Allocation of growth rate of real national income per person employed among the sources of growth

	PERCENTAGE POINTS IN GROWTH RATE			PER CENT OF GROWTH RATE			
	1909–29[a] (Commerce)	1929–57	1960–80[b]	1909–29[a] (Commerce)	1909–29[a] (Kendrick-Kuznets)	1929–57	1960–80[b]
Real national income	1.22	1.60	1.62	100	100	100	100
Increase in total inputs per person employed	.66	.67	.48	54	42	42	30
Labor, adjusted for quality change	.42	.57	.37	34	27	36	23
Effect of shorter hours on quality of a man-year's work	.00	−.20	−.35	0	0	−12	−22
Annual hours	−.23	−.53	−.42	−19	−15	−33	−26
Effect of shorter hours on quality of a man-hour's work	.23	.33	.07	19	15	21	4
Education	.35	.67	.64	29	23	42	40
Increased experience and better utilization of women workers	.06	.11	.09	5	4	7	6
Changes in age-sex composition of labor force	.01	−.01	−.01	1	1	−1	−1
Land	−.11	−.05	−.04	−9	−7	−3	−2
Capital	.35	.15	.15	29	22	9	9
Nonfarm residential structures	.07	.01	NA	6	4	1	NA
Other structures and equipment	.17	.10	NA	14	11	6	NA
Inventories	.08	.03	NA	6	5	2	NA
U.S.-owned assets abroad	.02	.01	NA	2	1	1	NA
Foreign assets in U.S.	.01	.00	NA	1	1	0	NA
Increase in output per unit of input	.56	.93	1.14	46	58	58	70
Restrictions against optimum use of resources	NA	−.07	.00	NA	NA	−4	0
Reduced waste of labor in agriculture	NA	.02	.02	NA	NA	1	1
Industry shift from agriculture	NA	.05	.01	NA	NA	3	1
Advance of knowledge	NA	.58	.75	NA	NA	36	46
Change in lag in application of knowledge	NA	.01	.03	NA	NA	1	2
Economies of scale—independent growth of local markets	NA	.07	.05	NA	NA	4	3
Economies of scale—growth of national market	.28	.27	.28	23	20	17	17

[a] "Commerce" and "Kendrick-Kuznets" headings refer only to the growth rate of total product. Contributions in percentage points under the Kendrick-Kuznets heading would be identical with those shown under the Commerce heading except for "real national income," 1.57, "output per unit of input," .91, and "economies of scale—growth of national market," .32.

[b] Growth rate based on high-employment projection.

NA: Not available.

Note: Contributions in percentage points are adjusted so that the sum of appropriate detail equals totals. Per cents of the growth rate have not been so adjusted.

considered, but concluded that zero was the best estimate of their contribution.[2]

Finally, I repeat that these results are experimental and tentative, and that I hope they will be improved by further research.[3]

THE 1929-57 PERIOD

Consider first the sources of growth in measured national income or product during the period of nearly three decades from 1929 to 1957. The broadest statement that can be made is that the increase in the quantity and quality of inputs was responsible for 68 per cent of total growth and the increase in productivity for 32 per cent. This result is meaningful only by reference to the particular classification I have employed. Consequently, it is most useful now to turn directly to the individual sources.

1. The changes that occurred in employment and working hours accounted for 27 per cent of total growth. The increase in employment would have contributed an amount equal to 34 per cent of the actual growth rate had hours not been shortened, but the shortening of hours provided an offset equal to 7 per cent of the total growth rate. This offset would have been much larger—18 per cent—if the shortening of hours had not led directly to an increase in the amount of work done in an hour. But such an increase (my estimates imply) did occur, and was sufficient to contribute 11 per cent to the growth rate, even after allowance for the fact that capital goods were used less intensively as a result of the shorter workweek for labor.

2. The quality of the labor force was greatly improved because its members at the end of the period had received much more education than had its members at the beginning of the period. This contributed 23 per cent of the total growth of national product. This improvement in the quality of the labor force reflected changes that had been made in education of the young before the period began more than it did improvements made after 1929, although the latter were not unimportant.

3. The average woman worker contributes less to production, and the average child worker very much less, than the average adult male. Between 1929 and 1957 the proportion of children in the labor force was reduced and

[2] This reminder is especially pertinent for any reader who may view the main value of these tables to be the format provided him to enter his own estimates; he should recall the other possible candidates for inclusion in the list.

[3] The reader may wonder which of two interpretations to place upon the figures shown for the contribution to the growth rate, in percentage points, of each growth determinant in Tables 2 and 3. Is it the rate at which the national income would have grown if nothing had changed but that determinant? Or is it the amount by which the growth rate would have differed if everything else had changed as it actually did, but that determinant did not change? The latter is the correct interpretation. This follows from my use of periodic changes in weights in deriving the input series and my allocation of "interaction effects" among the sources. However, the answers to the two questions do not differ very much, and in drawing the distinction I do not mean to suggest precision in the estimates.

the proportion of women increased. The effects of these shifts in proportions, as such, upon the average quality of the labor force were almost offsetting and deducted less than one-half per cent from the growth rate.

However, by 1957 women were remaining in the labor force far longer than in 1929 and in consequence were, on the average, more experienced and effective workers. In addition, discrimination against the employment of women workers in jobs utilizing their maximum capacities had diminished so their skills were more effectively utilized. These developments were responsible for 4 per cent of the growth rate from 1929 to 1957.

Altogether, changes in the quantity and quality of labor were responsible for 54 per cent of economic growth in this period.

4. The increase in capital input contributed 15 per cent of total growth. Of this amount the increase in inventories contributed 3 per cent, that in nonfarm residences 2 per cent, and that in our net international investments less than 1 per cent. The remaining 10 per cent was the contribution of the increase in the services provided by structures other than nonfarm dwellings and by equipment.

5. The advance of all kinds of knowledge relevant to production, by permitting more to be produced with a given quantity of resources, contributed 20 per cent of total growth.

6. Three developments that increased the efficiency with which the economy operates together contributed 3 per cent of the growth rate. There was a reduction (relative to employment in the economy as a whole, not in farming) in the amount of labor used in agriculture in excess of the amount required for actual production. New knowledge was incorporated into the productive process a little faster. Adaptation by business to the widespread ownership of automobiles and to the increasing concentration of the population in urban areas broadened local markets (quite apart from the growth of the national economy), permitting increased output per unit of input.

7. A number of institutional changes that led to misallocation of resources or prevented their most efficient use subtracted 2 per cent from the growth rate. These are combined in Table 2 but were separately discussed in Chapter 17. The introduction of resale price maintenance laws was the most important.

8. Agricultural output had a lower value on the market than other output requiring the same use of resources in the base year (1954) of the real national product series. Consequently, a reduction in agriculture's share of resources actually utilized had the effect of raising the real national product. This development contributed 2 per cent of measured economic growth.

9. Economies of scale made possible by the increase in the size of the national economy (including the associated increases in the size of local and regional markets) contributed 9 per cent of economic growth from 1929 to 1957. This is, of course, a passive element in growth made possible by the

other developments. Consequently, its contribution could, if desired, be re-allocated among the active ingredients in proportion to their contributions to growth. This would be comparable to the procedure I have used in appraising the potential effects of altering any of the active ingredients.

In summary, five sources contributed an amount equal to 101 per cent of the growth rate, out of a total of 109 per cent contributed by all sources making a positive contribution. These were increased employment (34 per cent); increased education (23); increased capital input (15); the advance of knowledge (20); and economies of scale associated with the growth of the national market (9). The reduction of working hours accounted for minus 7 of the total "contribution" of minus 9 per cent to the growth rate provided by sources adverse to growth, and increased restrictions against the optimum use of resources for the remainder.

THE 1909–29 PERIOD

The sources of growth from 1909 to 1929 can best be compared with those in the subsequent period by use of contributions measured in percentage points in the growth rate, as shown in the left half of Table 2. This is partly to abstract from the difference in the total growth rate, but it is especially necessary because the total growth rate in the earlier period, from which the percentages of the total are computed, is itself particularly uncertain. The chief differences between the two periods were the following:

1. Changes in employment and hours contributed much more—1.11 percentage points as against .80—in the earlier than in the later period. Employment increased more rapidly. Hours reduction was slower and had no adverse effect upon output because it was fully offset by the resulting increase in the amount of work done in an hour.

2. The increase in the educational background of the labor force contributed only .35 percentage points to the growth rate in the 1909–29 period as compared with .67 in 1929–57.

3. Capital input increased more rapidly in the earlier period and contributed .73 percentage points to the growth rate as compared with .43 points from 1929 to 1957. The sharpest drops, in relative terms, were in the contributions of inventories and housing. That of "other structures and equipment" was from .41 to .28.

4. All the growth sources affecting output per unit of input together contributed .93 percentage points to the 1929–57 growth rate. Based on a total growth rate computed from the Commerce national product estimates they contributed .56 points in 1909–29, but if the total growth rate is computed from the Kendrick-Kuznets estimates they contributed .91 points. No conclusion as to their relative contribution in the two periods is possible.

THE 1960–80 GROWTH RATE

My projection implies that only five sources will contribute to the 1960–80 high-employment growth rate an amount that differs importantly from their contributions to the 1929–57 rate.

1. Changes in employment and hours will contribute .98 percentage points to the growth rate as against .80 from 1929 to 1957. Employment will grow much more rapidly. The projected rate at which hours will be shortened is much below the 1929–57 rate, but its impact on output will be larger because much less of an offset can be expected in the form of increased work per hour.

2. The contribution of increased capital is foreseen as .49 percentage points as against .43 in 1929–57.

3. I assume that changes in restrictions against the optimum allocation and use of resources will be neutral in the future, whereas they subtracted .07 percentage points from the 1929–57 growth rate.

4. The shift of utilized resources from agriculture that is foreseen will contribute only .01 percentage points to the growth rate as against .05 from 1929 to 1957.

5. The advance of knowledge is seen as contributing .75 percentage points in the future as against .58 from 1929 to 1957.

The contribution anticipated from each of the other sources of growth differs by .03 percentage points or less from its contribution in the 1929–57 period.

The Sources of Growth of National Income Per Person Employed

A different, and in some ways more illuminating, perspective on these developments is provided by an examination of the sources of increase in real national income per person employed, given in Table 3.[4] This measure is more closely associated with living standards. By simply taking into account, in addition, changes in the ratio of employment to population one could proceed to an explanation of changes in real national income per capita.[5] Allowance for other changes for which data are readily available would allow one to proceed to an explanation of additional measures, such as per capita disposable income or consumption.

[4] It will be recalled that employment is measured on a full-time equivalent basis.
[5] ... the 1929–57 growth rate of real GNP per capita was 1.69 while that of real GNP per person employed was 1.60 per cent per annum. Hence, .09 percentage points of the per capita rate was due to an increased ratio of employment to population. The sources of the remaining 1.60 per cent are as given in Table 3.

It may be noted, first, that the increase in inputs, including labor input, per person employed contributed 42 per cent and the increase in output per unit of input 58 per cent of the total growth rate of national income per person employed. The latter is, of course, much larger than the corresponding percentage in the growth rate of total income.

Negative elements are more important in the growth of income per person employed than of total income. It is convenient to consider first the sources that made a positive contribution to the 1929–57 growth rate, and then those that exercised an adverse influence.

1. Improved education of the labor force contributed an amount equal to 42 per cent of the total increase in national income per person employed.

2. The greater experience and better utilization of women workers contributed 7 per cent.

3. The increase in capital input per person employed contributed an amount equal to 9 per cent of the growth rate, of which 6 per cent was due to the increased services provided by structures (excluding nonfarm resi dences) and equipment, 2 per cent to inventories, and 1 per cent to the increase in assets owned abroad and in nonfarm residences.

Capital input per person employed is a somewhat abstract idea, for much of the labor force works with no private capital and much of the capital provides services with little or no labor, or United States labor, but it is the appropriate concept to explain the increase in measured national income per person employed. The likelihood that the contribution of capital is under-stated as a result of biased price indexes for construction should be recalled.

4. Various changes that permitted the economy to operate more efficiently, including the shift of fully employed resources out of agriculture, and the independent growth of local markets, were responsible for an amount equal to 9 per cent of the growth rate.

5. The advance of knowledge contributed an amount equal to 36 per cent of the growth rate.

6. Economies of scale associated with the growth of the national market contributed an amount equal to 17 per cent of the growth rate of national income per person employed.

These positive elements together contributed 1.93 percentage points to the 1.60 percentage point growth rate of national income per person employed; the sum of their contributions thus equaled 121 per cent of the total growth rate actually achieved.

Four developments adverse to growth provided the offsets. Shorter hours subtracted an amount equivalent to 12 per cent of the actual growth rate, the reduction in the quantity of land per person employed 3 per cent, increased restrictions against the most efficient allocation and use of resources 4 per cent, and changes in the age-sex composition of the labor force 1 per cent.

THE 1909–29 PERIOD

Several sources operated toward producing a higher growth rate of real national product per person employed from 1909 to 1929 than from 1929 to 1957. The shortening of hours deducted nothing from the growth rate as against .20 from 1929 to 1957. Increased capital input contributed .35 points as against .15; the contribution of each type of capital distinguished was larger in the earlier period. Changes in the age-sex composition of the labor force added .01 points whereas they deducted .01 in the later period. Economies of scale associated with the growth of the national market contributed .28 or .32 (depending on whether it is calculated from the Commerce or the Kendrick-Kuznets national product series) as against .27.

Against these, several sources tended to produce a lower rate in the 1909–29 period. Improved education contributed only .35 percentage points as against .67 later. Greater experience and better utilization of women contributed .06 points as against .11. The decline in the quantity of land per person employed subtracted .11 percentage points as against .05, partly because employment increased more rapidly but also because land was a more important factor of production in the earlier period.

As with the growth rate of total income, the relative contribution in the two periods of the advance of knowledge and other changes affecting output per unit of input depends upon the total growth rate selected.

THE 1960–80 PERIOD

The projection of high-employment national product from 1960 to 1980 implies a growth rate of national income per person employed of 1.62 per cent as against 1.60 per cent from 1929 to 1957. To achieve this rate it relies upon the advance of knowledge to contribute 46 per cent of the total as compared with only 36 per cent in 1929–57; it foresees an increase of .17 percentage points in the contribution of this source. In comparison with the 1929–57 period, the absence of increased restrictions against the most efficient allocation and use of resources would contribute .07 points to a higher future rate, a reduction in the lag of average practice behind the best known .02 points, the lessened importance of a fixed quantity of land .01 points, and economies of scale associated with growth of the national market .01 points.

The projection implies that all other sources of growth will contribute either the same or a smaller amount to growth per person employed in 1960–80 than they did in 1929–57. Hours shortening, even though the pace of reduction is assumed to be much slower, will subtract .15 percentage points more than it did in the earlier period. Other changes, though individually small, in total are adverse to the extent of .11 percentage points. Education will contribute .03 points less, changes in the experience and utilization of women .02 points less, the shift of surplus labor from farming .04 points less, the independent growth of local markets .02 points less, and the growth of capital input the same amount (even though capital input will be increasing more rapidly, because its importance in total income is smaller).

Unless knowledge does in fact advance more rapidly than in the past and further institutional impediments to efficient production are avoided a reduced growth rate in output per man will have to be expected.

Summary

Whatever period we examine, it is clear that economic growth, occurring within the general institutional setting of a democratic, largely free-enterprise society, has stemmed and will stem mainly from an increased labor force, more education, more capital, and the advance of knowledge, with economies of scale exercising an important, but essentially passive, re-enforcing influence. Since 1929 the shortening of working hours has exercised an increasingly restrictive influence on the growth of output.

It is reasonable to conclude that these are also the growth determinants that ought to be examined most carefully in projecting the national product; and that would have to be influenced to change the future growth rate very much over an extended period of time. Smaller, but nonetheless worthwhile, contributions may also reasonably be sought in other directions.

6

Technical Progress, Capital Formation, and Economic Growth

Theories of economic growth have gone through several stages of progress and refinement. Robert M. Solow, Professor of Economics at the Massachusetts Institute of Technology, has contributed much to this field. One of his contributions is the notion that technical progress, as an outgrowth of expanded knowledge, may be embodied in investment in new capital equipment. Even though Solow's approach to knowledge and productivity differs markedly from the analysis of human capital represented in the works

ROBERT M. SOLOW

of Denison and Schultz, the methodology and implications of this selection are clear. Embodiment of technology, whether directly or indirectly cognizant of human capital, affects the relative significance one attaches to factor inputs and capital requirements in the growth process. Further, elements determining technical change such as human resource quality are critical to the growth process and our understanding of it.

Introduction

The goal of this paper is an answer to the question: How much fixed investment is necessary to support alternative rates of growth of potential output in the United States in the near future? Notice that I said "necessary to support" and not "sufficient to generate." I believe that a high rate of capital formation is required if the growth of aggregate productivity and

Reprinted from Robert M. Solow, "Technical Progress, Capital Formation, and Economic Growth," *American Economic Review Proceedings* 52 (May 1962), pp. 76–92, with the permission of the author and publisher.

output is to accelerate, but I do not believe that it is all that is required. Notice also that I said "potential output" and not "realized output." The relation between investment and output is two sided, as I think I once heard my friend Evsey Domar say, and I am concerned here with the supply side only. Whether any particular required rate of investment will be accompanied by a high enough level of final demand to use the resulting capacity is another question. And how a particular required rate of investment can in fact be induced is yet another. Neither will be answered in this paper.

I shall try to deduce an answer to my question by estimating an aggregate production function, because I do not know any other way to go about it. One aggregate production function is pretty much like another, I admit, and this one has only a few distinctive markings. They are: (1) the data differ a little from those normally used in this kind of enterprise; (2) it is assumed that *all* technological progress needs to be "embodied" in newly produced capital goods before there can be any effect on output; (3) a sharp distinction is drawn between actual output and potential output, and the method includes a built-in estimate of the gap between them.

The next section of the paper sets out the assumptions of this approach. Then I shall briefly describe the data, present some alternative estimates of the production function, and draw the implications for capital requirements.

Assumptions and Theory

I assume that new technology can be introduced into the production process *only* through gross investment in new plant and equipment. This is certainly not literally true. No one knows whether it is more or less true than the exactly opposite assumption that technical progress makes new and old capital goods more productive in the same way and in the same proportion. I have worked both sides of the street in different papers, and I will produce estimates in both assumptions in this paper. That seems to me to be the moral equivalent of Edward Denison's suspiciously round assumption that half of new technology is the "embodied" kind and half the "disembodied" kind. The most casual kind of reflection suggests to me that embodied technological progress is by a substantial margin the more important kind.

Suppose that capital goods produced in any year are 100λ per cent more productive than those produced the year before. Suppose also that if a gross investment of $I(v)$ is made in year v, the amount surviving in a later year t will be $B(t-v)$. Under the further assumption that labor and machines of various vintages are arranged in such a way as to yield maximum output (or equivalently that all workers receive the same wage regardless of the age of their equipment) it can be shown that the stock of surviving capital goods of different vintages and productivity can be summarized for production-function purposes in an "equivalent stock of capital." The equivalent stock of capital adds up the survivors of each vintage after weighting them by the appropriate productivity improvement factor. To be precise, the equivalent stock of capital in year t is

$$(1) \qquad \mathcal{J}(t) = \sum_{v=-\infty} (1+\lambda)^v B(t-v) I(v)$$

Potential output is a function of the available equivalent stock of capital and the available input of labor $N(t)$, say

$$(2) \qquad P(t) = F(\mathcal{J}(t), N(t))$$

No explicit mention of technical progress is needed; it is already wrapped up in $\mathcal{J}$. What we observe, however, is not $P(t)$ but actual output $A(t)$. It is tempting to try to make some estimate of potential output and then to use it in estimating the production function. But since what one expects from the production function is a statement about potential output, it seems a little circular to impose an independently calculated measure of potential output to begin with. I have tried to get around this difficulty by a device which owes a lot to some of Arthur Okun's ideas.

Actual output falls below potential output because employment is less than the available supply of labor and because some capital stands idle. There is a logical pitfall here. If it is assumed—as I have tacitly done in (2)—that labor and already existing capital are substitutable for each other, then in principle capital should never be idle unless its marginal value product has fallen to zero (if depreciation occurs with use rather than with time, I should say marginal net product). Otherwise it would pay to use more capital with the current input of labor; the extra product would provide at least some quasi-rent. Yet we believe there to be such a thing as idle capacity in periods of economic slack. The paradox is easily resolved in a model which permits virtual substitution of labor and capital *before* capital goods take concrete form, but not after. I have analyzed such a model [3] but I do not at the moment see any direct way of using it in empirical work. So I shall simply assume, as an approximation, that the ratio of actual to potential output is a function of the unemployment rate. (The unemployment rate I shall be using is the difference between the "full employment" supply of man-hours and the number of man-hours actually worked, expressed as a ratio of the full employment supply. It differs from the ordinary labor-force concept in a number of ways—for example it can become negative, and did so in 1942–44, because the number of man-hours worked exceeded the normal supply.) If I let $u(t)$ stand for the unemployment rate:

$$(3) \qquad A(t) = f(u(t)) P(t) = f(u) F(\mathcal{J}, N)$$

With a convenient choice of functional forms for $f(u)$ and $F(\mathcal{J}, N)$, I can hope simultaneously to estimate the production function for potential output, and the curve which relates the degree of slack to the unemployment rate. The raw materials are time series of actual output, the full employment supply of labor, and the equivalent stock of capital, to be described in a moment.

To simplify computations, I have used the Cobb-Douglas function with constant returns to scale for $F(\mathcal{J}, \mathcal{N})$. For $f(u)$ I have used what amounts to the half of a normal curve lying to the right of the peak. This choice has the double advantage of being workable and of having the right general shape. One would want, I think, to have a kind of diminishing returns to the reduction of unemployment after a point, and this occurs as the normal curve flattens out near its peak. Also, any linear approximation near usual unemployment levels tends to show actual output dropping to zero when the unemployment rate reaches 30 per cent or so, and the normal curve avoids this.

With those specializations, my production function now reads:

(4) $$A = a 10^{b+cu+du^2} \mathcal{J}^\alpha \mathcal{N}^{1-\alpha}$$

though I shall fit it in the form:

(4') $$A/\mathcal{N} = a 10^{b+cu+du^2} (\mathcal{J}/\mathcal{N})^\alpha.$$

or

(4'') $$\log(A/\mathcal{N}) = \log a + b + cu + du^2 + \alpha \log(\mathcal{J}/\mathcal{N}).$$

In (4'') there are two constant terms, one belonging to F and one to f. They can be separated as soon as I make a statistical definition of "full employment." It happens that the measure of unemployment used in this paper coincides numerically with the usual labor force measure when they are both equal to about 4 per cent. That figure has become, at least temporarily, the conventional description of full employment, and I adopt it here. Now I must have actual output equal to potential output at full employment. This implies

$$f(.04) = 1 \quad \text{or} \quad b + .04c + (.04)^2 d = 0$$

From estimates of c and d I can calculate b, and then from (4'') I can find a.

With all constants estimated it is possible to ask and answer such questions as: given the expected increase in the supply of man-hours, and given the already determinate mortality of existing capital, how much gross investment is necessary to increase *potential* output by 3 or 4 or 5 per cent in the next year?

Data

Several time series measuring the "equivalent stock of capital" were constructed along the lines of equation (1), with alternative trial values of λ.

The case $\lambda = 0$ is, of course, the plain stock of capital. All are expressed in 1954 prices. Stock and equivalent stock figures were computed separately for plant and equipment—sometimes using different values of λ for each component, on the chance that equipment improves in productivity more rapidly than plant—with mortality calculated according to the schedules devised by George Terborgh. Because the plant and equipment series are quite highly correlated, I did not try to use them as separate inputs in the production function. Instead, every stock of capital or equivalent stock of capital figure in my regressions is actually the sum of a stock of plant and a stock of equipment, each generated from gross investment data with its own mortality curve and its own value of λ. The investment series used is consistent with "producers' durable goods" plus "other construction" in the national accounts, with the exception that religious, educational, hospital and institutional construction are excluded. (Dwellings are excluded from the stock of capital, which is intended to be a measure of privately-owned business plant and equipment.)

The output concept comparable to this measure of capital stock is gross national product minus the product originating in general government, government enterprises, households and institutions, rest of the world, and services of houses: This defines a reasonably close approximation to the output produced by the privately-owned stock of plant and equipment. It is expressed in 1954 prices.

The series for "full employment man-hours" is essentially due to Knowles [2]. This is based on the age and sex distribution of the population together with smoothed trends in participation rates and annual hours worked. Some minor adjustments were made, particularly to eliminate government employees since the output and capital series are restricted to the private business economy. Analogous adjustments were made to the BLS series on man-hours worked in the private economy, to restrict the coverage approximately to that involved in the other data used in the analysis.

Estimated Production Functions

Equation (1) defines the equivalent stock of capital for any constant rate of increase in the productivity of capital goods. As noted earlier, I have experimented with different improvement factors for plant and equipment separately and then added the two series. The regression results I shall report here use the following six combinations:

	J_0	J_1	J_2	J_3	J_4	J_5
λ plant	0	.02	.02	.02	.03	.03
λ equipment	0	.02	.03	.04	.03	.04

The multiple regressions themselves are given in the following table: The parameters are designated as in (4), with standard errors following in parentheses, except that $f(u)$ was actually estimated as $10^{b+cu+d(u+.130)^2}$.

Inspection of Table 1 yields some obvious generalizations.

(a) From the similarity of the estimated values of α for the equations with J_2 and J_4 and for those with J_3 and J_5, it seems clear that more depends on the improvement factor for equipment than on that for plant. This is associated with the fact that between 1929 and 1961 the ordinary stock of plant increased by about 50 per cent while the stock of equipment grew by almost 170 per cent.

(b) The estimated elasticity of output with respect to the equivalent stock of capital declines as the improvement factor (particularly that for equipment) increases, for obvious reasons.

(c) Very low values for the improvement factor lead to implausible values for α. One gets nonsense results unless considerable weight is given to technological progress.

(d) The estimated curve relating realized to potential output is not very sensitive to alternative assumptions about the improvement factor.

Table 1

	log a	b	c	d	α	R^2	Standard error of estimate
J_0	−.4179	.0460	−.1244 (.2016)	−1.344 (.413)	1.2377 (.0993)	.9622	.0322
J_1	−.3934	.0395	−.2814 (.1524)	− .979 (.315)	.6323 (.0364)	.9789	.0241
J_2	−.3328	.0382	−.3187 (.1465)	− .879 (.304)	.4990 (.0274)	.9806	.0230
J_3	−.2956	.0370	−.3386 (.1398)	− .813 (.291)	.4026 (.0221)	.9825	.0220
J_4	−.3888	.0387	−.3097 (.1427)	− .909 (.295)	.5054 (.0270)	.9816	.0225
J_5	−.0375	.0375	−.3319 (.1381)	− .838 (.287)	.4160 (.0214)	.9828	.0217

(e) The multiple correlation is a little higher and the standard error of estimate a little smaller for the larger values of λ. But because the estimates of α change in an offsetting way, goodness of fit is a poor way of distinguishing among neighboring values of λ.

It will be interesting to compare the conclusions flowing from estimates of (4) with those derived on the assumption that all technological progress is "disembodied," falling alike on new and old capital goods and therefore not requiring investment to generate an increase in productivity. For this purpose I have also estimated the production functions.

(5) $A = a(1+\mu)^t J_0{}^\alpha N^{1-\alpha} 10^{b+cu+d(u+.130)^2}$

with the result

(5′) $A = 1.10(1.025)^t J_0{}^{.11} N^{.89} 10^{.0365 - .251u - .888(u+.130)^2}$.

The squared correlation is .9945. The elasticity of output with respect to J_0 is about equal to its standard error. Essentially, output per man-hour just rises at $2\frac{1}{2}$ per cent a year.

Actual and Potential Output

A useful by-product of this procedure is a built-in estimate of the ratio of actual to potential output as a function of the unemployment rate. It must be remembered that the measure of unemployment I am using is not the conventional one. I define the unemployment rate in any year as the difference between the estimated full employment supply of man-hours and the number of man-hours actually worked, expressed as a fraction of the full employment supply of man-hours. This should be in principle a better measure of the excess supply of labor, for two reasons. In the first place, when the demand for labor is slack some people leave the measured labor force although they would willingly take work if they thought work was available. This kind of "unemployment" represents excess capacity. Second, involuntary part-time work, though it does not show up as unemployment in the official statistics, does affect the alternative concept. On the other hand, the usual labor force statistics undoubtedly contain less error than the ones used here.

A plot of the two measures of the unemployment rate against each other shows that most points fall along a smooth nonlinear curve. It happens by chance that the two measures coincide approximately at an unemployment rate of 4 per cent, which is the conventional definition of "full employment" I am using. Columns 1 and 2 of Table 2 give a few selected corresponding values of u (the unemployment rate used in this paper) and u^* (the usual labor force unemployment rate).

It is also the case, mentioned earlier, that the regression equations using different equivalent stocks give very similar curves relating the ratio of actual to potential output to the unemployment rate. The ratios corresponding to J_4 and J_5, and those corresponding to equation (5) are given in columns 3, 4, and 5 of Table 2.

Table 2

u	u^*	A/P J_4	A/P J_5	A/P (5)	A/P Okun's Law
−.13	.01	1.200	1.203	1.172	1.096
−.03	.02	1.094	1.094	1.084	1.064
.00	.03	1.054	1.054	1.051	1.032
.02	.035	1.028	1.025	1.027	1.016
.04	.04	1.000	1.000	1.000	1.000
.06	.05	.971	.971	.976	.968
.08	.06	.941	.942	.949	.936
.10	.07	.911	.912	.921	.904
.27	.21	.645	.652	.671	.456

The only other systematic attempt to relate the gap between actual and potential output to the unemployment rate is Okun's Law [1] which states that the percentage excess of potential over actual output is 3.2 times the excess of the (conventional) unemployment rate over 4 per cent. In my notation, Okun's Law states that

$$\frac{P-A}{P} = 3.2(u^* - .04)$$

Okun himself, it should be noted, has used this relation only for the period since 1955. The ratio of actual to potential output read from this equation is shown in the last column of Table 2.

It is altogether remarkable that Okun's Law and the approach used in this paper give very similar results for conventional unemployment rates between 3 and 7 per cent, despite the fact that they are based on entirely different data (and the fact that u relates to private employment and u^* to total). It is only natural that they should differ for extremely high unemployment rates and extremely low ones. I introduced the possibility of considerable curvature into this approach because I wanted to allow for diminishing returns as the unemployment rate becomes very low. But as Table 2 shows, at very low levels of unemployment, the approach in this paper indicates a greater excess of actual over normal full employment potential than does Okun's Law. The required curvature is actually in the equations; the apparent paradox arises because the man-hours figures allow for the super-normal increase in labor force and hours worked during the war years of very low unemployment.

Investment Requirements for Economic Growth

With the unemployment rate fixed at $u = .04$, any one of the estimated production functions states that potential output is constrained by the currently available input of labor and by the whole history of capital formation. If the American economy can and must move along such a function in the next few years, the growth of productive potential is tied in a specific way to the growth of the labor supply and the rate of investment. Movements in the supply of hours of work are usually taken as given. That leaves the volume of investment as the most important determinant of growth which is actually open to influence by policy. (There is also the equally important possibility of influencing the rate of technological progress, λ; but that leads to an entirely different set of questions.)

The movement of full employment man-hours for the entire economy in the next few years can be estimated with reasonable accuracy from demographic trends. It is less easy to estimate the supply of man-hours to the private economy, because that is less purely a matter of demography. Public employment has been gaining relative to private employment in recent years, and since there is no reason to expect a reversal of this trend, it is safe to conclude that the supply of labor to the private economy will rise more slowly than the total. With the labor force expected to grow at about 1.7 per cent per year and average annual hours worked declining at an annual rate of some 0.3–0.4 per cent, the supply of potential man-hours is likely to increase at about 1.3–1.4 per cent a year in the near future. This is a more rapid rate of increase than in the decade just past. But the supply of labor to the private economy will rise more slowly than that. Between 1950 and 1960, our series for the supply of potential man-hours to the private economy rose at an average annual rate between 0.4 and 0.5 per cent. For looking ahead, I have made alternative calculations with an annual increase in labor supply of 0.65 per cent and 1.0 per cent.

With this growth in labor input, a substantial amount of investment is needed just to keep capital per man-hour constant. Suppose that some $2\frac{1}{2}$ per cent of the capital stock is retired each year. (I am speaking now of the ordinary capital stock, with $\lambda = 0$.) Then with a capital-output ratio of about $1\frac{3}{4}$, $4\frac{1}{2}$ per cent of private GNP must be invested just to replace worn-out capital, and between $5\frac{1}{2}$ and 6 per cent of GNP must be invested (depending on the assumed rate of growth of the labor force) to keep capital per man-hour constant. A slightly higher rate of investment would be needed to keep capital per worker from falling.

When we deal with an equivalent stock of capital the calculations are a little more complicated but the results not very different. The annual mortality of "equivalent capital" can be calculated. For J_3 and J_5 it runs just over 3 per cent of the equivalent stock; for J_4 it is about $2\frac{1}{2}$ per cent. The capital-output ratio is much higher because the improvement factor makes the equivalent stock considerably higher than the capital stock itself. Working against this is the fact that a dollar's worth of investment is more potent, creating more than "a dollar's worth" of equivalent capital.

Generally speaking, the result is that the maintenance of capital intensity —and the accompanying achievement of low rates of growth of output— can be obtained with a somewhat slighter investment burden than consideration of the ordinary stock of capital would suggest.

To attain a high rate of growth of output, the equivalent stock of capital must grow faster than the input of labor. Additional investment now performs a function beyond the widening process as the labor force increases and the conventional deepening process as the capital-intensity of production increases. The third function is, of course, what one might call quickening: the carrying into production of new technology as represented by the improvement factor. Table 3 shows—for 1960–61 values of the variables—the percentage of business GNP which must be invested gross to permit different rates of growth of output. The calculations are shown for J_3, J_4, and J_5 with the two alternative rates of growth of the labor force mentioned earlier.

In interpreting these figures it should be remembered that the output concept used here covers about 80 per cent of the total gross national product. Also the omission of various kinds of institutional construction reduces the gross investment total to about 93 per cent of "producers' durable equipment" plus "other construction" in the national accounts. Thus an investment quota corresponding to the ratio of business fixed investment to GNP would be about 86 per cent of the number given in Table 3. With this adjustment, the estimates in the table seem to be of the right order of magnitude. They suggest that a necessary condition for increasing the rate of growth of output from about $3\frac{1}{2}$ per cent annually to $4\frac{1}{2}$ per cent annually may be a 20–25 per cent increase in the investment quota from the range 10–11 per cent of business GNP to the range 12–14 per cent of business GNP. J_4 gives both a lower required investment quota and a smaller relative increase to get from $3\frac{1}{2}$ to $4\frac{1}{2}$ per cent growth than do J_3 and J_5. Alternative improvement factors have only a minor effect on the implied investment requirements because the estimated elasticity changes to make a partial compensation.

Rough calculations show that to maintain an accelerated rate of growth throughout a decade requires a slowly rising savings-investment quota. But the rise is slow and the average investment quota only slightly above the initial figure shown in Table 3.

Table 3—Investment quotas for alternative growth rates

Growth rate	3%	3½%	4%	4½%	5%
J_3					
Slow growth in man-hours	9.9	11.2	12.4	13.8	15.0
Fast growth in man-hours	9.2	10.4	11.7	13.1	14.3
J_4					
Slow growth in man-hours	9.0	10.2	11.4	12.5	13.7
Fast growth in man-hours	8.5	9.8	10.9	12.0	13.2
J_5					
Slow growth in man-hours	10.1	11.3	12.6	13.9	15.3
Fast growth in man-hours	9.4	10.8	12.0	13.3	14.7

By comparison, the production function (5), which makes technological change a pure "residual," gives altogether different results. The high time trend—a residual increase in output of $2\frac{1}{2}$ per cent annually with labor and capital constant—and the low elasticity of output with respect to capital imply that a fairly rapid rate of growth of output per man-hour is achievable with very little investment but that a visibly higher rate of growth can be supported only by an unrealistically high investment rate. For example, with the slower rate of growth of the labor force, (5) says that a 3 per cent increase in potential output is achievable with a slight decrease in the capital stock. The gross investment implied is about $3\frac{1}{2}$ per cent of potential output; the net investment is actually negative. But to lift the rate of growth to 4 per cent a year would require an investment quota of almost 20 per cent of potential output. These implications seem wholly unrealistic to me, and they suggest that the "embodied" model is a better one. But I must admit that there is nothing in the analysis I have given which "proves" that (4) is a better model of production than (5).

Entirely apart from all statistical difficulties, one must admit the possibility that our economy is not free to move back and forth along a production function like (4) or even (5). An attempt to accelerate movement out along the function may have the effect of shifting the function itself. For one thing, a sharply higher rate of investment may bring about premature scrapping of old equipment. Second, there may be limits even in a mature economy to the speed with which the system can adjust to large inflows of new capital. Third, a change in the investment quota is itself a change in the composition of output; changes in the composition of output may also have the effect of shifting the function bodily, though it would be difficult to make an a priori judgment about the nature of the shift. This reflection suggests the wisdom of trying to make such analyses of the productivity of investment sector by sector. This would place a greater strain on the availability of data, but might in compensation yield important conclusions about the best sectoral composition of investment.

Conclusion

Capital formation is not the only source of growth in productivity. Investment is at best a necessary condition for growth, surely not a sufficient condition. Recent study has indicated the importance of such activities as research, education, and public health. But while economists are now convinced of the significance of these factors in the process of economic growth, we are still a long way from having any quantitative estimate of the pay-off to society of resources devoted to research, education, and improvements in allocative efficiency. Since such estimates must form the foundation for a national allocation of resources in the interests of economic growth, their provision by hook or by crook presents a research problem of great theoretical and practical interest. The object of this paper is to make a start in that job for the much easier and prosaic case of tangible capital formation.

References

[1] "The American Economy in 1961: Problems and Policies," in "January 1961 Economic Report of the President and the Economic Situation and Outlook," hearings before the Joint Economic Committee (87th Cong., 1st sess., 1961), pp. 324, 375.

[2] James W. Knowles, "Potential Economic Growth in the United States," Study Paper No. 20, prepared for the Joint Economic Committee in connection with the Study of Employment, Growth and Price Levels (86th Cong., 2d sess., 1960).

[3] Robert M. Solow, "Substitution and Fixed Proportions in the Theory of Capital," *Rev. of Econ. Studies*, 1962.

7

Investment in Humans, Technological Diffusion, and Economic Growth

Professors Richard R. Nelson of Yale University and Edmund S. Phelps of the University of Pennsylvania discuss how technological progress and investment in human resources are interrelated in the economic growth process in the following selection. These authors specify a direct relationship between returns to educational investments in human capital and technical progress. Given interactions of this sort, simplified human resource quality indices may reflect poorly the relationships between growth in output and the contributions of educational investments to the growth process.

RICHARD R. NELSON
EDMUND S. PHELPS

I Introduction

Most economic theorists have embraced the principle that certain kinds of education—the three R's, vocational training, and higher education—equip a man to perform certain jobs or functions, or enable a man to perform a given function more effectively. The principle seems a sound one. Underlying it, perhaps, is the theory that education enhances one's ability to receive, decode, and understand information, and that information processing and interpretation is important for performing or learning to perform many jobs.

In applying this principle we find it fruitful to rank jobs or functions according to the degree to which they require adaptation to change or

Reprinted from Richard R. Nelson and Edmund S. Phelps, "Investment in Humans, Technological Diffusion, and Economic Growth," *American Economic Review Proceedings* 56 (May 1966), pp. 69–75, with the permission of the authors and publisher.

require learning in the performance of the function. At the bottom of this scale are functions which are highly routinized: e.g., running a power saw or diagnosing a malfunction in an automobile. In these functions, the discriminations to be made and the operations based on them remain relatively constant over time. In the other direction on this scale we have, for example, innovative functions which demand keeping abreast of improving technology. Even a highly routinized job may require considerable education to master the necessary discriminations and skills. But probably education is especially important to those functions requiring adaptation to change. Here it is necessary to learn to follow and to understand new technological developments.

Thus far, economic growth theory has concentrated on the role of education as it relates to the completely routinized job. In its usual, rather general form, the theory postulates a production function which states how maximum current output depends upon the current services of tangible capital goods, the current number of men performing each of these jobs, the current educational attainments of each of these job-holders, and time. To simplify matters, some analysts have specified a production function in which output depends upon tangible capital and "effective labor"; the latter is a weighted sum of the number of workers, the weight assigned to each worker being an increasing function of that worker's educational attainment. This specification assumes that highly educated men are perfect substitutes for less educated men (in the technical sense that the marginal rate of substitution between them is constant). Actually, it is possible that educated men are more substitutable for certain capital goods than for other labor; they permit production with less complex machines. However, the exact specification of the production function does not concern us. The pertinent feature of this kind of production function is this: The "marginal productivity" of education, which is a function of the inputs and the current technology, can remain positive forever even if the technology is stationary. In the models we shall later introduce, education has a positive payoff only if the technology is always improving.

We shall consider now the importance of education for a particular function requiring great adaptation to change. We then propose two models which these considerations suggest.

II   The Hypothesis

We suggest that, in a technologically progressive or dynamic economy, production management is a function requiring adaptation to change and that the more educated a manager is, the quicker will he be to introduce new techniques of production. To put the hypothesis simply, educated people make good innovators, so that education speeds the process of technological diffusion.

Evidence for this hypothesis can be found in the experience of United States agriculture.[1] It is clear that the farmer with a relatively high level of education has tended to adopt productive innovations earlier than the farmer with relatively little education. We submit that this is because the greater education of the more educated farmer has increased his ability to understand and evaluate the information on new products and processes disseminated by the Department of Agriculture, the farm journals, the radio, seed and equipment companies, and so on.[2] The better educated farmer is quicker to adopt profitable new processes and products since, for him, the expected payoff from innovation is likely to be greater and the risk likely to be smaller; for he is better able to discriminate between promising and umpromising ideas, and hence less likely to make mistakes. The less educated farmer, for whom the information in technical journals means less, is prudent to delay the introduction of a new technique until he has concrete evidence of its profitability, like the fact that his more educated friends have adopted the technique with success.

This phenomenon, that education speeds technological diffusion, may take different forms outside of agriculture. In large, industrial corporations, in which there is a fine division of labor, the function of keeping abreast of technological improvements (though perhaps not the ultimate responsibility for innovation) may be assigned to scientists. In this case, their education is obviously important; but so too is the education and sophistication of top management which must make the final decisions.[3]

So much for our broad hypothesis and the evidence supporting it. We shall consider now two specific models of the process of technological diffusion and the role of education.

III Two Models of Technological Diffusion

We shall adopt a postulate about the factor-saving character of technical progress which permits us to speak meaningfully about the "level" or

[1] See E. M. Rogers, *Diffusion of Innovations* (Free Press, 1962), especially Chap. 6.

[2] To be sure, some of the correlation described between education and diffusion may be spurious. Some farmers are undoubtedly both progressive and educated because they come from progressive and prosperous farming families that could afford to give them an education. But there is no question that educated farmers do read technical, innovation-describing literature more than do less educated farmers—and presumably because they find it profitable to do so.

[3] For an interesting essay on science policy, in which it is argued that Britain's growth has suffered from a shortage of scientists in management, that too small a fraction of scientists are engaged in using (rather than adding to) the existing stock of knowledge, see C. F. Carter and B. R. Williams, "Government Scientific Policy and the Growth of the British Economy," *The Manchester School*, Sept., 1964.

"index" of technology. Specifically, we suppose that technical progress is Harrod-neutral everywhere (i.e., for all capital-labor ratios), so that progress can be described as purely labor-augmenting. This means that if output, Q, is a function of capital, K, labor, L, and time, t, the production function may be written

$$(1) \qquad Q(t) = F[K(t),\, A(t)L(t)]$$

In (1), the variable $A(t)$ is our index of technology in practice. If we interpret (1) as a vintage production function in which $K(t)$ is the quantity of currently purchased capital, $L(t)$ the labor working with it, and $Q(t)$ the output producible from it, then $A(t)$ measures the best-practice level of technology, the average technology level "embodied" in the representative assortment of capital goods currently being purchased. Alternatively, we could suppose that all technical progress is wholly "disembodied" and that (1) is the "aggregate" production function for the firm, industry or economy and $A(t)$ is the average index of technology common to all vintages of capital, old and new.

In addition to this concept, we introduce the notion of the theoretical level of technology, $T(t)$. This is defined as the best-practice level of technology that would prevail if technological diffusion were completely instantaneous. It is a measure of the stock of knowledge or body of techniques that is available to innovators. We shall suppose that the theoretical technology level advances exogenously at a constant exponential rate λ:

$$(2) \qquad T(t) = T_0 e^{\lambda t}, \quad \lambda > 0$$

FIRST MODEL

Our first model is as simple a one as we can invent. It states that the time lag between the creation of a new technique and its adoptions is a decreasing function of some index of average educational attainment, h, of those in a position to innovate. (We may think of h as denoting the degree of human capital intensity.) Letting w denote the lag, we can represent this notion as follows:

$$(3) \qquad A(t) = T(t - w(h)), \quad w'(h) < 0$$

The level of technology in practice equals the theoretical level of technology w years ago, w a decreasing function of h.

Substitution of (2) in (3) yields

$$(4) \qquad A(t) = T_0 e^{\lambda[t - w(h)]}$$

If h is constant, two results follow from (4). First, the index of technology in practice grows at the same rate, λ, as the index of theoretical technology. Second, the "level" or path of the technology in practice is an increasing function of h, since an increase of h shortens the lag between $T(t)$ and $A(t)$.

An important feature of this model is that, *ceteris paribus*, the return to education is greater the faster the theoretical level of technology has been advancing. As equation (5) shows, the effect upon $A(t)$ of a marginal increase of h is an increasing function of λ, given $A(t)$, and is positive only if $\lambda > 0$.

(5)
$$\frac{\delta A(t)}{\delta h} = -\lambda w'(h) T_0 e^{\lambda[t-w(h)]}$$

$$= -\lambda w'(h) A(t)$$

The same property is displayed by the "marginal productivity of educational attainment." Using (1) and (4) we have

(6)
$$Q(t) = F[K(t), T_0 e^{\lambda[t-w(h)]}L(t)]$$

Hence,

(7)
$$\frac{\delta Q(t)}{\delta h} = \lambda T_0 e^{\lambda[t-w(h)]}L(t)[-w'(h)]F_2$$

$$= -\lambda w'(h) \times \text{Wage Bill}$$

Thus the marginal productivity of education is an increasing function of λ, given the current wage bill, and is positive only if $\lambda > 0$. This feature is not found in the conventional treatment of education described at the beginning of this paper.

The first model is not altogether satisfactory. It is unreasonable to suppose that the lag of the best-practice level behind the theoretical level of technology is independent of the profitability of the new techniques not yet introduced. Further, it is somewhat unrealistic to suppose that an increase of educational attainments instantaneously reduces the lag. In these respects, our second model is somewhat more realistic.

SECOND MODEL

Our second model states that the rate at which the latest, theoretical technology is realized in improved technological practice depends upon educational attainment and upon the gap between the theoretical level of technology and the level of technology in practice. Specifically,

(8)
$$A(t) = \Phi(h)[T(t) - A(t)]$$

or equivalently

(8')
$$\frac{A(t)}{A(t)} = \Phi(h)\left[\frac{T(t)-A(t)}{A(t)}\right], \quad \Phi(0)=0, \quad \Phi'(h)>0$$

According to this hypothesis, the rate of increase of the technology in practice (not the level) is an increasing function of education attainment and proportional to the "gap," $(T(t)-A(t))/A(t)$.

Some results parallel to those in the first model can be obtained if we again postulate exponential growth of $T(t)$, as in (2), and constancy of h. First in the long run, if h is positive, the rate of increase of the level of technology in practice, $\dot{A}(t)/A(t)$, settles down to the value λ, independently of the index of education attainment. The reason is this: if, say, the level of h is sufficiently large that $\dot{A}(t)/A(t) > \lambda$ initially, then the gap narrowed; but the narrowing of the gap reduces $\dot{A}(t)/A(t)$; the gap continues to narrow until, in the limit, $\dot{A}(t)/A(t)$ has fallen to the value λ at which point the system is an equilibrium with a constant gap.

Another result is that the asymptotic or equilibrium gap is a decreasing function of educational attainment. Thus increased educational attainment increases the path of the technology in practice in the long run.

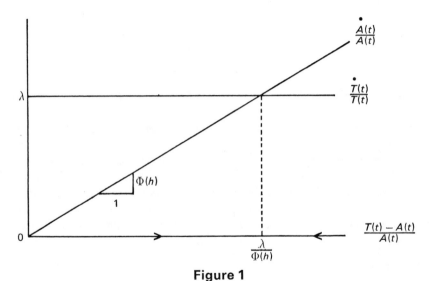

Figure 1

Both these results are shown by Figure 1 and by (9), which is the solution to our differential equation (8), given (2):

$$(9) \qquad A(t) = \left(A_0 - \frac{\Phi}{\Phi + \lambda} T_0 \right) e^{-\Phi t} + \frac{\Phi}{\Phi + \lambda} T_0 e^{\lambda t}$$

As both (9) and Figure 1 imply, the equilibrium path of the technology in practice is given by

$$(10) \qquad A^*(t) = \frac{\Phi(h)}{\Phi(h) + \lambda} T_0 e^{\lambda t}$$

the equilibrium gap is given by

$$(11) \qquad \frac{T(t) - A^*(t)}{A^*(t)} = \frac{\lambda}{\Phi(h)}$$

In a technologically stagnant economy $(\lambda=0)$, the gap approaches zero for every $h>0$. In a technologically progressive economy $(\lambda=0)$, there is a positive equilibrium gap for every h and λ. The equilibrium gap is increasing in λ and decreasing in h.

In the first model it was seen that the marginal productivity of educational attainment is an increasing function of λ and positive only if $\lambda>0$. That is also true of the second model in the long run (once the effect of an increase of h has had time to influence the level of $A(t)$ as well as its rate of change). Equation (12) shows that the elasticity of the long-run equilibrium level of technology in practice, $A^*(t)$, with respect to h is increasing in λ:

$$(12) \qquad \frac{\delta A^*(t)}{\delta h} \frac{h}{A^*(t)} = \left[\frac{h \Phi'(h)}{\Phi(h)} \right] \left[\frac{\lambda}{\Phi(h)+\lambda} \right]$$

This indicates that the payoff to increased educational attainment is greater the more technologically progressive is the economy.

These are only partial models and excessively simple ones. No machinery has been given for determining educational attainment.[4] The theoretical level of technology has been treated as exogenous. Finally, it might be useful to build a model which combines elements of both the first and second model: the rate of technical progress in practice may depend both upon the length of time during which a new technique has been in existence and upon its profitability. But we hope that these two models may be a useful starting point.

IV Concluding Remarks

The general subject at this session is the relationship between capital structure and technological progress. Recalling that the process of education can be viewed as an act of investment in people that educated people are bearers of human capital, we see that this paper has relevance to that subject. For, according to the models presented here, the rate of return to education is greater the more technologically progressive is the economy. This suggests that the progressiveness of the technology has implications for the optimal capital structure in the broad sense. In particular, it may be that society should build more human capital relative to tangible capital the more dynamic is the technology.

Another point of relevance for social investment policy may be mentioned. If innovations produce externalities, because they show the way to imitators, then education—by its stimulation of innovation—also yields

[4] This is done in a paper by Phelps which develops a Golden Rule of Education. It is shown that Golden Rule growth requires more education the more technologically progressive is the economy.

externalities. Hence, the way of viewing the role of education in economic growth set forth here seems to indicate another possible source of a divergence between the private and social rate of return to education.

Finally, the connection between education and growth which we have discussed has a significant implication for the proper analysis of economic growth. Our view suggests that the usual, straightforward insertion of some index of educational attainment in the production function may constitute a gross misspecification of the relation between education and the dynamics of production.

8

Embodied Technology, the Asymptotic Behavior of Capital's Age, and Soviet Growth

The methodology of economic growth analysis and the embodiment thesis discussed by Robert M. Solow earlier are illustrated empirically by Professor Earl R. Brubaker of the University of Wisconsin in an attempt better to understand Soviet economic growth. Although similar to other studies of the American economic growth experience, Brubaker's approach and conclusions regarding

EARL R. BRUBAKER

the relative importance of human capital are different in discernible ways. Even though the size and specific character of the growth residual remains uncertain in many respects, it is equally as apparent that more refined analysis of inputs to the growth process does extend our knowledge.

I Some Basic Measurements

One of the most fascinating aspects of Soviet economic development has been the remarkable pace in growth of aggregate output maintained over the substantial period of more than three decades. The pace has been remarkable, though not completely unprecedented, and there need be little doubt about its authenticity. Thanks largely to Professors Abram Bergson, Warren Eason, and Raymond Powell, to Dr. Richard Moorsteen, and to Nancy Nimitz there exists a carefully prepared and consistent record of

Reprinted from Earl R. Brubaker, "Embodied Technology, the Asymptotic Behavior of Capital's Age, and Soviet Growth," *Review of Economics and Statistics* 50 (August 1968), pp. 304–11, with the permission of the author and publisher.

Soviet Russia's gross national product, capital stock, and labor inputs for the period 1928 through 1961 [4] [13]. In table 1 a portion of this basic record on Soviet economic development is reproduced. The primary purpose of this paper is to explore the usefulness of the hypothesis of embodied technical change for providing insight into sources of the growth in output.

II Alternative Aggregate Production Functions and Soviet Growth

In essence the problem involves interpreting the data, explicitly or implicitly, in terms of an aggregate production function.

Although we shall be focussing on a function accounting for the possible impact of embodied technical change, it will be useful as a preliminary to analyze the record in terms of: (1) a Cobb-Douglas function with dis-embodied technical change, and (2) a function amended further to account for changes in the stock of human capital arising from expenditures on formal education.

THE COBB-DOUGLAS INTERPRETATION

Making a number of customary assumptions[1] equation (1) may be derived from the traditional Cobb-Douglas function:

$$\frac{\Delta 0}{0} = \frac{\Delta A}{A} + b\,\frac{\Delta L}{L} + (1-b)\,\frac{\Delta K}{K} \tag{1}$$

where 0 represents gross national product; L and K are labor and capital inputs, respectively; A is an unexplained residual; and b and $(1-b)$ are

Table 1—USSR: growth of GNP and factor inputs[a]

Period	GNP	Employment (adjusted for changes in hours)	Fixed capital stock	Inventories	Livestock	Agricultural land
1928–1937	11.9[b]	2.5	8.8	5.4	−4.6	2.0
1937–1940[c]	5.7	8.5	10.3	9.2	6.3	3.6
1940–1950	2.0	1.4	2.2	2.3	−0.4	−0.3
1950–1958	7.9	1.4	9.3	7.0	2.9	3.7
1958–1961	6.0	−1.2	10.2	11.7	3.7	1.5
1928–1961	6.7	2.1	7.1	5.7	0.2	1.7

[a] Percentage change per year. Unless otherwise indicated data are from [13, pp. 315, 337–338, 361–362, 365–366]. For some variables it has been necessary to select one of a number of conceptually different time series lest the calculations become unwieldy. Fuller discussion of the choices is available from the author on request. As a practical matter, with few exceptions, the pertinent measures differ little from one another, so that the basic record, its interpretation, and our basic conclusions will be essentially the same no matter which we choose. There is, however, a notable exception. The rate of growth of output for 1928–1937 reproduced here, Bergson's measure in ruble factor costs of 1928, amounts to 11.9 per cent a year contrasted with only 6.2 per cent a year as measured by Moorsteen and Powell in ruble factor costs of 1937. With the substitution of Bergson's measure for 1928–1937 the series presumably approximates better the growth of Soviet capacity to produce a late period mix [4, pp. 31–34] [13, pp. 2–4].

[b] [4, p. 217].

[c] Data reflect territorial changes.

[1] It is not at all clear that these assumptions are appropriate or even relevant to the Soviet economy. At any rate equation (1) might quite plausibly be hypothesized directly.

partial elasticities of output with respect to labor and capital.[2] Thus $\Delta 0/0$ is the relative change in GNP; $\Delta L/L$ and $\Delta K/K$ are the relative changes in labor and capital inputs; and $\Delta A/A$ is the relative change in the residual.

Using data from the basic record and estimates[3] for b and $(1-b)$, $\Delta A/A$ can be calculated as a residual from equation (1):

Period	$\dfrac{\Delta A}{A}$	$\dfrac{\Delta A/A}{\Delta 0/0}$	Period	$\dfrac{\Delta A}{A}$	$\dfrac{\Delta A/A}{\Delta 0/0}$
1928–1937	8.3	0.70	1950–1958	4.4	0.56
1937–1940	−2.7	—	1958–1961	3.9	0.65
1940–1950	0.6	0.30	1928–1961	3.5	0.52

Notice the striking variation in $\Delta A/A$. Notice also that for periods other than 1937–1940 and 1940–1950 $\Delta A/A$ is called upon to explain something on the order of two-thirds of the rate of growth of GNP, a result quite similar to Nelson's [14] calculations for the United States. The generally large size of $\Delta A/A$ suggests that the Cobb-Douglas interpretation including only disembodied technical change leaves much to be explained about Soviet growth.

THE COBB-DOUGLAS FUNCTION AMENDED TO INCLUDE HUMAN CAPITAL

Today most economists would agree with Professor Theodore Schultz that human capital may well be an important reason for our large unexplained residual. Fortunately, we now have systematic evidence on a very important aspect of the stock of human capital in the USSR. Professor Nicholas DeWitt in his unpublished Ph.D. dissertation has prepared estimates of capital embodied in the Soviet labor force due to accumulated expenditures on formal education [8]. From this point forward references to educational capital, H in the notation, are to this large, but admittedly limited, aspect.[4] DeWitt's estimates cover the period 1928–1958, and his

[2] The measured shares of incomes to the factors often serve as estimates of these elasticities, and something akin to that procedure is employed in the present analysis.

[3] The computations were accomplished by obtaining a weighted average of the growth rates for the inputs as presented in table 1. Thus, agricultural land, like inventories and livestock, may be regarded as a particular form of capital. Plausible "synthetic" income shares may be estimated for the Soviet economy. Computations by Moorsteen and Powell [13, p. 371] for 1937 suggest that relative shares weighted 0.70 for labor and 0.30 for capital may approximate fairly closely the "true" values. The weight for capital may be distributed among fixed capital—0.206, inventories—0.067, and livestock—0.027 [13, p. 160]. The weight for agricultural land is estimated by analogy with the United States at 40 per cent of agricultural labor, or, with all labor 0.70, at 0.087 [13, pp. 255–256]. Finally, with weights adjusted to sum to 1.0 we obtain: labor—0.644, capital—0.276, and land—0.080.

[4] Professor David Granick has cogently argued that a vital feature of Soviet industrialization was the emphasis on bringing "... very large numbers of raw peasant youth into direct contact with machinery in the environment of large factories" developing through "learning by doing" the discipline and skills needed in an industrial labor force. If we were able to quantify the formation of human capital by this means, we would have to introduce the results both on the output and the input sides of our accounts [9, pp. 156–157]. Furthermore no allowance has been made for changes in the quality of educational capital. Cf. footnote 13.

methods have been used to extend the series of 1965 [15, p. 296]. The
pertinent results of these calculations are taken as approximations to the
values for the time periods considered here.

Period	ΔH/H	Period	ΔH/H
1928–1940	13.8	1958–1961	4.6
1940–1950	4.4	1928–1961	8.4
1950–1958	7.0		

Clearly for the entire period the stock of educational capital has grown at
impressive rates, and where these rates exceed those for labor inputs, the
effect will be to reduce[5] the computed $\Delta A/A$. Formally equation (1) simply
is expanded to include $\Delta H/H$ as follows:

$$\Delta 0/0 = \Delta A^*/A^* + b'(\Delta L/L) + (1-b)\Delta K/K + c(\Delta H/H) \tag{2}$$

where $\Delta A^*/A^*$ is a residual net of the effects of investment in education, b' is
a new elasticity of output with respect to labor, and c is the elasticity of
output with respect to educational capital. If estimates of b' and c can be
obtained, $\Delta A^*/A^*$ may be calculated as a residual in equation (2). Following
DeWitt one might assume that part of labor's share in national income is
appropriately attributable to investment in education, and, rather arbitrarily,
that the rate of return on such investment equals that on physical capital.
Implied values for b' and c are 0.59 and 0.055 respectively.[6] Associated
values for $\Delta A^*/A^*$ are:

Period	$\frac{\Delta A^*}{A^*}$	$\frac{\Delta A^*/A^*}{\Delta A/A}$	Period	$\frac{\Delta A^*}{A^*}$	$\frac{\Delta A^*/A^*}{\Delta A/A}$
1928–1937[a]	7.8	0.94	1950–1958	4.1	0.94
1937–1940[a]	−2.8	—	1958–1961	3.7	0.90
1940–1950	0.4	0.68	1928–1961	3.2	0.91

[a] The rate shown for $\Delta H/H$ during 1928–1940 is taken as an approximation to the correct values for both sub-periods.

Comparing $\Delta A^*/A^*$ with $\Delta A/A$ we see that for the periods other than 1937–
1940 and 1940–1950 at least 90 per cent of the residual remains.

THE HYPOTHESIS OF EMBODIED TECHNICAL CHANGE

Professor Robert M. Solow's hypothesis of embodied technical change
[17] [18] as elaborated by Nelson may provide additional insight into the
possible nature of the residual, $\Delta A/A$. Although some doubts have been
expressed about the embodiment hypothesis in its usual form [13, pp. 306–
307], relatively thorough and rigorous investigation of the implications of
accepting it in the Soviet case may help to clarify its usefulness for interpreting both Soviet economic growth and economic growth in general.

[5] Because part of labor's weight is reallocated to H.
[6] See [13, pp. 248, 315, 337–338].

Following Nelson,[7] then, we further break down $\Delta A/A$ to obtain the following approximation.

$$\frac{\Delta 0}{0} \approx \left[\frac{\Delta A'}{A'} + d\lambda - \frac{d\lambda\Delta\bar{a}_t}{1+\lambda(-\Delta\bar{a}_t)} \right] + b'\frac{\Delta L}{L} + c\frac{\Delta H}{H} + e\frac{\Delta M}{M} + d\frac{\Delta K'}{K'} \qquad (3)$$

where $\Delta A'/A'$ is relative growth in factor productivity attributable neither to growth of educational capital nor to embodied technical change; $\Delta K'/K'$ is the rate of growth of fixed capital; $\Delta M/M$ is the rate of growth of other capital; d and e are the partial elasticities of output with respect to K' and M; λ is the relative growth in the quality of K'; and $\bar{a}_t$ is the average age of K'. The third term in the brackets on the right-hand side of (3) indicates that $\Delta A^*/A^*$ will tend to be inversely related to $\Delta\bar{a}$. This relationship is of considerable interest as it will be possible to present some substantial evidence on $\Delta\bar{a}$. At any rate, equation (3) contains three new variables, so that if outside information can be obtained about any two of them, it may be possible to compute values for the third.

In fact Moorsteen and Powell [13, p. 336] present some interesting evidence on $\bar{a}$:

Year	$\bar{a}$ (years)	Year	$\bar{a}$ (years)
1928	17.3	1950	15.3
1937	13.9	1958	11.6
1940	13.4	1961	10.4

Also there is precedent for simply assuming that $\Delta A'/A'$ equals zero. This assumption might be called a partial embodiment assumption since it implies that all of $\Delta A^*/A^*$ results from changes in design technology that need to be embodied in new capital items. It is a bit less extreme than the widely discussed complete embodiment assumption, which requires that all of $\Delta A/A$ be due to improvement in capital design. With $\Delta A'/A'=0$ and the estimates of $\bar{a}$ by Moorsteen and Powell, it is indeed possible to compute values of λ.

Before presenting the implied values for λ it will be useful to consider briefly the essential fashion in which $\Delta K'/K'$ and n, the service life of capital items, affect the pattern of change in average age of a capital stock. To make the analysis easily manageable we assume that the service life of *all* capital items is given by n and that investment and retirements both take place at the beginning of the year. Then $\bar{a}_t$ may be defined:

---

[7] Nelson [14, p. 582, footnote 17] takes 1 as approximately equal to $1 + \lambda(\bar{a}_0 - \bar{a}_t)$ in deriving $\frac{\Delta\mathcal{J}}{\mathcal{J}} = \frac{\Delta K}{K} + \lambda - \lambda\Delta\bar{a}$. Without this approximation we obtain $\frac{\Delta\mathcal{J}}{\mathcal{J}} = \frac{\Delta K'}{K'} + \lambda - \frac{\lambda\Delta\bar{a}}{1+\lambda(-\Delta\bar{a})}$. The latter expression was used because of the relatively large values for $\Delta\bar{a}$ in the Soviet case. As it turns out, this refinement makes little difference in the values of λ computed here.

$$\bar{a}_t = \frac{0I_t + 1I_{t-1} + 2I_{t-2} + \ldots (n-1)I_{t-(n-1)}}{K'_t} \tag{4}$$

where I is gross investment. If I, and K', flow at a constant rate, r, it may be shown that the equilibrium average age,[8] $\bar{a}_e$, is given by:

$$\bar{a}_e = \frac{1}{r} + \frac{n}{1 - (1+r)^n} \tag{5}$$

Some examples using measurements of the Soviet economy may provide additional insight into Soviet growth. First we calculate values for $\bar{a}_e$ assuming: (1) that values of r equal the rates of growth of capital stock measured for 1928–1937, 1950–1958, and 1958–1961, and (2) that n equals 44 years.[9] The results are, respectively, 10.3, 9.8, and 9.2 years. In other words, to the extent that reality corresponded to the model, Soviet fixed capital stock growing at a rate of 8.8 per cent a year would have tended toward an eventual average age of 10.3 years. Notice the difference between the equilibrium average age of 10.3 years and the 17.3 years measured for 1928. The declining $\bar{a}$ measured during 1928–1937 may be thought of as a movement from the high initial value in 1928 toward a new equilibrium implied by the new rapid rate of growth of capital stock. By 1937 substantial progress had been made in pursuit of the new equilibrium. The decline continued during 1937–1940. But then during 1940–1950 $\Delta K'/K'$ dropped drastically because of sharply reduced investment and substantial wartime destruction. As $\bar{a}_e$ rose correspondingly, the pursuit of an equilibrium average age proceeded from below. The average age climbed again to as much as 15.8 years in the early postwar period, but when $\Delta K'/K'$ accelerated again in 1950–1958 the corresponding $\bar{a}_e$ fell to 9.8 years. By 1958 the measured $\bar{a}$ had approached to within 1.8 years of the equilibrium age. The further acceleration of $\Delta K'/K'$ in 1958–1961 again reduced $\bar{a}_e$ but only by 0.6 years thereby prolonging the pursuit.

Finally it is of interest to note the asymptotic behavior of $\bar{a}_t$. Specifically $\bar{a}_t$ tends to approach $\bar{a}_e$ the more rapidly (in absolute terms which are important for boosts to factor productivity) the greater the difference between them. Consider, for example, the movement of a capital stock from age 17.3 years toward an equilibrium value of 10.3 as in the Soviet case from 1928–1937. Suppose that for the 44 years preceding 1928, both I and K' were

[8] Note that this $\bar{a}_e$ is an equilibrium value in only a restricted sense. It assumes that the economy is able to sustain growth of investment at the constant rate, r. This in turn could involve a constantly changing ratio of investment to GNP. Such changes might not be possible indefinitely, so that many values of $\bar{a}_e$ would not represent true long-run equilibrium values.

[9] Following Moorsteen and Powell [13, p. 67] we use investment weights to average service lives for equipment, structures, and installation [13, pp. 65–67, 387]. Here, however, 1937 rather than 1934 investment weights were used.

growing at 2.7 per cent a year, i.e., a rate consistent with an $\bar{a}_e$ of 17.3. Suppose further that $\Delta K'/K'$ accelerates to r' equal to 8.8 per cent a year. By examining the movement from year to year it will be possible to discern a pattern in the approach of $\bar{a}_t$ toward a new $\bar{a}_e$. It may be shown that $\bar{a}_t$ and $\bar{a}_{t-1}$ are related as follows:

$$\bar{a}_t = \frac{K'_{t-1}}{K'_t} + \frac{K'_{t-1}}{K'_t}(\bar{a}_{-1}) - \frac{I_{t-n}}{K'_t}n. \tag{6}$$

The right-hand side of (6) indicates opposing tendencies with regard to the difference between $\bar{a}_t$ and $\bar{a}_{t-1}$. K'_{t-1}/K'_t is fixed at $1/1+r'$, so that the first term states that $\bar{a}_t$ will tend to be older than $\bar{a}_{t-1}$ by about one year for normal values of r'. The third term must be negative and tends to counter the effect of the first term. The second term, which suggests that $\bar{a}_t$ will be $1/1+r'$ times as large as $\bar{a}_{t-1}$, may reinforce the first or the third term depending on the numerical value for r. In our example K'_{t-1}/K'_t is less than one, so that if only the first term influenced the change $\bar{a}_t$ would tend to exceed $\bar{a}_{t-1}$ by a little less than one year. The second and third terms tend, however, to offset that increase by an amount equal to $(1-1/1+r')\bar{a}_{t-1} + \frac{I_{t-n}}{K'_t}n$. In fact the second and third terms more than offset the first and $\bar{a}_t < \bar{a}_{t-1}$. In the successive years the offset diminishes as $\bar{a}_t$ approaches the new $\bar{a}_e$. The absolute value of $(1-1/1+r')\bar{a}_{t-1}$ declines with $\bar{a}_{t-1}$. $\frac{I_{t-n}}{K'_t}$ declines in a geometric ratio $(1+r/1+r')$. Thus in our example $\bar{a}_t$ would fall by one year between 1928 and 1929 but by only 0.35 years between 1936 and 1937.

According to the embodiment hypothesis, then, acceleration of $\Delta K'/K'$ may provide an initial spurt of growth not simply because of the faster rate growth of capital, but also because of a boost to factor productivity due to a decline in $\bar{a}$. This boost is likely to be largest immediately following the acceleration of $\Delta K'/K'$. Even though $\Delta K'/K'$ is maintained at the new high rate the boost to factor productivity will tend to decline as $\bar{a}_t$ continues to approach $\bar{a}_e$ but in ever smaller steps.

The observed pattern of decline in $\bar{a}$ in the Soviet economy is, of course, not so smooth. Rates of growth of I and K' varied substantially from year-to-year, and retirements apparently followed an especially peculiar pattern. A tendency toward declining reductions in $\bar{a}$ was, nevertheless, clearly visible. As may be seen from the data presented above, the decline in $\bar{a}$ during 1937–1940 amounted to only 0.17 years per year compared with 0.38 years per year in 1928–1937. Similarly, the decline in $\bar{a}$ during 1958–1961 amounted to 0.40 years per year compared with 0.46 years per year in 1950–1958. By the beginning of 1961 the average age of capital had reached a level so low, 10.4 years, that further rapid reductions appeared unlikely.

Now let us use the available measurements of $\bar{a}$ as an ingredient in computing a final residual, λ:

Period	λ	Period	λ
1928–1937	30.4	1950–1958	15.1
1937–1940	−12.3	1958–1961	14.1
1940–1950	2.5		

At first the numerical values may appear implausibly high. It must be recalled, however, that our model has thrown the entire burden of explaining the residual growth in output upon a variable that refers to the quality of a single input with a weight of less than twenty per cent. Furthermore the values of λ do not appear so extreme when compared with similar values, seven to nine per cent a year, computed from data on the American economy.[10]

Values of λ for the periods spanning 1928–1950 strongly suggest the importance of factors other than annual increments in the quality of capital. In 1937–1940 the implied numerical values for λ are negative, and this is clearly most improbable. The low value for 1940–1950 probably is a consequence of the disruptive effects of the war. The indicated 2.5 per cent a year is, nevertheless, not clearly absurd, since under conditions prevalent in the Soviet Union during World War II progress in civilian design technology could hardly have approached the rates achieved in the peace time periods. Finally, the admittedly high value for 1928–1937 also must reflect the diverse impact of substantial forces other than design technology.[11] Such forces of possible high potence include collectivization, purges [3, p. 25], reduction of unemployment, and the shift of labor from low productivity agriculture to relatively high productivity industry [2, p. 498]. There are also factors such as the possible overstatement of growth in output because of remaining distortions in the 1928 price structure [13, p. 286] and possible understatement of the decline in the average age of capital immediately following 1928 [13, p. 99]. On the other hand, there seems to be a consensus among students of the Soviet economy that technical advance may have been especially facilitated by extensive "borrowing" from abroad during the 1930's [3, p. 25] [10, pp. 19, 25] [16, p. 174]. For this reason at least we

[10] The data are not strictly comparable since the computations for the United States have attributed improvements in the quality of labor to λ, while the values of λ computed here for the USSR reflect the attempt to account for the influence of the growth in educational capital. The incomparability is not gross, however, since for the USSR $\Delta A^*/A^*$ is generally not vastly different from $\Delta A/A$. Thus the differences between the United States and the USSR in the values for λ seem to correspond fairly closely to the differences in the values of $\Delta A/A$, although, of course, the more rapid declines in $\bar{a}$ in the USSR also would remove part of the burden of explanation from λ. See [14, p. 584] for values of $\Delta A/A$ for the United States.

[11] It should also be recalled that our measure of output for this period, though presumably the best available approximation to growth in capacity to produce a late period mix, is strongly affected by index number relativity.

might not be particularly surprised by a value for λ substantially greater for 1928–1937 than for 1950–1961.

Because of the residual nature of λ as computed here it would seem best to regard the numerical values for "normal" periods, 1928–1937, 1950–1958, and 1958–1961 as upper limits[12] for an approximation to the conceptual λ. Values computed for 1937–1940 and 1940–1950, on the other hand, do not seem to be appropriate limits of any sort.

SOURCES OF SOVIET GROWTH

Our final interpretation includes eight variables hypothesized to have some influence on the rate of growth of GNP. It may be of interest to compare quantitative approximations to the relative importance of the various sources of Soviet economic growth under this model of production. Inspection of table 2, which summarizes our results, suggests the following points. First, in "normal" periods growth of fixed capital stock has been increasingly important as a source of Soviet growth. Second, a dominant factor, generally positive, has been the quality of fixed capital. This result must, however, be viewed skeptically, since λ was calculated as a residual reflecting the influence of all variables not specified in the interpretation. The large size of λ is still, to a degree, a measure of our remaining ignorance. Finally, note the stable contribution, about 15 per cent of the growth rate, of the declining average age of capital.

An interesting implication of the interpretation hypothesizing embodied technical change is that an important source of Soviet growth in "normal" periods has been reductions in the average age of capital. Moreover, considering the asymptotic behavior of $\bar{a}$ and the already low value of $\bar{a}$ attained by 1961, the distinct possibility arises that further boosts to productivity from this source might well tend to diminish in subsequent periods, perhaps to virtually nothing. Indeed, Professor Judith Thornton [19] has pointed that $\Delta K'/K'$, an important determinant of $\bar{a}$, may well have grown during 1928–1940 and again during 1950–1961 at high, and eventually unsustainable, rates since they have required a rising ratio of investment to GNP. Reductions in $\Delta K'/K'$ could induce increases in $\bar{a}$ and, to the extent that the embodiment model approximates reality, increases in $\bar{a}$ in turn may provide a significant drag on growth of factor productivity.

III Conclusion

In summary we first presented fundamental portions of the basic record on Soviet economic growth as compiled by Western scholars. Second, we interpreted the data within the analytical framework of a Cobb-Douglas

---

[12] Assuming the net impact of all other forces affecting the residual is positive.

Table 2—Sources of Soviet economic growth, 1928–1961

Sources of Soviet growth	PERCENTAGE POINTS					PER CENT OF GROWTH RATE				
	1928–37	1937–40	1940–50	1950–58	1958–61	1928–37	1937–40	1940–50	1950–58	1958–61
Labor	1.47	5.01	0.82	0.82	−0.71	12.35	87.89	41.00	10.38	−11.83
Educational Capital	0.76	0.76	0.24	0.39	0.25	6.39	13.33	12.00	4.94	4.17
Fixed Capital Stock	1.67	1.96	0.42	1.77	1.94	14.03	34.39	21.00	22.41	32.33
Inventories	0.33	0.57	0.14	0.43	0.73	2.77	10.00	7.00	5.44	12.17
Livestock	−0.12	0.16	−0.01	0.07	0.09	−1.01	2.81	−0.50	0.89	1.50
Agricultural Land	0.16	0.29	−0.02	0.30	0.12	1.34	5.09	−1.00	3.80	2.00
Growth in Quality of Fixed Capital	5.77	−2.34	0.47	2.87	2.69	48.49	−41.05	23.50	36.32	44.83
Changes in the Age of Fixed Capital Stock	1.66	−0.70	−0.09	1.24	1.02	13.95	−12.28	−4.50	15.69	17.00
Gross National Product	11.9	5.7	2.0	7.9	6.0	100	100	100	100	100

a Components may not sum exactly to totals because of rounding.

function amended to include the effects of disembodied technical change. This interpretation left much of growth unexplained. Third, we amended our function to reflect investment in education, but about 90 per cent of the original residual still was unexplained. Fourth, we assumed that the remainder of the residual is due solely to design changes in physical capital, and we used the age of capital as a proxy for its quality. Then we calculated as a residual the average annual rates at which this capital quality appears to have changed between bench mark years. On the basis of these calculations we compiled a summary on some sources of Soviet growth. Finally, we analyzed the pattern of changes in the average age of Soviet capital and found that during "normal" periods it was approaching an "equilibrium" level in large steps that appeared likely to diminish with the passage of time. It seems that during "normal" periods such declines in average age may have provided a significant contribution to growth, and that this contribution may decline substantially as possibilities for further reductions in the average age of capital decline.

Of course the process of Soviet growth was far more complex than equations can currently show. We can be quite confident that many important sources of growth have not been mentioned. We have not discussed returns to scale. We have made no attempt to say anything about changes in social organization at any level, and these were at times drastic indeed. We have neglected learning by doing, and we have ignored interaction among supposedly independent variables. Few would be surprised, for example, to find a significant connection between investment in education and the change in quality of new capital.[13] We have had to make arbitrary assumptions about the elasticity of factor substitution. Recent estimates [1], [6], [11], [12] for the United States and for other economies suggest values substantially less than the unity frequently assumed, often more on the order of one-half. If our assumptions similarly overstate the value appropriate for the USSR, the very rapid growth of capital per man would have been more severely affected by diminishing returns than our calculations indicate. The list of

[13] To the extent that there is interaction between variables such as $\Delta H/H$ and λ, the estimates of the latter are likely to err. Specifically if we were confident that $\Delta H/H$ was the only variable having any influence on λ, then, as Nelson has shown, the rate of return on H should reflect its contribution to output and any remaining residual would have to be attributed to factors other than technology. It would be an error to include H as an explanatory variable and then identify the residual with embodied technical change. Actually, of course, we have little knowledge of the sources of change in λ. It is plausible to argue that H may in some way affect λ, but that is far from saying that H is its sole determinant. In fact λ could be a more important determinant of H than H is of λ. In this event the estimates of H may themselves suffer from failure to account for fundamental changes in quality. As knowledge advances so does the curriculum in the schools, and consequently, the mere number of years of schooling may seriously understate the "true" growth in educational attainment. Finally there may be other "complementarities" involved in the model. For example it has been suggested that there is reason to expect that λ and $\Delta K/K$ also may interact. See [14, p. 591] for a discussion of these and other such interactions.

deficiences could, of course, continue, but its purpose has already been fulfilled. In conclusion, we have been forced, at times, to strong assumptions, to analogy with the American economy, and to other crude approximations. These circumstances warrant great caution in making claims for this interpretation. It is only one of a very large set. Yet the current interpretation seems relatively rigorous, plausible, promising, and, at a minimum, worthy of consideration.

References

[1] Arrow, K. J., H. B. Chenery, B. S. Minhas, and R. M. Solow, "Capital-Labor Substitution and Economic Efficiency," *Review of Economics and Statistics*, 43 (Aug. 1961), 225–250.

[2] Balassa, B., "The Dynamic Efficiency of the Soviet Economy," *American Economic Review*, Proceedings, 54 (May 1964), 490–505.

[3] Bergson, A., "National Income," in A. Bergson and S. Kuznets, eds., *Economic Trends in the Soviet Union*. (Cambridge: Harvard University Press, 1963).

[4] Bergson, A., *The Real National Income of Soviet Russia Since 1928*. (Cambridge: Harvard University Press, 1961).

[5] Cohn, S. H., "Soviet Growth Retardation: Trends in Resource Availability and Efficiency," in Joint Economic Committee, *New Directions in the Soviet Economy*, Washington, 1966.

[6] David, P. A., and Th. Van de Klundert, "Biased Efficiency Growth and Capital-Labor Substitution in the U.S., 1899–1960," *American Economic Review*, 55 (June 1965), 357–394.

[7] Denison, E. F., *The Sources of Economic Growth in the United States and the Alternatives Before Us*. Supplementary Paper No. 13. New York, Committee on Econom'c Development, 1962.

[8] DeWitt, N., *Costs and Returns to Education in the U.S.S.R.* Unpublished Ph.D. dissertation, Harvard University, 1962.

[9] Granick, D., "On Patterns of Technological Choice in Soviet Industry," *American Economic Review*, Proceedings, 52 (May 1962), 149–157.

[10] Grossman, G., "National Income,"

in A. Bergson, ed., *Soviet Economic Growth*. (Evanston: Row, Peterson and Company, 1953).

[11] Kendrick, J. W., and R. Sato, "Factor Prices, Productivity, and Economic Growth," *American Economic Review*, 53 (Dec. 1963), 974–1003.

[12] Kravis, I. B., "Relative Income Shares in Fact and Theory," *American Economic Review*, 49 (Dec. 1959), 917–949.

[13] Moorsteen, R., and R. P. Powell, *The Soviet Capital Stock, 1928–1962*. (Homewood: Richard D. Irwin, Inc., 1966).

[14] Nelson, R. R., "Aggregate Production Functions and Medium-Range Growth Projections, *American Economic Review*, 54 (Sept. 1964), 575–606.

[15] Noren, J. H., "Soviet Industry Trends in Output, Inputs, and Productivity," in Joint Economic Committee, *New Directions in the Soviet Economy*, Washington, 1966.

[16] Powell, R. P., "Industrial Production," in A. Bergson and S. Kuznets, eds., *Economic Trends in the Soviet Union*. (Cambridge: Harvard University Press, 1963).

[17] Solow, R. M., "Investment and Technical Change," in *Mathematical Methods in the Social Sciences*. (Stanford: Stanford University Press, 1959).

[18] ———, "Technical Progress, Capital Formation, and Economic Growth," *American Economic Review*, Proceedings, 52 (May 1962), 76–86.

[19] Thornton, J., "Factors in the Recent Decline in Soviet Growth," *Slavic Review*, 25 (Mar. 1966), 101–119.

[20] TsSU, *Narodnoe khoziaistvo SSSR v 1965 godu*. Moscow 1966.

Benefit-Cost Analysis

of Human Capital

Investments

The Purpose and Nature
of Benefit-Cost Analysis

Benefit-cost analysis may be useful in comparing alternative public programs which compete for government funds even though the methodology entails many pitfalls if naively used. Assuming that it is desirable to squeeze as much output from scarce resources as is feasible, a general theoretical criterion for defining an optimum is needed. With no budget constraint, an optimum would require investment in any given program until *marginal* program benefits (dB) and costs (dC) are equal, at which point net benefits are maximized:

$$\frac{dB}{dg} = \frac{dC}{dg} \text{ or } \frac{dB/dg}{dC/dg} = 1.0$$

However, there is normally some kind of budget constraint, and alternative investments must be evaluated. Under these circumstances, an optimum is obtained when equal marginal benefits per marginal dollar outlay for programs $g, h, \ldots n$, are obtained:

$$\frac{dB/dg}{dC/dg} = \frac{dB/dh}{dC/dh} \cdots \frac{dB/dn}{dC/dn}$$

Marginal benefit-cost analysis must also be accompanied by discounting. In its simplest form, benefits (B) are compared to costs (C), all of which are converted to present values (v) to derive Bv/Cv ratios. Moreover, one can estimate the unknown benefits required given some cutoff ratio (X) of benefits to costs (e.g., $Bv/Cv = X$; $Bv = X \cdot Cv$). An alternative procedure is the derivation of the internal rate of return (r), which is that rate of discount which equates the present value of benefits and costs. As in solving for benefit-cost analysis, one can solve for the unknown benefits required given specification of the other two terms—Cv and r. Unlike benefit-cost analysis, the rate of return is not a constant since it reflects the cost of capital.

Roland N. McKean **9**, Robert Dorfman **10**, and Arthur Maass **11** discuss benefit-cost analysis in general terms as it relates to decision making in the public sector. Another selection written by Otto Eckstein **12** is concerned with the "proper" rate of discount.

9

The Unseen Hand in Government

Increasing participation by all levels of government in the economic affairs of society raises difficult issues. Economists have developed an intricate theory of resource allocation for the private sector of the market economy. Unfortunately, very little progress has been made in improving our understanding of the process of allocating resources in the public sector where the price system plays a muted role at best. Roland N. McKean, Professor of

ROLAND N. McKEAN

Economics at the University of Virginia, develops the thesis that an "unseen hand" driven by power and bargaining guides resource allocation in the public sector. The author's cogent plea for greater attention to problems of choice and resource allocation are as applicable to the large and rapidly growing education industry as to other categories of government.

For a long time economists have given a great deal of attention to the "invisible hand" that guides resource allocation in the private sector of the economy. We have spelled out a theory of the firm, models of the private sector, conditions for achieving a limited kind of optimality, and formidable lists of limitations on the functioning of the mechanism. With the growth of government, we should probably devote more effort to understanding the mechanism that guides resource allocation in the public sector of the economy. We need a theory of government to supplement our theory of the firm, and more insights into the limitations of the invisible hand in the governmental sector. In this article I wish to take at least a few additional steps in these directions.

Reprinted from Roland N. McKean, "The Unseen Hand in Government," *American Economic Review* 55 (June 1965), pp. 496–507, with the permission of the author and publisher.

I The Private Sector

It is usually said that the necessary conditions for Pareto optimality are met when the marginal private cost of each output (MPC) equals marginal private benefit (MPB), marginal total benefit (MTB), and marginal total cost (MTC).[1] That is, we would like to have the "welfare equation" satisfied:

$$MTC = MPC = MPB = MTB.$$

With appropriate institutional arrangements, the price mechanism guides individual decisions so that they tend to yield this result. As many persons have emphasized, however, there are numerous limitations on the performance of this mechanism in the private sector. A degree of monopoly power leads to inequalities in the "welfare equation." Externalities lead to other inequalities.[2] Vaccinations bestow benefits on nonusers of this service, and vapors emitted by vehicles inflict costs on others that are not felt by those who take the actions. These spillover effects arise because it is sometimes uneconomical, or even impossible, to define and enforce property rights in an appropriate fashion, e.g., so that people could charge automobile drivers for damaging their rights to smog-free and noise-free air. (In the long run, one of the most important externalities may be the discrepancy between the private and total costs of having additional children. As a consequence, if we solve enough technological problems, we may ultimately have population congestion that rivals automobile congestion.) Also, it is often said that the actions of firms to increase profits leads to the concentration of power in great corporations, yielding a spillover impairment of freedom.

Another point that is sometimes raised is that firms really engage in satisficing rather than utility-maximizing, producing different outcomes from those corresponding to the welfare equation. (Actually, satisficing and utility-maximizing may turn out to be identical as soon as one recognizes that there is uncertainty, that acquiring information is costly, and that re-examining all the alternatives every five minutes would be expensive.) Another limitation frequently cited is that there is not perfect knowledge and that misinformation or lack of information leads us far from economic efficiency (as it might be conceived, in these circumstances, by some omniscient observer).

[1] Although it may be a small semantic issue, I prefer to talk of "total" costs and benefits, which suggest that they are felt by individuals, instead of "social" costs and benefits, which may sound as though some mysterious entity like the state feels these effects.

[2] Doing anything about them sometimes costs more than it would gain, in which case the "departure from optimality" is much like our failure to have a world free of disease and boll weevils. See the excellent discussion of such matters by Harold Demsetz in [5].

In certain kinds of advertising, firms devote resources to nullifying the efforts of other firms, much as people at parades stand on tiptoe to nullify the effects of others standing on tiptoe; and, especially if we ignore any stimuli to the introduction of new products, this type of advertising appears to yield something less than optimality. In addition, due to a variety of institutional constraints, there are restrictions on the ability of people to consider tradeoffs —there are tie-in sales, restrictions on entry into occupations, "throwaway TV" programs instead of pay-TV. Another troublesome blemish on the unseen hand is a special type of spillover—the fact that utility functions are not really independent. What Jones buys *does* affect my utility. As some see it, a final crushing blow is dealt by the theory of second-best. If all conditions for optimality are not fulfilled, we cannot always be certain that progress toward fulfilling particular conditions is truly desirable. All in all, there is a lot of palsy in the unseen hand, and it is no wonder that many persons look upon the private sector with some disapproval.

II The Public Sector

Before drawing hasty conclusions about what should be done, however, we should look at the public sector from these same standpoints. In the public sector too, choices are made by individuals. Politicians, executives, and agency heads are similar to managers of businesses; other personnel are laborers; and voters can perhaps be viewed as boards of directors. Inevitably each person has a separate utility function, a "parochial" viewpoint so to speak. These individuals do not arise each morning and ask, "what can I do today for Pareto optimality?" Like the rest of us, they are surely utility-maximizers.

This does not mean that they are selfish, brutish, or motivated solely by self-interest narrowly conceived. It simply means that individuals get satisfaction from a variety of things—material goods, play, helping others, performing tasks well, and so on—and that these things are to some extent substitutes for each other. As a consequence, if the cost to a person of one item increases, he will demand less of it and more of other items. If the benefit he feels from an item increases, he will demand more of it and less of other things. In government, if the cost to an official of one action increases, he will take less of it. If the gains that he feels increase, he will take more action of that sort.[3]

Also, in government as well as in the private sector, there is a mechanism that leads utility-maximizers to a pattern of decisions that is somewhat orderly and sensible. This mechanism is the bargaining process and, at

[3] One of the best presentations of the utility-maximization hypothesis is by Armen A. Alchian and William R. Allen [1, Ch. 2].

least in Western nations where many interests are represented, it has some similarities to the price mechanism in the private sector of the economy. The price system makes individuals feel many of the relevant costs and gains produced by their decisions. When a business firm takes action, it has to bargain with and compensate numerous persons who supply buildings, labor services, and other inputs. That is, if the firm's action uses up or damages property, the firm ordinarily has to buy the consent of the owners. Whenever the firm's action produces beneficial effects, the management tries to charge the beneficiaries. If all compensations are made and the firm still makes a profit, some persons are made better off without making others worse off. The greater the extent to which all these compensations are made, the less the extent to which the firm's costs and gains will diverge from total costs and gains.

In government the bargaining mechanism produces some of the same effects. If a public official's action will use up someone's property or damage certain interests, he will probably find a cost associated with that action. He will feel the complaints of those damaged or the inconvenience of trying to mollify them. Or, he may suffer embarrassing or expensive enmities among his colleagues or retaliation by other officials. He has to bargain with many people who are affected and, in one way or another, encounter costs if he makes decisions that impose sacrifices on others. From those who are benefited, on the other hand, he can bargain for compensation. The reward may be support in connection with other matters, reduced enmity, increased friendship or convenience, or some other kind of *quid pro quo*. The size and completeness of the compensations for both costs inflicted and gains bestowed depend upon bargaining strengths and circumstances (as they do in the private economy). And again the greater the extent to which these compensations are made, the less the extent to which the costs and gains felt by an official will diverge from total costs and gains.

Every decision or action, it might be noted, involves bargaining, tacit or explicit. When a senator considers voting to censure Senator McCarthy, he asks himself, "what will be the consequences?" If he decides to accept the reactions of others to a yes vote, *that* is his bargain. If he decides to refrain from voting or to vote "no," he accepts a different set of reactions, and *that* is his bargain.

As in the private sector, shifts in costs or gains (i.e., prices paid or received) cause shifts in behavior. As conditions change, the price of apples sometimes goes up and the price of oranges down. Consumers alter their behavior (though not necessarily their nature). Similarly, if a senator from Texas becomes President of the United States, the price or cost of some actions goes up and the cost of other actions goes down. For example, the cost of closing down a base in New York goes up, the cost of closing an installation in Texas goes down. The structure of rewards also alters. The rewards for a war on poverty in the entire United States go up, those for aid to constituents in a particular State go down. Thus a man who becomes President will take more nearly a national viewpoint—i.e., will acquire a greater "sense of responsibility"—though his nature need not change at all. The altered cost-reward structures are bound to affect his behavior. And, like the price system, this bargaining mechanism has many desirable effects. It might be called the "unseen hand in government."[4]

For these reasons, while the particular values, principles, or even whims of a government official occasionally play roles in his decisions, they do not usually play major roles in democratic governments. [The bargaining mechanisms limit the discretion of decision-makers.] Let us look at this side of the coin—the constraints on the authority of individual officials. Again the forces at work are akin to those that operate in the private sector. In a highly competitive industry, a business firm must give much attention to avoiding losses and increasing profits or it will fail. In these circumstances employees find that they must devote most of their efforts to achieving the firm's goals or be fired. In a public utility or nonprofit corporation, both managers and employees have greater leeway, but they too are limited in the extent to which altruistic, evil, or personal aims can guide their actions. In government also, while managers and other personnel have some discretion, they cannot flout the wishes of voters, superiors, and colleagues and hope to survive long. They certainly cannot do just whatever they wish. They must compromise with their principles, whether good or evil, and accept a great deal of guidance from the unseen hand.

The fact that individual decision-makers have parochial viewpoints does not mean that the pattern of decisions will inevitably be stupid or vicious. The right kind of bargaining process can make special interests and parochial viewpoints, which one might think would produce chaotic decisions, lead to an orderly and sensible pattern of choices. If well designed, the invisible hand can go a long way toward turning private "vice" into public virtue, in government as well as in the private sector.

The mechanism may seem like a Rube Goldberg device in comparison with a mathematical model of optimality, since government decision-making appears to cater to majorities of large groups rather than to fine differences in individual preferences, and it appears to respond to voters' views on packages of issues rather than on each individual issue. But the mechanism is not quite as imprecise as that. As for voters, minority views on particular issues carry some weight, because there is the threat that those voters, when considering the larger package of issues at election time, may shift their votes and in effect form a new coalition that has real power. Differential

[4] C. E. Lindblom has presented closely related arguments and has referred to "the hidden hand in government" [8]. For additional thoughts about the unseen hand and government spending, see [9].

intensity of feelings or different values attached to particular policies can carry weight for essentially the same reason. If a minority attaches a high value to a particular policy, it can sacrifice its feelings about other issues and join the coalition of its choice. Others react, as they see the "prices" being paid for various decisions, by accepting a little less of those items that are becoming relatively expensive and a little more of those items that are becoming relatively cheap. In legislative bodies, similarly, views on individual issues as opposed to a package, the views of minorities, and differences in the values attached to particular policies *do* help shape decisions, because some tradeoffs—giving up a vote on this issue for someone else's vote on that one, giving up some of one policy for more of another—are possible, and "shadow prices," so to speak, gradually emerge to reveal the costs and gains from various actions. With checks and balances, a multiplicity of interests represented in the bargaining process, and some possibilities for voluntary "exchange," the pattern of choices can cater to individual preferences better than may be suggested by the words "majority rule."[5]

This mechanism has *some* influence on most choices, though the extent of this influence varies greatly with circumstances.[6] In the aggregate these choices and decisions shape the allocation of resources at various levels. Consider first the allocation of resources between the private and public sectors. Suppose a larger share for government is under consideration. Senators and congressmen will become aware of constituents' views on this and other issues and will respond to prospective votes almost the way a board of directors responds to prospective profits. These legislators will "feel" many of the expected benefits and (probably to a lesser extent) the expected costs. The benefits are likely to be concentrated on a smaller group and be larger per-person-affected than are the costs (mainly taxes), but legislators will feel some pressure from both groups and will anticipate some reaction at election time from both groups.

Second, consider the allocation of resources within the public sector among programs and activities (comparable to the allocation of resources among industries). Officials can take home no profits, and they are spending other people's money; yet they may "feel" the major gains and costs because some tradeoffs are possible and crude "shadow prices" emerge from the bargaining process. An official finds that it *does* cost him something to expand his program—as well as bring rewards. Resources tend to be shifted toward programs in which marginal individual benefit (MIB) is

---

[5] For some provocative contributions to the development of a theory of government to supplement the theory of the firm, see the work of Buchanan, Downs, Olson, Tullock, and Williams [4] [6] [10] [11] [13].

[6] For example, such influence is much smaller wherever decision-makers are partially sheltered from the necessity of bargaining, e.g., the Supreme Court or agencies that are relatively independent. Such independent checks and balances, however, can often play a beneficial role in the over-all bargaining network.

greater than marginal individual cost (MIC), and bargaining helps make MIB equal to MTB and MIC equal to MTC. The hidden hand harnesses individual decisions so that they come a little closer to satisfying the welfare equation than they would if no such mechanism existed.

Finally, consider the utilization of resources within a program by lower-level officials (comparable to the allocation of resources by firms within an industry). The alternative methods of production that are considered depend upon constraints that proscribe certain of the alternatives and pressures that induce personnel to examine more or fewer alternatives. The costs and gains from each alternative, as perceived by government personnel, depend upon the criteria in terms of which personnel are judged, the importance of efficiency to survival of the agency or branch, and so on. Again the gears of the mechanism may appear to clank quite a bit; but rivalry and the bargaining process still work to internalize what would otherwise be externalities, and make gross inefficiency somewhat costly to government personnel. To some extent, flagrant inefficiency impairs an official's ability to bargain for promotion, larger budgets, freedom from investigation, and other desiderata. Compared with discretionary authority, then, the bargaining mechanism is again a valuable and unseen hand guiding resource utilization.

In the public sector too, however, we find that there are numerous limitations. We tend to blame faulty outcomes in government upon individuals, perhaps because some of them are in the limelight. We are prone to say that things go wrong because of stupidity, sloth, weak character, or some other personal inadequancy in particular government officials. Yet to a great extent, as in the private sector, there are limitations on the system that should make us expect faulty outcomes. We should understand these limitations better in trying to appraise alternative arrangements and devise improvements.

COUNTERPART OF MONOPOLY

The bargaining process is extremly imperfect in government. Monopoly models do not fit precisely, of course; for one thing utility-maximization by monopolies in the private sector implies a good deal of emphasis on obtaining higher profits, while in the public sector it implies a good deal of attention to obtaining higher budgets. Nonetheless there are somewhat analogous resource misallocations. An agency with strong bargaining power may not *restrict* its output inefficiently, but it will tend to seek approval of below-cost pricing and *expand* its output inefficiently. An agency with weak bargaining power is likely to find its activities curbed even if it would be economic to expand them. Pressure by voters and the unseen hand may tend to correct these situations, but in a slow and exceedingly imprecise fashion.

Another way in which the imperfect bargaining process in government distorts output is through the "holdout." Sometimes a project affecting several States or counties or other governmental units would be economic from the standpoint of total benefits and costs, yet uneconomic from the standpoint of any *one* of the governmental units. A deal would be mutually advantageous, and sometimes this happens. (In 1964 one city in Los Angeles County decided not to have its annual fireworks display, but an adjoining city said that it reaped benefits too, so after some bargaining, compensation was arranged, and the fireworks display was presented.) Yet often the last State or county refuses to bargain, hoping for a "free ride." Similar phenomena occur with respect to agencies within a single jurisdictional authority such as the federal government. Centralization, incidentally, may reduce the problem of the hold-out, but impairs the functioning of the bargaining mechanism in other ways.

Entry of new agencies to replace obsolete ones is probably more difficult than the entry of new firms with new ideas in private industries. Reservoir-building agencies are ardent spokesmen for conventional methods of producing water. There are relatively few spokesmen for certain alternative methods of increasing water supplies, such as shifting water from lower-valued uses to higher-valued uses, reclaiming waste water, or reducing losses from seepage, evaporation, and vegetation. For new methods or products to be *seriously* considered, it often requires entry by a new branch or agency and a chance for it to build up a clientele. But entry in the public sector is difficult, and it often takes a long time to drive obsolete activities into "bankruptcy."

So much for examples of the effects of "imperfect competition" in government. The point is merely that the counterparts of oligopoly and monopoly distort prices and outputs in the public as well as in the private sectors.

EXTERNALITIES

Another limitation on the unseen hand in government is the pervasiveness of externalities. Authorities who approve a new irrigation project can impose costs they do not feel on firms, individuals, and other government agencies. This can happen, for example, because irrigation introduces additional salts or pesticides into downstream or underground water supplies. Some projects even affect the porosity of soils and the underground flows of water. Sewage disposal may impose costs on others and education may bestow benefits on others that the bargaining process does not always cause local governments to feel in reaching these decisions.[7] Federal officials, in setting tariffs or price supports, are inflicting costs that the bargaining process does not make them feel very keenly.

It is difficult to assess the size of these externalities because officials feel

[7] For a provocative case study and discussion of spillovers in education, see [7].

costs and gains attributable to their choices mostly through bargaining pressures, and these are hard to measure. Parochial outlooks as such do not reveal what costs or gains are felt. In the private sector, a businessman does not say "I want to be sure and take into account *all* the costs to the nation," and an uncritical observer might conclude that there must therefore be tremendous externalities. But the price system compels the businessman to consider (most of) the costs he causes. In the public sector, similarly, a government official does not say, "I want to be sure and count all the costs to the nation." Again a naïve observer might conclude that there must therefore be great externalities. But the bargaining process compels the official to take at least many of the costs into account.

Still, while the net externalities are hard to assess, they appear to be widespread in government. Third parties who have little or no bargaining power are often affected. Or, another way to put the matter is to point out the peculiar, sometimes indeterminate, nature of property rights within government. (Who has the right to do what with various assets in the public sector has important implications just as it does in the private sector.) The common pool problem—the resource that is treated as though it is a free good—in the private sector is still more in evidence in the governmental sector. This is not to say that there should be a massive shift of activities from the government to the private sphere. It is simply to say that in terms of the "welfare equation" and Pareto optimality, the public sector too is in plenty of trouble.

As far as the concentration of power is concerned, utility-maximization in government surely generates this spillover to a greater extent than in the private sector. The ultimate possibilities of discretionary authority in government surely loom larger than those in the world of giant corporations. In one famous Jules Feiffer cartoon, an employee of the telephone company says: If you don't like our service, why don't you try one of our competitors?[8] This may appear to be a devastating thrust at the concentration of power in the private sector, but the same sort of cartoon could apply to many services provided by government.

OTHER IMPERFECTIONS

As for "satisficing" rather than maximizing, this is surely as applicable in government as it is in business. There are standards of performance, standards of water quality and housing, rules regarding the use of government cars, and rules of thumb regarding all manner of things. As in the private sector, rules of thumb are often better than not having them, since reviewing alternatives and acquiring information are costly activities [3].

[8] From *The Explainers* by Jules Feiffer. 1960. McGraw-Hill Book Company. Used by permission.

But they are there, and in that sense governments can be said to "satisfice" rather than maximize. Uncertainty, too, causes the same complications in the public sector that have been discussed so much with reference to the private sector. Even advertising is present in government, as agencies seek to hold or expand their clienteles [12, pp. 120–21].

Restrictions on tradeoffs, another point sometimes mentioned in connection with the private sector, pervade the government sphere. In order to control what is actually done in this environment, Congress must authorize appropriations for specified categories and prohibit significant transfers of resources without requests for reprogramming permission. Moreover reprogramming requests are not only an inconvenience; they are often frowned upon by Congress. Furthermore, the Departments, in order to control what is actually done, must "shred out" narrower categories and discourage transfers of resources among them. This means that substitution possibilities must often be neglected. As noted before, it may be better to have such rules of thumb or restrictions than not to have them, but their existence, like any similar phenomena in private industry, is a departure from the ideal.

There are other obstacles to the consideration of alternatives and tradeoffs in government. Small jurisdictions elect representatives at large, and there the wishes of minority groups, i.e., certain sets of alternatives, tend to be neglected. If a metropolitan government consisted of councilmen elected at large, or a state legislature consisted of assemblymen elected at large, the majority might well ignore the "needs" of minorities or local areas and the costs thrust upon them. The actual outcomes would depend upon the kind of behind-the-scenes logrolling mechanism that developed.

Finally, when we turn to the public sector, we do not escape the interdependence of utility functions or the troublesome implications of the theory of second-best. The success of Administrator Jones affects my utility function, and either deliberate or by-product favors to some voters affect the satisfaction of others. As for second-best, it is omnipresent. The full conditions for optimality in the public sector are definitely not fulfilled. We are destined to live in a world of Nth best and to wonder at times if apparent improvements really make us better off.

III Conclusions

What significance does the unseen hand in government, and its imperfection, have for us? First of all, just as background in thinking about government activities, we ought to keep in mind the existence of this invisible hand and the way it works. It tends to harness individual interests within government to carry out broader objectives. It keeps parochial viewpoints from yielding exclusively parochial policies. But we must keep in mind the formidable imperfections of the mechanism—the fact that there are major spillovers affecting parties who have inadequate voices in the bargaining process. Moreover, we should recognize that many questionable policies or choices are inherent in the institutional framework and should not be blamed on "bad" officials or bad luck. Where the bargaining process does not eliminate or offset serious spillovers, the cost-reward structures confronting officials tend to pull them toward wrong decisions.

As far as comparing the two sectors is concerned, the only thing that is obvious is that both are imperfect.[9] In fact the whole discussion underscores the limitations of Pareto optimality as a guide to policy. Actions that can clearly make some persons better off without making others worse off constitute a small set, and for a number of reasons we cannot possibly expect many governmental actions to be in that set. It may seem unfair and irrelevant, therefore, to appraise government choices in terms of the conditions for Pareto optimality. If this seems inappropriate, however, it is surely inappropriate also to call for government action wherever the conditions for economic efficiency are not fulfilled in the private sector. One ought not argue that the government should control an activity *because* the private sector does not bring about Pareto optimality and *then* regard it as irrelevant that government control does not bring about such optimality either.

We should not favor having an activity in one sector or under one particular regulatory arrangement *merely because the alternative is less than perfect*. Our choice must rest on the view reflected in a remark sometimes attributed to Maurice Chevalier: when asked how he felt about growing older, he is said to have replied, "It's not exactly ideal, but it's better than the alternative."

A more important point, perhaps, is the following: we should learn more about the unseen hand in government and its shortcomings in order to improve institutional arrangements affecting both sectors. We should study the anatomy of market failure, the anatomy of government failure, and the possibilities of improving the functioning of both. In the government sphere in particular, a better understanding of the unseen hand and its limitations may help us improve the bargaining framework that shapes public decisions.

---

[9] This is hardly a new thought. For one statement along this line, see Francis M. Bator's discussion of the fact that our real choice is among various imperfect arrangements [2, pp. 99–112].

References

[1] Armen A. Alchian and William R. Allen, *University Economics*. Belmont, California 1964.

[2] Francis M. Bator, *The Question of Government Spending*. New York 1960.

[3] William J. Baumol and Richard E. Quandt, "Rules of Thumb and Optimally Imperfect Decisions," *Am. Econ. Rev.*, March 1964, *54*, 23–46.

[4] James M. Buchanan and Gordon Tullock, *The Calculus of Consent*. Ann Arbor 1962.

[5] Harold Demsetz, "Some Implications of Property Right Costs," *Jour. Law and Econ.*, 1963, *6*, (forthcoming).

[6] Anthony Downs, *An Economic Theory of Democracy*. New York 1957.

[7] Werner Z. Hirsch, Elbert W. Segelhorst, and Morton J. Marcus, *Spillover of Public Education Costs and Benefits*, Institute of Government and Public Affairs, University of California at Los Angeles, 1964.

[8] C. E. Lindblom, "Bargaining: The Hidden Hand in Government," The RAND Corporation, RM-1434, Santa Monica 1955.

[9] Roland N. McKean, *Public Spending*, Economic Handbook Series, McGraw-Hill, New York, (in process).

[10] Mancur Olson, Jr., *A General Theory of Public Goods* (forthcoming).

[11] Gordon Tullock, *The Politics of Bureaucracy*. Washington, D.C., 1965.

[12] Aaron Wildavsky, *The Politics of the Budgetary Process*. Boston, 1964.

[13] Alan Williams, *Welfare Economics and Local Government* (in process).

10

The Benefit-Cost Framework

Robert Dorfman is Professor of Economics at Harvard University. Long interested in resource allocation problems in the public sector, he briefly sketches some of the major dimensions to benefit-cost analysis in this selection taken from a Brookings Institution volume which he edited. Many of the difficult measurement and conceptual prob-

ROBERT DORFMAN

lems enumerated by the author are not easily overcome, especially in studying returns to human capital investment. Nonetheless, benefit-cost analysis does serve as a worthwhile tool if used properly in studying allocation decisions in the public sector.

Incentives for Government Enterprise

Governments rush in where businessmen decline to tread. As a general rule, if a good or a service is desirable, it will also be profitable and thus will be provided by private enterprise. But there are important exceptions to this rule. Government initiative is, for example, called for in cases where investments that businessmen would deem unprofitable are socially worthwhile. These exceptions can arise from a number of circumstances: some relate to the conditions under which a product is distributed and consumed; some to the conditions of its production; some have other justifications.

CONDITIONS OF CONSUMPTION

The circumstances that favor government provision cluster around the concept of collectability or, rather, uncollectability. In the usual economic

Reprinted from Robert Dorfman, ed., *Measuring Benefits of Government Investment* (Washington, D.C.: The Brookings Institution, 1965), pp. 4–8, with the permission of the author and publisher.

transaction, the user is charged for the good or service he consumes, the amount he is willing to pay measures the value of the commodity to him, and, since his use of the commodity precludes anyone else from benefiting from it, the value of the commodity to the user is also its value to the entire society. This standard analysis of social value is not strictly valid for any transaction (there are always side effects), and for a few types of transactions it is too wide of the mark to be acceptable. The most important of these latter cases are (1) collective goods and (2) goods that are characterized by external economies of consumption: in neither case is the provider of the good able to collect from beneficiaries a charge commensurate with the benefits conferred.

In general, a *collective good* is a facility or service that is made freely available to all comers without user charge, either because to assess a charge on each occasion of use would be excessively cumbersome or because use is not voluntary or even clearly definable. It is, for example, not feasible or desirable to levy a charge on every shipmaster who sees a lighthouse, on every householder whose door the patrolman passes, or on every housewife when a health officer inspects a food market.

With rare exceptions, collective goods cannot be provided by private firms, because they do not induce a flow of income to the provider. Therefore the responsibility for providing them falls frequently—but not invariably— to the government. In addition to the examples cited above, some important collective goods are national defense, civil and criminal justice, streets and most highways, and outdoor recreational facilities. Other significant categories include the findings of scientific research, since even patients usually do not enable the scientist or his employer to collect from beneficiaries more than a portion of the benefits conferred, and aesthetic amenities, such as a fine building or a landscape that confers benefits on passersby for which they cannot be assessed. The important feature of collective goods for our purpose here is that, since they are not sold, there are no market prices to assist in appraising their value.

Collective goods are allied to *external economies of consumption* but the latter come into being in a different way. When a man is treated for a communicable disease the relief afforded him is only part of the social value; every resident of his community benefits from the reduced danger of infection. When a high school student is dissuaded from leaving school, his neighbors receive benefits (among them a reduction in potential delinquency) over and above the direct benefit to the boy and his family. In other words the consumer of a good or service is not the sole beneficiary, and the amount he is willing to pay does not measure the entire value of the good to society. The act of consumption, in effect, creates a collective good. In such instances it may be socially desirable to provide the good, although the amounts collectable from direct users do not suffice to cover production costs. Market prices are not, in those cases, adequate measures of social value.

CONDITIONS OF PRODUCTION

The circumstances that conduce to government initiative relate to economies of scale. Some activities can be performed economically only on such a very large scale that for private enterprise to undertake them is infeasible or undesirable. For example, without invoking governmental power, it is not practicable to assemble the large areas of property required for highways, urban redevelopment, or hydroelectric projects. Some natural monopolies, such as water supply, are retained by the government as an alternative to regulating private development. It is probable, however, that whatever the condition of production the government would not undertake a project unless important collective goods or external benefits were involved.

OTHER INCENTIVES

The supposition that private investors may take an unduly short view of the consequences of their investments is an important justification for all investments having to do with the preservation of natural resources and their orderly exploitation. It is pertinent also to investments in urban renewal and improvements. In a way, the justification is related to the collective goods theme: there is little reason to believe that current prices for urban property or rural woodlands reflect adequately the importance of these depletable resources to future generations. Society as a whole may assign quite different values to such resources than do the participants in current markets.

And sometimes government undertakings are stimulated by an incentive of a very different sort: the desire to influence the distribution of income. The desire for a regional redistribution, for example, is one of the explicit motivations for the Appalachia Program, and the desire for socioeconomic redistribution plays a large role in urban renewal programs. Appraising the social value of such redistributions presents peculiarly difficult problems.

Formulas for Comparing Benefits and Costs

As the above discussion of incentives suggests, the government tends to intervene in precisely those markets in which prices are either lacking or are seriously divergent from social values. It is inherent in government enterprises, therefore, that market prices cannot be used in appraising their social contributions. Still, some economic basis is needed for judging which potential government undertakings are worthwhile and which are not. Benefit-cost analysis provides this basis.

Benefit-cost analysis is closely analogous to the methods of investment project appraisal used by businessmen. The only difference is that estimates of social value are used in place of estimates of sales value when appropriate. There are in use a number of slightly different formulas for comparing benefits and costs of government undertakings; two of the most popular ones are sketched below.

The starting point of any of the formulas is a projection of the physical output of the undertaking, either in each year of its life or in some typical year of operation. If the undertaking is a highway, for example, there would have to be estimates of the number of passenger-car miles, truck miles, and bus miles to be traveled on it in each year or in a typical year. Next, there would have to be estimates of the unit social value of each of these physical outputs, be they passenger-car miles, kilowatt hours, or whatever. These two estimates induce at once an estimate of the gross social contribution of the enterprise in a single year.

At this point the different formulas begin to diverge. One approach is to perform the gross benefit calculation for a typical year and to make a parallel computation for social costs in a typical year. The costs consist of two major components: current costs—the typical year expenditures for operating and maintaining the facilities; and capital costs—a charge levied against a year's operations to amortize the initial expenses of construction and installation. The ratio of gross annual benefits to total annual costs is the benefit-cost ratio. This formula amounts to a businessman's calculation of the ratio of sales to cost of goods sold, or of a profit-sales ratio, except, of course, that the value of output used in a benefit-cost computation is the social, rather than the market, value.

An alternative formula subtracts current costs in each year, or in a typical year, from gross benefits to obtain an estimate of current net benefits. The current net benefits for each year are discounted back to the date of inception of the project and added up to obtain an estimate of the present value of discounted net benefits. The ratio of this figure to the estimated capital cost of the project is then the benefit-cost ratio. This formula is therefore analogous to a businessman's calculation of the rate of profit that can be earned by capital invested in the undertaking. Indeed, in sophisticated variants of this approach, an internal rate of return, which is a strict analog of a rate of profit, may be computed.

These brief sketches have excluded many technical questions that may have significant, and even decisive, influence on the outcome. For example, what rate of interest should be used in amortizing the capital expenses or in discounting back the net benefits? What account, if any, should be taken of off-site and secondary benefits? What allowance should be made for consumer surplus? How should any effects on the distribution of income be taken into account? Such questions are important and arise in all formulations of benefit-cost comparisons, and some of them are discussed in the papers in this volume.

Quite clearly, the precise formula used for consolidating and expressing the results of the analysis is a relatively superficial matter: properly interpreted all the formulas lead to the same conclusions. The heart of the matter lies in deciding what benefits should be included and how they should be valued. The debate about benefit-cost analysis centers on the question of whether the social value of benefits can be estimated reliably enough to justify the trouble and effort involved in a benefit-cost computation.

This issue cannot be resolved categorically. It is no accident that benefit-cost analysis had its origin and highest development in the field of water resources. That is the field in which government operations are most analogous to private business and in which the highest proportion of outputs —water and power—are saleable commodities bearing relevant market prices. And nonpriceable, almost intangible consequences, though present, are less obtrusive than in other spheres of government activity. . . .

11

Benefit-Cost Analysis: Its Relevance to Public Investment Decisions

Benefit-cost analysis is a partial response to the need for assessment of expenditure efficiency in the public sector. Arthur Maass, Professor of Economics at Harvard University, points out certain advantages and limitations to benefit-cost analysis and stresses the need for a more rational approach to

ARTHUR MAASS

decision making and resource allocation in the public sector. Among the several issues brought out by Maass is the need to recognize goals other than economic efficiency and to structure benefit-cost studies in a multiple objective context.

The United States government has for some time used benefit-cost analysis in the design and justification of dams and other water resources improvements. Currently the government is trying to adapt the technique to other public investment programs. At the request of the Bureau of the Budget, the Brookings Institution held a major conference on the topic in November 1963 with papers on applying benefit-cost analysis to urban highways, urban renewal, outdoor recreation, civil aviation, government research and development, and public health.[1] In 1965 the Bureau of the Budget established

Reprinted from Arthur Maass, "Benefit-Cost Analysis: Its Relevance to Public Investment Decisions," *Quarterly Journal of Economics* 80 (May 1966), pp. 208–26, with the permission of the author and publisher. Copyright 1966 by the President and Fellows of Harvard College.

[1] Robert Dorfman (ed.), *Measuring Benefits of Government Investments* (Washington: Brookings, 1965).

a special unit to adapt and apply benefit-cost and cost-effectiveness studies to a broad range of government programs. It is appropriate, therefore, to examine and evaluate this important branch of welfare economics.

What Is the Problem?

The major limitation of benefit-cost analysis, as it has been applied to public investments in the United States, is that it ranks projects and programs in terms only of economic efficiency. (At the national level this means that projects and programs are judged by the amount that they increase the national product.) But the objective of most public programs is not simply, not even principally, economic efficiency. The redistribution of income to classes or to regions is an important objective in government plans— witness the Appalachia Program; and there are other objectives, too, the promotion of national self-sufficiency, for example.

In other words, the objective functions of most government programs are complex; yet benefit-cost analysis has been adapted to only a single objective —economic efficiency. Thus, benefit-cost analysis may be largely irrelevant, or relevant to only a small part of the problem of evaluating public projects and programs. We should not settle for the current state of benefit-cost analysis, but rather find ways to make it applicable to the real issues of public investment.

Now in all complex objective functions for government programs, economic efficiency will be one term. A second is frequently income redistribution, as we have noted, to classes (e.g., the poor) or to regions (e.g., depressed areas). These two objectives may be complementary in some ways; a program designed to transfer income from the rest of the nation to Appalachia or from the wealthy to the poor may also increase national product.[2] But a government program that maximizes efficiency will not necessarily, indeed is not likely to, achieve a specified high level of income redistribution. Thus, a planner who is responsible for developing a program or project for both purposes will need to know the relative weights to assign to efficiency and income redistribution.

Assume that the problem is to design an irrigation project on an Indian Reservation so as to increase the income of the Indians as a group and to increase food production for the nation as a whole. The relation between

[2] For conditions under which regional redistribution in the United States can be achieved without any significant loss in economic efficiency, see Koichi Mera, "Efficiency and Equalization in Interregional Economic Development," unpublished Ph.D. thesis, Harvard University, 1965. For a more general statement of the relations between economic efficiency and income distribution, see Stephen A. Marglin, "Objectives of Water-Resource Development: A General Statement," in Arthur Maass, Maynard M. Hufschmidt, Robert Dorfman, Harold A. Thomas, Jr., Stephen A. Marglin, and Gordon Maskew Fair, *Design of Water-Resource Systems* (Cambridge: Harvard University Press, 1962), pp. 63–67.

income for the Indians (income redistribution) and food production (national economic efficiency) in this case can be stated in any one of three ways as follows:[3]

1. Maximize net income to the Indians, subject to a constraint that the ratio of efficiency benefits to efficiency costs is at least 1.0 to 1.0, or 0.9 to 1.0, or some other.

2. Maximize net benefits from food production in national terms—i.e., economic efficiency—subject to a constraint that the Indians net $X thousand per year.

3. Maximize a weighted sum of net benefits from economic efficiency and income redistribution in which $1 of income to the Indians is valued at $(1 + X)$ of efficiency. (In this case the X can be called a shadow premium on redistribution benefits.)

With proper values these three statements will be equivalent. Any constraint can be converted into a shadow price and any shadow price, into a constraint.

The efficiency benefits and costs of this two-term objective function can be measured fairly well by the art of benefit-cost analysis in its present state. There are problems, to be sure, resulting from such factors as the collective character of the benefits of many public programs, the need to measure costs in terms of resource displacements rather than market prices where these two measures diverge, the selection of an appropriate discount rate, various so-called effects; but great progress has been made on these in recent years.[4] Thus, all that is needed to solve the maximization equation is to specify the trade-off ratio between efficiency and income redistribution. If there is a way of finding this ratio, the maximization problem can be solved in any of its three forms, and we can design projects and programs that are responsive to a realistic two-factor objective function.

There is a way to determine the trade-off—through the political process. For the federal government my studies indicate that there is a capacity in the legislative process to make the trade-off decisions that can then govern the design of projects and programs. The President initiates the legislative process; the Congress examines the President's proposals in the light of alter-

[3] This example is adapted from Marglin, "Objectives of Water-Resource Development," *op. cit.*

[4] For a discussion of these problems as of 1961, see Chaps. 2 (Marglin), 3 (Dorfman), and 4 (Marglin) in Maass, Hufschmidt, *et al.*, *Design of Water-Resource Systems, op. cit.*; and Maynard M. Hufschmidt, John Krutilla, and Julius Margolis, with assistance of Stephen A. Marglin, "Report of Panel of Consultants to the Bureau of the Budget on Standards and Criteria for Formulating and Evaluating Federal Water Resources Developments" (Washington, June 30, 1961), mimeo. For examples of more recent developments see Peter O. Steiner, "The Role of Alternative Cost in Project Design and Selection," this *Journal* LXXIX (Aug. 1965), 417–30, and Kenneth J. Arrow, "Discounting and Public Investment Criteria," paper presented at Water Resources Conference, Fort Collins, Colorado, July 6, 1965.

natives and accepts, modifies, or rejects them. Thus, the experts in the executive departments need to develop data that show the effects on the design of programs and projects of different trade-off ratios. This the executive can do. The President needs to select one or a range of these ratios and thereby initiate formally the legislative process. This the President can do. And finally, the Congress, when presented with such data and such a presidential initiative, needs to and can, as we shall see, respond in order.

Ironically but understandably, the field of public investment for which the present benefit-cost technique is most advanced, water resources, is the field for which the political technique for determining trade-offs among efficiency and other objectives is most primitive. The legislative process for water resources consists principally of omnibus bills that authorize individual projects, rather than of legislation that sets standards and criteria. In the housing and urban renewal area, by contrast, standards and criteria, based on both income redistribution and economic efficiency, are determined in the legislative process, and benefit-cost analysis is primitive.

The problem is to combine the advanced state of the art of efficiency benefit-cost analysis, as found in water resources planning, with an equally sophisticated technique for relating efficiency benefits and costs to those stemming from other objectives.

Have Benefits Been Overestimated?

In this context it is interesting to examine the arguments over so-called secondary benefits and how they should be included, if at all, in project analyses. There is no such thing as a secondary benefit. A secondary benefit, as the phrase has been used in the benefit-cost literature, is in fact a benefit in support of an objective other than efficiency.[5] The word benefit (and the word cost, too) has no meaning by itself, but only in association with an objective; there are efficiency benefits, income redistribution benefits, and others. Thus, if the objective function for a public program involves more than economic efficiency—and it will in most cases—there is no legitimate reason for holding that the efficiency benefits are primary and should be included in the benefit-cost analysis whereas benefits in support of other objectives are secondary and should be mentioned, if at all, in separate subsidiary paragraphs of the survey report. Using the current language and current standards, most of the benefits to the Indians in the Indian irrigation project are secondary benefits. How silly!

In this context it is interesting also to examine the conclusion of many

[5] The term has been used also to describe a small class of *efficiency* benefits that are *induced* rather than *produced* directly, by the public investment, but this distinction is of questionable utility.

nongovernmental studies of government planning for water resources projects, namely, that benefits have been overestimated. Professor Hubert Marshall recently recited the evidences of chronic overestimation in a major address before the Western Resources Conference at Fort Collins.[6] The principal cause of such benefit "overestimation" is, I believe, the unreal restrictions placed on the analysis of projects by the unreal but virtual standard that the relation of efficiency benefits to efficiency costs is the indicator of a project's worth, when in fact the project is conceived and planned for objectives in addition to efficiency. In such an incongruous circumstance one might expect project planners to use a broad definition of efficiency benefits. The critics, either not understanding or unsympathetic to the planners' plight, have judged them by a more rigorous definition of efficiency.[7]

How Did We Get to Where We Are?

Why has benefit-cost analysis developed in this way? Certainly not because of any myopia on the part of the Congress, though executive officers are frequently quick to blame Congress for their ills. To be sure, we do not have adequate legislative objectives, standards, or trade-off ratios for the design and evaluation of water resources projects, but this is because the President has failed to initiate the legislative process, not because of a lack of receptivity to such initiatives by Congress. In fact certain committees of Congress, impatient with the President for not proposing legislation to set standards, have tried to initiate the legislative process themselves; but without cooperation from the executive they have failed, understandably.[8] The task of assembling and analyzing data, the necessary first step in the legislative process, is beyond the capacity of the Congress and its staffs in complex areas like this one. Insofar as there is a general standard for the design of water projects that has been approved by Congress in legislation, it is a thirty-year-old statement that "the benefits to whomsoever they may accrue should exceed the costs."[9] This standard, you will note, does not specify efficiency benefits, but "benefits to whomsoever they may accrue."

The executive agencies have painted themselves into the efficiency box. In 1950 the Subcommittee on Benefits and Costs of the Federal Inter-Agency

[6] Hubert Marshall, "Politics and Efficiency in Water Development," Fort Collins, Colorado, July 7, 1965.

[7] There are causes, in addition to what I consider to be the principal cause, for so-called benefit overestimation, and these, but not the principal cause, are given in Marshall's Fort Collins paper, *op. cit.*

[8] Arthur Maass, "System Design and the Political Process: A General Statement," in Maass, Hufschmidt, *et al., Design of Water-Resource Systems, op. cit.,* p. 588.

[9] The origin of this provision of the Flood Control Act of 1936 (49 Stat. 1570) did not, incidentally, come from a Presidential initiative.

River Basin Committee gave overwhelming emphasis to the efficiency ranking function in its now well-known "Green Book" report.[10] In 1952 the Bureau of the Budget, in a Budget Circular that neither required nor invited formal review and approval by the Congress, nailed this emphasis into national policy, adopting it as the standard by which the Bureau would review agency projects to determine their standing in the President's program.[11] And soon thereafter agency planning manuals were revised, where necessary to reflect this Budget Circular. In this way benefits to all became virtually restricted to benefits that increase national product.

The federal bureaucrats, it should be noted, were not acting in a vacuum; they were reflecting the doctrines of the new welfare economics which has focused entirely on economic efficiency. Non-efficiency considerations have been held to be outside the domain of the welfare economist. They have been called by such loaded names as inefficient, value-laden, altruistic, merit wants, uneconomical.[12]

What Changes in Economic Welfare Theory Are Needed?

From a practical point of view the new welfare economics has dealt exclusively with efficiency because for it, and not for other objectives, benefit and cost data are provided automatically by the market, though market prices sometimes have to be doctored. Theoretically, however, the preoccupation of present-day welfare economics, and its branch of benefit-cost analysis, with economic efficiency results from its very basic assumptions, and two of these in my view can and should be abandoned.

First is indifference to the distribution of income generated by a government program or project—the assumption that each dollar of income from the program is of equal social value regardless of who receives it. In benefit-cost analysis that maximizes efficiency, an extra dollar to a Texas oil man is as desirable socially as one to an Arkansas tenant farmer, and an additional dollar of benefits for Appalachia, West Virginia is no more worthwhile than one for Grosse Pointe, Michigan.

Few welfare economists support the social implications of this basic assumption, and they would compensate for them in one of two ways. Some

---

[10] U.S. Federal Inter-Agency River Basin Committee, Subcommittee on Benefits and Costs, *Proposed Practices for Economic Analysis of River Basin Projects* (May 1950).

[11] U.S. Bureau of the Budget, *Circular A–47*, Dec. 31, 1952.

[12] See for an example Richard A. Musgrave, *The Theory of Public Finance* (New York: McGraw-Hill, 1959). The first of these labels is perhaps correct technically, but even this cannot be said of the others, for efficiency is not necessarily either less or more value laden, or altruistic, or meritorious than other objectives.

hold that the professional planners should design projects and programs for economic efficiency, for which benefit-cost analysis can provide the necessary ranking function; and that thereafter these project designs can be doctored and modified by a political process to account for any "uneconomic" objectives.[13] But this response is unsatisfactory for reasons already given. Where government programs are intended for complex objectives they should be designed, where this is possible, for such objectives, not designed for one objective, which may not be the most important, and subsequently modified in an effort to account for others. Almost inevitably economic efficiency will be overweighted in such a scheme. How relevant is this type of planning for our Indian irrigation project? Furthermore, such a planning process calls on political institutions to perform a task for which they are not well equipped. Where the approval and modification of individual projects, rather than a debate on objectives and standards for designing projects in the first place, is the *principal* activity of the legislative process, decision-making for the nation can disintegrate into project-trading. In the legislature, for exmple, the voices of the whole house and of committees are muted at the expense of those of individual members, each making decisions for projects in his district and accepting reciprocally the decisions of his colleagues. Nor does the executive under these circumstances play a more general or high-minded role. The public investment decision process can be organized, hope-fully, to play to the strengths rather than to the weaknesses of political institutions.

An alternative response of some welfare economists to the inequitable social consequences of the basic assumption of indifference to income distribution is as follows. It is more efficient to redistribute income directly from one group of individuals to another, through government programs of taxation and subsidies, than to do so indirectly through government investment programs that are designed also to increase national product. If the government's objectives are, for example, to increase both national food production and income of the Indians, it should plan to accomplish these by two programs rather than by a single one. Government planners should design the most efficient program for increasing food production, which may mean additional irrigation facilities in the Imperial Valley of California where there are no Indians. Then, with taxes collected from the irrigators that represent their willingness to pay for their new benefits, the government should make subsidy payments to the Indians. In this way, so goes the argument, the government can achieve the best of both worlds. Best in this context means efficient, however, and there is no reason why a community need prefer the most efficient method for redistributing income, especially if it requires transferring cash from one group to another. As Marglin points out

[13] In essence this is what Dorfman proposes for West Pakistan. Robert Dorfman, "An Economic Strategy for West Pakistan," *Asian Survey*, III (May 1963), 217–23.

in his treatment of this subject, the means by which a desired distribution of income is achieved may be of great importance to the community.[14] In our example, the community would probably be willing to give up some efficiency to see the living standard of the Indians improved by their own labors rather than by the dole. In short, the community may quite properly want to realize multiple purposes through public investment projects and programs, and if benefit-cost analysis is to be of great use in planning these activities, then the basic assumption of indifference to their distributive consequences must be abandoned.

It should be noted, however, that where, as in the case of the Indian irrigation project, a government program produces benefits that can be sold or otherwise charged for, a desired redistribution of income can be achieved by both the quantity of benefits produced and the prices charged for them. For any given quantity of irrigation water, the smaller the repayment required from the Indians, the greater the income they will receive. Thus, when the agency men prepare data showing the effects on public programs of alternative trade-offs between economic efficiency and income redistribution, these alternatives should include different repayment possibilities.

The second basic assumption of the new welfare economics and of benefit-cost analysis that needs to be challenged is consumers sovereignty—reliance solely on market-exhibited preferences of individuals. This assumption, to be sure, provides normative significance for the familiar prescriptions of welfare economics on which the efficiency calculus is based—for example, that price ought to equal marginal costs. Nonetheless, it is not relevant to all public investment decisions, for an individual's market preference is a response in terms of what he believes to be good for his own economic interest, not for the community.

Each individual plays a number of roles in his life—social science literature is filled with studies of role differentiation—and each role can lead him to a unique response to a given choice situation. Thus an individual has the capacity to respond in a given case, to formulate his preferences, in several ways, including these two: (1) what he believes to be good for himself—largely his economic self-interest, and (2) what he believes to be good for the political community. The difference between these two can be defined in terms of

[14] Stephen A. Marglin, "Objectives of Water-Resource Development," *op. cit.*, pp. 17–18, 62–67. Jan Tinbergen, *On the Theory of Economic Policy* (Amsterdam: North Holland, 1952), observes that in the normal case *n* programs (or instruments) are required to maximize a welfare function that includes *n* objectives (or targets). But for his normal case Tinbergen assumes that only the results of the programs, not their qualitative characteristics, affect welfare, and that planners are free to select that level of achievement of each objective that maximizes the overall welfare function. This freedom is theirs only if *n* programs are available to the planners. Our discussion, on the other hand, proceeds from the assumptions that the qualitative characteristics of the programs affect welfare, and that the number of acceptable programs may be fewer than the number of objectives, which necessitates the trade-off among objectives. This would be an abnormal case in Tinbergen's formulation.

breadth of view. To the extent that an individual's response is community, rather than privately, oriented, it places greater emphasis on the individual's estimate of the consequences of his choice for the larger community.

Now, the response that an individual gives in any choice situation will depend in significant part on how the question is asked of him, and this means not simply the way a question is worded, but the total environment in which it is put and discussed. This can be illustrated with a small group experiment. Questions with relevance for the church (e.g., should birth control information be provided to married individuals who desire it?) were asked of Catholic students randomly divided into two groups. One group met in a small room where they were made aware of their common religious membership. The other group met in a large auditorium, along with hundreds of other students of many religions, where no effort was made to establish awareness of common religious beliefs. Although all of the students were instructed to respond with their "own personal opinions," there was a significant difference between the replies of the group that were aware of their common religious membership and the unaware group, the former approximating more closely the orthodox Catholic position against birth control.[15]

An individual's response depends, then, on the institutional environment in which the question is asked. Since the relevant reponse for public investment analysis is a community, not privately, oriented one, the great challenge for welfare economics is to frame questions in such a way as to elicit from individuals community oriented answers. The market is an institution designed to elicit privately oriented responses from individuals and to relate these responses to each other. For the federal government the electoral, legislative, and administrative processes together constitute the institution designed to elicit community oriented responses. The Maass-Cooper model describes these processes within such a context.[16]

Although several welfare economists have recognized explicitly that individuals play several roles and that these roles influence preferences, they go on to say that in making decisions relating to social welfare each individual uses a composite utility function, a total net position representing a balance of all of his roles.[17] This last hypothesis, which is not supported by experimental evidence, is unfortunate. It misses the point that an individual will

[15] W. W. Charters, Jr. and Theodore M. Newcomb, "Some Attitudinal Effects of Experimentally Increased Salience of a Membership Group," in Eleanor E. Maccoby, Theodore M. Newcomb, and Eugene L. Hartley, *Readings in Social Psychology* (New York: Henry Holt, 1958), pp. 276–81.

[16] Arthur Maass, "System Design and the Political Process: A General Statement," *op. cit.*

[17] Anthony Downs, "The Public Interest: Its Meaning in a Democracy," *Social Research*, Vol. 29 (Spring 1962), pp. 18–20, 27–32; Gerhard Colm, "The Public Interest: Essential Key to Public Policy," in C. J. Friedrich (ed.), *The Public Interest* (New York: Atherton, 1962), p. 121; Jerome Rothenberg, *The Measurement of Social Welfare* (Englewood Cliffs, N.J.: Prentice-Hall, 1961), pp. 296–97.

respond differently depending on how the question is asked of him, and it fails to give proper emphasis to the differentiation of institutions for putting the question—e.g., the market institution to elicit private oriented responses and political institutions for those which are community oriented.

Ideally we want the community, not market, responses of individuals with respect to both factors in our complex objective function—economic efficiency and income redistribution. Fortunately, however, market-determined prices are a fairly good surrogate for the economic efficiency factor, providing adjustments are made for so-called externalities and the like.[18] This is opportune. Were it not for the propriety of using market related prices for efficiency benefits and costs, benefit-cost analysis for public projects and programs would be beyond the capacity of available economic techniques and of political institutions as they operate today.

Some day, I am confident, we shall be able to use institutions that elicit community oriented responses to measure all factors in a complex objective function—efficiency, income redistribution, and others. The very recent search by a few economists, inspired largely by the work of Kenneth Arrow, for a new criterion of social welfare may contribute to this end.[19] The more modest proposal of this article is that we use political institutions to measure the trade-off ratio between a basically market-determined efficiency and the single most important nonefficiency objective of a government program, which is likely to be income redistribution but may be some other.

What Is the Evidence that Trade-offs Can Be Determined?

It remains to be demonstrated that there is a capacity in the legislative process to select trade-off ratios in a way that will be useful for the design of government programs and projects. As stated earlier, the legislative process involves three steps. First, the officials in the executive departments prepare data showing what would be the effects on programs and projects of alternative trade-offs between economic efficiency and another objective; second, the President, with these data in hand, selects a trade-off ratio and proposes it to Congress as the legislative standard; and third, Congress examines the President's proposal, in the light of the alternatives developed in the departments and of others that may come from outside sources, and accepts, rejects, or modifies it.

The first step should not involve great difficulties, especially in water resources where analysis of the efficiency factor is well advanced, although

---

[18] Marglin's 1962 analysis, *op. cit.*, is one demonstration of this.

[19] For an excellent summary of this research see Rothenberg, *op. cit.*

there will be obvious problems in areas where economic efficiency analysis is primitive. For continuing programs, the data necessary to initiate the legislative process need not relate to projects and programs being designed or to be designed; they can be drawn from projects already in operation and in some cases from hypothetical or prototype projects. Agency men can re-examine completed projects and programs and estimate how differently they would have been built and would have operated with different trade-offs among objectives. At the same time they can reflect in the data that they prepare for new investment programs information generated during previous planning periods, thereby using a sequential planning process.[20]

It is at the final, or Congressional, stage that doubters will raise most questions, and it is, of course, this stage that is most difficult to prove, because in the water resources area, for which the legislative initiative could be taken most clearly, the President has failed to act. To demonstrate Congress' capacity we must, therefore, turn to public investment programs for which standards have been set in legislation, and these are ones for which efficiency benefit-cost analysis is so rudimentary that it is necessary to examine the record very carefully for implicit evidence of a concern for trade-offs between efficiency and other objectives.

Legislation authorizing the National System of Interstate Highways, principally the Act of 1956, furnishes one example.[21] The legislation provides that the system should consist of 41,000 miles of roads which are identified generally as to location, and it sets design criteria for these roads. The criteria depart from those of earlier highway legislation in three important respects, apart from the taxing methods for financing the federal government's share of the costs. First, roads are to be designed for predicted traffic volumes of 1975, and the monetary authorizations are calculated from this standard.[22] Second, the federal-state matching ratio is changed from 50:50 to 90:10. Third, the formula for apportioning funds among the states is changed. The earlier formula for the primary system of roads was one-third on the basis of each of the following ratios: a state's population to the total U.S. population, a state's area to the total U.S. land area, a state's rural delivery and star routes to the total U.S. mileage of such roads. The new formula provides a single ratio: the estimated cost of completing the Interstate System within the borders of a state to the total estimated cost of completing the entire system by a fixed date, 1972.[23] This last criterion was agreed to after con-

[20] See Stephen A. Marglin, *Public Investment Criteria* (London: Allen and Unwin, 1966).

[21] My data are taken from David C. Major, "Decision Making for Public Investment in Water Resource Development in the United States," unpublished, PhD. thesis, Harvard University, 1965, Chap. 5. See this thesis for citations of statutes and reports referred to here.

[22] This design standard was amended in 1963 to provide for predicted traffic volumes twenty years from date of approval of project plans.

[23] The Act of 1956 contemplated completion by fiscal year 1969, but both estimated costs and year of completion were later amended.

siderable discussion involving numerous alternatives, but principally two: the one adopted and one that would continue to give considerable weight to a state's area and its population. As Major has shown, these alternatives represent, respectively, economic efficiency, or more properly a surrogate for efficiency, and income redistribution. Given the requirement of completing a given mileage, by a given date, to a given capacity (1975 traffic volume), an apportionment based on cost of completion would be efficient; and one based on such factors as a state's area would introduce other objectives into the program, namely, redistribution of income (largely federal construction funds) to rural states where traffic volumes and highway construction costs per mile are typically lower. This is especially true because the alternative provided that if a state received more funds than necessary to complete its portion of the Interstate System, it could divert a percentage of the excess for use on its other federally-aided roads.

A study of the legislative process in which these new program criteria, especially the third one, were adopted has some useful lessons for our inquiry. There was a vigorous and effective executive initiative of the process. The concept of uniform completion of an Interstate System in all states at approximately the same time appears to have been recommended first by a non-federal entity, the American Association of State Highway Officials. Thereafter the Bureau of Public Roads made a detailed factual study of the costs of building an Interstate System. The President, in an address before the 1954 Governors' Conference, proposed that the nation develop a new master plan for highways, and he appointed an Advisory Committee on a National Highway Program, chaired by General Lucius Clay, to prepare one. The Clay Committee used the Bureau of Public Roads report as its empirical base. It recommended the three design standards that were finally adopted, presenting them in the context of alternatives about which debate in the legislative process could and did revolve.[24] Both the BPR and the Clay reports were sent to the Congress, along with a Presidential recommendation. The discussion in Congress, in committee and on the floor, was informed and extensive. Information was available on the expected consequences in terms of investment of choosing alternative standards, the participants were aware of the nature of the choices they had to make, and their debate was rich in relevant arguments pro and con on the alternatives, especially on apportionment formulae.

What we have called economic efficiency in this case—i.e., the most efficient way of satisfying a fixed requirement—is of course quite different from economic efficiency as an objective in benefit-cost analysis for water resources, where it means to maximize the contribution of a project to

---

[24] The Clay report's proposals on tax policy and accounting procedures for financing the road system, which we do not discuss here, were altered significantly in the legislative process.

national product. The latter concept played no part in setting the standards for the highway program. The art of efficiency benefit-cost analysis is much less well developed for public investments in highways than in water resources developments, and this was even more true ten years ago than it is today. It is not unreasonable to suggest, from the record of the legislative process for the Interstate Highway System, that had data been available on real economic efficiency and on alternative trade-offs between it and income redistribution, these would have been used intelligently in setting standards.

Comparing the legislative processes for the Interstate Highway System and water resources, the former is less concerned with authorizing individual projects that have been designed and more concerned with setting standards for project design. To be sure, the highway act authorized 41,000 miles of roads and fixed their general locations. Design of the roads, including definite locations for them, was left, however, for administrative action insofar as the federal government was concerned.

In federal programs for housing and urban renewal, standards and design criteria have been set in the legislative process, and the recent legislative history of the rent supplement program is an instructive example.[25] In his Housing Message of 1965, President Johnson described a proposed program for rent supplement payments as "the most crucial new instrument in our effort to improve the American city." The federal government was to guarantee to certain private builders the payment of a significant part of the rent for housing units built for occupancy by moderate income families. These are families with incomes below the level necessary to obtain standard housing at area market prices, but above the level required for admission to publicly-owned low rent housing units. The rent payments were to be the difference between 20 per cent of a family's income (the proportion of income that a moderate income family is expected to allocate to housing) and the fair market rental of the standard housing to be built. The President proposed an authorization of $200 million over four years which was designed to encourage the construction of 500,000 new housing units in this period. The housing supported in this way would constitute some but not all of the rental units in new housing projects.

The Housing Act of 1961 had also included a program designed specifically for moderate income families, but this program had encountered

[25] Except where otherwise noted, the facts of this case are derived from legislative documents relating to the Housing and Urban Development Act of 1965: President's Message (H. Doc. 89–99); Hearings before Subcommittees on Housing of the House and Senate Committees on Banking and Currency (Mar.–Apr. 1965); Reports of House and Senate Committees on Banking and Currency (H. Report 89–365, S. Report 89–378); Debate in House and Senate (*Cong. Rec.* for June 28–30 and July 14–15); Conference Report (H. Report 89–679; Debate in House and Senate on adoption of Conference Report (*Cong. Rec.* for July 26–27). Dr. David C. Major has assisted in developing the facts and interpretation of this case.

certain problems that slowed its expected impact. Section 221d(3) of the 1961 Act provided for 100 per cent loans to qualified private builders at below-market interest rates. The low interest rates were to keep rents within the reach of moderate income families. The law provided, however, that the interest rate was to be the average rate on all outstanding marketable federal obligations. This was $3\frac{1}{8}$ per cent when the program began, but it had risen to approximately $4\frac{1}{8}$ per cent by mid 1965. This meant that rents would be significantly higher and beyond the capacity of most moderate income families. Another problem with the 1961 program was that the low interest mortgages constituted a heavy drain on the special assistance funds of the Federal National Mortgage Association (FNMA), the federal housing credit agency that purchased them. Because these mortgages were below market rates, FNMA could not issue against them debentures for sale in private capital markets, and they remained a 100 per cent charge on federal funds. Nonetheless the Administration recommended in 1965 that the 221d(3) program be continued for four years with a mortgage authorization of $1.5 billion, for about 125,000 new housing units. But this program was to be phased out if the rent supplement proposal worked as its backers hoped that it would.

The Administration had three principal objectives in proposing rent supplements. The first was to increase the number of housing starts. This derived from a desire to expand the national housing stock and a concern about the possibly failing health of the housing industry and the industry's impact on the national economy. We can equate this objective roughly with increasing national product, or economic efficiency. The government's housing experts found that there was a large untapped market for new housing among moderate income families, and that rent supplements for them would stimulate the rapid construction of substantial amounts of new housing.

The second principal objective of the Administration in recommending a rent supplement program was to give direct assistance to a large group of families with incomes above the public housing level but below the level needed to obtain standard housing at market prices. This objective we can equate with income redistribution—to moderate income families.

As for direct assistance to low income families, the Administration bill would authorize additional public housing units. Over a four year period 140,000 new units were to be built and 100,000 units purchased or leased from private owners and rehabilitated. Using the trickle down theory, the Administration could claim that all other housing programs that increased the national stock of standard housing would ultimately improve the housing of the poor, but certainly the primary and direct impact of the rent supplement program, insofar as its objective was income redistribution, favored moderate income families.

The Administration's rent supplement program contained, then, as one design criterion a trade-off ratio relating the objectives of efficiency and income redistribution and as a second, a specification of the group to be favored by the redistribution. The second criterion was explicit in the Administration's legislative initiative, though the first was largely implicit.

The Administration's third principal objective for the rent supplement program was "economic integration." Families being aided by the government would live in projects with families who would pay normal market rentals for their housing. In this respect the new program differed from most other federal housing programs for disadvantaged groups, for the latter promoted economic segregation. Only the poor live in public housing; all units in 221d(3) projects are for occupancy by designated groups. To encourage economic integration even where local authorities may oppose it, the Administration proposed that in certain cases projects supported by rent supplements need not conform to locally approved "workable programs" for housing development.

After hearings, and debates, and conferences, Congress modified drastically the Administration's design criteria for a rent supplement program. Briefly, the supplements are to be given for standard housing units that are to be occupied by low income families. As a result, both the trade-off ratio between efficiency and income redistribution and the impact of the redistribution itself have been changed.

The relative contributions of the program to increasing national product and to redistributing income have been altered because, with a given authorization or appropriation, there will be fewer housing starts if rents of low, rather than moderate, income families are supplemented. The unit costs of standard housing are the same in either case, but the supplement required to make up the difference between what the family can pay and what is needed to support the new housing varies greatly. The new law authorizes $150 million for rent supplements (rather than the $200 million proposed by the President). According to current (December 1965) estimates of housing experts, this $150 million would result in 350–375,000 housing starts over four years if it were available for the Administration's program of aiding moderate income families. As rent supplements for low income families, the same money will induce only 250–300,000 starts.[26]

As for the criterion that governs the group to be benefited, the relative impacts on low and moderate income families of the original and revised programs for rent supplements and closely related activities are shown in Table I.

[26] Under the Administration bill the rent supplement would be the difference between rent for standard housing and 20 per cent of a moderate-income family's income. Under the act as approved, the rent supplement is the difference between the same rent and 25 per cent of a *low*-income family's income. The two changes made by Congress work in opposite directions, but they do not offset each other.

Table I—Impact on low and moderate income families of certain provisions of 1965 Housing Act

Program	Administration proposal	Congressional action
	(all figures are thousands of housing units over four years)	
Low income		
Public housing	240	240
Trickle down from all programs that increase national stock of standard housing	ok	ok
Rent supplement program	zero	250–300
Moderate income		
Rent supplements	467–500	zero
221d(3)	125 (*but* problems in achieving this because of high interest rate and drain on FNMA funds)	125 (*and* this likely to be achieved because interest rate fixed at 3% and provision made for tapping private capital)

The impact of Congress' revisions on the Administration's third objective of economic integration is not so clear. Insofar as it is poor rather than moderate income families who are enabled to live in housing developments along with families that are able to pay normal rents, a more dramatic integration can be achieved. On the other hand, it is clear from the legislative history that Congress does not intend that the housing agency exempt any rent supplement projects from the "workable plan" requirement, which means that local controls will continue.

The housing case study, like that of the highway program, shows that there is a capacity in the legislative process to discuss and adopt standards and criteria to control the design of public projects and programs; that the Congress is prepared to focus its efforts on such standards and forego authorization of the projects themselves—public works for housing, urban renewal, and community facilities are not individually authorized by law; and that the legislative process for setting standards can be used to select trade-off ratios where a program has two objectives. On this latter point, the rent supplement case is a bit weak, to be sure. The Administration in its legislative initiative did not make sufficiently explicit the trade-off between economic efficiency and income redistribution that was involved in its proposal for approximately 500,000 new housing starts for the benefit of moderate income families. Administration witnesses failed to give a clear statement of how the two objectives were related and how the program would differ if alternative trade-off ratios were assumed. One reason for this failure is that efficiency benefit-cost analysis has not been perfected for housing programs as it has for water resources. Nonetheless, the Congress, in revewing the

President's program, managed to focus on the relevant design criteria and, after extensive consideration, including some confused debate, revised them in a way that apparently was consistent with its policy preferences. Also, the executive now has a legislated standard that it can use in redesigning the relevant housing programs. How much better the process would have been if the initiative had been better prepared!

The Lesson

To those in the executive departments of the United States government, the lessons of this article should be clear. If the subject is water resources, initiate a legislative proposal for setting a trade-off value between economic efficiency and the most important non-efficiency objective that is relevant to your agency's program. Once this is approved, you can forget about secondary benefits, probably be relieved from the repetitive and profession-wise insulting charges that you persistently overestimate benefits, and you can design projects that are more in accord with the nation's objectives. If the subject is highways, or housing, or most other public investment programs, perfect the efficiency benefit-cost technique for your agency's program. Once this is done, there should be no difficulty in deriving through the legis-lative process a trade-off between efficiency and another objective. As a result, the design and selection of projects will be more intelligent and the program should be more convicing to those who judge it.

After the agencies have learned how to work with two-term objective functions, they can try to solve for more complex ones. For the time being, however, purposes other than efficiency and the most important non-efficiency objective will need to be treated descriptively in the familiar "additional paragraphs" of program and project reports.

12

Interest Rate Policy for the Evaluation of Federal Programs

Distinctions between the private and social discount rate are extremely important if public sector investment alternatives are to be evaluated rationally. Otto Eckstein, a pioneer in the area of public sector resource allocation problems and Professor of Economics of Harvard University, discusses in this selection the issues involved in using an "appropriate"

OTTO ECKSTEIN

discount rate. The basic recommendation is that the discount rate used in benefit-cost studies should reflect the opportunity cost of public capital—a concept often violated in past public sector investment decisions.

These hearings of the Subcommittee on Economy in Government of the Joint Economic Committee are a milestone in Federal expenditure policy. Government investment in physical and human capital has increased enormously in the last 30 years, and the crisis in our cities makes a dramatic further growth of public investment very likely. If these investments are to be productive in accomplishing our national purposes they must be well planned, employing sensible economic principles and meaningful tests of performance.

Although it appears to be an abstract and highly technical matter, the choice of interest rate in planning is fundamental and important. The history of many economies, including our own, is replete with capital projects based on faulty interest rates, with disastrous results and enormous

Reprinted from Otto Eckstein, "Interest Rate Policy for the Evaluation of Federal Programs," testimony before the Subcommittee on Economy in Government, Joint Economic Committee, *Hearings*, 90th Congress, 2nd Session, 1968, pp. 50–57.

waste. Perhaps the most extreme example was the attempt by the Soviet Union to plan an industrialization process without the use of any interest rate—an absurd undertaking saved only by the ingenuity of technicians in introducing interest-like criteria under other names. Under Joseph Stalin the use of zero interest rates helped produce the worst of gigantism. Projects of enormous scale and capital intensity were started in the various regions of the Soviet Union. Because of their size and capital intensity, years went by with little payoff from these slowly progressing monuments. Even after their completion their returns were often modest. After Stalin's death, as the aspirations of the Russian people have begun to make themselves felt, his successors have sought a higher degree of rationality in economic calculations, and among other things have encouraged more systematic testing of capital investments in terms of their rate of return. Even for large investments a rate as high as 10 percent is prescribed today, and for less capital intensive projects the rates are higher.

Another interesting example can be found in the United Kingdom. Its premature investment in atomic energy for electric power reportedly can partly be blamed on the Government's use of a low interest rate in planning at a time in the early 1950's when capital was scarce.

In the United States the larger part of physical investment has been in private hands. While the actual capital market bears no more than a family resemblance to the perfect allocating mechanism of economic theory, it still provides a vital discipline to investment decisions to avoid the very grossest errors.

But in the public sector, interest rate policy perhaps has been just as remote from economic rationality as in the Soviet Union. In many fields of investment there is no use of interest rates at all. In the water resource areas the interest rates have been about 3 percent, leading to the usual results: excessive scale of development, excessive capital intensity, in other words, waste of the Nation's capital.

So long as Federal investment was no more than a few billion dollars a year, the waste that resulted from a 3-percent interest policy was a luxury that we could afford. But the magnitudes of the tasks before us have increased, and we expect more from economic policy than we used to do. As we attempt to bring economic rationality into the public sector generally, interest rate policy must be thoroughly reexamined. My testimony today will attempt to contribute to the discussion which will lead to the foundation of a sound and comprehensive interest rate policy for Federal investment programs.

I The Role of the Interest Rate in a Market Economy

Interest rates serve four essential functions in the market economy:

1. *The price for liquidity.*—The interest rates in the short-term money market are paid for the use of money for a brief period, usually less than a year. The variations of short-term interest rates are mainly determined by the interplay of swings in the financial needs of business and the Federal Government and the policy of the Federal Reserve System. These interest rates are not pertinent to the planning of long-lived public investments.

2. *The price and cost of long-term capital.*—Long-term interest rates are the price for borrowing long-term capital. As such, they serve to allocate that share of the Nation's savings which becomes available for long-term investment. They funnel savings into those uses in which they promise to yield a return greater than the interest rate. They also serve to keep capital out of uses which do not hold the promise of yielding the market rate of interest.

3. *Interest rate as a means of valuation of income and consumption at different points in time.*—Households can choose to consume their lifetime income in various time profiles by saving or borrowing. Typically, households borrow in their early years while acquiring a home and raising children, pass through a savings phase preparatory to retirement, and draw down their savings thereafter. The prices confronting households in these choices are the interest rate at which they can borrow, such as the interest rate on home mortgages, on installment credit or personal loans, and the rates at which they can lend, such as the interest rates on savings accounts, Government bonds and the return on common stocks.

4. *Interest rates as a way of compensating for the return for taking risks.*—Interest rates differ according to the riskiness of the loan or investment. The highly diverse structure of actual interest rates found in the economy is partly due to differences in risk as viewed by investors.

II Imperfections in Capital Markets

In a perfectly competitive, and perfectly functioning market economy, there would be only one interest rate for all risk-free loans of any given maturity. This interest rate would be faced by both the borrowers and the lenders. In this way, there would be an assurance that the return on marginal investments of businesses exactly equals the rewards for marginal savings made by households. The optimal total amount of saving and investment would be determined through free choice in this process, and, leaving errors aside, the optimal combination of investment projects in the economy would be undertaken.

Economists differ in their assessment of the degree of correspondence between this ideal picture and the actual market economy as we know it. My judgment is rather far out on the spectrum of imperfections: as I have stated earlier, I assume "The capital market to be imperfect, to be rife with rationing, ignorance, differential tax treatments, reluctance to finance investment from external funds, slow adjustment processes, et cetera, which destroy the normative significance of actual rates found in the market." These imperfections, once acknowledged, give rise to two further concepts for interest rates which have received much attention in the academic discussions of interest rates for evaluating public investments.

5. *The social rate of time preference.*—With no single market rate embodying marginal returns and marginal household preferences perfectly, and with the total savings of the economy not necessarily optimal, a new basis must be found for deriving a socially optimal interest rate. This problem is of particular significance in countries where investment is heavily government-determined, but it is of pertinence even in the United States.

Theorists have devoted considerable effort to the derivation of an optimal rate of social time preference, some would say an excessive rate. The rates have been derived from theoretical models of economic growth and postulated functions for the marginal utility of consumption over time. It is usually inferred from this literature that the rate of social time preference is low; that is, that the planner's interest rate should be low, giving full weight to the welfare of future generations and overriding the myopic desires of present individuals.

6. A second concept which arises from the imperfections of the capital market is *the opportunity cost of public capital:* In the absence of a perfect capital market no one single actual interest rate can be used as a test to assure that the return of a public project will exceed the return of whatever other investment—or consumption—is forgone in its stead. It therefore becomes necessary to identify, on the most realistic analysis possible, what actual other investments—or consumption—are forgone, and what their return would have been.

In examining these forgone opportunities, and then identifying the opportunity costs, one must ask these questions:

(a) Where would the resources have been used in the absence of the particular public investment—in the public sector or in the private sector?

(b) If the resources are drawn from the public sector, that is, if the particular public investment is at the expense of other public expenditures within a fixed budget, what return would have been earned?

(c) If the resources are drawn from the private sector, are they obtained through taxation or through additional Government borrowing? If general fiscal policy considerations require that the additional resources be obtained through taxation, one must postulate a specific set of tax changes in order to identify what private expenditures are forgone, and one must then measure the returns in those alternative uses. If general fiscal policy permits the public investment to be financed by public borrowing, one must trace what private investments are forgone because of this particular Government claim in the capital market.

(d) Does the public investment preempt a private opportunity at the physical site, or in the same product market, or in utilizing a scarce natural resource? If there is preemption of private investment, an additional test must be performed to assure that the public investment is superior to the preempted private opportunity.

Let me add that I would not include the possibility of preemption of private opportunities in deriving the interest rate itself. It is really a side test that must be performed on a project-by-project basis.

Let me examine quickly what I think is a theoretically correct solution in an imperfect economy and then evaluate if practically it is a solution.

III A Theoretically Correct Solution in an Imperfect Market Economy

A theoretically correct solution to the problem of the choice of interest rate for public investment planning in an imperfect market economy is as follows:

1. Identify the actual opportunities that are forgone and measure the flow of returns that would have been earned in the alternative use;

2. Apply the social rate of time preference to derive the present value of the returns forgone in the alternative use;

3. Undertake only those public investments which yield more present value per dollar of expenditure than the forgone alternatives.[1]

This formulation, which I sketched in my book, "Water Resource Development," translates into U.S. Government practice as follows:

1. Apply the social time preference rate of interest in the valuation of projects; but

2. Compute the benefit-cost ratio of the forgone opportunities in the private or public sector. If the interest rate is very low, if we assume the social time preference to be very low, the benefit-cost ratio of the forgone opportunities will be very high.

3. Undertake those public projects which have a benefit-cost ratio greater than the benefit-cost ratio of the forgone opportunities. With an

[1] This formulation does not deal with the optimal time schedule of public investments, the physical or economic interdependence of projects, adjustments for risk, or the intricate question of the symmetrical treatment of taxation.

interest rate of 3 percent, they would nowadays come to a benefit-cost ratio on the order of 2.

While this formulation is correct within the particular theoretical model, and I had high hopes for it 10 years ago, there are serious difficulties in applying the method. It is my present judgment that a more workable approach must be developed. The faults are these:

1. There is no generally agreed upon empirical basis for deriving the rate of social time preference. One can make plausible arguments in favor of high or low rates. When individuals have a chance to express their preferences about present versus future consumption they value the present highly. The willingness of households to borrow at interest rates in excess of 10 percent is a strong kind of evidence. I doubt that a rate of social time preference is defensible in a democratic society which is dramatically different from the interest rates revealed to be preferred by consumer saving and borrowing actions.

The theoretical argument has been advanced that the people may choose to redistribute income to future generations collectively—reflecting low social time preference—while expressing high time preference in their private actions. In other words that what they choose to do together, knowing that all will do it together through the tax system, they may choose to be more farsighted than they will in their individual family planning. While not refutable by logic, it is a fragile position. There is no evidence that it is true that people have such collective preferences; governments in underdeveloped countries have been known to misjudge the wishes of their people in taking this point of view, planning on a very capital intensive basis with low interest and then finding great local objection to the fact that the projects do not pay off.

2. Even if one accepts the argument of collective desire to redistribute income to the future—that is, even if one grants the theoretical argument in total, it is still very dubious that public investments are the most desirable method of accomplishing this goal. A higher rate of taxation reducing the Government deficit, lowering interest rates and permitting a higher rate of capital accumulation, whether private or public, is a far more direct and efficient method of making provision for the future than to provide a privileged access to cheap capital for a few kinds of economic activities which have no extraordinary growth potential.

IV Some Pragmatic Considerations

Before deriving a sound criterion for Federal public investments, that is, before we finally come to the hard issue of what is the right rate, if there is such a thing, let me set down a few postulates that will underlie my conclusions.

1. *The rate of return on capital in the United States is high.* We are able to keep the economy prosperous through fiscal and monetary management of aggregate demand; fluctuations around our natural growth trend are becoming smaller. If you compare the 1950's with the 1960's, the variations are smaller; if you compare prewar with postwar, the fluctuations are smaller. The rate of advance of technology remains very great; the computer —probably the greatest innovation since the introduction of the automobile 50 years ago—assures further rapid technological progress.

The recorded rates of return on capital are high in most major sectors of the economy. The only exception I can think of are railroads. The market rates of interest, which reflect long run forces of supply and demand for capital, are high and will probably remain so. As the Vietnam war draws to a close and is, at last, financed through higher taxes, the interest rates will diminish somewhat. But it is very unlikely that interest rates will fall to the plateau that prevailed in the early 1960's, when unemployment was $5\frac{1}{2}$ percent for 5 years and prices were stable, when the rate of investment was low and the Government deficits small.

2. *That the demands on public budgets will remain great so that the competition for budget money will remain stiff.* This means that the opportunity cost in the public sector will be high. Whatever criterion is used, it must reflect the overall Federal budget position, including the needs for large public investment in human resources, the considerable outlays for military purposes, and the needs for social overhead investments in a rapidly advancing economy.

3. Third, as a fundamental postulate, *the high productivity of capital must be reflected in the interest rate used for planning and evaluating public investments.* The two-step procedure discussed above, that of using high social time preference rates and revaluing opportunity costs at a social time preference rate, does not appear to be workable for our government. The logic that a low interest rate must be coupled with cutoff benefit-cost ratios on the order of 2 is too obscure for Government and general public discussion. The first part of the method, that low interest rates can be justified on social grounds, is attractive. But the pressures on agencies and their desire to promote their programs are such that they will never accept the second part of the method, that investment programs only be accepted if benefits exceed costs by a factor of 2.

If the two-stage procedure is not workable, the interest rate itself must reflect the high opportunity costs of capital in the private and in the public sector.

The operational question then becomes: What should that interest rate be?

V What Interest Rate for Public Investments?

Given these postulates, the social time preference approach is ruled out. With it is also ruled out any logic which would produce interest rates as low as 3 percent which are still applied in some Federal programs. There are no observable interest rates anywhere in the economy as low as this: Capital yields substantially more in all sectors, and households make their saving-borrowing choices also at much higher rates. This is not to argue that the social time preference consideration be eliminated completely in the derivation of the final rate, but the weight given to it must be very limited if resources are not to be grossly wasted.

The Government borrowing rate? This concept has some things to recommend it if it is used properly, but it cannot survive full theoretical scrutiny. On the one hand, it is the interest rate at which the Government, as an enterprise, is able to obtain capital by borrowing. It also is a measure of the pure, risk-free, long-term interest rate in the market. On the other hand, the rate is not appropriate because, in actual practice, public investment projects are not financed by borrowing but by taxation. The opportunity costs in the private or public sectors are likely to exceed the long-term Government borrowing rate.

Nonetheless, if the Government borrowing rate were applied correctly, it would yield a better answer than current practice. The trouble has been that the actual Federal interpretation, as spelled out for example in Senate Document 97, has been very different from a "businesslike" enterprise borrowing cost.

Senate Document 97 bases the rate on the average rate payable on outstanding U.S. securities having maturities of 15 years or more. Because of the $4\frac{1}{4}$ percent interest ceiling, the Treasury has been unable to issue any securities of longer maturity since April 18, 1963, and has issued no 10-year bonds, which is less than the 15 years postulated, since May 15, 1964. It has issued notes of medium term in recent years, most recently a 7-year issue on May 15, 1968, paying 6 percent. This issue is currently yielding 5.54 percent. In response to the improvement in the bond market after the tax rise, long-term Treasuries are yielding 5.1 percent, a yield made possible only by the complete lack of new issues, and the capital gains component in their yield. If the Treasury were to issue new 15-year debt today, assuming that the interest ceiling is eliminated, it would have to pay at least $5\frac{1}{2}$ percent.

The Government bond rate is a measure of pure interest, before allowance for risk. If it is to be the basis for policy, a risk premium must be added, either in the interest rate or elsewhere in the criterion.

VI The Opportunity Cost of Public Investment

Let me turn now to what I think is the correct method. To estimate opportunity cost of public capital obtained by taxation is an intricate, but feasible piece of analysis. In an earlier book, "Multiple Purpose River Development," with J. V. Krutilla, I presented such a study and obtained estimates of $5\frac{1}{2}$ to $5\frac{3}{4}$ percent under the conditions prevailing in 1955. I have not attempted to redo that exercise. The interest rate structure has moved up $2\frac{1}{2}$ percent since then—that is, most long rates have moved up by that amount, suggesting that the opportunity cost today is approximately 8 percent. I append the earlier study for the record, if the committee wishes, to indicate the method in detail.

VII Conclusion and Recommendation

The borrowing cost for long-term capital for the Federal Government is $5\frac{1}{2}$ percent—if the Government could borrow long term. The opportunity cost for tax-raised capital is about 8 percent. What, then, should be the interest rate for Federal investment planning?

In my judgment, both rates are of some pertinence, but the heavier weight should be placed on the opportunity cost estimate based on tax financing. The Government borrowing rate can be interpreted as the lower limit of the opportunity cost of borrowed capital, which is a part—albeit a small part—of Federal financing. Under contemporary circumstances, and subject to more detailed reestimation of opportunity cost, under today's interest rate conditions, an interest rate of about 7 to $7\frac{1}{2}$ percent is a proper rate for Federal planning to assure economic use of the Nation's capital.

My testimony has not dealt with the estimation of benefits or the selection of goals. I do not believe that all investments should pass a narrow test of economic efficiency. Programs of human investment and of urban reconstruction have important social and redistributive goals which justify some sacrifice of economic efficiency.

But nothing is gained by confusing sensible economic planning through an unrealistic interest rate policy. Let us quantify our social goals and allocate our scarce resources so they will yield a maximum social return.

13

Special Problems in the Economic Analysis of Education

Because alternative methods of evaluating public sector investments can produce different choices, it is important to understand the details of program evaluation techniques. In their recent study of investment in vocational education completed at Pennsylvania State University for the United States Department of Labor, Professors Hu, Kaufman, Lee, and Stromsdorfer summarize, compare, and evaluate differences in the present value, benefit-cost

TEH-WEI HU
JACOB J. KAUFMAN
MAW LIN LEE
ERNST W. STROMSDORFER

ratio, and rate-of-return method of analyzing human capital investments. Selection of *one* investment criterion for all public investment options is not feasible for reasons noted by the authors of this selection, an extract from their larger study.

... The application of cost-benefit and cost-effectiveness analysis in the area of education is, in general, subject to a number of broad conceptual problems and qualifications. This chapter indicates that additional issues in the specific application of the various investment criteria, such as the internal rate of return or the benefit-cost ratio, must be considered before investment techniques can be applied to the economic evaluation of education.

When costs and benefits are both directly measurable in money terms, these techniques can be used with few reservations. When either costs or

This extract is taken from *A Cost Effectiveness Study of Vocational Education* by Teh-wei Hu, Jacob J. Kaufman, Maw Lin Lee, and Ernst W. Stromsdorfer, The Pennsylvania State University Institute for Research on Human Resources (1969), pp. 35–66, with permission of the authors.

benefits are not directly or completely measurable in monetary terms these techniques can only give limited, albeit needed and valuable, insights into educational and other investments in man.

General Considerations

THE ELEMENTS OF ANALYSIS

There are four basic elements in cost-benefit analysis: costs, benefits, time, and the interest rate by which to discount the costs and benefits.[1] Both the costs and benefits of investment in education occur through time. Different investment alternatives are likely to have different time profiles. The purpose of discounting is to attach relative weights to these cost and benefit time profiles in order to account for the productivity of investment and social or private time preference. In some cases a premium is also added to the interest rate to account for risk. However, such a practice, while pragmatically expedient and commonly practiced, is only theoretically correct where risk is a geometrically compounding function of time. . . .

Discounting is theoretically justified for a number of reasons. The first is that the interest rate used in discounting represents the opportunity cost of investment funds: that is, invested wealth usually earns a positive rate of return. Thus, Y dollars invested today will yield $Y + X$ dollars at some time in the future due to the productivity of the investment. Therefore, reversing the process, to relate this *future* income to its *present* value, one must discount the future income stream to the present time when the investment decision is being contemplated. Second, future income is valued less than present income. People have a positive time preference, that is, they dislike postponing consumption.[2]

[1] Much of the discussion which follows is derived from the following: A. R. Prest and Ralph Turvey, "Cost Benefit Analysis: A Survey," *The Economic Journal*, December 1965; Roland N. McKean, *op. cit.*; Otto Eckstein, "A Survey of the Theory of Public Expenditure Criteria," in National Bureau of Economic Research, *Public Finances: Needs, Sources, and Utilization*, A Conference of the Universities—National Bureau of Economic Research (Princeton, New Jersey: Princeton University Press, 1961); Jack Hirshleifer, *et al., op. cit.*; Ezra Solomon, Editor, *The Management of Corporate Capital* (New York: The Free Press, 1959). For additional bibliography, see Mark Blaug, *A Selected Annotated Bibliography in the Economics of Education*, Education Libraries Bulletin, Supp. Eight, Institute of Education, University of London, London, England, 1964; also by the same author, *Economics of Education: A Selected Annotated Bibliography* (New York: Pergamon Press, 1966).

[2] See William J. Baumol, *Economic Theory and Operations Analysis*, 2nd. ed. (Englewood Cliffs, New Jersey: Prentice-Hall, 1961), pp. 410–413 for a brief exposition of the theoretical rationale of time preference.

Investment Criteria

There is a variety of investment criteria which are available to the education decision maker. At the simplest level of analysis *benefit differentials* and *cost differentials* can be estimated. *The pay-back period can also be estimated. The net expected present value, the cost-benefit ratio, the ratio of differences in marginal benefits among programs to differences in marginal costs among programs, the expected annual net benefit, and the expected internal rate of return* can be calculated. Under certain conditions, these last four measures are equivalent and provide the same guidance to investment decision making. The conditions are noted later and exceptions to these comprise the bulk of this discussion.

THE CORRECT CRITERION

In general, the most correct criterion for making choices among competing investment alternatives is the criterion of maximizing the difference between the present value of benefits and the present value of costs. However, there are both practical and theoretical conditions which either commonly exist or can be devised which demonstrate that no single investment decision criterion is theoretically correct for all investment situations.[3] This discussion concentrates on only three of the above criteria: the expected internal rate of return; the expected net present value; and the cost-benefit ratio. The other measures are dealt with in only cursory fashion.

COST AND BENEFIT DIFFERENTIALS

Cost and benefit differentials represent a necessary but incomplete stage of economic analysis. These differentials are useful to show the configuration of the data and to provide the inputs to the proper (for a given set of constraints) investment criterion. However, alone they are not a useful guide to decision-making. Yet, one commonly perceives misunderstanding of this fact. For instance, a given project A, costing X dollars more than an alternative project B, is averred (by its advocates) to be of "higher quality" or (by its detractors) to be "too costly." But "higher quality" or "too costly" in what sense? Both these statements, taken by themselves, are nonsense in terms of economic efficiency. Costs and benefits must always be related to each other. More specifically, marginal costs must be related to marginal benefits. If the marginal or extra costs of two alternative programs are the same, but one has higher benefits than the other, it is possible to assert, other things equal, that the project with the larger net benefit is, in an

[3] See, especially Jack Hirshleifer, "On the Theory of Optimal Investment Decision," *Journal of Political Economy*, August 1958, pp. 329–352, and Martin J. Bailey, "Formal Criteria for Investment Decisions," *Journal of Political Economy*, October 1959, pp. 476–488.

economic efficiency sense, better than that with the smaller. But how much better and whether only one or both programs are efficient investments cannot be determined without further analysis. And, the confusion becomes even greater when one must make a choice between investing in a high cost-high benefit program and a low cost-low benefit program.

For instance, which is the greater educational investment between two projects each having a 20 year life span: project A which has an initial cost outlay of $200 and yields an annual benefit of $50 or project B which has an initial cost outlay of $1200 and an average annual benefit of $200? The first may be better than the second; the second may be better than the first.

THE PAY-BACK PERIOD

The pay-back period is a simple ratio of total costs, C, to constant marginal benefit, b, with the constant benefit measured over a given time unit such as a month or year. Thus, C/b equals the pay-back period.[4] This simple index relates costs and benefits to each other and different programs can be crudely judged as to their relative effectiveness. The criterion is to select the investment with the shortest pay-back period. For example, using the illustrative data of project A above yields a pay-back period of four years ($200/$50). Under the same set of assumptions, the pay-back period for B is six years. Thus, by this criterion one should select project A over B, other things equal.

A more general formulation for the pay-back period which accounts for non-constant benefits or costs is as follows:

$$\sum_{t=0}^{n} b_t - \sum_{t=0}^{n} c_t = 0, \text{ such that } t \text{ is minimized} \tag{1}$$

where b and c are marginal benefits and costs and t is the number of time periods.

The pay-back criterion, however, suffers from a variety of conceptual flaws. First, it ignores the fact that costs and benefits of competing investment alternatives are distributed through time and have different time profiles. Discounting is necessary to make the different cost-benefit profiles commensurable. Second, the absolute size of net benefits between alternatives may differ but the use of the ratio will obscure this. Third, as with the expected internal rate of return, the pay-back criterion breaks down completely in those cases where investment alternatives are mutually exclusive.

In light of these criticisms, consider again projects A and B mentioned above. The pay-back criterion directs one to invest in A and not in B.

---

[4] Under certain conditions the reciprocal of the pay-back period is equal to the expected internal rate of return. For this to occur, all costs must occur in the initial time period, and benefits must be constant and continue infinitely. See Myron J. Gordon, "The Payoff Period and the Rate of Profit," in Solomon, *op. cit.*, pp. 48–55.

Assume the life of A and B is 20 years for each. Clearly, if A and B are mutually exclusive and both are discounted over 20 years at a discount rate of 6 percent, the total net discounted benefits of B would be greater than those of A, \$2292 — \$1200 versus \$573 — \$200. A decision to invest in A under such conditions would result in a loss to total economic welfare. Thus, the pay-back period criterion has serious conceptual limitations as a decision-making tool and is not highly recommended.

A Consideration of Three Criteria

The expected net present value criterion and its variant, expected annual net present value, the cost-benefit ratio, and the expected internal rate of return will often provide the same results in terms of the proper ranking of alternative investments. However, the expected internal rate of return rule is not always conceptually equivalent to the total net expected present value and annual net present benefits rules. These three rules are conceptually equivalent only under some fairly severe assumptions.

These assumptions are:

> ... if and only if (a) capital markets are perfectly competitive; (b) all available projects are completely divisible; (c) there is no interdependency among projects; and, (d) all net returns can be reinvested at their own internal rates of return up to the terminal date of the longest-lived project.[5]

The appropriateness of these three criteria is analyzed below in terms of their possible deviations from these conditions.

FORMAL STATEMENT OF THE CRITERIA

The net expected present value criterion can be stated as follows.[6]

Given the assumptions above and given the appropriate interest rate by which to discount, one should adopt any project for which the present value of the discounted stream of net benefits is greater than zero. Or, if more than one project has net discounted benefits greater than zero at the given rate of interest, adopt that project with the highest present value of net benefits. If funds still exist to invest, adopt the project with the next highest present value, and so on, until funds are exhausted or projects with positive or zero net present values are exhausted.

Computationally, an equation for achieving this measure is as follows:

    [5] See Mark Blaug, "An Economic Interpretation of the Private Demand for Education," *Economica*, May 1966, p. 168.
    [6] Most of the following formulas are based on Hirshleifer, *et al., op. cit.*

$$V_0 = \frac{s_0}{(1+i)^0} + \frac{s_1}{(1+i)^1} + \frac{s_2}{(1+i)^2} + \ldots + \frac{s_t}{(1+i)^t} \qquad (2)$$

Where:

V_0 is total net present value, i is the rate of interest used to discount; t is the time period; s_t is the sum of benefits, b_t, less costs, c_t.

This formula accounts for the fact that costs may occur in other than the very beginning of the income stream. If conditions affecting the value of the interest rate are expected to change over the time span of the income stream, different values for the interest rate can be inserted at such points.

Using the illustrative data for project A above and given the following assumptions: $i = 6$ percent, $t = 20$; $b_t = \$50$; $c_t = \$200$; and the cost outlay occurs at the very inception of the investment period—the present value of benefits for project A is:

$$V_0 = \frac{\$0 - \$200}{(1+.06)^0} + \frac{\$50 - 0}{(1+.06)^1} + \frac{\$50 - 0}{(1+.06)^2} + \ldots + \frac{\$50 - 0}{(1+.06)^{20}} \qquad (2a)$$

$$V_0 = \frac{-\$200}{1} + \frac{\$50}{1.060} + \frac{\$50}{1.124} + \ldots + \frac{\$50}{3.207} \qquad (2b)$$

$$V_0 = -\$200 + \$47.17 + \$44.48 + \ldots + \$15.59 = \$374 \qquad (2c)$$

And, V_0 for project B is $1,092, where the assumptions are the same as above except that $b_t = \$200$ and $c_t = \$1,200$.

Therefore, if 6 percent is the proper social opportunity cost rate of investment funds, then in pure economic efficiency terms, assuming *monetary* benefits are a proper index of *social* benefits, project B ($1,092) should be preferred over project A ($374).

If the benefit stream is constant from its inception and continues to infinity, the total present value of benefits can simply be denoted as:

$$V_0 = \frac{s}{i} \qquad (3)$$

where:

i is the chosen rate of interest used to discount and s is the level of net annual benefit. Here, benefits must begin at time 1 and all costs, C_0, must be incurred at time zero, the immediate inception of the project. Then, $V_0 - C_0$ must be zero or greater in order to invest in the given project. Thus, the net present value of benefits for project A is $833 - $200, or $633, while for project B it is $3,333 - $1,200, or $2,133. The use of higher interest rates in discounting will substantially reduce the disparity between the results of equation (2) and those of equation (3). Thus, at just a 10 percent rate of discount V_0 becomes $500 for project A and $2,000 for project B, with $V_0 - C_0$ for projects A and B being $300 and $800, respectively. Clearly, the rate of interest by which to discount becomes crucial in cost-benefit analysis since the higher the rate the more severely are the more distant benefits or costs discounted relative to more current benefits or costs.

If the net benefit stream is constant but finite, beginning at time 1 and ending at time t, the discounting formula is:

$$V_0 = s \frac{(1+i)^t - 1}{i(1+i)^t} \qquad (4)$$

where the symbols are interpreted the same as in equation (2) above. Thus, for project A,

$$V_0 = 50 \frac{(1+.06)^{20} - 1}{.06(1+.06)^{20}} \qquad (4a)$$

$$V_0 = 50 \frac{3,207 - 1}{.06(3.207)} \qquad (4b)$$

$$V_0 = \frac{2.207}{.1924} = 574 \qquad (4c)$$

and, net benefits are $574 - $200, or $374.

EXPECTED ANNUAL NET PRESENT BENEFIT

This rule yields investment decision results identical to the expected net present value criterion. The rule is

... based upon the principle of finding the level net stream that corresponds to the actual stream of costs and benefits associated with the project.[7]

The formula is as follows:

$$s = \frac{V_0 i (1+i)^t}{(1+i)^t - 1} \qquad (5)$$

where

$$V_0 = s \frac{(1+i)^t - 1}{i(1+i)^t}$$

and the rest of the symbols are interpreted as in equation (2) above.

In terms of investment decision-making this rule states that, at the chosen rate of interest, one should

... select all projects where the constant annuity with the same present value as benefits exceeds the constant annuity (of the same duration) with the same present value as costs.[8]

[7] *Ibid.*, p. 155.
[8] Prest and Turvey, *op. cit.*, p. 703.

For both this rule and the expected net present benefits rule, costs, c, and benefits, b, can be estimated separately, simply by substituting either of these two values in equations (2), (4) and (5) where s occurs. Also, V_0 in equations (4) and (5) becomes C_0 or B_0, respectively. Next, the discounted total costs or cost annuity, C_0 or c, respectively, is subtracted from the discounted total benefits or benefit annuity, B_0 or b, respectively. Then, for an investment to occur, the difference, $B_0 - C_0$ or $b - c$, must be zero or greater. One useful aspect of the expected annual net present benefit rule is that, if only costs (or benefits) are known, annual discounted costs (or benefits) can be estimated. A judgment can then be made as to the likelihood that expected annual net present benefits (or costs) will be as great or greater than their cost (benefit) counterparts.

Using the hypothetical data for project A one has:

$$c = \frac{C_0 i (1+i)^t}{(1+i)^t - 1} \tag{5a}$$

$$c = \frac{\$200(.06)(1.06)^{20}}{(1.06)^{20} - 1} = \$17.42; \text{ and,} \tag{5b}$$

$$b = \frac{B_0 i (1+i)^t}{(1+i)^t - 1} \tag{5c}$$

$$b = \frac{\$574(.06)(1.06)^{20}}{(1.06)^{20} - 1} = \$50.00 \tag{5d}$$

The respective figures for project B are $c = \$104.52$ and $b = \$199.63$. Thus, in each case, b is greater than c at the chosen interest rate and, in pure economic efficiency terms, assuming monetary benefits are an appropriate index of social benefits, it pays to invest in either project, but project B is more desirable than project A.

THE BENEFIT-COST RATIO

The benefit-cost ratio tells the decision-maker to invest in those projects for which the ratio of the present value of benefits to the present value of costs is greater than unity. The equation for this rule is as follows:[9]

$$\frac{\dfrac{b_0}{(1+i)^0} + \dfrac{b_1}{(1+i)^1} + \dfrac{b_2}{(1+i)^2} + \ldots + \dfrac{b_t}{(1+i)^t}}{\dfrac{c_0}{(1+i)^0} + \dfrac{c_1}{(1+i)^1} + \dfrac{c_2}{(1+i)^2} + \ldots + \dfrac{c_t}{(1+i)^t}} > 1 \tag{6}$$

The symbols are interpreted in the same manner as in equation (1) above.

Applying equation (6), the data for project A above give the following results:

[9] *Ibid.*, p. 703.

$$\frac{\dfrac{\$0}{(1+.06)^0}+\dfrac{\$50}{(1+.06)^1}+\dfrac{\$50}{(1+.06)^2}+\cdots+\dfrac{\$50}{(1+.06)^{20}}}{\dfrac{\$200}{(1+.06)^0}+\dfrac{0}{(1+.06)^1}+\dfrac{0}{(1+.06)^2}+\cdots+\dfrac{0}{(1+.06)^{20}}} \qquad (6a)$$

$$=\frac{\$574}{\$200}=2.87$$

The ratio for project B is \$2,292/\$1,200 or 1.91. By this criterion, project A is preferred over project B as long as the two projects are not mutually exclusive.

THE RATIO OF DIFFERENCE IN MARGINAL BENEFITS AMONG PROGRAMS TO DIFFERENCE IN MARGINAL COSTS AMONG PROGRAMS

A variation on the benefit-cost ratio is the ratio of the difference in marginal benefits to the difference in marginal costs between two alternative projects. Equation (7) expresses this ratio algebraically as follows:

$$\frac{\dfrac{b_{X_0}-b_{Y_0}}{(1+i)^0}+\dfrac{b_{X_1}-b_{Y_1}}{(1+i)^1}+\dfrac{b_{X_2}-b_{Y_2}}{(1+i)^2}+\cdots+\dfrac{b_{X_t}-b_{Y_t}}{(1+i)^t}}{\dfrac{c_{X_0}-c_{Y_0}}{(1+i)^0}+\dfrac{c_{X_1}-c_{Y_1}}{(1+i)^1}+\dfrac{c_{X_2}-c_{Y_2}}{(1+i)^2}+\cdots+\dfrac{c_{X_t}-c_{Y_t}}{(1+i)^t}}>1 \qquad (7)$$

where, as above, b and c refer to marginal benefits and costs, i is the rate of interest used in discounting, t is the number of time periods, and the subscripts X and Y refer to projects X and Y, respectively.

Briefly stated, this rule says that as long as the ratio of net discounted benefit differences to net discounted cost differences is greater than one, then additional public funds should be invested in project X in preference to project Y.[10]

[10] To be more specific, the following cases indicate the direction in which an extra dollar of public funds for educational expenditures should be spent. Equation (7) can be expressed as follows:

$$\frac{B_X-B_Y}{C_X-C_Y}>1$$

where capital B and C represent the summation of the discounted b's and c's. The condition of equation (7) holds true *if and only if*:

1. $B_X>B_Y$ and $C_X>C_Y$, then additional dollars of public funds should be devoted to project X; or
2. $B_X<B_Y$ and $C_X<C_Y$, then additional dollars of public funds should be devoted to project Y.

The more generalized version for equation (7) is

$$B_X-B_Y>C_X-C_Y$$

Under this generalized version, not only cases 1 and 2 can be applied, but also the following cases can hold:

3. if $B_X>B_Y$ and $C_X<C_Y$, then additional dollars of public funds should be devoted to project X; or
4. if $B_X<B_Y$ and $C_X>C_Y$, then additional dollars of public funds should be devoted to project Y.

An additional problem with this variation in the benefit-cost ratio criterion should be noted. Even though it is rational to invest extra public funds in project X as long as the ratio expressed by equation (7) is greater than 1, this does not necessarily imply that the marginal internal rate of return to project X is equal to or greater than the social opportunity cost rate of capital. Indeed, the marginal internal rate of return to project X could be less than the social opportunity cost rate of capital. Project X may even be suffering net losses. Even so, project Y will be suffering even greater losses, so that a shift of expenditure from project Y to project X (or, the expenditure of an additional dollar on project X instead of project Y), will still result in maximizing net benefits, in this case, by minimizing losses.

THE EXPECTED INTERNAL RATE OF RETURN

The result of calculating a rate of return is a simple percentage which can be compared against that interest rate which represents an acceptable rate of social or private investment return. Briefly defined, the internal rate of return is that interest rate which makes the discounted value of costs equal to the discounted value of benefits. One question for this measure is as follows:

$$E(r) = \sum_{t=0}^{n} (b_t - c_t)(1+r)^t = 0 \tag{8}$$

where: r is the expected internal rate of return; b is the benefit per time period; c is the cost per time period; and t is a subscript denoting the time periods.

In practice, equation (8) is relatively difficult to use and depends for its solution on a technique of successive approximation. However, the use of an electronic computer makes the solution of such a polynomial equation relatively straightforward at least in terms of the physical effort required.

A variant of this equation is the following:[11]

$$c \cdot \sum_{t=0}^{n} \frac{1}{(1+r)^t} = b \cdot \sum_{t=0}^{n} \frac{1}{(1+r)^t} \tag{9}$$

where: r is the expected internal rate of return; c is the average cost per time period and assumed constant for all time periods; b is the average benefit per time period and assumed constant for all succeeding time periods; and t denotes the number of time periods. This equation also depends for its solution on a technique of successive approximation.

However, if costs are assumed constant during the training period and if benefits are assumed constant and extend to infinity, equation (9) reduces to equation (10) below and the rate of return can easily be obtained as follows:[12]

$$r = (1 + b/c)^{1/t} - 1 \tag{10}$$

---

[11] Jacob Mincer, "On-the-Job Training: Costs, Returns, and Implications," *Journal of Political Economy, Supplement,* October 1962, p. 64.

[12] *Ibid.,* p. 64.

where r is the expected internal rate of return, t is the number of time periods of education in whatever units chosen, (years, months, etc.) and b and c are the marginal benefit and marginal cost per unit of time (years, months, etc.) and assumed constant. The assumption of an infinite discounting stream creates an error which tends to become negligible as the actual benefit stream becomes longer.

Using the above hypothetical data, but changing our assumptions so that all investment outlays occur at the end of time period one, yields the following result:

For project A,

$$r=[1+(\$50/\$200)]^{1}-1 \qquad (10a)$$
$$=(1+.25)-1$$
$$=.25$$

Multiplying .25 by 100 yields the rate of return of 25 percent. For project B the rate of return is 16.7 percent.

An even simpler equation for estimating the rate of return can be used if one assumes that both benefits and costs are constant, that costs occur only in the *initial* t time periods, and that the level benefit stream extends to infinity. The equation,

$$r=b/C \qquad (11)$$

then applies, where r is the expected internal rate of return, b is the constant benefit per unit of time accruing to the investment and C is total costs over t time periods.[13] Note that this simplified formulation is the reciprocal of the pay-back period discussed previously. For the hypothetical data above, the results of equation (10) and (11) happen to be the same. This would not be the case, though, if cost outlays occurred for more than one time period.

In terms of providing advice to the investment decision-maker, if the social opportunity cost rate of investment funds were as low as 16.7 percent, both programs would be worthwhile. If the social opportunity cost rate of investment funds were as high as 25 percent, only project A would pay. And, if the social opportunity cost rate of investment funds were just 6 percent, both would pay, as the examples above on total and annual net discounted benefits show. Again, this analysis assumes that monetary benefits are a valid index of social benefits. If all costs have been accounted for, but social benefits are higher than monetary benefits, then the monetary rates of return would understate the social rates of return.

Finally, for equations (6), (8), (9), (10), and (11), if either costs or benefits are equal to zero, the criterion breaks down.[14] For zero costs, the

---

[13] See Becker, *op. cit.*, p. 107.
[14] The qualifications for equation (7) are discussed in footnote 10.

situation is mathematically undefined. Zero costs imply an infinite benefit-cost ratio or infinite internal rate of return. If benefits are negative (there are losses) and costs are positive, equations (6), (8), (9), and (10), the benefit-cost ratio and the internal rate of return, give correct advice, a negative ratio or rate of return, as the case may be. But equation (8) and (9) can yield imaginary numbers. Mathematical problems also exist for equations (6), (8), (9), (10), and (11) where benefits are positive and costs are negative, that is, where there are subsidies. But, the subsidy case should not be considered as an investment decision-making situation; what one is essentially dealing with is a gift. When benefits and costs are negative, mathematical problems also exist, but one is still in a gift and not an investment situation.

A Critique of the Three Criteria

Much controversy exists over what constitutes the proper investment criterion. The discussion in the literature centers around a critique of the present value and the internal rate of return criteria. The benefit-cost ratio is not widely considered. This latter fact is especially significant in light of federal government practice to employ the benefit-cost ratio as an investment criterion.[15]

Many writers argue that the present value rule is most correct since it automatically assures that the present value of benefits is at a maximum. However, to repeat, both the present value and the internal rate of return criterion will result in the proper and identical investment decision given that: capital markets are perfectly competitive; investment alternatives are not interdependent; all relevant investment choices are completely divisible so that marginal adjustments can be made; and all net returns are reinvested at the original rate of return or higher up to the end of the project with the longest benefit stream. In this context both are correct and neither is to be preferred over the other.[16] However, it is unlikely that these conditions will ever be met simultaneously. The real world imposes constraints such that each of these rules can, at times, give advice which, if followed, will result in the investor not maximizing the present value of net benefits. The following sections consider these constraints in turn. A subsequent section indicates the problems which exist with the benefit-cost ratio.

[15] See, for instance, the discussions in the following: U.S. Congress, Joint Economic Committee, Subcommittee on Economy in Government, "Interest Rate Guidelines for Federal Decision-making," *Hearings*, 90th Congress, 2nd Session, January 29, 1968 (Washington: U.S. Government Printing Office, 1968).

[16] It is important to note again that, as Bailey and Hirshleifer have demonstrated, there are theoretical situations where both rules can give incorrect results.

Where two projects are mutually exclusive, the use of the rate of return criterion breaks down. It is possible under this condition of interdependency to invest in an activity which has a higher internal rate of return but lower present value than an alternative project. This criticism is quite relevant from the view of an individual contemplating an investment in himself. When an individual makes a decision which commits him to some irrevocable course of action for a specified period of time, he eliminates all other actions he may have taken at that point and for the period which is subsequently committed. If he decides to take training as a carpenter, he usually cannot simultaneously decide to take training as a psychiatrist. In short, one can think of the human as a site or locus upon which, in general, only one type of training can occur at a given point in time. Thus, educational or occupational investments in human beings have the general characteristic of being mutually exclusive.

This criticism of the internal rate of return is just as binding from the social standpoint but the relative magnitude of the consequences stemming from it are probably not as serious. For example, if the construction of a comprehensive high school on one end of town proves to be an economic mistake, one can always construct an area vocational-technical school on a different site in another part of town. Or, an incorrect investment in an individual A does not preclude a correct investment decision to be made with respect to an individual B, since, while one individual is not divisible, a group of individuals is.

SUCCESSIVE COST OUTLAYS

More than one cost outlay occurring over time will result in more than one rate of return being estimated for the same benefit-cost stream. The same number of rates can exist as there are inflection points where the cost stream switches to a benefit stream and vice-versa. No one of these rates is conceptually correct.

From the private standpoint the occurrence of multiple cost outlays is a theoretical possibility due to the risk of unemployment. The individual can perceive at least part of the expenditure necessary to maintain him during periods of long-term cyclical unemployment as costs incurred to maintain his productive capacity in a given skill. . . .

Finally, from both society's and the private viewpoint, if the person had to reinvest in himself due to the fact that technological change had destroyed the economic relevance of his previous skill, this new investment cost and the benefits flowing from it should be treated as an entirely new cost-benefit sequence.

Investment in vocational education over time will likely change the distribution of income and hence, other things equal, will also change the social opportunity cost of investment funds which depends, in part, on the distribution of income. In this case, a uniquely calculated rate of return becomes conceptually irrelevant since it does not reflect the changing social opportunity cost rate of investment funds.

Constraints that Invalidate the Present Value Criterion

MULTIPLE INTEREST RATES

An individual may invest in himself by using personal savings, borrowed funds, or by reducing current consumption. A different private interest rate may be relevant to each of these sources of funds. Assuming the individual did not use some weighted rate of interest to represent these two interest rates and the rate of time preference he attaches to foregone consumption, but instead chose to discount the costs and benefits of different alternatives by each rate, the ranking of alternatives at one rate may differ from the ranking of alternatives at the others. It is then unclear as to which relative ranking is the correct one.

In addition, in many practical situations when a single unambiguous rate cannot be chosen, advice is often given that more than one rate of interest should be used in order to provide a range of estimates of discounted costs and benefits. This again may result in a switch in the differential rankings of alternatives vis-à-vis the different rates. The result will be that choice between investment alternatives will become indeterminate if one attempts to employ both rankings.

A suggested solution to this switching problem involves the selection of that interest rate which makes the net present values of the set of alternatives all equal.[17] This rate then serves as the cut-off point in selecting the appropriate ranking, and hence, the appropriate investment. . . .

BUDGET CONSTRAINT

The present value rule will sometimes prove to be invalid when a budget constraint or investment discontinuities face the decision-maker. If one follows the advice to invest first in that activity which has the highest present value, it may well be that some alternative combination of investments will prove possible, each of which requires a smaller investment outlay but which, when taken together, yield a summed present value greater than the single larger investment. For example, given a constraint of $1000 on

---

[17] This rate is known as Fisher's rate of return.

the amount that can be invested, project C, requiring a $900 outlay, may yield a present value of $1100 while the set of projects D and E requiring outlays of $400 and $600, respectively, yield present values of $600 and $800, respectively. Present value for a single project is highest for C and it would be chosen over either D or E if one were to follow the rule stated above. But due to the budget constraint and project discontinuity, choosing C precludes additional investment in D or E, each of which have higher internal rates of return than C. Thus, the proper strategy when budget constraints or discontinuities occur, then, as long as the alternatives are not mutually exclusive, is to exhaust the budget by choosing the *set* of alternatives with the highest internal rates of return. This will actually maximize present value for the *set* of investments. In this case, one should invest in D and E, to gain a total present value of $1400 as contrasted with only $1100 for C.

Such a constraint is a major problem from the standpoint of the individual seeking to invest in himself. As investors, students have limited access to investment sources. Also, students are relatively unproven in the labor market so that there is a great deal of risk and uncertainty concerning the benefit stream of an investment in them. Capital markets are relatively imperfect in the area of human resource investment due, in part, to the unwillingness of creditors to accept a person's own self as loan collateral as well as the quasi-illegality of indenturing oneself. The capital created by the investment in education is real but it is embodied in and cannot be separated from the human agent. It cannot be used as collateral in the same way that physical capital can. High risk and liquidity premiums would have to be charged in addition to the opportunity cost rate of capital if the capital market were to make funds generally available to investors in this area.[18]

Institutional constraints are such that these very high interest rates are not charged. Instead, lower rates are set and the pool of investment funds is rationed among those projects which qualify at the lower interest rates. As a result, investment funds are not generally available to finance one's self-investment at the secondary education level.

Personal loans *are* made strictly on a person's representation that his actual or expected income stream and, hence, his expected capital value, is of sufficient size and certainty of being realized that he can pay back the loan. Thus, in such cases the loan is made on the basis of accepting the person's expected capital value as collateral, but this practice occurs normally *after* and *not before* the person seeking the loan has created the capital value which is embodied in him. In line with this, most student loans made by banks are offered mainly as a public service and are made

[18] See Becker, *op. cit.*, p. 55.

on the basis of the parents' expected income stream and not on the basis of the great expectations of the student seeking the loan.

Hence, the individual is generally faced with investment budget constraints which do not allow him perfect choice among all possible investment alternatives. He may have access to sufficient funds to contemplate training as a carpenter but not as an electronics technician.

Investment budgets are also constrained from a governmental standpoint, though disagreement exists as to the exact nature and seriousness of this constraint. Legislative limits are set upon amounts to be spent by school districts and other governmental units, for limited and specified periods. Even though new funds are voted for new budget periods and the budget periods continue through time, a short-run constraint exists which can be repeated indefinitely.

Only in the broadest sense does a constraint exist for the economy as a whole for it is difficult to conceive of a given investment in this area of education which would be so large as to absorb a significant proportion of the gross national product.

Constraints that Invalidate the Benefit-Cost Ratio Criterion

The benefit-cost ratio has some of the operational shortcomings of both the expected net present value rule and the expected internal rate of return. Like the expected net present value rule, its use will cause problems if more than one interest rate is used to discount. That is, the choice of the most efficient investment alternative may switch. However, if budget constraints or discontinuities, or both, occur, then the benefit-cost ratio like the internal rate of return is preferred over the present value criterion. Given the interest rate used to discount, choice of those investments with the highest ratios will maximize net present benefits. But, if investments are mutually exclusive, the use of the benefit-cost ratio, as with the expected internal rate of return, may give an incorrect result unless the returns from the investment are reinvested at an interest rate at least as high as that yielded by the next best alternative and at least through that time period represented by the investment alternative having the longest time profile of costs and benefits.

The numerical examples in Table 1 display the difficulty involved in relying on the benefit-cost ratio as the "correct" criterion. The interest rate used to discount controls the ranking of alternatives. Neither the internal rate of return nor the benefit-cost ratio alone gives the explicit clue as to the correct answer. Y has a higher internal rate of return than X. X has a higher benefit-cost ratio than Y, given a 4 percent interest rate, but the B/C ratio is reversed for X and Y given the 6 percent interest rate. To resolve the conflict an inspection of the net present value is needed! If the market rate of interest is 6 percent, then Z is preferred since investment in four Z projects gives a present value of $7.84 compared to $2.89 for X and $2.88 for two Y projects. The ranking remains the same at 8 percent as at 6 percent, but the present values of X and Y are negative while Z is just at the decision margin.[19]

Table 1—Comparison of three investment criteria: internal rate of return, present value of net benefits, and benefit-cost ratio

					INTEREST RATE FOR DISCOUNTING					
	COST BENEFIT			Internal rate of return	4%		6%		8%	
Invest-ment	Time 0	Time 1	Time 2		B-C	B/C	B-C	B/C	B-C	B/C
X	$100	$53.00	$56.18	6%	$2.89	1.058	$0.00	1.000	−$2.67	0.972
Y	$ 50	$53.50	$00.00	7%	$1.44	1.029	$0.47	1.009	−$0.46	0.991
Z	$ 25	$00.00	$29.16	8%	$1.96	1.078	$0.95	1.038	$0.00	1.000

Assumptions: The investment budget is constrained at $100. Investments B and C can be duplicated in order to exhaust the budget.
Source: Hypothetical data.

The resolution to this switching problem under conditions of budget constraint is to discount at only one interest rate. Note that this single rate is not necessarily the social or private interest rate representing the opportunity cost of capital. The proper rate is the highest marginal rate of return on that set of investment projects which just exhausts the investment budget. Then, those projects in the chosen set which are discounted at this rate must have a present value of zero or greater. Any project with a present value of less than zero when discounted at this marginal rate should be excluded. In addition, the benefits from this investment set should be reinvested at that marginal rate of return, or a higher one. The method for finding the investment set with the highest marginal rate of return is to discount the array of investment alternatives at different interest rates until that set of investment alternatives is found which just exhausts the investment budget.[20] One then chooses the set with the highest rate. However, this technique can be cumbersome and impractical if there are a large number of alternatives and interdependency exists among them. With interdependency, an extremely large number of possible combinations of these alternatives can exist, all of which must be tested.

It is important to note that the budget could conceivably be so constrained that the number of investment projects would be insufficient to include those which would lower the marginal rate of return down to the

---

[19] Other numerical examples where the benefit-cost ratio is shown to be misleading are in McKean, *op. cit.*, pp. 107–113.

[20] These arguments are substantially drawn from McKean, *op. cit.*, Chapters 5 and 7, and Hirshleifer, *et al.*, *op. cit.*, Appendix to Chapter VII.

social or private opportunity cost rate of capital. If the social rate is used in a situation where it is less than the marginal internal rate, then projects will likely be adopted which will not result in maximizing net present value.

However, Hirshleifer points out that even this rule, while a useful and plausible one under conditions of capital rationing or budget constraint, is not strictly correct. First of all, the marginal project may not have an unambiguous rate of return. Second, even if there is an unambiguous internal rate of return, one may choose the wrong course of action, unless consideration is made of the earning value of resources yielded by each project as well as the market rate of interest by which intertemporal shift of benefits of a given benefit stream can be undertaken.[21]

In summary, given the qualifications above, when there is capital rationing (and this is probably a common situation for an individual contemplating investment in himself), the benefit-cost ratio is the proper criterion for investment decision-making, since by choosing the set of investments with the highest ratios he will thereby maximize net present value. When there is no budget constraint, and for society (not a governmental unit) this is usually the case, adopting those projects with the maximum net present value is the proper course of action. The choice of rules for a community or governmental unit should depend on whether or not there is a budget constraint. . . .

Summary

In appraising the operational effectiveness of cost-benefit analysis, the following list of factors should be kept in mind.

1. Discounting the stream of benefits and costs must be performed.
2. The relevant value for the social opportunity cost rate of investment funds probably lies in a range of from 6 to 10 percent.
3. The use of an artificially low rate of interest when discounting may not increase the total amount of investment. It may just result in the displacement of some high return investments by low return investments, with a resulting loss in present and future economic welfare.
4. Although the fundamental goal is always to maximize the net present value of benefits, there is no one correct investment criterion for all investment situations. This is true both in a theoretical and an operational sense. The constraints involving a given investment situation should be examined and the rule most relevant to that situation applied.

[21] Hirshleifer, et al., op. cit., p. 171. The numerical example given clarifies these two points. Actually, the examples given by McKean take account of these two factors also, but he does not stress them to the degree they are stressed in Hirshleifer. See McKean, op. cit., pp. 82–83.

Part
Three
CONTINUED

Analytical problems
and Dissenting Views

The benefit-cost articles presented through the first half of Part Three reveal that the task of measurement is not easy. For example, benefits from additional investment in education may accrue directly to the individual in the form of higher earnings and indirectly to his children who have a higher probability of obtaining additional education. Furthermore, some benefits are external, or "spillover" to other individuals in society. The prevention of crime or eradication of disease may possess significant spillover content (external benefits) for society just as does the collection of garbage. Benefit-cost variables also may be noneconomic in character and approximated in money terms with grave difficulty, if at all. Difficulties are also encountered in determining the extent to which natural ability, motivation and socio-economic status are intercorrelated with higher levels of education. Still another problem derives from the fact that investment in health and education has a consumption component of unknown magnitude.

The noneconomic, indirect, and social effects of both costs and returns to investments in human capital are discussed by the authors of the following selections who present an impressive critique of the human capital concept. Teh-wei Hu, Jacob J. Kaufman, Maw Lin Lee, and Ernst W. Stromsdorfer **13** explain the methodological problems empirical studies encounter. The selections written by Jack Wiseman **14** and Thomas Balogh and Paul P. Streeten **15** question the desirability of measuring investment returns to human capital investment, and Neil W. Chamberlain **16** questions the validity of the human capital concept.

14

Cost-Benefit Analysis in Education

Cost-benefit analysis is no panacea to those concerned with the economics of manpower and education. Indeed, some authorities, including the author of this selection, are uncertain as to the usefulness of this technique for decision making in the public sector. The "extra-economic" characteristics of human capital formation typically are ignored in the evaluation of human capital investments. This constitutes a serious weakness according to

JACK WISEMAN

Professor Jack Wiseman, currently Director of Social and Economic Research at the University of York (England). In addition to considering problems related to assessing individual returns to education and social benefits and costs, Wiseman suggests that market oriented studies of human investment may be of real value to students of the economics of education.

A conference of this kind is properly concerned with the improvement of decisions about public policy. I have consequently taken as my problem the relation between studies of "investment" in education and the rationale of policy decisions. This is not to suggest that I would wish such studies to be judged, or to be judged solely, by their ability to illuminate policy questions: I agree with Professor Schultz[1] that research cannot expect to begin by "asking the right questions," since the discovery of those questions may itself be an end-consequence of the research. At the same time, many of those

Reprinted from Jack Wiseman, "Cost-Benefit Analysis in Education," *Southern Economic Journal* 32 (July 1965), pp. 1–14, with the permission of the author and publisher.

[1] Theodore W. Schultz, *The Economic Value of an Education* (New York: Colombia University Press, 1963).

concerned with "human resource" studies do believe their work to be relevant to public policy: Professor Schultz says also that such studies are "... laying the foundations for an economic growth policy which assigns a major role to schooling. . . ."

In these circumstances, it might be thought not unreasonable to expect that "human investment" studies would reduce the importance of policy disagreements about education, or at the least permit the more precise specification of the nature of such disagreements and hence facilitate their resolution. But superficial observation suggests that the growth of analytical understanding and empirical information has been accompanied by continuing (increasing?) disagreement among economists, and between economists and others, about such fundamental matters of education policy as the "right" size and character of public finance of education provision.

In asking why this should be so, and suggesting how the areas of disagreement might be reduced, I shall try from time to time to suggest how my argument relates to the special problems of the South. But I pretend to no expertise in this domestic problem, and in any case, my concern is rather with the identification of some of the questions to which we need answers than with the provision of answers (policy prescriptions) that I could believe to be universally and unambiguously acceptable. At least some of the issues to be considered incorporate choices between, and/or the weighting of, policy ends: and I do not pretend that I know how to provide technical solutions to problems of this kind.

It is also not my intention simply to be critical of existing "human resource" studies. In my view, recent developments and interest in the study of human resources, associated particularly with the pioneering studies of Professor Schultz and now the concern of an increasing number of specialists, have already resulted in tremendous analytical illumination and in much ingenious and fruitful empirical research. Indeed, I would regard the evolving integration of "human resource" studies with the existing corpus of economic analysis as one of the major breakthroughs of the last few decades. Further, few of the individual problems to which I shall draw attention are unfamiliar. But they are not commonly brought together in a policy context, and I believe that the attempt to do so may be illuminating both about the nature and interpretation of cost-benefit studies themselves and about the general difficulties of policy decisions concerned with the use and development of human resources.

Some Problems of Benefit-Cost Studies

This section is not concerned with any particular study, but assumes a general acquaintance with the relevant literature and a general understanding of the procedures used in benefit-cost studies of human resource problems. Nor is it intended as an exhaustive critique: the sole purpose is to direct attention to some of my own problems and confusions concerning the use of benefit-cost studies to guide public policy.[2]

ECONOMIC AND OTHER "VALUES"

It is widely recognized that education serves ends (variously designated as "cultural," "spiritual," etc.) not normally thought of as economic. This is not generally regarded as destructive of the utility of economic studies (and, presumably, their policy relevance): it is in the nature of theory to abstract from some attributes of a problem, and to do so is not inconsistent with these attributes being thought important. Equally, the fact that these attributes exist does not in a logical sense destroy the relevance of studies of the chosen problem. Thus, Balogh and Streeten, e.g., in a paper generally critical of "human investment" studies, argue that it is mistaken to object to the economist's "sordidly mercenary" approach because it involves a "perversion of values": at the least, we might learn something about what the pursuit of these "other values" is costing us.[3]

However, while I would agree that there is no *necessary* conflict between the study of the economic implications of education provision and any particular view of its other attributes, I would argue that the way we *in fact* study education as an investment perforce involves us in confusions between the two. Further, these confusions are of particular importance in a policy context. The point is of sufficient importance to merit elucidation in another form. Essentially the (implicit or explicit) justification for distinguishing the economic implications of education from its other attributes is on grounds of division of labor: we can leave the consideration of other aspects to those qualified to deal with them, and these independent functions can then be "integrated" or "co-ordinated" at the policy level into a common "education policy" framework. After all, this is the rationale of division of labor elsewhere: the efficiency of the specialization of functions depends upon the possibility of co-ordinating the results. But while this may be what economists like to think they are doing, it is questionable whether it is what they are in fact doing. Rather, we study one aspect of a common process, admit the "indivisibility" of that process (i.e., that economics is not distinct from culture but an aspect of it), but shift on to others the responsibility of discovering how the piece that we have elected to study and quantify fits into the organic whole. Lee R. Martin provides us with a useful illustration (though there are numerous others): "The writer pleads guilty," he says,

---

[2] An exhaustive list of relevant studies, as well as a very valuable survey of the literature, is provided by T. W. Schultz (see note 2). I have also been fortunate enough to be able to read Gary S. Becker's study *Investment in Education*, now awaiting publication by N.B.E.R.

[3] T. Balogh and P. P. Streeten, "The Coefficient of Ignorance," *Bulletin of the Oxford University Institute of Economics and Statistics*, May 1963, p. 104.

"to having—however unintentionally—implied a technological elite and the superior utility of technical knowledge, but it is difficult to over-estimate the importance of humanistic or social values in an advanced civilization. Although the writer senses intuitively [*sic*] the overwhelming importance of these factors, he leaves their discussion to better qualified scholars."[4] These same superior creatures would presumably also be left to spell out the (logical and empirical) relationships between these "overwhelmingly important" factors and the economic magnitudes that the author believes economists should study. This attitude is not only too modest: it is also unreasonable, and in the event impossible of fulfillment.

Of course, the reason for the difficulty has not gone unrecognized: the same education which changes the economic attributes of an individual simultaneously changes his "extra-economic" characteristics. Also, that change is inseparable from the person undergoing it. A person who makes an "educational investment" in himself can sell the fruits of that investment, but cannot market the asset itself: in Mrs. Robinson's phrase, the present capital value of future personal earnings has a metaphysical but not an actual financial meaning.[5] Similarly, the "non-economic" consequences of education are in effect changes in the human personality. These also clearly inhere in the person educated, though of course they may *affect* others.

In fact, as the following sections argue, the consequence of these difficulties has been that studies of human investment have not been (and perhaps cannot be) free of implicit or explicit propositions about other values: it is for this reason that they have produced less policy accord than might have been expected.

We shall consider first the problems of assessing the returns from education to individuals, then turn to social benefits and costs: both throw up questions of the kind described.

THE RETURNS TO INDIVIDUALS FROM EDUCATION

Benefits. It is conceptually possible to discover the "gain" that an individual obtains from some specified type of education by comparing the changes in his income-stream that result from the education with the costs that he must incur in order to obtain it. Ideally, the economist's interest is in measuring "real" rather than monetary returns. On the benefit side, this means that "psychic" returns as well as monetary ones must be considered, or, to use an alternative terminology, that we treat education as a form of consumption as well as a form of investment for the individual.

---

[4] Lee R. Martin, "Research Needed on the Contribution of Human, Social and Community Capital to Economic Growth," *Journal of Farm Economics*, February 1963, p. 82, n. 10.

[5] Joan Robinson, *The Accumulation of Capital* (London: Macmillan, 1965), pp. 11–12 ·

No one has suggested any direct method of evaluating "psychic" returns (which accrue to other kinds of resource-use as well as "human investment" uses), and the indirect methods are not very satisfactory. A possible procedure is to use the relative growth of human and physical capital to make inferences about the "real returns" to education, and then to use the difference between this and the money returns to assess the relative "psychic returns" to education and to physical capital. But even long-run information about growth of capital of various types is capable of a wide variety of possible explanations (changes in risk attitudes, in actual rates of return to different kinds of capital, and so on) about which we have very little information as yet. Further, the results so far would seem in any case to be statistically inconclusive, in that the evidence could be compatible with either lower or higher psychic returns to education than to physical capital. Finally, the evidence throws no light on the "spread" of psychic returns between individuals: and it will shortly be appreciated that for our present purposes this is not a trivial omission.

While "psychic returns" associated with any kind of resource-use are difficult to evaluate, there are special problems in the case of education (and other "human investments") that complicate the question further. In the first place, there is a fundamental fashion in which the two types of psychic return differ in character. A man may obtain a "psychic" (consumption) return from "running his own business," or from owning land. In such cases, we can distinguish the source of the return, and identify the time-period over which it accrues (the period of control of the business or ownership of the land). In the case of education, it has already been pointed out that the education process is indivisible and also that the "asset" cannot be separated from the consumer of its services.

In the second place, "consumption" of education has at least two forms. It may consist in the enjoyment obtained from the "education process" during that period of becoming educated (i.e., using the facilities of an educational institution) which simultaneously improves the individual's expectations of future earnings, and it may consist in the "psychic returns," obtained from having been educated, but enjoyed during the rest of the individual's life. Most writers believe both types of return to be relevant, and it is frequently suggested that they can be distinguished by considering the first as a form of current consumption and the second as consumption of the services of a durable consumption good (the earlier education). However, the analogy is a dubious one: apart from the difficulty of distinguishing the capital from the return to it, the character and "value" of the long-run "psychic returns" to individuals from education are unusual, to say the least.

It is the essence of the education process that it changes attitudes, expectations and preference patterns: it takes Beatlemaniacs and turns them into Bach lovers. In the nature of things, the *ex ante* process of valuation of the "consumption" return to education by individuals is usually going to be different from the valuation that these individuals would make *ex post:* there are indeed arguments that it is a central purpose of the educational process to produce such a change. Be that as it may, there is clearly an awkward question to be answered. For our graduated student now gets psychic returns from having been educated to appreciate Bach. But he can no longer tolerate the Beatles. Should we not deduct the (notional) "loss" of consumption that this latter change implies? Or should we abandon the attempt to measure psychic returns as fruitless? Or should we treat only the *ex post* valuation (at what point?) as relevant, despite the fact that it has been created by the education itself?

It might appear that the position could be recovered by recourse to the old philosophical conundrum: How does a pig know whether it is better to be a pig than a philosopher? And how does a philosopher know? J. S. Mill would have answered this by arguing, essentially, that the philosopher was in a better position to choose than the pig, because he better understood the alternatives placed before him. Essentially similar "choice-widening" propositions have begun to appear in the literature of the new welfare economics. However, in my view they fit the character of education but poorly: the process is one of *changing* tastes rather than (or as well as) of widening the range of choices. An education cannot be kept like a row of (subjective) suits in a closet, so that a man can retain the (Beatle) suit he began with, add others to it in the process of education, but remain free to return to the original clothing whenever he so chooses.

One popular way to deal with the intractability to measurement of education "consumption" is to assert that the education of a person's tastes must have an unambiguously positive continuing value to him.[6] (The illiterate native is always "happier" for being introduced to the education system of an industrial society.) If we assign some positive value to consumption, then we can treat the other returns to education as "investment" returns. Apart from its arbitrariness, such a procedure leaves some important questions unanswered. Is the assertion that "consumption" returns are positive a logical proposition, or a personal value judgement? Is there no relation between the precise form of education, the methods by which it is provided and the "psychic" returns to it?[7]

[6] See e.g. Schultz, *op. cit.*, p. 51 n.

[7] The reader will perhaps recognize the close resemblance between the special case here being argued and the general approach to the relation between economic and other values that permeates the work of Frank H. Knight. I believe the work of Professor Knight to be sufficiently germane to merit quotation at length:

"To state the fundamental issue briefly at the outset, are the motives with which economics has to do—which is to say human motives in general—'wants,' 'desires' of a character which can adequately be treated as *facts* in the scientific sense, or are they 'value,' or 'oughts,' of an essentially different character not amenable to scientific description or logical manipulation? For if it is the intrinsic nature of a thing to grow and change, it cannot

A similar point has been made by Shaffer, who draws attention to the fact that some school attendance in the U.S.A. is compulsory, and hence outside the area of private decision-making.[8] Schultz dismissed this as irrelevant to problems of measurement: the "investment" rate of return to those educated, he says, is unaffected by the way they obtained access to (educational) resources, in the same way that the value of a physical investment is unaffected by its being publicly or privately financed.[9] But while this rejoinder is not without any substance, it is nevertheless seriously misleading. The problem of assessing the "consumption" value of publicly-provided goods not rationed by prices is a central one in public finance, and the present problem is in part an extension of this one. Further, whatever may be the position concerning "investment" return, it is clear that the "consumption" value of education must be related to the opportunity-cost

---

serve as a scientific datum. A science must have a 'static' subject-matter; it must talk about things which will 'stay put'; otherwise its statements will not remain true after they are made and there will be no point to making them. Economics has always treated desires or motives as facts, of a character susceptible to statement in propositions, and sufficiently stable during the period of the activity which they prompt to be treated as causes of that activity in a scientific sense. It has thus viewed life as a process of satisfying desires. If this is true then life is a matter of economics; only if it is untrue, or a very inadequate view of the truth, only if the 'creation of value' is distinctly more than the satisfaction of desire, is there room for ethics in a sense logically separable from economics." *The Ethics of Competition* (New York & London: Harper & Brothers, 1935), p. 21.

"The facts, as emphasized, are altogether against accepting any balance-sheet view of life; they point rather toward an evaluation of a far subtler sort than the addition and subtraction of homogeneous items, toward an ethics along the line of aesthetic criticism, whose canons are of another sort than scientific laws and are not quite intellectually satisfying. We cannot accept want-satisfaction as a final criterion of value because we do not in fact regard our wants as final; instead of resting in the view that there is no disputing about tastes, we dispute about them more than anything else; our most difficult problem in valuation is the evaluation of our wants themselves and our most troublesome want is the desire for wants of the 'right' kind." *Ibid.*, pp. 41–2.

"But man is also a problem-solving entity at the higher level of critical deliberation about ends, or free choice of ends on the basis of thinking, illustrated by the pursuit of truth. That is, he is a being who seeks, and in a real sense creates, values. The essential significance of this is the fact that man is interested in changing himself, even to changing the ultimate core of his being. This is the meaning of being active. It makes a categorical distinction between men and all other objects of knowledge. We cannot be sure that other objects are not conscious, or even that they are devoid of will; but if they have any conscious, will-attitude toward themselves it is limited, as far as we can tell, to the *perserverare in esse suo.* They do not strive to change their own nature or character—or, indeed to 'convert' fellow-members of their species; and in so far as scientific categories apply, they do not undergo change at all, in their ultimate nature. In contrast with natural objects— even with the higher animals—man is unique in that he is dissatisfied with himself; he is the discontented animal, the romantic, argumentative, aspiring animal. Consequently, his behaviour can only in part be described by scientific principles or laws." *Freedom and Reform* (New York & London: Harper & Brothers, 1947), pp. 236–7.

[8] Harry G. Shaffer, "Investment in Human Capital: Comment," *American Economic Review*, December 1961.

[9] Theodore W. Schultz, "Investment in Human Capital: Reply," *American Economic Review*, December 1961.

situation of the individuals being educated. That situation is determined by the available alternatives, and compulsory schooling clearly affects these, e.g., by ruling out (or increasing the costs of) such alternatives to school as going fishing. This argument in turn leads naturally to one that is perhaps more fundamental for present purposes: whose valuations are or should we be measuring? If there is compulsion to attend school, this would suggest that the community does not accept the valuations placed upon education by children and/or parents. It is clear that the valuation of their education by children will be different from its valuation by others and may well be negative for many of them at some ages. If they were free to choose, they would "consume" different amounts and types of education from those that their parents would choose, and these latter in turn would differ from the "valuations" of society as decided by the government.[10] Whose valuations are we to count?

There is a clear sense in which a decision whether and how to make education compulsory is a decision about whose valuations are relevant to policy. When we measure the "returns" to education, that is, we measure the results of a given method or provision. Thus to assert that the method chosen (incorporating e.g. some type of compulsion) is irrelevant to the measured magnitudes is not only to assert that the same situation could have been produced by other means (e.g., without compulsion), but also that the "consumption" value of the education itself is unaffected by the division of rights and obligations for education between children, parents, and governments.[11] Insofar as this assertion is unacceptable, it follows that the difficulties of distinguishing "consumption" and "investment" returns to education are not simply technical, but are related also to existing policies and to some system of "social" values.

It should now be apparent that we are concerned with something more than a philosophical quibble. *The measured "returns" to educational spending are intimately connected with the nature of access to educational resources, and this in turn is intimately related to the value of education to individuals, families, and society. If we are to translate statistics into policy, we must be prepared to show what difference we think would be made to our data if educational policies were changed in character (as well as if existing policies were extended or contracted), and/or to specify those social values (such as the rights and obligations of families), that we believe to be ineluctable.*

Costs The interesting problems from our present point of view concern the "costs" of earnings foregone in obtaining education. Up to a point, the disagreement about whether or not such earnings are a "real" cost is a sham

---

[10] I.e., the community's "valuation" of the consumption of education by individuals. We are not at this point concerned with indirect ("social") returns.

[11] Would it be entirely unfair to suggest that such a view is most likely to appeal to the better educated, who have more than one reason to overvalue education—and to point out that it is this better-educated group that is primarily concerned in the policy debate?

fight, in that the "right" solution must depend upon the actual and postulated alternative conditions being considered. There are, however, two ways in which problems of policy become entangled with those of valuation: both can be treated briefly since the argument follows the same line as that of the previous section.

The first problem has already been indicated. The calculation of foregone earnings involves an answer to the question "What would have happened if the students being educated had been less or differently educated?" This must depend upon the alternative situation postulated, so that to answer the question precisely *implies* the elucidation of the alternative (education and other) policies that would pertain in the new situation. A common means of escape from this problem is to assume (implicitly or explicitly) that the adjustment would be "marginal," in the sense that methods of educational provisions are considered unchanged, and the numbers of persons "moving" in and out of education are treated as too small to affect relative earnings in different occupations, etc. This "solution," however, fits badly with the aggregative methods of computation used: it also makes the results of dubious value for policy if the changes being considered are global in character (such as the general introduction of equal educational opportunity for non-whites in the South), and/or affect *methods* as well as volume of education provision.

The second problem concerns the treatment of leisure. One way to "pay" for education may be to take less leisure than "would" have been taken had the individual taken a job not involving education. Thus the "opportunity-cost" of obtaining education is not just foregone earnings, but the sum of this and foregone leisure, somehow valued in money. Up to a point, this is a technical rather than a conceptual matter. The difficulties of including leisure in calculations of income or output are well-known, and those concerned with "human investment" estimates are scarcely to be blamed for not resolving this difficulty within their chosen field. But there are some additional considerations. One aspect of the "taste-changing" consequences of education is likely to be a change in leisure-preference, so that changes in the distribution of time between education, work for income, and leisure may reflect not just the "constant" opportunity-cost situation of the individual but also the influence of increasing "consumption" of education upon him.[12] Again, the character of the opportunity-cost of leisure is clearly related to the general nature of access to educational resources: a comparison of Britain (where the student once admitted to a university is generally provided with a living allowance) and the U.S.A. is a sufficient illustration of this.

[12] Machlup has drawn attention to the positive correlation between amount of education and hours of work in the U.S.A. See *The Production and Distribution of Knowledge in the United States* (Princeton, N.J.: Princeton University Press, 1962), p. 112.

In sum, computations of the "costs" of education to individuals unavoidably contain more or less implicit assumptions about *methods* as well as volume of education provision, and the implications of these need to be spelled out in detail if statistical information about rates of return is to be given a policy construction.

SOCIAL RETURNS FROM EDUCATION

The costs of, and benefits from, education provision to society differ from the returns to individuals. The nature of these "social" gains and losses has been usefully classified, e.g. by Weisbrod.[13] Also, while it is generally agreed that the social effects of education are difficult to quantify, it has been argued that upper and lower limits can be set—e.g., by using before-tax differentials to measure the lower limit, and the "residual factor" in growth studies such as Denison's to measure the upper one.[14] Existing studies suggest that the difference between the two is uncomfortably large. But what concerns us more in the present context is that the procedure ignores important qualitative problems of the education process.[15]

For present purposes, it is pointful to adopt a classification of social costs and benefits that is less detailed and differently specified than those just referred to. The most useful distinction for us is between those benefits and costs that can (conceptually at least) be attributed to economic units (individuals, households, etc.), in the sense that those units would be willing to pay rather than forego the relevant benefit, and those "social" gains from education that do not have this characteristic. The first group comprises all those benefits (costs) that the individual being educated does not capture, but which clearly accrue to others. There are two broad (polar) types of such benefits (costs). One is the type that accrues to specific and identifiable economic units (e.g., the income of A is raised as a result of the education of B). The other is generalized: it is the "public good" economic benefit that the community at large obtains from B having been educated, the benefit being "consumed" by the community at large and not directly imputable to individuals. While both these types of indirect consequence of education are difficult to assess, the problems are technical rather than philosophical: we are fairly clear about what we want to measure but at a loss as to how to do it. But failing agreed means of measurement, it must remain doubtful

---

[13] Burton A. Weisbrod, *External Benefits of Public Education* (Princeton University: Industrial Relations Section Research Reports, no. 105, 1964).

[14] Edward F. Denison, *The Sources of Economic Growth in the United States and the Alternatives Before Us* (New York: Committee for Economic Development, 1962).

[15] I have discussed these matters further in a joint paper with Alan T. Peacock, "Economic Growth and the Principles of Educational Finance in Developed Countries," Paper for O.E.C.D. Conference on the Finance of Education, September 1964. See also Harold W. Groves, *Education and Economic Growth* (Washington, D.C.: National Education Association, 1961).

what light recognition of the existence of social costs and benefits (externalities) of these types can throw upon the problems of education policy. Coase, Buchanan, and others[16] have demonstrated, conclusively in my view, that the existence of externalities provides no *a priori* reason to believe that resource-allocation will be affected in any particular way, or e.g. that such allocation would be improved (and economic growth encouraged?) were the gainers and losers in fact penalized and compensated. Further, it has to be recognized that the way benefits and costs are allocated between persons is determined by the institutional arrangements through which access to education is provided: we therefore cannot hope to relate these kinds of externalities to policy decisions save by their incorporation in a model (analytical framework) that embraces those institutional arrangements.

The other broad group of social "benefits" is even more indirect, but there is ample evidence that economists interested in "human investment" attach great importance to it. It consists in the "gains to society" that education confers by encouraging "cultural advance," improving the "character" of the community, the "quality" of leadership and of economic and social decisions, and so on. The essential matter here is that it is fundamentally open to question whether these are "values" at all in the economist's sense, and whether they are even conceptually measurable.[17] Thus, Musgrave for example argues for the reservation of education policy decisions to the educated, on grounds that they understand the "value" of education better than others.[18] If we accept this, our benefit-cost study presumably would include the "valuations" only of the "informed." But what should we put in as a measure of the "costs" (e.g., by restriction of choice) imposed on others? Another version emphasizes the social value of an informed society and electorate. But informed about what? All Russian schoolchildren learn about communism, and an interpretation of capitalism that stigmatizes it as evil. American children seem to learn the opposite. Which electorate is being the better "informed" through education? Who is competent to "value" these social "benefits"? These are problems that have defied political philosophers for generations. I am not so foolish as to criticize economists for not providing agreed answers to them. But neither am I happy to see them swept into a dust-bag labelled "other social benefits." Our statistical observations about the returns to education as an investment are built upon the actual answers that have been and are being given to questions like these: we should recognize this rather than try to deal with the difficulty by a taxonomic evasion.

[16] The recent literature is summarized in R. Turvey, "On Divergences between Social Cost and Private Cost," *Economica*, August 1963.

[17] Were the social "values" of pre-nineteenth century Germany enhanced by subsequent emphasis on education?

[18] R. A. Musgrave, *Theory of Public Finance* (New York: McGraw Hill, 1959), pp. 13–15.

The affinity of these arguments with the ones put forward in earlier sections is clear, as is the conclusion. Unless it can be clearly demonstrated that there are "social costs" that are "economic" (and quantifiable) in a sense distinguishable from "social values" of other kinds, the results of "human investment" studies must be difficult to translate into policy recommendations.

This is the more true since it must now be clear that there is no unique (or simple) relation between "social" and "private" returns to education. For example, a given volume of public expenditure for educational purposes must be expected to affect private "investment" and "returns" differentially according to the manner in which it is spent.[19]

Failing agreed solutions to such problems, our only recourse is to acknowledge that "social benefits" if broadly defined, are (at least in part) not an "economic" category at all in the ordinary sense, to recognize that there is a relation between the (notionally) measurable aspects of eduction as a social investment and the broader social context and institutional environment within which the education is provided, and to avoid allowing personal value judgements to masquerade as objective propositions or potentially quantifiable magnitudes.

Conclusions and Suggestions

It is one thing to parade one's own difficulties and confusions, quite another to make positive suggestions for future progress, and to relate the argument to a specific issue such as education policy in the South. But the discussion does suggest some kinds of future development that would be fruitful, and also throws some light upon our specific policy problem. The proposals divide conveniently into two groups, concerned respectively with the further development and policy-orientation of benefit-cost studies, and with the need for more comparative and other studies adopting alternative approaches to education provision.

THE BEARING OF BENEFIT–COST STUDIES ON POLICY MAKING

I have already made clear that I do not wish to suggest that the study of "human investment" through such things as education has or can have no value. On the contrary, I believe the conception to be fruitful of understanding: to take an example of direct interest to myself, I would expect these developments to produce radical changes in our approach to public finance. But it is consistent with this to be concerned about the bearing of actual studies upon public policy. I have argued that there are serious

[19] For examples, see Schultz, *The Economic Value of an Education*, and Balogh and Streeten, *op. cit.*

interpretative problems awaiting answers, and I would suggest that many economists are themselves ambivalent in their interpretation of the results of "human investment" studies.

The basic need might be put in the form that the parameters of benefit-cost studies in this field are insufficiently specified for their policy scope and relevance to be assessed, particularly by non-economists. But this formulation perhaps gives the problem too technical a flavor; the parameters in question incorporate e.g. distinctions between *ends* and *means* of a particularly difficult kind (is public provision of education an end in itself or a means to other ends, and if the latter, precisely what other ends?), and/or the attachment of "values" to attributes of education that lie outside any direct economic nexus. The economist cannot be expected to provide impeccable answers to such questions: but this does not justify his pushing the problems aside, and I have argued that in any case he is unable to do so. It is sensible to distinguish conceptually between value judgements, *a priori* propositions, and "scientific" (empirically tested) statements. But it is futile to pretend that benefit-cost studies can be so organized that they incorporate statements only of the last type, leaving the others to be made by whoever cares to make use of the economist's "scientific" information. If this neat distinction is not possible, then it will be both intellectually more satisfactory and practically more rewarding to accept the situation, and to devote time and thought to spelling out the nature of the "social," etc., characteristics of empirical studies that we believe to influence the observed magnitudes.

In fact, I do not think it can be denied that economists not infrequently have particular but implicit "social ends" in mind when interpreting "human investment" studies. For example, if it is "reasonable" to divide the costs of education into a "consumption" and an "investment" component, it would seem reasonable also to make the same distinction in deciding public policies concerned to meet these costs. But such an inference is not usually made or pursued: methods of finance are either ignored or policy concerning them is debated on quite different "social" grounds. Similar questions arise in the interpretation of statistics of the returns to education of whites and non-whites. Thus, Shaffer has pointed out that if education is treated as an investment for purposes of policy decision, then a higher rate of return to whites than to non-whites would seem to provide an argument for shifting (education) resources from the latter group to the former.[20] Criticism of this position has been concerned less to deny the validity of the inference *qua* inference than to argue about the statistics.[21] But let us suppose Shaffer's data to be accurate, for purposes of argument. How many economists would accept his policy inference? If we do not, and we wish to be listened to, then do we not have an obligation to set out *in*

[20] Shaffer, *op. cit.*
[21] Schultz, "Investment in Human Capital: A Reply," *loc. cit.*

advance the other policy objectives (such as non-discrimination, in some sense, in access to education) that we intend to treat as constraints?[22] Further refinement of statistics is no substitute for such explicit value judgments. Rather, it is likely to invite the unkind and generally unjustified comment that we start from our conclusions and pursue our statistics simply to the point at which "the correlation is good enough."

Of course, we can take the position that we are concerned only to present the evidence: it is for others to use it. But it has been the tenor of my argument that empirical studies are not easily to be separated from the general social and educational environment concerned: such a detached attitude will become plausible only if we can reach a point at which it is possible unambiguously to solve the valuation problems I have described, and to predict the economic consequences of changes in the *environment* as well as of changes in the *volume* of education provision. (In the case for example of the education of non-whites is it not clear that the economist's contribution to policy-making is concerned at least as much with the consequences of methods of provision as with those of the size of educational spending?) Given the difficulties to which I have drawn attention (and particularly the relation between the things we treat as "values" and existing social arrangements), I would expect such a day to be long in coming. In the meantime, it is pointful to try to improve the methods by which we assess returns to "investment in education," but I would suggest that it is also important, given the difficulties, to put some of our capital into other baskets. These complementary approaches are the concern of the next (and final) section.

THE EDUCATION "MARKET"

Interest in benefit-cost studies of education is clearly not unrelated to the way education is commonly provided, and particularly to the degree of absence or inhibition of market arrangements. While many of those interested in "human investment" would accept the relevance of (market) institutional arrangements to their studies, the argument is sometimes made that to examine such arrangements for economic policy purposes is not particularly pointful because "education is not a commodity like soap." If this means that there may be social values involved in decisions about the production and distribution of education that are not involved in the production and distribution of soap, it is of course true enough. But, equally, there is an

---

[22] Of course, this argument is not confined to education policy but is general in scope: economists are perhaps less ready to give it explicit recognition than they might be. For example, monopoly policy involves not only views about the relation between monopoly power, resource allocation, technical progress, and so on; but also an attitude to the preservation of freedom of choice as an end in itself. But it properly diminishes the influence of economists' arguments if they invoke their judgments of value on this last issue only after all other ("technical") arguments have been used.

important sense in which education *is* a commodity (economic good) like any other: those who object to its being so considered not uncommonly also seize on evidence of high (economic) rates of return to argue for increased educational spending. In my view (and I do not suggest that it would not be shared by many others), there is point in studying education provision in particular environments as a resource-allocation process. Indeed (as other writers have recognized), such studies are probably a necessary complement to benefit-cost analyses, and may prove to be the most fruitful approach that we have available to us to qualitative problems concerned with such matters for example as the relation between *methods* of education provision (which determine the character of the "market") and the value of education as an investment and as a stimulus to economic growth.

Essentially, "market-oriented" studies have to be concerned with the behavior of individuals, families, governments and other social groups as producers or consumers of education: they examine the behavior of the "knowledge industry" in which the educated are the consumers, and schools and other relevant enterprises the "producers." Studies adopting this general approach already exist, and can be described in four broad (but overlapping) groups.

(a) Studies concerned with actual methods of provision. These need to be descriptive, institutional and quantitative, and to distinguish relevant types of education rather than treat it as a global magnitude, as would an applied study of the steel industry. But they also need to be analytic, in the sense that they are concerned to relate the results to the structure of the market (and e.g. to assess the consequences of changes in that structure), to defined criteria of "efficiency," and to such extra-economic "values" (ends) as seem relevant. I would regard Machlup's study of U.S. arrangements as a pioneering effort in this field.

(b) Normative studies such as those of Friedman,[23] Peacock and Wiseman,[24] and Johnson[25] concerned to set out the relations between particular (market, etc.) systems of education provision and postulated economic and social goals. While such studies may have some limited empirical content, their contribution lies rather in the stimulus they provide for the clearer specification of ends and means in the making of education policy. The need for this clearer specification has already been argued to be a significant problem in the policy interpretation of benefit-cost studies.

[23] M. Friedman, "The Role of the Government in Education," in *Economics and the Public Interest*, Robert A. Solo, ed. (New Brunswick, N.J.: Rutgers University Press, 1955).

[24] Alan T. Peacock and J. Wiseman, *Education for Democrats* (London: Institute of Economic Affairs, 1964).

[25] Harry G. Johnson, "The Social Policy of an Opulent Society," in *Money, Trade and Economic Growth* (Cambridge, Mass.: Harvard University Press, 1962).

(c) Broader, but still "market-oriented" studies. I have in mind here studies related to a wider and different social context, which nevertheless throw incidental light upon the implications of particular methods of education provision. There are two studies of this kind that are of topical interest: Becker's study of the economics of discrimination,[26] and Hutt's[27] recently published study of the economics of the color bar in South Africa. This latter sets out to argue that the economic inferiority of the non-whites has been perpetuated and reinforced by institutional arrangements affecting (inhibiting) the operation of markets. While little is provided by way of quantification, Hutt nevertheless argues a convincing case, in my view, for the nature of the ends-means relations that have produced the results he describes. Certainly, he illuminates the character of public policy in the relevant area, and demands refutation. This is not to argue that more statistical data would have detracted from the study, but rather to reinforce the argument that such studies and quantitative research into "human investment" are powerfully complementary rather than substitutable activities.

We should also include in this section studies of voting systems after the pattern of Buchanan and Tullock.[28] If education has important "social" characteristics, then we must expect education decisions to be made at least partly through the political process. Consequently, we need to learn more not only about the individual (private) " consumption" and "investment" demand for education, but also about the relation (e.g.) between voting systems and the (public) demand for it.

(d) While (international and inter-regional) comparisons of returns to "human investment" are already under way, less interest has yet been evinced in the comparative study of institutional arrangements. This is an obvious necessity internationally, if we are not simply to produce "education tables" capable of as wide a variety of policy interpretations as are the present "growth tables." It is also relevant to the problems of the South: the spelling out of the precise nature of the different barriers to educational opportunity facing whites and non-whites, and attempts to assess (even if only qualitatively) the likely results of their removal, is an obvious and valuable way of supplementing more aggregate studies.

If further argument for such comparative-market-institutional studies is needed, it may be worth pondering upon the lack of success which has so far attended attempts to relate educational policies and historical growth rates. Might not greater understanding of differences in methods of education provision help to resolve this problem?

[26] Gary S. Becker, *The Economics of Discrimination* (Chicago, Ill.: University of Chicago Press, 1957).

[27] W. H. Hutt, *The Economics of the Colour Bar* (London: Institute of Economic Affairs, 1964).

[28] J. M. Buchanan and G. Tullock, *The Calculus of Consent* (Ann Arbor, Mich.: University of Michigan Press, 1962).

In conclusion, let me repeat that I do not believe these alternative approaches to contain a panacea. Rather, I am very uncertain as to how useful a policy tool benefit-cost studies *alone* can ever become, and suggest therefore (on the same grounds that others have argued for a liberal rather than a narrow technical education system because of uncertainty about future demands for labor) that we should not neglect these complementary approaches.

15

The Coefficient of Ignorance

The authors of this selection express concern that recent studies of educational investments in human capital in developed countries may mislead less developed nations. Thomas Balogh and Paul P. Streeten, of the University of Oxford and the University of Sussex respectively, suggest that investment analysis must be cognizant of factors frequently slighted in manpower planning and human capital research. Use of elegant econometric models to trans-

THOMAS BALOGH
PAUL P. STREETEN

form a statistical coefficient of ignorance to one of knowledge, allegedly required for economic development, may be misleading. Instead of devoting singular attention to studies of returns to education in the aggregate, much more attention needs to be devoted to the types of skills and the details of manpower planning.

Carefully directed social expenditure can have a much higher total yield (including all secondary effects) than types of expenditure which may result in some imposing visible structure, but whose effects on output in other sectors of the economy are zero or negative. Expenditures on the health, education and feeding of workers, on the provision of information, the creation of skills, etc., can raise output considerably, if properly directed and linked with improved equipment and appropriate institutional reforms. But these expenditures have for long been recalcitrant to theoretical treatment because

1. they are permissive, creating opportunities for output growth without being its sufficient condition.

Reprinted from T. Balogh and P. P. Streeten, "The Coefficient of Ignorance," *Bulletin of the Oxford University Institute of Economics and Statistics* 25 (May 1963), pp. 99–107, with the permission of the authors and publisher.

2. their direct output is often not easily measurable.
3. their effects are widely diffused.
4. their effects are spread over a long time.
5. there exists no determinate functional relationship between inputs and outputs, partly because success is contingent on complementary measures.
6. independent value, as well as instrumental value, is attached to both the initial expenditure and the resultant flow of satisfactions.
7. considerations of "deserved social rewards" enter into the determination of costs (e.g., teachers' salaries).
8. they cut across the traditional distinction between investment and consumption (on which many growth theories are built), according to which a sacrifice in current consumption can make future consumption greater than it would otherwise have been.
9. they are frequently correlated with other causes of higher productivity from which they are not easily separated.

Although many of these considerations apply, perhaps to a lesser extent, also to expenditure on physical capital, they are more glaring when social expenditure is considered and therefore social expenditures have been, until recently, unpopular with model builders. But the bias which emphasizes allegedly measurable, separable and determinate, and neglects other types of relationship is unwarranted. Actions about whose results it is possible to make only the vaguest guesses may be much more important than actions whose trivial effects are supposed to be precisely foreseeable. The challenge of estimating the returns on certain types of social expenditure has been accepted, but in the process of analyzing them the same mistakes have been made which have vitiated the use of more traditional concepts and relations, both in analysis and in their application to development planning.

In the last few years models have been constructed which attempt to isolate the contribution to growth made by expenditure on research, education, health, provision of information, etc. The starting point has usually been the addition of one term to the Cobb Douglas production function. $Y = aK^{\alpha}L^{\beta}H^{\gamma}$ where Y is national income, K capital, L labor and H a ragbag term for "human factor" including "improved knowledge," improved health and skills, better organization and management, economies of scale, external economies, changes in the composition of output, etc., the terms a, α, β and γ are constants, and $\alpha + \beta = 1$. Thus whatever is not caught in variations of K and L is attributed to H. "Improvement in knowledge" is a name for what has rightly been called "coefficient of our ignorance."[1]

[1] Mr. E. F. Denison, in his book *The Sources of Economic Growth* (Committee for Economic Development, 1962) simultaneously assumes a linear homogeneous production function and perfect competition in order to use average return per unit of factor as a measure of its marginal value product, and attributes a substantial proportion of "residual" growth to economies of scale.

Whatever the value of these models for advanced Western countries, and however welcome the attempt to get away from preoccupation with physical investment, their application to the problems of underdeveloped countries has bred confusion.[2]

The reasoning behind these new models can be briefly summarized in this way: the increased use of one factor of production, while others are kept constant and "knowledge" and "skills" are given, will yield diminishing marginal returns. If the growth of national product over several decades is such that the expansion of land, labor and capital does not account for the whole increase, the remainder must be due to "investment in human beings."

Another approach has attempted to estimate the returns in the form of higher earnings to the educated in relation to expenditure on their education in the U.S.A. Both these approaches and others have seemed to show that the returns to this type of "investment" are substantially above the returns to physical investment. The conclusion is then drawn that expenditure on education and on other ways of improving knowledge and skills should be carried out by planners in other countries, and particularly in underdeveloped countries.[3]

The pitfalls and fallacies in this admittedly over-simplified chain of reasoning are too numerous to be discussed here in detail. In the models of an aggregate production function a relationship, based on static economic

[2] For a brief discussion of and reference to these attempts, see John Vaizey, *The Economics of Education* (London 1962) chapter III. For criticism of the application of these models to underdeveloped countries, see T. Balogh, "Balance in Educational Planning: Some Fallacies in Current Thought," *The Times Educational Supplement*, June 8th, 1962, and "Misconceived Educational Programmes in Africa," *Universities Quarterly*, 1962.

[3] Thus Mr. Adiseshia, Unesco's Acting Director-General at a United Nations Association in Cambridge said: "So my thesis is that accelerated economic growth is, to a large degree, a function of adequate and commensurate development of human resources . . . the expenditure in formal education, in training, in mass media and in research and development leads to increased returns both to the individual and to the community. . . . The return from education over a 12-year period to the individual, expressed in terms of the relation between the amount invested by him and/or his parents and his higher earnings in the future, can be averaged at 16 per cent gross or, if allowance is made for income forgone while at school or college, the net average would be 11 per cent. Similarly, a two-year training course increases future earnings by around 6 per cent gross or 3 per cent net." *War on Want* (Pergamon Press, 1962).

Paul G. Hoffman, the head of the United Nations Special Fund, was reported in the *New York Times* of October 21st, 1962, to have said: "Possibly the greatest change in my own thinking is my widening recognition of the financial return from secondary education. Leadership must come from people with at least 12 years of schooling." John Vaizey, in a letter to *The Times*, March 14th, 1963, quoting the study of Edward F. Denison. "Of an average percentage rate of growth in G.N.P. from 1929 to 1957 of 2.93, education contributed 0.67—far more than any other factor. In 1957 the typical United States male adult worker over 25 years of age had two and a half times more education than his counterpart in 1910. The implications for Britain are obvious. . . ." The recent emphasis on expenditure on education has occasionally been accompanied by an equally unwarranted depreciation of the importance of physical capital.

models, is *assumed* between capital, labor and output; the historically *observed* relationship in *advanced* countries is seen to diverge widely from the *assumed* relationship, and the difference is *postulated* to be due solely to "improvements in knowledge." This conclusion is then bodily *transferred* to a totally different technical, historical, cultural, religious, institutional and political setting. Even if improved knowledge were a necessary condition for production growth, it might yield output only if incorporated in machines, exploited in specific ways, or combined with other policies, but not if occurring in isolation. Nor is education a homogeneous input. The teaching of Sanscrit has different results from the teaching of land cultivation. The teaching of book-keeping may increase the efficiency of manual labor, while the teaching of certain religions may reduce it. Isolation of "education" from other measures ignores the importance of coordinating policies, and aggregating all types of "education" obscures the type of education required for development. The concept therefore suffers both from illegitimate isolation and from misplaced aggregation.[4]

Similar objections must be raised to the models attempting to calculate the returns to education by discounting the excess earnings of the educated over those of the uneducated. The American data, which are mostly used, do not provide evidence as to whether expenditure on education is *cause* or *effect* of superior incomes; they do not show, even if we could assume it to be a condition of higher earnings, whether it is a *sufficient* or a *necessary* condition of growth,[5] and they do not separate *monopolistic* and *other forces* influencing differential earnings which are correlated with, but not caused by, differential education.

The calculations based on these data ignore both the indirect (financial and non-financial) returns accruing to others than the educated individual, and the direct non-financial returns to the individual. On the other hand, they pay a good deal of attention to "income forgone during study" which constitutes a large proportion of the costs of "investment." But neither the income forgone by other groups in society (housewives, voluntary workers, people such as some university teachers—accepting a lower income than they could get in other occupations), nor the non-financial benefits enjoyed during education are estimated. Since the time-flow over a lifetime of the earnings of the educated is quite different from that of the uneducated lifetime earnings now must be calculated as returns on education in the nineteen-twenties. To conclude from those returns anything about today's returns is like identifying a crystal radio set with Telstar.

Assuming that the ratio of returns to costs reflected something significant, it would be rash to attribute it to education. Expenditure on education is

---

[4] See Paul Streeten, "The Use and Abuse of Models in Development Planning," in K. Martin and J. Knapp (Ed.), *The Teaching of Development Economics* (Frank Cass, Ltd., 1967).

[5] Industrialisation in Britain preceded general compulsory education.

highly correlated to income and wealth of parents, to ability and motivation, to educational opportunities such as urban residence and proximity to educational centers, to access to well-paid jobs through family and other connections, any one of which could, either by itself or in conjunction with any of the others, account for the superior earnings.

But monopolistic elements enter not only in the differential advantages enjoyed by the children of wealthy parents, but also in reaping the rewards of an education. How much of the differential earnings of lawyers and doctors is due to "investment in men" and how much to restrictive practices concealed as requirements of qualifications? Much of the higher earnings is not a return on education but a monopoly rent on (1) the scarcity of parents who can afford to educate their children well and (2) the restrictions on members permitted into a profession in which existing members have a financial interest in maintaining scarcity.

If anybody attempted to use these models for calculating the returns to education in many underdeveloped countries, he would discover even higher rates of return. All this would show, however, is that pay scales in the civil service, in universities and in the professions are still governed by the traditional standards of a feudal or colonial aristocracy and by natural or artificial restrictions. It would provide no clue as to how public money ought to be distributed between "investment" in "physical capital" and in "people."

This approach, though logically weak, not only appeals to the snobbery and flatters the self-esteem of the educated, appearing to provide an economic justification of existing income differentials, but also buttresses vested interests. The specific measures that would be required to make expenditure on technical and agricultural education effective are painful, they violate vested interests and run into numerous inhibitions of the planners and obstacles put up by the planned. What a relief then to be served by econometricians with an elegant model, and how convenient to elevate a statistical residual to the engine of development, thus converting ignorance into "knowledge." Instead of having to specify *which type of education combined with what other measures* (such as investment in improved methods of cultivation, provision of the right equipment), creating skills and ability and willingness to work efficiently, and *complemented by what other* policies reforming attitudes and institutions (land reform, reform of the credit system, the civil service, price guarantees, transport), one item is singled out, either as the necessary and sufficient condition, or as a principal strategic variable of development. But the wrong kind of education, unaccompanied by the required complementary actions, can check or reverse the process of development. An unemployed or unemployable intelligentsia can be a source of revolutionary rather than economic activity, and young people brought up to despise manual work can reinforce the resistances to development.[6] Growth rates derived from the experience of the United States cannot be used to calculate the returns on education in the entirely different setting of underdeveloped countries. The same "input" could result in refusal to work on farms, an increase in urban unemployment, subversion and collapse. The wrong type of education can also produce a ruling elite which gives the wrong kind of advice, as well as setting up ideals that stand in the way of development. It can encourage ignorance of and contempt for the professional and technical qualifications which are a condition of economic development.[7]

Aggregation of all "investment in human capital" and its separation from "investment in physical capital" not only obscures the complementary nature of most subgroups of the two, but also serves as an intellectual and moral escape mechanism from unpleasant social and political difficulties.

New types of models are beginning to appear in which the returns yielded by expenditure on research and development, on training in management and administration, perhaps even on psychological treatment to transform tradition-bound into "achievement-motivated" personalities are calculated. But as long as crucial distinctions are blurred by aggregation, crucial connection severed by isolation, and historical and geographical differences neglected, the results will be useless or misleading.

One group of critics have attacked the sordidly mercenary approach to activities of high intrinsic value, saying that it is a perversion of values to calculate rates of return on what is, or should be, the ultimate end of all production. But these criticisms miss the point. The chief conclusion of most of the recent researches is that not enough is spent on education. The high independent value of education itself and of the consequent flow of independently (i.e., not instrumentally) valued satisfactions may be used as an argument against not spending enough, but it cannot be used as an argument against spending at least as much as would yield a return equal to that on physical capital. It could, of course, be said that once mercenary calculations are admitted, the relative values of different kinds of education

---

[6] "Wilfrid Malenbaum, for instance, found that unemployment in India varies directly with the degree of higher education. See 'Urban Unemployment in India,' *Pacific Affairs*, XXX, No. 2, June 1957, p. 146." Quoted in Gustav Ranis, "Economic Development: A Suggested Approach," *Kyklos*, Vol. XII, 1959, Fasc. 3, p. 445. In Mexico experiments have shown that investment in rural schools may not result in increased production or changed attitudes. For a discussion of the hostility to development generated by education and intellectuals see Joseph A. Schumpeter, *Capitalism, Socialism and Democracy*, pp. 152 ff.

[7] The importance of the *type* and *composition* in contrast to the *total* of social expenditure is particularly glaring in the field of health: expenditure on death control which simply reduces mortality rates has a negative effect on per capita growth rates in many underdeveloped countries, whereas expenditure on birth control and improved health which raises vigour and reduces apathy has a positive effect. The same is true of expenditure on education. Education which breeds religious aversion and snobbery yields a selection mechanism and policies which have income-depressing effects.

will be assessed by the wrong standards, and that the sense of the *value* of education will be lost, the more accurately its *price* is known. Already some authors argue that the returns on education in certain countries are lower than those on physical capital.

But the fact that we attach both independent and instrumental value to certain activities and that we attempt to estimate, if and when this is possible, the instrumental value, need not detract from the independent value. If the two reinforce each other, there can be no cause for complaint, and if they don't, it is surely rational to know the costs of policies promoting independent values.

The objection to the models is therefore not that they degrade education and equate human beings to machines. Better knowledge of the productive potential of human beings would raise, not lower, human dignity, human choice and human freedom. The objection is that the models approach the problem in the wrong way.

The faulty isolation of one tributary to the stream of production and the aggregation of different channels, some of which flow in opposite directions, some of which are stagnant and some of which do not contain any liquid, does not imply a disparagement of the need for detailed quantitative planning, including the planning of education, which has particularly long gestation periods. Whether a particular theoretical model is worth constructing depends upon whether we can give sufficient precision to the definition of the parameters and the variables and whether we can estimate the numerical relations between them. The rigor which is claimed for mathematical models is an illusion if the terms which they contain have no clear reference to the relevant items.

In the process of criticizing misplaced aggregation, such as that which lumps all education into a single category, we are led to the formulation of less general concepts: education is subdivided according to where it takes place, in what subjects, at what level and to whom. The purpose of such decomposition, disaggregation and subdivision is not to restrict analysis to less general concepts. We are, indeed, first trying to get rid of ragbag terms which do not correspond to anything observable and to replace them by "boxes" that can be "filled." But as the boxes are being filled and as we gain fuller empirical knowledge, we may look forward to the formulation of new aggregates and to the recomposition of the decomposed material in a different form. The new "packages" or "boxes" will differ from the old. Some of the new distinctions will cut across the old ones.[8] Thus when we examine the forces determining labor utilization in underdeveloped countries ("unemployment" and "under-employment" are as misleading as "education"), we shall discover that certain forms of education improve

[8] See Paul Streeten, "The Use and Abuse of Models in Development Planning," *op. cit.*— Ed.

the quality of work and its efficiency, as well as, by improving hygiene and sanitation, the duration of work. Capital equipment may extend the duration (cooperation enforcing discipline) and efficiency. Instead of separating "equipment" from "labor" and aggregating each, we may arrive at a new abstraction in which skill and knowledge are infused through the introduction of machines.[9]

The formulation of long-term plans of economic development for underdeveloped countries which must incorporate the planning of education, must meet, in addition to these conceptual, certain other requirements.

1. A long-term plan must embrace a study of how and how far traditional educational patterns have contributed to the failure of social and economic progress in the past. The study must discover whether the attitudes which are hostile to economic progress have been the result of a specific structure of education, and what modifications of that structure are needed to accelerate development. In both the formerly British and the formerly French territories a disdain of technical education has grown up which has been strengthened by the low status of technical schools and the restricted openings for their pupils. So long as the Civil Service and the appointments controlled or influenced by it are the preserve of the non-technically educated, the best ability will be diverted into non-technical education. This will both justify and strengthen the initial disdain and render progress more difficult. On the basis of this study of obstacles a new educational structure can be planned which will raise the status of those who meet the requirements of accelerated growth. Thus both diversion of the best talent and an increase in the supply of the required skills will be achieved.

2. The second requirement is a concrete idea of the size and composition of long-term development, based upon knowledge of the concrete endowments of the economy and a clear formulation of specific objectives and ideals. From these the future pattern of manpower distribution can be derived and thus an indication of the measures and the timing needed for educational development. The long gestation period of much education and training requires that starts are made now in order to reap results after 15, 20 and 25 years. Neither general formulae of ill-defined and irrelevant aggregates and their unverifiable relationships, nor even the occupational composition experienced at comparable stages of development in advanced

[9] An interesting attempt to construct a model in which all productivity change is embodied in new investment was made by Professor Robert M. Solow, who, in the words of Arthur Smithies, "is like a Pied Piper who can play different tunes." This particular tune is the exact opposite to those which separate "disembodied" knowledge and other improvements from capital accumulation ("Technical Progress, Capital Formation and Economic Growth," *Papers and Proceedings, American Economic Review*, May 1962, pp. 76–86). Professor Kenneth Arrow and Messrs. N. Kaldor and J. A. Mirrlees also have proposed a model of this type in *Review of Economic Studies*, June 1962.

industrial countries are of much use.[10] Past experience of non-Soviet countries relates to spontaneous growth (or its failure). It cannot be assumed
that deliberate efforts to accelerate growth by a series of policies would
show the same requirements. The problem is to overcome *specific* difficulties,
which differ from country to country and from time to time, while historical
experience from now advanced countries points to broadly *similar* categories.
From the long-term plan the quantities and types of educated personnel
in detailed categories can be derived. Since changes in technology, demand,
international policies, etc., will continually change these requirements, the
long-term plan should be a "rolling" plan, reviewed continually and at
least annually, and adapted to new information. It should provide the
framework for the five-year (or seven-year) plans and for the annual budgets,
so that policies which will not bear fruit until after more than five or seven
years do not get neglected. To avoid superimposing new rigidities upon
often already rigid economies, all three plans, the annual budget, the
"plan" and the perspective plan should be reviewed continually, and
carried forward, so that they apply always to the next year, five years,
fifteen years.

3. A number of measures will have to be taken which lie outside the
scope of conventional economic considerations. Thus if training takes place
abroad, the return of the trained men will have to be insured; if they have
acquired the required skills, it will be necessary that they use them in
isolated rural areas and reluctance to live there has to be overcome; the
type of training provided must fit the available technology and not be
appropriate to a more advanced form, etc.

4. Because of the narrow margins of tolerance and the closeness of many
underdeveloped countries to misery and starvation, it is crucially important
that minimum needs are estimated and that the required combination of
measures are planned and executed. Failure to execute complementary
measures can spell disaster. The isolation of "educational" expenditure
distracts attention from the urgent need, not only to select the right type of
education, but also to combine it with the provisions of better seeds, drainage

---

[10] The most promising approach is that adopted by Mr. Pitambar Pant of the Indian
Planning Commission: "To conclude, planning for education involves careful analysis of a
number of issues . . . [the] planning [of education] should be approached from the point
of view of long-term objectives of the society. In other words, the objectives and programs
of education should be related to the requirements of the future plans. Secondly, it is not
very meaningful to talk in terms of aggregates, when the equation of supply and demand
has to be worked for each separate category of personnel. For only to a limited extent are
these variously qualified graduates interchangeable. A comprehensive plan should identify
clearly the various categories of trained manpower required, and it is the main function
of the educational process to give to properly selected boys and girls the best education
and suitable environment to fit them for creative endeavor in the future." *Indian Journal of
Public Administration*, Vol. VII, No. 3, p. 330. (Such manpower planning cannot take the
place of, but should be supplemented by, appropriate forms of cost-benefit analysis.)

and fertilizers, with land reform and price stabilization, with improvements in transport and birth control, with a reform of recruitment to the Civil Service and business management. The waste involved in not planning for the required complementarities, and pushing education too far, can be catastrophic.

5. The detailed planning of education and training will have to make explicit political judgments about the distribution of the benefits between classes and over time. One of the costs of raising output later above what it would otherwise have been is the use of resources now to support the educational system required at a later stage. Since the social rate of time discount will tend to be high in countries where many are on the verge of starvation, extreme care is required in the expenditure on education. Financially conservative advice will be politically difficult and unpopular and may in many areas give rise to accusations of racial discrimination. Efforts are therefore needed to remove prejudices against quick-yielding and applied types of education. Education has to be used to get the right kind of education accepted. The larger the area for which collective planning can be initiated, the greater will be the scope for, and the less will be the danger of, indivisible highly specialized institutions which are expensive, not directly related to current progress, but imposing and prestige-yielding. The division of labor, in this field too, is limited by the extent of the market, and the larger and richer the area the more scope is there for specialized units conducting "basic" research. Although it is true that the practical use of "pure" research is unpredictable and that conscious direction of education and research to "applied" field does not always yield higher returns earlier than some initially "pure" research, it cannot be denied that it takes time between a discovery, its application by engineers and its exploitation by entrepreneurs and their followers. Only a large and rich economy with a low rate of time discount can afford to devote much energy to basic or pure scholarship. It must not be forgotten, moreover, that the adaptation of *known* techniques by poor developing countries could raise substantially their real income. Training rather than research would yield maximum returns.

The choice of the distribution over time is related to the choice between types of education with a high ratio of instrumental to independent value and those with a low ratio. The pursuit of knowledge for its own sake, wherever it may lead, is highly valued in many cultures, but it is not costless. This decision will in turn depend upon the political judgments made about the rate of growth of real income compared with that of leisure and the form in which leisure is to be enjoyed. These political value judgments will not be given once for all, but will themselves change as the plan is executed. But without a specification of concrete valuations and concrete manpower requirements, the calculation of "returns to education" suppresses these value judgments in a pseudo-scientific formulation, buries the factual judgments in misplaced aggregation and severs crucial connections by illegitimate isolation.

16

Some Second Thoughts
on the Concept of Human Capital

More than one notable economist has doubts about the human capital concept. Neil Chamberlain, Professor of Economics at Columbia University, reviewed recent developments on this subject in his 1967 presidential address to the Industrial Relations Research Association. Warning against the use of statistical wizardry to mask shallow assumptions, Chamberlain suggests that extreme care is in order in dealing

NEIL W. CHAMBERLAIN

with the concept of human capital that is central to contemporary manpower problems. He concedes the human capital approach to be a valuable one, but maintains that it is by no means an adequate analytical approach for the variety of manpower problems in society today.

The subject of manpower, with which our meetings deal this year, has followed a shifting and sometimes shifty path. Without trying to chart its twistings, turnings, and switchbacks, I shall confine my remarks to one aspect which is freighted with considerable consequence. If, considering the range of disciplines and interests represented in our Association, I speak too much like an economist, I hope you will forgive me for pursuing the specialization I know best. In any event, the aspect I propose to deal with has implications broader than are encompassed by one profession.

I am concerned with the effects of trying to make "scientific" (by which so many today seem merely to mean quantitative) the search for

Reprinted from Neil W. Chamberlain, "Some Second Thoughts on the Concept of Human Capital." Paper included in the *Proceedings of the Twentieth Annual Winter Meeting of the Industrial Relations Research Association*, December 28–29, 1967, pp. 1–13. With permission of the author and publisher.

understanding of social problems, including manpower problems, with an accompanying disposition to disdain forms of analysis which do not precipitate numbers and even to disregard problems which do not lean themselves readily to some system of accounts. The result has been to move the field of economics along lines that reflect a preoccupation with measurement and to deflect it from the more fundamental, often elusive, and always difficult conceptual problems with which the field tried to come to grips, however sloppily, in the past. No greater opprobrium can be cast on an economist today than to label him philosophical and speculative, as though the problems with which economists wrestle can be adequately dealt with on a nonphilosophic and nonspeculative basis.

But I am getting ahead of myself and anticipating my closing remarks. Let me back up a bit to take a quick and admittedly superficial look at some of the developments in the manpower field which are related to my theme. I shall go back no farther than fifty years or so, to remind you first of the fight by the American Federation of Labor to have incorporated in the Clayton Act of 1914 a declaration by the United States Congress that the labor of a human being is not a commodity or an article of commerce.

Economists have been inclined to snigger over that episode as one betraying the naivete of a paranoid labor movement. No one ever suggested, they commented then and have commented since, that workers were a commodity. But the labor services which they offer are a factor in the production process, like capital, and there is a market for such services, out of which arises a price or set of prices attaching to them. The worker sells his services without selling himself, and no political body can by fiat alter the commodity-like nature of that transaction. If economists speak, abstractly, of labor as a factor of production, and of markets for labor, they do not equate the disembodied labor with very much embodied workers. Their theoretical analysis is not intended as a doctrine supporting what has sometimes been referred to by unionists as "wage slavery."

Behind the misunderstanding that persisted as professional economists and professional unionists spoke past each other (no one could accuse them of engaging in a dialogue!) was a genuine issue which has never been wholly resolved. Granting that the economist's abstract formulation was not intended to *describe* a state of affairs (for one thing, that would have reduced them to being institutionalists, which to the representative economist meant something on a par with a poor sociologist), its effect *was* to render familiar, and ultimately acceptable by familiarity, the very thing that workers protested—that the sale of services to an employer involved in some unmeasurable degree the sale of the worker himself. How can labor services be disembodied from the person supplying them except by a construct of the imagination? The conception of labor as a factor of production did carry with it all the connotations and consequences of an impersonal market for people that Karl Polanyi portrayed so vividly in *The Great Transformation*. The unionist's view of the process that turned him from a craftsman producing a whole product which he sold for a price—not his time, but his product—as a form of wage slavery becomes more understandable despite the hyperbole of the phrase.

Actually, it was specialization of labor carried to the point of fragmenting the craftsman's art which was responsible—a technological matter. When a worker performed only a piece of a job he no longer had a product to sell, but only his time, spent in ways which someone else determined for him.

But all this is familiar territory, and there is no point in dwelling on it further. Suffice it to add that the Clayton Act declaration came towards the close of this conversion of labor into a "commodity" for sale, when its words could serve only as an epitaph for a lost cause. We are all wage workers now, or most of us, anyway, managers and professionals as well as production and clerical employees, selling ourselves with our services. In this respect we do not differ at all from the Communist countries which weep copious ideological tears over our condition.

With a leap of the mind—a species of acrobatics at which we have all become adept—let us now skip over three decades or so and place ourselves in the midst of World War II. The armed forces have drained off ten million persons at the same time that the economy is operating under a forced draft such as it had never previously experienced. A new sense of the importance of manpower potential and of manpower development follows naturally. People can be trained to do work which they—and others—would never have believed themselves capable of. Rosie the Riveter becomes a national figure, both actually and symbolically.

Partly as a consequence of this experience, and even more as a reflection of the increased postwar interest of economists in the processes of economic growth, a new concept began to make its way into the professional parlance—education as an investment in human resources. Whether the concern is over the means by which a backward economy can achieve and accelerate a forward movement, or over the requirements if an already advanced economy is to retain its vigor rather than stagnate, the quality of the contribution of its people is a—indeed, *the*—critical factor, and one which need not be taken as given. If, to be fair to the past, the idea was not spanking new, it nevertheless came with a fresh impact that made it novel and intriguing to the present generation of economists. I suppose that Professor Theodore Schultz of the University of Chicago, as much as any one person, can be credited with sparking this conception through his presidential address at the American Economic Association meetings in 1960.

The truth that expenditures on human beings are productive of something more than personal satisfaction or a sense of personal completeness is an important one. An outlay on education can also increase the economic productivity of those instructed, giving rise to a stream of returns higher than what they would otherwise have been. Who would dispute what everyone now accepts as self-evident? Education is thus a form of investment, just like an investment in improved capital equipment. In fact, human beings represent a species of physical capital, just like the machines with which they collaborate. Each gives rise to an ongoing stream of productive services. The value of that stream can be modified by improving the quality of both. In the case of human capital—manpower—such improvement need not be restricted to education: health and environmental conditioning for example are also likely to play their part.

The basic insight of this approach, as long as it is confined to picturesque analogy, recommends it to anyone concerned with the very important problems of helping individuals to improve their material productivity and societies to expand their GNP. These are worthy aims which require no subtle justification. Material wealth can be instrumental and is often essential in achieving a satisfying life, the "good" life. On the whole, people and societies of affluence are more likely to be liberated in spirit than people and societies frustrated with poverty.

But when the analogy of human capital to other forms of capital is pressed too far, not only does it break down on purely logical grounds but it invites conclusions which are both dangerous to social welfare and demeaning to the economics profession. It carries the abstract conception of the disembodiment of labor one stage further than where the Clayton Act controversy left it. If workers are not only suppliers of current services but also capital equipment from whom issue a stream of services whose value depends in part on how they are "tooled up" (educated), then the value of such an investment can be compared directly with the value of other investments. Appropriate—that is, economic—choices can be made depending on relative rates of return on competing investments. Expenditures on education can be laid alongside expenditures on road systems, irrigation projects, public housing or baseball stadia to determine which provides the higher payoff. Social choice can then be governed by the maximizing principle in its simplest form, that more is to be preferred to less.

Some advocates of the investment-in-human-capital approach consider this comparability a victory on the side of human welfare conceived in its broadest, not only material terms. Aha, they say, if we can induce legislators and city councilmen, and businessmen and other taxpayers, to recognize that education can pay dividends no less than a postal system or power project, or for that matter than a factory or farm, the chances are improved for getting appropriations for schools. Education becomes not only a matter of social welfare but a business proposition.

This use of the analogy as a kind of legislative ploy has a certain appeal because of the undeniable core of truth which the analogy reveals. But there is another side of the matter which is a darker side. As soon as one talks about investments, he invites a consideration of any one investment with the alternative possibilities. And as soon as he speaks of returns on investment the comparison among these runs in terms of relative rates. It is difficult to get away from the accountants' logic. Even Professor Schultz, who in addition to being the pioneer is one of the most sophisticated in this field, has lent his support to this next step. Although he expresses some reservations because not all of the more important forms of capital have been identified, he nevertheless believes that "thinking in terms of the rate of return is fundamental."[1]

Understandably, then, within the last few years there has emerged a series of research studies attempting to measure the rate of return on investment in education, both from the standpoint of an individual making such an investment and from that of a society. In doctoral dissertations the subject has steadily moved up the popularity ladder. There has been able exposition of some of the difficulties encountered in making such estimates, just as the accounting literature over the years has offered excellent analyses of some of the subtleties involved in calculating the actual or expected returns on more traditional forms of business investment. In both cases the user of the resulting measures is put on notice as to their deficiencies, but there is no suggestion that there is anything wrong with the concept itself. If investment occurs, it obviously has, or is intended to have, some return. The return is the measure of its value. In weighing competing investments, one can only weigh competing returns, calculated as rates. How else?

And so, in adopting as we have the conception of human capital, and education as investment in human capital, not as analogy but as categorical identity, we put education in the position of having to *defend* its value in the form of a rate of pecuniary return. We may recognize and allude to certain incommensurable values which it also has, but if it *is* investment in capital we cannot evade the accountants' justifiable insistence that while the incommensurables may be held in mind and may even be allowed to tip the scales, they come on top of the rate of return, which is the fundamental base and basis for decision. Economists have responded to the challenge by turning accountants, and have produced the desired measures—admittedly crude at this stage but hopefully to be refined later. In a way that the calculation of rates of return on business and industrial capital never managed to do, the measurement and refinement of rates of return on human capital have aroused the ardor and zeal of numerous members of the economics profession.

In part, I suspect, the phenomenon is traceable to the fact that the

[1] T. W. Schultz, "The Rate of Return in Allocating Investment Resources to Education." *Journal of Human Resources*, Summer 1967, p. 295.

concept of human capital has come into vogue at precisely the period when the profession at large had been swept into a strong current of quantification. Here was something to be measured, a rate to be calculated, and moreover the subject was one to which social welfare overtones attached. The conjuncture was fortuitously perfect.

It is against this contemporary trend that I would like to raise two objections, one based on an old-fashioned—or may I say time-honored?— philosophical conviction, the other on purely logical grounds. They are more closely related than they may at first appear. Let me take the philosophical issue first, though I will be returning to it later.

The fact that economic resources must of necessity be allocated to a variety of purposes if they are to be achieved does not automatically invoke an economic calculus, PPBS to the contrary notwithstanding. There are some allocations we make on faith rather than by rational calculation. To weigh on a pecuniary scale whether the benefits are equal to the costs, or to calculate what constitutes the rate of return, of an investment in democratic government, racial non-discrimination, a healthy human environment, and let me include education as well, is to look at all values through money-colored glasses. It is no justification to say that these become economic matters because we could conceivably put all our resources into any one of these ends, and therefore we must make decisions of degree—an allocation problem. The use of scarce resources carries with it no license for the economist to reshape articles of faith into rationalist maximizing decisions.

Admittedly the line is not clear that divides objectives which we might call ends from those we refer to as means. The inextricability of ends and means poses a philosophical question as old as the Garden of Eden. But to resolve that question by treating all choices as means, convertible on measurable terms, is to make a mockery of the human story. I can more readily accept a social accountant's effort to value secretarial schooling than I can his attempt to estimate the worth of education generally. Some values come with a moral content that preclude—or should preclude—our putting them on the same scale with groceries, to see where the marginal trade-off lies, or to measure the value of one in terms of the other. By the *indiscriminate* application of his pecuniary measuring rod the economist can belittle both himself and his profession. To reduce human beings, whose good is the ultimate end of all society if there is any ultimate end, to forms of capital earning returns is indiscrimination rampant.

But to calculate a rate of return, it is said, is not the same thing as to make a choice on the basis of comparative rates. It simply provides additional and pertinent information. If it is found that graduate education, for example, gives a comparatively low yield, this does not mean that society cannot invoke any other values it wishes and still invest in graduate education. On the other hand, if it is found that graduate education has a high rate of return, this is either economic reinforcement for a decision which still might have been made on other grounds or possibly persuasive of an investment which might otherwise not have been made.

The logic is a little loose. If the calculated rate has some persuasive effect when it is high, it can equally have a persuasive effect when the yield is "demonstrated" to be low. Why else are rates of return computed? Is investment in human resources the same as investment in inanimate plant and equipment, or is it not? If it is (which seems to be the direction of current thinking, seeking to establish a generic concept which will embrace all forms), then the economic calculus should be expected to have its influence, and the fears I express are justified. If it is not the same thing, then it stands revealed as analogy rather than identity, with all the dangers of analogical reasoning, including those I have suggested.

But let me pass, for the moment, from this point, which might leave us unprofitably arguing the extent to which values are economic or noneconomic, to one which seems to involve no such classificatory problem. Assuming for the moment that expenditures on education *can* be regarded as an investment, I am concerned with the now widespread notion that a rate of return can then be calculated. Here we are dealing with a matter that can be appraised on purely logical grounds or analytical feasibility.

As I have already noted, perhaps the most frequently cited reason for estimates of rates of return, as for cost-benefit analysis quite generally, is that it contributes to an efficient allocation of resources. The sums which are spent on education are already so great that we should know what we are getting for our money, it is said, or on the other hand it is sometimes held that we might well be investing more in education or at least certain forms of education if we were aware of the high returns deriving from such expenditures. The weighing of one outlay against competing outlays involves a judgment in efficiency of resource use which has been the economist's stock in trade for many generations.

But that preoccupation has always been premised on a stability of tastes and resources and an exclusion of exogenous forces, which is to say, change-creating forces. When one deals with social investments which not only are made under conditions of uncertainty but which are themselves intended to be change-creating, there is no firm basis for calculating their payoff. In the face of futurity and purposiveness (to use two favorite terms of one of our intellectual forebears, John R. Commons), calculations which are geared to the past, however refined analytically, make little sense.

There are two elements here which are distinguishable. Let me first consider the uncertainty elements, based on the inscrutability of the future. Since none of us is gifted with prophetic vision, we cannot foretell whether the future will prove economically wise the decisions we made today. We can only look to the future, keeping the past in mind, and conjecture as to the spectrum of likely effects which may issue from present actions. If judgments of this sort involve efficiency, it is in a very special and peculiar sense, certainly not the traditional marginalist meaning. Any implication that such an exercise leads to efficiency in resource allocation is crudely misleading.

The future value of investment in educated citizenry, whether one is speaking in terms of marginal or total expenditures, will depend, among other things, on the kind of a world in which such educated individuals will live—a world which will be partially, though not wholly, of their own making but the outlines of which are at best conjectural and speculative. The future values to which these pieces of human capital will give rise individually and collectively cannot in fact be known at the time of the investment in their education.

If the uncertain future of a society turns out to be composed largely of making or resisting war, the future value of a present educational system which stresses extended work in the arts will be quite different—and perhaps significantly less—than the future of a type of education emphasizing discipline and physical culture, chauvinistic ideology, and applied science and technology. If a society invests in the education of an elite leadership, the future value of that education will depend, among other things, on whether the future society will accept that leadership, or, as in the case of the Belgian Congo a few years back, exterminate it.

These are matters which are not now predictable, in any scientific sense, and they cannot be made predictable by the expedient of adopting a "most likely" set of assumptions. For one thing, there seldom exists any agreement even among the experts as to the appropriate assumptions concerning the future, and there is certainly no objective basis for isolating such assumptions. The uncertainty element is inherent in futurity insofar as it relates to human affairs.

In this respect, investment in education is of course subject to the same limitations as other forms of investment. All are subject to the uncertain impact of a changing environment, ruling out the measurability of their returns, in any meaningful sense of that term, and leaving them conjectural no matter how refined the effort at quantification.

But there is a second respect—the element of purposiveness—which afflicts investment in education (and certain other types of public investment, as well) more severely than it does traditional investments in producer goods.

This element of purposiveness may take the form of a conscious effort by those responsible for the investment to change the social environment in which the investment comes to fruition, in ways which are designed to augment the value of the stream of services issuing from it. The public and its political representatives may have a vision of a future which differs from the present, and which the social investment in question is in part intended to help realize, thus itself creating the context which is controlling of its value.

To take a specific example, educational patterns which are aimed at achieving less invidious discrimination among races will add to the stream of values flowing from a better educated Negro population. In the absence of such an influence (whether from education or some other source), the same investment in improved education for Negroes is almost certain to have a lower value, though how much lower is a matter of conjecture which is not rendered any more certain by quantification.

Here we are dealing with a future whose speculative characteristics are due not only to unpredictable exogenous events but also to the unpredictable effects of change-inducing actions by the resource-users themselves, those who are endogenous to the system. Indeterminacy is not only environmental to the decision-makers but embedded in their decisions. The very investment decisions which are made, or related decisions, may modify—perhaps unconsciously but often purposively, and sometimes at cross-purposes—the environment in which those investments come to fruition and which will be partially determinative of their value.

But the purposive element of social investment has an even deeper significance. It may involve not simply an effort to change the environment in ways which uncertainly affect the value of the stream of services to which the investment gives rise. Purposiveness may render literally unmeasurable the values from an investment in a way which has nothing to do with uncertainty, and in this respect the very concept of investment in human capital is especially vulnerable.

A society, or some sector of a society, through its agents, may will to change its characteristics not because this is expected to increase the return from its investment but because a change is wanted for its own sake. Educational expenditures aimed at eradicating invidious inter-racial discrimination may be made not because this is expected to improve the returns on educational investment in minority groups but because the public has come, for other reasons, to want that kind of a society. And how does one measure the rate of return on that kind of investment in education? How does one measure the satisfactions or utilities people derive from one social environment in contrast to another?

The value of an educated citizenry—national income accounting notwithstanding—is not given solely by the bricks and mortar which a society produces but by the institutions which it creates with the bricks and mortar. If the education provided by a people leads to a more productive economic machine but it comes to fruition in a hierarchic, technocratic, militaristic society, to which it has in some indeterminable but realistic sense contributed, the value of the education must be calculated differently than if the end product is equally productive but along lines which are humanistic and permissive. One does not have to make value judgments to call attention to the existence of such differential values, but he does have to make value judgments if he wishes to "measure" them.

I hope that no one misconstrues that what I am saying is that economists *should* make estimates of the pecuniary value of future states of society which education contributes to making. I hope equally that no one construes that I am suggesting that economists should sell short their major accomplishments in the field of public economic policy by substituting murky philosophizing and shallow sociology for "rigorous" analysis. My concern is rather that the admitted successes which economics has enjoyed may ill-advisedly encourage more ambitious adventures which purport to be "hard", realistic, and rigorous but which in fact incorporate implicit, murky, and shallow assumptions as to social values without an appreciation of that fact.

If economists want to be "scientific" and therefore quantitative, they are obliged to stick to a short enough run for the phenomena with which they work to stay relatively fixed—where changes are so moderate or incremental as not to invalidate logic based on a continuity of circumstance. If economists want to deal with a farther future, which increasingly involves not only change but change which is planned for, they are obliged to work with other standards than efficiency and with methods that are judgmental and strategy oriented rather than scientific.

In my own judgment, both approaches are desirable. We need efficiency-based decisions to help us achieve as much value as we can from a present which we can reasonably regard as having a steady state, and for such decisions quantitative analysis growing out of the recent past acts as a more reliable guide than guesswork. But we also need strategic decisions anchored in a future which is planned to be different from the present, towards which we draw ourselves by purposeful action. For this latter category of decisions, including many investment decisions, no amount of quantitative analysis will ever suffice, and guesses—if by that we mean informed judgment—are a better guide than econometrics.

I hope that you will grant me that this is not an anti-intellectual or obscurantist point of view. It is simply a recognition that everything does *not* have its calculable price or value, in any accounting sense, and that choice problems must proceed in the face of that difficulty. Preoccupation with accounting calculations of a discounted stream of future values as a basis for deciding whether or not educational investment or expenditures on manpower should be made, or in what form, is simply misguided. We must always, of course, question the value of specific programs and estimate their likely results, but we need the courage and intellectual honesty to make such assessments rest, in the final analysis, on our own best judgments. We cannot escape that uncomfortable necessity by taking refuge in numbers which—whatever the relevance of their underlying logic to the past—are uncertainly relevant to the future but are nevertheless supposed, somehow, to be influential over society's allocative choices.

This is perhaps doubly so in the case of education, which, like health, is a consumer as well as a producer goods. In private conversation and correspondence Professor Carl Stevens has repeatedly called my attention to the fact that education is a peculiarly important kind of consumer good, again like health, in that in addition to being appreciated in its own right it has the synergistic effect of influencing the utility to be had from many other consumer goods. Moreover, in the case of education, once again like health, the categories of consumer and producer utilities are not necessarily competitive, so that more utility on one account does not necessarily mean less on the other. Consumer satisfaction may go hand in hand with producer gain. Both these characteristics contribute to the problem of attaching meaningful values to the end product of the investment, and both these characteristics are responsive to the unceasing flow of cultural and technological change.

I come back to the intuitive wisdom that the naive labor leaders fought to incorporate in the Clayton Act. If labor is not a commodity because it cannot be separated from the human being who markets it, or, more precisely, if it is not *only* a commodity, neither is it an investment good, for the same reason. It is the tastes—the vision—of the "human capital" itself which guides the investment in itself. Economists, as well as others, can assist the human capital to see its own potentials, singly and collectively, and to make choices, within the framework of basic social values, which are rooted in an uncertain but hopeful future rather than constrained by some past performance. That future, because it is uncertain, is not to be determined by how some factitious rate of return on some marginal social investment compares with the rate derivable from competing public works projects.

And so, on this second ground, as well as on the first, I would like to register one protest against the implicit but prevalent view that the ultimate in economics is to put a number on everything, to derive equations which will yield determinate solutions. There is a place, and an important place, for such an approach, but it is not coextensive with the field. There is also a fascination in working with problems which are no less real because indeterminate, and no less demanding of choice because there is no efficient solution.

Human Capital Formation Through Education, Health, and Mobility

Returns to Education

Having examined several supporters and the defenders of human capital analysis, we turn now to some sample studies of the methodology discussed earlier. Although these studies are representative of some of the most recent and best empirical efforts to date, it is apparent that many of the criticisms presented in Part Three apply to them. The difficulties in sorting out non-economic, external, and indirect benefits and costs are severe—particularly since social values are desired. Perhaps the best one can do, given the contemporary state of the art, is to use the rate-of-return approach in such a way as to narrow down the range of speculation about benefit-cost related variables by studying measurable economic magnitudes. In a general sense this allows one to identify or surrogate value for the noneconomic, external, and indirect dimensions of investments in human capital.

Our focus momentarily is human capital formation through investment in education—a relationship discussed in the income-educational context by Herman P. Miller **17**. Following examination of the relationship between education and income, there are presented two recent empirical studies on rates of return to educational investments—one by Giora Hanoch **18** and the other by Orley Ashenfelter and Joseph D. Mooney **19**. We then examine some indirect noneconomic social relationships related to investment in education in Burton A. Weisbrod's contribution **20**.

17

Lifetime Income and
Economic Growth

The quality and quantity of basic data relevant to human capital economics is in no small measure the result of Herman P. Miller's long association with the Bureau of the Census. Now Chief, Population Division, Bureau of the Census, Miller differentiates between income gains owing to economic growth and those owing to age in this study of

HERMAN P. MILLER

income differentials by age and educational attainment level. The distinction drawn is an important one for those using age-earnings profiles by level of education because lifetime earnings are subject to distinct age-profile and time-productivity changes.

The purpose of this article is to show that the usual procedure for estimating lifetime income based on cross-section surveys tends to produce underestimates because of the failure to take future growth into account. Estimates based on cohort analyses produce quite different results. Census data show that the differences in real income for a given age cohort in two sucessive decennial censuses (e.g., men 25 to 34 years old in 1950 and 35 to 44 years old in 1960) are far greater than those obtained for men in the same age groups at a given point in time. The main reason for the difference is that the income measures obtained ten years apart reflect economic growth which is entirely excluded from the cross-section surveys. The use of income averages by age based on the cross-section surveys therefore produces lower values than would be obtained by the use of averages based on successive censuses.

Reprinted from Herman P. Miller, "Lifetime Income and Economic Growth," *American Economic Review* 55 (September 1965), pp. 834–44, with the permission of the author and publisher.

Moreover, the impact of growth appears to be greater for young men than for those past the prime working years. This fact suggests an additional source of downward bias in the currently available estimates, since the discounting procedures used to convert estimated lifetime income to present values attach greater weight to incomes expected early in life than to those expected later on.

These conclusions are, of course, subject to the limitation that they are based on only two points in time. Several decennial censuses would be needed to verify whether the rates of change in average income obtained are stable over time. The rates for any one decade could be affected by factors such as differences in the size of the cohorts. Almost all of the labor force in 1950 and 1960 were born in an era of declining birth rates. Hence one might expect a tight labor supply in the younger age groups. This might be reversed by 1970–80 when the younger cohorts will be far more numerous relative to older ones.

I Shortcomings of Cross-Section Estimates

The procedure generally used to estimate the present value of income received during a working lifetime for a given subgroup in the population can be summarized as follows [2, p. 47]:

$$V_{18} = \sum_{n=18}^{75} \frac{Y_n W_n P_n}{(1+r)^{n-18}}$$

In this formula Y_n is the average income at age n; W_n is the proportion of persons at age n with income; P_n is the probability of surviving at least one year at age n; r is the discount rate; and n is the working lifetime span, here defined as 18–75 years. The income averages generally come from household surveys conducted with a cross section of the population at a given point in time. Since the average incomes based on these surveys are generally tabulated only for age groups (e.g., 35–44 years) rather than for single years of age, it is assumed that the average income for the entire age group applies to each of the single years of age within the group.

Perhaps the major shortcoming of the model is that it assumes no future increases in average income.[1] The model recognizes that each individual may

---

[1] This model has several other shortcomings which are not discussed in the present report. First, it assumes that there will be no future increases in life expectancy during the working years. This is a rather doubtful assumption in the light of historical evidence, but it is probably not critical because the likelihood of surviving an additional year during the prime ages of working life is already quite high. More serious is the fact that it assumes the same discount rate for all socioeconomic groups. This procedure may be valid if the purpose is to provide a single estimate of lifetime income from an over-all standpoint. In that case, we would wish to use the rate that would best reveal the present value from a single stand-

expect his own income to rise as he gains in experience, seniority, and other factors that produce income differences among age groups at a given point in time. It fails to recognize, however, that "in a growing economy every individual may expect an upward trend in his own earning superimposed on the cross-sectional pattern for a given year" [1, p. 27].

So long as the model is used as a standardization procedure with the age distribution of the population held constant, it can yield meaningful comparisons among subgroups in the population. Very often, however, the results are treated as actual approximations of lifetime income rather than as statistical abstractions. That is, the figures are used to suggest the actual amount of income in current dollars, discounted to represent present values, that might result from a given investment. In such cases, the figures are interpreted as if they really represent the best estimate of the present value of the stream of income that a given subgroup might expect to receive over a lifetime. Under these circumstances, a case can be made for including the returns associated with economic growth as part of the total because they represent income that the individual may realistically expect to receive. The fact that their receipt is independent of any action on his part is unimportant in this case because the objective is to measure the returns *associated* with the investment, and not only those *caused* by the investment.

Under other circumstances, however, the decision as to whether or not to include such returns does become more complicated. This is particularly true when returns to different types of investments are being considered or when comparisons are made between different groups. For example, in one recent study the cost of preventing school dropouts was compared with the estimated amount by which the lifetime income of school dropouts might be increased if they were induced to stay in school [3]. In this kind of application it could be argued that returns to lifetime income associated with growth should not be included unless it can be demonstrated that these returns are *caused* by education or that they accrue differentially to the various education groups and therefore affect comparisons that may be made among them.[2] If the income measure associated with education were free of all such extraneous

---

point. If, however, the purpose is to show the estimate that individuals or particular groups may be considering when they make their decisions, different discount rates for different socioeconomic groups may be appropriate. Studies of poverty show that one of the major problems low-income families have is their inability to plan for the future, to recognize the future implications of present actions. It is very likely, for example, that college graduates discount the future at a far lower rate than high school graduates. If this is the case, the present value of a future stream of income is likely to be far higher for them than for the high school group.

[2] Table 2 suggests that economic growth affects higher education groups more than the lower ones; but, even if all education groups were equally affected by economic growth, we might still want to include the contribution caused by growth in those cases where the cost of investing in an additional year of education is compared with the amount of return associated with that investment.

factors as differences in innate ability, quality of schooling and discrimination, it would be reasonable to exclude income gains associated with economic growth. But, if the income figure for each education group shows only the *association* between income and education, with other factors included, there is little reason to exclude income associated with economic growth. Where global comparisons are made and the growth factor is omitted, the results are misleading because the estimating procedure understates the present value of lifetime income.

II Differential Impact
of Economic Growth on Age Groups

Empirical evidence based on the 1950 and 1960 Censuses, which is presented below, suggests that the relative increases in income associated with economic growth appear to be greater in the early years of working life than they are once the age of peak income is passed. Since the procedure generally used to estimate lifetime income counts income received early in life more nearly at its full value than income received in the later years, failure to include increases due to growth provides an additional source of downward bias in the estimates. Caution must be exercised in interpreting the data because they are based on experience during a single decade. Nevertheless, the figures do suggest that all groups do not share equally in economic growth and that the young tend to benefit more than others. The reasons why this should be so are not entirely clear. However, young workers are more mobile than others in the labor force. They are not as much tied down by family responsibility, home ownership, seniority, and other factors which reduce mobility. Therefore, they are more likely to move into new areas and new industries where wages tend to be higher and opportunities for rapid advancement are greater. Conversely, having been in the labor force a relatively short time, they are less likely to be trapped in declining industries where incomes may be dropping despite the over-all growth in the economy. The newer entrants into the labor force may also be better trained than those who have been employed for a decade or more, having been exposed to more modern methods of education and training. It is also possible that employers prefer younger workers even when they have the same ability as older workers because of their interest in potentials for growth. For these and other reasons, the evidence regarding the differential impact of economic growth for different age groups, based on the experience during the 'fifties, seems reasonable. In view of this fact, it might be reasonable to modify the estimating procedure described at the outset along the following lines:

$$V_{18} = \sum_{n=18}^{45} \frac{Y_n W_n P_{n(1+x)}}{(1+r)^{n-18}} + \sum_{n=46}^{75} \frac{Y_n W_n P_{n(1+y)}}{(1+r)^{n-18}}$$

The symbols are used here with the same meaning they had at the outset with the following exception. Since gains in income associated with economic growth appear to be greater up to age 45 than they are later on (see Table 1) the estimating procedure is broken into two parts, one representing incomes received till age 45, and the other, incomes received from age 45 to 75. The growth factors x and y represent the gains in income associated with economic growth for age groups 18–45 and 46–75.

As previously noted, the model assumes that all relationships which exist at the time the estimates are made will remain unchanged in the future. If, for example, the supply of college graduates is increased more rapidly than the demand for them, their incomes relative to others might be changed and, as a result, their expected lifetime incomes will change. Changes in technology, tastes, international relations, and many other factors could alter the results. Since these potential changes cannot be predicted, it is assumed that, on balance, their effect is neutral.

III Graphic Presentation
of Cohort and Cross-Section Data

Some of the basic issues involved in this paper can perhaps best be demonstrated by use of a numerical example. If the lifetime income of college graduates were estimated on the basis of the experience of 1949, using the formula described at the outset, $4,891 would have been used as the average for the 25–34 year age group and $8,595 would have been used for the 35–44 year group (see Table 1). These values are based on the cross-section data on income received during 1949 that were collected in the 1950 Census. They represent differences in income associated only with age (i.e., experience, seniority, and similar factors) and are independent of changes in the economy over time. In other words, on the basis of the cross-section data for 1949 that were collected in the 1950 Census it could be said that the increase in average income between age 30 (the average for 25–34) and age 40 was $3,704, representing a gain of 76 per cent for the decade or 7.6 per cent per year. The variation of income with age based on cross-section data has been measured annually during the past 15 years and has been found to be quite stable. The relationship does not appear to be affected in any appreciable way by cyclical changes in the level of economic activity. Therefore it could be deduced that the relationship between income and age reflected in the cross-section data provides a measure of the extent to which experience, seniority, loss of work due to illness, and similar factors associated with age have an impact on individual income.

An alternative way of estimating the income change between ages 30 and

Table 1—Change in mean income for selected cohorts of males, by years of school completed, color, and region, for the U.S.: 1949 and 1959 [a]

Color, region, and years of school completed	COHORT OF 1915–1924			COHORT OF 1905–1914			COHORT OF 1895–1904			COHORT OF 1885–1895		
	25–34 in 1950	35–44 in 1960	Percent change	35–44 in 1950	45–54 in 1960	Percent change	45–54 in 1950	55–64 in 1960	Percent change	55–64 in 1950	65–74 in 1960	Percent change
All Classes Total	$3,556	$6,212	75	$4,396	$6,136	40	$4,540	$5,522	22	$4,008	$3,415	−15
Elem: Less than 8 years	2,295	3,564	55	2,719	3,625	33	2,938	3,501	19	2,776	2,202	−21
8 years	3,077	4,705	53	3,660	4,854	33	3,925	4,644	18	3,662	2,967	−19
High School: 1–3 years	3,440	5,465	59	4,154	5,681	37	4,535	5,614	24	4,268	3,965	−7
4 years	3,920	6,379	63	4,868	6,697	38	5,702	6,746	18	5,531	4,527	−18
College: 1–3 years	4,121	7,854	91	6,035	8,679	44	6,852	8,817	29	6,277	5,386	−14
4 years or more	4,891	11,088	127	8,595	11,590	35	9,853	11,039	12	9,292	8,123	−13
White Total	3,705	6,508	76	4,627	6,449	39	4,782	5,802	21	4,172	3,571	−14
Elem: Less than 8 years	2,527	3,918	55	3,011	3,961	32	3,218	3,781	17	2,959	2,327	−21
8 years	3,154	4,845	54	3,738	4,958	33	3,986	4,718	18	3,699	2,994	−19
High School: 1–3 years	3,537	5,650	60	4,254	5,820	37	4,627	5,729	24	4,326	4,035	−7
4 years	3,971	6,494	64	4,939	6,807	38	5,794	6,867	19	5,611	4,602	−18
College: 1–3 years	4,181	8,023	92	6,140	8,835	44	6,976	9,001	29	6,370	5,463	−14
4 years or more	4,939	11,263	128	8,716	11,747	35	9,992	11,181	12	9,411	8,226	−13
Nonwhite Total	2,123	3,465	63	2,240	3,113	39	2,157	2,674	24	1,854	1,650	−11
Elem: Less than 8 years	1,730	2,590	50	1,887	2,539	35	1,869	2,272	22	1,609	1,431	−11
8 years	2,244	3,416	52	2,449	3,358	37	2,522	3,126	24	2,334	2,084	−11
High School: 1–3 years	2,384	3,728	56	2,644	3,618	37	2,700	3,357	24	2,402	2,243	−7
4 years	2,710	4,299	59	2,998	4,090	36	2,983	3,753	26	2,707	2,466	−9
College: 1–3 years	2,732	4,625	69	3,289	4,527	38	3,273	4,114	26	3,046	2,624	−14
4 years or more	3,133	6,366	103	4,371	6,803	56	4,613	6,297	37	3,985	4,850	+22
North and West All Classes Total	3,786	6,603	74	4,748	6,606	39	4,886	5,926	21	4,281	3,627	−15
Elem: Less than 8 years	2,828	4,246	50	3,321	4,321	30	3,459	4,066	18	3,166	2,465	−22
8 years	3,235	4,920	52	3,813	5,054	33	4,060	4,814	19	3,761	3,056	−19
High School: 1–3 years	3,567	5,690	60	4,303	5,935	38	4,675	5,859	25	4,423	4,083	−8
4 years	3,965	6,520	64	4,893	6,818	39	5,740	6,832	19	5,577	5,069	−9
College: 1–3 years	4,168	8,023	92	6,074	8,823	45	6,886	8,901	29	6,338	5,490	−13
4 years or more	4,869	11,395	134	8,702	11,851	36	9,997	11,309	13	9,435	8,322	−12

Table 1 (continued)

Color, region, and years of school completed	COHORT OF 1915–1924			COHORT OF 1905–1914			COHORT OF 1895–1904			COHORT OF 1885–1895		
	25–34 in 1950	35–44 in 1960	Percent change	35–44 in 1950	45–54 in 1960	Percent change	45–54 in 1950	55–64 in 1960	Percent change	55–64 in 1950	65–74 in 1960	Percent change
North and West (cont'd.)												
White Total	$3,848	$6,776	76	$4,853	$6,774	40	$4,993	$6,072	22	$4,342	$3,693	−15
Elem: Less than 8 years	2,905	4,409	52	3,440	4,476	30	3,570	4,184	17	3,220	2,501	−22
8 years	3,272	5,004	53	3,856	5,117	33	4,097	4,861	19	3,782	3,072	−19
High School: 1–3 years	3,628	5,817	60	4,371	6,034	38	4,736	5,943	25	4,468	4,133	−7
4 years	4,003	6,609	65	4,947	6,902	40	5,811	6,932	19	5,643	5,154	−9
College: 1–3 years	4,205	8,169	94	6,154	8,942	45	6,980	9,056	30	6,398	5,545	−13
4 years or more	4,898	11,530	135	8,768	11,940	36	10,083	11,409	13	9,503	8,390	−12
Nonwhite Total	2,711	4,309	59	2,921	4,002	37	2,834	3,531	25	2,589	2,216	−14
Elem: Less than 8 years	2,460	3,548	44	2,645	3,494	32	2,547	3,159	24	2,330	1,985	−15
8 years	2,633	3,905	48	2,832	3,849	36	2,866	3,556	24	2,743	2,362	−14
High School: 1–3 years	2,695	4,242	57	2,966	4,116	39	3,066	3,885	27	2,732	2,582	−5
4 years	2,932	4,731	61	3,217	4,530	41	3,261	4,151	27	2,932	2,660	−9
College: 1–3 years	3,060	5,047	65	3,494	5,117	46	3,608	4,569	27	3,581	2,797	−22
4 years or more	3,355	7,061	110	4,975	8,161	64	4,935	7,142	45	4,514	5,147	+14
South												
All Classes Total	3,033	5,255	73	3,573	4,978	39	3,639	4,434	22	3,189	2,641	−17
Elem: Less than 8 years	1,970	2,991	52	2,208	2,869	30	2,236	2,598	16	2,009	1,696	−16
8 years	2,634	4,042	53	3,081	4,085	33	3,290	3,868	18	3,081	2,581	−16
High School: 1–3 years	3,132	4,825	54	3,750	4,917	31	4,132	4,843	17	3,721	3,618	−3
4 years	3,737	5,901	58	4,776	6,281	32	5,541	6,455	16	5,331	4,275	−20
College: 1–3 years	3,986	7,372	85	5,922	8,246	39	6,750	8,567	27	6,109	5,114	−16
4 years or more	4,956	10,270	107	8,086	12,504	55	9,349	10,191	9	8,799	7,577	−14
White Total	3,327	5,778	74	4,011	5,535	38	4,126	4,973	21	3,577	2,934	−18
Elem: Less than 8 years	2,229	3,418	53	2,532	3,266	29	2,575	2,970	15	2,285	1,899	−17
8 years	2,786	4,304	54	3,248	4,296	32	3,421	4,022	18	3,184	3,218	+1
High School: 1–3 years	3,300	5,141	56	3,919	5,143	31	4,296	5,033	17	3,844	3,738	+3
4 years	3,841	6,096	59	4,917	6,475	32	5,719	6,649	16	5,470	4,383	−20
College: 1–3 years	4,109	7,602	85	6,095	8,507	40	6,964	8,837	27	6,292	5,244	−17
4 years or more	5,063	10,547	108	8,370	12,973	55	9,660	10,445	8	9,088	7,760	−15
Nonwhite Total	1,725	2,585	50	1,802	2,349	30	1,720	1,930	12	1,435	1,305	−9
Elem: Less than 8 years	1,516	2,132	41	1,614	2,031	26	1,575	1,732	10	1,319	1,163	−12
8 years	1,858	2,699	45	1,979	2,613	32	1,992	2,305	16	1,697	1,692	−2
High School: 1–3 years	2,003	2,900	45	2,212	2,819	27	2,187	2,441	12	2,006	1,764	−12
4 years	2,241	3,304	47	2,549	3,188	25	2,364	2,772	17	2,141	2,054	−4
College: 1–3 years	2,248	3,657	63	2,951	3,512	19	2,724	3,188	17	2,386	2,437	+2
4 years or more	2,900	5,313	83	3,748	5,586	49	4,287	5,273	23	3,609	3,979	+10

a Mean income in 1959 dollars. The Consumer Price Index was used as the price deflator. Figures shown for 1950 represent income in 1949; figures shown for 1960 represent income in 1959.

Source: Unpublished data of the Bureau of the Census.

40 is to compare the incomes (measured in constant dollars) of college graduates 25–34 years old in 1949 ($4,891) with those of college graduates 35–44
years old in 1959 ($11,088). This procedure provides a more valid measure of
the change in income over time than the one described above because it permits the comparison of average incomes for the same group of men at two
different points in time whereas the cross-section data permit only a comparison of two different groups of men at the same point in time. On the basis of
the cohort approach, it could be said that the average income of college
graduates increased by $6,197, representing a gain of 127 per cent for the
decade or about 12.7 per cent per year. This increase consists of two separately identifiable elements. One of these elements is the increase in income due
to experience, seniority, and other factors associated with age. On the basis of
the cross-section data previously described, it might be roughly estimated
that about 7.6 percentage points of the total increase for this age group is due
to the variation of income with age. This factor, incidentally, is taken into
account in the traditional method of estimating lifetime income because it is
reflected in the averages used in the formula described at the outset. There is,
however, a second component of 5.1 per cent per year which is not taken into
account in the traditional method of estimating lifetime income. This component represents the increase in average income over time for this cohort due
to changes in productivity, in the industrial and occupational mix of the
labor force, in the geographic distribution of the labor force, and similar
factors that are associated with changes in the economy as a whole.

A visual presentation of the problem discussed above is presented in
Figure 1. According to the formulation described at the outset, the values used
to estimate lifetime income are based on the cross-section data shown at
points A ($8,595) and C ($9,853). The difference between these two points
represents the variation due to age (i.e., experience, seniority, etc.) that the
economy is willing to pay for a given resource (college graduates) at a given
point in time (1959). Another way of looking at this problem is to see how
much the economy is willing to pay for the same resource at two different
points in time. This information is provided by points A ($8,595) and B
($11,590). If it is assumed that the conditions of supply were unchanged
between 1949 and 1959, it can be concluded on the basis of this evidence
that because of the increased experience of this group of college graduates
and because of the change in the entire economy during the decade, the
annual income for this group increased from $8,595 to $11,590. The difference between points A and B ($2,995) represents the *total change* due to both
the increase in experience and the growth in the economy, whereas the
difference between points A and C ($1,258) represents the increase due to
age alone. Therefore, the difference between points B and C ($1,737) rep-
resents the increment associated with economic growth. The age component
of the increase is included in the current techniques for estimating lifetime

income. The component identified as being associated with economic growth
is not included.

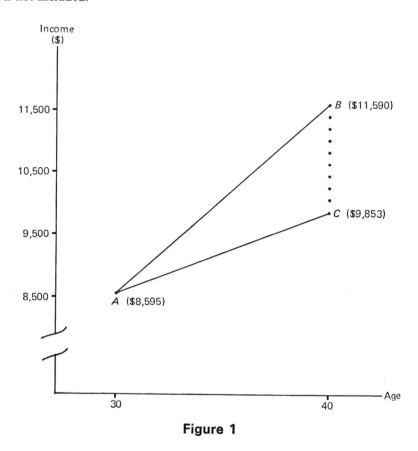

Figure 1

IV Summary of Components
of Income Change by Age Groups

A summary of the components of change in income for various subgroups
in the population is shown in Table 2. The key factor to note here is that for
each color and education group, the greatest gains in income are experienced
by the younger age groups. Thus, for example, to continue with the illustration of college graduates previously used, it can be noted that the cohort of
men born between 1915–24 (i.e., those who were 25–34 years old in 1950 and
35–44 years old in 1960) had annual increases in income of 12.7 per cent,
whereas men who were 10 years older had annual increases of only 3.5 per
cent during the same period; and those who were 20 years older had annual

Table 2—Components of change in mean income for selected cohorts of males, by color and years of school completed for the U.S., by region: 1949 and 1959

Color, region, and years of school completed	ANNUAL RATE OF INCREASE IN INCOME BETWEEN AGE 25-34 AND AGE 35-44			ANNUAL RATE OF INCREASE IN INCOME BETWEEN AGE 35-44 AND AGE 45-54			ANNUAL RATE OF INCREASE IN INCOME BETWEEN AGE 45-54 AND AGE 55-64		
	Based on cross-section data (change associated with age) (1)	Based on cohort data (total change over the decade) (2)	Difference (2)−(1) (change due to economic growth) (3)	Based on cross-section data (change associated with age) (1)	Based on cohort data (total change over the decade) (2)	Difference (2)−(1) (change due to economic growth) (3)	Based on cross-section data (change associated with age) (1)	Based on cohort data (total change over the decade) (2)	Difference (2)−(1) (change due to economic growth) (3)
United States									
All Classes Total	2.4	7.5	5.1	0.3	4.0	3.7	−1.3	2.2	3.5
Elem: Less than 8 years	1.8	5.5	3.7	0.8	3.3	2.5	−0.6	1.9	2.5
8 years	1.9	5.3	3.4	0.7	3.3	2.6	−0.7	1.8	2.5
High School: 1–3 years	2.1	5.9	3.8	0.9	3.7	2.8	−0.6	2.4	3.0
4 years	2.4	6.3	3.9	1.7	3.8	2.1	−0.3	1.8	2.1
College: 1–3 years	4.6	9.1	4.5	1.4	4.4	3.0	−0.9	2.9	3.8
4 years or more	7.6	12.7	5.1	1.5	3.5	2.0	−0.6	1.2	1.8
White Total	2.5	7.6	5.1	0.3	3.9	3.6	−1.5	2.1	3.6
Elem: Less than 8 years	1.9	5.5	3.6	0.7	3.2	2.5	−0.9	1.7	2.6
8 years	1.9	5.4	3.5	0.7	3.3	2.6	−0.8	1.8	2.6
High School: 1–3 years	2.0	6.0	4.0	0.9	3.7	2.8	−0.7	2.4	3.1
4 years	2.4	6.4	4.0	1.7	3.8	2.1	−0.3	1.9	2.2
College: 1–3 years	4.7	9.2	4.5	1.4	4.4	3.0	−1.0	2.9	3.9
4 years or more	7.6	12.8	5.2	1.5	3.5	2.0	−0.6	1.2	1.8
Nonwhite Total	0.6	6.3	5.7	−0.4	3.9	4.3	−1.6	2.4	4.0
Elem: Less than 8 years	0.9	5.0	4.1	−0.1	3.5	3.6	−1.6	2.2	3.8
8 years	0.9	5.2	4.3	0.3	3.7	3.4	−0.8	2.4	3.2
High School: 1–3 years	1.1	5.6	4.5	0.2	3.7	3.5	−1.2	2.4	3.6
4 years	1.1	5.9	4.8	—	3.6	3.6	−1.0	2.6	3.6
College: 1–3 years	2.0	6.9	4.9	—	3.8	3.8	−0.7	2.6	3.3
4 years or more	4.0	10.3	6.3	0.6	5.6	5.0	−1.6	3.7	5.3
North and West									
All Classes Total	2.5	7.4	4.9	0.3	3.9	3.6	−1.4	2.1	3.6
Elem: Less than 8 years	1.7	5.0	3.3	0.4	3.0	2.6	−0.9	1.8	2.7
8 years	1.8	5.2	3.4	0.6	3.3	2.7	−0.8	1.9	2.7
High School: 1–3 years	2.1	6.0	3.9	0.9	3.8	2.9	−0.6	2.5	3.1
4 years	2.3	6.4	4.1	1.7	3.9	2.2	−0.3	1.9	2.2
College: 1–3 years	4.6	9.2	4.6	1.3	4.5	3.2	−0.9	2.9	3.8
4 years or more	5.5	13.4	5.5	1.5	3.6	2.1	−0.6	1.3	1.9

Table 2 (continued)

Color, region, and years of school completed	ANNUAL RATE OF INCREASE IN INCOME BETWEEN AGE 25–34 AND AGE 35–44			ANNUAL RATE OF INCREASE IN INCOME BETWEEN AGE 35–44 AND AGE 45–54			ANNUAL RATE OF INCREASE IN INCOME BETWEEN AGE 45–54 AND AGE 55–64		
	Based on cross-section data (change associated with age) (1)	Based on cohort data (total change over the decade) (2)	Difference (2)–(1) (change due to economic growth) (3)	Based on cross-section data (change associated with age) (1)	Based on cohort data (total change over the decade) (2)	Difference (2)–(1) (change due to economic growth) (3)	Based on cross-section data (change associated with age) (1)	Based on cohort data (total change over the decade) (2)	Difference (2)–(1) (change due to economic growth) (3)
White Total	2.6	7.6	5.0	0.3	4.0	3.7	−1.5	2.2	3.7
Elem: Less than 8 years	1.8	5.2	3.4	0.4	3.0	2.6	−1.1	1.7	2.8
8 years	1.8	5.3	3.5	0.6	3.3	2.7	−0.8	1.9	2.7
High School: 1–3 years	2.0	6.0	4.0	0.8	3.8	3.0	−0.6	2.5	3.1
4 years	2.4	6.5	4.1	1.7	4.0	2.3	−0.3	1.9	2.2
College: 1–3 years	4.6	9.4	4.8	1.3	4.5	3.2	−0.9	3.0	3.9
4 years or more	7.9	13.5	5.6	1.5	3.6	2.1	−0.6	1.3	1.9
Nonwhite Total	0.8	5.9	5.1	−0.3	3.7	4.0	−0.9	2.5	3.4
Elem: Less than 8 years	0.8	4.4	3.6	−0.4	3.2	3.6	−0.9	2.4	3.3
8 years	0.8	4.8	4.0	0.1	3.6	3.5	−0.4	2.4	2.8
High School: 1–3 years	1.0	5.7	4.7	0.3	3.9	3.6	−1.2	2.7	3.9
4 years	1.0	6.1	5.1	0.1	4.1	4.0	−1.1	2.7	3.8
College: 1–3 years	1.4	6.5	5.1	0.3	4.6	4.3	−0.1	2.7	2.8
4 years or more	4.8	11.0	6.2	−0.1	6.4	6.5	−0.9	4.5	5.4
South									
All Classes Total	1.8	7.3	5.8	0.2	3.9	3.7	−1.4	2.2	3.6
Elem: Less than 8 years	1.2	5.2	4.0	0.1	3.0	2.9	−1.1	1.6	2.7
8 years	1.7	5.3	3.6	0.7	3.3	2.6	−0.7	1.8	2.5
High School: 1–3 years	2.0	5.4	3.4	1.0	3.1	2.1	−1.1	1.7	2.8
4 years	2.8	5.8	3.0	1.6	3.2	1.6	−0.4	1.6	2.0
College: 1–3 years	4.9	8.5	3.6	1.4	3.9	2.5	−1.0	2.7	3.7
4 years or more	6.3	10.7	4.4	1.6	5.5	3.9	−0.6	0.9	1.5
White Total	2.1	7.4	5.3	0.3	3.8	3.5	−1.5	2.1	3.6
Elem: Less than 8 years	1.4	5.3	3.9	0.2	2.9	2.7	−1.3	1.5	2.8
8 years	1.7	5.4	3.7	0.5	3.2	2.7	−0.7	1.8	2.5
High School: 1–3 years	1.9	5.6	3.7	1.0	3.1	2.1	−1.2	1.7	2.9
4 years	2.8	5.9	3.1	1.6	3.2	1.6	−0.5	1.6	2.1
College: 1–3 years	4.8	8.5	3.7	1.4	4.0	2.6	−1.1	2.7	3.8
4 years or more	6.5	10.8	4.3	1.5	5.5	4.0	−0.6	0.8	1.4
Nonwhite Total	0.4	5.0	4.6	−0.5	3.0	3.5	−2.0	1.2	3.2
Elem: Less than 8 years	0.6	4.1	3.5	−0.2	2.6	2.8	−1.9	1.0	2.9
8 years	0.7	4.5	3.8	−0.1	3.2	3.1	−1.7	1.6	3.3
High School: 1–3 years	1.0	4.5	3.5	−0.8	2.7	2.8	−0.9	1.2	2.1
4 years	1.4	4.7	3.3	−0.8	2.5	3.3	−1.0	1.7	2.7
College: 1–3 years	3.1	6.3	3.2	−0.8	1.9	2.7	−1.4	1.7	3.1
4 years or more	2.9	8.3	5.4	1.4	4.9	3.5	−1.9	2.3	4.2

gains of only 1.2 per cent. If, instead of using cohorts, cross-section data had been used, they would have revealed that differences associated with age accounted for an annual increase of 7.6 per cent between the average ages of 30 and 40; 1.5 per cent increase between the average ages of 40 and 50; and a decrease of about 0.6 per cent between ages 50 and 60. When the age component of the total increase is taken into account, it appears that economic growth accounted for a 5.1 per cent annual increase in income between ages 30 and 40; a 2.0 per cent increase between ages 40 and 50; and a 1.8 per cent increase between ages 50 and 60. Since the latter element is not taken into account in traditional measures of estimating lifetime income, it appears that its inclusion would add to the expected income gains of younger men and would therefore have an important bearing on the estimates of expected lifetime income.

A second point of interest in Table 2 is the fact that income gains associated with economic growth appear to be somewhat greater for nonwhites than for whites. Over all, the income gains associated with growth were 5.7 per cent per year for nonwhites as compared with 5.1 per cent for whites between the ages of 30 and 40. The corresponding differences between ages 40 and 50 were 4.3 per cent for nonwhites and 3.6 per cent for whites; and between ages 50 and 60 the gains were 4.0 per cent for nonwhites and 3.6 per cent for whites. Most of these differences are eliminated, however, when the figures are examined separately for the North and West and for the South, suggesting, therefore, that the apparently greater gains for nonwhites associated with economic growth are largely due to their migration from the South.

References

[1] H. S. Houthakker, "Education and Income," *Rev. Econ. Stat.*, Feb. 1959, *41*, 24–28.

[2] Burton A. Weisbrod, *External Benefits of Public Education*. Princeton, 1964.

[3] ———, "Preventing High School Dropouts," in R. Dorfman, ed., *Measuring Benefits of Government Investments*, Brookings Institution, 1965.

18

An Economic Analysis
of Earnings and Schooling

Using 1960 census data, Giora
Hanoch, Professor of Economics at
The Hebrew University, Jerusalem,
Israel, analyzes earnings by age,
education, race, and region in the
United States. On the basis of these
data, private internal rates of return
on investment in schooling are
determined. Hanoch also comments
on data and technical problems

GIORA HANOCH

encountered in his analysis. These
problems include ability adjustments, nonpecuniary returns, and
identification of social rates of return.
The data presented include marginal
rates of return and differential
rates of return for whites and non-
whites in the United States.

The flow of net earnings (y) that an individual expects to receive at a given time is assumed to be a function of his age (t), his schooling level (s), and various additional factors, lumped together throughout the following discussion in a vector of variables $(\mathcal{Z})$. Thus, the earnings function $y(t,s;\mathcal{Z})$ embodies all the information concerning the lifetime earnings of an individual or a homogeneous group, with given characteristics $(\mathcal{Z})$ for any acquired schooling level (s), apart from random fluctuations (the expected value of which is assumed to be zero).

The marginal effect of the s'th school year on earnings at age t can then be approximated by the difference: $D_t(s,\mathcal{Z}) = y_t(s,\mathcal{Z}) - y_t(s-1,\mathcal{Z})$,

From Giora Hanoch, "An Economic Analysis of Earnings and Schooling," *Journal of Human Resources* 2 (Summer 1967) (© 1967 by the Regents of the University of Wisconsin), pp. 310–329. Used by permission of the author and publisher.

where the differences D_t are normally negative at first, during the schooling years, and later positive. The marginal internal rate of return (R) to the s'th school year is determined by

$$\sum_{t=0}^{N} (1+R)^{-t} \cdot D_t(s,\mathcal{Z}) = 0$$

where the (constant) rate of discount (R) sets the present value of the sum of all the D_t equal to zero.

If the earnings function $y(t,s;\mathcal{Z})$ can be estimated within a group homogeneous with respect to the $\mathcal{Z}$ variables—in which there are nevertheless variations in the actual schooling (s) owing to varying tastes and supply conditions—then the schedule of internal rates of return $R(s)$ can be derived and can be identified as the demand of the group for investment in education. A modest attempt to approximate this procedure empirically will be carried out and analyzed.

I Estimates of Income-Age Profiles

The 1/1,000 sample of the 1960 Census, including more than 57,000 males over age 14, provides an unparalleled opportunity to simultaneously analyze the impact of a variety of factors on the earnings of a number of homogeneous subgroups, without being severely restricted by statistical considerations concerning sample fluctuations and unreliable estimates. Nevertheless, one should constantly keep in mind that statistical biases do not diminish with large sample size, and that large-scale data sources coupled with modern computer speed cannot be substitutes for caution, scrutiny, and judgment.

It is outside the scope of this presentation to review the various experiments which have been carried out or to describe in detail the considerations involved in choosing an appropriate functional form for the earnings function which incorporates a satisfactory set of variables.[1] However, some of the key methodological issues deserve mention. First, the selection of variables is important—i.e., whether to include as explanatory variables (in the set $\mathcal{Z}$) of the earnings function variables which are themselves related to schooling and age. For example, given extensive mobility across occupation and industry lines, which depends in turn upon age and schooling, there is

---

[1] A more detailed discussion of the preparatory analyses and some of the considerations involved in this process is found in Hanoch, "Personal Earnings and Investment in Schooling," Ph.D. dissertation, University of Chicago, 1965. Hereinafter referred to as *Thesis*.

a real question as to the meaning of "holding constant" these variables in a regression analysis.[2]

Empirically, there is no variable which would strictly satisfy all the requirements imposed by theory. No variable (except race, perhaps) is truly exogeneous, is uncorrelated with the residuals of earnings, and is not subject to any degree of choice by the individual (implying some simultaneous-equations bias in a cross-section, resulting from dependence on the individual's earnings and schooling). Hence, one must weigh the benefits against the undesirable aspects of including each set of variables, experiment with the results, and finally makes the arbitrary but unavoidable educated choice.

A similar problem concerning the form of the earnings function is the extent to which interactions among variables must be considered. This could be done either by explicitly defining some interaction variables (e.g., as a product of two variables), or by splitting the sample into subgroups, thus allowing for full interactions between the classifying factor and all the remaining explanatory variables.

And finally, additional questions arise with regard to the presentation of each variable which is quantitative in nature (e.g., earnings, age, schooling, size of place): should it appear in a continuous form (linear or logarithmic), or be represented by a group of characteristic or dummy variables, defined on intervals of its range. A qualitative factor can be represented only by a set of dummy variables, but the size and number of its subgroups are still open to arbitrary determination, which may affect the resulting estimates.

The final choices of subgroups and variables on which our estimates are based are described briefly below. The sample of individuals not attending school in 1959 was divided into 24 groups defined by race (white or nonwhite), region (South or non-South) and age (14–24, 25–34, 35–44,

---

[2] If, on the one hand, occupation and industry are to be excluded from the analysis, the elements of ability, nonpecuniary returns, and motivations associated with these classifications will be lost. On the other hand, a high degree of mobility exists among occupations and among industries, and this mobility depends strongly on schooling and on age. Thus, "holding constant" the occupation or the industry allows only for intragroup differentials of earnings. It eliminates the effects of schooling and age on interoccupational or interindustry differentials. In other words, an individual who completed more years in school would expect to move upward in the occupational scale and perhaps to work in a better-paying industry. This is in fact the main channel by which he can realize returns on his additional investment in education. If he were to be restricted to the same occupation group or industry, he would have much less opportunity to increase his income. This could probably be more effectively resolved by use of a simultaneous-equations model to explain both earnings and occupational structure. However, it would require additional information on ability and on other factors which was not available. As a result, it was decided to exclude occupation and industry variables from the equations and thus avoid serious biases in the estimated coefficients of schooling which, after all, are the target estimates of this analysis

45–54, 55–64, 65 and over). Table 1 summarizes the size and some characteristics of these groups.

Table 1—Earnings and schooling by race/region and age: all males (except age 14–24 in school), 1959[a]

Race-region Age	No. persons	No. with no earnings	Mean earnings (dollars)[b]	Mean schooling (years)
Total	50,211	7675	4242	10.0
Whites/North	33,005	4745	4700	10.4
14–24	3719	393	2466	11.0
25–34	6345	232	5058	11.8
35–44	7179	282	6326	11.3
45–54	6232	326	6042	10.3
55–64	4519	535	5019	9.1
65–99	5011	2977	1620	7.6
Whites/South	12,186	1956	3838	9.6
14–24	1762	244	1885	10.2
25–34	2382	96	4306	11.0
35–44	2612	120	5373	10.4
45–54	2161	176	4949	9.5
55–64	1579	266	4099	8.5
65–99	1690	1054	1179	7.3
Nonwhites/North	2357	431	2941	8.4
14–24	326	77	1588	10.1
25–34	536	59	3216	10.3
35–44	557	46	3927	9.4
45–54	441	48	3390	7.7
55–64	260	59	2795	6.3
65–99	237	142	1185	5.4
Nonwhites/South	2663	543	1586	6.6
14–24	467	81	1087	8.4
25–34	511	54	2006	8.4
35–44	533	52	2130	7.0
45–54	478	48	1993	5.9
55–64	325	71	1493	4.7
65–99	349	237	338	3.7

[a] Source: *Thesis*, Table 2.
[b] Mean earnings for all persons, including persons with no earnings.

Within each of the groups we estimated a separate linear regression equation of earnings (in dollars, including zero for persons with no earnings) on 23 explanatory variables, most of which were in dummy-variable form. These include (1) seven schooling-group variables (representing differences between eight school levels); (2) age (both a continuous variable for exact age and a dummy variable defined on the lower half of the group's age interval—e.g., a variable having the value 1 for age 25–29 and 0 for age 30–34 within a group of age 25–34);[3] (3) type of residence—size

---

[3] The inclusion of both a continuous and a dummy form allows for two linear segments with a common slope but different intercepts.

of place (in logs), and dummy variables for six groups defined as urban–rural–nonfarm–rural farm, inside or outside a metropolitan area; (4) origin (foreign-born parents, born in a different region); (5) mobility (length of time in a given place, change of residence since 1955, and also birth in a different region), and some family attributes—(6) marital status, (7) size of family, (8) number of children.[4]

The next step in estimating the earnings function was to combine the fragmentary results of the separate regressions into a unified earnings-age profile for each school level, within each of the four major race-region groups. First the net earnings (y) are estimated within each age-schooling group, by choosing appropriate values for the other explanatory variables $(\mathcal{Z})$ in each regression equation.

There are two types of $\mathcal{Z}$-variables: (1) variables expected to vary with age, which should not be "held constant" among age groups (e.g., marital status, number of children); these were given their mean value in the specific age group considered; and (2) variables which may be correlated with age fortuitously in the given cross-sectional sample but which are not intrinsically associated with age (e.g., type of residence and origin variables). These were given the mean value of the total race-region group—i.e., of all age groups combined. It was decided not to hold constant any variable among race-regions, but to regard the race-regions as independent populations. Thus, $\mathcal{Z}$ is held constant among schooling groups in a given race-region, and sometimes among its various age groups; but comparisons are not made with another race-region by fixing a constant distribution of type of residence or family characteristics, e.g., in all race-regions.[5]

Using these methods and values, we estimated eight different earnings-age profiles, corresponding to the eight school levels, within each race-region. Each of these profiles, in turn, was constructed from disconnected linear segments, representing the relation between earnings and age for that school level, as estimated by the specific age-group regression. It does not seem reasonable to assume that such a collection of fragmentary segments may adequately represent the expected earnings function $y(s,t;\mathcal{Z})$. If it is desired to quantify and formalize an individual's vague expectations about his future earnings at given alternative school levels, or if the earnings function were to represent the average behavior for a relatively large and stable homogeneous group, then smooth and well-behaved profiles could be expected. Because there is no reason to believe that the discontinuities and

[4] See *Thesis*, Table 3 and Appendix A, for detailed definitions of variables and some regression results.

[5] Such a procedure would, however, be appropriate for other purposes, such as the analysis of net regional or racial differentials in earnings. But for the estimation of internal rates of return it is more reasonable to assume that an individual who forms his expectations about earnings at future ages will base these expectations on conditions prevailing among people of his own race and region rather than among the total U.S. population.

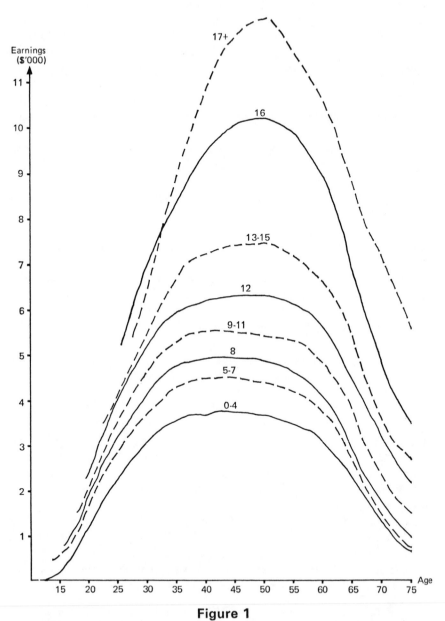

Figure 1
Estimated Earnings by Age and Schooling: Whites/North

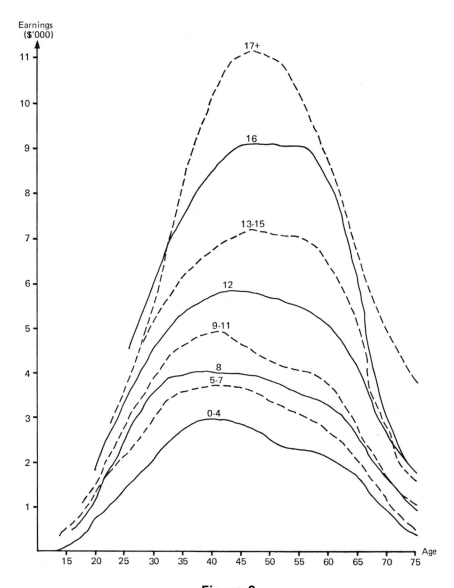

Figure 2
Estimated Earnings by Age and Schooling: Whites/South

irregularities manifested by the estimated profiles represent any real and stable phenomenon, the profiles were transformed into smooth curves by using moving averages of the original estimated earnings at each single year of age. The form of the moving average was a simple mean of ten years, centered at the sixth year. This achieved reasonable smoothness, while preserving the general shape of the original profiles.

These estimated profiles, which serve as our best estimates of the earnings function of persons out of school, are summarized in Table 2, which shows, for each schooling level in a race-region, the smoothed estimated profiles at selected ages. Figures 1 and 2 describe the complete profiles for whites, in the North and the South, respectively.

Earnings are given, on the average, only for ages above those when each school level is completed. To estimate the average postcompletion ages, the age distribution of persons enrolled in school was computed for each level completed. The integral age closest to the mean, plus one year, was selected as the age of entrance to the labor market. These ages are as follows:

Years of school completed:	0–4	5–7	8	9–11	12	13–15	16	17+
Age at first year out of school:	10	14	16	18	20	23	26	28

To complete this estimation of the earnings function, the earnings profiles should be supplemented with estimates of two types of earnings of persons attending school: the positive earnings of students who work during the school year or during vacations, and the negative, direct, private costs of education. In principle these estimates could be made separately and then combined to give average net earnings.

We did not have adequate data concerning the direct costs of education, classified by age, school level, race, and region, ordinarily required for this sort of analysis. In fact, even such detailed data would not be sufficient for our purposes, because such costs would have to be adjusted for other factors, as was done for earnings out of school. For example, it would be desirable to adjust the costs for differences in type and size of place of residence, for origin, or for mobility. Refined data of this nature might be derived from a special detailed survey of individual schooling expenditures or by the compilation of the required information in a future census. Making use of the crude data available today seems neither useful nor desirable, since it may only bias and blur our results. However, other studies based on more aggregative and crude data revealed that the average, direct, private costs of one year in school are nearly equal to the average yearly earnings of

Table 2—Estimated expected earnings at selected ages by schooling in race-region: persons out of school, 1959[a]

				YEARS OF SCHOOL COMPLETED				
Age	0–4	5–7	8	9–11	12	13–15	16	17+
				Whites/North				
14	69	253						
18	670	1073	1174	1306				
22	1574	2131	2301	2519	2930			
27	2570	3160	3498	3924	4461	4558	5602	
37	3672	4397	4809	5398	6052	7019	8713	9578
47	3717	4466	4967	5478	6281	7745	10,109	12,138
57	3404	4092	4506	5292	6023	7393	9677	11,398
67	1840	2083	2382	3079	3897	4493	5969	8019
77	465	514	733	1213	1916	2151	3101	4931
				Whites/South				
14	46	332						
18	429	957	926	1151				
22	1020	1745	1828	2052	2454			
27	1767	2655	3022	3233	3847	4246	4965	
37	2860	3665	4004	4780	5520	6448	7992	9027
47	2775	3658	3950	4572	5802	7215	9109	11,146
57	2365	3060	3633	4008	5475	7018	8981	9665
67	1257	1595	2073	2258	3370	3611	4228	5905
77	230	415	727	820	1584	1332	1357	3258
				Nonwhites/North				
14	63	571						
18	510	1338	646	757				
22	1586	2175	1529	1736	2122			
27	3021	2711	2337	2705	3201	2866	3249	
37	2879	3310	3197	3618	3989	3876	5146	7834
47	2898	3362	3412	3608	4305	4183	4480	9129
57	2503	2763	3674	2984	3361	3551	2543	6561
67	1385	1409	1942	1917	1896	1983	1139	2241
77	697	625	824	1191	1100	1085	514	557
				Nonwhites/South				
14	91	340						
18	475	823	607	757				
22	960	1280	1146	1284	1420			
27	1459	1691	1775	1874	1976	1832	2169	
37	1924	1870	2159	2166	2597	2679	3986	3112
47	1785	1969	2197	2134	2868	2621	3260	3920
57	1495	1654	2128	2144	2091	2275	1827	4178
67	572	635	970	819	667	1725	575	2724
77	171	212	391	199	169	1178	171	1664

[a] Source: *Thesis*, Table 4. At spaces with no entry, persons of that age are enrolled in school. In dollars.

students, especially at the college level.[6] There is good reason to believe that these two magnitudes move in the same direction:

First, the higher the level of schooling, the higher the private costs and the higher the average student earnings. In elementary school, both costs (in public schools, which include a large majority of the elementary school students) and earnings are negligible. In high school, both increase— usually concomitantly with the class attended. In college, many students have sizeable earnings, especially during the summer quarter; but costs are also high.[7]

Second, student earnings and their average, direct, private costs tend to vary in the same direction among population groups. For example, non-whites usually spend less than whites on tuition and on other direct-cost items, and they enroll in higher proportions than do whites in the less expensive public schools; but their earnings are also lower, owing to lower wages and limited employment opportunities.

In view of the lack of detailed cost data and the apparent proximity of the two magnitudes, we assumed that earnings and direct costs cancel each other out in each of the student groups analyzed here at all levels of schooling. This implies that the net earnings during school are expected to equal zero in all cases, as indeed we assumed throughout the following analysis.[8]

It is not easy to evaluate the quality of the resulting estimates given in Table 2. The statistical process of their derivation is so complicated that appropriate confidence intervals could not be estimated by any direct method, although some extended simulation analysis would be useful in clarifying this aspect. However, statistical variability appears to be of a second order of importance, relative to more basic omissions and in-adequacies of the data and of the estimation procedure. The most signi-ficant deficiencies of these estimates are discussed below, relative to the evaluation of rates of return to schooling derived from these estimates.

However, the limitations, reservations, and shortcomings (some of which seem unsurmountable in any empirical study), should not be over-emphasized to the point of discarding meaningful and valuable information

[6] Gary S. Becker, *Human Capital*, Columbia University Press, 1964 (referred to as *Becker*), Chap. iv, p. 75, and Appendix A, sec. 2. The earnings of college students are estimated by Becker to amount to 25 percent of the earnings of high school graduates not attending school. The remaining 75 percent are "foregone earnings," which constitute 76 percent of total cost. Hence, total costs are about equal to total earnings out of school, and direct costs are about equal to earnings during school.

[7] In graduate school, however, earnings from all sources may exceed direct private costs, because many students receive fellowships and scholarships.

[8] However, if better data about direct costs became available, it would be desirable to match them with data concerning students' earnings. For this purpose, estimates of student earnings were carried out separately, but are not given here. Cf. *Thesis*, Table 5, and pp. 64–68.

ın the name of purity. One can fill only a few gaps at a time, utilizing whatever information is available, while acknowledging its limitations and interpreting the results accordingly.

II Rates of Return and the Demand for Schooling

The earnings-age profiles estimated above for various schooling levels are used to derive the internal rates of return in Table 3.

Table 3—Estimates of private internal rates of return among schooling levels by race and region [a]

Higher schooling level in each comparison	\multicolumn{7}{c}{LOWER SCHOOLING LEVEL IN EACH COMPARISON}
	0–4	5–7	8	9–11	12	13–15	16
\multicolumn{8}{c}{Whites/North}
5–7	[b]						
8	[b]	.218					
9–11	.474	.185	.163				
12	.331	.175	.161	.160			
13–15	.196	.125	.111	.097	.071		
16	.170	.124	.115	.107	.096	.122	
17+	.144	.110	.103	.096	.087	.095	.070
\multicolumn{8}{c}{Whites/South}
5–7	[b]						
8	[b]	.144					
9–11	.662	.162	.182				
12	.441	.172	.186	.188			
13–15	.274	.139	.138	.127	.093		
16	.216	.131	.128	.120	.101	.110	
17+	.179	.118	.114	.107	.092	.091	.073
\multicolumn{8}{c}{Nonwhites/North}
5–7	[b]						
8	.06	.01					
9–11	.13	.03	.23				
12	.18	.06	.23	.22			
13–15	.07	.03	.07	.04	[c]		
16	(.07)	(.03)	(.07)	(.04)	[d]	(.08)	
17+	(.12)	(.09)	(.13)	(.12)	(.10)	(.16)	(.23)
\multicolumn{8}{c}{Nonwhites/South}
5–7	.89						
8	.27	.06					
9–11	.22	.06	.10				
12	.17	.08	.11	.12			
13–15	(.13)	(.08)	(.09)	(.09)	(.07)		
16	(.11)	(.07)	(.08)	(.08)	(.06)	(.07)	
17+	(.08)	(.06)	(.06)	(.06)	(.05)	(.06)	(.05)

[a] Adjusted for various factors. Source: *Thesis*, Table 6. Numbers in parentheses were based on too few observations to be reliable.

[b] Rate was above 1 (extremely high in most cases).

[c] Negative rate (−.05).

[d] Multiple solutions, with no rate between −0.1 and 1.0.

For each pair of schooling levels in a major race-region group, the rate indicated in the table is the average rate of return on the amount of schooling, which is the difference between the two levels. It is that rate of discount which equates the present values of the two corresponding earning streams at a given age. When related to adjacent schooling levels (e.g., eight and nine-to-11 years of school), it could be regarded as a marginal rate of return, where the marginal unit is the difference in years between adjacent levels (two years, in most cases). Hence, the relation between the rates appearing on a diagonal in Table 3 and the amount of schooling in the corresponding row could be regarded as approximating the marginal efficiency of investment in schooling, when investment is measured in school years.[9] It is, therefore, the demand for schooling in that group.

Before the results of Table 3 are interpreted, some of the technical and conceptual shortcomings and deficiencies of these results should be examined.

A unique solution for an internal rate obtains only where the two profiles intersect just once. In some cases of multiple intersections, we chose arbitrarily the economically meaningful solution and discarded irrelevant solutions such as negative rates.[10]

Cases of multiple solutions are more common among groups of nonwhites for two reasons. First, the higher sampling variability of the estimated profiles increases the probability of intersecting profiles. Second, smaller earning differences, which are associated with lower returns to schooling, decrease the stability of the solutions, increase their sensitivity to minor variations in the earnings profiles, and hence also increase the probability of multiple intersections. Any irregularity in the estimated earnings function is reflected and even emphasized by computing internal rates of return. The estimated profiles of nonwhites are less reliable statistically (owing to much smaller sample sizes, but apparently also to the lower quality of the data); but they also seem closer to one another, because of generally lower returns to schooling in these groups.

In general, we would be inclined to have more confidence in the earnings profiles estimated above than in the numerical values of the internal rates discussed here. The values computed for internal rates seem to be highly sensitive to exactly those elements of the earnings profiles which are the least accurate and the most vulnerable to omissions and biases—i.e.,

---

[9] The rates in each column can be interpreted as a schedule of average productivity. The quantitative relations between marginal and average rates are similar to the relations found in general between average and marginal magnitudes.

[10] These obtain whenever the earnings differences between the two schooling groups reverse their normal sign at old age, and these future "losses" are weighed more heavily than current or near-future "gains." In a money-economy with positive interest rates this is not acceptable, although such negative old-age differences are definitely possible—e.g., if persons with higher education retire earlier than less educated persons.

mainly the measured net earnings at young ages, during the schooling period and shortly thereafter. In addition to the lack of data on schooling costs and the crude assumptions used here instead, reporting errors are more common among youngsters, whose employment and wages are less stable. Their reported earnings in the year of leaving the school are applicable in many cases to only a fraction of the year, or to a partial source of earnings. The computed rates are also sensitive to the exact length of the schooling period and the exact age of entry into the labor force—both determined here on the basis of crude estimates.[11] The general under-reporting of earnings may also bias the results, especially if associated with the level of schooling.

In addition to these statistical and technical reservations, many remaining conceptual and theoretical qualifications require clarification before these results can be used for economic analysis. It is not our intention to dwell at length on these qualifications, nor do we intend to use outside information and additional assumptions to modify the numerical results with various adjustments and corrections. Because of inadequate data, such adjustments cannot be complete; however, a partial adjustment may increase rather than decrease the over-all bias. Furthermore, adjustments and modifications may also mask the results of this particular sample, introducing a higher degree of arbitrariness, subjective judgment, and uncertainty concerning the source and reliability of these results.[12] For all these reasons, it seems preferable to list briefly the important biases, but to leave the numerical results intact.

The more important biases inherent in the estimated profiles and rates of return are those associated with ability. There is probably a significant positive correlation between ability to earn income—a combination of natural and acquired ability traits—and the level of schooling achieved. This obviously leads to a positive bias in the differentials between schooling levels and in rates of return to schooling.

Nonpecuniary returns (positive or negative), which are not measured as earnings, are another source of serious bias. Some of the variables used to estimate the earning function may have partially accounted for such factors (e.g., type of residence), but only to a limited extent. The consumption aspect of the schooling activity itself is also a form of nonpecuniary element. The over-all effect of all the various forms of nonpecuniary elements

---

[11] This, however, seems to be less arbitrary than the procedure chosen in various studies, where it is assumed that one school year corresponds to one actual year of age, with no allowance for late-comers and older graduates. In fact, the difference in ages of completion may account for many of the differences in estimated rates of return between this and other studies. See *Becker*, p. 162.

[12] However, the interested reader may estimate approximately the effect of each kind of adjustment on the resulting internal rates by inspecting its effect on the rates in another study in which such an adjustment was actually carried out.

on the rates of return is unknown and difficult to evaluate, especially because many of these elements are not measurable or even quantifiable (such as status, satisfaction from learning, etc.).

Additional modifications of the rates of return are required in principle to adjust for mortality, for expected secular growth in incomes, for improvements over time in productivity and in the quality of schooling, for cyclical variations in earnings, for expected changes in relative supply and demand of various skills, for the progressive taxation of earnings, and for differences in the cost of living. These modifications, applied to the cross-sectional results, would accord with the theory that individuals and groups base their expectations about earnings not on conditions at a point in time among different age and schooling groups, but rather on the economic experience of cohorts over their lifetime.

Finally, it should be emphasized that the rates of return estimated and analyzed here are strictly private rates of return. Extensive modifications are required if one wishes to derive from them social rates of return, which take into account the considerable external effects of schooling.

Keeping in mind the drawbacks and limitations of these rates of return (Table 3), one may first examine the rates within the groups of whites. Although their order of magnitude is lower than usually claimed, it is considerably higher than rates of interest in the market and somewhat higher than average rates of return generally estimated for nonhuman capital.[13] The average rate for high school (relative to grade school or to high school dropouts: 12 against 8 or 9–11 years of school) is 16 percent for whites in the North and 19 percent in the South.[14]

College dropouts (13–15 vs. 12 years) showed relatively low marginal rates, as would be expected—7 and 9 percent in the North and South, respectively. The completion of college (16 vs. 13–15 years) shows return rates of 12 and 11 percent, respectively, although the average rate between college and high school (16 vs. 12) is only about 10 percent in both regions.[15]

The marginal rate of return to graduate school (dropouts and graduates, 17+ vs. 16 years) is surprisingly low: 7 percent in both regions. The

[13] See George S. Stigler, *Capital and Rates of Return in Manufacturing Industries* (Princeton: NBER, 1963).

[14] Becker estimated rates of 16 percent for 1939 and 20 percent for 1949 cohorts of white males. The rates estimated by him for 1956, 1958, and 1959 were 25, 28, and 28 percent, respectively, for all males. The methods used were extremely crude, however, and based on survey rather than census data. The rate for 1959 was roughly estimated by inspection of earning differences between a survey in 1958 and summary tables of the 1960 Census (*Becker*, p. 128).

[15] Becker estimates this as 15 percent for all males. (*Ibid.*) However, besides all the other differences in detail, sources, and methods, the rates are not comparable owing to his inclusion of all graduate school entrants and graduates in the college-graduate group (*Ibid.*, p. 74).

assumption that direct costs equal student earnings may require more qualification in this case than at other levels, because many more students in graduate school get tuition scholarships and fellowships which are currently not reported as earnings. Nevertheless, it seems clear that the high earnings foregone by these students during school attendance reduce the attraction of graduate school as an economic investment, in spite of the large future returns.

Returns to the very low levels of education (5–7 and 8 vs. 0–4) are extremely high, mainly because of the negligible magnitude of both direct and indirect school costs at these levels. In fact, all levels of schooling, including graduate school, seem to bear very high returns relative to the level of virtually no education (0–4 years, the first column in the table). However, adjustment for differential ability might reduce these rates considerably.

In contrast, the last year of grade school bears significantly lower marginal returns than the fifth-to-seventh years, especially in the South. The marginal rates are 21.8 percent in the North, but only 14.4 in the South. The latter figure may reflect the fact that young boys dropping out of grade school before completion often stay home or are unemployed in most of the country, but go to work in the South, thus increasing the foregone earnings component of costs and reducing the estimated rates of return.

Except for this last case, there seems to be a definite tendency for rates of return to whites to be higher in the South than in the North.[16] This probably reflects the relative shortage of skills in the South. Another explanation may be found in the lower costs per school year in the South, as explained below. However, the difference in the rates among regions is negligible at the university level (especially 17+ vs. 16 years).

The internal rates of return for nonwhites are generally low and relatively erratic, as was anticipated in view of the irregular nature of the estimated earnings profiles in these groups. Additional data and more extensive analysis might indicate whether these results merit any serious consideration.

The marginal rates appearing in the diagonals of Table 3, particularly the far more reliable rates estimated for whites, reveal a downward trend— i.e., the higher the amount of schooling, the lower the marginal internal rate. This seems to verify the conjecture that the marginal efficiency of investment in schooling is decreasing. Individuals would thus tend to increase their amount of schooling if the supply of investment funds shifted to the right, or if the marginal internal discount rate applicable to them were to decrease.

[16] This is also a main finding in: Gary S. Becker and Barry R. Chiswick, "Education and the Distribution of Earnings," *American Economic Review* (May 1966, pp. 358–69).

So far, the analysis has been restricted to the investment in education measured by a single dimension—namely, years of school. To convert the marginal efficiency schedule or the demand for schooling to conform with common economic usage, the estimated internal rates of return should be related to the amount invested in dollars.[17] This transformation could be effected by attributing to each level of schooling the total direct and indirect cost of completing that level—i.e., the total amount of money invested. This would give rise to a different schedule, in which the investment-axis would be transformed from years into dollars. A schedule thus transformed should be cautiously interpreted, however. It is valid only for the "extensive" margin of investment in schooling and not for the "intensive" margin—i.e., it depicts the internal rate as a function of the money invested if variations in this amount occur by varying the number of school years completed. If, on the other hand, increases in the total amount invested by an individual occur through increases in the amount invested *per school year* (e.g., by a rise in tuitions or in the wages and employment opportunities of comparable persons outside the school—constituting a rise in foregone earnings—or by increase in the average distance traveled to school), then the rates of return applicable to these increasing investments may be totally different from the rates estimated here. This is because many additional restrictions are imposed on the one margin that are not imposed on the other. In most instances, changes in costs per year are not subject to a student's determination and choice; individuals may be forced out of an optimal position into one with larger deviations from the desired rate of return than those imposed in the other margin (of changing the number of school years). In some respects, however, individuals may be responsible for the "intensity" of costs per year (e.g., by transferring to a more expensive school or by hiring a private tutor), in which case they would probably equate the marginal rate in both margins.[18] In such situations the demand estimated above, expressed in dollars, would be applicable to intensive variations as well.

The discussion above was intended not as a digression from the main course of this analysis, but to clarify the comparison of demand schedules estimated for distinct groups. Attention is focused here on the differences between the four major race-region groups. One may assume for the sake

[17] Actual estimates of total costs for each level, as implied by the estimated earnings function, were not presented here—in view of the crude nature of the assumption about direct costs. They may be estimated on the basis of the earnings profiles given in *Thesis*, Table 4. However, the numerical values of these costs are immaterial for the present general discussion.

An extensive discussion of the correct measurement of these costs is given by *Becker*, pp. 39–48.

[18] That is, if we assume that individuals are in equilibrium on the extensive margin—e.g., that they have the desired number of school years.

of simplification that the following features obtain for the demand curves of the four race-region groups, abstracting from the necessary qualifications and modifications: (1) all these curves are downward-sloping; (2) in each region the schedule for whites is higher than for nonwhites; and (3) among whites, rates of return are higher in the South than in the North at low and medium school levels. It is also assumed that the intensive margin (of increasing costs per year of school) gives rise to the same schedules as the extensive margin (of increasing the number of years of school).

Given these assumptions and broad generalizations, one may inquire what factors cause the levels of marginal efficiency of investment to vary among different groups with the same number of school years invested? These may be classified into three major types of factors: quality of schooling, marginal market discrimination, and ability—in a broad sense.

The first factor—quality of schooling—implies differences among groups in the financial value of the units "years of school." These may represent differences in private investment per school year, differences in social investment accompanying them, or differences in the efficiency of these investments.[19]

The private investment for the same number of school years may be less for one group than for another. Hence, conversion of the schooling axis from units of years to dollars of private investment will shift to the *left* —or decrease—the demand schedule of the group with the lower costs per school year.[20] This might explain the higher rates of return estimated for whites in the South, compared with the North, since private costs per school year are probably lower in the South. Thus, rates corresponding to *equal investment in dollars* may be approximately equal in the two regions. Similarly, the discrepancy between whites and nonwhites in rates of return for equal investment is probably *greater* than that measured for equal schooling, because nonwhite students have, on the average, lower costs per year and thus get more school years per dollar privately invested. A conversion of the investment axis to dollars would cause a relative shift to the *left* of the lower nonwhite schedule, so that a larger difference between the rates of return would obtain at a given financial investment.

Presumably, social investment is positively correlated with private investment per school year, and perhaps also with the efficiency, or embodied quality, of these investments—all three factors being associated with "quality." Hence, standardizing the amount invested by its conversion

[19] Efficiency may be defined here as real inputs applied in a school year, per unit of money spent on that year. It is *not* the marginal efficiency of investment as measured by its effect on incomes. A definition of quality of schooling based on the marginal returns from schooling would defeat its own purpose, of course.

[20] In addition to a shift in the level, this transformation would most probably change the slope and the shape of the schedules, because of a correlation between cost-differentials and schooling. This, however, will not affect the general conclusions drawn here.

from units of school years to units of comparable quality (i.e., the comparable real amount of inputs to the school) will again shift to the left the demand for schooling of the lower-quality groups who have invested less per year (e.g., nonwhites). When the differences between the private rates of return to the two groups is evaluated at an equal amount of "standard schooling," it is *greater* than when evaluated at an equal number of years. Surprisingly, therefore, it appears that differences in the quality of schooling cannot "explain away" the fact that rates of return for whites are higher than for nonwhites.[21]

The second factor, market discrimination, depresses one group's private rates of return if the market price paid for services decreases, relative to the price paid for comparable services to the other groups, as the level of education increases. It is important to note, however, that if discrimination affects all school levels equally, its existence per se ("average discrimination") may not affect the rates of return at all. Discrimination may even increase the marginal rate of return if foregone earnings are depressed by the same (absolute) amount as earnings at every age and school level. It is only an *increase in the degree of discrimination* with increased education, or a *marginal* discrimination, which can diminish the rate of return from schooling.[22] Thus, one may conclude that, if nonwhites' rates of return and demand for schooling are lower than those for whites because of discrimination in the labor market, this must be a *marginal* discrimination which is greater for persons with more education than for those with less. Whether such marginal discrimination exists is open to further study and requires additional information.

Ability, the third factor which causes differences between rates of return among race-region groups, comprises all the inherited and acquired traits which differ among groups and which are neither acquired in school nor eliminated by the schooling process—as far as these traits affect the efficient utilization of a real investment toward increasing earnings. Education and training outside the school, motivation, innate ability, taste—in short, all social, psychological, and biological factors affecting a group's economic efficiency—should be included. If one is inclined to emphasize the environmental and social factors, then the disparity between rates of return to schooling in the two racial groups can be attributed entirely to some form of discrimination against nonwhites occurring in the schools, in the current labor market, or in the accumulated social burden.

---

[21] The conclusion in the text is valid only when the true marginal efficiency curve, correctly adjusted for biases and for dynamic elements, is indeed downward-sloping, both for the "extensive" margin and the for "intensive" one. If investment in social outlays *per year* of schooling is in a stage of rising marginal efficiency, this and similar results would not obtain. I am indebted to Professor T. W. Schultz for drawing my attention to this point.

[22] Cf. *Becker*, pp. 96–100.

III Conclusions

In conclusion, it should be stressed that the above estimates and analysis refer to *private* rates of return and the private demand for schooling. The application of these to society requires modification of the estimated rates of return to take into account social costs and benefits, as well as the establishment of a criterion (such as a social rate of discount) for evaluating these social rates of return and for determining the desirability of additional schooling for a given group. However, any policy measures based on this evaluation must be made according to the determinants of private interest and return rates—so as to induce individuals to adapt their own behavior pattern to the socially desirable one. Hence, it is clear that the individual private rates and the associated private demand functions for schooling are essential data for the evaluation and determination of social decisions. The present study should thus be construed as a modest basis for a more complete analysis of income-determination and of decisions about education, from both the private and the social points of view.

19

Some Evidence on the Private Returns to Graduate Education

Burgeoning enrollments in graduate schools constitute a major change in most universities across the country in recent years. In the following selection, Professor Orley Ashenfelter of Princeton University and the late Joseph Mooney evaluate the private rate of return to graduate education. The data used are drawn from Woodrow Wilson Fellows

ORLEY ASHENFELTER
JOSEPH D. MOONEY

recently attending graduate school. This article, instructive in a methodological as well as factual context, distinguishes between internal rates of return for Ph.D.'s in the humanities, social sciences, and natural sciences.

I Introduction

The objective of this study is to present estimates of the private rates of return to various levels and types ("products") of graduate education in the arts and sciences. Although the seminal work of T. W. Schultz and Gary Becker spawned a good deal of research on the "economics of education," the lack of adequate data has heretofore severely limited work in the area of graduate education. Probably, the most novel contribution of this study stems from the nature and characteristics of our sample. The sample consists entirely of respondents who have experienced some graduate education and who are of approximately equal intellectual ability. In a later section, the characteristics of the sample will be delineated in more detail.

Reprinted from Orley Ashenfelter and Joseph D. Mooney, "Some Evidence on the Private Returns to Graduate Education," *Southern Economic Journal* 35 (January 1969), pp. 247–56, with the permission of the authors and publisher.

Why should a study of the returns to graduate education be undertaken at this juncture? In the first place, graduate enrollments in the arts and sciences have expanded very rapidly in recent years.[1] The decision to attend graduate school or not has become an increasingly relevant one for a growing segment of Bachelor Degree holders. Hopefully, some of the economic ramifications of this decision will be illuminated by the results of this study. Secondly, throughout the "returns to education" literature there runs a lament about the need for a sample of people of approximately equal intellectual ability in order to perform correctly the typical "returns to education" analysis. Although certain previous studies have made Herculean attempts to control for ability in order to isolate the effects of education *per se* on earnings, none of these has been entirely satisfactory. This study is the first to examine a cohort of highly talented and more or less equally able respondents.

The format of the paper is as follows: Section II is a brief summary of the limited research in this area, Section III discusses the nature of the sample, Section IV examines methodology and the basic rate of return and present value results and Section V concludes with a summary of our findings and their major implications.

II Summary of Existing Research

In one of the earliest attempts to estimate the returns to graduate education, Shane Hunt (1963) used the Time Magazine College Graduate Study of 1947. By means of a number of ingenious adjustments, Hunt tries to control for such factors as ability level and occupation in constructing his estimates of the returns to graduate education. For high ability people, Hunt finds that the private rates of return to $3\frac{1}{4}$ years of graduate education range from 1% (occupation-education) to 3.2% (occupation-business) with government work in the middle at 1.8%. The basic fault with this part of Hunt's study (which he readily admits) is his small sample size. Hunt's sample contains information on only 221 persons with the equivalent of $3\frac{1}{2}$ years of graduate education. After he controls for such variables as ability and occupation, the number of observations in the relevant cells is extremely small. Furthermore, he is simply unable to control for field of graduate study or graduate degree level. Lastly, because he uses the 1947 *Time* data, many of those in his sample had been to graduate school over 30 years ago. The authors believe that there is a genuine question about the relevance of his findings with respect to graduate education *today*.

---

[1] According to estimates provided by the National Science Foundation, graduate enrollments in the arts and sciences increased from 73,178 in 1954 to 218,855 in 1964. Thus, graduate enrollments virtually tripled in one decade.

Giora Hanoch (1965, 1967) presents more up-to-date estimates of the private internal rate of return to graduate education. Using the 1/1000 sample from the 1960 census and running multiple regressions with a number of relevant control variables, Hanoch is able to construct earnings profiles for those with 17+ years of education.[2] Hanoch's best estimate of the "internal" private rate of return to 17+ years of education (i.e., as compared with only 16 years) is approximately 7%. Although our results based on survey data are generally consistent with Hanoch's results based on census data, there are many questions left unanswered by his study. In particular, the nature of the census data does not allow explicit consideration of different combinations of graduate degree level and graduate schooling as separate types of educational investment. Hence, questions about the profitability of different lengths of graduate training, of different types of graduate degrees attained, and of graduate work within disciplines simply cannot be raised. Hanoch's estimate of the rate of return to 17+ years of schooling can therefore best be considered as a rate of return to an average of many different types and lengths of graduate study.

Finally, a report by Irene Butter (1966) has recently become available. This study is largely concerned with estimation of the total resource costs of graduate education in four academic disciplines (Physics, Zoology, Sociology, and English). Drawing on salary data from the National Science Foundation's *National Register of Scientific and Technical Personnel* (1964), Butter computes social internal rates of return to Ph.D. holders in these same disciplines and occupations. Her most refined estimates of the social internal rates of return for Ph.D.'s over B.A.'s, averaged across occupations are .1% (English), 1.9% (Sociology), 5.2% (Physics) and 8.0% (Zoology). Since the goal of this study was to estimate social internal rates of return, almost nothing is said about the issue of private internal rates of return or the concomitant economic implications regarding a personal investment in graduate schooling.

III The Sample

Our sample consists of a cohort of recent Woodrow Wilson Fellows—. all males and all elected from 1958 to 1960. Woodrow Wilson fellowships are awarded to first year graduate students in the arts and sciences— approximately 75 percent of all awards given to graduate students in the Humanities and Social Sciences and the remainder to those in the Natural Sciences. The selection procedure is carried out nationwide (regional quotas

[2] Hanoch's estimates of the coefficients for the age variables for those with 17+ years of education were derived after controlling for the following variables: Race, Geographic Region, Residence, Size of Place of Residence, Length of Time in Place, Family Size, Number of Children, Marital Status, Foreign Born and Born in South.

being used to some extent), and, aside from the obvious academic qualifications, candidates need only express an interest in college teaching as a future career in order to qualify for a fellowship.

Fortunately, the Woodrow Wilson National Fellowship Foundation of Princeton, New Jersey, maintains detailed background records on all Fellows and keeps their records current by means of an annual mail questionnaire. Longitudinal information for each Fellow is thus available on the number of years spent in residence at a graduate school, the year in which a degree was received, the Fellows' present employment, his field of graduate study, etc. In mid-1966, all male Woodrow Wilson Fellows who were members of the three classes elected from 1958 to 1960 were asked via a mail questionnaire their first and present annual salaries. After a number of unusable responses were deleted, a sample of 1,322 people resulted.[3]

What are the advantages of this sample for a "returns to education" study? We believe that there are two general characteristics of this sample which make it ideal for use in a study of this kind. The essential homogeneity of this group is its first advantageous characteristic. All members possessed excellent undergraduate academic credentials.[4] In addition to this implicit control for ability, the respondents in this sample were of the same sex, generally the same age, and relatively recent entrants to the labor force.

The second important aspect of this sample pertains to the detailed information available on each respondent. We knew the occupation of the respondent, when and if he got a graduate degree, how long he spent in graduate school, his primary field of graduate study, how long he had been working full time, and relevant salary information. Blessed with such detailed information, we were able to estimate income differences for various groups after controlling for the relevant variables at our disposal. Also, we could permit interactions to occur among such variables as degree level, field

---

[3] Details on the non-respondents to the salary questionnaire are contained in Ashenfelter and Mooney (1968). On the basis of the information at our disposal, we have no reason to believe that any significant biases are introduced by the lack of salary data on the non-respondents.

[4] The computation of income differentials in this paper is based on our full sample of over 1,300 persons. In another paper the authors have shown that a variable explicitly measuring variations in ability within the sample was a significant determinant of income. The ability variable, however, was available for only about half of the observations in our sample and it was decided that more efficient parameter estimates could be obtained by dropping the ability variable and concentrating on the full sample. It is clear that this entails a specification error which will lead to bias in estimating the effects of education on income only if the variable left out is correlated with the included explanatory variables (see Arthur S. Goldberger, 1964, pp. 194–197). Not very surprisingly—since the sample is so very homogeneous—our measure of ability is almost orthogonal to the other independent variables in the regressions. The coefficient of determination between the dummy variables representing years of education and the ability variable, for example, is only .01. Further, a direct analysis of the specification error for the data available showed it to be small (see Ashenfelter and Mooney, 1968).

of study, and occupations so that we could determine, for example, whether the differential income due to obtaining a Ph.D. was independent of the field of study or occupation that a person entered.

The drawback to the use of this sample for estimating *lifetime* returns to educational investment is, of course, that it contains observations on only the first few years of the lifetime income profile. This is a serious problem which admits of no easy solution. If cross-sectional observations were available on the complete lifetime income profile, the individuals involved would generally not be homogeneous with respect to variables which the investigator cannot control (e.g., ability). Worse yet, there is some doubt whether a given educational attainment, as measured, would be similar from individual to individual. As mentioned in the next section, we have attempted to overcome this difficulty by the judicious combination of sample information with various assumptions about the shape of lifetime income profiles.

IV Methodology and Findings

METHODOLOGY

Since we had salary data for a group which on the average had been working only 2–3 years, the lack of a lifetime income profile represented a genuine problem. There are at least two possible solutions to this problem. First, it is possible to make careful estimates of the income differences for different groups at a particular point in time and then simply extrapolate this difference (the difference can also be allowed to grow or decline at a fixed rate) over their working lifetimes. The use of a number of alternative discount rates will then yield an array of present value estimates. This reasonable but crude approach is used for certain analyses in this paper. Secondly, if lifetime income profiles were available for people of different educational levels, one could combine this information on the shape of the profiles with more detailed sample information on their levels in order to arrive at fairly accurate *hypothetical* lifetime income profiles. Although reliable longitudinal income data for a large cohort of people with different educational levels is not available, it is possible to construct lifetime earnings profiles from the cross-section data available in the 1/1000 sample of the 1960 Census. Fortunately, from the authors' point of view this exercise has already been done by Giora Hanoch (1965, 1967). The great advantage of this source of data is that it allows one to consider complex interactions between age and various levels of education. Hence, one can concentrate on careful estimation of the time-profile of lifetime earnings.[5]

[5] The specific earnings-age profiles in Hanoch's study which we used were for whites in the North with 16 and 17+ years of education.

We next had to find a way to combine the results of our regressions with Hanoch's estimated earnings profiles. The first step was to "squeeze" the information on the shape of the earnings profiles into regression equations by fitting successively higher order polynomials in age. Using the joint criteria of goodness and randomness of fit (as judged by the conventional R^2 and the Durbin-Watson statistic), the authors settled on the following cubic expressions for those with 16 and 17 + years of schooling respectively:

$$\Upsilon = -19.255 + 1.3786A - .0189(A)^2 + .000061(A)^3 \tag{1}$$
$$R^2 = .977 \qquad D - W = 1.41$$

$$\Upsilon = -48.603 + 3.0108A - .0467(A)^2 + .000216(A)^3 \tag{2}$$
$$R^2 = .993 \qquad D - W = 1.55$$

where Υ is annual earnings (measured in thousands of dollars) and A is age. As would be expected, the maximum for equation (1) which takes place at age 47, occurs before the maximum for equation (2), which takes place at age 49.

Second, we estimated a regression equation with our own sample in order to arrive at projected income differences due to different combinations of schooling and degree level attainment during the early years of the lifetime earning process.[6] This regression contained dummy variables to control for Field of Graduate Study (Natural Sciences, Social Sciences, Humanities), Profession (College Teacher, Business and Government), and Number of Years Working. Since it did not appear meaningful to consider years of graduate education separately from graduate degree attained when estimating such an equation, a dummy variable for each possible combination of degree (B.A., Masters, Ph.D.) and length of graduate schooling (0–5 years) was inserted into the regression.[7] Multiplying the appropriate control variable regression coefficients by their sample means allowed the computation of average incomes for different degree-schooling educational combinations.[8] Use of the Years of Work coefficients also allowed us to obtain sliding estimates of gross foregone earnings which differed for each year of the educational process. Net foregone earnings were computed by subtracting

[6] Since the authors have reported elsewhere similar regressions, with associated measures of significance, intercorrelation, etc., (see Ashenfelter and Mooney, 1968) it was decided not to include these results here since they are unwieldy (the regression contains 21 independent variables) and not of central importance to the purpose of this paper. Full details of this regression, and other underlying the results herein, are available from the authors upon request.

[7] In order to increase the sample size of our basic reference group, those Bachelor degree holders with either zero or one year of recorded graduate education were grouped together. Careful inspection of the data by the authors suggested this introduced only a minor distortion of reality.

[8] Since sample means of dummy variables are proportions (i.e., of persons in the sample falling in the appropriate class), we are actually computing a weighted average.

$2,500 per year from the preceding estimates: a stipend of $1,500 for the academic year plus average summer earnings of $1,000.[9]

Finally, we recomputed the intercept terms of the cubic approximations to lifetime incomes by evaluating them at the relevant school leaving age plus two years (the average amount of work experience in the sample) and forcing the intercept of the cubic to take on a value which equated our independent estimate of the earnings profile for the first working years with the cubic approximation. The procedure maintains the same shape for the estimated lifetime earnings profile and only adjusts its level.[10]

PRESENT VALUE ESTIMATES

Figure 1 presents the incremental present value estimates at age 21 for graduate programs of varying lengths over the B.A. The discounting period has been taken through age 70 and no adjustments have been made for mortality or personal income taxes. It should be noted that these results pertain to Ph.D.'s who are "average" with respect to fields of graduate study and profession. In a sense, these represent our most general results. The major findings can be summarized briefly:

(a) Viewed as a investment project, the 3-year Ph.D. is unequivocally the most attractive program. At all relevant discount rates, the incremental present value of the 3-year Ph.D. is greater than that of any other program. The reason for this stems from the fact that our regression equation suggested no incremental income gains to the four or five year Ph.D. program compared to the foregone earnings associated with an additional year or two in graduate school.

(b) The 4-year Ph.D. program, a length of time for the Ph.D. which has become the goal of many graduate schools, fares rather well by comparison with the optimal three-year Ph.D. program (see Table I), while the five-year Ph.D. program is a relatively poor investment.

(c) Finally, we considered M.A.'s with two years of schooling separately because we felt that this group would contain largely those persons who were engaged from the outset in terminal programs. The comparison between the M.A. of 2 years with the Ph.D. of 5 years is extremely interesting. The choice between acquisition of an M.A. in 2 years and continuation in graduate school with the hope of acquiring a Ph.D. in 5 years or so is probably a very relevant one for many graduate students. In this context, our

[9] The $1,500 stipend equals the Woodrow Wilson Fellowship stipend and the $1,000 figure was our best estimate of summer earnings for graduate students.

[10] Symbolically, we pick $P(A) + K$ so that $P(A^0 + 2) + K = Y^0$, where $P(A)$ is the original cubic in age, A^0 is the school leaving age, K is a constant to be determined, and Y^0 is our estimate of the average income for a particular educational class at age $A^0 + 2$. Since $P(A)$ and $P(A) + K$ have identical derivatives the shapes of the two curves will be identical. We have assumed throughout that B.A.'s start work at 23, 3-year Ph.D.'s at 26, 4-year Ph.D.'s at 27, 5-year Ph.D.'s at 28, and M.A.'s at 25.

results depict a very plausible possibility: namely, at low discount rates, the Ph.D. in 5 years is more attractive financially than the M.A. in 2 years and vice-versa at higher discount rates. The crossing of the M.A. and 5-year Ph.D. curves depicts an interesting conceptual point. At interest rates below 5.4%, the 5-year Ph.D. program is unequivocally more profitable. However, the internal rate of return for the M.A. in 2 years is slightly higher than that for the 5-year Ph.D.

Private Internal Rates of Return

It is a simple matter to move from these present value estimates to estimates of the private internal rates of return. The private internal rate of return is simply that discount rate which equates the differential present value of income between doctorates and B.A.'s to zero. In Figure 1, the internal rate of return is represented by the point at which the curve of present value estimates crosses the horizontal axis. The upper half of Table 1 presents our original estimates of the private internal rates of

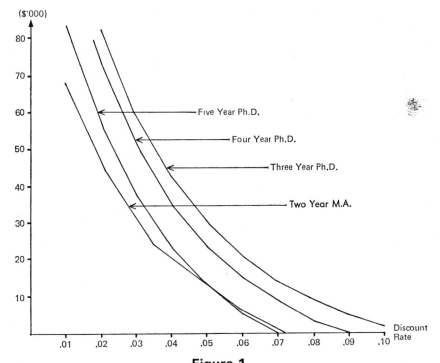

Figure 1
Incremental Present Values of Various Ph.D. and M.A. Programs over the B.A.

return to doctorate programs of varying lengths along with the confidence bands for these estimates. Even though our sample was one characterized by virtually "full information," we were well aware of the number of assumptions we had to make before arriving at our point estimates. Consequently, it was felt that a more realistic picture of the rates of return would be provided by constructing a confidence band bracketing the point estimates. These bands appear in parentheses below the point estimates in Table I.[11]

Table I—Private rates of return to Ph.D.'s and M.A.'s (and 95% confidence bands)

WITH ESTIMATED CURVILINEAR LIFETIME INCOME DIFFERENTIALS AVERAGE RATES BY DEGREE ONLY		
	M.A.	Ph.D.
B.A.	.065	0.088
	(.052, .079)	(.075, .100)

	BY DEGREE AND YEARS OF SCHOOLING			
	M.A. (2 yrs.)	Ph.D. (3 yrs.)	Ph.D. (4 yrs.)	Ph.D. (5 yrs.)
B.A.	.075	.108	.091	.071
	(.050, .101)	(.082, .135)	(.070, .113)	(.052, .089)

WITH ESTIMATED LINEAR LIFETIME INCOME DIFFERENTIALS AVERAGE RATES BY DEGREE ONLY		
	M.A.	Ph.D.
B.A.	.016	.063
	(−.050, .049)	(.041, .083)

	BY DEGREE AND YEARS OF SCHOOLING			
	M.A.	Ph.D. (3 yrs.)	Ph.D. (4 yrs.)	Ph.D. (5 yrs.)
B.A.	.048	.105	.070	.035
	(−...., .113)	(.057, .146)	(.030, .102)	(−.008, .064)

Since these results follow directly from our estimates of present values, it is not surprising that the internal rate of return for 3-year Ph.D.'s, (10.8%), is highest and that for the 5-year Ph.D. is lowest (7.1%). The most striking aspect of these results is their over-all high value. At the outset of this study, the authors believed that negative rates of return were well within the realm

[11] We call our interval estimates confidence "bands" because they should not be confused with true confidence "intervals," which can be defined only when exact knowledge of the distribution of the rate of return estimator is known. Our confidence bands were estimated by allowing the estimated lifetime earnings differences to vary by ± 2 standard errors and computing the two additional rates of return. A better, but still approximate estimator is derived in Hillier (1963).

of possibility. Recall that Hunt's estimates ranged from 1 to 3%, Hanoch's was 7%, and Butter's estimates of the social rates of return ranged from .1% to 8.0%. Clearly our estimates are generally rather high relative to those of other researchers.

As a result, we decided to reestimate the differential discounted income streams in the more orthodox fashion. Foregone earnings were estimated in exactly the same fashion described above. From our regressions, we could also estimate the present average income differential between a Ph.D. of 3, 4 or 5 years and a B.A. holding constant the same variables mentioned previously. The differential was then assumed to be constant over the remainder of their working life (22–70 years of age, 49 years in all). This method represents a naive approach for it assumes no change in the absolute income differentials of Ph.D.'s and B.A.'s.

The results can be quickly summarized. The absolute values of the present value estimates were reduced sharply. However, the shapes of the present value graphs remained essentially unchanged. The private rates of return were reduced across every cell (see the bottom half of Table I). The results contained in Table II suggest that a Master's degree in the arts and sciences has a very low rate of return compared to the B.A.[12]

Table II—Private rates of return for Ph.D.'s over B.A.'s by field and profession

| | PROFESSION | |
Field	College teacher	Non college teacher
Natural Science	.086	.066
Social Science	.053	.098
Humanities	.007	N.A.

Lastly, we will present our estimates of the internal rates of return to an "average" Ph.D. recipient by Field of Graduate Study and Profession (College Teacher vs. all others). By an "average" Ph.D. recipient, we mean anyone who has taken anywhere from 2 to 5 years to acquire a Ph.D. and who has been working from 1 to 5 years. The Bachelor degree holders with whom they are compared are first degree holders with "zero" years of graduate education in those fields and professions. Those in Table II who were not College Teachers and were in the Natural Sciences or Social Sciences were largely working in industrial research or for the government. There

[12] In computing the rates of return in Table I, the cubic approximation for those with 17+ years of education was applied to both Ph.D. holders and M.A.'s. It is possible that this curve overestimates the earnings patterns for M.A.'s and thereby yields the rather high rates of return for M.A.'s depicted in Table I.

were simply too few Ph.D.'s in the Humanities who were not college teachers to estimate an internal rate of return for this group.

The methodology employed in arriving at the results in Table II was the same as that used for computing the results of the bottom half of Table I. We did not use our general cubic approximations to the earnings profiles for these specific groups. Foregone earnings were estimated from regressions in which Field of Graduate Study, Degree Level, and Profession were allowed to interact. The reference group consisted of Bachelor degree holders in a particular Field and Profession who had "zero" years of graduate education.

The group with the highest internal rate of return consists of Ph.D.'s in Social Sciences who are not college teachers. Many on this group are working for non-profit research organizations (Rand, Institute for Defense Analysis, etc.) which pay on the average higher salaries than universities—at least at this early stage of their working life. At the other end of the spectrum, the rate of return for Ph.D.'s in the Humanities who are college-teachers is very low (.007). Before concluding this section, the authors would like to add that their confidence in the reliability of the results is somewhat less for Ph.D.'s by Field and Profession than the results for all Ph.D.'s. The reason for this ebbing of confidence is straightforward. The cell sizes rapidly become small as soon as we begin to control for such things as Field and Profession. Consequently, the statistical reliability of the estimates suffers accordingly.

V   Implications and Conclusions

For purposes of generalizing the results in this study, there is a drawback associated with the high ability level of our sample. Their high ability level *per se* probably imparts an upward bias to our estimates of the rates of return. In addition, from other sources of information available to the authors, it is known that male Woodrow Wilson Fellows tend to cluster at a relatively small number of high-quality prestigious graduate schools. It would follow that the economic returns to Woodrow Wilson Fellows would again be higher than the returns to the average graduate student as a result of this higher quality graduate education. In sum, the combination of greater individual ability and higher quality of graduate education undoubtedly produces an upward bias to our results.

Despite differences in sample, methodology and time period, it is interesting to note the general consistency of the rates of return presented in this study with those limited results of Hanoch and Butter already cited. The preponderance of evidence suggests rates of return to graduate education in the arts and sciences in the range 5–11%.[13] Furthermore, the rates of return

[13] The exception is, of course, Hunt's results obtained for a 1947 sample, *op. cit.* Taking his results at face value suggests an upward trend in rates of return to graduate education which is fully consistent with the phenomenal growth in this area of education.

presented in this paper seem to fit roughly into the general pattern of educational investment yields suggested by other authors. Conceptually, one would expect a decline in the rates of return to successively higher levels of education. Other authors (Hansen, 1963 and Hunt, 1963) have generally found the return to four years of college to lie in the range 11–15%. Returns to graduate education in the range 5–11% are clearly consistent with these results.

On the whole we must conclude that the returns to graduate education are fairly substantial. An exception is the generally low return (.7%) found for people in the Humanities. This brings us to the more general issue embodied in the question, "Why do so many people continue the educational process in a field where the pecuniary rewards to further education are so low?" One answer might stem from the fact that Humanists have few employment opportunities outside the University in which they could make use of their professional training. Hence, one might argue that a short-run disequilibrium exists in the Humanities field which allows universities to pay rather low salaries to Humanists without fear of losing them to other types of employers. It is clear that this answer will not do, however, if one considers the differentially low returns that exist in the Humanities to be an equilibrium position. A second answer falls under the rubric, "psychic benefits," which many people claim they receive from an academic position in the Humanities. Presumably, these psychic benefits take the form of longer vacations, stimulating colleagues, idyllic geographic settings, and the pure undiluted pleasure of stimulating young minds. Since there are literally thousands of graduate students in the Humanities who aspire to become college teachers and who probably have some idea of the low financial rewards which await them, there is probably something to this notion of large psychic benefits to an academician.[14]

From the financial investment point of view, how long should one remain as a full-time graduate student? After 4 years in graduate school, the internal rate of return (regardless of field or occupation) declines very rapidly. On the basis of the composite picture contained in this paper, we would assert that the internal rate of return to an average 5-year Ph.D. is approximately 5%. If, for some reason, one does not acquire a Ph.D. after 5 full years in graduate school, the rate of return is quite likely negative. Yet, many students obviously spend more than 4 years in graduate school as a full-time student. Why does this happen? Two possible reasons come to mind. If that 5th year in graduate school means that a person is permanently deferred from military service, an obligation which apparently has high pecuniary and non-pecuniary costs for many individuals, the fifth year graduate student may

[14] A recent study by Marsh and Stafford (1967) provides evidence that professional attitudes toward work and occupation on the part of academicians tend to be a compensatory substitute for monetary returns in the choice of occupation and institutional setting.

not be acting irrationally from an economic point of view. Secondly, some portion of graduate education undoubtedly represents a consumption good for certain individuals. They "enjoy" graduate school and thus linger on after it has become patently clear that graduate education is a poor pecuniary investment.

In conclusion, it should be noted that nowhere in this article did we try to ascertain whether or not the behavioral responses of students accord with the pattern of rates of return presented in this paper. Of course, the importance of these rates of return as allocative signals in the area of education ultimately depends on whether or not students respond to them. Adequate behavioral models for testing student responses are in the embryonic stage of development at this time. Determination of the relevant investment horizon for students, the treatment of uncertainty, and the selection of the relevant earnings variable or rate of return are merely a few of the variables which have to be included in such models and which greatly complicate their construction.[15] In spite of these conceptual difficulties, we believe that the effort expended in formulating adequate behavioral models represents the most important type of research currently being undertaken in this area.

References

Ashenfelter, Orley and Mooney, J. D. "Graduate Education, Ability and Earnings," *Review of Economics and Statistics*, February 1968, pp. 78–86.

Butter, Irene H. *Economics of Graduate Education: An Exploratory Study*—U.S. Department of Health, Education, and Welfare, Office of Education, (November 1966).

Goldberger, Arthur, *Econometric Theory* (New York: John Wiley and Sons, 1964).

Hanoch, Giora, "Personal Earnings and Investment in Schooling," Ph.D. dissertation, University of Chicago, 1965.

———, "Personal Earnings and Investment in Schooling," *Journal of Human Resources*, Summer 1967, pp. 310–329.

Hansen, W. Lee, "Total and Private Rates of Return to Investment in Schooling," *Journal of Political Economy*, April 1963, pp. 128–140.

Hillier, Frederick S. "The Derivation of Probabilistic Information for the Evaluation of Risky Investments," *Management Science*, April 1963, pp. 443–457.

Hunt, Shane, "Income Determinants for College Graduates and the Return to Educational Investment," *Yale Economic Essays* (Fall 1963), pp. 305–357.

Marsh, John and Stafford, Frank, "Income Foregone: The Effects of Values on Pecuniary Behavior," manuscript (National Opinion Research Center, University of Chicago, 1966).

Wilkinson, Bruce, "Present Values of Lifetime Earnings for Different Occupations," in *Journal of Political Economy*, December 1966, pp. 556–573.

Schultz, T. W. "The Rate of Return in Allocating Investment Resources to Education," *Journal of Human Resources*, (Summer 1967), pp. 293–309.

[15] See T. W. Schultz (1967), pp. 302–305, for a more complete discussion of these issues, and Wilkinson (1966) for some preliminary work.

20

Education and Investment in Human Capital

Burton A. Weisbrod, Professor of Economics at the University of Wisconsin, is a frequent visitor to the edges of knowledge in human resource economics. In the following selection he describes several non-economic and external benefits derived from educational investments in human capital. Many studies concerned with the benefits of investment in education concen-

BURTON A. WEISBROD

trate on the economic effect of education on earnings, only briefly identifying nonpecuniary and external benefits. Weisbrod's classic paper emphasizes a variety of benefits from educational investments in human capital in addition to the readily observed direct financial returns to the individual.

I

As technological developments have altered production techniques, types of mechanical equipment, and varieties of outputs, society has begun to recognize that economic progress involves not only changes in machinery but also in men—not only expenditures on equipment but also on people. Investment in people makes it possible to take advantage of technical progress as well as to continue that progress. Improvements in health make investment in education more rewarding by extending life expectancy. Investment in education expands and extends knowledge, leading to advances which raise productivity and improve health. With investment in

Reprinted from Burton A. Weisbrod, "Education and Investment in Human Capital," *Journal of Political Economy* 70 (October 1962), pp. 106–23, with the permission of the author and publisher. Copyright 1962 by The University of Chicago.

human capital and non-human capital both contributing to economic growth and welfare and in what is probably an interdependent manners more attention should be paid to the adequacy of the level of expenditure, on people.

The principal forms of direct investment in the productivity and well-being of people are: health, learning (both in school and on the job), and location (migration). Formal education and health constitute two large components of public and private spending in the United States. Private expenditures alone for hospital and physician services were over $18 billion in 1959, having risen from $8.6 billion in 1950.[1] Public education expenditures rose to $19.3 billion in 1960 from $7.3 billion at the turn of the decade.[2] Priced at cost, gross investment in education in the United States has risen from 9 per cent of gross physical investment in 1900 to 34 per cent in 1956.[3]

Investment in future productivity is occurring increasingly outside the private market and in intangible forms. Our traditional conception of investment as a private market phenomenon and only as tangible plant, machinery and equipment must give way to a broader concept which allows not only for government investment but also for intangible investment in the quality of human capital.

Most economic analysis of return from education has focused on the contribution of education to earning capacity (and, presumably, to production capacity). While this has been valuable, it is only part of the picture, and perhaps not even a large part. Even aside from market imperfections, which create inequalities between wage rates and marginal productivity, earnings are an incomplete measure of the productivity of education to the extent that production occurs outside the market. In addition, emphasis on incremental earnings attributable to education disregards external effects. Schooling benefits many persons other than the student. It benefits the student's future children, who will receive informal education in the home; and it benefits neighbors, who may be affected favorably by the social values developed in children by the schools and even by the quietness of the neighborhood while the schools are in session. Schooling benefits employers seeking a trained labor force; and it benefits the society at large by developing the basis for an informed electorate. Compulsory school attendance and public (rather than private) support for education in the United States both suggest that external economies from either the production or consumption of education are believed to be important.[4]

---

[1] United States Department of Health, Education and Welfare, *Health, Education and Welfare Trends, 1961* (Washington: Government Printing Office, 1961), p. 23.

[2] *Ibid.*, p. 53.

[3] T. W. Schultz, "Capital Formation by Education," *Journal of Political Economy,* December, 1960, p. 583.

[4] Similarly, but perhaps more clearly, compulsory smallpox vaccination together with public provision of vaccine reflects external economies of "consumption" of the vaccine.

From the vantage point of one interested in Pareto optimal resource allocation, it is essential to consider all benefits from some action (as well as all costs). Whether the benefits (or costs) involve explicit financial payments, or whether they are internal to, or external from, a particular decision-maker is irrelevant.

In the private sector of the economy, private benefits from goods and services are reflected in consumer demand; assuming economic rationality, competition, and the absence of external effects, private producers will meet the demand in a socially optimum manner. But when goods and services either have significant external effects or are indivisible (in the sense that consumption by one person does not reduce consumption opportunities for others—as, for example, national defense), the private market is inadequate. If the public sector attempts to provide the service, and if consumer sovereignty is to reign, the extent of consumer demand must be judged. Thus arises the need for benefit-cost analysis.

Within the benefit-cost framework this paper focuses principal attention on the ways by which a society benefits from formal education, discussing much more briefly some of the ways by which it incurs costs in providing education. It is worth emphasizing that analyzing benefits (or costs) does not preclude specifying which people reap the returns (or incur the costs). We shall attempt to identify the benefits of education by recognizing the beneficiaries of the educational process.

In the discussion which follows, a "benefit" of education will refer to anything that pushes outward the utility possibility function for the society. Included would be (1) anything which increases production possibilities, such as increased labor productivity; (2) anything which reduces costs and thereby makes resources available for more productive uses, such as increased employment opportunities, which may release resources from law enforcement by cutting crime rates; and (3) anything which increases welfare possibilities directly, such as development of public-spiritedness or social consciousness of one's neighbor. Anything which merely alters relative prices without affecting total utility opportunities for the group under consideration will not be deemed a social benefit (or loss). For example, if expanded education reduces the number of household servants, so that the wage rates of those remaining rise, this rise would not constitute either a benefit or loss from education but rather a financial transfer. Without making interpersonal utility comparisons we cannot say more. Of course, the increased productivity of those with the additional education is a benefit of type 1.

In addition to an analysis of the forms of education benefits and the nature of the beneficiaries, I shall investigate opportunities for quantifying these returns and some implications of the benefits analysis for the financing of education.[5] In Section II, I shall consider benefits which the individual receives in the form of market opportunities—including additional earnings resulting from increased productivity and benefits which the individual receives in ways other than earnings. In Section III, I shall consider benefits which the individual does not capture but which accrue to other persons. Benefits from elementary, secondary, and higher education will receive attention.

II

In this section we examine those benefits of education (or returns from education) which are realized directly by the student. One form of such benefits is the "financial return" accompanying additional education. A second form is the "financial option" return. Previously unconsidered, this benefit involves the value of the opportunity to obtain still further education. Third are the non-monetary "opportunity options," involving the broadened individual employment choices which education permits; fourth are the opportunities for "hedging" against the vicissitudes of technological change. And fifth are the non-market benefits.

DIRECT FINANCIAL RETURN

Census Bureau data relating level of earnings to level of educational attainment show an unmistakable positive correlation. A number of investigators have estimated the percentage return from investment in education by attributing these observed earnings differentials to education.[6] Some have attempted to adjust for or, at least, to recognize factors other than education which affect earnings and which are positively correlated with level of education. These include intelligence, ambition, informal education in the home, number of hours worked, family wealth, and social mobility. One factor which I believe has not been considered is that a positive correlation of educational attainment with family wealth suggests that those with more education may live longer and consequently tend to

[5] While I shall refer throughout this paper to the research of others I should like to mention particularly the excellent survey recently completed by Alice M. Rivlin; see her "Research in the Economics of Higher Education: Progress and Problems," in Selma J. Mushkin (ed.), *Economics of Higher Education* (hereinafter cited as *"Higher Education"*) (Washington: United States Department of Health, Education, and Welfare [forthcoming]).

[6] On the relation between educational attainment and earnings, see G. Becker, "Underinvestment in College Education?" *American Economic Review, Proceedings*, May, 1960, pp. 346–54; H. S. Houthakker, "Education and Income," *Review of Economics and Statistics*, February, 1959, pp. 24–28; H. P. Miller, "Annual and Lifetime Income in Relation to Education," *American Economic Review*, December, 1960, pp. 962–86; E. F. Renshaw, "Estimating the Returns to Education," *Review of Economics and Statistics*, August, 1960, pp. 318–24.

receive greater lifetime incomes, education aside, although it is true that longer life is not synonymous with longer working life. We are led to the presumption that, in general, persons who have obtained more education would have greater earnings than persons with less education, even without the additional schooling.[7] At the same time, at least one study has attempted to isolate some of the non-education variables affecting earnings, with the finding that median salaries rose with additional amounts of post-high-school education, even after adjustments were made for (1) level of high-school class rank, (2) intelligence-test scores, and (3) father's occupation.[8] Apparently at least part of the additional earnings of the more educated population are the results of their education.

Although earning differentials attributable to education may be of considerable significance to the recipients, the social significance depends upon the relationship between earnings and marginal productivities. However, we know that market imperfections may make earnings a poor measure of one's contribution to output and that in a growing economy cross-section age-earnings data will understate future earnings. Mary Jean Bowman has suggested that older workers may receive more than their marginal productivity because status and seniority rules may maintain income although their productivity is falling.[9] But even assuming that earnings equal current marginal productivity, estimation of lifetime productivity from cross-section earnings data tends to understate future productivity of today's young men; this is true because in a growing society each new cohort of people into the labor force comes with better education and knowledge. These two examples suggest that the observed current earnings of men are less than fully satisfactory as reflections of future marginal productivity. Much work remains before we can feel confident of our ability to measure adequately the productivity return to education. Perhaps more serious, because apparently it has not been recognized, is a methodological limitation to previous estimates of the financial return to education.

FINANCIAL OPTION RETURN

Given our interest in resource allocation, we should like to know what financial return from additional education a person can expect. I suggested above that earnings differentials associated with education-attainment differentials would have to be adjusted for differences in ability, ambition,

[7] See D. S. Bridgman, "Problems in Estimating the Monetary Value of College Education," *Review of Economics and Statistics, Supplement,* August, 1960, p. 181.

[8] Dael Wolfle, "Economics and Educational Values," *Review of Economics and Statistics, Supplement,* August, 1960, pp. 178–79. See also his *America's Resources of Specialized Talent* (New York, Harper & Bros., 1954); and Wolfle and Joseph G. Smith, "The Occupational Value of Education for Superior High School Graduates," *Journal of Higher Education,* 1956, pp. 201–13.

[9] "Human Capital: Concepts and Measures," in Mushkin (ed.), *Higher Education.*

and other variables before we could isolate the education effects; and that an adjustment for systematic differences between earnings and productivity would also be required. Let us assume that these adjustments have been made and that we have computed the present values of expected future earnings of an average person with J and with K years of education, *ceteris paribus*; it is my contention that this would be an erroneously low estimate of the gross return which may be expected from the additional education. The value of the additional education may be thought of as having two components: (*a*) the additional earnings resulting from completion of a given level of education (properly discounted to the present, of course) and (*b*) the value of the "option" to obtain still further education and the rewards accompanying it. It is (*b*) which I wish to elaborate upon here.

In formula (1) below, the first term represents the rate of return over cost for education unit j, as computed in the usual manner; it is the difference between the present value of expected future earnings of a person who has attained, but not exceeded, level j, and the present value of expected future earnings of a person without education j, as a percentage of the additional cost of obtaining j. This is the rate of return as computed heretofore.

Subsequent terms in the formula measure the option value of completing j and should be understood as follows: each of the R^* are rates of return on incremental education α, computed in the manner described in the paragraph above. $\bar{R}$ is the opportunity cost of expenditure on education in terms of the percentage return obtainable from the next best investment opportunity, so that $R^*_\alpha - \bar{R}$ indicates any "supernormal" percentage return. $C_\alpha =$ the marginal social cost of obtaining the incremental education α (where each cost ratio, C_α/C_j, is a weighting factor, permitting the percentage returns on the costs of various levels of education to be added), and P_α is the probability that a person who has attained level j will go on to various higher levels.

$$R_j = R^*_j + (R^*_k - \bar{R})\frac{C_k}{C_j} \cdot P_k$$

$$+ (R^*_l - \bar{R})\frac{C_l}{C_j} \cdot P_l + \ldots$$

$$+ (R^*_z - \bar{R})\frac{C_z}{C_j} \cdot P_z = R^*_j \tag{1}$$

$$+ \sum_{\alpha=k}^{z} (R^*_\alpha - \bar{R})\frac{C_\alpha}{C_j} \cdot P_\alpha$$

Thus, for example, a decision to obtain a high-school education involves not only the likelihood of obtaining the additional earnings typically realized by a high-school graduate but also involves the value of the opportunity to pursue a college education.[10] The value of the option to obtain additional education will tend to be greater the more elementary the education. For the "highest" level of formal education, the value of the option is clearly zero,[11] except insofar as the education provides the option to pursue independent work.

The option-value approach attributes to investment in one level of schooling a portion of the additional return over cost which can be obtained from further education—specifically, that portion which is in excess of the opportunity cost rate of return. Although part of the return from college education is indeed attributed to high-school education, there is no double-counting involved. In fact, the procedure is the same as that involved in the valuation of any asset, where the decision to retain or discard it may be made at various times in the life of the asset. Consider the following case: a machine is offered for sale. The seller, anxious to make the sale, offers an inducement to the buyer in the form of a discount on the purchase of a replacement machine when the present one wears out. Analyzing the prospective buyer's current decision, we see that he is being offered a combination of (1) a machine now, and (2) a discount (or option) "ticket" for possible future use. Both may have value, and both should be considered by the prospective buyer.

Let us assume that the machine has been purchased and used, and the owner is now deciding whether he should buy a replacement. Needless to say, the rate of return expected from the prospective machine will be a function of its cost net of the discount. The profit-maximizing buyer will compare the rate of return on the net cost and compare it with the opportunity cost of capital. Thus, in a real sense, the discount ticket has entered into two decisions: to buy the original machine and to buy the replacement. But this is not equivalent to any erroneous double-counting.

The machine discount-ticket analogy also makes clear the point that the value of the option (or discount) cannot be negative. If a greater rate of return (or discount) is available elsewhere, the value of the option merely becomes zero, as long as it need not be used. Thus, as long as a high-school graduate need not go on to college the value of the option to go on cannot be negative. It is formally conceivable, however, that a positive option value of elementary-school education could consist of a negative value for the high-school component and a larger positive value for the college component.

---

[10] Research by Jacob Mincer suggests that additional schooling also provides opportunities to obtain additional on-the-job training (see his "On-the-Job Training: Costs, Returns, and Some Implications"). The value of this opportunity should be included in the financial option approach developed here.

[11] Thus, for estimating the return from college or graduate education, omission of the value of the option may not be quantitatively significant. At the same time, since the return from higher education as previously estimated seems to be close to the return on business investments, recognition of the value of the option might tip the balance.

Formula (1) indicates that the value of the option to pursue additional schooling depends upon (1) the probability of its being exercised and (2) the expected value if exercised. Without further information, factor 1 may be estimated by the proportion of persons completing a particular level of education who go on to a higher level. The expected value of the option if exercised, factor 2, is any excess of the return on that increment of education over the return obtainable on the best comparable alternative investment, where the latter may be assumed to equal, say, 5 per cent. Actually, the "excess" returns should be discounted back to the decision date from the time the higher education level would begin, but to illustrate the point simply I shall disregard this, at least to begin with.

According to some recent estimates reported elsewhere, the return to the individual on total high-school costs (including foregone earnings) for white urban males in 1939[12] was approximately 14 per cent and the return on college costs for those who graduated was estimated at 9 per cent.[13] We might assume the return to be somewhat lower—say, 8 per cent—for those who did not complete their college training.[14] Then with approximately 44 per cent of high-school male graduates beginning college and 24 per cent graduating,[15] the a priori expected return on a social investment in high-school education in 1939 was, substituting in equation (1) above, 17.4 per cent, as shown in equation (2). . . .

$$\underset{\substack{\text{High-School}\\ \text{Graduates}}}{14} \quad + \quad \underset{\text{College Graduates}}{(9\text{--}5)\ (2.70)\ (.24)} \quad + \quad \underset{\substack{\text{Some College}\\ \text{(Assumed}=2\text{ years)}}}{(8\text{--}5)\ (1.35)\ (.20)} \qquad (2)$$

$$= 14 + 2.6 + 0.8 = 17.4 \text{ per cent.}$$

$$\underset{\substack{\text{Grade-School}\\ \text{Graduates}}}{35} \quad + \quad \underset{\text{High-School Graduates}}{(14\text{--}5)\ (2.3)\ (.67)} \quad + \quad \underset{\text{College Graduates}}{(9\text{--}5)\ (6.3)\ (.16)} \quad + \quad \underset{\substack{\text{Some College}\\ \text{(Assumed}=2\text{ years)}}}{(8\text{--}5)\ (3.1)\ (.13)} \qquad (3)$$

$$= 35 + 13.9 + 3.8 + 1.2 = 53.9 \text{ per cent.}$$

[12] T. W. Schultz, "Education and Economic Growth," *Social Forces Influencing American Education* (hereinafter cited as "Economic Growth") (Chicago: National Society for the Study of Education, 1961), chap. iii, referring to G. S. Becker's work. H. H. Villard has seriously disagreed with these estimates. See his "Discussion" of Becker's "Underinvestment in College Education?" in *American Economic Review, Proceedings*, May, 1960, pp. 375–78. See also W. L. Hansen, "Rate of Return on Human versus Non-human Investment" (draft paper, October, 1960).

[13] Schultz, "Economic Growth," p. 78.

[14] While this paper deals with education benefits, quantitative comparison of benefits with costs are made to help assess the relative magnitudes of benefits. In doing this I do not intend to imply complete satisfaction with the cost estimates. The appendix of this paper presents some of the issues involved in defining and measuring social costs.

[15] Computed from 1960 data for males of ages 25–29, in United States Bureau of the Census, *Current Population Reports: Population Characteristics, Projections of Educational Attainments in the United States, 1960–1980* (hereinafter cited as "*Educational Attainments*") (Series P-20, No. 91 [January 12, 1959, p. 8, Table 2]).

To reiterate, the first term, 14, is the estimated percentage return to high-school education. In subsequent terms, the first element is an estimate of the return in excess of alternatives, obtainable on additional education; the second element is the total cost of the additional education as a proportion of the cost of high-school education;[16] the third element is the proportion of high-school graduates who obtain the additional education. If the returns to college education were discounted back four years to the date at which high-school education was initiated, at a 5 per cent discount rate the expected return to high-school education would drop to $14 + 2.1 + 0.7 = 16.8$, instead of 17.4 per cent.

In the example above it was assumed that a decision to complete high school would be realized with certainty. Other assumptions could be fitted easily into the framework. And if knowledge existed regarding the prospective high-school student's college plans, then *average* probabilities of his continuation should not be used.

If the option value of education has been overlooked by parents as it has been by economists there would be a tendency toward underinvestment in education. If time horizons are short so that, for example, a prospective high-school student and his parents sometimes fail to consider that a few years later the child may wish he could be going on to college, there will be a systematic downward bias to the valuation of education by individuals. Even disregarding graduate education, the option value of high-school education increased the rate of return on high-school costs from 14 to 17 per cent, considering only the "monetary" returns. For grade-school education, recognition of the value of the option to obtain additional education increases the expected 1939 return even more substantially above the previous estimate of 35 per cent[17] (see eq. (3). . . .

The option turns out to be quite valuable indeed, increasing the return on elementary education from 35 to 54 per cent. It could be argued in this case that whether the return is 35 per cent or 54 per cent[18] is relatively immaterial for policy purposes, both being considerably greater than

[16] Computed from data in Schultz, "Economic Growth," p. 79.

[17] Again disregarding the discounting. The 35 per cent estimate is from Schultz, "Economic Growth," p. 81. Relative costs were estimated from the same source (p. 79), except that Schultz's elementary-school cost figure was doubled, since it applied to only four years of school. The proportions of children continuing on to higher education were estimated from *Educational Attainments*, p. 8.

In this paper I do not discuss any option value for college education; however, there may be a positive option value related to opportunities for graduate study and additional on-the-job training.

[18] Previous estimates of rates of return represented a discounting of costs and returns back to the beginning of that particular level of schooling; since our time bench mark is the beginning of grade school, the values of the high-school and college options should be discounted back to the beginning of grade school. Doing so, at a discount rate of 5 per cent, reduces the 54 per cent return to $35 + 9.5 + 2.1 + 0.7 = 47.3$. The return would almost certainly be larger if persons obtaining only some high-school education were considered.

available alternatives. However, given the state of our confidence in the previously computed rates of return, it is comforting to see the estimates moved further from the decision-making margin. Of course, in addition to these returns, assuming they are attributable solely to education, are the non-market returns to education, including the direct consumption value of learning and the opportunity to lead the "full life."

NON-FINANCIAL OPTIONS

The words "option" and "opportunity" have appeared in the discussion above a number of times. Indeed, it seems that in many respects the value of education is a function of the additional options which became available to a person having it—job options, income-leisure-security options, additional-schooling options, on-the-job learning options, way-of-life options.

Recognizing the existence of such options suggests a possible means of estimating the monetary equivalent value of non-monetary returns from education. Thus, the college graduate who chooses to go to graduate school and then enter academic life may be assumed to obtain a total (not merely monetary) return on his graduate education costs at least equal to what he could have obtained from a comparable alternative investment. In general, added education permits widened job choices, and to some extent people with more education will choose employment which provides non-monetary rewards (for example, greater security) at the expense of monetary rewards. To the extent that this is correct and that knowledge of alternatives exists, previous estimates of the individual returns to education, utilizing incremental earnings figures for people with two different levels of education, have had a downward bias. If monetary returns from, say, graduate education turn out to be less than comparable alternative returns, the difference would be a minimum measure of non-monetary returns, though not necessarily of the employment-associated return alone.

"HEDGING" OPTION

There is another respect in which education provides a person with options: the increased ability to adjust to changing job opportunities. With a rapid pace of technological change, adaptability (which may be a noteworthy output of additional education) becomes important. Education may be viewed as a type of private (and social) hedge against technological displacement of skills. New technology often requires new skills and knowledge;[19] and those persons having more education are likely to be in a

---

[19] This view seems to be shared by H. Coombs, who states that "there will be many unpredictable shifts in the proportions needed of specific categories of . . . manpower. Thus, it will be important . . . to enlarge the total supply of high ability manpower available for all purposes" ("Some Economic Aspects of Educational Developments," in International Association of Universities, *Some Economic Aspects of Educational Development in Europe* [Paris: International Universities Bureau, 1961], p. 78).

position to adjust more easily than those with less education, and to reap the returns from education which the new technology has made possible. This line of reasoning suggests that a more general academic curriculum is desirable since it permits greater flexibility than a curriculum which requires earlier specialization.

Insofar as the return resulting from greater flexibility is realized in the form of earnings, it will be reflected directly in the estimated monetary value of education. The hedging option has additional value, however, to the extent that people have a preference for greater security and stability of earnings.

The hypothesis that added schooling develops added labor-force flexibility and thereby facilitates adjustments to changing skill requirements suggests the following implication: the greater the level of an individual's formal education attainment, the more he can benefit from additional on-the-job training, and, therefore, the more on-the-job training he will obtain. Jacob Mincer's data support this view;[20] through time, investment in learning on the job is increasingly being concentrated on persons with education beyond elementary school. He estimates that in all three years, 1939, 1949, and 1958, on-the-job training costs per person were positively correlated with the level of education. Moreover, a trend is observable—in 1939, on-the-job training costs per person with elementary education were 38 per cent of costs per college-educated person; in 1949 they were 30 per cent; and by 1958, 28 per cent. Over the twenty-year period, training costs per capita for elementary-educated persons actually declined (in constant dollars), while they climbed 13 per cent for college-trained persons.

NON-MARKET RETURNS

So far we have discussed the return to education which is realized by the individual in terms of his employment conditions. But some of the value of education to the individual accrues in other forms. For example, the fruits of literacy—an output of elementary education—include, in addition to consumption aspects, the implicit value of its non-market use. To illustrate: when a person prepares his own income tax return he performs a service made possible by his literacy. Were this service provided through the market, it would be priced and included in national income.[21]

---

[20] *Op. cit.*, Tables 1 and 2. But E. F. Renshaw predicts that the principal educational requirements of the 1960's, with respect to the labor force, will be directed toward trade schools and apprenticeship programs ("Investment in Human Capital" [unpublished manuscript, 1960], p. 13).

[21] It could be argued that the service (like many others in national income and product) is not a final output, but a cost item (cost of tax collection), and thus should not be included in estimates of production; but since it is often difficult to distinguish clearly outputs from inputs in our national accounts, and since our national income and product accounts principally measure effort expended, it would be interesting to make some estimate of the

Assume that roughly fifty million of the sixty million personal income-tax returns filed per year are prepared by the taxpayer himself. At a value of $5.00 per return, a low estimate of an average charge by an accountant for preparing a not-too-complex return, we arrive at an annual market value of the tax-return services performed by taxpayers for themselves of $250 million. Relative to Schultz's estimate of total elementary-school costs of $7.8 billion in 1956,[22] this suggests a current-year return of 3.2 per cent of the current investment in literacy! And this is only one, obviously minor, form of return from literacy which the individual enjoys.

This attempt to place a value on a particular use of literacy is subject to at least the following criticism: were it not for widespread literacy in this country we would probably not have the present type of income-tax system operating, and, therefore, we would adjust to illiteracy in a less costly way than having others (say, accountants) prepare tens of millions of returns. The adjustment might involve government tax assessments or a resort to another type of tax such as one on expenditures. This suggests that the literacy value estimate above is on the high side, in terms of the alternative tax collection cost in the absence of literacy.

I have attempted a very rough estimate of the alternative cost of collecting an alternative form of tax—a sales tax—which would not require such a literate population, in order to compare it with the collection cost of the income tax.[23] The assumption is that a principal reason for the relative tax-collection efficiency of the income tax is the work performed by the taxpayer in preparing his own return. For the year 1940, the all-states average cost of collecting state personal income taxes was $1.50 per $100 collected, while the comparable figure for the general sales taxes of states was $2.00 per $100 collected. In the same year, collection costs per $100

---

market-value equivalent of the services performed by a person in preparing his own income-tax return.

Inclusion of the value of this non-market production as an educational benefit presupposes that this represents a net increase in the value of the individual's total non-market activities and that the opportunity cost of performing additional non-market production is essentially zero.

Richard Goode has suggested that, although the failure to consider non-market production leads to understatement of the return to education, "nevertheless, there seems to be little danger that this omission will lead to an undervaluation of educational benefits in comparing time periods, countries, and population groups with different amounts of formal education." He presents "the hypothesis that the greater the amount of formal education the greater the proportion of goods and services acquired through the market. If this is true, estimates based on money earnings or national income statistics may exaggerate the contribution of education to real income differentials or growth."

[22] "Economic Growth," p. 64, Table 5.

[23] This disregards the different distributive effects of the two forms of tax.

[24] James W. Martain, "Costs of Tax Administration: Statistics of Public Expenses," *Bulletin of the National Tax Association*, February, 1944, pp. 132–47, as cited in Charles A. Benson, *The Economics of Public Education* (Boston, Houghton-Mifflin Co., 1961), p. 145.

of federal personal income tax were estimated at $1.68,[24] while there was, of course, no federal sales tax.[25]

In the absence of a superior alternative I have assumed that, as was true for the state tax-collection costs presented above, a federal sales tax would cost one-third more to collect than the federal personal income tax. Assuming the 1960 Internal Revenue Service estimate of collection costs, of approximately forty cents per $100, to apply to the personal income tax, then a one-third increase in the cost of collecting $50 billion (1959 individual income-tax receipts) would involve an additional $66 million—approximately 0.8 per cent of elementary-school costs.[26]

III

In this section we consider the benefits of education which are external to the student. If all the benefits of education accrued to the student, then, assuming utility-maximizing behavior and access to capital markets, there would be little reason for public concern about the adequacy of education expenditures—unless publicly supported education were an efficient way of altering the personal distribution of income in a desired way.

Income redistribution effects aside, it seems clear that access to the capital market is imperfect and also that a child, even at high-school or college age, is in a poor position to make sensible long-run decisions regarding the amount or type of education, though advice from teachers, counselors, and parents may improve the decision. But these imperfections hardly appear to justify the massive public expenditures in support of education—more than $19 billion in 1960, including capital outlays.[27] We are led to the position that, to understand why education is of public concern as well as to project demand for education and determine whether expanded education is warranted on allocative-efficiency grounds, we should pay more attention to identifying and quantifying external benefits of education.[28] This section of the paper suggests a framework for analyzing these benefits and considers opportunities for measurement.

As economists, our interest in external benefits is typically related to the question of whether all benefits (as well as costs) of some action are taken

[25] Estimation of collection costs is subject to the common difficulty of the allocation of joint costs; furthermore, we really know little about scale economies in tax collection, or about the difference in degree of enforcement of state and federal taxes, so that it is dangerous to apply state cost figures to the federal level.

[26] Actually we should note that a number of years of education is required to develop "literate" people but also that, once developed, they presumably retain the knowledge. Were we to take into account the number of tax returns an average person may be expected to file during his lifetime, a higher rate of return would appear.

[27] *Health, Education and Welfare Trends, 1961, op. cit.*, pp. 52, 53.

[28] It is true, however, that economies of scale (with respect to the number of students) would also be a sufficient explanation for the public interest in education.

into account by the decision-maker. The issue is whether the benefits are or are not captured by the decision-maker, since the assumption of profit maximization has the implication that benefits will be recognized by the decision-maker if, but only if, he is able to obtain them. Insofar as parents and children make joint decisions on purchases of education, with none of them being a very expert, experienced buyer, those benefits which are less apparent and indirect are likely to be overlooked. Parents thinking of their children may even neglect the less direct benefits to themselves, discussed below. Moreover, benefits to non-family members are probably not considered at all.

In principle, the recipients of external benefits from some activity (for example, education) should be willing to subsidize the activity and, indeed, should seek to subsidize it. The voting mechanism and taxation provide the means for subsidization. Analysis of voting behavior may shed some light on the question whether external benefits are recognized and have an effect on decisions. But regardless whether or not subsidies are actually paid by "outsiders," we need to identify and measure the magnitudes of external benefits to determine the rate of return on resources devoted to education.

Persons receiving external benefits from a student's education may be divided into three broad groups, though the same people may be in more than one: (1) residence-related beneficiaries—those who benefit by virtue of some relationship between their place of residence and that of the subject; (2) employment-related beneficiaries—those who benefit by virtue of some employment relationship with the subject; (3) society in general.

RESIDENCE-RELATED BENEFICIARIES

Current Family of the Subject   While the purpose of schooling is obviously education, the manner in which it is provided may result in incidental, and even accidental, by-products; in the case of elementary education, such a by-product is child care. Schools make it possible for mothers who would otherwise be supervising their youngsters to do other things. For those mothers who choose to work, we have an estimate of the productivity of the child-care services—their earnings. This rests on the assumption that the mothers would not work if a sitter had to be hired but do work when the child is in school. If mothers would make other child-care arrangements in the absence of schools, then a better measure of value than earnings obtained would be the cost of hiring a baby sitter or making some alternative custodial arrangement.

In March, 1956, there were 3.5 million working mothers in the United States with children six to eleven years of age.[29] Assuming that as few as

---

[29] United States Bureau of the Census, *Marital and Family Status of Workers: 1956* (Series P-50, No. 73 [April, 1957]), p. 11, Table 3.

one million of these mothers would not work except for the schools (the others being willing to let their children stay with hired persons or simply care for themselves), and assuming $2,000 as the earnings of each mother during the school year, the value of the child-care services of elementary school may be estimated as roughly $2 billion per year.[30] Estimating total resource costs (excluding capital outlays but including implicit interest and depreciation) of public and private elementary schools in 1956 at $7.8 billion,[31] we reach the startling conclusion that elementary-school support provided a return of 25 per cent of cost in the by-product form of child-care services alone.[32] This disregards the value of these services to mothers who do not choose to work; since the value is certainly greater than zero, the total value of the child-care is even more than 25 per cent of cost.

The increased production from working mothers tends to offset the foregone production from students in school. Various writers have emphasized students' foregone earnings as a cost of education, and have debated its magnitude,[33] but have not considered the fact that some mothers' earnings are made possible by the fact that children forego earnings to remain in school.

Future Family of the Subject   When the student reaches adulthood and becomes a parent, the children will benefit from his or her education by virtue of the informal education which the children receive in the home. The presence and relevance of such education is recognized, but to my knowledge no attempts to estimate its value have been made. If scores on achievement tests could be related to educational attainments of parents, adjusting for variation in students' ability, we might obtain some information about the extent of education in the home. This might be translated into equivalent years in school, to which a value, perhaps average cost, could be attributed.

If we think of the investment-consumption distinction as involving whether or not benefits accrue in the "present" (consumption) or in the "future" (investment), then education has an investment component in the form of these intergeneration benefits.[34] If we generalize the conception of

[30] For those mothers who would be willing to hire baby sitters, obtainable for, perhaps, $1,000 per year, the value of the school child-care services is this alternative cost of $1,000, instead of $2,000. Of the 3.5 million working mothers with children six to eleven years old, approximately 1.5 million also had children twelve to seventeen. Some of the older children could conceivably care for the younger ones; but even considering the remaining 2 million, the assumption that one-half would not work except for the care provided by schools seems plausible and even conservative.

[31] Schultz, "Economic Growth," p. 85.

[32] If working mothers employ housekeepers as substitutes and if they incur other additional costs in working (for example, transportation and additional clothes), these added costs should be deducted from the gross returns.

[33] See Appendix below.

[34] Schultz has also recognized this point: "The education of women . . . reduces the subsequent effective costs of education because of the critical role that mothers play in motivating their children to obtain an education and to perform well while they are attend-

investment to include not only intertemporal benefits,[35] but also interpersonal benefits, then the child-care role of schools, discussed above, represents an investment in the productivity of mothers. Similarly, other interpersonal benefits examined below will constitute investment aspects of educational expenditures.

Neighbors As we consider more extended groups, beginning with the individual receiving the education and then his family (present and future), we come to his neighbors. Education affects them at least in the following ways: by inculcating acceptable social values and behavior norms in the community children and by providing children with alternatives to un-supervised activities which may have antisocial consequences. The second is essentially of short-period significance—during the time the child is of school age. The first effect is clearly of long-period consequence, following the student as he grows, and as he moves. As the student achieves adulthood, and as he migrates, the social values developed in part through his education continue to affect his "neighbors."[36]

The hypothesis that education does affect neighbors might be tested by studying voting behavior on school issues among non-parents. We might expect that their voting would be influenced by the extent to which students emigrate after completion of school, so that any potential external benefits or costs to neighbors would be realized by persons in other communities. Perhaps some notion of the magnitude of external, neighborhood benefits— at least to the extent they are recognized—could be obtained in this manner.

Taxpayers Related to the effects of education on neighbors are the effects on those who pay (directly or indirectly) for the consequences of the lack of education. For example, insofar as lack of education leads to employment difficulties and crime, law enforcement costs will tend to be high. Thus may education provide social benefits by reducing the need for incurring these "avoidance costs," to the advantage of taxpayers.

Education also benefits taxpayers in other communities. The migration of poorly educated persons having behavioral patterns and educational attainments differing from those prevailing in the new areas may necessitate additional effort and expense to permit the in-migrant children to adjust to

---

ing school. Thus, if we could get at the factors underlying the perpetuation of education, it is likely that we would discover that the education of many persons not in the labor force contributes heavily to the effective perpetuation of the stock of education. To the extent that this is true, some part of the education not in the labor force contributes to this invest-ment process" ("Economic Growth," pp. 74–75).

[35] Tax implications of the existence of intertemporal education returns have been dis-cused by R. Goode, "Educational Expenditures and Income Tax," in Mushkin (ed.), *Higher Education*.

[36] One writer points out: "Education has effects on the caliber of voluntary community activities: choral groups, drama, clubs, local art shows, etc." (Benson, *op. cit.*, p. 349).

the new school conditions.[37] Thus, people in areas of in-migration have a stake in the education of children in the areas of out-migration. People who are or may be in the same fiscal unit with an individual have a financial stake in his education.

EMPLOYMENT-RELATED BENEFICIARIES

The education of one worker may have favorable external effects on the productivity of others. Where production involves the co-operative effort of workers, flexibility and adaptability of one worker will redound to the advantage of others. Productivity of each member of the group influences the productivity of each other member. In such a case, each worker has a financial interest in the education of his fellow workers. Again, the relevance of this interdependence for the present context rests on the assumption that education develops the properties of flexibility and adaptability. Further analysis is required to determine the extent to which the assumption is valid, and if it is, to estimate its significance.

Employers may also have a financial interest in the schooling and training of their employees. Much of education improves the quality of the labor force and thereby bestows some benefits to employers of the workers insofar as market imperfections or the "specific"[38] nature of the education result in failure of the employer to pay the marginal revenue product of a worker.

SOCIETY IN GENERAL

Some of the benefits from education are enjoyed by individuals and groups that are reasonably identifiable, as we have seen. But some of the benefits are distributed broadly either spatially or temporarily, so that the nature of individual beneficiaries is obscure. These shall be considered under the heading, "Society in General," which thus becomes somewhat of a residual category of benefits.

Literacy is not only of value to the individual possessing it and to employers but also is of value to others. Without widespread literacy the significance of books, newspapers, and similar media for the transmission of information would dwindle; and it seems fair to say that the communication of information is of vital importance to the maintenance of competition and,

[37] See, for example, C. F. Schmid, V. A. Miller, and B. Abu-Laban, "Impact of Recent Negro Migration on Seattle Schools," *International Population Conference Papers* (Vienna: Union International pour l'Étude Scientifique de la Population, 1959), pp. 674–83.

[38] As the term is used by Gary S. Becker "specific" training is that which raises the marginal productivity of the worker in one firm more than it raises his productivity in other firms. By contrast, "general" training raises marginal productivity equally in many firms. Since, under competitive conditions, wage rates are determined by workers' marginal productivities in other firms, a worker with "specific" training would be expected to receive a wage less than his actual marginal revenue productivity but more than his alternative productivity. . . .

indeed, to the existence of a market economy, as well as to the maintenance of political democracy.

Along the same lines it should be noted that the substantial role played by checking deposits in our economy requires, among other things, generalized literacy and competence with arithmetic operations. It is not necessary to argue the issue of cause versus effect, but only to recognize the essentiality of literacy—a principal output of elementary education—to the present state of our economic development. Nor does saying this deny the possibility that other factors were also indispensable to growth.

Equality of opportunity seems to be a frequently expressed social goal. Education plays a prominent role in discussions of this goal, since the financial and other obstacles to education confronted by some people are important barriers to its achievement.[39] If equality of opportunity is a social goal, then education pays social returns over and above the private returns to the recipients of the education.

Although the long-term effect of education on future earnings is surely the most powerful income distribution consequence of education,[40] there are also some short-term effects. These occur through the provision by schools of things traditionally considered to be private consumer goods and services—including subsidized lunch programs, musical instrument lessons, and driver-training courses.

Earlier we distinguished between the output of education in the form of the student's training and the output of the system or means by which the training was accomplished—the latter being illustrated by custodial or child-care services. The same distinction may be made with respect to higher education, the point being that the training of students is not the only output of schools; a joint product is the research activity of college and university faculties, from which society reaps benefits. It is undoubtedly true that were it not for the higher-education system the volume of basic research would be smaller. A question exists regarding the extent to which the value of the research is reflected in salaries and, thereby, in private returns. The relation of education to research and of research to social returns deserves more attention from economists.[41]

---

[39] Even if it were true that educating everyone would widen the personal distribution of earnings compared with what it would be with less education, it would not follow that additional education for some people would worsen their relative or absolute economic position.

[40] The relation between education and income distribution has been studied by J. Mincer ("Investment in Human Capital and Personal Income Distribution," *Journal of Political Economy*, August, 1958, pp. 281–302) and L. Soltow ("The Distribution of Income Related to Changes in the Distributions of Education, Age and Occupation," *Review of Economics and Statistics*, November, 1960, pp. 450–53).

[41] For an interesting study of returns from research see Z. Griliches, "Research Costs and Social Returns: Hybrid Corn and Related Innovations," *Journal of Political Economy*, October, 1958, pp. 419–31.

Training of persons in particular kinds of skills may result in important external benefits if there are bottlenecks to economic development. In the context of underdeveloped economies, one writer, while particularly noting the political significance of primary and higher education, and the prestige significance of the latter, argues: "Secondary education is essential to the training of 'medium' personnel (elementary teachers, monitors, officials, middle classes). The shortage of such people is today a real obstacle to economic development."[42] But without perfect capital markets and appropriate subsidization programs, these socially valuable people may be unable to capture for themselves the full value of their contribution. Therefore, their earnings would understate the full benefits of their education.

IV

In the preceding pages I have asked: "Who receive the benefits from education?" In addition, I have considered some of the limited possibilities for quantifying certain of the benefits. As plans are developed for future research I urge that more attention be directed to the spatial and temporal dimensions of these benefits.

While much work remains, we might summarize our findings. We have noted that some of the benefits of education are realized at the time the education is being received (that is, in the "short" run); others, after the formal education has been completed (that is, in the "long" run). Benefits to mothers, in terms of the child-care role of schools, and benefits to neighbors in keeping children "off the streets" are realized while the education is being obtained. Any benefits associated with subsequent employment of the students as well as benefits to the student's future children are realized later.

We have found, further, that benefits from education occur not only at various times but also in various places. The benefits of education do not necessarily accrue to people in the area or in the school district which financed the child's education. In particular, some of the benefits depend upon the individual's place of residence, which may change. Location of many residence-related benefits as well as employment-related benefits will be determined partly by population migration, though this is not generally true of benefits to family members and to society as a whole. While it is not necessarily true that total benefits will depend upon one's location, the point is that the particular beneficiaries will be a function of the location of the individual. Thus, the process of migration is a process of spatial shifting of some of the external effects of education.

[42] Michael Debeauvals, "Economic Problems of Education in the Underdeveloped Countries," in International Association of Universities, *op. cit.*, pp. 116–17.

Some interesting questions are raised simply by the recognition that external benefits of education exist, and that they are not all in broad, amorphous form; that is, that to some extent these benefits accrue to particular, rather well-defined, groups. Thus, to the extent that the education system at the elementary level is producing child-care services as an output, benefit-principle taxation would suggest that families of the children might pay for these benefits.[43] In general, a desire to use this taxation principle would imply attempts to identify various groups of education beneficiaries and to assess taxes in recognition of the distribution of benefits.[44]

It seems to me that there is a legitimate question concerning the justice of requiring broad, public support for education insofar as the benefits are narrow and private, except as an income-redistributive device. For example, to the extent that there is really no educational sacrifice involved in having children attend split-shift classes, so that the real motive for the abolition of split-shifts is to make life more comfortable for mothers who have all of their children in school at the same time, then a question of equity arises: should non-parents be expected to share the costs associated with the provision of these child-care services for parents? The answer may not be an unequivocal "no," but the question deserves further consideration. Except for lack of information, or a disavowal of benefit-principle taxation, there is little rationale for failure of our education-tax system to recognize the existence of particular groups of beneficiaries.

There is another strong reason in addition to the alleged justice of benefit-principle taxation for identifying benefits and beneficiaries. To the extent that the distribution of tax burdens for the support of education differs substantially from the distribution of education benefits, it is likely that education will be either undersupported or oversupported from an allocative-efficiency standpoint, given the existing preference structure and distribution of income and wealth.[45]

Both with respect to equity and to efficiency in education finance, the increasing phenomenon of migration needs to be recognized. Insofar as some of the benefits of education depend upon the location of the individual and insofar as this location is a variable over his lifetime, some of the benefits from education accrue to people who have played no part at all in the financing of this particular person's education. This would seem to be especially pertinent with respect to areas of substantial net in- or out-migration. Areas experiencing net in-migration might be expected, on benefit-principle grounds, to subsidize areas of net out-migration, particularly if highly productive people are involved. Subsidy in the opposite

---

[43] This point came out in a discussion with Julius Margolis.

[44] This is not to argue that the benefit principle, in contrast to the ability-to-pay or some other principle, should necessarily prevail.

[45] However, an objective of education may be to change the distribution.

direction might be justified insofar as the in-migrants to an area are relatively unproductive compared to its out-migrants. Needless to say, there are good and powerful arguments in favor of keeping all the financing of education at a local level. However, a thorough analysis of the issue would seem to require recognition of the points raised here.

The analytical approach to benefit identification employed in this paper is one of many alternatives; it does appear to have the advantage of focusing on the time and the location of education benefits, and these are relevant to the study both of efficiency in the allocation of resources between education and other ends and of equity in the financing of education.

It is clear that even with much additional effort we shall be unable to measure all the relevant benefits of education. At the same time the following four points are worth noting, and they summarize the views expressed in this paper: (1) identification of benefits is the logical step prior to measurement and, therefore, recognizing the forms of benefits represents some progress; (2) determination of what it is we are trying to measure will make it easier to develop useful quantification methods; (3) some reasonable measures of some education benefits are possible; (4) even partial measurement may disclose benefits sufficiently sizable to indicate a profitable investment, so that consideration of the non-measured benefits would, a fortiori, support the expenditure decision.

In any event, and however difficult the measurement task is, it remains true that education expenditure decisions will be made, and they will be made on the basis of whatever information is available.

Appendix: Costs of Education

The objective here is to consider briefly, at the conceptual level, some of the issues involved in estimating costs of education. There is no doubt that a complete picture of the cost of education would include all foregone opportunities, whether or not reflected by actual expenditures. Thus, the attempt to measure foregone production by looking at foregone earnings of students in school is fully appropriate. There is, of course, the difficult question of how to estimate the foregone earnings—in particular, whether they may be estimated by looking at the earnings of people of comparable age and sex who were not in school.

One of the issues is whether those in school are not, in general, more able and ambitious, so that their opportunity cost of schooling exceeds the earnings by their "drop-out" counterparts. Another involves the effect on earnings (actually, on the value of marginal productivity) of a large influx to the labor market, such as would occur if all college, or all high-school, students entered the labor force.

But it seems to me that this latter issue is beside the point. Studies involving cost and benefits of education are surely not directed to the question whether there should or should not be education. Rather the issue is the profitability or productivity of reasonably small increments or decrements to education. The issue is whether fewer or more people should be encouraged to go further in school. Only marginal changes are being contemplated.

Still on the subject of estimating foregone production among students by estimating foregone earnings, there is the additional question of the validity of using earnings of employed people when there is a question whether resources released from the schools would or would not find employment. Thus, the view is not uncommon that measuring foregone earnings of students by the earnings of presently employed people is satisfactory only if there is little unemployment.[46] This question arises frequently, especially when public investment is being considered. Thus, it inevitably arises when the economic efficiency of public health expenditures is being discussed; would the additional labor resources made available by an improvement in public health be able to find employment? And with regard to education, would labor resources released from schools be able to find employment?

It seems to me to be analytically unwise to mix study of the allocative efficiency of additional expenditures on education with study of the efficiency of monetary and fiscal policy in maintaining full employment. I would like to urge that in looking at the question of whether to invest more in education, we consider what students could earn and produce, not what they might actually earn or produce, as affected by unemployment. The efficiency of educational expenditures in dealing with unemployment is a quite different question from the efficiency of education as an allocation problem. Although there might be short-run transitional unemployment associated with some movement of students into the labor force, the basic issue of investment in people through education is of the long run.[47]

The alternative production foregone because of education also involves the government services used by educational institutions. Since many of these services are rendered without charge to the schools, they are generally, and mistakenly, omitted from discussion of costs. Recognition by R. C. Blitz of the relevance of these services to estimation of education costs is a valid and important point.[48] However, estimating the social cost of these services as equal to the value of the property and sales taxes which the schools would have paid had they not been exempt is conceptually inappropriate (albeit perhaps pragmatically reasonable). To the extent that the services rendered to schools by governments are "pure public services," the actual marginal cost of providing these services to the school is zero. The essence of "pure" public services is that everyone may enjoy them in common, and the consumption by one person does not subtract from the amount available to others. For example, it is not at all clear how much additional police or fire services will be required in a community by virtue of the fact that there is a school within its limits.

At the same time, services performed by governments are never entirely of a

[46] See, for example, Rivlin, op. cit., p. 12.

[47] Mary Jean Bowman shares this view: "Such validity, if any, as may attach to it [the view that marginal social opportunity costs of education are zero when unemployment is serious] is in any case limited to short term marginal valuations, whereas we are interested in long-term averages and aggregates. When long-term aggregate human capital formation is the focus, social opportunity costs are not zero even with chronic unemployment" ("Human Capital: Concepts and Measures," in Mushkin [ed.], Higher Education).

[48] "The Nation's Education Outlay," in Mushkin (ed.), Higher Education.

"pure public service" nature—particularly in the long run (for example, public libraries, which are frequently used by students)—so the marginal cost of providing them to a school will, in general, exceed zero. But the marginal cost is likely to be below average cost and, therefore, to be below the estimated foregone property and sales taxes, which are related to average costs of providing public services.

Since social costs represent alternatives foregone, it is certainly not correct to include among the costs of education costs which would have been incurred anyway; therefore, all the food, shelter, and clothing costs of students while they are at school should not be considered a cost of education.[49] At the same time, if any of these maintenance costs are higher for students than they would be were the children not in school, then these additional costs are justifiably charged against the education process. If additional clothing, laundry, and transportation costs are incurred by virtue of a person being a student, these incremental costs are quite relevant to the issue of the productivity of investment in education. Such cost may be particularly high for college students living away from home, though they may not equal zero for college students living at home, or for elementary- or high-school students.

[49] See discussion by Rivlin, *loc. cit.*, pp. 11–12, correctly criticizing the study by Harold F. Clark and Ruth E. Sobokov for including them.

Part
Four

CONTINUED

Health and Mobility

Does human capital formation occur in ways other than investment in formal schooling? The all too obvious answer is, yes. On-the-job training, informal "learning by doing," improved health, greater mobility, better job information, and amelioration of discrimination and poverty are additional ways in which improved human capital formation may occur.

Even though health investment is an obvious dimension to human capital formation, improved health also nicely illustrates that things left unsaid may alter the character of benefit-cost conclusions dramatically. Suppose, for example, that the eradication of disease increases longevity in an under-developed country already plagued with overpopulation problems. Are net "social" benefits negative or positive, and at what price are they obtained? Or take the case of interstate migration in the United States. To what extent does the depopulation of rural America, which has consistently exhibited an unfavorable balance on the human capital account, subsidize a rapidly growing urban America? Or does this rural-urban flow lead to urban diseconomies of scale?

The selection by Herbert E. Klarman **21** is a general review of benefit-cost analysis in the health field. This is followed by an article by Selma J. Mushkin and Burton A. Weisbrod **22** which measures the stock of health capital in the 1960 American work force. The interregional transfer of human capital has many economic implications for personal and aggregate economic welfare—a topic ably discussed by Mary Jean Bowman and Robert G. Myers **23**.

21

Present Status of Cost-Benefit Analysis in the Health Field

Improvement in the quality of manpower is by no means the exclusive province of education. Investments in health are an important aspect of human capital formation. Moreover, tools of economic analysis can be and are applied to this form of human capital investment. Herbert

HERBERT E. KLARMAN

Klarman, Professor of Public Health Administration at The Johns Hopkins University, reveals this in his review of cost-benefit studies in health economics. He also suggests more discriminatory uses of this tool.

So much has been written in recent years about the application of cost-benefit analysis to the health field that almost every point that might be made has been made [1]. The task before us now is to discriminate, to choose among the several elements of the procedure, discarding some and changing the relative emphasis of others; to combine them into a useful analytical tool; and to try to apply this tool to concrete problems in order to advance—and justify—the best possible programs.

It is only fair to observe that policy decisions were made prior to the advent of cost-benefit analysis. Some of these decisions must have been correct under the circumstances then prevailing and others might even meet the more stringent test of a retrospective review.

Reprinted from Herbert E. Klarman, "Present Status of Cost-Benefit Analysis in the Health Field," *American Journal of Public Health* 57 (November 1967), pp. 1948–53, with the permission of the author and publisher, The American Public Health Association, Inc.

The Nature of Cost-Benefit Analysis

Looking ahead, cost-benefit analysis aims to measure all the consequences of a program or policy, including so-called spillover effects. However, some of the consequences are difficult to predict and some are difficult to measure. Among the most difficult to predict are drastic shifts in people's expectations and behavior, as exemplified by changes in the birth rate after World War II. Among the most difficult to measure are the intangible aspects of human life and experience, including the sheer value of human life or of good health.

With respect to the value of human life—apart from livelihood—it has been suggested recently that the meaningful question is to inquire into the willingness of persons to pay for a specified reduction in the statistical probability of dying [2].

Sometimes it is proposed that cost-benefit analysis be applied to problems that may not require it [3]. In the absence of appreciable spillover (or external) effects or of complex bundles of outputs, there is no need to employ an elaborate analytical apparatus. Thus if the problem consists of a comparison between two programs that promise identical outputs at different costs, the cheaper one is clearly preferred. In this case the comparison of programs has been reduced to a comparison of costs. If one can conceive of two hospitals with certain specified characteristics and size as being identical, then a comparison of costs suffices.

Essentially cost-benefit analysis entails a comparison of costs and benefits for a series of programs thought of as alternatives or competitors for public funds. The cost side of the equation consists of the projected expenditures, such as are itemized in a budget. The benefits are those future losses that will be averted by the success of the program. There are three categories of benefit: (1) savings in the use of health resources, (2) gains in economic output, and (3) satisfactions from better health. Unlike manpower, equipment, or supplies, money is not a tangible economic resource. It is neither a cost nor a potential benefit. The transfer of money in the absence of production represents a transfer in command over resources, not a cost.

A frequent source of confusion to readers of the cost-benefit literature is that cost and benefit are usually not measured at the same time and that the so-called costs of a disease being measured are really the projected benefits, on the implicit assumption that the disease will be totally eliminated or eradicated. To view the costs and benefits of a program simultaneously, or at least to state clearly which section of the analysis is under consideration, serves to lessen this source of confusion.

The assumption of eradication, if unrealistic, can lead to a faulty approach to the problem facing the decision-maker. Most often the choice is not between doing everything and doing nothing but between doing more than is currently being done, or less, and by how much. The appropriate analysis is in terms of increments of resources, their cost, and prospective returns. An existing program, say a water supply fit for drinking, is essential for community life. It may or may not pay to spend additional money to make it still purer, in order to serve other purposes, such as recreation. It should be understood that to say it is not worth while to spend more on a given program is not the same as to say that current expenditures are being wasted [4].

Differential Difficulties in Measurement

Cost-benefit analysis, an offspring of welfare economics and public finance, the former an abstruse branch of economic theory and the latter the applied study of government expenditures and taxation, has been developed as a tool of quantitative analysis. The difficulties of performing measurements outside the market economy are many, as has been pointed out [5]. The temptation is great to measure what appears to be objective and reproducible, rather than what is really sought. It is so much more practicable to measure the prospective value of human output than the value of health itself that the former is calculated with precision and the latter tends to be disregarded. It is so much easier to ascertain the production loss due to mortality than that due to debility, that again the former is measured with care, and the latter neglected and lost from view.

None of this would matter in the competition among programs for the health dollar if the several elements of loss (or prospective benefit) were approximately constant proportions of the total loss for each disease. Sometimes economists make this assumption for convenience of analysis [6]. The assumption is not realistic, of course, for the mortality loss is relatively small for most mental diseases and high for some cancer sites. In some mental diseases and arthritis, morbidity generates a loss in output while in skin diseases the loss is largely in personal comfort and in self-esteem. It goes without saying that if the assumption is unrealistic, the implications of the analysis may be misleading.

The sovereign public may wish to pursue the goals of comfort or enjoyment, as well as any other. It is not for the economic analyst to make definitive value judgments but to explore the implications of alternative values.

It is a distortion, moreover, as well as an oversimplification, of the task of economics to view additions to the national income as the sole or principal economic benefit of a health services program. The goal of production is consumer satisfaction, including the enjoyment of leisure. The limitations of a truncated view of economics are most obvious in dealing with health services for children. In our society a child is scarcely to be viewed as an object of investment [2].

Recent Developments and Applications

It is admittedly a complex technical task to try to measure some of the elements that are not being measured now. Yet it is fair to note that the elements that are now being measured so readily and with elegance were but recently measured with difficulty and a high degree of approximation. Examples of substantial improvement come readily to mind, such as the employment of average earnings figures classified by sex, race, age, and now, level of education [7]. There is no reason to despair over the prospects of technological progress in this field, provided we know what to seek and pursue it with diligence.

In the past two or three years, calculations have been performed by Conley on vocational rehabilitation [8]; by Klarman on heart disease [9]; by Rice on heart disease, cancer, and stroke; by Rice again on all diseases, divided into 20-odd diagnostic categories; and by Rice very recently on the value of human life [7]. Theoretical contributions were also made by Mushkin, linking health with education [10], and by a group of economists convened by the De Bakey Commission to discuss the economics of medical research [4]. In October, 1966, Yett circulated a compendium of work under way in health economics, which reports on cost-benefit analyses applied to mental illness, artificial heart devices, birth control, and air pollution [11].

Papers presented at two conferences on government expenditures sponsored by the Brookings Institution bear to varying degrees on the problems encountered in the health field [1, 2, 5, 10], as do two recent British publications [12].

A noteworthy event in the application of cost-benefit analysis is the effort mounted last summer to employ cost-effectiveness in preparing the budget of the Department of Health, Education, and Welfare for fiscal year 1967–1968. Health services programs were included, with costs and benefits calculated simultaneously. I am not in a position to present a formal evaluation of this attempt. My impression is that the results varied, task force by task force [13]. Among the factors responsible for variation are the problem area, the specific programs evaluated, and the availability of full-time staff.

The application of cost-benefit analysis as a crash program is almost bound to present the weakest case for the technic. In the long run such an attempt, if properly exploited, is bound to be a step forward in the rational allocation of resources among health services. It results in a more complete listing of factors to be taken into account in budgeting a program than would otherwise be the case. It compels one to recognize how much or how little is known about the several factors. Finally, it can lead to a formulation of approaches and methods to obtain the knowledge that is needed but lacking. Arranging the available information in systematic fashion throws light on the question of priorities for pursuing such knowledge.

Valuation and Outcome

The problems of measurement to be pursued fall into two areas. It is for the economist, employing all of his traditional tools plus those of the operations researcher and the psychologist, to try to measure the value of the consumption aspects of health services. Among the approaches that have been proposed and attempted are those of insurance or game theory, expenditures for an analogous disease at old age, jury verdicts, the implications of past decisions on public expenditures, and the sheer listing of known consequences without quantification or valuation [14].

It remains for epidemiology and the clinical trial to determine the effects produced by health services. It is futile for the economist to attach values to programs when the physical units are not known. In Karl Evang's phrase this would be akin to "prognosis without diagnosis," a weakness that he attributes to economists.

It is no great mystery why knowledge concerning the end results of rendering health services is sometimes lacking. Among the factors that have been listed are: medicine is not an exact science and physicians disagree; prolonged longitudinal studies do not offer attractive careers; the presence of asymptomatic disease in control groups affects the criterion for evaluation; the possibility of inducing iatrogenic disease; the simultaneous presence of multiple diseases [15].

The best results will accrue from a dialogue between the economist and the physician, such as was initiated by Fuchs in the spring of 1966. He reviewed the literature on the current capabilities of medicine to improve health, disease by disease, and presented it to physicians for criticism and emendation [16].

In any event, better decisions will be made if all elements of a problem are specified, those not being measured as well as those that are. Just a listing will serve as a reminder that the elements not measured have a value greater than zero [17].

If an automobile accident is prevented, the benefit from a given expenditure must be greater than that following a full cure after treatment, even if the obvious effects on tangible costs were identical, for at least two reasons. One, anxiety on the part of close relatives is avoided. Two, there is no damage to vital organs, obviating any concern over residual effects.

A complete listing will also help to keep germane the benefits attributed to a proposed program. For example, if a principal benefit of the new regional complexes were the promotion of area-wide coordination of health services [18], rather than the provision of better and more services for patients with heart disease, cancer, or stroke, then it would be appropriate to ask whether this instrument would be best suited to that purpose.

Addendum on Medical Research

Cost-benefit analysis, when applied to medical research, presents certain special aspects [19]. In the language of economics, the output of basic research is a public good, because it is not appropriable by the producer. It offers great externalities in production because knowledge, once obtained, is easy to reproduce. Since knowledge crosses geographic boundaries easily, there are widespread benefits. These characteristics reflect differences in degree from health services, perhaps not differences in kind.

Unique characteristics of research are the uncertainty of outcome of any project and even uncertainty where its results will be applied. A good example of the latter is the reduction in patient-load in mental hospitals achieved through knowledge gained from research in earth molds, nutrition, and circulation of the blood.

The estimated benefits of research are the product of the probability of success in research multiplied by the probability of a specified reduction in the calculated economic loss when services are offered and used.

Scarcity and Futurity

The fact that this paper was prepared for a meeting of the American Public Health Association has certain implications. One is recognition of economic considerations in making health services decisions. It is no longer necessary to argue that economic resources are scarce (relative to wants), that all desirable social objectives cannot be pursued simultaneously, and that every society, however wealthy, must choose between what it will and will not do [20]. An obvious proviso to accepting the contribution of economic analysis is that it be done competently and that it will have relevance to the real world.

Such a posture is appropriate for the public policy-maker or the public health administrator. The clinician caring for his own patients is not expected to assume this posture and should not. He must continue to act as if human life and health were invaluable. It is for society to introduce the constraints that make this objective unattainable, if only to diffuse the awful responsibility for decisions affecting life and death [2].

A corollary to the proposition that sound economic analysis can make a contribution to health services policy is that the rate of discount will reduce the weight accorded to future streams of benefit and cost, thereby permitting each stream to be expressed as a single value, the present or capital value [21]. There is no other way to allocate resources over time. In socialist economies, where there is no private property or income therefrom, a rate of interest is nevertheless charged, so that capital may be rationed among industries. I do not understand why some public health students find the process of discounting so distasteful. Of course, discounting is an academic matter when the time interval under consideration is short, say two or three years.

A more valid point is that economists have failed to provide sufficient guidance on the level of the discount rate to be employed. There are some good reasons for this failure [22], but students of public health should not be compelled to make this decision, as well as the others.

Programs are directed to the future, and they are analyzed in terms of present knowledge, as projected. Thus an allowance is built in for economic growth, which serves as a partial offset to the operation of the discount rate. Sometimes the change in medical care prices is projected relative to other prices. But some things cannot be projected, particularly the effects of changes in technology still to be born or changes in the forms of delivering services still to be conceived. If the time span is long enough, say more than five years, provision for the flexibility of a program becomes desirable and a justified addition to its cost [23].

I have said little about procedures or technics for making calculations. Such matters are best handled in the course of describing actual calculations, and precise procedures are being steadily reported [7, 8, 9]. Indeed, there is some danger of premature codification of accepted procedures, without regard for the reasons that certain conventions were adopted by a student working on a particular problem. One convention that may yet prove troublesome is the assumption of full employment, in the fact of evidence that many disabled persons do not find jobs after rehabilitation [24]. The last word has probably not been said about measuring the value of the housewife's services at the wage of a full-time maid. Alternative procedures are in terms of what it takes to replace the housewife at home [25] or what it takes to bring her into the labor market.

Tasks Ahead

The tasks ahead appear to be as follows:

1. To try to calculate both the costs and benefits of specific programs, always looking ahead and looking out for side effects. We shall learn the technic by doing.
2. To formulate the problems in a manner that will clearly point to the kinds of data required, and to ask for the compilation of data where they do not now exist.
3. To enlist the efforts of investigators and program analysts from various disciplines to help develop and bring to bear the methods of measurement and analysis required.
4. To continue to strive for good judgment in making decisions when major elements of the cost-benefit calculation are missing, as they frequently are.

References

[1] Klarman, Herbert E. The Economics of Health. Irvington-on-Hudson, N.Y.: Columbia University Press, 1965, pp. 162–173; also, for more complete citations, Klarman, Herbert E. "Syphilis Control Programs." In: Dorfman, Robert, ed., Measuring Benefits of Government Investments. Brookings Institution, Washington, D.C., 1965, pp. 367–410; p. 369.

[2] Schelling, Thomas C. The Life You Save May Be Your Own. Paper presented at the Second Conference on Government Expenditures. Brookings Institution, Washington, D.C. (Sept. 15–16), 1966 (processed).

[3] Llewellyn-Davies, Richard. Facilities and Equipment for Health Services. Millbank Mem. Fund Quart. 49,3:249–272, 266–268 (July), 1966, Pt. 2.

[4] Klarman, Herbert E. "Conference on the Economics of Medical Research." Report of President's Commission on Heart Disease, Cancer, and Stroke. Vol. 2, Gov. Ptg. Office, Washington, D.C., 1965, pp. 631–44; p. 635.

[5] McKean, Ronald N. The Use of Shadow Prices in Evaluating Federal Expenditure Programs. Paper presented at the Second Conference on Government Expenditures, The Brookings Institution, Washington, D.C. (Sept. 15–16), 1966 (processed).

[6] Weisbrod, Burton A. Economics of Public Health. Philadelphia, Pa.: University of Pennsylvania Press, 1961, pp. 95–98.

[7a] Rice, Dorothy P. Economic Costs of Cardiovascular Diseases and Cancer, 1962. Health Economic Ser. No. 5, Gov. Ptg. Office, Washington, D.C., 1965. (Reprinted from Report of President's Commission On Heart Disease, Cancer and Stroke. Vol. 2. Washington, D.C.: Gov. Ptg. Office, 1965, pp. 439–630.)

[7b] ———. Estimating the Cost of Illness. Health Economic Ser. No. 6. Washington, D.C.: Gov. Ptg. Office, 1966.

[7c] ———. The Economic Value of Human Life. A.J.P.H. 57,11:1954 (Nov.), 1967.

[8] Conley, Ronald W. The Economics of Vocational Rehabilitation. Baltimore, Md.: Johns Hopkins Press, 1965.

[9] Klarman, Herbert E. "Socioeconomic Impact of Heart Disease." In: Second National Conference on Cardiovascular Disease, The Heart and Circulation, Vol. 2. Washington, D.C.: Federation of American Societies for Experimental Biology, 1965, pp. 693–707.

[10] Mushkin, Selma. Comments on Klarman's "Syphilis Control Programs." See reference 1 above, pp. 410–414.

[11] Yett, Donald E. Research on Health Economics. Published by the author, at the University of Southern California, Los Angeles (Oct.), 1966 (processed).

[12] Peters, G. H. Cost-Benefit Analysis and Public Expenditure. Eaton Paper 8, The Institute of Economic Affairs, London, 1966. Prest, A. R. and Turvey, R. Cost-Benefit Analysis: A Survey. The Economic Journal 75,300:683-735 (Dec.), 1965.

[13] Department of Health, Education, and Welfare, Program Analysis Group on Selected Disease Control Programs.
a. Application of Benefit-Cost Analysis to Motor Vehicle Accidents. Office of Assistant Secretary for Program Coordination (Aug.), 1966.
b. Public Health Programs for Arthritis. Division of Chronic Diseases, U.S. Public Health Service (Sept.), 1966.
c. An Analysis of Planning, Programming, and Budgeting in Cancer Control. Cancer Control Branch, Division of Chronic Diseases, U.S. Public Health Service (Oct.), 1966.

[14] Klarman, Herbert E. "Socioeconomic Impact of Heart Disease," pp. 700-701; also Feldstein, Martin S. Measuring the Costs and Benefits of Health Services, World Health Organization, Regional Office for Europe, Copenhagen (June), 1966 (processed).

[15] ———. "Socioeconomic Impact of Heart Disease," op. cit., p. 698.

[16] Fuchs, Victor R. "The Contribution of Health Services to the American Economy." Millbank Mem. Fund Quart. 49,4 (Oct.), 1966: pt. 2.

[17] Klarman, "Conference on the Economics of Medical Research," op. cit., p. 638.

[18] Roemer, Milton I. Letter to the Editor. A.J.P.H. 56,4:562-563 (Apr.), 1966.

[19] Klarman, "Socioeconomic Impact of Heart Disease," op. cit., pp. 703-704.

[20] Stigler, George J. The Theory of Price (rev. ed.). New York: Macmillan, 1952, p. 2.

[21] Rice, Dorothy P. Letter to the Editor. A.J.P.H. 56,4:564-565 (Apr.), 1966.

[22] Klarman, "Syphilis Control Programs," op. cit., pp. 371-374.

[23] ———. Some Technical Problems in Areawide Planning for Hospital Care. J. Chronic Dis. 17,9:735-747, 740 (Sept.), 1964.

[24] Conley, The Economics of Vocational Rehabilitation, op. cit., p. 137.

[25] Weisbrod, Economics of Public Health, op. cit., pp. 114-119.

Investment in Health—Lifetime Health Expenditures on the 1960 Work Force

What is the magnitude of aggregate investment in health in the American labor force? Selma J. Mushkin, currently with the Urban Institute, and Burton A. Weisbrod, Professor of Economics at the University of Wisconsin, explain a variety of conceptual and methodological problems encountered in valuing the

SELMA J. MUSHKIN
BURTON A. WEISBROD

health capital stock. They estimate that investment in health for the 1960 labor force was $204 billion, considering both private and public outlays.

What are the sources of economic growth? Recent attempts to explore this question have all led to the view that emphasis on quantitative increases in the traditional land, labor, and capital is mistaken—that much of our economic growth appears to have been a function of other factors: qualitative changes in resources, changes in production functions, and economies of scale.

Recently an increasing amount of economic research has been directed to the changes occurring in the quality of labor resources. The hypothesis is that labor productivity is rising in part because the capabilities of workers, quite apart from cooperating resources, are improving. People who are healthier and better educated can produce more. Moreover, a healthier

Reprinted from Selma J. Mushkin and Burton A. Weisbrod, "Investment in Health—Lifetime Health Expenditures on the 1960 Work Force," *Kyklos* 16 (April 1963), pp. 533–97, with the permission of the authors and publisher.

person can benefit more from education, and an educated person can benefit more from training on the job. In these ways the economy's production-possibility frontier is pushed outward. Health and education expenditures are principal means by which the quality of labor resources can be improved. These improvements in quality represent the application of capital to labor; thus, we might refer to the resulting resource as a hybrid of labor and capital —human capital. Any attempt to determine the sources of economic growth would be incomplete if changes in the quality of human capital were neglected.

Answers to the questions of how much of the U.S. economic growth can be attributed to each form of investment in human capital still elude us.[1] In this paper we shall attempt to take a small step in the direction of determining how much economic growth can be traced to investment in the health of our population. Specifically, we shall estimate the value of privately and publicly-provided resources which have been devoted to the health of persons employed in 1960, over their lifetimes. We shall then see how the magnitude of these expenditures on health compares with the corresponding expenditures on schooling. We shall also compare the magnitude of health resources embodied in the 1960 work force and the resources in the 1960 stock of physical capital. In the process we shall note changes through time in the pattern of private health expenditures by age, and in the mix of private and public expenditures on health.

Looking at health expenditures as investment in productivity does not deny the consumption value of better health for its own sake. It does, however, assume that whatever the motivation of those financing health expenditures, there are effects on productivity.

Every health expenditure cannot be considered investment in human capital—at least in the sense of contributing to production and economic growth—just as every education expenditure cannot.[2] But the dividing line between a health (or education) expenditure that contributes to enlarged output and one that does not is difficult to draw. Cosmetic surgery, to take one illustration, may be elective surgery in a medical sense, but may affect an individual's productivity markedly by influencing his attitude toward other people. Health expenditures for the care of the dying and of those with permanent and total disabilities may be considered as the clearest cases of

[1] Investment in human capital through health, schooling, on-the-job training, migration, and market information was the subject of a recent conference of the National Bureau of Economic Research. The papers presented there appeared as a supplement to the October 1962 issue of the *Journal of Political Economy*.

[2] It is by no means clear that the study of world geography, ancient history, or music appreciation, to cite but a few examples, will contribute to worker productivity, although they may contribute much to one's enjoyment of life. In his "Capital Formation by Education," T. W. Schultz produces estimates of total resource costs of education, but he notes, properly, the remaining task of allocating these costs between consumption and investment. (*Journal of Political Economy*, December 1960, *68*, 571–583.)

consumption outlays which do not improve the quality of labor resources, and thus, do not increase future labor productivity.

Our interest in the sources of economic growth leads us to investigate the influence of health expenditures on the nation's output, by studying the lifetime health expenditures on the 1960 work force. The procedure employed considers *none* of the health expenditures on persons who were not in the 1960 work force (employed labor force)—although to the extent that production occurs outside the market (e.g., by women in the home), the contribution of improved health to real output will be understated by an analysis limited to market output; and the procedure considers *all* of the lifetime health expenditures by, or on, persons in the work force. In this latter respect we are tending to overstate the investment (future output-increasing) component of these expenditures because of the consumption aspect discussed above. Furthermore, we do not account for depreciation. Since a person's working-life expectancy declines as he ages, the present value of the additional future output resulting from previous health expenditures generally declines also. In this paper we investigate the medical care investment at its original cost rather than at its present value. At the same time, we may be tending either to understate or overstate total investment by focusing only on current work-force members, including temporary members while disregarding temporary non-members. These biases in our results are analogous to those present in previous estimates of the stock of investment in people through education: all education costs incurred for working persons, but only for working persons, have been considered generally as investment; there has been no explicit consideration of which education expenditures have contributed to market productivity; and the investment (i.e., expenditures) has been valued at undepreciated cost.[3]

There are at least two objectives which one might have in mind when one considers estimating the stock of health investment in human capital: (1) to determine the percentage rate of return being realized on the resources which were required to produce the stock; and (2) to determine the amount of past or future increases in output (economic growth) which may be attributable to the existing stock. Each objective requires a different definition of the stock. For (1) it is necessary to include not only the value of investment which was successful in raising productivity, but also the value of unsuccessful investment including that on persons who had been expected to be in the labor force, but who either did not enter, or left prematurely. For objective (2), however, it is necessary to consider only investment which was medically successful in influencing the number and productivity

[3] G. S. Becker, "Underinvestment in College Education?" *American Economic Review, Proceedings*, May 1960, *50*, 346–354; T. W. Schultz, "Education and Economic Growth," Offprint of Chapter III, *Social Forces Influencing American Education*, 1961, Chicago, National Society for the Study of Education.

of workers and which, therefore, contributed (or will contribute) to aggregate economic growth. An analogy may be helpful. If one is interested in discovering the rate of return on past investment on oil drilling, one should consider the total resource inputs including those which produced only dry wells. But if one is interested in the future output of oil one should consider only the successful investment, disregarding the costs of dry wells.

In the present paper we are considering the health stock in the latter sense—as a contributor to economic growth. Consequently, for our purpose the appropriate definition of the stock would exclude the value of health inputs which were devoted to persons who did not or will not, contribute to output. Of course, people enter and leave the work force constantly; by considering the health stock in those persons who were in the work force in a particular year, as described below, we assumed implicitly that any of them who were *in* the work force temporarily were matched by an equal number of persons of the same ages who were out temporarily.

Before we proceed to estimate the "health stock" in the work force, we need to decide on an appropriate definition of health expenditures. Although it is true that food, shelter, clothing, and recreation all have an impact on one's health (just as many things other than schooling contribute to one's "education"), we shall define health expenditures more narrowly to include both private and public outlays on traditional health services: physician services, hospital care, dental services, and drugs, and such public health expenditures as those on environmental health, medical research, and sanitation.

Now we turn to the principal question to which we sought an answer: how much has been spent for health services for persons in the 1960 work force? First we estimated private expenditures. The beginning step was to take reported estimates of the age distribution of the 1960 work force using figures for the average number of employed persons by age. The average age was assumed to be the mid-point of each age interval except for persons 70 years old or over who were assumed to be age 70.

Private medical care expenditures were then traced back through the years of life of each age cohort, starting with the mid-point of each age group, and continuing back to the date of birth. For example, for those in the age group 14 to 15 (14.5 mid-point), expenditures were traced from 1960 to 1946. For those 70 and over expenditures were traced from 1960 to 1890. No distinction was made between expenditures for males and females because of data limitations.

Average expenditures for each of 14 age groups during the years elapsing from birth to 1960 were estimated under the assumption that the pattern of relative expenditures by age remained unchanged within each of three periods of time, 1956–1960, 1943–1956, and 1890–1943. In other words, it was assumed that during each period, average expenditures at each age increased or decreased in the same proportion as the change in per capita private expenditures for health care. The 1957/58 Health Information Foundation study of the medical care spending pattern by age was used for the period 1956–1960, and the earlier 1952/53 study by the same organization was used for the years 1943–1956. The earliest study of private health expenditures by age available to us was the 1928–1931 study of the Committee on Costs of Medical Care. The pattern of expenditure in this study was applied for the entire period 1890–1943. All three age-expenditure functions are presented in Table 1 and Chart 1.

Table 1—Average (mean) gross expenditures for all personal health services per individual, by age, 12-month period

Age group	1928–1931 $	1952/53 $	1957/58 $
All ages	25	66	94
0–5	12	28	48
5–9	19		
10–14	17		
15–19	16		
6–17		38	49
20–24	28		
25–34	33		
18–34		70	98
35–44	29		
45–64	30		
35–54		80	108
55–64		96	129
65 and over	32	102	177

Sources: 1928–1931 data: I. S. Falk, Margaret C. Klem and Nathan Sinai, *The Incidence of Illness and the Receipt and Costs of Medical Care Among Representative Families*, Committee on Costs of Medical Care, 1933—1952/53 and 1957/58 data: O. W. Anderson, P. Collette, and J. Feldman, *Family Expenditure Patterns for Personal Health Services*, Health Information Foundation, New York, n.d., p. 11.

In deriving the estimated expenditure at each age level for a specific year, the base year data on medical care expenditures by age were adjusted to reflect the change in per capita medical care expenditures. The 1928–1931 age-expenditure pattern was applied up to 1943, for it was about that year that introduction of antibiotics, early ambulation in surgical cases, and prepayment marked the beginnings of a radical change in personal expenditure patterns for medical care.

The per capita expenditure estimates used in estimating each year's expenditures by age group were in turn derived from a number of sources. For 1948 to 1960 the estimates used were those developed by the Social Security Administration and published in the *Social Security Bulletin* of December 1960. Personal medical care expenditures include all private expenditures for medical care and voluntary health insurance: hospital services, physicians services, medical services, and dental services and miscellaneous health services. The per capita expenditures for the period 1929 to 1948 were computed from *National Income, (1951 edition) Supplement to the Survey of Current Business.* The data reported in the *Supplement* are the estimated medical-care-expenses component of personal expenditures developed as part of the national product estimates. The aggregates reported were converted to per capita amounts by dividing by the census estimates of the civilian population for July of each year.

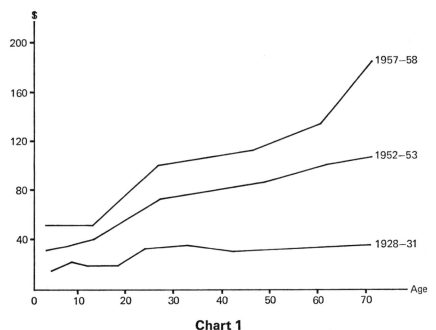

Chart 1
Mean Gross Expenditures for Personal Health Services Per Person, by Age, 12-Month Period, 1928–1931, 1952/53, and 1957/58

For selected years between 1909 and 1929 estimates of personal medical care expenses as summarized in *Historical Statistics of the United States* were used. Again these figures were converted to per capita amounts and the percentage changes between the base period, 1928–1931, and each of the years 1909 to 1929 were calculated as a step toward adjusting expenditures for each age cohort. For the years for which no estimates were reported in *Historical Statistics*, estimates of aggregate personal expenditures for medical care were developed by assuming a gradual change in the proportion of personal income devoted to medical care.

For ... 1890–1901, per capita expenditures for personal medical care were estimated from material reported in the Aldridge Report for 1890[4] and the Bureau of Labor Statistics Report for 1901.[5] Average family expenditures for medical care were converted to expenditures per family member and, in turn, to national aggregates by multiplying the expenditure per member by the total population. For both 1890 and 1901 the percent of personal income devoted to medical care outlays was calculated in order to estimate medical expenditures for the intervening years, and for the years between 1902 and 1909, when another estimate was available. Relative expenditures by age were assumed to be similar to those indicated in the 1928–1931 study—an assumption not wholly unrealistic in view of the relatively unchanged state of the medical arts during this period.

Having derived the average expenditures at each age in this way over the years 1890–1960, the second step in the computation was to add the expenditures for each of the age cohorts from the year of birth to 1960, in effect accumulating the expenditures made at the prices prevailing in the years in which expenditures were incurred. These cumulative expenditures were then multiplied by the number of persons in the work force in 1960 by age, to derive Table 2.

No adjustment of the data was made to exclude items of expenditure attributable to the extraordinary expenses of those in each age cohort who became permanently disabled or who died. That is, average expenditures by

Table 2—Estimate of health program stock (private outlays, only) of 1960 work force (current prices)

Age group	Persons in work force (in thousands)	Average health expenditures over lifetime $	Aggregate health investment (in millions) $
14–15	904	579.00	523.0
16–17	1,769	650.00	1,150.0
18–19	2,360	726.50	1,714.5
20–24	6,120	839.00	5,134.7
25–29	6,386	1,018.50	6,504.1
30–34	7,244	1,207.50	8,747.1
35–39	7,881	1,445.00	11,388.0
40–44	7,717	1,674.00	12,918.3
45–49	7,637	1,883.00	14,380.5
50–54	6,600	2,067.50	13,645.5
55–59	5,238	2,255.50	11,814.3
60–64	3,752	2,406.00	9,027.3
65–69	1,715	2,527.00	4,333.8
70 and over	1,358	2,587.50	3,513.8
Total	66,681		104,794.9

[4] *Report on Wholesale Prices and Wages*, Volume 5, Table 8.

[5] 18th Annual Report of the Commissioner of Labor. *Cost of Living and Retail Prices of Food*, Government Printing Office, 1901.

age for *all* persons were used to estimate expenditures for persons in the work force, and so our figures may be somewhat too high. There was one exception to our failure to adjust; namely, persons in the work force who were *over* 60 years of age were assumed to have average expenditures similar to those of persons of age 60, as a rough adjustment to exclude extraordinary expenses of the aged.

The costs of medical care during birth were not considered separately. In effect the costs of birth were included in the expenditure figures for adults. This tends to diminish the estimated expenditures for health care for the younger members of the work force in 1960 and to increase them somewhat for older members, compared with the estimates which would result from attributing costs of birth to the newborn.

Next the private-health-stock estimates from Table 2 were converted to 1960 prices; the results appear in Table 3. The price adjustments used were obtained as follows: For the period 1926–1960 the medical care price index of the Bureau of Labor Statistics (adjusted to a 1960 base) was used. For the period 1890 to 1926, a medical care price index was constructed in this manner:

(1) The Douglas index for all consumer prices for the period 1890 to 1926 was converted from an 1890–1899 base to a 1947–1949 base by splicing the Douglas and BLS indexes so that an index of all consumer prices (241 for 1926 on an 1890–1899 base) was converted to a 1947–1949 index (75.6 for 1926).[6]

(2) The 1926 relationship between the medical care price index and the 'all' consumer price index was assumed to be maintained throughout the period 1890–1926, except (a) medical care prices were assumed to be more rigid and to lag behind all consumer price changes, as suggested by the 1930–1940 experience; and (b) increases in medical care prices during World War I were assumed to have been in the same ratio to the increases in all consumer prices as they were during World War II.

(3) Estimated medical care prices on the 1947–1949 base were converted to 1960 price equivalents.

Average medical expenditures for each year 1890–1960, price-adjusted in this way, were cumulated for each age cohort. The cumulative expenditures for each age group, and the total (privately financed) health-program stock for the 1960 work force are shown in Table 3. The private health stock in the 1960 work force—that is, the lifetime private health expenditure of this group—was approximately $162 billion in 1960 prices, or $105 billion in current prices. The $162 billion was equivalent to $2,426 per member of the work force.

---

[6] US Bureau of Census, *Historical Statistics of the United States, Colonial Times to 1957*, Washington, DC, 1960, p. 127.

Table 3—Estimate of health program stock (private outlays, only) of 1960 work force (1960 prices)

Age group	Persons in work force (in thousands)	Average health expenditures over lifetime (1960 prices) $	Aggregate health stock (in millions) $
14–15	904	714	645.5
16–17	1,769	824	1,457.7
18–19	2,360	940	3,384.0
20–24	6,120	1,122	6,866.6
25–29	6,386	1,388	8,863.8
30–34	7,244	1,712	12,401.7
35–39	7,881	2,128	16,770.8
40–44	7,717	2,526	19,493.1
45–49	7,637	2,924	22,330.6
50–54	6,600	3,305	21,813.0
55–59	5,238	3,715	19,459.2
60–64	3,752	3,991	14,974.2
65–69	1,715	4,255	7,297.3
70 and over	1,358	4,442	6,032.2
Total	66,681		161,789.7

Next we wished to account for the *public* investment in the health of the work force. The amount of health services financed through the public sector was estimated from Census Bureau data on total public outlays (federal, state and local) for health and hospitals. Estimates are available from this source annually since 1952 and prior to that time biennially for the period beginning with 1932. Earlier censuses of governments were taken in 1902, 1913, 1922 and 1927.

Because of the importance of water-borne diseases at the turn of the century expenditures for sanitary engineering activities were included along with health and hospital expenditures as public health outlays in the first decades of the analysis. Health and hospital outlays were interpolated for years in which data were not available.

Persons in the 1960 work force were traced back to their date of birth, and beginning with those dates, per capita outlays for public health were allocated to them. In 1960 the work force accounted for 37 percent of the total population. Despite the fact that only 41.0 million of the 66.7 million in the 1960 work force were born in, or prior to, 1929 these 41.0 million persons accounted for 40 percent of the total 1929 population. Members of the 1960 work force accounted for 25 percent of the 1913 population and for roughly 4 percent of the population in the latter part of the 1890's.

Use of a single figure for per capita public expenditures on health and hospitals for persons at every age involves a bias upward because of the relatively large share of public expenditures which were actually for persons in the older age groups who were not in the work force, for persons with terminal illness, or for persons with mental illness who were not returned to the labor force. Perhaps as much as 20–25 percent of all public expenditures were made for these special groups who are not in the work force, so that our estimates of public outlays made on behalf of members of the 1960 work force overstate the investment in these work force members.

Per capita public expenditures were adjusted to a 1960 price level using the same price index applied to private expenditures. While the consumer price index may not be an entirely appropriate index for deflating governmental outlays in view of differences in the composition of public and private expenditures for health care, a superior index was not available.

Table 4 shows the "total" public plus private lifetime health expenditures on the 1960 work force both in current and in 1960 dollars. Omitted from the "total" are expenditures by employers for in-plant health services and expenditures by charitable organizations for direct provision of health care and research; the sum of these two items was around $110 million in 1929, and $930 million in 1959.[7]

Table 4—Total health program stock 1960 work force (in billions)

	Current dollars $	1960 dollars $
Total	132.5	203.9
Private	104.8	161.9
Public	27.7	42.0

The measured total health expenditure in the 1960 work force is seen in Table 4 to be almost $204 billion in 1960 prices. This may be compared with the estimated $535 billion of total *educational* expenditures embodied in the 1957 labor force.[8] Thus, about 38 cents of health resources have been devoted to the labor force for each $1 of educational resources. The size of the total health expenditure, which we are calling a health stock—a form of human capital—may also be compared with the total stock of reproducible *tangible* (non-human) wealth. Doing so, we find that the $204 billion health stock is the equivalent of 16 percent of the $1,270 billion of reproducible tangible assets in 1957.[9]

On definitional grounds, the health stock is more comparable with the education stock than either is comparable with the physical capital stock. The latter reflects the estimated depreciation of assets over their expected

---

[7] Ida C. Merriam, "Social Welfare Expenditures, 1958/59," *Social Security Bulletin*, November 1960, *23*, 43.

[8] Schultz, "Education and Economic Growth," *op. cit.*, p. 71. Educational capital in the labor force includes estimated earnings foregone by students attending school.

[9] *Ibid.*, from the estimate by Raymond W. Goldsmith and adjusted by Schultz to 1956 prices.

lifetimes; but the health and the education stock estimates implicitly assume no depreciation until a person has dropped from the work force, at which time he is suddenly depreciated completely.

Another objection to comparison of the physical capital stock with our estimate of the health stock (or with estimates by others of the education stock) is that some expenditures on physical capital are normally considered as "maintenance," and thus are neither counted as investment nor included in the capital stock. But all health (and education) expenditures have been included in the estimates of the health (and education) stock, including any expenditures that might be termed "maintenance."

The different treatment of maintenance expenditures may be more apparent than real. Maintenance of physical capital prolongs its life, and thereby reduces annual depreciation. The result is that the reported stock of physical capital *net* of depreciation is larger than it would be if maintenance expenditures were lower. If depreciation were reduced by the exact amount of maintenance expenditures this would be equivalent to counting the maintenance as investment. Thus, the treatment of maintenance on human and non-human capital may be reasonably consistent after all.

The $204 billion health stock shown in Table 4 amounts to $3,058 per member of the work force. This compares with the estimate by T. W. Schultz that the cost (or stock) of *education* per labor force member, in 1957, was $7,663;[10] and it compares with the stock of *physical* capital of approximately $19,000 per member of the 1960 work force ($1,270 billion/67 million work force).

Moreover, our evidence on the changing age pattern of private health expenditures suggests that the health investment per worker is growing. According to Table 1, the average individual spent $25 per year on his health around 1930, but by 1957/58 he was spending $94 per year. Assuming that health expenditures increased in the same proportion at each age, and that the age distribution of the population was constant, we can say that the per capita health expenditures over the lifetime of the average person increased in the ratio of $94/$25, or 276 percent. If we adjust these expenditure figures for the change in the level of medical care prices,[11] the increase is reduced to 100 percent.

While the health stock per capita was increasing 100 percent in constant prices between 1930 and 1957, the stock of education per capita was increasing less than 85 percent,[12] and the stock of reproducible non-human

---

[10] *Ibid.*, p. 70.

[11] The medical care price index rose from 74.2 in 1930 to 138.0 in 1957 (US Bureau of the Census, *Historical Statistics of the United States, Colonial Times to 1957*, Washington, DC, 1960, pp. 125, 126).

[12] Obtained by dividing Schultz's estimates of the educational stock of the population 14 years and older (*op. cit.*, p. 73) by the population sizes in each year, and then computing the percentage increase.

wealth per capita was increasing 24 percent,[13] also in constant prices.

When health capital ($204 billion in 1960) is added to earlier estimates of educational capital ($535 billion in 1957) we find that human capital in these two forms total almost $740 billion, which amounts to nearly 60 percent of the stock of reproducible physical capital ($1,270 billion in 1957). And perhaps more significantly the total stock of human capital is about equal to the aggregate stock of reproducible physical capital used in farming, industry and commerce (total reproducible tangible property less residential real estate and consumer durable goods).[14]

Estimating the amount of resources devoted to the health of the work force is a first step toward determining their contribution to economic growth. So far we have found that the resources devoted to the health of the 1960 work force have been substantial by comparison with the resource-costs of schooling and with the stock of physical capital. The return on the investment in health takes the forms of increased output resulting from (1) increased life expectancy and, thus, a larger labor force; and from (2) increased productivity per man-hour (in addition to the consumption value of better health). Of course, other factors affect life expectancy and productivity. Growing income, partly resulting from investment in physical capital and in human capital in forms other than health have raised real incomes and, thereby, resulted in improved diets, housing and clothing. Advances in etiology have aided people in avoiding unhealthful circumstances. These changes have lead to improved health, independently of the level of "health" expenditures.

We need to determine how much of health expenditures can be considered as investment, and then to determine the changes through time in the stock of health capital in the work force. This would aid an attempt to discover the amount of increased output which can be attributed to the effects of health expenditures on the productivity of the labor supply.

Summary

Our interest in the sources of economic growth leads us to investigate the influence of health expenditures on the nation's output, by studying the stock of health capital in the labour force. Estimating the investment in people through health programmes is a first step toward determining the

---

[13] Obtained by dividing Raymond W. Goldsmith's estimates, as adjusted to 1956 prices by Schultz ("Education and Economic Growth," *op. cit.*, p. 73), by the population sizes in each year, and then computing the percentage increase.

[14] Derived from wealth estimates by type of reproducible capital assets; Raymond W. Goldsmith, *Statistical Appendix to the National Wealth of the United States in the Postwar Period*, New York, National Bureau of Economic Research, February 1961.

productivity of the resources used, i.e., toward determining the rate of return on the investment in health. We consider expenditures made for or by members of the work force throughout their lifetime to have been investment in health and measure this investment both at current and constant prices.

The measured total health stock in the 1960 work force of the United States, in 1960 prices, is estimated at $204 billion—a figure which may be compared with the estimated $535 billion of *educational* capital in the 1957 labour force. Thus, about 38 cents of health capital is embodied in the labour force for each $1 of educational capital.

23

Schooling, Experience, and Gains and Losses in Human Capital Through Migration

Regional transfers of human capital, once viewed in the simple context of a quantitative enumeration of migrants, takes on a new dimension in this selection. Export-import relationships between human capital flows may be of increasing importance in the private and social contexts to regional development and social welfare. Professors Bowman and Myers, both of whom are associated with the Comparative

MARY JEAN BOWMAN
ROBERT G. MYERS

Education Center at the University of Chicago, suggest many new dimensions to manpower mobility in this selection. Regional and demographic problems and public policy may benefit substantially in the future from research suggestions and data needs identified in this selection.

Introduction

Since the revival of the concept of human capital in the 1950's, many areas of economic research, including the economics of migration, have undergone a rethinking. Although neither the idea of human capital nor its application to migration can be termed "new," current estimating procedures and their economic applications are much more sophisticated

Reprinted from Mary Jean Bowman and Robert G. Myers, "Schooling, Experience, and Gains and Losses in Human Capital Through Migration," *Journal of the American Statistical Association* 62 (September 1967), pp. 875–98, with the permission of the authors and publisher.

than earlier ones.[1] In considerable part new approaches and greater sophistication reflect improvements in the quality and availability of data. However, new appreciation of critical problems is always some jumps ahead of the data—and also, we might add, behind them.

We will first sketch briefly several recent treatments of human capital in migration. Some of their methodological implications will become evident in a reexamination of one-way migration that takes into account place and timing of schooling and work experience. We turn then to the more complex analysis required when we include remigration possibilities. Along the way suggestions will be made for useful new tabulations of 1960 census data together with some pleas or hopes for the 1970 census.

In discussing the relation between "Migration and Economic Opportunity," we might emphasize migration as a means of responding to economic opportunity or as a means for creating economic opportunity. Heretofore more attention has been given to the passive view of migration as an allocative mechanism than to the view of migration as playing a dynamic training role. But migrants often move out and return with new skills, and in-migrants bring and transfer know-how. We emphasize these linkages among investments in schooling, experience, and migration. We present decision models incorporating various migration and remigration sequences and argue their value as tools for analysis of migration behavior, human resource policies, the transfer of know-how, and the diffusion of development.

Recent Applications of Human Investment Models to Migration

MIGRATION AS A PRIVATE INVESTMENT

In a 1962 article, Larry Sjaastad[2] looked at migration primarily as a form of private, rational decision-making—as a private investment that

---

[1] In the 19th Century, estimates of human capital gains and losses were made for the United States, England, and Germany, using both present values and cost replacement methods. Discussions of the estimates and methods may be found in: Richmond Mayo-Smith, *Emigration and Immigration*, New York: Scribner's Sons, 1892, Chapter VI, and in Grace Abbott, ed., *Historical Aspects of the Immigration Problem, Selected Documents*, Chicago: The University of Chicago Press, 1926, 370–81. Discussions of "Human Capital" and attempts to measure it in other contexts go back to Wm. Petty if not earlier. For perspectives on this history see E. A. J. Johnson, "The Place of Learning, Science, Vocational Training, and 'Art' in Pre-Smithian Economic Thought," in the *Journal of Economic History*, XXIV (June, 1964), 129–144. Also, Rudolf Blitz, "Education, the Nature of Man, and the Division of Labor," and "Education in the Writings of Malthus, Senior, McCulloch and J. S. Mill," (English language revisions of an article in Spanish), forthcoming in UNESCO, *Readings in Education and Economic Development* (1967), and B. F. Kiker, "The Historical Roots of the Concept of Human Capital," *Journal of Political Economy*, LXXIV, No. 5 (October 1966), 481–499.

[2] Larry Sjaastad, "The Costs and Returns of Human Migration," *The Journal of Political Economy*, LXX, No. 5, Part 2 (October, 1962), 80–93.

entails costs and engenders increments to lifetime earnings streams. To oversimplify, people discount expected earnings streams to set present values on themselves for alternative courses of action: migration or remaining put. In theory, people will move if they can increase their present value by an amount greater than the cost of moving. This added value might be attained if, by moving, a person finds a better market for his existing skills, upgrading himself within his occupation, or if migration provides an opportunity for him to change occupations, thereby acquiring a new skill and increasing his remuneration. Sjaastad emphasizes occupational change in attempting to analyze rural-urban migration and to account for observed age patterns in such migration.

Costs, according to Sjaastad, include direct costs of moving, earnings foregone while moving, earnings foregone while searching for employment and training for a new position. He gave special emphasis to the training or retraining costs of urban newcomers, which are identified with the initial excess of foregone rural earnings over realized urban wages. Returns (benefits) are the expected income stream at the destination.[3]

Sjaastad's primary concern was with the efficiency of migration as a process of resource allocation. He argued that much of the seemingly non-rational response or lack of response to economic incentives to move is really a matter of measurement methods which look at net migration rather than gross figures. He also criticized failures to disaggregate populations sufficiently before associating them with differential opportunities and earnings. In order to identify statistically the potential earnings streams of migrants at places of origin and destination, Sjaastad suggested that comparisons must be made among more homogeneous sub-groupings, specifying in particular use of age-occupational classifications. (Curiously, he said nothing about classifications by schooling.)

Statistical averages of costs and earnings for each population category are used as proxy measures in a decision model that is fundamentally individualistic. Despite his work with the Upper Midwest Project, Sjaastad's interest in spatial resource allocation remains spatially neutral; hence we find neither aggregated human capital measures nor "regionalism." The important thing is the micro-economic allocative process.

MIGRATION AND A RATIONALE OF COMMUNITY INVESTMENTS IN EDUCATION

In his treatment of migration, Burton Weisbrod[4] takes a very different tack—even though he starts from the same base in human investment

---

[3] In his theoretical formulation, Sjaastad also considers "psychic" costs and benefits.

[4] Burton Weisbrod, *External Benefits of Public Education*, Princeton, N.J.: Industrial Relations Section, Princeton University, 1964.

theory as Sjaastad and, like Sjaastad, computes "human capital" in present value terms.

Weisbrod sets up a model in which the community is treated not only as an aggregative entity that receives benefits and incurs costs, but also as a decision-making unit analogous to the individual decision-maker of micro-economic theory. The decision on which he focuses is local community investment in schooling. He is concerned with how migration will affect benefits accruing to the community from investments in education, and hence with how it affects the cost-benefit balances that would determine rational investment decisions. He argues that rational community behavior in this context will lead to under-investment in education on a national scale because of "spill-over" effects—"external benefits" of a community's investments that accrue to other communities. This treatment of the community as a decision unit has been attacked from several sides.[5] However, the empirical part of Weisbrod's work is relevant to aggregative analysis of human capital gains and losses, flights of the imagination quite aside.

A careful study of Weisbrod's method for computing "spill-overs" points up the problems involved in assigning values to human capital flows. In working from incremental income[6] streams associated with varying levels of educational attainment through high school graduation, he assumes, for instance, that the relevant income streams for valuing both *in* and *out* migrants of given age, race, and sex are the same. All those who migrate to and from the Clayton, Missouri community are valued at non-South rates, regardless of their origin or the location of their previous education. This is an empirical compromise dictated by data limitations, and is discussed by the author at some length.

COST VALUATIONS OF INTERNATIONAL MIGRATION

Grubel and Scott[7] focus on international migration of "human capital," and on arguments concerning "brain drains." Although they discuss individual decision-making in a framework similar to Sjaastad's, in their published work they emphasize the effects of out-migration on social wel-

---

[5] In particular, see A. G. Holtman's, "A Note on Public Education and Spillovers through Migration," *Journal of Political Economy*, LXXIV, No. 5 (October, 1966), 524–25.

[6] Census cross-classifications are by income, not earnings. There are substantial difficulties involved in establishing a "correct" figure for such groups as proprietors. Neither income nor earnings is quite accurate.

[7] See the following three articles of Herbert Grubel and Anthony Scott: (1) "The International Flow of Human Capital, the Brain Drain," *American Economic Review, Papers and Proceedings*, LVI, No. 2 (May 1966), 268–274, (2) "The Immigration of Scientists and Engineers to the United States," *The Journal of Political Economy*, LXXIV, No. 4 (August 1966), and (3) "The Characteristics of Foreigners in the U.S. Economics Profession," *American Economic Review*, forthcoming.

fare. There is no community decision unit, such as Weisbrod's; in fact, they discard aggregates and GNP in theoretical presentations. Social welfare they define as the *per capita* incomes of all initial residents, whatever their place of residence after migration.

However, appealing as the welfare measure they suggest may be, it is no accident that in the end Grubel and Scott make no attempt at direct empirical assessments in such a framework; the practical difficulties are manifold. Instead, they go to quite the other extreme of empirical pragmatism. Not only do they forsake their welfare concept for an aggregative type of social assessment, but they also by-pass human capital measurement in present value terms, choosing to use cost assessments instead.[8]

National gains are measured by the cost-savings realized in acquiring human capital formed elsewhere without paying for its formation. National losses are incurred when a nation pays for the formation of human capital that others then acquire free.

Using figures from an annual census of foreign students in the United States, interesting estimates are derived for United States gains and losses. The value of the gain (saving in costs) to the United States of acquiring "non-returning foreign students" is taken as what it would have cost to "produce" an American equivalent. Against these cost-savings are set the costs incurred by the United States in providing education for all foreign students. Similar human capital estimates are made for scientists and engineers who have migrated to the United States.[9]

Measurement of human capital in cost terms as a way of assessing the resources that have gone into the making of a man is one thing. Using cost valuations in assessing gains and losses through migration is quite another. Serious distortions are apt to occur when reproduction cost estimates exceed present value. Thus a fallacious cost view of human capital can explain many of the complaints that have been so common concerning Southern or Appalachian losses through migration.[10]

PRESENT VALUE ESTIMATES OF INTERREGIONAL MIGRATION

Rashi Fein,[11] like Weisbrod, was concerned with the measurement of aggregate human capital gains and losses of spatially defined units—in

[8] Herbert Grubel, "Non-returning Foreign Students and the Cost of Student Exchange," *International Educational and Cultural Exchange* (a publication of the U.S. Advisory Commission on International Educational and Cultural Affairs), Spring, 1966.

[9] Herbert Grubel and Anthony Scott, "The Immigration of Scientists and Engineers to the United States," *loc. cit.*

[10] This, by the way, is where Grubel and Scott's social welfare view of effects on per capita incomes could prove especially fruitful—and empirically operational up to useful approximations.

[11] Rashi Fein, "Educational Patterns in Southern Migration," *The Southern Economic Journal*, XXXII, No. 1, Part 2 (July 1965), 106–124.

Fein's case, regions within the United States. Like Weisbrod, Fein used a present value measure of human capital (discounting future income streams at 5 per cent). There is no decision theory in Fein's analysis, however, and he draws no inferences for public policy.

Fein's first task, a considerable one, was to lay out the census data in a form that would permit examination of gross 1955–60 migration streams for males. Male migrant flows are disaggregated by age, race, and educational attainment. Focusing on the South and its sub-regions, he then computes net in- or outflows for each age-race-education category. To get estimates of social net capital gains or losses associated with migration he first multiplies net flows by average discounted values of Southern income streams associated with each age-race-education category. These sub-aggregates are then summed to give the overall net gain or loss to the region. Present values have, in effect, become weightings for the various statistical categories. Although this procedure preserves the disaggregation by sex, age, race, and schooling, the distinction between characteristics of inflows and outflows is unfortunately lost in the procedure for valuing human capital. We will come back to this later.

Alternative Earnings Streams and One-way Migration

From the above discussions of recent work, it is evident that analysis of migration in human investment terms has opened up over a wide front. There are at once common elements and sharp distinctions in problem foci, in theoretical frameworks applied, in the kinds of compromises made in using incomplete and sometimes inappropriate sets of data. Back of all this are some fundamental theoretical problems in decision theory on the one hand, some critical issues for public policy on the other. Theory and policy are in fact quite closely related. It is with such basic questions in mind that we ask: Which earnings streams are the relevant ones in *either* private or social assessments of migration? Whichever the viewpoint, identification of the conceptually appropriate future earnings streams is a necessary first step. We start in this section with the simplest case—one-way migration. This in fact is the only case for which earnings streams have been examined in anything we have seen.

THE NET FLOW FALLACY AND ESTIMATES OF HUMAN-CAPITAL GAINS AND LOSSES

In estimating human-capital gains and losses in the South, Fein took a short cut. As noted earlier, instead of valuing the gross inflows and out-flows he took the net flows for each age-race-schooling category of males, computing the aggregate present values of these net flows on the basis of

Southern life-income patterns. To the extent that he was dealing with flows among regions within the South he had no alternative; the needed income data are not available for sub-regions. Ideally we would want such figures, and we would want to maintain clear distinctions among parts of the South, for it is a very heterogeneous region. However, when it comes to flows between Southern and other regions the situation is changed; we have data on life-income streams by race, sex, age, and schooling that can differentiate at least on this gross-regional dichotomy.

Weisbrod also used a single set of values in his study of gains and losses through migration into and out of the Clayton school district, in Missouri. However, our chief criticism of this aspect of his work is that he did not check for the sensitivity of his results to his valuation procedure. Since he was only incidentally interested in his quantitative results, and was not posing the more substantive and analytical questions concerning migration in which we are most interested, this omission is understandable, even if regrettable.

We assume, with Sjaastad, that an individual will not normally migrate unless his potential discounted earnings stream in the new area is going to be at least as high as that at the area of origin. When the average stream for the area of destination is obviously lower than that in the area of origin, but people move anyway, this would suggest that the rational in-migrant is not typical of the area into which he is moving. When this happens even within particular race-sex-age-schooling categories, the fallacy of using average incomes at the lower income destination for migrants to that area is underlined. Until data that distinguish migrants are available there can be no firm answer as to what is happening, and how. At present we can only hypothesize, meanwhile making some crude estimates as to what alternative hypotheses may imply.

The potential importance of taking market differences into account can be illustrated by making some simple calculations. The distribution of schooling among 1955–60 out-migrants from the South as a whole is very close to the distribution of schooling among 1955–60 migrants into the South. However, except at college levels, incomes of white males with the same years of schooling are higher in the North than in the South. After a bit of rough pencil-and-paper work we picked $40,000 as an average present-value figure for income streams of white male Southerners leaving the South and $50,000 for white male migrants from other regions into the South.

Valuing in-migrants at their place of origin (Table 1, b) rather than at their destination (as Fein did, Table 1, a) results in a substantial increase in the estimated gain, both in relative and in absolute terms. Raising or lowering per-migrant present values or varying the ratio between non-Southern and Southern present values would change our numbers but not our argument. From the perspective of the South, Fein's method sets a minimum for net gains, while valuing both in- and out-migrants at their origin sets a maximum.[12]

Table 1—Alternative estimates of net human capital gains from migration for the United States South; 1950–60

	Number migrating	Present value (per migrant)	Total value (millions)	Net human capital gain (millions)
Out Migration	554,900	40,000	22,196	—
In Migration:				
a. Valued at destination	579,100	40,000	23,164	968
b. Valued at origin	579,100	50,000	28,955	6759

We have not considered what proportion of the in-migrants may have been unsuccessful returning Southerners, or what proportion of the out-migrants were originally from the North. Our estimates are still gross over-simplifications. Until data that distinguish migrants and their associated income streams are available, there can be no firm answer.

Typically applications of human investment models to migration have suffered from insufficient disaggregation of the population of migrants, though industrious scholars in and outside of the Census Bureau are beginning to remedy the most serious gaps. It is obvious by now that within-each-region disaggregation by age, sex, race, educational attainment, and income (preferably earnings) is needed. Both Weisbrod and Fein recognize this and adjust their human capital estimates accordingly. Actually for the 5 per cent sample of the 1960 census we have, within South and within North, cross tabulations of all these variables plus 1960 occupations. However, there is no breakdown that would separate out migrants within each of these cells.

A possibility we would very much like to see followed up in 1970 would be refinement of the regional tables on incomes by sex, race, age, and schooling of 1960 residents in order to distinguish the new migrants (1955–60) from others, and each of these groups in turn by place of birth and occupation—ideally both at origin and destination. Obviously this will be possible only if all these items are obtained on the 25 per cent sample.

Suppose we had all of this information. What else should we know to distinguish migrants and their earnings in a meaningful way? It is obvious that many other factors affect productivity and earnings streams of any

[12] The figures for numbers migrating in and out of the South, exclusive of intra-South migration, are taken from William N. Parker's comment on the Rashi Fein article (see footnote 11), in *The Southern Economic Journal*, XXXII, No. 1, Part 2 (July, 1965), 126, Table I.

given population of migrants. Ability, attitudes toward work, quality of schooling, environmental experiences as a youth, and job experience differentials will all be reflected in differential earnings streams. Important also are labor market imperfections that may partially segregate migrant from native populations of the same race, sex, age, and reported years of schooling.

Concerning ability and attitudes we will be brief. We can reasonably assume that the ability distribution for a given age, race, sex, education category of the population will not differ much among regions; hence we need not be concerned on this score with places of origin of migrants. However, in these pages we go further to make the more vulnerable assumption that the average ability of migrants is no different from that of non-migrants once disaggregation has established homogeneity of population sub-groups in other critical respects. The saving feature of this assumption is the critical disaggregation presupposed; there can be no presumption that within each population sub-category mobility will be correlated either positively or negatively with ability.[13] Differences in attitudes toward work are a problem that we will simply have to ignore for the present. It should be noted, however, that both ability and attitudes can be objectively assessed, and for special migrant groups this has been done.

Experience and quality of schooling differentials are at the heart of our analysis, and command more careful attention.

SCHOOLING AND EXPERIENCE

School-quality differences can be critical in the economics of migration from many points of view, one, but only one, of which is estimation of regional gains or losses in human capital through migration. If the distributions of quality of schooling among men of the same race and age with the same reported schooling were the same in one region as in another (or in urban as in rural areas), we could forget about this problem. However, despite large within-area differences in quality of schools there are also large and significant differences between rural and urban schools and between schools in one region as against another.

To get at effects of differences in average quality of schooling we need to know where the migrant was schooled (ideally for secondary school by sub-region or state and by type of community). Present census data do not permit disaggregation by locus of schooling even on a broad regional basis. However, one could make some assumptions about the location of both schooling and previous job experience by looking at place of birth, place

[13] See, for example, Donald J. Bogue, "International Migration," in Philip M. Hauser and Otis Dudley Duncan (ed.), *The Study of Population*, Chicago: University of Chicago Press, 1959, especially pp. 504–5.

of 1955 residence, and 1960 residence in relation to age at the time of migration.

The first component of experience, a very important one, is the learning that goes on outside of school during school years. There is ample evidence to show that youth from rural communities start at a disadvantage when they come to the city; the extent of the disadvantage varies with the nature of the rural area. This is one among many reasons why data concerning location at the time when a young man attended secondary school (or if he stopped short of that, where he last attended elementary school) would be more valuable than information concerning where he attended college.[14] In fact we strongly urge inclusion in the 1970 census of information concerning the state and type of community in which a man resided at the time when he last attended school below the college level (or alternatively, at, say, age 16).

The importance of what men learn on the job has been reappraised recently and given new theoretical respectability in the economics journals. If we accept Mincer's estimates, over a life-time investments in learning on the job typically exceed investments in schooling in the United States today.[15] In any case, whatever the relative magnitudes, learning through on-the-job training and experience is a major component in the formation of human competencies. Given this fact, we must ask what and how much of such learning has been built into which groups of migrants.

Taking it for granted that we will not be working with full life histories —such data would swamp us in any case—what might we hypothesize as the best statistical clues to sort out categories of migrants (and non-migrants) by experience? Obviously age is part of the picture. So is schooling if we look at the national scene, since over-all there is a positive correlation between schooling and on-the-job training and learning. However, this is much too crude an approximation. How do people of the same age and years of schooling differ in competencies acquired at work? As a first step we would look for two kinds of information: what a man was doing (his occupation) prior to migration, and where he was doing it.

---

[14] The critical importance of community characteristics in determining differences among schools in distributions of achievement has been well documented. See, for example, H. T. James, J. Alan Thomas and Harold J. Dyck, *Wealth, Expenditure and Decision-Making for Education*, in U.S. Department of Health, Education, and Welfare, Cooperative Research Project No. 1241, Stanford (School of Education), 1963, and Charles Benson, *et al.*, "State and Local Fiscal Relationships in Public Education in California," State of California Senate Fact Finding Committee on Revenue and Taxation, *Report*, Sacramento, March, 1965.

[15] Jacob Mincer, "On-the-Job Training: Costs, Returns, and Some Implications," *The Journal of Political Economy*, LXX, No. 5, Part 2 (October, 1962), 50–79.

At any given time, however, the aggregate on-the-job training embodied in the labor force will be the lower figure, since young people who have completed school have yet to accumulate the learning on-the-job that Mincer measures by opportunity costs.

The 1960 census does not provide information on prior occupations, and collection of data on past occupations is both difficult and expensive; however, this possibility has been considered for the 1970 census. If collection of such data proves feasible for a large enough sample, it will open up a range of possibilities for hypothesis testing that must challenge many researchers on both migration and the economics of education.

There can be no doubt that work opportunities and with them opportunities for on-the-job training and learning vary substantially from one place to another. This is glaringly obvious if we look across nations on a world scale. It is sufficiently evident within the United States, and even if we control for age, sex, and prior schooling. There is a strong presumption that knowledge of the location in which men have acquired their work experience will improve statistical predictions of their competencies. How far a migrant's previous experiential learning may be transferable to his new setting is another matter. Undoubtedly there is selectivity in such transferability; he can move into the new environment carrying his experience with him only to the extent that the new environment gives scope for its use. This may contribute to differentiation of labor markets between natives and in-migrants, especially in the middle and higher occupational brackets. It is a reasonable generalization that unless a man can take enough of his acquired competencies with him to ensure earnings at least as high as those he would receive at home, our "average" migrant will not move —at least not if he already has a substantial investment in such competencies and there is a demand for them at home. For youth who have little or no such investment the problem does not arise. Rather, the question may be, where can I go to get the best learning and long-term income opportunities?

We may systematize these comments concerning effects on potential earnings associated with location of schooling and experience by setting up a rough typology of schooling-work combinations as between two regions, A and B. Within any age, sex, race, educational, and, ideally, prior occupational grouping of migrants who moved from place A to place B, we would distinguish the following (still deferring consideration of temporary migration and return):

1. Those born in A, but who migrated to B for schooling and work.
2. Those born in A and schooled in A, but who migrated to B as soon as their formal schooling was completed and who have worked only in B.
3. Those born in A and schooled in A who remained to work for some time in A, but moved to B before they were 40, continuing to work in B thereafter.
4. Those born in A and schooled in A who worked in A to at least the age of 40, migrating to B after that age.

1. The first category of individuals might be expected to have an age-

earnings profile very close to or even the same as comparable life-time B residents of the same race, sex, age, years of schooling—and perhaps prior occupation—because all schooling and work experience is in B.

2. Those in the second category were schooled in A but their entire work experience is in B. We would expect their average earnings profiles to fall somewhere between those of life-time residents of A and of B, but closer to the latter. Deviations from average B earnings streams would be greater the greater the regional differences in average quality of schooling.[16] It will be greater the greater the differences between out-of-school environment of the migrant's adolescent years (rural or urban, and where) and the environment into which he is moving. Related to this, though partially independent of it, is also the extent to which migrants from A enter labor markets in B that are distinct from those in which lifetime residents of B sell their services.

3. Migrants in category 3 should also, on the average, have future income streams falling somewhere between those of lifetime residents of A and of B. The older they are at migration and the more experience they bring with them, the closer we should expect them to be to the lifetime residents of their area of origin. Here (as also in case 2), if migrants to B work in branch organizations which have head offices in and are operated by individuals from A, their earnings streams should approximate A-type earnings. This is merely an extreme of differentiated labor markets— islands of A located within the geographic boundaries of B. On the other hand, the younger the migrant the larger the part of his experience he will accumulate in B (segregation of labor markets aside), and the more clearly will his future income stream approach the B pattern.

4. If the movement to region B comes after age 40, it is probable that earnings in B will be similar to those in A where schooling and work experience were obtained. Non-economic locational preferences for B aside, the A income potential should in fact give us a minimum estimate of earning streams in B. We assume that a rational person established in a career in A will not move after age 40 unless he can earn at least as much in his new location virtually from the start. Although there are exceptions, there is sufficient empirical evidence to show that after age 40 most men are recouping investments in themselves rather than making new ones, intuitive reasoning quite aside.

A fifth category which is really a special case of the fourth has quite different implications, however. Suppose an individual born in A, schooled and with his work experience in A, whose skill has become obsolete after age 40 (or somewhat earlier). In this case the migrating individual has

---

[16] This makes the further assumption that migrants average the same schooling quality as comparable non-migrants in their area of origin.

suffered a severe "human capital loss." He has little or no learned competence to apply in either A or B, and his expected future earnings stream cannot be measured by an average in either area. Though a special case, this is an important one, which merits the special study that is beginning to be given to it.

PACKAGE MIGRATION AND THE TRANSFER OF EXPERIENCE

In discussing the locus of schooling and experience as related to likely future income streams of migrants we commented upon the possibilities— in some cases the strong likelihood—that there would be some differentiation of markets in which migrants and non-migrants resident in a given area sell their services. We specified further that this differentiation could and does occur even among men of the same race, age, and years of schooling. Even if we went all the way from regions down to state economic areas in an attempt to assure greater homogeneity we would not necessarily get rid of such labor market differentiation.

Taking the more dramatic in-migrant labor market segments to illustrate the extreme case, there are "Northern firms" in the deep South, firms from the United States in Sao Paulo, French firms in the Ivory coast. Traditionally such "foreign" firms have preferred to import talent from their area of origin rather than to employ locals who lack not only the technical know-how acquired on a job but also, equally important, know-how with respect to how a modern Northern organization operates.[17] (In addition the Northern high school graduate is likely to be better schooled than the Southern.) Many of the men who have been brought into the South when a Northern firm established a branch there would not otherwise have migrated; there would have been no opportunities for them to work in the South at jobs in which they could use their Northern skills and experience. Transfer of those skills would not have been possible. Conversely, the firm would not have moved into the South had it not been possible to bring Northerners with know-how along. This is what we mean by "package migration."[18]

To the extent that migration is associated with these segmentalized labor market structures, differences in earnings stream between migrants

[17] Roy L. Lassiter reports Southern Business preference for Northerners with high school education or more in "The Experience of Selected Manufacturing Firms with the Availability, Skills and Training of Manufacturing Workers in Florida," Occasional Paper No. 1, Bureau of Economic and Business Research, College of Business Administration, University of Florida, 1961. The reluctance of U.S. firms abroad to employ local management is illustrated by John Shearer in his *High-Level Manpower in Overseas Subsidiaries: Experience in Brazil and Mexico*, Princeton, New Jersey: Industrial Relations Section, Princeton University, 1960, especially Chapter VI.

[18] For some related discussions of transfer of know-how, see Mary Jean Bowman, "From Guilds to Infant Training Industries," in C. A. Anderson and Mary Jean Bowman, eds., *Education and Economic Development*, Chicago: Aldine Publishing Company, 1965, pp. 98–129.

and permanent residents should appear. However, this assumes further that there are not parallel opportunities of a very different kind to which the local population has the readier access. When a traditional elite, experienced in its own culture and perhaps protected by other barriers to entry[19] exists along with a "foreign" class of high-salary professionals and technicians, income data alone will conceal important differences between the new and native populations. How far this pattern characterizes the South is not entirely clear, though the statistics on education, occupation, and income by region do suggest that it exists in some degree and is not uniform. Such a pattern is unstable, however. It fades away with development. Ultimately, we suspect, it is eroded more by the progress of native populations at the middle level than by any direct impact at the top.

As the number of "Northern" firms in the "South" multiplies, and as a few and then a few more Southerners filter into and through these enterprises at the middle levels, the transfer of skill and experience from North to South becomes easier. Migrants now come in greater numbers without any special prior association with the enterprises in which they find jobs. The process of diffusion of development is well under way.

How much validity there may be in this theorizing concerning relations between migration and the process of diffusion of development remains to be seen. Existing evidence is spotty. But there is clearly a challenge to test hypotheses of this kind. To what extent are Southern labor markets differentiated or even sharply segmentalized? For any given race, age, and schooling, how do earnings of Southerners working in Southern-type firms compare with those in Northern-type firms in the South? How do earnings of similar individuals in Northern firms in the North compare with those in Northern firms in the South? Looking at the shapes of income streams and applying Mincer's method of analyzing on-the-job learning, do we find that Northern profiles transfer to the South intact? If there are differences between Northern firms in the South and Southern firms with respect to training and learning opportunities, who is reaping the benefits— migrants from the North (temporary or permanent) or locals? Over time are profiles in Southern firms changing—and can we observe this in cross-section by comparing the border South with the deep South? Turning to data on occupations, types of firms quite aside, are occupation and occupation-earnings patterns quite different among migrants into the South and native Southerners of comparable race-sex-age-schooling categories? Are these differences persistent, and repeated over large parts of the South, or are they changing?

Many of these questions concerning segmentalization of labor markets,

---

[19] However, the high incomes of the "traditional" or native elite groups may be largely property income (for instance, Southern farmers with college education) or their salaries may be bureaucratic sinecures (as in many developing areas).

transferability of experience, the relative role of experience and schooling in shaping productivity, and the processes of diffusing skills might be tested by using human capital models and U.S. census data.[20]

Migration and Re-migration

The common tendency to treat migration as though it were a once-and-for-all affair, often combined with a definition of migration that in itself suggests permanency, has many unfortunate results.

One of the more obvious of these may be faulty assessments of "brain drains" and gains (the latter rarely noted). It is evident that once re-migration is considered, new difficulties arise in such assessments. Are the migrants college students returning home, prodigal sons, disappointed job-seekers, retrained workers, retiring elders, or former political "outs" who are now "in"?

Further, how does the human capital value of these re-migrants differ from what it was when they first migrated? This question points to a more basic weakness of one-way migration simplifications; they disregard the duration of migration. There is a continuum from brief periods away at school or on a short-term job assignment to permanent residence at destination. To disregard temporary migration is to disregard the important linkages among private investments, on-the-job learning, and migration which, when coupled with regional differentials in quality and availability of schooling and experiential learning, can provide extremely important channels for the transfer and local acquisition of know-how. A developing country seeking to build up its cohorts of qualified people is faced with important choices as to how this can best be done. How many and which sorts of individuals should be sent for study and/or for work experience "abroad"? How many will return? What about the importing of outside experts on a temporary basis? How can these choices be evaluated from the points of view of the receiving and of the sending nations? What about problems of recruiting such men, of the strategies of inducing higher rates of return among those subsidized for study or training abroad, or in another

---

[20] In the 1970 census and thereafter, social security numbers may be included, making possible special studies that can be linked into census information for the same individuals. This should allow many kinds of research on migration that have not been feasible previously without incurring prohibitive costs. For example, a special survey might obtain rosters of individuals working in Southern firms and in Northern firms in the South. By matching, these individuals could be located in the census and their age, schooling, and migrant status identified. Such data would permit analysis of the degree of labor market differentiation and of native Southerners and immigrants of comparable age and education employed in establishments with Southern and Northern managers. Many other possibilities, including migration sequences as revealed by social security data, come to mind.

region of the United States? Human investment decision models that incorporate re-migration sequences can aid in such evaluations. We will develop this theme shortly. First, however, we look briefly into the quantitative importance of re-migration as return to the sub-regions (Divisions) of birth within the United States and a few distinctive patterns in these respects.

THE QUANTITAVE IMPORTANCE OF RE-MIGRATION IN THE UNITED STATES

Although U.S. census publications do not permit breakdowns by earnings, sex, age, schooling, occupations for migrants—let alone re-migrants—they do permit a partial assessment of the extent of re-migration. This is made possible by the tabulations of 1960 division of residence against residence in 1955 and according to whether division of birth was or was not the same as that of residence in 1960. We selected three divisions as illustrations and computed for selected age and education groups the proportions of the white male 1955–60 in-migrants who were coming "back home" and of out-migrants who were returning to the division in which they were born. The results are shown in Tables 2 and 3.

The most striking feature of Table 2 is the generally high rates of return to division of origin. The only exception is the migrants into the Pacific Division, only a small proportion of whom were returning to the part of the country in which they were born. This is, of course, to be expected. Almost equally striking in the Pacific ratios is the extremely high proportion of the younger out-migrants who were returning to their home divisions and virtually regardless of educational attainment levels—though the proportion is less extreme for college graduates. As Table 3 shows, the ratio of in- to out-migrants among young college men is exceptionally high for the Pacific Division, though in all age and schooling groups that division had net inflows.

At the opposite extreme is the East South Central region, which had net outflows in every case. The differences in the gross in and out movements were small, however. The most interesting thing to us in the East South Central figures is the rising proportion of in-migrants who were returning home as we move down from college graduates to the high school drop-outs. This pattern is repeated for every age group. We strongly suspect that had we computed ratios below high school 1–3 those ratios would have been even higher than for men with one to three years in high school. Here a very distinctive migration and re-migration phenomenon is evident. It should come as no surprise, for this is a manifestation of "the poverty problem" in one of its most serious and difficult forms—and of the failures of migration to solve problems of Galbraith's "insular poverty" where men have become obsolete or have never been sufficiently equipped to enter into jobs that offer opportunities for new training or learning.

Table 2—Return migration rates among 1955–60 migrants into and out of the East South Central, East North Central, and Pacific Divisions: white males in selected age and schooling categories

Schooling	PROPORTION OF 1955–60 IN-MIGRANTS WHO WERE RETURNING TO DIVISION OF BIRTH 1960 AGE			PROPORTION OF 1955–60 OUT-MIGRANTS WHO WERE RETURNING TO DIVISION OF BIRTH 1960 AGE		
	25–29	30–34	35–39	25–29	30–34	35–39
			East South Central			
Highschool 1–3	.59	.56	.53	.24	.18	.17
Highschool 4	.52	.42	.36	.32	.23	.23
College 1–3	.46	.35	.26	.37	.26	.23
College 4	.32	.32	.28	.30	.30	.27
			East North Central			
Highschool 1–3	.43	.30	.27	.29	.29	.26
Highschool 4	.56	.36	.30	.25	.21	.19
College 1–3	.53	.34	.30	.22	.18	.18
College 4	.40	.34	.30	.18	.21	.20
			Pacific			
Highschool 1–3	.09	.06	.05	.60	.46	.47
Highschool 4	.10	.07	.07	.61	.42	.36
College 1–3	.15	.09	.09	.60	.38	.30
College 4	.11	.12	.09	.46	.37	.30

Source: Computed from data in the 1960 U.S. Census of Population, *Lifetime and Recent Migration*, PC (2) 2D, Table 8. Ratios are computed excluding persons for whom residence was not reported.

The least predictable of the results, at least to us, were those for youth returning to the East North Central Division. Even though this has not been a growing area, we had expected that lower proportions of in-migrants would be returnees. Even the lowest ratios are around 30 per cent. It is interesting that the highest ratios are for young men, and are associated with absolute net inflows, while in the older age categories the East North Central Division was a net loser in each of the age-schooling groups we examined. Such findings invite further speculation, but we resist that temptation in favor of a more generalized (and safer) procedure—the presentation of migration and re-migration decision models with some of their analytical and policy potentials.

DECISION MODELS FOR MIGRATION AND RE-MIGRATION

The interpretation of migration behavior in economic terms and the analysis of potential strategies in social policy require something more than aggregative estimates of gains and losses.

Table 3—Number of 1955-60 white male in-migrants and out-migrants for whom residence was reported: the East South Central, East North Central, and Pacific Divisions

Schooling	1955-60 IN-MIGRANTS 1960 AGE			1955-60 OUT-MIGRANTS 1960 AGE		
	25-29	30-34	35-39	25-29	30-34	35-39
			East South Central			
Highschool 1-3	7300	5750	4280	9585	6955	5145
Highschool 4	13367	7960	6716	16279	9296	7690
College 1-3	6781	4067	3441	8064	4573	3679
College 4	9752	7485	5372	13743	9577	6303
			East North Central			
Highschool 1-3	18305	10884	7455	15488	15558	13185
Highschool 4	36831	14659	12030	25922	21715	20856
College 1-3	17920	8615	6752	13918	11793	10456
College 4	33906	24707	15326	31472	28233	20950
			Pacific			
Highschool 1-3	22146	20800	16556	14764	10011	7453
Highschool 4	36646	27640	26411	31305	14452	13301
College 1-3	22645	14578	12942	16439	7592	7432
College 4	35438	27629	19899	16825	13764	9626

Source: Same as Table 1.

With this in mind, we have developed models that begin with the individual viewpoint but are transformed into social decision models as parameter values are readjusted to allow for cost and income transfer, as individually expected earnings are replaced by socially expected or realized productive contributions, and as probability values are applied to allow for rates of return and non-return of migrants. The models allow choices with respect to locus, duration, and sequences of schooling and experiential learning. Relevant earnings streams are those of an "average individual" within a sex, race, age, and initial educational attainment and occupation category.[21] Our presentation is necessarily summary.[22]

[21] The models could of course be generalized to incorporate nonpecuniary benefits and returns or to disaggregate down to the individual decision maker with all his personal and environmental characteristics. However, we have limited the model to include only key economic variables and to keep it potentially operational data-wise.

[22] The models used here are part of a family of such models for analysis of investment in human resources (and before that in business economics). Their relation to Gary Becker's approach is evident. (See his "Investment in Human Capital," *The Journal of Political Economy*, LXX, No. 5, Part 2 (October, 1962) and his *Human Capital*, Columbia University Press, 1964). However, for our purposes, comparison of present values taking an assumed external discount rate is more flexible and is generally more appropriate than the "internal rates of return." Use of the "internal rate of return" method entails unnecessarily restrictive assumptions. (See also footnote 23.)

The following notation is used:

a—age at the first decision point relating to migration

b—date of actual or intended out-migration

m—age at return from residence abroad

n—retirement age

R_t—expected earnings in the year t at the place of origin prior to (or in the absence of) any migration

D_t—expected earnings abroad in the year t

Y_t—expected earnings in the year t at the place of origin for migrant returnees $(t > m - a)$

C_t—direct cost in the year t of schooling or training in the area of origin

K_t—direct cost in the year t of schooling or training abroad

Z_t^0—direct cost of out-migration incurred in year t

Z_t^h—direct cost of return migration incurred in year t

r—discount rate

V—present value of future income streams

j—superscript denoting a particular race, age, sex, school attainment, and occupation (if any) at time a

We limit ourselves to the following possible migration sequences:

1. Remain in the area of origin permanently (no migration)

$$V_1^j = \sum_{t=a}^{n} \frac{R_t - C_t}{(1+r)^{-a}} \tag{1}$$

2. Migrate immediately and remain permanently in the area of destination

$$V_2^j = \sum_{=a}^{n} \frac{D_t - K_t - Z_t^0}{(1+r)^{t-a}} \tag{2}$$

3. Migrate immediately, remain temporarily in the area of destination, then return to the area of origin

$$V_3^j = \sum_{t=a}^{m-1} \frac{D_t - K_t - Z_t^0}{(1+r)^{t-a}} + \sum_{t=m}^{n} \frac{Y_t - Z_t^h}{(1+r)^{t-a}} \tag{3}$$

4. Remain temporarily in the area of origin, then migrate permanently

$$V_4^j = \sum_{t=a}^{b-1} \frac{R_t - C_t}{(1+r)^{t-a}} + \sum_{t=b}^{n} \frac{D_t - K_t - Z_t^0}{(1+r)^{t-a}} \tag{4}$$

5. Remain temporarily in the area of origin, migrate and remain temporarily in the area of destination, then return to the area of origin

$$V_5^j = \sum_{t=a}^{b-1} \frac{R_t - C_t}{(1+r)^{t-a}} + \sum_{t=b}^{m-1} \frac{D_t - K_t - Z_t^0}{(1+r)^{t-a}} + \sum_{t=m}^{n} \frac{Y_t - Z_t^h}{(1+r)^{t-a}} \tag{5}$$

These models could be generalized to admit unlimited numbers of moves (or migration), of learning situations, and of successive cost-benefit relationships. Also, the external interest rates used could be varied to allow for shifts in relevant criterion or reservation rates.[23]

Individual Choices   An individual has many alternatives within each of the five sequences. To illustrate the complexity of choice, we begin with sequence one, the simplest case.[24] Think of a high school graduate deciding about his future. He must weigh going to work immediately against spending, one, two, five, or more years in school during which his earnings are low or zero. He must weigh schooling now against schooling later. If he is in the United States he is faced with a bewildering array of institutional settings. Each of the above carries implications for cost streams (C_t) and for future earnings (R_t).

Each of the schooling choices can be associated with a set of alternative occupational and job choices with varied amounts of experimental learning. The potential occupation and/or job choice implies visualizing a series of future yearly earnings (R values). These separate streams may differ in their present value and in the amount of associated experiential learning.

A person may choose between positions with higher learning potential which pay little at first but will bring higher pay later and positions with less or negligible potential which pay well at first but promise little or no earnings increase in the future.[25] The relation of experiential learning to

[23] In some cases this could lead to incorrect optimizing solutions even with the present-value, external rate method; but such cases entail very special forms of preference functions. [See Martin J. Bailey, "Formal Criteria for Investment Decisions," *Journal of Political Economy*, LXVII, No. 5 (October, 1959), 476–488.] Over the past decade a number of economists have been pressing these problems on the frontiers of capital theory proper, though spill-over of these analyses to discussions of investments in Human Resource Development have been tardy. Bruce Wilkinson, who builds his argument on Hirshleifer, is an exception. [See Bruce W. Wilkinson, "Present Values of Life-Time Earnings for Different Occupations," *Journal of Political Economy*, LXXIV, No. 6 (December, 1966), 556–572, and J. Hirshleifer, "On the Theory of Optimal Investment Decision," *Journal of Political Economy*, LXVI, No. 4 (August, 1958), 329–52.] Valerian Harvey demonstrates the advantages of using both internal rate-of-return and present value schedules in an assessment of *Economic Aspects of Teachers' Salaries* in Quebec (Chicago Ph.D. dissertation, 1967).

[24] Though this complexity is further compounded by various kinds and degrees of uncertainty, we follow here the common practice of abstracting from uncertainty. This simplification is necessary for expositional purposes but should not be taken to imply that effects of uncertainty and ignorance are unimportant either in individual behavior or in social policy-making. (See also footnote 25.)

[25] Note that this description of choices, and our use of present value comparisons, requires no assumption with respect to year-to-year choices of alternatives or constancy of internal rates of return to successive self-investments such as Mincer used (*op. cit.*). For some remarks on Mincer's as one of a broader set of models that varies the length of a contract term, see M. J. Bowman, "The Costing of Human Resource Development" in E. A. G. Robinson and J. E. Vaizey, eds., *The Economics of Education* (Proceedings of the 1963 Conference of the International Economics Association), London and New York: Macmillan and Co., 1966. A few aspects of decision-making with respect to human resource formation under uncertainty are also included in that article.

earnings stream differences and the place of experiential learning in our models is less observable than that of schooling. Schooling obviously involves foregone earnings: most students do not work or they have earnings far below what they might have if employed full-time. And schooling also carries direct costs—tuition, books, fees—that are only too evident to all who have paid them at one time or another. However, costs to an individual of experiential learning, embedded as they are in the earnings streams and usually involving less contrast in earnings, are less conspicuous even when they are cumulatively substantial.[26]

From the above it is apparent that even within sequence one, there are potentially almost an infinity of schooling and experience mixes from which to choose, each with its earnings stream and associated costs. Within sequence two, the possibilities for mixing schooling and experience are increased as a geographical dimension is introduced; within sequence three, the number of possibilities is further multiplied as the geographical progression becomes more complicated; and so forth.

In theory, one could identify the costs and earnings streams for every conceivable combination within and between each of the five migration sequences and select that one giving the highest present value. However, many combinations can be immediately discarded as unpromising ones. Furthermore, in practice any one individual will be constrained by his native ability, his interests, his financial situation, behavior of acquaintances, etc. The possibilities actually considered are reduced to the most promising and feasible ones, even to choices among two or three specific combinations for which costs and benefits are weighed and compared.

The most interesting aspect of this exercise for analysis of migration concerns how the locale of schooling and/or experiential learning up to any given age affects subsequent income streams for each work location which might be chosen after that age.

How great are the differences in particular cases? How stable are they? What explains them? How fully do they, in turn, explain migrant behavior? By what processes and how rapidly are they changed in the wake of migration? These questions are key ones for a positive economics that would go beyond traditional resource allocation to merge decision theory into a theory of development dynamics.

Social Choices and Migration Probabilities   Now, suppose we shift our viewpoint to a social one, for instance that of a regional or national body which

---

[26] Stress here is on cost *to the individual* because we are speaking of an individual decision. There is no need to assume year-to-year matching of incomes and productivity even in social assessments, however, since only the present value enters into our social decision models; more than one income sequence can yield the same present value. Becker's "general" learning will cause no trouble. Some part of what he terms "specific" on-the-job training will escape measurement in the estimations of present values of income streams accruing to individuals.

is deciding whether or not to subsidize study outside the area. Social gains and losses may be evaluated by using the same basic models used for individual decisions. However, the costs and returns are now those to the society. For example, all costs of educational services (teacher time, physical facilities, etc.) are real social costs, even though subsidies may reduce or eliminate such costs to the individual. In this section we assume that market prices (wages, etc.) coincide with social shadow prices.[27]

Permanent migration, as in sequences 2 and 4, is commonly regarded as unambiguous loss from a social viewpoint. This position, which assumes that to add to the productivity of an area an individual must be physically present, has been challenged.[28] However, in most cases policy-makers are concerned with the problem of non-return and regard physical presence as a crucial consideration from the national or regional point of view.

Temporary migration, as in sequences 3, and 5, when viewed socially as a training alternative, requires a major adjustment.[29] Unless a government coerces in some way, it cannot insure that those trained at home will stay at home or that those trained abroad will necessarily return. Therefore it is necessary to allow for the possibility that students trained at home will emigrate and that students trained outside will not return. This is done by including probabilities in the models.

As an example, we focus on comparisons between longer and shorter periods of training abroad. Let α_t^m be the probability that students trained outside the area for $(m-a)$ years will return before age t. To illustrate, sequence three then becomes:

$$V_{3m}^j = \sum_{t=m}^{n} \frac{\alpha_t^m \Upsilon_t^m - \alpha_t^m Z_t^h}{(1+r)^{t-a}} - \sum_{t=a}^{m-1} \frac{K_t + Z_t^0}{(1+r)^{t-a}} \tag{6}$$

For each value of $(m-a)$ there will be a different set of income variables, Υ_t^m, and the probabilities of return, α_t^m. The probability set α_t^m is likely to be

[27] Evidently the use of shadow pricing for public cost and benefit assessments will sometimes be required—where there are substantial discrepancies between present values of what men will be paid and what they will produce over ensuing years; this is why, earlier, we spoke of transformations from "individual earnings" to productive contributions. The discussion in this section identifies "social" returns with returns to the entire society, as measured by national product. Often foundations may take similar ultimate goals as a basis for decisions to allocate funds to one or another type of educational project in one or another location. Narrower definitions of "social" that balance flows into and out of one versus another public exchequer are a very different matter.

[28] For a listing and discussion of contributions to the area of origin which might be made from outside the area, see Harry Johnson, "Economics of the 'Brain Drain': The Canadian Case," *Minerva*, III, No. 3 (Spring, 1965), 299–311, and Herbert Grubel and Anthony Scott, "The International Flow of Human Capital, the Brain Drain," *op. cit.* An allowance for such contributions could, in principle, be incorporated in the social present value equations though it poses some elusive measurement problems.

[29] One of the authors—Myers—has been developing implications of this approach more fully. Our discussion here is limited by space considerations.

a declining function of $(m-a)$; the rate at which α_r^m declines will be one of the critical elements in the comparison of social net returns from longer or shorter periods of training abroad. In this form the equation refers to one individual (or a fraction thereof) but with appropriate identification of Υ, K, and $\mathcal{Z}$ it is also a marginal social benefit-cost summation. (Any part of costs for training or travel borne by other than the area of origin would of course be deducted from the K and $\mathcal{Z}$ figures.)

Another type of comparison involves locus of training for any given training period as, for instance, in a comparison of sequences 1 and 3. A concrete example is the argument over establishing local medical schools (versus training doctors abroad or out-of-state). The answer will depend on rates of migration and retention as well as on the relative cost and quality of the training in each locality. The argument usually given is that probabilities of retention for those trained at home so exceed the probability of return for those trained elsewhere as to outweigh all other considerations. From a "nationalistic" or "localistic" point of view, the economic validity of this argument will depend, among other things, upon who bears the costs of training in the alternative locales.

Another practically important issue is whether and how long students sent overseas should be allowed or encouraged to stay beyond formal schooling in order to acquire experience. The solution will depend, in part, on what "wastage" from non-return is associated with the experiential learning. This "wastage" is incorporated into our social decision model by introducing the migration probabilities.

The dependence of social policy upon understanding individual behavior is particularly evident in attempts to decrease wastage by influencing rates of out-migration and re-migration. Also, knowledge of how migration probabilities vary with individual characteristics within each schooling-work alternative would provide guidelines for efficient selection of individuals to the training programs, further reducing wastage.

Long Versus Short-Term Importations of Highly Qualified Manpower As a final example of human capital models applied to migration, we turn to decisions in developing nations concerning imported skills. We by-pass comparison of more training of local people against more importing of outside talent to focus on models weighing three alternatives in the purchase of foreign experts' services: a one-man, long-term contract, a sequence of short-term contracts to several people, and a system of two year rotations between two individuals.

When decisions involve a continuous series of replacements, the succession of short income streams can be regarded as one long one. The equivalence is not complete, however. The sharpest contrasts and associated problems can be most clearly illustrated by looking at human capital migration from the point of view of the developing nations and their needs for highly qualified manpower from the more advanced economies.

There is much discussion today of alternatives and combinations in the flow of high-level manpower for shorter or longer stays in the developing nations. In the terminology of the previous section, should a man be kept abroad for a period $(m-a)=2$ or for, say, $(m-a)=5$, or 10, or even 20 years? For that matter, what about double appointments in which two individuals alternate with each other at home and abroad?

In this discussion, present value refers to the value of imported services to the importing country, independent of the supply prices of these services. We will look at how supply conditions may affect optimal choice. Note that previously we used observed incomes as measures of both demand and supply prices in market equilibrium.

Let us designate the present value to the importing country, X, of a single individual for 10 years as V_x^1, that of two individuals who replace each other every two years over a period of 10 years as V_x^2, and that of a sequence of five individuals staying two years each as V_x^5. In the third case, on our assumption that each successive individual is the twin of his predecessor D_t for $t=1$ will have the same current year value as D_t where $t=3$, 5, 7, or 9 and D_t where $t=2$ will have the same value as where $t=4$, 6, 8, or 10. We make the simplifying assumption that the importing country pays for all travel expenses. Let these travel expenses be represented by:

$$Z^j = \sum_{t=a}^{a+10} \frac{Z_t^0}{(1+r)^{t-a}} + \sum_{t=a}^{a+10} \frac{Z_t^h}{(1+r)^{t-a}}$$

Also, let $D_{1,t}$ represent the earnings of individual 1 in year t, $D_{2,t}$ represent the earnings of individual 2 in year t and so forth.

Then the maximum present values and hence the amounts that the importing country would be justified in paying for the production streams generated by each of these alternatives can be represented as follows:

$$V_x^1 = \sum_{t=a}^{a+10} \frac{D_t^1}{(1+r)^{t-a}} + Z^1 \tag{7}$$

$$
\begin{aligned}
V_x^2 = &\left[\frac{D_{1,1}^2}{(1+r)} + \frac{D_{1,2}^2}{(1+r)^2}\right] + \left[\frac{D_{2,3}^2}{(1+r)^3} + \frac{D_{2,4}^2}{(1+r)^4}\right] \\
&+ \left[\frac{D_{1,5}^2}{(1+r)^5} + \frac{D_{1,6}^2}{(1+r)^6}\right] + \left[\frac{D_{2,7}^2}{(1+r)^7} + \frac{D_{2,8}^2}{(1+r)^8}\right] \\
&+ \left[\frac{D_{1,9}^2}{(1+r)^9} + \frac{D_{1,10}^2}{(1+r)^{10}}\right] + Z^2
\end{aligned} \tag{8}
$$

$$
\begin{aligned}
V_x^5 = &\left[\frac{D_{1,1}^5}{(1+r)} + \frac{D_{1,2}^5}{(1+r)^2}\right] + \left[\frac{D_{2,3}^5}{(1+r)^3} + \frac{D_{2,4}^5}{(1+r)^4}\right] \\
&+ \left[\frac{D_{3,5}^3}{(1+r)^5} + \frac{D_{3,6}^5}{(1+r)^6}\right] + \left[\frac{D_{4,7}^5}{(1+r)^7} + \frac{D_{4,8}^5}{(1+r)^8}\right]
\end{aligned}
$$

$$+\left[\frac{D_{5,9}^5}{(1+r)^9}+\frac{D_{5,10}^5}{(1+r)^{10}}\right]+\zeta^5 \tag{9}$$

Assuming successive twins for V_x^5 with $D_{1,1}=D_{2,3}=D_{3,5}=D_{4,7}=D_{5,9}$ and $D_{1,2}=D_{2,4}=D_{3,4}=D_{4,6}=D_{5,10}$ we have:

$$V_x^5=D_{1,1}\Sigma\left[\frac{1}{(1+r)}+\frac{1}{(1+r)^3}+\frac{1}{(1+r)^5}+\frac{1}{(1+r)^7}+\frac{1}{(1+r)^9}\right]$$

$$+D_{1,2}\Sigma\left[\frac{1}{(1+r)^2}+\frac{1}{(1+r)^4}+\frac{1}{(1+r)^6}+\frac{1}{(1+r)^8}+\frac{1}{(1+r)^{10}}\right]+\zeta^5 \tag{10}$$

We can simplify in comparing these alternatives by assuming that the amounts and timing of travel costs paid by the receiving country are the same in all three cases. This is evidently the case as between V_x^2 and V_x^5, and it is consistent enough with common practice respecting travel allowances for vacation at home in the case of expatriates on long-term appointments. Which alternative will yield the highest present value then depends upon the summations of sets of terms incorporating the D's.

If there is any learning on the job at all, the V_x^5 stream will clearly have the lowest present value. In fact, if we had made any allowance for direct outlays on training, this disadvantage of the V_x^5 stream would be still more apparent. There is good reason for the widespread concern over the cutting off of so many technical assistance activities at two years per man, and even stronger reason for the increasingly firm attempts to adhere to a two-year minimum, to permit men to learn about the situation in a strange environment and to attain a reasonably high level of effectiveness in it. Two year appointments may serve very well when there is a special job that needs to be done by a man with unusual qualifications, after which the requirements of the task are less demanding—in other words, when the calibre of the first man has to be higher than that of his successors. But that is a different sort of situation, and not the "successive twin" case with which we started and by which we defined V_x^5.

Comparison between V_x^1 and V_x^2 must be a bit more subtle. In case V_x^1 there is the advantage of continuity on the job in country X, but offsetting this is loss of contact with dynamic centers of activity in the expert's home country; he tends to fall progressively further behind his colleagues there. Case V_x^2 has the advantage that experiences in the home country and in the importing country may well feed into each other, to enhance a man's effectiveness in both. This is one of the arguments in favor of developing career opportunities in technical assistance by establishing supernumerary university posts (double staffing) in selected fields and locations.

If V_x^5 is so likely to be the inferior choice for value to the importing country, why is this alternative so common in practice? Evidently there are two reasons. First is the political reaction to colonial experience and the desire to avoid entrenchment of foreigners who might build up too much power in the country. In many cases ex-colonial countries have quite deliberately made a trade-off between economic and political ends by their policies with respect to expatriates. However, this phase of the transition is fading, and with this change the economic decision models may have greater potential impact on policies. In strictly economic terms, what can be said for V_x^2? To properly evaluate V_x^1, V_x^2, and V_x^5 we also need to know the supply prices involved. It seems clear that set against the lower present values of a V_x^5 stream are lower recruitment costs; it is easier to get good men for a short than for a long time, and primarily for two reasons: First, the pace of learning in the first year is likely to be especially high, and what is learned over a two-year period may have more transferability to the job market in the expert's home country than the learning that cumulates with longer time abroad. He loses little, if anything, in carrying this learning home with him. Second, he has suffered less loss in getting out of touch and losing contacts with colleagues at home when his stay is not too prolonged. (In addition, a reasonably short term abroad may be enticing for quite non-economic considerations that would pall if the stay were extended.) Thus set over against the lower value of the V_x^5 stream is the greater ease and lower cost of maintaining it.

This brings us back to V_x^1 against V_x^2 once again. Let us take another look at V_x^1. Unless a man becomes a permanent migrant, he is likely to suffer a disadvantage when he returns home after a long stay abroad. He has foregone learning opportunities suited to his home country, and the experience he has accumulated in his years abroad often has limited transferability back into an advanced industrial nation. (In lesser degree this may happen with migration from North to South in the United States, unless the migrant is associated with a Northern or a Northern-type firm.) In order to attract a man for 10 years, it would be necessary to pay him a very high salary to compensate for this accumulation of obsolescence. There is evidently a point at which long-term stays abroad must become permanent ones if they are to prove beneficial both to the receiving country and to the individual involved.

V_x^2 is quite another matter. In this case the learning process continues and contacts at home are maintained. No special bribe need be paid to attract a man into such a career. On balance it looks very much as though V_x^2 might come out as the best alternative in a large proportion of cases. Systematic application of human investment decision models to particular cases will help sort these alternatives out. They just might lead to some important innovations in technical assistance and in relations between Universities and the Department of State.

In Conclusion

1. *Current methods of calculating human capital gains and losses from migration take a too simplistic view of migration.*

a. Even adhering for the moment to the prevalent treatment of migration as if it were a one-way affair, it is of the greatest importance that gross flows be analyzed: the critical problems and evidence concerning the effects of migration are concealed when net flows only are assessed—even when the latter are broken down into finely disaggregated population categories.

b. Re-migration is important quantitatively. Furthermore, disregard of re-migration leads to serious misinterpretations of even the gross flows and even when the latter are disaggregated on a number of key variables. The importance of analyzing re-migration is underlined where regions differ in quality of schooling and experiential opportunities and where there is rotating migration of obsolescent and undereducated men.

2. *Human investment decision models provide useful conceptual and empirical tools when applied to migration, from both individual and social perspective.*

a. The models add insight into motivations of migrants. Understanding migrant behavior provides points of leverage for channeling migration to social purposes, and provides a means of determining to what extent the socially rational may coincide or conflict with effects of individual behavior that are rational.

b. Social decisions involving the locus of training may be put in a cost-benefit framework and evaluated. Major decisions such as whether to train elsewhere or at home can be weighed. Losses from non-return and their probabilities can be valued and included in assessing investment alternatives. The potential gains from policies to reduce rates of non-return could also be estimated.

c. Migration, coupled with regional differentials in quality of schooling and experience, can be examined as it relates to the diffusion of know-how among regions or nations. Of particular interest would be application of human capital concepts to understanding "package migration" as an agent of change.

d. Effects of social decisions to import manpower on a short-term continuous replacement basis, an alternating basis, or a long-term basis can be sorted out using human capital investment models. For each situation, individual decision models provide estimates of outlays necessary to attract the talent desired. Costs and benefits can be compared to determine the best alternative.

3. *Availability of census tapes with data for samples large enough to permit refined breakdowns would permit new kinds of research on critical aspects of migration as a human investment.* Potential contributions to both theoretical developments in the social sciences and to public policy formation are substantial.

a. Even if no data other than those collected in 1960 were obtained, larger samples would permit multiple breakdowns that distinguish migrant status by origin, destination, and place of birth for Divisions, within existing categories on age-sex-race-income-education-occupation tables.

b. All too sizeable a list of other items might be suggested, but we will use restraint. A high priority item would be occupation just prior to migration, but we recognize that occupation data are costly. Home residence of college students is presumably being included. We would be interested in dates of migration, together with state and type of community in which a migrant last resided, but we would not want to give up the identification of residence and other traits at a fixed time interval (5 years) before the census. Obviously not all these things can be done.

c. Because of the importance we attach to it, we list separately information concerning residence when last attending high school (or, for those who never entered high school, elementary school). Alternatively, the question could be asked for age 16, though this might be more difficult for some to answer. State of residence and type of community would both be desirable; together they should provide valuable indexes of the combined effects of quality of schooling and experiential learning from adolescent environment. Such information could be extremely useful not only in analysis of migration but in many other aspects of the economics of human resource development and utilization.

Environmental

Investments

in Human Capital

Poverty and Discrimination Economics

The decade of the 1960s will be remembered for many reasons, not the least of which will be the quickened American conscience concerning discrimination and the coexistence of poverty amidst plenty. The problems of discrimination, minority groups, and the poor are not confined to economics, nor are they solely a result of inadequate human capital formation. Yet, the connections between human capital embodied in the poor and the economics of discrimination reflected by income variance between whites and nonwhites is direct and all too obvious. It is where poverty and discrimination are concerned that issues of "quality" and noneconomic externalities such as equal opportunity surface in a most visible manner. The dearth of our knowledge and data on such matters in a form amenable to the quantitative manipulation so dear to economists is remarkable as well as unfortunate. Again, this forces economic analysts to take as givens important variables badly in need of more definitive identification.

After discussing the magnitude of poverty and the direction of public policies in an extract reprinted from the 1969 *Economic Report of the President*

24, the selections by John P. Formby **25** and Walter Fogel **26** examine the problem of economic discrimination from an empirical vantage point.

24

Combating Poverty
in a Prosperous Economy

A new awareness of the coexistence of poverty and prosperity in the America of the 1960s must be regarded as one characteristic feature of that decade. In the 1969 *Economic Report of the President*, the Council of Economic Advisers describe the past progress and current magnitude of poverty. Chairman Arthur Okun

COUNCIL OF
ECONOMIC ADVISERS

and Council Members Merton Peck and Warren Smith review the problems of the poor, including education and training in their assessment of the prospect of future relief in this domestic war.

. . . the policy of the United States [is] to eliminate the paradox of poverty in the midst of plenty in this Nation by opening to everyone the opportunity for education and training, the opportunity to work, and the opportunity to live in decency and dignity.

For over four years the United States has had an explicit national commitment to eliminate poverty in our society, a commitment enunciated by the President in the State of the Union Message of 1964 and confirmed by the Congress in the above words later that year in the Economic Opportunity Act.

Americans are increasingly prosperous. Median family income in the United States (in constant 1967 prices) rose from $6,210 in 1959 to $7,974 in 1967, a gain of 28 percent in 8 years. Yet many families are still not able to attain minimum living standards. A preliminary estimate indicates that in 1968 about 22 million people lived in households with incomes below the

Reprinted from Council of Economic Advisers, "Combating Poverty in a Prosperous Economy," *Annual Report of the Council of Economic Advisers* (January 1969), pp. 151–55 and 161–63.

"poverty lines." While this is far fewer than in the past—more than 40 million were similarly situated in 1960—too many Americans remain poor.

This chapter examines the recent progress in reducing poverty, the nature of the task that remains, and the strategies available for eliminating poverty.

The Extent of Poverty

A family is "poor" if its income is insufficient to buy enough food, clothing, shelter, and health services to meet minimum requirements. Universally acceptable standards for determining these minimum needs are impossible to formulate since the line between physical necessities and amenities is imprecise.

The social and psychological aspects of poverty further complicate efforts to measure poverty. As average incomes rise, society amends its assessment of basic needs. Individuals who cannot afford more than a small fraction of the items enjoyed by the majority are likely to feel deprived. Consequently, an absolute standard that seems appropriate today will inevitably be rejected tomorrow, just as we now reject poverty definitions appropriate a century ago.

Even a rough measure of progress in reducing poverty requires an explicit definition, although the line drawn is unavoidably arbitrary. In its 1964 Annual Report, the Council used a poverty line of $3,000 annual family income. Since 1965, the Council has employed the more refined definition of poverty developed by the Social Security Administration (SSA).

The SSA poverty lines reflect the differing consumption requirements of families based on their size and composition, the age of members, and whether their residence is farm or nonfarm. The calculations center around the U.S. Department of Agriculture's Economy Food Plan, which in December 1967 added up to a per capita weekly food outlay of $4.90. For families of three or more, the SSA measure assumes all other family needs can be obtained for an amount equal to twice the family's food requirement. In 1967, the nonfarm poverty threshold for an average four-person family was $3,335 as compared to a median income, for families of that size, of $8,995. Poverty lines for different types of households are shown in Table 1.

The problems of low-income families neither begin nor end at any arbitrary poverty line. A sharp decline in poverty may be a misleading indicator of progress if a large number of families are raised just above the poverty line. Accordingly, the SSA has also developed a "near poor" standard averaging about one-third higher than the poverty line but still less than one-half of median income for many types of families. Near-poor income standards are shown in Table 1.

The SSA poverty definitions have some limitations. Since they are multiples of food costs, the poverty lines change only when food prices change, and these prices do not necessarily parallel the prices of other essentials. Regional differences in living costs are not reflected in the poverty line. The income data take no account of income in kind such as health care, subsidized housing, and foodstuffs (except for food grown on farms). No adjustment is made for either net assets or fluctuating incomes, and yet families with savings or temporary income interruptions have different problems than the chronically poor.

Table 1—Poverty and near-poverty income lines, 1967

Household characteristic[a]	Poverty income line	Near-poverty income line
Nonfarm households:		
1 member	$1,635	$1,985
65 years and over	1,565	1,890
Under 65 years	1,685	2,045
2 members	2,115	2,855
Head 65 years and over	1,970	2,655
Head under 65 years	2,185	2,945
3 members	2,600	3,425
4 members	3,335	4,345
5 members	3,930	5,080
6 members	4,410	5,700
7 members or more	5,430	6,945
Farm households:		
1 member	1,145	1,390
65 years and over	1,095	1,330
Under 65 years	1,195	1,450
2 members	1,475	1,990
Head 65 years and over	1,380	1,870
Head under 65 years	1,535	2,075
3 members	1,815	2,400
4 members	2,345	3,060
5 members	2,755	3,565
6 members	3,090	3,995
7 members or more	3,790	4,850

[a] Households are defined here as the total of families and unrelated individuals.

Note.—Poverty and near-poverty income standards are defined by the Social Security Administration; they take into account family size, composition, and place of residence. Income lines are adjusted to take account of price changes during the year.

Source: Department of Health, Education, and Welfare.

These problems are currently under study in an effort to refine the poverty concept. A different threshold could affect the distribution of measured poverty among various groups but would probably show much the same trend in total poverty over the long run.

POVERTY TRENDS

With the general rise in family incomes in the postwar period, the incidence of poverty—the percentage of persons in poor households relative to the total population—has declined sharply from 30 to less than 12 percent (see Chart 1). The number of persons in poverty declined about 20 million over the past 20 years, including a drop of 12 million since 1963—an estimated 4 million in 1968 alone.

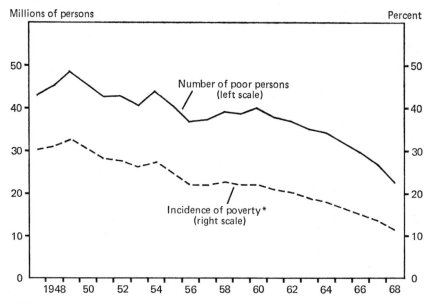

* Poor persons as percent of total noninstitutional population.

Note: Poverty is defined by the Social Security Administration poverty-income standard.

Sources: Department of Commerce, Department of Health, Education, and Welfare, Office of Economic Opportunity, and Council of Economic Advisers.

Chart 1
Number of Poor Persons and Incidence of Poverty

Along with the reduction in the number of poor households, the "poverty gap"—the difference between the actual incomes of the poor and the incomes necessary to place them above the poverty line—has been reduced. The poverty gap fell from $13.7 billion in 1959 to $9.7 billion in 1967, measured in current dollars.

Distribution by Community Type The incidence of poverty is highest—23 percent—in those rural areas not in metropolitan counties, with the heaviest concentrations in the South and Appalachia. The incidence is also quite high—19 percent—in the smaller cities and towns outside of major metropolitan areas. In the central cities, the incidence is 16 percent and in their suburbs about 9 percent.

Racial and Ethnic Distribution   Most of the poor are white. In 1967 (the latest year for which detailed data on the poor are available), 71 percent of all poor families and 83 percent of all poor unrelated individuals were white. The incidence of poverty is far higher among nonwhites: about one household in three compared with about one in seven among whites.

Of the 2.4 million nonwhite households in poverty, 2.3 million are Negroes; the remainder are mostly the original Americans—Indians and Eskimos. A 1964 survey revealed that 74 percent of the 55,000 families living on Indian and Eskimo reservations had incomes under $3,000.

Only recently has the reduction of poverty among nonwhites matched the reduction among whites. Between 1959 and 1962, the number of whites in poverty declined 2.8 million, but during the same period the number of poor nonwhites rose by 0.9 million. Between 1962 and 1967, white poverty was reduced another 7 million or about 28 percent, while poverty among nonwhites fell by 3.2 million—also about 28 percent.

The relative position of nonwhite families, after deteriorating in the late 1950's has improved since 1961. (See Appendix Table B–20.*) Only since 1966 has nonwhite median family income as a fraction of white median family income surpassed its previous peak of 57 percent in 1952. Unemployment among nonwhite men age 25 to 54 has recently fallen below 1951–53 levels, but unemployment rates for nonwhite women and nonwhite teenage males are much higher than during the early 1950's.

Most poor white families in the United States are not members of identifiable ethnic groups; however, two groups—Mexican-Americans, living largely in southwestern States, and Puerto Ricans, concentrated in New York City—exhibit disproportionately high incidences of poverty. In 1966, unemployment rates among Mexican-Americans in southwestern cities ranged between 8 percent and 13 percent, two to three times the national average. Subemployment—the sum of unemployment, employment producing earnings too low to provide an escape from poverty, and nonparticipation in the labor force by individuals who have given up hope of finding work—ranged from 42 to 47 percent in the Mexican-American sections of south-western cities. And while Puerto Ricans constitute only about 8 percent of the New York City population, they have been estimated to represent over one-third of the recipients of welfare and about one-third of all occupants of substandard housing.

STRATEGIES FOR REDUCING POVERTY

A program for reducing poverty has four principal economic dimensions.

First, sustained high employment and economic growth—key objectives of economic policy for a wide variety of reasons—are prime essentials.

* This reference is to the Data Appendix published annually in The Economic Report of the President.

Second, education, training, medical assistance, and access to well-paying jobs are needed by many of the poor to escape from chronic unemployment and low-paying dead end jobs.

Third, three-fifths of the heads of poor households cannot easily enter the labor force because of age or disability, or because they are mothers with sole responsibility for the care of young children. Some workers with large families are not likely—even with training and other types of employment assistance—to earn an income sufficient to pull their families out of poverty. Because increased employment opportunities will not eliminate poverty among these groups, some form of income maintenance is required.

Fourth, poverty is concentrated in "pockets"—city "ghettos" and certain rural areas. The numbers of poor in poverty pockets can be reduced by promoting public and private investment in these communities and by providing relocation assistance to those with employment opportunities elsewhere.

In addition to economic policies, social and psychological strategies have an important role to play. These include information about family planning for those who request it, legal assistance, and the encouragement of self-help organizations. Such programs lie outside the purview of this Report.

Prosperity and the Reduction of Poverty

Virtually all the progress in reducing poverty over the past 20 years has occurred during periods of general prosperity. In three periods of sustained economic expansion—1949–53, 1954–56, and 1961 to the present—the annual decline in the number of individuals in poverty averaged two million or more a year. In contrast, during recessions the number of poor people has increased. The brief recession of 1954 wiped out half of the gains of the preceding 4-year expansion, and several successive years of sluggish economic performance in the late 1950's increased the number of persons in poverty to about the level of 7 years earlier. (See Chart 1.)

EFFECTS OF PROSPERITY

Poor families are affected unequally by economic growth and high employment, depending upon their ability to take advantage of expanded employment opportunities. Recent trends in poverty reduction for different groups are shown in Table 2.

Households with Heads of Working Age   Economic expansion has caused significant reductions in poverty among households headed by a working-age man. Tightening labor markets raise wages for the poor who are employed, and provide better employment opportunities for the unemployed and for those with very low-paying or part-time jobs. Furthermore, when prosperity

Table 2—Number of poor households and incidence of poverty, selected years, 1959–67

Characteristic of head of household	1959	1961	1964	1966[a] Originally published	Revised	1967
Number of poor households :[b]			*Millions*			
Total	13.4	13.0	11.9	10.9	10.7	10.2
Head 65 years and over	3.9	3.9	3.8	3.9	4.0	3.8
Unrelated individuals	2.5	2.5	2.8	2.7	2.7	2.7
Families[c]	1.4	1.3	1.1	1.2	1.2	1.1
Head under 65 years	9.4	9.1	8.0	7.0	6.8	6.4
Unrelated individuals	2.6	2.4	2.3	2.1	2.1	2.2
White	1.9	1.8	1.8	1.6	1.6	1.6
Male	.6	.6	.6	.5	.6	.5
Female	1.3	1.2	1.2	1.1	1.0	1.1
Nonwhite	.7	.7	.5	.5	.5	.5
Male	.3	.3	.2	.2	.2	.2
Female	.4	.4	.3	.3	.3	.3
Families[d]	6.8	6.7	5.7	4.9	4.7	4.2
White	4.9	4.7	4.0	3.3	3.1	2.8
Male	3.8	3.7	3.0	2.3	2.2	2.0
Female	1.1	1.0	1.0	1.0	.9	.8
Nonwhite	1.9	2.0	1.7	1.6	1.5	1.4
Male	1.3	1.3	1.1	.9	.9	.7
Female	.6	.7	.6	.7	.7	.7
Incidence of poverty :[e]			*Percentage*			
Total households[b]	24.0	22.6	19.9	17.8	17.5	16.2
Head 65 years and over	48.6	43.8	40.0	38.5	38.9	36.3
Unrelated individuals	68.1	64.4	59.9	55.3	56.3	53.4
Families[c]	32.5	27.2	21.6	23.0	23.1	20.3
Head under 65 years	19.8	18.8	16.0	13.7	13.3	12.2
Unrelated individuals	36.8	33.9	31.0	28.3	28.7	27.0
White	32.9	29.7	28.3	25.8	25.5	24.4
Male	24.6	22.8	22.0	20.1	21.0	18.0
Female	39.1	35.2	33.0	30.0	28.8	29.0
Nonwhite	54.8	55.0	45.1	41.7	45.3	40.1
Male	47.1	45.5	34.6	29.1	35.5	29.4
Female	63.5	66.8	58.1	54.1	55.1	51.7
Families[d]	16.8	16.1	13.3	11.2	10.6	9.5
White	13.4	12.6	10.4	8.4	7.9	7.1
Male	11.4	10.7	8.5	6.5	6.1	5.4
Female	35.9	33.9	31.2	29.1	27.9	25.3
Nonwhite	48.6	47.8	27.8	34.3	33.4	29.9
Male	42.1	40.2	32.3	25.9	25.1	20.9
Female	71.3	72.8	62.4	61.2	60.3	54.9

[a] The revised estimates differ slightly from those originally published because of the use of a somewhat different estimating procedure. For an explanation of the two methods, see "Current Population Reports" Series P–60, No. 54.

[b] Households are defined here as the total of families and unrelated individuals.

[c] Consists only of two-person families whose head is 65 years or over. All other families included in "head under 65 years."

[d] All families other than two-person families whose head is 65 years or over.

[e] Poor households as percent of total households in the category.

Note.—Poverty is defined by the Social Security Administration poverty-income standard; it takes into account family size, composition, and place of residence. Poverty-income lines are adjusted to take account of price changes during the period.

Detail will not necessarily add to totals because of rounding.

Sources: Department of Commerce and Department of Health, Education, and Welfare.

pushes unemployment rates to low levels among skilled workers, business is more inclined to train poorly qualified workers for skilled jobs. From 1964 to 1966, the number of poor households headed by a working-age man with work experience fell 400,000 a year; in contrast, there had been no decline from 1959 to 1961.

The number of poor households headed by a working-age woman with job experience has not changed during the 1960's. The decline in the incidence of poverty among this group reflected a rise in the total number of households headed by working-age women.

Prosperity is less effective in reducing poverty among households headed by women for several reasons. Women are far less likely to be employed than men; only about three-fifths of the women who head families have some job experience, compared to about 90 percent for male family heads. Many women who head families, being the adult solely responsible for young children, are unable to accept full-time employment unless day care is provided for their children. Furthermore, women are far less likely to escape poverty even if they do work, because their employment is less steady and they earn lower wages. Nonwhite families are more than twice as likely— and white families are more than three times as likely—to be poor if headed by a woman than if headed by a man.

Elderly Households During the 1960's, the number of poor elderly households fell slightly, while the incidence of poverty among this group decreased substantially. High employment has some immediate effect on poverty among the aged by providing more jobs for elderly individuals wishing to continue work. This opportunity is particularly important for those with retirement income below the poverty line.

Over the longer run, prosperity permits more workers to accumulate assets and to achieve higher pension rights prior to retirement. At present, an individual earning the minimum wage and working full-time in a job covered by social security is entitled to old-age benefits of approximately $120 a month upon retirement—only about $10 a month below the poverty line.

Reflecting both the higher lifetime earnings of the aged and statutory improvements, social security retirement benefits have increased greatly and have been the most important factor in reducing poverty among the elderly. Since 1961, legislation has increased social security retirement benefits 21 percent across the board,—substantially greater than the increase in consumer prices. The minimum benefit increased 37 percent.

The Disabled The ill and disabled have benefited least from recent prosperity and other efforts to alleviate poverty. Although the *incidence* of poverty among households whose heads are under 65 and not working for health reasons fell from 1959 to 1967, the *number* actually rose. Some disabled can be retrained, and these individuals can obtain jobs more readily when unemployment is low. But many who are ill or disabled cannot take advantage of job opportunities.

The Near-Poor   Table 3 shows the number of households and the number of persons who were in the near-poor category in 1959 and 1967.

The compositions of the poor and the near-poor categories differ considerably. Most striking is the difference in the proportion of nonelderly households headed by a working-age woman. These households account for 46 percent of all nonelderly poor households; among the near-poor, they account for 22 percent. Except for the elderly, most near-poor families are headed by men who are employed, but at low wages.

Table 3—Number of near-poor households and incidence of near-poverty by age and sex of head of household, 1959 and 1967

Age and sex of head of household	NUMBER (millions)		INCIDENCE OF NEAR-POVERTY (percent)[a]	
	1959	1967	1959	1967
Near-poor households[b]	4.3	3.7	7.7	5.9
Families	3.8	2.9	8.3	5.8
Head 65 years and over[c]	.7	.8	15.2	14.0
Head under 65 years[d]	3.1	2.1	7.6	4.8
Male head	3.4	2.4	8.4	5.5
Female head	.4	.5	8.2	8.7
Unrelated individuals	.5	.8	5.1	6.0
Head 65 years and over	.2	.5	6.1	9.1
Head under 65 years	.3	.3	4.6	4.0
Male head	.2	.3	5.5	5.8
Female head	.3	.5	4.9	6.1
Addendum:				
Near-poor persons	15.8	12.0	9.0	6.1

[a] Near-poor households as percent of total number of households in the category; near-poor persons as percent of total persons.

[b] Households are defined here as the total of families and unrelated individuals.

[c] Consists only of two-person families whose head is 65 years or over. All other families included in "head under 65 years."

[d] All families other than two-person families whose head is 65 years or over.

Note.—Near-poverty is defined by the Social Security Administration near-poverty-income standards; it takes into account family size, composition, and place of residence. Near-poverty-income lines are adjusted to take account of price changes during the period.

Detail will not necessarily add to totals because of rounding.

Sources: Department of Commerce and Department of Health, Education, and Welfare.

The number of near-poor showed a considerable decline between 1959 and 1967. Many who rose from poverty were added to the near-poor, but at the same time an even larger number of the former near-poor moved to a higher income level.

PROSPECTS FOR FURTHER PROGRESS

As indicated above, prosperity has played a key role in reducing poverty and is essential to further progress. But sustained growth and high employment—in the absence of other more direct efforts to help the poor—cannot maintain the recent rate of decline in poverty.

If the 1961–68 reductions in the number of poor persons could be continued, poverty would be eliminated entirely in about 10 years. If the record of 1968 could be continued, poverty would be eliminated in about 5½ years. Maintenance of these rapid reductions will become increasingly difficult because, as poverty declines, an increasing fraction of the remaining poor are members of households whose economic status is least affected by prosperity. Households headed by women with children, disabled persons, or elderly persons accounted for 6.0 million or 59 percent of all poor households in 1967.

Much of the progress in the 1960's has been due to the lowering of the unemployment rate. As that rate fell, further declines were increasingly effective. The hard-core unemployed, the educationally disadvantaged, and the victims of discrimination are the last to be hired during a return to high employment and the first to be fired during a slowdown. Upgrading the unskilled and uneducated to fill shortages in skilled labor takes time. Consequently, if high employment is maintained, these adjustments will continue to reduce poverty, but their effects will gradually diminish. In the absence of increased direct assistance to the poor or further reductions in unemployment, present annual declines in poverty must be expected to become smaller.

The elimination of poverty will be long in coming if the incomes of the poor grow only at the same pace as the incomes of other households. If the real income (including transfer payments) of each poor household were to grow at 3 percent a year—approximately the average gain for all households during normal conditions of economic growth—eliminating only half of poverty would take 12 years for poor families and 17 years for unrelated individuals. To shorten substantially the period needed to reduce poverty, the incomes of the poor must grow faster than average income—some redistribution to the poor must be made from the benefits of growth.

INCOME DISTRIBUTION

Only a relatively small redistribution of the benefits of growth is needed to speed greatly the reduction in poverty. If the approximately 85 percent of households that are not poor and receive about 95 percent of total income are willing to make only a small sacrifice of the estimated 3 percent yearly growth in their real income per capita, the prospects for poverty reduction can be greatly transformed. If the increase in real income for the nonpoor is lowered merely from 3 percent to 2½ percent a year and if that differential of about $2.8 billion annually is effectively transferred to those in poverty, then family incomes for those now poor can grow about 12 percent annually. This redistribution would eliminate the 1967 "poverty gap" of $9.7 billion in less than 4 years. Since any program of redistribution would be likely to reach some of the near-poor and might raise some poor families substantially above the poverty line before others are affected, perhaps a better projection of the time required would be 6 to 8 years.

The rapid reductions in poverty during the 1960's paralleled a significant rise in the share of total family income going to the lowest income groups. In part, this shift in distribution has been accomplished by increased employment of poor adults at higher wages.

The combined effect of the tax and transfer payment systems at all levels of Government also operates to redistribute income to the poor. The net gain or burden from the public sector for any group depends on the difference between all the benefits received from government expenditures and all the taxes paid. Many programs—like national defense—have benefits that are difficult to allocate by groups; however, the benefits of transfer payments—such as social security benefits, welfare payments, and unemployment compensation—can be allocated and compared with the tax burden. The impact of Federal, State, and local taxes and of transfer payments on the distribution of income in 1965 is shown in Chart 2.

The tax system by itself redistributes income away from the poor. As a share of income, higher taxes are paid by households in the lower income classes than by those with incomes between $6,000 and $15,000. This reflects the heavy tax burden on low-income families from State and local taxes—primarily sales, excise, and property taxes. Federal taxes also contribute to this burden through the social security payroll tax.

The poor receive nearly as much from transfer payments as from all other sources. While these payments do not go exclusively to the poor, they do have a powerful redistributive impact. The ratio of receipts to household income (excluding transfers) is very high in the lowest income classes. As household incomes rise, the proportion of transfers to other income falls sharply.

When government transfer payments and taxes are combined, the concentration of transfer payments in the lower income groups much more than offsets their tax burden. But since average transfer payments fall rapidly as income rises, the excess of taxes over transfer payments as a fraction of income rises much more sharply from $0 to $4,000 than in higher income classes.

Education, Jobs, and Training

Education and training measures can improve job opportunities for the poor and their children.

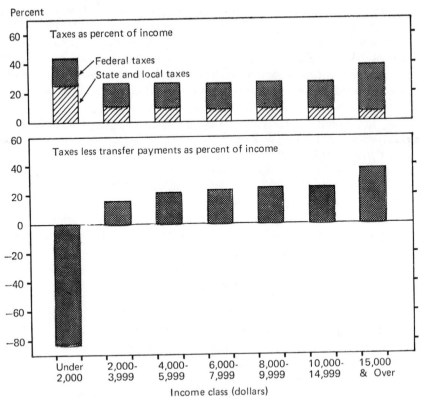

Source: Council of Economic Advisers, based on data from a variety of sources.
Description available on request.

Chart 2
Taxes and Transfer Payments as Percent of Income (Excluding Transfers), by Income Class, 1965

Education can help prevent the children of the poor from remaining poor when they grow up. They are already better schooled than their parents. About three-fourths of poor youths between 16 and 21 either are attending school or are high school graduates, whereas more than half of their parents had no high school education. Yet these youths still have less schooling than their more fortunate contemporaries, 90 percent of whom are in school or are high school graduates.

Although most poor children of all ages are now in school, inferior facilities and poorly qualified teachers lower the value of the education many of them receive. Even schools equivalent to those of the prosperous would not yield equal education. Poverty imposes handicaps that children of more prosperous families do not have.

Children of the poor are less likely to receive good health care and good nutrition, both of which affect success in school. They are also less likely to receive the verbal and intellectual stimulation in their early years that prepares them to master school work. They start school somewhat behind other youngsters, and they receive less parental assistance. Since school does not meet the challenge of helping them catch up, it becomes a place of defeat, leading many to drop out.

Poor children from minority groups suffer another handicap, segregation. More than 60 percent of all Negro pupils in the first grade attend elementary schools in which at least 90 percent of the students are Negro. Not only are facilities and instruction inferior in many of these schools, but studies of educational performance suggests that segregation itself has an adverse effect on school performance.

If poor children are to have equal opportunity to compete successfully for good jobs, they need special help in the preschool years. They also need compensatory education, with expenditures exceeding those made on other pupils. Finally, they need financial help and other encouragement to stay in school and continue their education.

Major efforts have been made to upgrade education provided children of the poor in programs such as the Elementary and Secondary Education Act, the Economic Opportunity Act, and the Vocational Education Amendments of 1968. Head Start, Title I of the Elementary Education Act, and Follow Through are comprehensive programs, combining health care, nutrition, and the involvement of the child's family, as well as education. Most of these special Federal efforts have been in operation for 3 years or less. While too little experience has been gained to allow a full evaluation, enough positive results are evident to justify continuing the programs. . . .

25

The Extent of Wage and Salary Discrimination Against Non-White Labor

Do nonwhites pay a "price" or tax as members of a predominantly white society and, if so, what is the magnitude of the economic cost borne by the black community? John Formby, Professor of Economics at the University of North Carolina at Greensboro, examines this issue in a dynamic context. As one might expect, the losses are substantial, numbering in the billions of dollars in 1959. The economic costs of discrimination vary by region, sex, and educational attainment, as the author observes. Formby's conclusion that nonwhite human capital experiences greater economic discrimination as human capital content increases carries with it important implications for future human capital investments for this society.

JOHN P. FORMBY

The cost of racial discrimination may have several meanings. To the anthropologist the differences in length of life between Negroes and whites may be interpreted as the cost of discrimination. Another approach might be to calculate the cost of discrimination as the total income differential between Negroes and whites and the additional costs to society of a higher incidence of Negro juvenile delinquency, crime, and occupancy in prison. In economic terms the cost of economic discrimination is perhaps best defined as the net value of output to the economy as a whole which is foregone because of the

Reprinted from John P. Formby, "The Extent of Wage and Salary Discrimination Against Non-White Labor," *Southern Economic Journal* 35 (October 1968), pp. 140–50, with the permission of the author and publisher.

misallocation of resources associated with discrimination. A useful distinction, however, can be drawn between the current discriminatory treatment of minority groups in the market place with its resulting costs and the cumulative impact of past discrimination resulting in lower productivity of non-white factors of production. The former can be thought of as the cost of market discrimination and the latter as the current cost of past discrimination.

This paper is concerned with market discrimination against non-white wage and salary earners. This aspect of market discrimination is measured by the net wage and salary income differentials between perfectly substitutable white and non-white labor. In order to avoid confusing these income differentials with the more inclusive concept of the cost of market discrimination, the differentials are interpreted as measures of the extent of wage and salary discrimination against non-white labor.

Given this definition the purposes of the paper are: (1) to present calculations of the extent of wage and salary discrimination against non-whites between the ages 22 and 64 for the years 1949 and 1959; (2) to show the changes in such discrimination over this interval; (3) to show regional differences in the extent of wage and salary discrimination; and (4) to show the relation between the extent of wage and salary discrimination and human capital. No attempt is made to explain the changes in discrimination or the differential treatment of non-whites with differing amounts of human capital. The only discrimination of concern here is wage and salary discrimination against non-white labor.[1] For example, the paper does not attempt to assess the impact of discrimination against all women—only non-white women and only in regard to their color—not their sex. Similarly, the paper does not attempt to measure the market discrimination against non-white capital.

The Theory of Market Discrimination

Professor Gary S. Becker's path breaking study of market discrimination[2] relates the cost of discrimination to incomes earned in the market place. According to Becker, economic discrimination occurs when a majority group (whites) discriminates against a minority group (non-whites) and such discrimination reduces the minority group's income. Economic discrimination manifests itself in a reduction in the quantity of white capital employed with non-white labor. This reduces the income of non-white labor and white capital while raising the income of white labor and non-white capital.

---

[1] More than 95 per cent of non-whites are Negroes (99 per cent in the South). Consequently, when we refer to non-whites we are for all practical purposes referring to Negroes.

[2] Gary S. Becker, *The Economics of Discrimination* (Chicago, 1957).

Professor Becker shows that non-white pecuniary losses from discrimination will be greater than whites' pecuniary gains.[3]

The cost of economic discrimination viewed within the confines of this theory includes only the net reduction of pecuniary total income caused by discrimination, that is, the amount by which discrimination reduces non-white incomes less white gains from discrimination. Any estimate of the cost of market discrimination which does not compare incomes of non-whites and whites who are perfect substitutes in production and which does not allow for possible white gains from discrimination may be unreliable at best and possibly significantly misleading.[4]

In *The Economics of Discrimination* Professor Becker estimated the cost of market discrimination by using a production function of the Cobb-Douglas form, $X = KL^rC^{1-r}$. The cost of market discrimination can be calculated from this production function if exponents, ratio of white to non-white labor, ratio of white to non-white capital (including human capital), actual amount of white capital employed with non-white labor, and actual non-white income are known. The ratio of white to non-white capital (including human capital) and the amount of white capital employed with non-white labor are not known. Of course, reasonable assumptions about these values are possible; and estimates of the cost can be made.[5] However, even with reasonable assumptions the margin of error in the estimate is not known with any precision. In addition, it is exceptionally difficult to use this method to estimate regional costs of discrimination, changes in discrimination over time or to show the relation between discrimination and human capital. The major purpose of this paper is to present estimates of the extent of wage and salary discrimination which is not subject to these shortcomings.

Data Used and Problems Associated With the Estimates

The 1950 and 1960 United States Census of Population data on income by color, sex, age, education, and region for the years 1949 and 1959 can be utilized in constructing estimates of the extent of wage and salary discrimination which employ Becker's concepts as a starting point.

Professor Becker treats white and non-white labor in matched age-education categories as perfect substitutes in production.[6] Generalizing this

---

[3] *Ibid.*, pp. 15 and 29.

[4] Professor Becker vociferously criticized E. Roper's rough approximation of the cost of discrimination for not considering substitutability, *ibid.*, p. 21 and ff. 16.

[5] Professor Becker assumed the ratio of white to non-white capital was 150:1; and that discrimination reduced the amount of white capital employed with non-white labor by 40 per cent. These assumptions yield the estimate that non-white incomes would rise by 16 per cent if discrimination ceased, *ibid.*, p. 21.

[6] *Ibid.*, p. 91.

for all age-education categories, the extent of wage and salary discrimination can be measured by computing the amount that total non-white incomes would be if non-whites in a matched category had received the same income as whites and then subtracting actual non-white income. This procedure for determining the size of the income differential can be summarized as:

$$CD_u = \sum_{i=1}^{n} N_i(\bar{W}_i - \bar{N}_i) \qquad (1)$$

where CD_u represents the upper limit estimate of the extent of wage and salary discrimination for all matched categories; n is the total number of matched categories; $\bar{W}$ is the mean income of whites in the matched categories; N is the total number of non-whites in the matched categories; and $\bar{N}$ is the mean income of non-whites in the matched categories. Since white labor may benefit from market discrimination, calculations utilizing equation (1) actually represent upper limit estimates of the extent of wage and salary discrimination. If a complete absence of wage and salary discrimination caused non-white income in a matched category to rise to the levels of whites in that category but also caused the income of whites in the category to fall, then the income differential, assuming no decrease in white income, overstates the extent of wage and salary discrimination. It is not possible to compute how much the income of white labor would fall in the absence of discrimination (i.e., white gains). However, an indirect method of showing maximum gains of white labor is to compute a lower limit estimate of the extent of wage and salary discrimination:

$$CD_k = \sum_{i=1}^{n} N_i(\bar{T}_i - \bar{N}_i) \qquad (2)$$

where CD_k represents lower limit estimates of the extent of discrimination and $\bar{T}$ represents the mean incomes of all workers, including both white and non-white, in the matched categories. Since non-whites presumably lose more from discrimination than whites gain from discrimination, one can conclude that the mean income of all workers in matched categories, reflecting the repressed income of non-whites and the inflated income of whites, is the lowest possible mean income of workers in the absence of wage and salary discrimination. This means, in effect, that the mean income of all workers can be used in computing a lower limit estimate of the extent of discrimination.

Census income data for the years 1949–1959 yielding the information needed to calculate the income differentials as outlined by Equations one and two are available by sex for the United States and the South. However, data are for non-whites and for the total population (whites and non-whites) not for whites alone. The mean income of whites by age-education categories is necessary to derive the upper limit estimates. White mean incomes were estimated by subtracting the non-white incomes by matched categories from the comparable categories for the total population. Estimates for the North and West were made by subtracting the income differentials by matched categories in the South from the income differentials in comparable categories for the United States.

For 1959, 54 age-education categories (6 age groups and 9 education levels) were used for each of the two sexes in each of the three regions (South, United States, and North and West) and for each of the three color groups (whites, non-whites, and total population). A total of 972 distinct age-education categories were used for 1959 ($54 \times 2 \times 3 \times 3$). For 1949, 48 age-education categories were used yielding a total of 864. Thus, for both years 1,836 distinct age-education categories were used. Within each age-education category for 1959 there are 10 income classes and 12 classes for 1949. The extent of wage and salary discrimination for a particular sex, region, educational, or age level is calculated by summing the income differentials in the appropriate categories.[7] In each case non-white males were compared to white males; and non-white females were compared with white females.

Census data are in the form of open-ended frequency distributions. To derive estimates of the mean income of a particular age-education category requires the mean income of the open-ended class. Pareto curves for the three highest income classes of frequency distributions were fitted for all 22 to 64 year olds by sex, region, and color for 1949 and 1959.[8] The mean income for these distributions were then estimated from the slope of the Pareto curves. The mean income of open-ended classes of various age-education categories was then estimated from the set of values derived from Pareto curve estimates. For example, the fit of the Pareto curve showed the mean income of non-white males, aged 22 to 64 with incomes over $15,000 in the South in 1959, to be $22,032. The mean income of open-ended classes for all age-education categories for the South, non-white males in 1959 (54 in all) was then assumed to be $22,032.

The reliability of the census data is a second problem. Herman P. Miller, Chief Economic Statistician for the Bureau of the Census, has stated one aspect of this problem succinctly: "Everybody lies to the census man." No doubt many people do lie; and, unfortunately, there is no way of knowing

---

[7] The Council of Economic Advisers has estimated the cost of discrimination by essentially assuming whites and non-whites in the same education category are perfect substitutes in production. This ignores the differences in age and the different relation between age and education of the two groups. Their estimates differ from the present in another sense. The Council uses census income. In this paper wage and salary income is used. For a description of the Council's technique see, *The Economic Cost of Discrimination*, Council of Economic Advisers, Staff Memorandum, March 26, 1965. Mimeo.

[8] Only the three upper income classes were used because a Pareto curve fitted for all income classes leads to overstatement of the mean. The mean of all income classes below $7,000 was assumed to be the midpoint; for the $7,000 to $9,999 class $8,200 was used; and $12,000 for the $10,000 to $14,999 class.

how much they lie or of improving the reliability of the data once the lies are published. The census income data by color, sex, age, and education are deprived by sampling; and there are sampling errors involved.[9] However, the very large number of age-education categories involved in this study made it infeasible to attempt to show statistically the effect of these sampling errors on the results. The 1950 census data are for the 48 coterminous states, while the 1960 census data include Alaska and Hawaii. For this reason, the cost of discrimination for 1949 and 1959 are not strictly comparable. However, the addition of the small number of non-whites in Alaska and Hawaii is not likely to affect comparisons significantly.

Another, and very serious, problem involves the income concept ideally suited for determining the extent of wage and salary discrimination versus the income concept available. Given the three census income concepts, the preferred measure is wage and salary income. It does not reflect non-white deficiency in terms of non-human, wealth-producing income to the extent of other census income concepts. Unfortunately, wage and salary income is not available by color. Census "income" which includes wage and salary income, self-employment income, and "other income" was used as a primary basis for estimating the extent of discrimination. Within each matched category the census "income" derived was reduced by the ratio of total wage and salary income-to-total income; thus yielding an estimate of the income differential in terms of wage and salary income. Wage and salary income of non-whites is understated; and, therefore, the extent of wage and salary discrimination is overstated by this procedure if the ratio of non-white wage and salary income-to-non-white income was greater than the ratio of total wage and salary income-to-total "income." Since whites as a group have greater amounts of non-human, wealth-producing income than non-whites as a group and since non-whites are under represented in professional services relative to whites, the extent of discrimination was undoubtedly overstated for both 1949 and 1959. No doubt there was a greater overstatement in the case of males than females because the great bulk of all female "income" comes from wages and salaries. Therefore, in this one sense estimates of the extent of market discrimination against females are likely to be more reliable than those for males. It is not possible to estimate the amount of overstatement of the extent of discrimination caused by the use of census "income."

The fourth problem associated with the estimates is that whites and non-whites are assumed to be perfect substitutes in production. This assumption is legitimate only if one of the two following conditions is met: there are no differentials in the quality of white and non-white education; or given regional, urban, and rural residence patterns, and the amount of wage and

[9] The 1960 census income data by color, age, and education are based on a 5 per cent sample, while the 1950 data are based on a $3\frac{1}{3}$ per cent sample.

salary discrimination occurring, differences in the quality of education between the two groups have no appreciable impact upon current income earned in the market place. To contend that there is no differential in quality of education is palpably incorrect. The second possibility must be stated as an hypothesis, and it must be noted that scant evidence exists which can be used to test it. To the author's knowledge, Becker is the only person who has attempted to test it. He presents evidence which indicates quality differences have no significant impact on current income.[10] Quality differences may, however, have a significant impact upon current income. If this is the case, the calculations presented in this paper show not only income differentials caused by wage and salary discrimination but also other kinds of discrimination, e.g., discrimination in education, and the cumulative impact of past discriminations which resulted in inferior education.

The Extent of Discrimination in 1949 and 1959

Table 1 presents upper and lower limit aggregate estimates of the extent of wage and salary discrimination against non-whites aged 22 to 64 in 1949 and 1959. In order to make comparisons, per capita estimates in constant 1959 dollars are also included. The $6.57 billion upper limit aggregate

Table 1—Upper and lower limit estimates of the extent of wage and salary discrimination against non-whites aged 22–64[a]

Income differential due to wage and salary discrimination	UNITED STATES		SOUTH		NORTH AND WEST	
	1949	1959	1949	1959	1949	1959
Lower limit estimate:						
Aggregate (millions)	3,315	5,614	1,545	2,612	1,770	3,001
Per capita	619	765	467	683	864	853
Percent change in per capita, 1949–59		+23.5		+46.3		−1.3
Upper limit estimate:						
Aggregate (millions)	4.019	6,573	2,123	3,365	1,896	3,208
Per capita	750	896	642	880	925	912
Percent change in per capita, 1949–59		+19.5		+37.1		−1.4

[a] By region in constant 1959 dollars.
Source: U.S. Bureau of Census. *U.S. Census of Population: 1960. Subject Reports. Educational Attainment. Final Report PC (2)-5B.* U.S. Gov't. Printing Office, Washington, D.C., 1963, Table 6, pp. 88–113 and Table 7, pp. 112–135. And U.S. Bureau of the Census. *U.S. Census of Population: 1950,* Vol. IV, *Special Reports,* Part 5, Chapter B, Education. U.S. Gov't. Printing Office, Washington, D.C., 1953. Table 12, pp. 108–27.

estimate of the extent of wage and salary discrimination for the United States in 1959 is 14.6 per cent or almost $1 billion greater than the lower limit estimate. In per capita (non-white) terms for 1959 the upper limit estimate

---

[10] Becker, *op. cit.*, pp. 93 and 94.

is $896 and the lower limit is $765, a difference of $131. In 1949 for the United States the difference in aggregate upper and lower limit estimates is a little over $700 million. In per capita terms, the difference is $131—a sum exactly equal to the per capita difference in 1959.

Table 1 shows that in terms of the upper limit estimate the South accounted for 51 per cent of aggregate wage and salary discrimination in 1959 and 53 per cent in 1949. At the lower limit, the South accounted for approximately 47 per cent in both years. The South, however, accounted for 52 percent of the non-white population aged 22 to 64 in 1959 and 62 per cent in 1949. Per capita wage and salary discrimination was greater in the North and West than in the South in both 1949 and 1959.

The tables below show more detailed information concerning the extent of wage and salary discrimination and changes in it. They include only upper limit estimates. The lower limit estimates show only what non-white labor would gain if discrimination ceased less what whites would lose, assuming rising non-white total wage and salary income is exactly matched by falling total white income in each age-education category, so that the mean income of all workers remains exactly equal to what it was with discrimination. The upper limit estimates, on the other hand, show only differentials in income and ignore possible white losses.

The rationale for presenting only upper limit estimates in the tables below is pragmatic. Table 1 shows that while the difference in upper and lower limit aggregate estimates is significant; it also shows the difference is relatively narrow. Hence one is justified in using a single estimate.

Changes in the Extent of Wage and Salary Discrimination

Table 1 shows that between 1949 and 1959 the upper limit aggregate measure of the extent of discrimination in constant 1959 dollars[11] increased by $2.5 billion.[12] The non-white population aged 22 to 64 during the same period increased by almost two million. Correcting for population and price changes by putting data in constant per capita dollars yields comparable measures of the income differentials. Changes in the per capita wage and salary income differentials then measure changes in the extent of wage and salary discrimination. However, an alternative measure of changes in discrimination is relevant. Discrimination reduces income, and the changes in

---

[11] The GNP deflator series was used to put 1949 income differentials in terms of 1959 prices.

[12] The changing age-distribution of the non-white population between 1949 and 1959 accounted for approximately 2.7 per cent ($68 million) of the aggregate increase.

the degree of income reduction may be taken as a measure of the change in discrimination. For example, assume per capita non-white potential income (what non-white labor would receive in the absence of market discrimination and taken as equal to white income in an age-education category) in year 1 is $100 and the per capita income differential is $40. In year 2 per capita potential income is $200, and the per capita income differential is $50. In absolute terms wage and salary discrimination has increased by 25 per cent (from $40 to $50). However, in year 1 discrimination reduced income by 40 per cent, ($40/$100); and in year 2 it reduced income by 25 per cent, ($50/$200). The relative impact of discrimination on income in year 2 is less than the impact in year 1. In relative terms discrimination can be said to have decreased between year 1 and year 2 by 37.5 per cent.

The changes in per capita income differentials can be termed the absolute measure of change in wage and salary discrimination. The change in the per cent by which wage and salary discrimination reduces potential income is termed the relative measure of change in discrimination. Table 2 shows changes in discrimination between 1949 and 1959 in the form of indexes of

Table 2—Absolute *a* **and relative** *b* **indexes of the extent of wage and salary discrimination by region and sex (1949=100)**

	ABSOLUTE		RELATIVE	
	1959	Change 1949–59	1959	Change 1949–59
United States*c*	119.5	+19.5	89.1	−10.9
South	137.1	+37.1	101.3	+1.3
North and west*c*	98.6	−1.4	79.9	−20.1
Males				
United States	137.2	+37.2	94.8	−5.2
South	156.5	+56.5	107.1	+7.1
North and west	114.1	+14.1	86.0	−14.0
Females				
United States	87.2	−12.8	73.6	−26.4
South	108.7	+8.7	89.5	−10.5
North and west	62.7	−37.3	57.9	−42.1

a Absolute discrimination is the per capita income differential between whites and non-whites. The base in each case is the 1949 per capita income differential of the regional group in question, e.g., for South males the base is 1949 per capita income differential between white and non-white males in the South.
b The base for the relative index of discrimination is the ratio of the per capita income differential-to-per capita potential income for each regional group in question.
c Weighted averages of males and females.
Source: Same as Table 1.

absolute and relative discrimination, with 1949 as the base of 100. For the absolute index, the 1949 value of the per capita income differential for the regional-sex group in question is the base. For the relative index, the base is 1949 per capita income differential as a per cent of potential income for the regional-sex group in question.

The absolute index shows that the extent of wage and salary discrimination in the United States increased by 19.5 per cent, 37.5 per cent in the
South, and decreased by 1.4 per cent in the North and West. For males
alone the absolute index rose in both the South and the North and West.
For females the decrease in the absolute index in the North and West offsets
the rise in the South so that for the United States as a whole there was a 12.8
per cent decrease. Similarly, the decrease in the absolute female index in the
North and West offsets the increase in the male index with the result that for
the North and West there was an over-all decline of 1.4 per cent for both
sexes. In brief, the decrease in the extent of discrimination against non-white
females in the North and West accounts for all the negative signs in Table 2
under the heading, Changes in Absolute Discrimination.

Table 2 shows negative signs for changes in the index of relative discrimination between 1949 and 1959 for three out of four regional-sex groups,
North and West males (-14.0), South females (-10.5), and North and
West females (-42.1). The relative index for South males rose by 7.1 per
cent. The increase for South males more than offsets the decrease for females
with the result that wage and salary discrimination against both sexes combined rose slightly in the South.

Comparison of the absolute and relative indexes shows both measures
moving in the same direction for two of the four regional-sex groups. Both
indexes show decreases for North and West females; while both indexes
show increases for South males. We can conclude that between 1949 and
1959, whichever measure of change in the extent of discrimination is used,
wage and salary discrimination against South males increased and against
North and West females decreased. For North and West males and South
females the absolute index shows an increase, and the relative index shows a
decrease. Similarly, the absolute index for both sexes in the United States
shows an increase while the relative index shows a decline.

Both measures of change in discrimination are useful. However, it is the
contention of the author that the absolute measure is more significant.
Non-whites, 95 per cent of whom are Negroes (99 per cent in the South), are
the nation's largest minority and are a disadvantaged people. They are over
concentrated in the poverty group.[13] One reason for this poverty is wage and
salary discrimination. Thus, wage and salary discrimination is intimately
related to the economic welfare of this group and shows the differences
between their income and whites'. If the welfare implications of market
discrimination are emphasized, then it seems that the best measure of changes
in wage and salary discrimination is the absolute index.[14] This leads to the

[13] c.f. Alan Batchelder, "Poverty: The Special Case of the Negro," *American Economic
Review*, May 1965, pp. 530–49.

[14] This is correct only if absolute income and not relative income is used as the measure
of poverty.

conclusion that there were significant increases in the extent of wage and salary discrimination in three out of four regional-sex groups and almost a 20 per cent rise in discrimination in the United States as a whole.

Regional Differences in the Extent of Discrimination

In attempting to answer the question, does the South discriminate more than the North and West, a problem similar to the two different measures of changes in the extent of discrimination is encountered. Per capita income differentials represent an absolute measure of the extent of wage and salary discrimination (i.e., the reduction in income); while the per capita income differential as a per cent of potential income can be interpreted as a relative measure of the extent of regional wage and salary discrimination. Table 3 shows that in 1959 there were greater absolute and relative measures of the extent of discrimination against non-white females in the South than in the North and West.

Table 3—Per capita income differentials of whites and non-whites and potential income of non-whites aged 22–64 by sex and region for 1949 and 1959

	(1) Per capita potential	(2) Per capita income differentials (absolute)	(3) Col. 2 as a % of Col. 1 (relative)
1959			
Males			
North and west	4235	1323	31.2
South	2883	1136	39.4
Females			
North and west	2154	346	16.1
South	1611	562	34.9
1949			
Males			
North and west	3195	1160	36.8
South	1974	726	36.3
Females			
North and west	1989	552	27.8
South	1327	517	39.0

Source: Same as Table 1. Table in constant 1959 dollars.

The results are unambiguous. There was more wage and salary discrimination against non-white females in the South than in North and West. In 1949, however, the measures of the extent of discrimination were mixed. The relative measure indicates there was more discrimination in the South; while the absolute measure shows greater discrimination in the North and West. For non-white males the measures are mixed in both 1949 and 1959.

The absolute measure shows there was more discrimination against North and West males than against South males. The relative measures are approximately equal in 1949, but for 1959 the relative measure indicates more discrimination in the South than in the North and West.

The Extent of Discrimination and Human Capital

Formal education as measured by the number of school years completed is not the only source of human capital. To assume that it is belies much of the recent research into the sources of human capital.[15] However, formal education is a readily-available measure and is undoubtedly a more important determinant than any other single measure. Consequently, the number of school years completed is used as the measure of human capital in this paper. The absence of formal education represents no investment in human capital. Five ranges of formal education correspond to the following quantities of human capital; one to eight years of school completed shows low human capital; nine to 11 years of school completed shows moderately low human capital; 12 years of school completed shows a medium quantity of human capital; and 13 to 15 years of school completed can be interpreted as showing high human capital; and 16 or more years of school completed shows a very high quantity of human capital.

Table 4—Per capita potential income and income differentials[a] of males by region and education for 1949 and 1959

Years of school completed	UNITED STATES			SOUTH			NORTH AND WEST		
	Potential (1)	PID[a] (2)	2÷1[b] (3)	Potential (4)	PID[a] (5)	5÷4[b] (6)	Potential (7)	PID[a] (8)	8÷7[b] (9)
1949									
None	1762	689	.39	1227	285	.23	3725	2170	.58
1–8	2164	754	.35	1758	588	.33	3308	1111	.34
9–11	2808	1011	.36	2579	1083	.41	2993	953	.32
12	3250	1214	.37	3126	1462	.47	3311	1094	.33
13–15	3657	1582	.43	3511	1786	.51	3758	1439	.38
16+	5443	2631	.48	5366	2844	.53	5521	2417	.44
1959									
None	2083	646	.31	1494	336	.23	3390	1334	.39
1–8	2927	942	.32	2420	854	.35	3706	1077	.29
9–11	3882	1385	.36	3427	1481	.43	4198	1318	.31
12	4318	1511	.35	3919	1781	.45	4527	1379	.31
13–15	5005	1998	.40	4669	2313	.50	5176	1837	.36
16+	6865	2809	.41	6720	3246	.48	6960	2522	.36

[a] Per capita income differentials is denoted by PID. Table is in constant 1959 dollars.
[b] Shows the ratio of per capita income differential-to-per capita potential income.
Source: Same as Table 1.

[15] For a discussion of human capital, see Gary S. Becker, *Human Capital* (New York: 1964).

Table 4 shows per capita potential income and per capita income differentials and the ratio of per capita income differentials-to-per capita potential income for males by region and the above education categories. Table 5 shows the same information for females. The ratio of per capita income differentials-to-per capita potential income is a measure of the extent of wage and salary discrimination against non-whites with varying amounts of human capital. If the ratio rises as human capital increases, this indicates that wage and salary discrimination against non-whites rises as they acquire more human capital. If the ratio falls as human capital increases, then discrimination is less as more human capital is acquired. The four regional-sex groups show four different relations between human capital and discrimination. For South males in 1949 and 1959 the ratio rises as human capital

Table 5—Per capita potential income and income differentials[a] of females by region and education for 1949 and 1959

Years of school completed	UNITED STATES			SOUTH			NORTH AND WEST		
	Potential (1)	PID[a] (2)	2÷1[b] (3)	Potential (4)	PID[a] (5)	5÷4[b] (6)	Potential (7)	PID[a] (8)	8÷7[b] (9)
1949									
None	1342	712	.53	838	298	.36	3273	2294	.70
1–8	1386	529	.38	1143	474	.42	1962	661	.34
9–11	1595	497	.31	1482	634	.43	1713	355	.21
12	1999	564	.28	1925	811	.42	2044	414	.20
13–15	2187	580	.27	2180	711	.33	2195	427	.20
16+	2769	383	.14	2674	374	.14	2947	401	.14
1959									
None	1197	348	.29	867	198	.23	1941	683	.35
1–8	1538	502	.33	1299	505	.39	1964	497	.25
9–11	1844	508	.28	1690	697	.41	1981	339	.17
12	2211	456	.21	2140	874	.41	2253	211	.09
13–15	2455	343	.14	2391	706	.30	2492	132	.05
16+	3307	104	.03	3121	54	.02	3558	172	.05

[a] Per capita income differential is denoted by PID. Table in constant 1959 dollars.
[b] Shows the ratio of per capita income differential-to-per capita potential income.
Source: Same as Table 1.

increases showing that wage and salary discrimination increases as human capital increases. For females in the North and West in 1949 and 1959 the ratio of per capita income differentials-to-per capita potential income falls as human capital rises, showing an inverse relationship between the discrimination and human capital. For North and West males the ratio is highest for those with no formal education but roughly constant for other levels of human capital. For South females the relationship between wage and salary discrimination and human capital can be described as inverted u-shaped being lowest for those with no human capital and those with very high human capital. There was less wage and salary discrimination against South females with very high human capital than any other regional, education-age group studied. The income differential between whites and non-whites in this group was only $54 and the ratio of per capita income differential-to-potential income only .02.

In a few age-education categories in 1959 non-white females with very high human capital received greater incomes than whites. This means that whites were discriminated against; or stated differently, there was negative discrimination against non-whites. The age-education categories where negative discrimination was found are: for South females with 16 years of school completed in the age groups 25–29, 30–34, 35–44, and with 17 or more years of school completed in the age groups 30–34, and 35–44; for North and West females with 16 years of school completed in the age groups 30–34, and 35–44, and those with 17 or more years of school completed in the age group 30–34. Thus, negative discrimination occurred in five age-education categories in the case of South females and three for North and West females.[16]

Summary and Conclusions

The upper limit estimate of the extent of wage and salary discrimination is the aggregate income differential between whites and non-whites in matched age-education categories. Measured in this fashion the extent of wage and salary discrimination adjusted for price changes increased from $4 billion in 1949 to $6.6 billion for 1959. In per capita terms the income differential rose from $750 to $896, an increase of almost 20 per cent.

The percentage change in per capita income differentials measures the absolute change in the extent of wage and salary discrimination. The extent of discimination in absolute terms increased by 37 per cent in the South (56 per cent for males and 14 per cent for females) and decreased by 1.4 per cent in the North and West (+14 per cent for males and −37 per cent for females). Changes in per capita income differentials as a per cent of potential income measures the relative change in the extent of discrimination. For South males the relative change was 7.1 per cent, for South females −10.5 per cent, for North and West males −14 per cent, and for North and West females −42 per cent. Whichever measure of change in discrimination is used, it is found that wage and salary discrimination increased between 1949 and 1959 for South males and decreased for North and West females.

The ratio of per capita income differentials-to-per capita potential income for non-whites with zero, 1–8, 9–11, 12, 13–15, and 16+ years of school completed shows the relation between wage and salary discrimination and

[16] Marshall R. Colberg has shown that "earnings of non-white teachers relative to whites are high and in many states higher than whites. No doubt the concentration of non-white females with very high human capital in teaching accounts for the negative discrimination in the above age-education categories. See *Human Capital in Southern Development, 1939–1959* (Chapel Hill, 1965).

human capital. If the ratio rises as human capital rises, then the higher the human capital the greater the discrimination. If the ratio falls as human capital rises, the reverse holds. For males there is a direct relationship between human capital and discrimination and an inverse relation for females.

26

The Effect of Low Educational Attainment on Incomes: A Comparative Study of Selected Ethnic Groups

Minority ethnic groups tend to embody less educational investment per capita than does the white majority—a difference sometimes used to "explain" lower minority incomes. Professor Walter Fogel of the University of California explodes any such illusions and shows that *any* given level of human capital formation through educational investment for "nonanglos" is valued

WALTER FOGEL

less than the "anglo" counterpart. Less than one-half of observed income differentials between these two groups can be explained by educational attainment differences. The remainder is the product of multiple factors, which include motivation, discrimination, and educational quality.

The economic value of education and the welfare of low income minority groups are topics which have recently received a great deal of general attention and some scholarly study. The two subjects, however, have not been brought together to provide more systematic knowledge of the economic value of education to a wide range of ethnic groups in our

Reprinted from Walter Fogel, "The Effect of Low Educational Attainment on Incomes: A Comparative Study of Selected Ethnic Groups," *Journal of Human Resources* 1 (Fall 1966) (© 1967 by the Regents of the University of Wisconsin), pp. 22–40. By permission of the author and publisher.

society. Most of the existing analyses focus on the white-nonwhite dichotomy.[1]

Part of the reason for this deficiency is that little relevant information is available for groups other than white and nonwhite. However, some pertinent though limited data on a number of ethnic groups have appeared in publications resulting from the 1960 *Census of Population*. The objective of this article is to utilize these data for an examination of the effects of educational attainment levels on the economic welfare of selected minority groups which are usually considered to be members of the disadvantaged segment of our population. The groups for which the Census provides suitable data include persons with Spanish surnames (primarily Mexican-Americans), Puerto Ricans, and the following nonwhite populations: Chinese, Filipinos, American Indians, Japanese, and Negroes.

Recent research has demonstrated conclusively that schooling has a substantial income value for those who obtain it, or it has confirmed earlier findings to this effect. High levels of educational attainment lead to desirable occupations upon entry into the labor force, increase the chances for job promotion, and insure relative stability of employment and earnings.[2] There are reasons to expect, however, that in our society a given number of years of schooling has less income value for members of disadvantaged minority groups than for the majority population. The majority population is better able to pay for educational inputs, such as physical facilities, teachers, and cultural programs; and the consequent better quality of their education undoubtedly pays off in income. In addition, discrimination against some minority groups prevents them from obtaining the same high wage jobs and profitable business investments which are available to similarly educated majority persons.

Moreover, because persons with equivalent schooling differ in abilities and motivations, they are employed in activities, occupations, industries, and regions which provide income in varying amounts. We do not know the relevant differences in abilities and motivations between the majority and minority populations, nor, indeed, whether there are any; but certainly such differences may exist and may cause variations in incomes among members of these populations who have equivalent schooling.

Such influences, the first two of which would appear to bring about greater income benefits from education for the majority population than for

---

[1] See, for example, Gary S. Becker, *The Economics of Discrimination* (Chicago: University of Chicago Press, 1957) and *Human Capital* (New York: National Bureau of Economic Research, 1964), Ch. 4; Morton Zeman, "A Comparative Analysis of White-Nonwhite Income Differentials," (Chicago: University of Chicago, Department of Economics, unpublished Ph.D. dissertation, 1955); and Paul M. Siegel, "On the Cost of Being a Negro," *Sociological Inquiry* (Spring 1965), pp. 41–57.

[2] See, for example, J. N. Morgan et al., *Income and Welfare in the U.S.* (New York: McGraw-Hill, 1962), Ch. 23.

the minority, also suggest differences in the relationships of education to income among the various ethnic groups which comprise the disadvantaged minority population. *Within* this segment of our society, however, variation in educational quality, and thus the importance of this variable in accounting for discrepancies in education-income relationships, would seem to be less than the differences in educational quality which exist between the majority and the aggregate disadvantaged minority populations. This is true to the extent that the quality of educational inputs provided for a group in society depends upon its income, for by definition disadvantaged groups have similar average incomes. It is also true to the extent that stimulation from school associates, competitive and collaborative, is associated with the quality of education, since residential concentration brings about some *de facto* school segregation for most low income ethnic groups, and thereby limits the socio-cultural peer environment to which members of these groups are exposed while in school.

With respect to discrimination, there are theoretical and empirical justifications for thinking that the connection between education and income varies among the disadvantaged minority groups because discrimination is greater against some groups than against others and thus affects the incremental income payoff from schooling in varying degrees. The "visible dissimilarity" proposition of race relations sociology suggests that, *ceteris paribus*, the rate of assimilation of an ethnic group into the host society is more rapid the greater the physical similarity between its members and persons of the majority population.[3] The South African experience provides some support for this hypothesis. The racial order of social and political "privilege" bestowed by the white population of that country goes from Coloureds, who are of mixed race and have the most white-like physical characteristics of any of the minority groups, to Indians (Asian), down to "black Africans."[4] Judgments of physical similarities and dissimilarities are, of course, subjectively as well as objectively influenced; but in the U.S. there is probably considerable agreement that, in general, Mexican-Americans and Puerto Ricans are physically more like majority persons than are Negroes. There also may be agreement, though much weaker, that Orientals fall between Spanish-speaking persons and Negroes in this regard. Surveys of the willingness of the U.S. majority population to accept social relationships with various minority groups have indicated a similar ordering of prejudice—greatest toward Negroes and perhaps slightly greater against

[3] Robin Williams, Jr., *The Reduction of Inter-Group Tensions* (New York: Social Science Research Council, 1947), pp. 54–56; see also Gordon W. Allport, *The Nature of Prejudice* (Boston: The Beacon Press, 1954), Ch. 8.

[4] See W. H. Hutt, *The Economics of the Colour Bar* (London: Institute of Economic Affairs, 1964); Sheila T. L. Van der Horst, "The Effects of Industrialization on Race Relations in South Africa," in Guy Hunter, ed., *Industrialization and Race Relations* (New York: Oxford University Press, 1965), pp. 97–140.

Orientals than against Mexican-Americans and American Indians.[5]

On the other hand, the common hypothesis that prejudice against some minority groups is an increasing function of their relative population in a community[6] leads to slightly different predictions of the ethnic order of discrimination. In most large metropolitan centers Negroes are the largest disadvantaged minority population, though in a number of urban centers in the East and Southwest, Spanish-speaking persons—principally Mexican-Americans and Puerto Ricans—are also relatively numerous. Oriental and Indian groups in most regions form very small fractions of the population. In this case, according to the relative size hypothesis, discrimination should be greater against Negroes and Spanish-speaking groups than against Orientals and Indians. However, Becker found that the importance of the relative size of nonwhite populations in accounting for differences in market discrimination among Southern cities was small, though statistically significant.[7]

There is not sufficient information available about the occupational abilities and motivations of different ethnic groups even to speculate about how these factors may influence the education-income relationships of the different disadvantaged minorities. One could assume that this lack of knowledge implies minor ethnic differences in occupational abilities and motivations; otherwise their existence would be widely recognized, even if not precisely measured. Such an assumption, however, is dubious, since occupational abilities and interests and their independent effects on personal income are not easily observed.

Lacking additional relevant information, our expectations of variation in the education-income relation among the minority groups considered in this report are formed on the basis of the previous discussion of discrimination. It is expected that given amounts of education provide the largest incomes to the Spanish-speaking groups and the smallest to Negroes. The income value of education for the other groups we deal with—American Indians, Chinese, Filipinos, and Japanese—would appear to be of intermediate degree: greater than for Negroes, but less than for Spanish-speaking persons, at least if we follow our inclinations and give more weight to the visible dissimilarity hypothesis.

The empirical portion of this article is devoted primarily to presenting estimates of the importance of educational attainment in explaining the income position of ethnic groups relative to the majority population.[8] The

[5] Emory S. Bogardus, "Changes in Racial Distances," *International Journal of Opinion and Attitude Research* (December 1947), pp. 55–62; see also Alphonse Pickney, "Prejudice toward Mexican and Negro Americans: A Comparison," *Phylon* (Winter 1963), pp. 353–59.

[6] See Allport, *op. cit.*, pp. 227–28.

[7] *The Economics of Discrimination, op. cit.*, pp. 104–07.

[8] Data availability dictated the use of total incomes for the analysis. Included in this measure are wage and salary earnings, earnings from self-employment, money income from

estimates provide evidence relevant to two general hypotheses from the previous discussion: (1) that educational attainment "explains" much less than all the income differences existing between the majority and minority populations, and (2) that within the disadvantaged minority population the incomes associated with given levels of educational attainment will differ in size according to the ethnic rank order suggested in the preceding paragraph.

The "residual" or unexplained differences between majority and minority incomes will show the influence of the other variables which have been discussed—educational quality, occupational abilities and motivations, and discrimination in labor and capital markets. There will be no attempt to estimate separately the importance of any of these residual influences, and, indeed, it may not even be possible to do so with the available information. Nevertheless, the discussion has suggested, and recent studies confirm, that discrimination is important in racial and ethnic income differences which cannot be accounted for by educational attainment and certain demographic factors.[9] The residuals thus provide relevant evidence for the discrimination hypotheses which have been mentioned.

Simple Relationships Between Education and Income

It may be helpful to present some perspective on the ethnic populations considered in this study. Table 1 provides 1960 figures on population and education and 1959 income data for these groups. The groups are ranked by median school years completed to show the crude relationship between income and education.

It is evident that there are some large differences in schooling and income among these ethnic populations. There does appear to be a tendency for median income to rise as educational attainment increases; however, since the figures do not account for age, locational, and other differences among the groups, no firm conclusions can be drawn.

---

property, and transfer income. Median total incomes of males in the U.S. are about two per cent larger than median earnings (from wage and salary and self-employment) for both the total and nonwhite populations. Cf. Table 208 in *U.S. Census of Population, 1960; Detailed Characteristics, U.S. Summary*, and Tables 25 and 26 in *U.S. Census of Population, 1960; Subject Reports, Occupational Characteristics*.

[9] See Morgan et al., *op. cit.*, pp. 48 and 56; Werner Z. Hirsch and Elbert W. Segelhorst, "Incremental Benefits of Public Education," *Review of Economics and Statistics* (November 1965), pp. 392–99; and Leonard W. Weiss, "Concentration and Labor Earnings," *American Economic Review* (March 1966), p. 106. The race variable (nonwhite-white) was significantly associated (in a statistical sense) with earnings or income in all three of these studies, even when the influence of a number of other earnings-related variables were held constant. For similar findings with respect to unemployment, see Harry J. Gilman, "Economic Discrimination and Unemployment," *American Economic Review* (December 1965), pp. 1077–96.

Table 2 allows a closer look at the education-income relation among minority groups. Figures for the West are presented because half or more of the population of each group listed except Negroes lives in that region.

Table 1—Education, income, and population by ethnic group (United States males age 14 and over, 1960[a])

Ethnic group	Median school years completed	Median income	Male population age 14 and over (thousands)
Japanese	12.2	$4,304	157
Chinese	10.7	3,471	96
White[b]	10.6	4,337	55,036
Puerto Rican	8.4	2,935	280
Indian	8.4	1,792	163
Negro	8.3	2,254	5,713
Filipino	8.3	3,053	84
Spanish surname[c]	8.1	2,804	1,057

Source: U.S. Census of Population, 1960.
[a] Income figures are for 1959.
[b] Includes persons with Spanish surname and almost all Puerto Ricans.
[c] The 1960 Census enumerated the Spanish surname group for only five states: Arizona, California, Colorado, New Mexico and Texas.

Data are given for urban males, age 35–44, thus controlling for age and urban-rural status as well as for region. This table makes it clear that, in general, higher incomes are associated with higher educational attainment among disadvantaged ethnic populations. The major exception to the pattern is the group composed of "white persons with Spanish surname", the

Table 2—Education and income by ethnic group (urban males in the West, age 35–44)

Ethnic group[a]	Median school years completed	Median income
Japanese	12.4	$5,687
Chinese	12.3	5,490
Indian	10.5	4,115
Negro	10.4	4,369
Spanish surname[b]	9.2	5,065
Filipino	9.2	3,938

Source: U.S. Census of Population, 1960.
[a] The most comparable data available for whites combine urban and rural persons. These are: median school years completed 12.5; median income $6,431.
[b] For four states: Arizona, Colorado, California, and New Mexico. The only state with a sizeable Spanish surname population which is omitted is Texas, since Texas is not in the Western region.

vast majority of such persons in the Western region are "Mexican-Americans." Their median income is well above those of Indians and Negroes, even though their median educational attainment is more than a year lower.

Standardizing for Education

The extent to which large incomes are associated with higher educational attainments is easily determined for the white and total nonwhite populations from Census tabulations of incomes by number of school years completed. Comparable data are not available for any of the groups included in Table 2.[10] An alternative approach for these groups is to compare their median incomes with that of the majority—in this case the "Anglo" population—after the incomes of all groups have been standardized for the effects of educational attainment. The Anglo population for this study consists of all whites, less the Spanish surname and Puerto Rican groups.

Because of the data limitations, standardizing for education has had to be done indirectly. The procedure was to compute an index of income for each ethnic group (males) from median incomes for eight levels of educational attainment, each weighted by the number of persons who had completed the corresponding level of educational attainment. The form of the calculation was:

$$\frac{\Sigma_i(a_iS_i)}{\Sigma_ia_i}$$

for Anglos, and

$$\frac{\Sigma_i(m_iS_i)}{\Sigma_im_i}$$

for the minority groups.

The a_i and m_i refer to the number of males in each educational attainment class from 0 through 16 and over.[11] The S_i are median incomes for the schooling classes, from either the nonwhite or total population as explained below.

Index incomes of ethnic groups computed in this manner (with the S_i constant for all groups) are lower than the similarly computed Anglo index income only because education distributions are more concentrated toward the low end of the range of school years completed (age differences were adjusted to remove their effects from the educational attainment distributions). Ratios of these index incomes, Anglo to ethnic group, show what will be called, for simplicity, the "educational effect"—the amount by which Anglo income exceeds that of each ethnic group because of the lower

[10] Income by educational attainment for these groups is available from the 1/1000 sample of the Bureau of the Census (see *U.S. Census of Population and Housing: 1960, One-In-A-Thousand Sample Description and Technical Documentation*). However, the sampling variances associated with the data for the smaller population groups—Indian, Chinese, Filipinos, and Japanese—are too large to permit use of these data for my purposes.

[11] The "school years completed" classes used by the Census are 0, 1–4, 5–7, 8, 1–3 and 4 years of high school, and 1–3 and 4 or more years of college.

schooling of the latter. These ratios, then, are the educational adjustment factors—the factors by which the actual income of each group must be multiplied in order to remove the income effects of its low schooling.

Two sets of schooling class incomes (S_i) were available for use in the calculations, those for nonwhites and those for the total population. A choice of one or the other involved a problem analogous to that of the appropriate price weights for quantity indexes. Since it was not possible to establish unequivocally that one set is more appropriate for our purposes than another, both were used and two sets of estimates are given in this article. The estimates made with the nonwhite schooling class incomes are more appropriate for the total nonwhite and Negro populations, but whether this is also true for the other groups is uncertain.[12]

In order to eliminate the influences of regional variations on the results, all calculations were performed on state units. It would also have been desirable to work only with urban populations, since both schooling and incomes are lower in rural than in urban areas. This could not be done, however, since appropriate urban data were not available for most of the minority groups. But, with the exception of Indians and, to a lesser extent, Filipinos, the urban proportions of the populations included in this study were quite similar, so that estimation errors resulting from failure to control for this factor are likely to be small.

[12] The percentage increments in income which accompany increases in schooling are greater for the total population than for nonwhites (among nonwhites there is a smaller relative difference between the incomes associated with any two schooling classes). Therefore, compared to the results obtained with schooling class incomes for nonwhites, use of total population schooling class incomes raises the computed indexes more for Anglos than for the minority groups, since a larger proportion of the former have completed high levels of schooling. This results in a larger adjustment of minority incomes. For the total nonwhite minority population, and for Negroes (who make up more than 90 per cent of all nonwhites in the United States), the total population schooling class incomes almost certainly overestimate the adjustment for education. This is because they incorporate the assumption that improvements in the educational attainment of these groups would raise the income increments which their members can obtain between each step of the schooling ladder. That may, indeed, occur; or, alternatively, even when Negroes as a group have as much schooling as Anglos, incremental gains for Negroes from each additional year of schooling may still be smaller than those found in the Anglo population. Even if their education-income relation does become "steeper," this will be as much a result of other changes in our society as of increases in Negro schooling relative to Anglos—changes which permit nonwhites and Negroes with high educational attainment to obtain the same jobs and, thus, the same incomes as those received by similarly educated Anglos. Therefore, use of total population schooling class incomes to obtain education adjustments for nonwhite and Negro incomes would attribute to education income differences which are the effects of other factors. For the other minority populations included in this study, however, there is some inferential evidence that their income-education relation is "steeper" than that of Negroes and all nonwhites; that is, it is perhaps closer to the relationship found in the total population. For further information, see Lyle W. Shannon and Elaine Krass, "The Urban Adjustment of Immigrants: The Relationships of Education to Occupation and Total Family Income," *Pacific Sociological Review* (Spring 1963), pp. 37–47; also see evidence cited below in the text. Since we cannot be certain which set of schooling class incomes is more appropriate for these groups, results obtained with both sets are presented.

Even though these steps were taken to arrive at the "pure" education effect, it is, of course, true that the variation in the schooling class incomes which were used to compute the index incomes may not be completely independent of factors other than schooling, e.g., the correlation between education and intelligence. Lack of data prevented any additional controls in this regard. Therefore, the results shown should be considered as *maximum* estimates of the importance of educational attainment in accounting for the minority-Anglo income differences, in contrast to an actual explanatory value which is, no doubt, somewhat less.

Table 3—Adjustments of 1959 ethnic group relative incomes for differences in educational attainment distributions (males, age 25 and over)

	(1)	(2)		(3) Adjusted		(4)	
		Education adjustment factors		relative income (columns 1 × 2)		Explanatory contribution (per cent)[d]	
Ethnic group	Relative income[a]	NW[b]	TP[c]	NW	TP	NW	TP
California							
Nonwhite	.65	1.11	1.16	.72	.75	20	29
Spanish surname	.73	1.21	1.32	.88	.96	56	85
Texas							
Nonwhite	.45	1.24	1.35	.56	.61	20	29
Spanish surname	.47	1.53	1.73	.72	.81	47	64
Illinois							
Nonwhite	.69	1.09	1.15	.75	.79	19	32
Puerto Rican	.59	1.19	1.34	.70	.79	27	49
New York							
Nonwhite	.64	1.08	1.15	.69	.74	14	28
Puerto Rican	.55	1.18	1.33	.65	.73	22	40

[a] Ethnic group ÷ Anglo. All incomes were standardized for age, using the age classes 25–34, 35–44, 45–64, 65 and over.
[b] Abbreviation for nonwhite. Figures are indexes of relative income (Anglo ÷ ethnic group) from schooling distributions (standardized for age) and nonwhite schooling class median incomes. See text for explanation.
[c] Abbreviation for total population. Figures are indexes of relative income (Anglo ÷ ethnic group) from schooling distributions and total population schooling class median incomes. See text for explanation.
[d] Per cent of the difference between the unadjusted income of Anglos and of each ethnic group (from column 1) which is removed by the educational adjustment.

Turning now to the results, column (1) of Table 3 shows the 1959 ethnic group median incomes as proportions of Anglo income (after standardization for age). The numbers in column (2) of the table are the educational adjustment factors. They were obtained from computation of indexes in the form previously shown, with the Anglo index expressed as a proportion of the index for each ethnic group. The larger these numbers, the greater the differences between Anglo and ethnic group schooling distributions. As previously explained, these figures are the multiples by which Anglo median income exceeds those of the ethnic groups because of the lower schooling of the latter.

Column (3) gives the 1959 median income of each ethnic group as a proportion of Anglo income after adjustment for the low educational attainment of the group. It can be seen that in most cases adjustment for schooling differences still leaves these incomes well below those of Anglos, even when the total population weights are used for the adjustment.[13]

Column (4) shows the proportions of the 1959 Anglo-ethnic groups income differences which are accounted for by schooling differences. Schooling explains more than half of the income differences only for the Spanish surname populations in California and Texas.[14]

Among the groups shown in Table 3, education is a better explanation for the low income status of Spanish surname persons than for that of the other groups. In 1959 actual incomes of Spanish surname males were above those of nonwhites in both California and Texas (column 1), even though the educational attainment levels of the former were much lower (column 2); thus, adjusted Spanish surname incomes exceed those of nonwhites by even greater margins. Education adjustments are also larger for Puerto Ricans than for nonwhites; however, the adjusted incomes of the two groups are similar in both Illinois and New York.

Results for Other Minority Groups

The previous analysis can be extended to consider separately each of the nonwhite populations enumerated in the 1960 Census, as well as the Spanish surname group. It is necessary to restrict our attention for this purpose to the state of California, for most of the nonwhite groups are not enumerated for the other states included in Table 3. It is also not inappropriate to do so since one-third or more of the persons with Spanish surnames or of Oriental origin live in that state.

The results of the standardization for education, as previously described, are shown in Table 4. From column (2) it can be seen that the distribution of educational attainment within most ethnic populations is such as to produce income levels which are 12 to 14 per cent below those of Anglos. Two groups must be excepted from this statement. The educational attainment of Spanish surname males is considerably lower than that of all others,

---

[13] Since income and education data from the *U.S. Census of Population, 1960* are from a 25 per cent sample, there are sampling errors associated with the relative incomes shown in column 3. Based on standard error tables published in the Census, all differences between the adjusted incomes of Anglos and those of the ethnic groups are significant at the 1% confidence level. This is also true for the differences between the incomes (relative) of nonwhite and Spanish surname persons; however, the nonwhite-Puerto Rican differences are not statistically significant (at the 5% level).

[14] Within each state, all differences between the figures in column 4 are statistically reliable at the 5% confidence level or above.

and the Japanese educational distribution is almost equivalent to that of Anglos.

The adjusted income ratios in column (3) show Spanish surname income closest to that of Anglos. The Japanese adjusted income, of course, is no higher than the unadjusted. Column (4) discloses in precise terms what we have already inferred: that the amount of the Anglo-ethnic group income differences which can be accounted for by educational attainment is zero for the Japanese, very sizeable for the Spanish surname population, and rather modest for all others.[15]

Table 4 *ᵃ—Adjustments of 1959 ethnic group relative incomes for differences in educational attainment distributions, California (males, age 25 and over)*

	(1)	(2)		(3)		(4)	
		Education adjustment factors		Adjusted relative income (columns 1 × 2)		Explanatory contribution (per cent)	
Ethnic group	Relative income	NW	TP	NW	TP	NW	TP
Spanish surname	.73	1.21	1.32	.88	.96	56	85
Chinese	.69	1.13	1.19	.78	.82	29	42
Filipino	.54	1.14	1.21	.61	.65	15	24
Indian	.57	1.14	1.21	.65	.69	19	28
Japanese	.81	1.00	1.00	.81	.81	0	0
Negro	.64	1.12	1.18	.72	.76	22	33

ᵃ All notes in Table 3 also apply to this table.

The most important findings from the data in Tables 3 and 4 are that the extent to which educational attainment can explain the existing income differences between Anglos and the selected ethnic populations varies considerably, but is rather limited for most of these populations. Schooling is most important in accounting for higher Anglo income in the case of Spanish surname persons; for all other groups it accounts for less than half of the gap between their incomes and those of Anglos.

To the extent that differences in the adjusted relative incomes shown in Tables 3 and 4 reflect differences in discrimination, they give some support to the visible dissimilarity hypothesis. As stated earlier, this hypothesis applied to the groups included in this study would seem to predict that the Spanish speaking groups would have the largest incomes after adjustments for education, and that Negroes would have the smallest. These predictions are supported by the California results if we exclude Filipinos

[15] Differences between the adjusted incomes of Indians and Filipinos and between those of Chinese and Japanese are statistically not significant (at the 5% level); all other ethnic differences are reliable at the 5% confidence level or above. In column 4 all differences are significant at or above the 5% confidence level except those between Indians and Filipinos and between Indians and Negroes.

and Indians, whose adjusted incomes are undoubtedly adversely affected by atypical residence and occupational distributions (rural and farm labor). They are also supported by the more limited data available for Texas. But in Illinois and New York, the education adjusted incomes of nonwhites and Puerto Ricans are not significantly different. This mixed support suggests that the physical dissimilarity factor must be supplemented by other variables to adequately explain differences in the intensity of discrimination against ethnic groups. It may be noted that the relative size hypothesis is not supported by the results. As an illustration of this, Puerto Ricans are a much smaller proportion of Illinois' population than nonwhites; the hypothesis would predict larger incomes for the Puerto Ricans in this situation, but the two groups have approximately the same incomes after adjustment for education.

Other Evidence

Recent research by others has produced findings which complement the above results. In a simple regression of median income on median school years completed by males 25 and over for 16 Standard Metropolitan Statistical Areas in five Southwest states, sizeable differences between Spanish surname persons and nonwhites were obtained. For the Spanish surname group, 1959 annual income was found to increase by $529 with each year of school completed; for nonwhites, the increase was $449 ($r^2$ was .82 for the Spanish surname population and .44 for the nonwhites). These results agree with those just presented, though with the small sample size the difference between the coefficients for the two groups are not statistically significant.[16]

The second bit of evidence comes from a factor analysis of Census tract variables in Los Angeles County.[17] From this analysis (most of which was unrelated to the subject of this article) it was evident that higher educational attainment had different implications for the Spanish surname minority than for nonwhites. The results are particularly interesting because they show relationships between education and a number of welfare indicators other than income. The correlations are presented in Table 5. Education is more strongly associated with almost all of the variables in Table 5 for Spanish surname persons than for nonwhites (85 per cent of whom were Negroes in this study). The expected relations are almost uniformly found for both Anglos and persons with Spanish surname, but not

[16] These results were provided by the staff of the Mexican-American Study Project, UCLA.

[17] See Leland S. Burns and Alvin Harman, *Profile of the Los Angeles Metropolis—Its People and Its Homes, Part 5, The Complex Metropolis* (Los Angeles: University of California, Graduate School of Business Administration, Real Estate Research Program, forthcoming).

for nonwhites—on residence, housing, and employment, as well as income variables. Of course, if better education does not provide much higher income, it is unlikely to be associated with better employment or housing either.[18]

Table 5—Simple correlations between school years completed and other variables (Anglos, Spanish surname and nonwhites, Los Angeles County) (census tracts)

CORRELATION COEFFICIENTS[a]

Variables	Anglos	Spanish surname	Nonwhites
Housing units with all plumbing	.624	.561	.194
Rooms per housing unit	.461	.380	.023
Housing units renter-occupied	−.421	−.330	−.085
Households with high population density	.647	.613	.127
Nonwhite and Spanish surname population	−.735	−.594	−.174
Income of group	.690	.523	.264
Income of Anglos	.690	.539	.001
College enrolled population	.417	.314	.086
Fertility ratio	−.451	−.440	−.076
Value of real property	.668	.586	.029
Gross rental	.634	.570	.032
Availability of two or more autos	.661	.534	.077
Use of bus transportation	−.523	−.352	−.111
Employment in food and kindred manufacturing	−.429	−.340	−.061
Employment in other nondurable manufacturing	−.476	−.302	−.041
Employment in transportation	−.334	−.289	.024
Employment in educational services	.493	.379	.112
Employment in professional services	.575	.495	−.009

[a] Pearson. Coefficients of .05 are statistically significant at the 1 per cent level of confidence.

Changes Over Time

The data in Tables 3 and 4 aptly demonstrate that disadvantaged minorities will not obtain equality of income with the majority population by matching the majority on educational attainment alone. This is shown by the relative incomes of the ethnic groups, which remain low even after their educational attainment is standardized to that of Anglos, and, without standardization, by the low incomes of the Japanese who have already attained Anglo levels of schooling. In view of the Japanese experience especially, it would be helpful for purposes of formulating and evaluating policy to know something about the dynamics of the income-education relation for disadvantaged ethnic groups. How long does it take before discrete improvements in schooling are reflected in larger incomes?

[18] It is of interest to note that simple correlations between incomes of each of the groups and the variables in Table 5 differ for nonwhites and Spanish surname persons in the same manner as do the correlations with school attainment. In particular, this suggests that nonwhites with high incomes face greater discrimination when they attempt to improve their housing. Of course, other explanations are also possible.

In order to gain at least a modicum of insight into this question, limited aspects of intertemporal change in income and education for ethnic groups were investigated. These efforts were frustrated in part because of problems of data comparability in different census years. Some results were obtained, however, and are worth presenting. The first investigation was of the Japanese experience over time. For how long has the schooling of Japanese in this country been equal to that of the majority population, and what changes in Japanese relative income have occurred in this period? Approximate answers to these questions are given in Table 6.

Table 6—Education and income: Japanese and reference populations (U.S. and California urban males, 1940–60[a])

United States

	MEDIAN SCHOOL YEARS COMPLETED		MEDIAN INCOME		Ratio of Japanese to white income
	Japanese	Whites	Japanese	Whites	
1940 (age 25 and up)	10.1	8.7			
1950 (age 25 and up)	12.3	10.3	$1945[b]	$2278[b]	.85
1960 (age 14 and up)	12.3	11.2	4532	4800	.94

California

	MEDIAN SCHOOL YEARS COMPLETED		MEDIAN INCOME		Ratio of Japanese to all male income
	Japanese	All males	Japanese	All males	
1940 (age 25 and up)	9.9	10.1			
1950 (age 25 and up)	12.2	11.7	$1962[b]	$2268[b]	.87
1960 (age 14 and up)	12.4	11.9	4615	5156	.90

Source: *U.S. Census of Population*, designated years.
[a] Income data are for 1949 and 1959, unadjusted for age differences.
[b] These median incomes are for males and females combined age 14 and up. Incomes of Japanese available only on this basis.

The educational attainment of Japanese urban males in the United States, as measured by median school years completed, has been as high as that of whites at least since 1940 (no data for earlier years are available) and it was more than one year higher in 1960. Their 1959 income was less than that of whites, even after 20 years of educational parity, but their relative income position did improve between 1949 and 1959.[19] The California data, free from the influence of regional differences in population distributions and changes, present a similar picture, though the improvement in Japanese relative income over the decade was less in California than in the United States as a whole.[20]

[19] The last part of this statement must be taken with caution, since relative incomes for 1949 had to be computed from incomes for males and females combined.

[20] The effect of the "relocation" of the Japanese from the West Coast during World War II on their income progress and present income levels is not known.

The other inquiry into intertemporal movements provided measures of changes in income and educational attainment since 1949 for all ethnic groups previously considered. This approach was predicated on the deliberately simple premise that income change would be related to change in schooling. Unfortunately, the income changes shown in Table 7 are necessarily for males and females combined. It is unlikely, however, that data for males only would have produced substantially different results.

Table 7—Percentage changes in education and income, 1950–60[a], and median educational attainment 1950 (selected ethnic groups, California urban males)

| | | PERCENTAGE INCREASE, 1950–60[a] | |
Ethnic group	Median school years completed in 1950	Median school years completed	Median income[b]
Chinese	8.0	38	64
Negroes	8.7	18	59
Filipinos	8.2	17	54
Indians	8.8	16	57
Spanish surname	8.1	14	72
All males	11.7	2	60
Japanese	12.2	2	82

Source: U.S. Census of Population, 1950 and 1960.
[a] Income changes are for 1949–59.
[b] These are changes in incomes of males and females combined, since incomes of the minority ethnic groups were available only on this basis in 1949. In general, 60–70 per cent of all income earners in any year are males, so that males provide the major enumeration basis for the income data underlying these figures.

In the decade covered by the data, ethnic ranking on increases in income did not correspond very closely with ranking on schooling changes. The group with the smallest income gains, Filipinos, improved their education about as much as all but one of the other groups. The Chinese had easily the greatest improvement in schooling, but ranked only moderately high on income change. Interestingly, the Japanese hardly improved their educational attainment at all, since it was so high at the beginning of the period, but they ranked first in income gains.

Though the high schooling level of Japanese in 1950 was followed by the largest income improvement of any group, 1950 level of schooling and 1949–1959 income gains were not very sensitively related for the other minorities. In the case of the Spanish surname population, their increase in median income was the second largest of all the ethnic groups included in Table 7, while their 1950 schooling level was near the bottom of the list.

It appears from these two pieces of evidence that in a time period of a decade, or perhaps longer, ethnic group gains in income bear little relationship to improvements in their schooling, and that achievement of majority levels of income is delayed until long after the ethnic group has matched majority educational attainments. This finding complements Glazer's observation that for many years Orientals and Jews in the United States were employed in jobs not commensurate with their educational qualifications; but these qualifications were available and were used to bring substantial economic progress after the decline in labor market discrimination which followed World War II.[21] It is, of course, quite likely that high educational attainment itself has much to do with lessening the intensity, generality, and effectiveness of discrimination against an ethnic minority, and with subsequent economic gains.

However, from the experience of the Japanese population in the U.S. it appears that even substantially higher levels of schooling for disadvantaged groups would not open doors to higher incomes nearly to the same extent or as quickly as they do for Anglos. The Japanese experience, admittedly, is just one piece of evidence relative to change in income and education, but it seems a fairly strong one. It is not likely that the low income of the Japanese in California can be explained by such income-related factors as educational quality, motivation, native ability, and inability to obtain capital; deficiencies in these dimensions seem rarely to be associated with persons of Japanese origin, even in a casual manner.

In addition to the discrimination "breakthrough" waiting period, the income gains which can be expected from increased schooling depend upon the existing labor market position and schooling level of a group. This can be illustrated with the Spanish surname population, which presently enjoys high relative income (among those shown in Table 4) with low educational attainment. Such a situation can exist because males of this ethnic population have had fair success in obtaining middle-wage jobs which do not have formal schooling requirements. Over eighty percent of the Spanish surname males in California are employed in manual and service occupations,[22] where educational attainment usually has only peripheral importance for obtaining employment and promotion. Moderate gains in educational attainment are not likely to lower this proportion and raise incomes greatly because, given the present low level of schooling for Spanish surname persons, moderate gains will not be sufficient to qualify many of this group for nonmanual employment, where so many of the high incomes are.

Finally, income gains to a group lag behind attainment of high schooling levels because income in our society is partly dependent upon age. Young persons entering the labor force can raise the education level of a group immediately, but an income impact will not result until the incomes of these persons rise above the average income of the group. This will occur, through job advancement, as the young persons age. An illustration of this

---

[21] Nathan Glazer and Daniel Moynihan, *Beyond the Melting Pot* (Cambridge, Mass.: MIT Press, 1963), p. 44.

[22] *U.S. Census of Population, 1960; Subject Reports, Persons of Spanish Surname*, Table 6.

process is found in the fact that the 1959 median income of male high school graduates of age 25 and over in the United States was higher than that of males with one to three years of college who were in the age class 25–29.[23]

Summary

This article has provided quantitative estimates of the importance of educational attainment in accounting for the income differences between Anglos and members of disadvantaged ethnic groups. Except for the Spanish surname population of the Southwest, educational attainment accounted for less than half of the difference between the 1959 median income of each group and that of Anglos. The income differences which remain after adjusting for education were not analyzed, but undoubtedly result from multiple causes, of which educational quality and especially discrimination would seem to be most important.

These influences also prevent proportionate gains in income from immediately following improvements in the educational attainment of a disadvantaged ethnic group. Many members of minority groups are forced to endure a frustrating waiting period until they are able to obtain incomes which are appropriate to their education. This lag between income and education can be understood in part to be a result of the fact that in our society the flow of causation is frequently from income to education rather than in the reverse direction. In spite of this, minority persons may be able to match the majority in education, but they will not obtain comparable incomes if they do not have access to income opportunities which are available to similarly educated members of the majority population.

Among the ethnic groups considered in this study, the Spanish surname populations had the highest incomes after adjustment for education. Next in rank were the Chinese and Japanese, and then Puerto Ricans and Negroes. Indians and Filipinos had the lowest adjusted incomes, partly due to the rural character of their residence locations and occupations. These results offer some support for the proposition that market discrimination is directly related to the observable physical dissimilarity between the ethnic group and the majority population.

---

[23] *U.S. Census of Population, 1960; Subject Reports, Educational Attainment,* Table 6.

Part
Five
CONTINUED

Manpower Retraining and the Disadvantaged

The manpower revolution of the 1960s, accompanied as it was by nearly an entire decade of economic prosperity, is characterized in part by concern for the coexistence of labor surpluses and shortages. The socio-economic imperative for closing the manpower-skill gap, particularly for the identifiable disadvantaged, continues to be fueled by technological change and educational drop-outs. It is not surprising, therefore, that retraining human resources became a part of public policy in the 1960s.

Is there a payoff from manpower retraining directed toward dis-advantaged Americans, and what problems are encountered in evaluating these efforts? Although several economists have examined these questions and reported upon their research, only a small sample of these studies can be reproduced here. The two empirical studies on manpower retraining presented by Gerald G. Somers and Ernst W. Stromsdorfer 27 and Worth Bateman 28 identify the problems encountered in such an effort and are suggestive of methodological approaches that may be useful. David O. Sewell's evaluation 29 of benefit-cost analysis of manpower retraining programs is an equally valuable contribution because many of the difficulties encountered in retraining and in economic evaluation of retraining programs are clearly identified.

27

A Benefit-Cost Analysis of Manpower Retraining

Manpower training is a problem area which has assumed new importance in the decade of the 1960s—a development reflected by the public policy of this period. Somers and Stromsdorfer investigate the economic gains associated with retraining efforts in West Virginia. Gerald G. Somers is Professor of Industrial Relations at the University of Wisconsin where Ernst W. Stromsdorfer has recently been visiting

GERALD G. SOMERS
ERNST W. STROMSDORFER

Associate Professor on leave from Pennsylvania State University. Using a benefit-cost framework, the authors conclude that the manpower retraining experience reported upon here represents a worthwhile investment from a private and social viewpoint.

Introduction

Government-sponsored retraining of the unemployed may be viewed as the major development in U.S. labor market policies of the 1960's. In addition to recently-enacted state and local programs, retraining has been assigned a central role in such federal legislation as the Area Redevelopment Act (ARA) (1961), the Manpower Development and Training Act (MDTA) (1962), the Trade Expansion Act (1962), amendments to the vocational education system and to the MDTA (1963), and the Economic Opportunity Act of 1964.

Reprinted from Gerald G. Somers and Ernst W. Stromsdorfer, "A Benefit-Cost Analysis of Manpower Retraining," paper included in the *Proceedings of the Seventeenth Annual Winter Meeting of the Industrial Relations Research Association* (1964), pp. 1–14, with permission of the authors and publisher.

In view of the hundreds of millions of dollars now being allocated to these retraining programs, an evaluation of the investment is timely. While recognizing the political, social and psychological benefits which may result from training the unemployed, this paper stresses questions which are more familiar to the economist: What are the gains in employment and earnings relative to the direct costs and opportunity costs of retraining? How do trainees fare in comparison with nontrainees? How long does it take the trainee and society to recoup the cost of retraining? What are the returns of the retraining investment?

SOME METHODOLOGICAL CONSIDERATIONS

Although extensive national data on ARA and MDTA trainees have been published, such data do not lend themselves to the detailed evaluation called for here. National data on the employment experience of trainees are classified by personal characteristics and other variables, but no basis is provided for comparisons with control groups of nontrainees; nor is information available on the income of the trainees before, during, or after their training.

Because of these limitations in the national data, primary emphasis in this paper is placed on our surveys of trainees and nontrainees in West Virginia. Five groups of workers were interviewed in 1962 and were followed up by mail questionnaires and additional interviews in 1963 and 1964. These groups were composed of (a) 501 trainees who took ARA courses or Area Vocational Training Program (AVP) courses set up for training the unemployed under West Virginia state legislation; (b) 233 "dropouts" who withdrew from their courses before completion; (c) 65 who did not report for training after having been accepted (DNR's); (d) 127 "rejects" whose applications for training were not accepted; and (e) 453 "nontrainees" selected by random methods from those in the local employment service files. The nontrainees, our basic control group, were workers who did not apply for training even though they had experienced unemployment immediately prior to that time when most of the trainees entered their courses.

The respondents were located in three areas typical of depressed employment conditions in West Virginia; Charleston-Huntington, an urban-industrial area; McDowell County, predominantly coal-mining; and Harrison-Monongalia Counties, a mixed mining, industrial and agricultural area. All trainees in selected courses in these areas were interviewed. The courses were typical of course offerings in West Virginia and the national retraining programs. They included auto repair, construction trades, electrical maintenance, machine tool operators, riveters, welders; and for women, nurses aides, typists, stenographers and waitresses.

In analyzing the employment gains of the trainees, comparisons were made with each of the four other groups of respondents. In determining the monetary gains of the trainees, the nontrainees were used as the control group. In particular, the opportunity costs incurred during training and the gains in income attributable to retraining were derived from comparisons with the income of the nontrainees during and after the training period.

At the outset, a few major limitations should be noted:

1. The samples are small, cover only particular courses in a few selected areas of the country, and in a few instances are insufficient to provide meaningful results within cross-classifications even for these areas.

2. Because of the nature of the selection of the control groups, they cannot be said to have the same personal characteristics as the trainees. Although the direction of bias is clear in the case of the "rejects," it is not so clear in comparisons with "dropouts," DNR's and nontrainees. Some of these workers lacked ambition and motivation, but others felt that their qualifications and opportunities were good enough to make training unnecessary. At any rate, an effort is made to control for some of these personal differences in the analyses which follow.

3. There are advantages and disadvantages in the use of the nontrainees' experience as a basis for determining the opportunity cost of training and as a basis for determining the income gain derived by the trainees from their training. The obvious alternative would be to base these calculations on comparisons with the earnings experience of the trainees themselves prior to their courses. This would reduce the disadvantages resulting from the differing personal characteristics of the trainees and the nontrainees. But our analyses have indicated that the average prior earnings of the trainees vary markedly with the time period selected. Many worked in high-paying coal mining occupations for years before the period of unemployment which induced them to enroll for training. During the period of unemployment just prior to their training, on the other hand, the earnings (other than government payments) of these workers were zero or close to zero. Moreover, changes occurred in the labor market situation in the years following completion of their courses. These changes would obscure the advantages derived from training if the calculation were based on a comparison of the trainees' pretraining and post-training experience.

4. Since the trainees and nontrainees may have been competing for scarce jobs in the post-training period, gains derived by the trainees may have been at the expense of the nontrainees. It was not possible to determine the degree of such interdependence. To the extent that it occurred, the benefits enjoyed by the trainees may not constitute a net employment gain for society as a whole.

5. Finally, it has not been possible to distinguish the effects of the specialized skill acquired in the training course from other advantages derived from completion of the course. Even when they were not hired in occupations for which they were trained, the training may have had a

crucial influence on the trainees' future employment success. They gained some versatility, and many employers preferred them because these workers had demonstrated sufficient ambition and sense of discipline to enter and complete a training course. Therefore, the following discussion is couched in terms of the benefits of the overall training experience rather than the benefits derived from the acquisition of a particular skill.

The Benefits of Retraining

THE GAINS IN EMPLOYMENT

National reports on the achievements of ARA and MDTA retraining place almost exclusive stress on the gains in employment. These reports indicate that between 70 and 75 per cent of the institutional trainees have found jobs, almost all in training-related occupations. Since almost 90 per cent of the MDTA trainees were fully unemployed just prior to their training, and over 40 per cent had been unemployed for more than 15 weeks, MDTA officials naturally take pride in this accomplishment. Moreover, virtually all of the workers placed in on-the-job training under MDTA auspices, have been employed.[1]

Although it may be presumed that training played an important role in the employment success of these workers, definitive proof of such a role is lacking in the national reports. We know that the trainees were younger and better-educated than the average of the unemployed;[2] and a study of MDTA placements in 1963 indicates that the post-training employment rate declined progressively with increasing age and greater length of previous unemployment.[3] Furthermore, the national data provide no time-period analysis and no comparisons with nontrainee control groups.

A lengthier follow-up and comparisons with control groups have been incorporated in analyses of the more limited West Virginia sample. Efforts to isolate the employment effects of the retraining variable have also been made in cross-classifications within common age, sex, education and previous-unemployment categories; and by means of regression analysis including these and other variables.[4]

[1] Data provided by the U. S. Department of Labor, Bureau of Employment Security. See also, *Manpower Research and Training under the M.D.T.A.* A Report by the Secretary of Labor, Washington, March 1964, pp. 33, 51, 168.

[2] *Ibid.*, pp. 19–21.

[3] Data provided by U. S. Department of Labor, Bureau of Employment Security. The national data are discussed in greater detail in Somers, "Retraining: An Evaluation of Gains and Costs," Conference on Unemployment Research, Boulder, Colorado, June 1964, to be published by John Wiley & Sons in 1965.

[4] Detailed tabulations on the employment effects of retraining in West Virginia are included in the chapter by Gibbard and Somers in *Retraining the Unemployed, op. cit.* Copies of these tables and detailed tables pertaining to the earnings-cost analysis can be obtained by writing to Retraining Research Project, Department of Economics, University of Wisconsin, Madison 53706.

Some of the principal findings on the effects of retraining on employment in the West Virginia surveys are as follows:

1. In the summer of 1962, 60 per cent of the "trainees" were employed, compared with 56 per cent of the "dropouts" and approximately one-third of the rejects, DNR's and nontrainees.
2. One year later, employment rates had increased for all groups, with a trainee employment rate of about 71 per cent and a continued, albeit narrower, gap between trainees and the nontrainees, rejects and DNR's.
3. About 12 per cent of those who had completed training were not in the labor force in the summer of 1962. The proportion was roughly similar among nontrainees, rejects and DNR's. In all groups, women had much higher rates of labor force withdrawal than men.
4. In both 1962 and 1963, the trainees had a higher rate of employment than nontrainees, rejects and DNR's in the same age category, in the same education category, and in the same previous-labor-force-experience category (including labor-force status and length of unemployment).

These findings of a consistent employment advantage of trainees over "similarly-situated" control groups are buttressed by regression analysis. To give a further indication of the impact of retraining on employment success after training, the five training statuses were introduced as the final variable in a regression in which we had previously controlled for the impact of age, sex, race, education and a variety of other socio-demographic variables. The dependent variable was the per cent of time employed in the 12 month period following the end of training.[5]

As is shown in Table 1, the worker's "Training Status" (that is, position as a "Trainee," Dropout, "DNR," "Reject" or "Nontrainee") is the second most significant variable in explaining post-training employment success.

In addition to training status, the only other variable groups significant at a .05 level of significance or above are "Previous Labor Force Experience" (including length of unemployment just prior to training), "Regular Occupation" (skill category of customary occupation prior to training), and "Labor Market Area" (one of the three West Virginia areas cited earlier).

It is understandable that the trainee's pre-training labor force and employment status would be a significant predictor of his post-training employment experience. The pretraining status reflects the composite of his characteristics and labor market qualifications. As noted above, however, trainees have greater employment success in comparison with nontrainees

[5] The independent variables in this study are all of a binary nature. That is, they assume a value of *one* or *zero*, depending on whether or not a respondent falls into a particular category in question. The dependent variable is the per cent of time employed in the 12 month period following the end of the retraining period. Thus, the range of this variable is constrained between the limits of 0 and 100. One must bear both these facts in mind when interpreting the tests of significance.

in each of the prior labor force categories. Thus, in many cases retraining has helped workers to escape a lengthy history of previous unemployment.

Training Status, when introduced as the last variable in the regression, increases $\bar{R}^2$ by 3.23 percentage points, or 25 per cent, after the intervening influence of the other socio-economic variables had been included. In the

Table 1—Impact of socio-economic and retraining variables on percentage of time employed in 12-month period following end of retraining [a]

Variable [b]	F-Statistic
Age	2.10
Sex	1.72
Race	2.41
Education	2.44
Marital Status	0.24
Labor Force Experience Prior to Retraining	17.25**
Regular Occupation	2.11*
Labor Market Area	2.94*
Previous Training [c]	1.18
Mobility of Respondent [d]	2.95
Year Training Ended [e]	1.48
Quarter Training Ended [e]	0.30
Training Status [f]	10.85**

* = Significant at .05 level.
** = Significant at .01 level.
[a] n = 1065 $\bar{R}^2$ = .1605** Std. Error = 47.58 Constant = 62.88 (8.11).
[b] The breakdown of the variables into sub-sets is omitted in this table.
[c] The presence or absence of formal training at any time prior to the ARA or AVP training period.
[d] Distance between address in Summer 1962 and Summer 1963.
[e] Year or quarter the ARA or AVP training ended (for those who completed training only).
[f] Trainee, Dropout, Reject, Did Not Report, or Nontrainee for ARA or AVP training.

12 month time span following retraining the trainees were employed 64.14 per cent of the one-year period or 7.6 months on the average. The nontrainees were employed an average of only 4.7 months.[6] Thus, we see that, in the West Virginia sample trainees had a significantly greater employment success than the nontrainee control groups.

THE GAIN IN EARNINGS

Since government-sponsored retraining was primarily prompted by excessive unemployment, it is understandable that the employment effects of retraining have considerable political significance and that government reports give major emphasis to employment gains.[7] But economists are

[6] The partial regression coefficients and their standard errors (in parentheses) for the four training statuses are as follows: dropout, -5.10 (4.94); rejects, -27.66 (6.62); did not report, -20.80 (7.56); and, nontrainees, -28.83 (6.62).

[7] Income from unemployment compensation, public assistance and other government sources is not included in this section, but these social payments are considered in the discussion of costs and returns in following sections.

equally concerned with the effects on earnings. Comparison of the trainees earnings with those of nontrainees reveal that the trainees experienced significant gains.

Three different post-training time periods were used to measure the average monthly gains or losses in earnings of white workers who completed their training in 1962. First, an 18 month period following the quarter in which training ended in 1962 was used to maximize the number of observations for a single time period. Next, the maximum time period, available after the end of retraining—18, 21, or 24 months depending on the quarter in which training ended—was used to maximize the length of time in which the impact of retraining could be felt. Finally, an estimation was made of earnings differentials in the first quarter of 1964, the last quarter for which data were available at the time of writing. In this period, the greatest time lapse after retraining permitted observation of the labor force experience of our sample following the transition, readjustment and, in some cases, migration of the trainees.

As is seen in Table 2, male trainees earned substantially more per month than nontrainees in each of the estimation periods; and societal estimates were higher than individual estimates. Societal estimates were also higher for females, but the advantage of female trainees over nontrainees was relatively small. Given the 18 month post-training estimation period, the average monthly gain of the male trainees over their nontrainee counterparts was $61 based on individual concepts and $69 based on societal concepts. For the same period, the average monthly gain is only eight dollars per month for females, given individual measurement concepts, and $15 based on societal concepts.[8]

Costs and Returns

As has been noted in the discussion of methodological considerations, the differential in post-training earnings enjoyed by the trainees, like their advantage in employment, cannot all be attributed to their retraining. However, given the controls attempted in this survey, it is reasonable to assume that their retraining played some significant role in providing the noted advantages of trainees relative to nontrainees. Based on this assumption, it is instructive to relate income gains to training costs and estimate returns on the retraining investment.

[8] For greater detail on methods and findings on earnings and costs, see the paper by Glen G. Cain and Ernst W. Stromsdorfer, "An Economic Evaluation of Government Retraining of the Unemployed in West Virginia," in *Retraining the Unemployed: Case Studies of the Current Experience, op. cit.*

COSTS OF RETRAINING

Generalizations concerning training costs are hazardous because of the wide variations in costs depending on the sponsoring agency, length of course, occupational content, training facilities, trainee qualifications, provision of allowances, and concepts concerning opportunity costs. The average cost per trainee reported for those in institutional programs of the MDTA is $1300. For those in on-the-job training programs, the per-trainee cost is approximately one fourth that amount. These include the direct costs of instruction and facilities as well as training allowances; but they exclude opportunity costs.[9]

Table 2—Average monthly differential in earnings of trainees vis-à-vis nontrainees for selected time periods after end of training, individual and societal estimation[a]

Sex	18 MONTH POST-TRAINING PERIOD		MAXIMUM POST-TRAINING PERIOD[b]		QUARTER, 1964 FIRST	
	Individual[c] estimation	Societal[d] estimation	Individual estimation	Societal estimation	Individual estimation	Societal estimation
Male Trainee N=164 Nontrainee N=188	61	69	65	76	74	94
Female Trainee N=95 Nontrainee N=60	8	15	6	11	0	11

[a] In dollars.

[b] This figure is a weighted average for three groups, those having a maximum of 18, 21 and 24 months post-training labor market experience.

[c] Net of taxes. Assumes those workers who voluntarily leave the labor force earn in imputed income during that time as much as they earned on the average in that job immediately preceding the time when they voluntarily left the labor force.

[d] Includes federal income taxes but no state taxes or Social Security. Zero earnings are imputed for that time when a worker is voluntarily out of the labor force.

The direct training costs and training allowances in the West Virginia ARA and AVP programs were considerably lower than those under MDTA. The courses were generally of shorter duration. Training allowances for ARA trainees, based on average state unemployment compensation, were lower than the national average; and no provisions for training allowances were included in the state AVP training. For the trainees included in the benefit-cost analysis, the average direct costs and training allowances for men totalled $502 and for women, $428. These costs were incurred by society rather than by the trainees.

[9] *Manpower Research and Training, op. cit.*, pp. 16, 48 and 165.

The opportunity costs of retraining—the income foregone during the training course—are less readily determined. Yet, these are the most important costs for the individual trainee. As has been noted above, the determination of the amount the trainees *could have* earned during their training period is based on the earnings of a comparable group (in age, sex, race and education) of nontrainees.

For society, during the period of the survey, the total opportunity costs for males were estimated to be $274 and for females, $122, bringing total training costs to an average of $776 for each male trainee and $550 for each female trainee. The *private* costs to the individual trainee represent only opportunity costs, including imputed earnings for voluntary not-in-the-labor-force status. The private costs averaged $300 for males and $145 for females.

THE PAY-BACK PERIOD

Table 3 relates gains in market earnings (see Table 2) to the costs of training by means of an average pay-back period expressed in months. The pay-back period is the length of time required for the differential gains in post-training earnings to offset the total costs of retraining. Generally speaking, the estimated pay-back periods are short. They are shorter for

Table 3—Average pay-back period in months for trainees[a]

	Individual			Society		
	AVERAGE PAY-BACK PERIOD IN MONTHS			AVERAGE PAY-BACK PERIOD IN MONTHS		
Benefit estimation periods	Male	Female	Average	Male	Female	Average
18 Month Post-Training Period	4.9	18.1	5.8	11.2	10.2	8.3
Maximum Post-Training Period	4.6	24.2	5.6	10.2	50.0	13.3
First Quarter, 1964, Period	4.1	0[b]	5.2	8.3	50.0	10.9

[a] The pay-back period represents the total costs divided by total monthly benefits for the group in question.
[b] Zero earnings benefits, implying that the investment costs will never be recouped.

the individual than for society, and much shorter for males than for females. For males, given the 18 month post-training estimation period, we have a pay-back period of 4.9 months based on individual concepts and 11.2 months based on societal concepts. For females, the figures are 18.1 and 36.2 months, respectively. Also, the pay-back period gets shorter for males and longer for females as time periods further removed from the end of training are used to measure earnings differentials. Only for females does the pay-back period exceed the earnings-estimation periods, thereby calling for the assumption that the earnings advantage enjoyed during the estimation period continues unchanged until the conclusion of the pay-back period.

NET EXPECTED CAPITAL VALUE INCREASES

Assuming a continuance of the trainee's earnings differential for the rest of his working life, it is possible to appraise the investment in training in terms of its contribution to the increase in the worker's capital value. Here, average monthly earnings gains along with data on changes in post-training social income are related to costs and the training period by means of a chosen rate of discount, thus estimating the present value of the net stream of future benefits to the trainee.[10]

The net expected capital increases are consistently greater for societal vis-à-vis individual estimation concepts. For the 18 month post-training estimation period the net average expected life-time capital increase for each trainee is $3,150, given a four per cent discount rate, and assuming a zero growth rate in average annual earnings. Under societal concepts, the corresponding figure is $6,640—about twice as great. The total gains for the members of our sample are $815,800 and $1,720,700 for the respective individual and societal concepts. But at the ten per cent discount rate the gains are much more modest, and, effectively, are cut in half. Given the 18 month estimation period and assuming a ten per cent discount rate and zero growth rate, the average net expected life-time capital increase is $1,600 and $3,230 for the respective individual and societal concepts. However, if we assume a two per cent growth rate the values are increased by about 20 to 25 per cent in every case. For instance, the total expected life-time gains at the four per cent discount using societal concepts increase from $1,720,700 to $2,327,500 while the average increases from $6,640 to $8,990 per worker over his lifetime.

Given the same initial outlay and discount rate, this type of evaluation of the returns to training is useful in comparing retraining with other alternative investments in labor markets or in evaluating other types of training.[11]

[10] The formula used is

$$V = \sum_{k=a}^{64} \frac{E_k}{(k+1-a)}$$
$$(1+r)$$

where,

V = the capital value; a, the average age at the beginning of training; E, the net earnings differential of trainees over nontrainees; and, r, the selected rate of discount.

[11] An alternative investment evaluation can be adopted by calculating an internal rate of return on the retraining investment. A derived formula for the rate of return is

$$r = \sqrt[t]{1 + \frac{E}{C}} - 1,$$

where t is the number of months of retraining, E is the net average monthly earnings differential received by the trainees (assumed constant in the future), and C is the average

Conclusions

Government-sponsored retraining of the unemployed began to emerge as a foremost Federal labor market policy in 1961. The infancy of the programs makes evaluation difficult, but the formative years are also the most important for an objective appraisal. The ARA and AVP programs in West Virginia, which are evaluated in this paper, were among the first to be initiated in the current move to retraining in the United States.

The West Virginia surveys indicate that the trainees enjoyed notable advantages in employment and earnings relative to "comparable" nontrainees. This was especially true for males, and less so for females. For the average male trainee, the costs of retraining were quickly repaid in increased earnings; and high capital values and rates of return followed in the retraining investment—for the trainee and for society.

Three obvious questions arise: First, can the post-training benefits enjoyed by the trainees be wholly attributed to their retraining? Since the control groups of nontrainees were not identical with the trainees and since special efforts were often made to place the trainees, other, non-training factors undoubtedly intervened. The limitations of the survey have been discussed in detail. However, careful efforts have been made to control for these other variables whenever possible; and the preponderance of various types of evidence pointing in the same direction leads to the view that the retraining experience played an important role in the relative post-training success of the experimental group.

Second, can the favorable West Virginia experience be generalized for the nation as a whole, for the MDTA and other programs? Because of the peculiarities of the West Virginia situation, there are obvious hazards involved. At the same time, the background of the trainees was similar to that of many other displaced and unemployed workers; and the courses studied were typical of those established elsewhere. If the training costs were unusually low, so were the employment opportunities unusually meager in the depressed West Virginia communities. Certainly, there is little evidence in national data or studies in other areas which would lead to the conclusion that the favorable West Virginia experience was unique.[12]

---

cost per month during training. Using the average earnings differential of the trainees during the two years following the end of their training, the estimated social rate of return is 105.6% for male trainees and 24.0% for females. For additional details see Cain and Stromsdorfer, *op. cit.* The formula for r is taken from Jacob Mincer, "On-the-Job Training: Costs, Returns, and Some Implications," *Journal of Political Economy*, Supplement, LXX, No. 5, Part 2, October, 1962.

[12] See, for example, the case studies of retraining programs in Connecticut, Illinois, Massachusetts, Michigan, Pennsylvania, and Tennessee, in *Retraining the Unemployed* ... *op. cit.*

Finally, is retraining of the unemployed a sound social investment? In view of the small number of trainees relative to the number of unemployed in West Virginia and the nation as a whole, it is clear that retraining is only a partial answer to the problem of unemployment.[13] But individual trainees have obviously benefited economically from retraining, quite aside from any social and psychological gain. Additions have been made to the nation's skills and income. Even if it could be shown that retrained workers merely find employment that might otherwise go to the untrained, there are important political, economic, cultural and social values in the demonstration that individual workers can gain through retraining.

The dollars-and-cents focus of this evaluation has been necessarily limited; but even within this narrow framework, there is evidence that the benefit and potential benefits of manpower retraining substantially outweigh the costs.

---

[13] Only 43,684 workers had completed ARA and MDTA training by January, 1964, at a time when there were 4,300,000 unemployed. Data provided by the U. S. Department of Labor, Bureau of Employment Security, and *Manpower Research and Retraining, op. cit.*, p. 33.

28

An Application
of Cost-Benefit Analysis
to the Work-Experience Program

Worth Bateman, now Vice President
of the Urban Institute, suggests
using a cost-benefit framework to
evaluate work-experience and training programs designed to enhance
both the employability and incomes
of public assistance recipients.
Although plagued with sparseness
of data, this selection briefly explains

WORTH BATEMAN

the methodological fundamentals of
the break-even concept. In addition,
the author reveals some of the data
and methodological problem spots
frequently encountered in empirical
applications of economic tools of
analysis.

Introduction

The Work-Experience and Training Program is one of many federally
supported programs which aims to reduce poverty and dependency by
raising individual capabilities for self-support. Funded under Title V of
the Economic Opportunity Act of 1964 and administered by the Department of Health, Education, and Welfare, the program seeks to increase the
employment and earnings potential of family heads who are recipients of
public assistance (primarily the adult recipients in families receiving Aid to

Reprinted from Worth Bateman, "An Application of Cost-Benefit Analysis to the Work-
Experience Program," *American Economic Review* 57 (May 1967), pp. 80–90, with the
permission of the author and publisher.

Families with Dependent Children, AFDC) and nonrecipients with similar characteristics.[1]

A variety of projects are funded in this program. Some are training projects utilizing the programs available under MDTA and the Vocational Education Act. Some provide adult basic education. Others are work-experience projects in which welfare clients and other needy persons are given jobs in public or nonprofit agencies. However, the majority of projects incorporate all these components.

The following profile shows some of the characteristics of the 101 thousand persons enrolled in the program in fiscal year 1966: participants are about equally divided between males and females; more than 60 percent of enrollees are married and over 90 percent are heads of households with four or more dependents; more than 80 percent are between 21 and 49 years old; nearly 30 percent are high school drop-outs; over half have completed eight grades or less of formal schooling; assistance payments made under AFDC, allowances provided under Title V of the Economic Opportunity Act, or General Assistance are the most important (and in most cases the only) sources of family income.

Thus, the program is focused on potentially employable poor persons with little formal education who are currently unemployed and who lack the means to support themselves and a comparatively large number of dependents. In comparison to the number currently enrolled in the program, this target population is large. Among public assistance recipients alone, it has been estimated that perhaps 250 to 350 thousand persons might be made self-supporting if given the proper training and other supporting services (e.g., day care for the children of AFDC mothers).[2] In addition, the universe of potential beneficiaries of the program includes many of the unemployed and employed poor who are not now recipients of public assistance.

The exclusive concern of this program with what Cain and Somers[3]

[1] According to a recent Welfare Administration report, Title V differs from other employment programs "in that it concentrates on developing an intervention program for the entire family, not just for the employable adult . . . [These individuals] have individual or family adjustment problems as well as educational and vocational training deficiencies which deter or preclude them from employment." Although employment is the ultimate goal, "the more proximate objectives center around improved individual and family functioning." Although it may, in fact, be necessary to overcome family problems as a condition for achieving the employment objective, there is no mention of improved individual and family functioning (whatever that may be) in the legislation authorizing expenditures for this program. This emphasis, in part, may be the natural consequence of having the Welfare Administration administer the program. See Abraham S. Levine, "Cost-Benefit Analysis of the Work-Experience Program," *Welfare in Review*, Aug.–Sept., 1966, pp. 1–9.

[2] Robert H. Mugge, "Demographic Analysis and Public Assistance," prepared for presentation at the Annual Meeting of the Population Association of America, New York City, Apr. 30, 1966.

[3] Glen Cain and Gerald Somers, "Retraining the Disadvantaged Worker" (Sept., 1966, mimeo.).

have called the "specially disadvantaged" reflects a pronounced change in emphasis of federally supported training programs in the last several years. The programs of the War on Poverty, of which this is one, are the most well-known examples of this change. At present, very little is known about the effectiveness of these programs in raising the earnings of the groups they serve.[4]

The purpose of this paper is to: (1) develop an analytical framework for evaluating the work-experience component of the program; and (2) to estimate its potential effectiveness in improving the capability for self-support.

Measures of Benefit

The benefits of the Work-Experience Program can be divided into two parts. First, there are the short-run or immediate benefits of a work-relief program—in part, the output produced by people working who would otherwise be unemployed. Second, there are the long-run benefits of reduced dependency and improved potential for economic independence and self-support. These benefits can be estimated by comparing the present value of expected future earnings of program participants before and after the training or with those of individuals with the same socioeconomic and demographic characteristics who have not participated in the program.[5]

Over any period of time, earnings will be equal to the product of the hourly wage rate which prevails for that period and the number of hours worked:

$$E_t = H_t W_t \tag{1}$$

where E_t represents the earnings in period t, H_t is the number of hours worked during period t, and W_t is the prevailing hourly wage rate over period t.[6]

[4] Cain and Somers report that on the basis of several case studies which they analyzed, the position of the disadvantaged worker is enhanced considerably when compared with their own pretraining experience and compared with disadvantaged workers who have not been trained. See Cain and Somers, *op. cit.*, and Gerald Somers, "The Experience with Retraining and Relocation," *Conference on Manpower Policy*, Berkeley Unemployment Project, New York City, June 20–22, 1966.

[5] This, of course, is not equivalent to the conceptually superior method of comparing the earnings and employment experience of given individuals with and without the training program. The validity of the results depends on how good the surrogate data are for the with-without data. See Burton A. Weisbrod, "Conceptual Issues in Evaluating Training Programs" (Feb. 14, 1966, mimeo.).

[6] If the wage rate for part-time work differed from that for full-time work (1) would have to be reformulated as follows:

$$E_t = (H_{ft} W_{ft} + H_{pt} W_{pt}) \tag{1'}$$

Where H_{ft} and H_{pt} are the number of hours worked full time and part time, respectively, and W_{ft} and W_{pt} are the wage rates for full- and part-time employment, respectively.

A change in earnings during period t can result from a change in the number of hours worked, from a change in the wage rate, or from a change in both:

$$\Delta E_t = H_t \Delta W_t + W_t \Delta H_t + \Delta W_t \Delta H_t \; [7] \tag{2}$$

The first term on the right-hand side of (2) can be thought of as a "wage effect," i.e., an increase in the value of employee productivity for a given number of hours worked; the second term can be thought of as an "employment effect" which, for a given wage rate, reflects additional time worked; and the third term an interaction term or "combination effect" resulting from a simultaneous change in both factors.

Assuming all improvements in expected lifetime earnings are attributable to program participation, the increase in the present value of expected lifetime earnings can be represented by:

$$\Delta E = \sum_{t=k}^{d} [S_t(H_t \Delta W_t + W_t \Delta H_t + \Delta W_t \Delta H_t)]\ldots(1+r)^{-(t-k)} \tag{3}$$

where S_t is the probability that individuals in year t will survive at least to year $t+1$; r is the discount rate; and d is the year when earnings are assumed to cease.

In the short run, the benefits of the program can be measured by the value of the additional output produced by those individuals in just the work-experience component of the program. Assuming a competitively determined wage rate and no external benefits, this would be just equal to the earned assistance payments since an individual works that number of hours which, when multiplied by the wage rate, equals the public assistance payment for which he is eligible. Of course, these wage rates are not determined entirely by competitive forces since, for the most part, individuals are placed on government payrolls. Moreover, even assuming competitively determined wage rates for regular government employees, it would not follow that the value of the marginal product of a participant necessarily equals the wage rate. If that were true, it would seem that employment

[7] Thus, a 10 percent increase in the number of hours worked has exactly the same impact on earnings as a 10 percent increase in wage rates. This alone has important policy implications since the same increase in earnings can be obtained through expenditures which increase the probability of employment or increase worker productivity. But the costs of doing so may be quite different. For example, in a simple model, we might have: $\Delta E = f(p)$, where p is the proportion of a given "human investment" budget spent on placement and referral activities (say like those of state employment offices) and $(1-p)$ is the proportion spent on productivity increasing activities (training programs, for example). Although we should maximize $f(p)$ for a given budget, it is not clear, a priori, that p will be less than or equal to one. Of course, the probability of employment is dependent not only on demand but also on willingness to work. The poor are little different in this regard than others. The higher the wage rate, *mutatis mutandis*, the higher the probability of employment. At very low wage rates, the supply curve may be very inelastic, and in the extreme case, it may be a discontinuous one. Below that point, the quantity of labor supplied would be zero.

could be obtained at that wage and the necessity for being placed in such a job under the auspices of the program would disappear.[8]

What is really required is an estimate of the social value of the marginal product (i.e., the aggregate amount which individuals would be willing to pay for this output if they revealed their preferences). This may diverge from the wage cost. For example, having the grass neatly cut and trimmed along the side of the road by work-experience enrollees may cost X. A well-manicured parkway is a public good for which individuals using it may be willing together to pay more or less.

This may be represented by:

$$SVMP_t = \alpha\beta R_t H_t \qquad (4)$$

where $SVMP$ is the social value of the marginal product; α is the ratio of the value of the marginal product of a work-experience enrollee to that of nonenrollees who could be used to perform the work; β is a factor reflecting the divergence of the $SVMP$ and the wage cost; R is the hourly wage rate; and H is the number of hours worked while enrolled in the project. If $\alpha < 1$, the $SVMP$ is reduced by using a work-experience participant to do the job rather than a more productive worker.

The sum of (3) and (4) is an estimate of the economic benefits of the program.[9]

[8] Except in those cases where governmental budget constraints prevent all activities being supported at a level where the social value of the marginal product equals marginal social cost; e.g., "public goods." See Paul Samuelson, "The Pure Theory of Public Expenditure," *Rev. of Econ. and Statis.*, Nov., 1954, pp. 387–89.

[9] Both the short- and long-run measures of benefit described above represent real returns to expenditures on the Work-Experience Program. There is a third category of real benefits accruing to the economy which might arise out of the income transfers made in this program (or put differently, from the payments made to enrollees for work performed on work-experience projects). Such income transfers may have an important investment component in the sense that the conditions in which children grow up have an important bearing on their income earning capacity as adults. Income transfers to poor families are, in part, investments in a better home environment, diet, and health, which in turn, enhance the long-range economic prospects of poor children. There are, of course, other benefits which might be realized from the program by participants and their families. These might include increased satisfaction, *mutatis mutandis*, of working rather than being idle, the benefits to children of seeing the example of a working parent, and the increase in family stability. (The program permits public assistance payments to be made to families where the male is present irrespective of whether a state had adopted the unemployed parent component of the AFDC Program. Unemployed or marginally employed heads of families not enrolled in the Work-Experience Program and residing in states without AFDC-UP may find that desertion is the only option available for supporting or improving the support of their families.) The most significant external benefits which have not been accounted for in (3) and (4) are the reduced welfare payments and increased tax revenues which result from an increased capability for self-support. Although these distributive effects are not additive to real returns, they are the consequence of a successful project and should be considered in Program evaluation. See Burton A. Weisbrod, "Preventing High School Dropouts," in Robert Dorfman, ed., *Measuring Benefits of Government Investments* (Brookings Institution, 1963), pp. 136–39; and also, "Income Redistribution Consequences of Government Expenditure Programs," Second Conference on Government Expenditures, Brookings Institution, Sept. 15–16, 1966.

Unfortunately, the complete lack of data prevented the benefit analysis from proceeding further than a mere formulation of how it should be done. The earnings profile of individuals enrolled in this program is unknown and the follow-up data on post-enrollment earnings is completely unreliable. It is also not possible to estimate the critical parameters in (4) from existing data.

The strategy adopted at this point was to estimate how much the expected income of participants would have to rise just to "break even." This requires an estimate of what the present value of future earnings of participants would have been in the absence of the program and an estimate of program costs. Although the latter are available, the earnings data of participants are not and have to be constructed.

There are a number of problems associated with making such estimates. The 1960 Census provides the most complete information on earnings, income, and labor force status by age, sex, color, and educational attainment. But the published reports of the 1960 Census also have gaps in information and deficiencies in the form reported critical to this analysis. The most serious of these is the absence of earnings data as distinct from income data for females.

Earnings data are clearly the most appropriate for this analysis. The income data in the 1960 Census include public assistance, social security, unemployment insurance, etc., which tend to narrow earnings differentials among various socioeconomic groups. This means that the use of income data would tend to bias the break-even estimates downward. For males, however, data are available from published sources in the 1960 Census on earnings, classified according to the selected control variables. Since the Census data are grouped by age class, average earnings by individual year of age were computed by imputing the average earnings of an age class to the mid-point of the class and then making linear interpolations between mid-points. This was done for white and nonwhite males in each education category. Earnings were arbitrarily assumed to stop at age 64.

In computing expected earnings in each age, education, and race category, an adjustment was made for the probability that an individual of a given age will survive to the next year by applying life table values by age, color, sex (no educational attainment) to the estimated earnings for each year of age.

Estimates of the expected probability of employment were obtained from the 1960 Census. At the present, it has not been possible to locate more recent information on labor force participation and unemployment rates classified according to the selected control variables. The effect of this procedure in the absence of any further adjustments is to bias the break-even points upward since overall employment conditions were less favourable in 1959 (the year for which earnings are reported in the 1960 Census) than currently.[10]

Measures of Costs

The estimate of costs made for this analysis is the additional cost for an individual participant which is incurred by the government (state and federal). While in general these are primarily additional administrative costs, work-related expenses, and public assistance payments, the actual estimate of these incremental costs varies by state, since these costs depend on what payments the individuals would have received from the government in the absence of the Work-Experience Program. This in turn depends on whether a state meets or falls short of meeting 100 percent of "need"[11] for public assistance recipients and whether the state has or does not have the Unemployed Parent (UP) component of the AFDC Program.[12]

[10] The 1959 male unemployment rate was 5.3 percent compared to 4.0 percent in 1965. For white males the rates were 4.6 percent and 3.6 percent and for nonwhite males 11.5 percent and 7.6 percent in 1959 and 1965, respectively. It should be pointed out that the estimate of average annual earnings which is desired for each age, education, and sex category is given by:

$$\left[\sum_i^n (WH)_i \right] (n+p+k)^{-1} \tag{6'}$$

where W is the hourly wage rate, H is the number of hours worked during the year, n is the average number of individuals in the labor force who had earnings during the year, p is the average number of individuals in the labor force during the year who had no earnings, and k is the average number of individuals who were not in the labor force. What we have estimated, on the other hand, is

$$\frac{\left[\sum_i^n (WH)_i \right]}{n} \frac{(n'+p')}{n'+p'+k'} \frac{n'}{n'+p'} = \frac{\left[\sum_i^n (WH)_i \right]}{n} \frac{n'}{n'+p'+k'} \tag{7'}$$

where all the terms in the expression are defined as above with the prime signifying that the observation is for a point in time rather than for a full year. The first term on the left-hand side of the equation is the average annual earnings reported in the Census. The second term is the labor force participation rates and the third term is the unemployment rate, the latter two observations being made at a point in time. Over the course of a year, $n'+p'+k'$ will, for all practical purposes, equal $n+p+k$. If $n'=n$, then (6') and (7') are equivalent. If n' is observed at a time of less than average unemployment, then $n'>n$. Of course, the converse is also true.

[11] Each state determines a level of "need" for public assistance recipients. The level of need is based on the prices of a market basket of goods and services deemed to be "adequate." The level established varies by family size and composition. Moreover, there is wide state by state variation in defined need and not all states allocate sufficient resources to public assistance programs to meet 100 percent of need. For example, Indiana defines need for an AFDC family of four to be about $225 per month whereas for the same size family, New York defines need to be about $255 per month. Although New York meets 100 percent of need, actual monthly payments in Indiana are about $110 or 48 percent of need.

[12] The 1962 amendments to the Social Security Act permitted federal matching of state expenditures for Aid to Families with Dependent Children where the male is unemployed. To date, only twenty-one states have adopted this provision of the law.

The table below shows the components of incremental costs according to the category into which a state falls.

Components of incremental costs of work-experience program

	States which meet less than 100 percent of need	States which meet or exceed 100 percent of need
I. States with AFDC-UP and AFDC	ΔC_{11} = Additional administrative costs + work-related expenses + additional public assistance payments necessary to meet 100 percent of need	ΔC_{12} = Additional administrative costs + work-related expenses
II. States with AFDC but no AFDC-UP		
a. AFDC	ΔC_{21} = Same as above	ΔC_{22} = Same as above
b. Male W-E participants	ΔC_{31} = Additional administrative costs + work-related expenses + 100 percent of public assistance payments	ΔC_{32} = Additional administrative costs + work-related expenses + 100 percent of public assistance payments

The additional administrative costs associated with program operations are self-explanatory and are a component of the incremental costs for all states. Work-related expenses such as transportation, clothing, etc., incurred only for program participants are also part of the marginal costs for all states.

Title V requires that work-experience participants receive payments equal to 100 percent of what the state defines as need for that individual and his family. In those states meeting 100 percent of need there are no additional public assistance costs incurred for welfare recipients participating in a work-experience project. However, public assistance recipients in states meeting less than 100 percent of need can increase their income by enrolling in a project. The federal government pays the difference between the state grant and state defined need.

In those states without AFDC-UP, unemployed male heads of families are not eligible for federally aided public assistance. Thus, for a male enrollee in a work-experience project in such a state, the incremental costs include the full public assistance grant for which he and his family become eligible.

Other things equal,[13] the relationship among the incremental costs shown in the table above is as follows:

$$\Delta C_{32} = \Delta C_{31} > \Delta C_{21} = \Delta C_{11} > \Delta C_{22} = \Delta C_{12} \tag{5}$$

and in the absence of differentials in benefits the benefit-cost ratios would rank from lowest to highest in the same order as presented in (5).

[13] That is, assuming no state-by-state variations in average need and payments per case, work-related expenses, and administrative costs.

The definition of program costs presented above raises a thorny problem when one recognizes the income redistribution objectives of this program which are held by many of its supporters. The costs per participant as defined above are viewed as an investment in present and future productivity. In a sense, this does involve implicitly a distribution objective with respect to income. It is possible, however, to go further than this and to insist that the program is merely a way of making a number of needy individuals eligible for public assistance who would not be otherwise because of existing or potential public hostility to the AFDC-UP Program. If that were true, one could argue that the straight public assistance component should not be counted as part of the incremental costs of the Program since income redistribution now is what is being bought and not exclusively improvements in productivity in the future. The redistributional objective is in a sense accomplished with the help of a ruse and a little work. If the program does raise future income and contribute something to current GNP at the same time, then that is all well and good; but the definition of the incremental costs of doing this, one could argue, should be the same as in those states with AFDC-UP meeting at least 100 percent of need (i.e., comprising only administrative costs and work-related expenses).

The definition of costs given above and the benefit-cost analysis made below would also be critically affected by many of the major income maintenance proposals currently under discussion. For example, the adoption of federal minimum standards for the current categorical public assistance programs and the compulsory adoption by states of the AFDC-UP Program[14] would reduce interstate differentials in public assistance costs of the Work-Experience Program. The same, of course, would be true if categorical public assistance programs were replaced entirely by a guaranteed annual income or negative income tax.[15]

Because of the dual nature of the objectives of this program, incremental costs were calculated: (1) including incremental public assistance costs and (2) excluding all public assistance costs. Costs were estimated for male work-experience participants in Pennsylvania, Michigan, Minnesota, and Kentucky.

"Break-Even" Analysis

The ratio of the incremental costs and the estimated present value of future earnings is an indication of how much earnings would have to rise

[14] Both of these measures were recommended in the *Report of the Advisory Council on Public Welfare* (June, 1966).

[15] For a discussion of these income maintenance programs, see the *Report of the Advisory Council on Public Welfare* and two recent articles in *The Public Interest:* James Tobin, "The Case for an Income Guarantee," Summer, 1966; and Alvin L. Schorr, "Against a Negative Income Tax," No. 5, Fall, 1966.

for the program to break even. The results for white males ages 25, 35, 45, and 55 for one state, Kentucky,[16] are shown in Table 1.

Table 1—Program costs, earnings, and break-even points for white male participants in the work-experience program—Kentucky

Age/education of participants		Program cost per participant Column (1)[a]	Estimated future earnings per participant without program Column (2)[b]	Per cent increase in future earnings required for program to break even (1) as percent of (2)
Age 25				
Elementary	0–7	$1,064	$56,577	1.9%
	8	1,064	75,938	1.4
High school	1–3	1,064	88,577	1.2
	4	1,064	99,652	1.1
Age 35				
Elementary	0–7	1,064	52,719	2.0
	8	1,064	69,555	1.5
High school	1–3	1,064	81,378	1.3
	4	1,064	91,596	1.2
Age 45				
Elementary	0–7	851	40,532	2.1
	8	1,064	53,041	2.0
High school	1–3	1,489	61,569	2.4
	4	851	68,977	1.2
Age 55				
Elementary	0–7	638	22,325	2.9
	8	851	29,149	2.9
High school	1–3	851	33,789	2.5
	4	1,064	37,694	2.8

[a] Includes public assistance costs.
[b] Computed from data in U.S. Bureau of the Census, *1960 Census of Population*, PC(2)-7B, Table 1 and PC(2)-5B, Table 4; and U.S. Public Health Service, National Vital Statistics Division, *Vital Statistics of the United States, 1961*, Vol. II-Sec. 2, *Life Tables*, Table 2–3. Future earnings were discounted at 4 percent.

The implication of this table is that, even when incremental public assistance costs are counted, only a small percentage increase in future earnings would be necessary to make the program break even. If work-experience can increase the present value of future earnings of participants by as much as 2 percent at younger ages or 3 percent at upper ages, it will pay for itself. If incremental public assistance costs are not counted as costs of work experience, then even small increases (less than .5 percent) would make the program break even.[17] However, in a world of constrained budgets, breaking even is not a sufficient condition for funding a project. If the desirability of funding this Program is to be weighed against other alternatives for which benefit-cost ratios have been estimated, is is necessary

[16] Because of the similarity of the results the break-even points for the other three states are not shown.

[17] It should be kept in mind that the earnings of work-experience enrollees are likely to be below the average which we have estimated from the Census for each age and education category. This biases the break-even points downward.

to make some guesses about the actual effectiveness of the program in raising future earnings.

We can get a somewhat better "feel" for the problem by considering that an individual earning $1.50 per hour, working forty hours per week, fifty weeks in the year, earns $3,000 per year. If we assume that an individual without work experience would continue to earn that sum for forty years, the present value (discounted at 4 percent) of his future earnings is about $59,000 (or roughly that of a white male 25 years old with 0–7 years of educational attainment; see Table 1, line 1). An increase of 25 cents an hour (i.e., a 17 percent increase) in his expected wage rate would imply under the assumption above an increase in the present value of his future earnings of about $10,000 or a benefit-cost ratio of 10:1.[18]

Although these data are suggestive of large potential payoff, the fundamental fact remains that such calculations are pure guesswork and the fragmentary program information which is available permits estimates which are only slightly superior.

A three-month follow-up survey of work-experience participants who had terminated their enrollment showed that the average monthly wage of those employed was about $250. But only 42 percent of those located whose records were reported correctly were employed; 58 percent were unemployed.[19] It is possible to make a crude estimate of what the rate of unemployment would have been in the absence of the program from data recently released by the Labor Department.[20] Public assistance recipients who had received training under the MDTA through February, 1965, had been unemployed 54 percent of the year prior to enrollment for training.[21] Assuming this is representative of the fraction who would be unemployed at any given time during the year, given the crudeness of the comparison, and the other factors (e.g., changes in aggregate demand for labor) which have not been accounted for, there would appear to be little difference between the employment record of Program participants before and after work experience. The post-training earnings of the employed MDTA trainees averaged about $250 a month, or the same as that of work-experience enrollees.

---

[18] This, of course, does not include an estimate of the social value of the marginal product while enrolled in the project.

[19] Of the total 14,221 terminees in the sample, only 8,370, or 59 percent, were located or had records which were reported correctly.

[20] U.S. Department of Labor, "Training of Public Assistance Recipients Under the MDTA," *Manpower Evaluation Report No. 6*, Apr., 1966.

[21] This is admittedly a very rough means of obtaining the needed control data. However, the characteristics of the MDTA public assistance trainees are not too dissimilar from those of the work-experience enrollees: they were about equally divided between males and females; they had approximately the same age distribution; they were preponderately the heads of families. The MDTA trainees, however, had a higher average level of educational attainment than did the work-experience enrollees.

The most significant differences between the public assistance recipients trained under MDTA and the work-experience participants was the much larger proportion of the former who were employed after training: 64 percent compared to 42 percent. This, however, is not surprising. The provision of work opportunities for individuals likely to suffer long periods of unemployment may be effective in preventing the loss of working skills demanded by almost all jobs. However, it seems doubtful that any significant increases in earning capabilities will be realized unless there are real opportunities for training and retraining. At present, however, the emphasis on manpower training in the Work-Experience Program is not great. In general, individuals are placed first in jobs available within state and local governmental units which, in many cases, do not provide any significant upgrading in the skills of the participants. The program could most likely be made more effective by infusing it with a much larger training component. This could be accomplished by expanding the MDTA programs of institutional and on-the-job training which are directed specifically to the disadvantaged. Of course, the costs would be substantially greater than the costs of work-relief.

29

A Critique of Cost-Benefit
Analyses of Training

David O. Sewell, Assistant Professor of Economics at Queen's University (Canada), investigates the impact of investments in manpower training and related programs intended to ameliorate poverty. Many of the problems encountered in applying benefit-cost analysis to human capital investment programs for the disadvantaged can be solved only with great difficulty, as Sewell notes in

DAVID O. SEWELL

this report originally prepared for the United States Department of Labor. Nevertheless, much can be gained from studying the cost-effectiveness of such programs according to Sewell, provided that indirect nonmonetary and external dimensions to benefits and cost are ultimately recognized.

Many hopes have been placed on investment in education as a strategy in the War on Poverty, and actual expenditures have reflected this emphasis. "Indirect" objectives have provided some of the rationale for educational programs: the belief that education fosters a more informed citizenry, reduces juvenile delinquency, and so forth. A more direct and probably more important objective has been that of raising the productivity and hence incomes of the currently poor.

Reprinted from David O. Sewell, "A Critique of Cost-Benefit Analyses of Training," *Monthly Labor Review* 90 (September 1967), pp. 45–51, Washington, D.C., with permission of the author.

The reader is also referred to two subsequent publications by the author, which contain slightly different views from those expressed in this article. See David Sewell, "Discussion" in Cost-Benefit Analysis of Manpower Policies: Proceedings of a North American Conference, ed. by G. G. Somers and W. D. Wood (Kingston, Ontario: Industrial Relations Centre, Queen's University, 1970), pp. 160–69; and *Training the Poor: A Benefit-Cost Analysis of Manpower Programs in the U.S. Antipoverty Program* (Kingston, Ontario: Industrial Relations Centre, Queen's University, 1971), 154 pp.

Independently conducted surveys of the cost-effectiveness of programs of the type incorporated in the War on Poverty are now beginning to appear. Contrary to expectations, there is little in these evaluations to justify optimism about the value of educational expenditures in general in ameliorating poverty and its related conditions. However, expenditures on vocational training are thought to constitute an exception to the general rule. Thus Ribich, after examining the "pay-off rates" of various educational measures and the related questions as to whether these are sufficient to justify a considerable emphasis on education in the poverty program, concludes that:

> Vocationally oriented training, at least in the form of recent manpower training programs, exhibits a higher rate of payoff than does general education. The rates are sufficiently in excess of those computed for improvements in general education that it is difficult to dismiss this result as an accident due entirely to the particular estimating techniques used ... With the exception of the job training programs, benefit-cost ratios were found to be generally less than unity. And, as suggested ... [by Ribich's earlier analysis] ... unweighted benefit-cost ratios would have to be something in excess of unity before it can be argued that education is clearly superior to transfers or other forms of direct help.[1]

Similarly, the Institute for Defense Analyses, in its report on federal poverty programs, asserts that:

> It appears that education and training programs, except for older workers, are quite promising for alleviating poverty ... the private returns to retrained workers are apparently substantial ... [and] training programs are a relatively inexpensive way to raise the incomes of lower income families.[2]

These generalizations are in turn based on three published benefit-cost analyses of training schemes, conducted in the States of Connecticut, Massachusetts, and West Virginia, and administered under the Manpower Development and Training Act (MDTA) of 1962, the Area Redevelopment Act (ARA) of 1961 (whose training provisions were later amalgamated into MDTA), or earlier state equivalents of such federal legislation. These schemes were all of a "neighborhood" nature, training workers in or close to the locality in which they lived, and all antedated the official War on Poverty.

It is immediately apparent that one cannot transfer the benefit-cost findings for the programs analyzed to some of the training schemes subsequently created in the War on Poverty. In the Job Corps, for instance, the

---

[1] Thomas I. Ribich, *Education and Poverty*, to be published by The Brookings Institution, Washington, D.C.

[2] *Federal Poverty Programs—Assessment and Recommendations*, Report R–116 (Arlington, Va., Institute for Defense Analyses, 1966).

clientele is much more youthful, is trained away from its home environment, and is provided with services in addition to training. And, correctly, reservations are usually expressed concerning the applicability of the earlier benefit-cost results to such vastly different training programs.

The point to be made here is rather more specific. Neighborhood training programs administered under MDTA or of a type similar to MDTA are an integral part of the War on Poverty. But the writer believes that it is totally incorrect to generalize from the training schemes mentioned above for which benefit-cost analyses have been performed to these training schemes dealing with the target population of the War on Poverty. Subsequent sections of this paper will document this hypothesis, and will also examine other more technical shortcomings of the published studies considered as benefit-cost analyses of training programs.

Alternative Incomes

An examination of data as to what trainees in the various schemes could have earned in the absence of training raises doubts as to whether they could be considered to be "poor." With regard to the Connecticut training programs, for instance, Borus estimates that the pretraining income of men in his sample was $2,626.[3] The crucial fact that must be taken into account, however, is that each man had only to support slightly over one extra person in addition to himself. Now, the more sophisticated calculations of the number of people in poverty in the United States, such as those of Mollie Orshansky, use a sliding scale relating family income to family size. If Orshansky's criteria as to what constitutes poverty are used, the Connecticut sample was far from being in the poverty group: an income of less than $2,050 is necessary to classify a nonfarm family of two (both under age 65) as being poor.[4]

Concerning the persons who entered the Massachusetts retraining

[3] Michael E. Borus, *The Economic Effectiveness of Retraining the Unemployed*, Research Report to the Federal Reserve Bank of Boston, No. 35 (Boston, Mass., The Federal Reserve Bank of Boston, 1966). The income of the women in the sample of Borus is simply irrelevant to the matter under consideration. Indeed, for all practical purposes, we cannot draw any benefit-cost conclusions concerning the training of women for subsequent employment from his data. This is because ". . . probably less than 20 per cent of the women in the sample were primary wage earners," the rest being housewives living with their husbands, and widows and single girls living with their families. The sewing machine operators' course in which these women were enrolled was later terminated, one of the reasons for this action being that "it attracted many women who were interested not in employment but rather in the home uses of the course."

[4] Mollie Orshansky, "Counting the Poor: Another Look at the Poverty Profile," *Social Security Bulletin*, January 1965, pp. 3–29; excerpted in *Monthly Labor Review*, March 1965, pp. 300–309.

schemes, Page reports an average income of $2,847 "without retraining."[5] Lacking data as to the number of dependents per trainee, we cannot judge whether this group would be poor by Orshansky's criteria. But we do have some additional information which throws a light on their individual circumstances. The Massachusetts training schemes had a feature unique among all the programs for which benefit-cost analyses were performed, in that trainees were charged tuition. The average amount of tuition paid by each trainee was $567. The true "opportunity costs" of participating in the programs, or the total amount of money sacrificed by each worker in the course of training, was the somewhat higher figure of $784.[6] It seems unlikely that trainees who could spare this large an amount of real income could also be classified as being below a poverty level which is, after all, based on subsistence income requirements.

Classification of the "Poor"

Deciding whether trainees can be classified as "poor" on the basis of their pretraining incomes is, however, slightly hazardous. An excellent illustration of this fact can be taken from the study of Somers and Stromsdorfer. Although no income data whatsoever are given, it is noted that:

> Many [of the trainees] worked in high paying coal mining occupations for years before the period of unemployment which induced them to enroll for training. During the period of unemployment just prior to their training, on the other hand, the earnings (other than government payments) of these people were zero or close to zero.[7]

This information raises a very relevant question. Should we consider a person as being poor if his income this year is under our poverty line, even though his income for many past years has annually exceeded this figure and may well exceed it again in the future? The obvious answer is no. It is clear that our primary concern is with those whose average annual "normal," "permanent," or "lifetime" incomes are below the annual income level we have selected as demarcating the poverty group. Clearly, income in any one

---

[5] David A. Page, "Retraining Under the Manpower Development Act: A Cost-Benefit Analysis," *Public Policy*, 1964.

[6] Ribich estimates the sum of what the average Massachusetts trainee could have earned during training plus tuition as being $2,361. Page's data reveals that the average retraining allowance was $1,577. Thus the true opportunity cost of retraining to the trainee was $2,361 minus $1,577, or $784.

[7] Gerald G. Somers and Ernst W. Stromsdorfer, *A Benefit-Cost Analysis of Manpower Retraining*, The University of Wisconsin Industrial Relations Research Institute Reprint Series, No. 64 (reprinted from the Proceedings of the Seventeenth Annual Meeting, Industrial Relations Research Association, 1964).

year can be a misleading indicator as to the numbers and composition of that part of the total population which is in this category.[8] We shall see, however, that there are other good reasons why the majority of trainees in the schemes for which benefit-cost analyses were performed cannot be classified as being poor in a permanent income sense.

Other Characteristics of Participants

When we turn to characteristics of the trainees other than income we perceive immediately that these groups are hardly typical of the poor. Some of the analysts compare the composition of trainees in their programs with that of the unemployed, or otherwise infer that the unemployed was the target group of the program they studied. Perhaps all that needs to be stressed here is that the populations of the poor and of the unemployed are not the same. But it will also be shown that, insofar as evidence concerning the composition of trainees in the programs is available, this composition was highly unrepresentative of the overall population of the unemployed.

One of the conclusions reached by Borus is that:

> The older, less educated, or long-time unemployed worker would, on the average, have a lower probability of utilizing and benefiting from the retraining than would other workers who entered the course.[9]

We can also suspect, from results in the Somers and Stromsdorfer study, that the returns to training women in general are low. Yet when Borus compares the characteristics of workers in his sample (all of whom qualified for training) with those of the unemployed labor force in Connecticut, we find that these

[8] There are other more technical reasons why income in any one year is an inadequate indicator of the population which is poor in a permanent income sense. According to the Institute for Defense Analyses, income data for any given year lead to an overestimate of numbers in this group because "In income classes below the average for all families, in any given year the number of families whose incomes are below normal for them exceeds the number with incomes above their normal level. In the following year, many of the families whose incomes were temporarily below a certain level, say $3,000 per year, will be closer to their normal income level and above $3,000 . . . The average normal income level of families whose income in any given year is $3,000 tends to be greater, perhaps $3,250."

[9] Michael E. Borus, "A Benefit-Cost Analysis of the Economic Effectiveness of Retraining the Unemployed," *Yale Economic Essays*, Fall 1964, pp. 371–430. As Borus points out, a number of labor force characteristics, such as education, marital status, labor force attachment, and number of dependents are highly correlated with the age of trainees. Thus the fact that the average age of the men in his sample was more than 15 years below that of the male civilian labor force has great significance, since the sample is automatically unrepresentative of the latter populations when these secondary or independent variables are considered. Thus, because the average age of the male sample was low, average educational attainment was significantly higher than the respective figures for the unemployed male labor force and the male labor force in general.

are precisely the groups that are underrepresented in the sample.[10] More-over, a good question arises as to why the sample is even being compared with the unemployed labor force in that State, since

> approximately one-third of the workers were either employed (mainly the men) or not in the labor force (mainly the women) at the time they took the aptitude test for retraining.

The last phrase in the quotation conveys the key to the whole question of representation in the training programs for which the benefit-cost analyses were performed. The accent should be on the fact that not all applicants for the training schemes were successful. As Borus remarks about the Connecticut training schemes, "the aptitude requirements appear to have been very important in determining eligibility for the courses." The rejection rate for these Connecticut courses varied from a low of 17 per cent to a high of 64 per cent. In the West Virginia training schemes surveyed by Somers and Stromsdorfer, "rejects" (presumably those who failed similar tests) amounted to the lesser proportion of 14 per cent of all applicants surveyed. No direct information is given regarding the selection procedures in the Massachusetts training programs analyzed by Page, but the inference is that they did not differ qualitatively from those employed in the other schemes surveyed, or those that were to be employed later in the first years of MDTA.[11]

Selection In versus Selection Out

Statistics compiled on the national level for characteristics of trainees in the early years of MDTA reveal the skewed distributions which can result from the use of such fairly stringent selection criteria. The significance of the selection tests is, of course, that the individuals who were least able or least amenable to training were thereby culled out of the training process. To use a simile frequently encountered in discussion of MDTA, the trainees represented the "cream" of the human material available for training. It is the contention of this paper that the experience of the great majority of the trainees in the early years of MDTA and, in particular, in the programs for which benefit-cost analyses have been performed is therefore of minor interest to the poverty program. They represent the group who might be expected to rise out of a temporary situation of having low incomes without

[10] Borus, *The Economic Effectiveness of Retraining the Unemployed*, op. cit.

[11] Thus in the conclusion to his paper, Page says that, "On the national scale similar results [to those in the Massachusetts training programs] may be expected from the MDA program, provided its administrators determine what jobs are reasonably certain to be available, and then select individuals for retraining who are unemployed or underemployed, and are willing, and *potentially well qualified*, to hold these positions." (Emphasis added.)

the aid of subsidized training. The selection criteria, on the other hand, excluded precisely those who might be expected to be "permanently" poor.

Something similar to the mechanism suggested in the last paragraph could easily have operated in the last few years. This has been a period of high aggregate demand and decreasing overall unemployment, and the type of unemployed person who was selected for the early MDTA programs could have been the major beneficiary of these trends.

Allocation of Training Slots

In the same period, however, high unemployment rates have persisted among certain groups of workers. The intention of the 1963 and 1966 amendments to MDTA and the guidelines for MDTA in fiscal 1967 has been to bring these groups into the program on a larger scale, without sacrificing the efficiency objective of the elimination of "skill shortages." Thus, the guidelines for 1967 stipulate that 65 per cent of all training slots are to be allocated to the "disadvantaged": among others, youths, nonwhite workers and other minority groups, persons with low academic achievement, the long-term unemployed, the rural poor, and older workers.[12]

The emphasis on training for the rural poor in this guideline is note-worthy. MDTA and the poverty program have recently been attacked in many quarters for their excessive concentration on urban problems. This urban bias also happens to be typical of all of the programs for which benefit-cost analyses were performed, with the possible exception of those studied by Somers and Stromsdorfer.

The gradual redirection of MDTA and the creation of similar training programs in the War on Poverty has meanwhile led other commentators to stress that "at present, very little is known about the effectiveness of these programs in raising the earnings of the groups they serve."[13] It should be noted that one of the writers subscribing to this viewpoint is Somers, a coauthor of one of the earlier cost-benefit analyses of training programs.[14] The tendency to describe the clientele of these programs as "the disad-vantaged" or the "specially disadvantaged" should also be noted. Whether

---

[12] The other 35 per cent of the training slots are to be allocated so as to meet the problem of emerging skill shortages, but again with the proviso that "These national goals have been developed in recognition of the fact that some of the disadvantaged may be suitable for training in skill shortage occupations. It is desirable to prepare disadvantaged workers for jobs in these occupations insofar as it is feasible to do so." Both this quotation and that in the text are from *Manpower Administration Notice No. 3–66*, Office of the Manpower Administrator, U.S. Department of Labor, April 1966.

[13] Worth Bateman, "An Application of Cost-Benefit Analysis to the Work-Experience Program," *American Economic Review* (May 1967), p. 81.

[14] Glen Cain and Gerald G. Somers, *Retraining the Disadvantaged Worker* (Madison, Wis., University of Wisconsin, 1966).

these are anything but euphemisms for describing that group which in a permanent income sense one could describe as *the* poor will be left to the reader to decide.

Techniques Used in Past Analyses

To some extent the published benefit-cost analyses may be viewed as a reaction to the information then (and now, predominantly) issued by interested agencies to illustrate the benefits of training. The latter generally consists of data illustrating the improvement in the employment record of trainees by a comparison between their pretraining status and their post-training status.

There are two predominant reasons why such calculations are considered unsatisfactory. In the first place, employment, while important, may not be *the* most important aspect of the trainee's experience which we are interested in examining. Any gain in income may be as important to the individual, and from the social point of view it is of interest to discover what contribution training programs can make to the objective of increasing national income. Another advantage of measuring the gain from training in terms of income is that we can then compare both gains and costs through the medium of the common *numeraire* of money.

The various analysts' choice of the income of participants as being the most important variable to be considered in benefit-cost evaluation of training schemes is thus not unreasonable. However, it should be noted that neither improvements in income nor employment exhaust the possible benefits that might result from these programs.

Before and After

The second objection to the usual method of estimating the gains from training is due to the before training/after training nature of the comparisons. Now, if we wish to isolate the gains from training, what we really want to know is how the participants in the training schemes fared after they had completed training compared with how they would have fared had they not undergone training. Before and after comparisons of the records of trainees may not satisfy this criterion, because cyclical conditions can change from the pretraining to the posttraining period, affecting the individual's economic prospects irrespective of whether he receives training or not.

While differences abound between the various studies in the particular techniques used to solve this second problem, most of the analysts made use of "control groups" with similar characteristics to those of the trainees.

Regression analysis was generally employed to allow for the effects of any remaining dissimilarities between the control group and the trainees. The income records of the trainees for a period of at least a year following training were next compared with those of the members of the control group, any differences being assumed attributable to the effects of training. Assumptions were then made as to the time period over which gains to training were assumed to persist, and any gains to training revealed by the short-run analysis were accordingly extrapolated into the future. The "present value" of all gains to training was then calculated by applying a discount rate to all benefits to training assumed to occur in future years. The final step was the comparison of the present value figure for benefits with that for the cost of training.

The Three Parties to Training

Costs and benefits to training were computed for three different parties in past studies: the individual trainees, society as whole, and the government. The calculations for the first two groups resemble those generally employed in both earlier and later empirical research on the returns to investment in education. Thus it is clear that if training results in a higher income, then benefits to the individual should be calculated net of any increases in taxes or decreases in transfer payments accompanying this higher income. Costs to the individual are "opportunity costs": the income that would otherwise accrue during the training period minus any wage or transfer payment allocated for participation, plus any excess personal expenses (such as transport costs) directly attributable to engaging in training.

The social calculation reflects our interest in training programs as measures designed to increase national output. The measurements of how far training satisfies this "efficiency" or "allocative" objective are a little more complex. There is wide agreement on one issue: that the benefits to society should include any increases in taxes paid as a result of training augmenting earning capacity. In other words, the gains from training to society are the total gains in real output. On the cost side, some differences exist in the treatment of subsidies or other transfer payments to trainees. The decision of Borus and Ribich to exclude such payments is surely correct, since they do not involve real costs to society.

Who Benefits from Training?

The reasoning in the various studies as to the parties who benefited from training carries certain implications for the social benefit-cost calculations which were apparently not realized by all authors of previous analyses.

Thus Borus views those who benefited from training as being the workers who used their training in subsequent employment. Page regards the "products" of the training programs he studied as being the workers who completed the courses and proceeded to use the training they had received in subsequent employment. Somers and Stromsdorfer are the only analysts who do not feel that employment in a training-related field is the criterion of whether workers benefited from training. Their argument is that:

> Even when they were not hired in occupations for which they were trained, the training may have had a crucial influence on the trainees' future employment success. They gained some versatility, and many employers preferred them because these workers had demonstrated sufficient ambition and sense of discipline to enter and complete a training course.

But it should be noted that Somers and Stromsdorfer still view the "product" of their programs as being the number of people who *graduated* from the programs.

These formulations of the benefits from training affect cost calculations for the programs. For, if we view the products of training programs as being the workers who use their training, the number of graduates or even more restrictively the number of graduates who proceed to use their training, consistency requires that we should also calculate costs on this basis. This is not, however, the procedure followed in the Somers and Stromsdorfer study, where costs are computed on a "per enrollee" basis.

Regarding the "object" of training schemes as being the production of graduates or workers who proceed to use their training could have some side-effects which may or may not be regarded as desirable. For instance, if the costs of processing and partially training dropouts are charged up as a cost of producing graduates, much more attention might be paid by project sponsors to ensuring that few potential dropouts enter the training schemes. This could be done by greater selectivity in recruitment. Such a procedure might be regarded, from one point of view, as being desirable. On the other hand, one feels that the adoption of this type of procedure would severely militate against the usefulness of MDTA schemes in helping the disadvantaged. As has already been demonstrated, this is precisely the group which is likely to be excluded from training programs if stringent selection criteria are used.

But have the authors of the various benefit-cost analyses reasoned correctly as to the minimum conditions which have to be fulfilled before it can be shown that retraining benefits a worker? In two of the studies, the trouble may simply arise from a variant of what Keats has called "the sheepskin psychosis": in this case the idea that the "product" of the training schemes is, at the lowest common denominator, the enrollee who completes training.

Now, the principal aim of training in an antipoverty context must be to raise the incomes of participants in the schemes by raising individual capabilities for self-support. The reasoning of Somers and Stromsdorfer—that a graduate may derive benefits from the training process even if he does not proceed to work in a training-related occupation—is persuasive. But there is no reason to stop here. It is obvious that some benefit might be derived from a course even though it is not formally completed. If, for instance, a trainee completes 14 weeks of an 18 week course and then obtains a job with another employer in which he proceeds to use the skill he was taught in the course, one implication we might draw is that the length of time required to complete training was originally overestimated. In such a case, we would surely credit the training scheme with an individual "success," even though formal completion requirements were not strictly adhered to.

Nor can a trainee who remained for a considerable length of time in a course and then obtained a job in which he made no use of the particular skills taught be automatically counted a "failure." For instance, the MITCE project [the project which is the subject of this proposal-Editor] lays considerable emphasis on accustoming its predominantly rural clients to the discipline and personal habits involved in successfully holding down a job in the nonagricultural sector of the economy. It could well be that some of these characteristics rub off onto MITCE trainees who fail to complete courses, and are subsequently of use to them in obtaining employment.

Effects on Output and Employment

A large thorn in all benefit-cost calculations—individual, social and governmental—is the type of assumption to be made about conditions in the job market in which training takes place. In making his calculations of the social gains from training, Borus does not subtract the income earned by the control group from the earnings of trainees as do, for instance, Somers and Stromsdorfer. The reasoning of Borus is based on two assumptions: that the jobs filled by trainees were in "skill-shortage" occupations and would otherwise not have been filled, and that the trainees were either previously unemployed or had jobs in which they could easily be replaced by previously unemployed workers. If these assumptions are correct, the whole of the income of the trainees in their new jobs represented a net gain to society.

The procedure of subtracting control group income from trainee income employed by Somers and Stromsdorfer and implicit in Page's study, however, only suggests that the gains from training to society are the sum of the gains in income to individual trainees from working more often and possibly at higher rates of pay after training.

Vacuum Effects

Neither of these assumptions could be described as polar. In another recent paper of which Borus is a coauthor,[15] it is pointed out that the social gains to training could be greater than the entire income of the trainee, if filling a skill-shortage job creates complementary demands for labor and hence raises the income of other workers. The process whereby other members of the labor force are "sucked" into jobs vacated by the trainees or complementary to those newly occupied by the trainees is described as a "vacuum effect." On the other hand, both Page and Somers and Stromsdorfer discuss in their papers the possibility that "trained" workers could simply be absorbing jobs which might otherwise go to unskilled workers.

Similar issues obviously also affect the benefit-cost calculations for the government and, less obviously, for the individual.[16] While the importance of such effects is evident, it is also clear that the weight to be attached to them cannot be decided a priori, but will vary with the individual project and conditions in the local job market.

Questions about how long the gains to training are likely to persist have also raised complications in past analyses. Some of these difficulties are directly attributable to the assumption of Borus and Page that the gains to training are linked to subsequent employment in training-related occupations. If, as has already been suggested, this criterion of the gains to training is too narrow and should be abandoned, then these associated difficulties also disappear. In any case, since the benefits provided are thought to mean the difference between the "employability" and "unemployability" of trainees in the nonrural sector of the economy, it seems entirely reasonable to calculate the gains from training on a lifetime basis.

Nonmonetary Benefits

Those who have viewed the process of education as "investment in human capital" and have sought to obtain estimates of the returns to this investment often have been accused of failing to measure a whole gamut of nonmonetary benefits deriving from education. This category of effects includes possible

[15] Einar Hardin and Michael E. Borus, "An Economic Evaluation of the Retraining Program in Michigan: Methodological Problems of Research," to be included in the forthcoming *1966 Proceedings of the American Statistical Association, Business and Economic Statistics Section.*

[16] Borus provides us with an illustration of the latter point in his analysis, when in calculating the benefits of training to the individual he allows for the possibility that nontrainees in his sample subsequently entered jobs which used skills taught in the training courses.

benefits to the individual such as increased psychic satisfaction, and possible benefits to society such as having a better educated electorate. Those benefit-cost analysts who have evaluated training schemes have continued in the supposed tradition of other empirical investigators of the returns to education: they pay lip-service to the presence of such "indirect" benefits, but do not attempt to measure them.

It should not be thought that these indirect effects have been ignored in the literature on human capital.[17] It is even a mistake to suggest that these factors are usually not treated in benefit-cost terms because a dollar sign cannot always be attached to their value: this underestimates the ingenuity of researchers in the field.[18] It is nevertheless true that more subjective measures would have to be employed in the evaluation of some of these benefits.

However, there is less need to be defensive about the failure to measure these effects in benefit-cost analyses of antipoverty training schemes, for two reasons. In the first place, many of the effects outlined above are thought to be particular advantages flowing from a general education rather than from vocational training.

Secondly, the context in which the programs are being conducted should be remembered. As Ribich says,

> The aim of the war [on poverty], after all, is essentially an economic one, and it is directed against a particular enemy—low incomes. Education, as well as other antipoverty tactics, may have a good many economic and noneconomic byproducts; but the matter of relative efficiency in raising the incomes of the poor would seem to be overshadowing.

These arguments constitute sufficient reasons, in our opinion, for concentrating on the monetary effects of training.

[17] See, for instance, Burton Weisbrod, *External Benefits of Public Education: An Economic Analysis* (Princeton, N.J., Princeton University, Industrial Relations Section, 1964).
[18] In this connection, Ribich's analysis of the effects of education on delinquency struck the writer as being especially noteworthy.

Manpower
and Educational
Planning

Investments in education and other forms of manpower development do not pertain to a timeless state or society. One of the basic features differentiating human from physical capital is the relatively longer lead-time requirements which the former demands. For this reason, and also because much of the formation of human capital is the responsibility of the public sector, manpower and educational planning takes on new significance. Advance planning and anticipation of economic and social change are prerequisite to fruitful investments in human capital for a nation, just as they are for corporations developing long-run plans. The national manpower and educational planning task, however, is complicated by the multiple objectives that prevail in this area. Mixed public and private decision making is inherent to manpower planning which is subject to human resource behavior. Moreover, estimation of the levels and stages of economic growth is also required where growth itself is a hypothesized function of human capital formation in the future.

The authors of the contributions that follow direct their attention to a broad range of related manpower and educational planning issues and problems in both developed and developing nations. Mary Jean Bowman **30** presents an overview of planning needs and techniques. Her study is followed by Gottfried Bombach's discussion **31** of manpower planning in developed nations. One of the key questions facing the developing nations is the optional amount of investment in education—an issue faced by Anthony Bottomley **32**. The concluding selection by Mark Blaug is a comparison of alternative approaches to educational planning **33**.

30

Perspectives on Education and Development

The rising popularity of analysis of human resources in relation to economic development must be handled carefully to avoid what Mary Jean Bowman of the University of Chicago terms a "manpower planning theology." Even though literacy increases appear to bear a historical relationship to patterns of development, Bowman notes that the "residual" approach can overexplain economic growth. Traditional rate-of-return studies serve many important purposes if used properly, and analyses of costs and benefits may be applied in an incentive and behavioral sense with validity. Manpower and educational planning, as currently practiced, tends to be a rigid technical bookkeeping process which too frequently fails to recognize the complementarity and substitution characteristics of human capital.

MARY JEAN BOWMAN

At no time since the mercantilists, with their emphasis on the importance of "art and ingenuity," has human resource development occupied so important a place in the main stream of economic thought as it does today. And never, I suspect, have so many battles raged concerning methods and interpretations in both research and planning practice. Meanwhile, we are at a stage when progress in understanding is almost unavoidably accompanied by the multiplication of confusion and of respectable but dangerous fallacy. Much of this multiplication, both positive and negative, emerges at the points at which researcher, policy maker and planning technician should converge.

Reprinted from Mary Jean Bowman, "Perspectives on Education and Development," *International Development Review* 6 (September 1964), pp. 3–7, with the permission of the author and publisher.

I am starting from the research end. What do we know that is so, what do we "know" that is *not* so, and how do we know these things? Planning practice starts with one or another set of assumed answers to many of the most critical questions. And what planners do, if it has any impact, in turn conditions the relationships the researcher is studying.

Given the vast scope of my topic and the recent proliferation of writing and talking about it, I shall have to be highly selective and unjustifiably dogmatic. In fact, I shall be deliberately dogmatic on some of the most disputed issues. Incidentally, I shall be particularly summary in disregarding the great diversity of subjects which are sometimes included under the label "manpower planning." My remarks will be organized under three main headings.

Education and National Income

I start on this one by making a set of assertions: In cross-country comparisons, both for all countries and for subsets classified by energy resources, Anderson and I found that per capita incomes in the 1930's explained enrollment rates in the 1950's much better than enrollment rates of the 1930's explained income in the 1950's. As of the 1950's, no country with less than a 40% adult literacy rate had a measured per capita income in excess of $200 with one exception, in which oil dominated the picture. Below 40% literacy, there was almost no education-income correlation. This suggests a minimum threshold educational diffusion level at about 40% as a precondition of development.

It is *not* true that the countries that first industrialized took off with literacy confined to a small minority. Anderson has accumulated evidence indicating male literacy rates of over 40% in England and France before the beginning stages of the factory system. In Russia at the end of the 19th century, education was lagging. Nevertheless, two thirds or more of the urban males were literates and, taking males and females together, urban literacy exceeded 40%.

It is not true that literacy is of relatively minor importance for agricultural progress. Moreover, progress in agriculture is a *sine qua non* for substantial, sustained growth. On this, I refer you to the new book by T. W. Schultz on *Transforming Traditional Agriculture*, which I consider a remarkable little work, outclassing his book and articles on education.

Though the 40% adult literacy I have reiterated may be a necessary condition for development, it is not a sufficient condition—and neither are higher levels of schooling. Even in the 1950's, there were a few Asian countries with over 40% literacy but incomes under $200. It is probable that in the 1960's and 1970's, there will be such low income countries with adult literacy as high as 60%, for the worldwide education drive is putting schooling out in front of other development efforts and strategies in many countries of the eastern hemisphere.

It is probably true that emergence today requires a higher level of schooling for more people than in earlier periods—even when we correct for the fact that generalizations to this effect typically make tacit assumptions of a much more rapid pace of change. The reasons for the higher schooling requirements are various, but I would note especially the importance of the transformation of communication systems and of the levels of education among the peoples of other countries with which the newly emergent must compete and interact. The necessary minima are higher, but they are not at 80 or 90% adult literacy. The extreme Addis Ababa and Karachi plans of priorities for universal primary education have no economic justification.

Most readers of this journal are probably familiar, at least to some extent, with the so-called "residual" and the efforts by Schultz and Denison to measure education's contributions to national income growth in the United States. The "residual" in this context is the part of national income growth that remains unexplained in econometric studies of aggregate inputs of labor and of physical capital as conventionally measured. Such work has come up with residuals in several European countries as well as in the United States running to over half of total income growth.

Though Schultz and Denison used quite different methods and were interested in different sets of problems, they converged in approximating what I have termed elsewhere a base-year rental-value measure of contributions of education to growth. This amounts to assuming that the income differential associated with a given differential in education in the base-year (after certain base-year adjustments for ability, parental status, etc.) will measure what the same level of education embodied in a member of the labor force will contribute to national product in other years. More technically, this is a constant marginal returns assumption. On this basis, Denison estimated for the period 1929–1957 increases in education per worker accounted for 23% of national income growth; this was about two fifths of the residual.

It is important to remind ourselves, when considering such estimates, that they do not in fact test anything about relations between inputs and outputs. Over the period 1929–1957 in the United States, the estimates have a very reasonable look. National income rose substantially and the estimates credited education with an important part of the increase but still left a plausible amount to be explained by unmeasured improvements in organization and in the quality of physical capital. These changes all worked together. But, things do not necessarily come out so neatly.

To take an extreme example, though results are very satisfactory for Russia since 1950, over the period from the middle 1920's to 1940 growth in per capita income is already over-explained by conventional inputs even without counting the substantial increases in per capita education at all. The Schultz-Denison type of treatment of education applied to this period in Russia would "explain" still more of what did *not* happen.

There is plenty of reason to expect equally nonsensical results if we apply such models over the coming decade or so in many developing countries—especially when initial education-related income differentials are large. Indeed, we are already seeing the evidence in the growing problems of urban unemployment in those countries.

Schultz and Denison do not generalize from their empirical findings for the United States. So to generalize is quite irresponsible. Nevertheless, their findings are being misapplied around the world—and sometimes by men of high levels of supposed expertise, certified under the wing of international agencies, as well as in the utterances of small politicos. The fact that what education can do depends upon other, complementary developments (as well as vice versa) is conveniently but unjustifiably ignored.

Generalization of education as a panacea can be dangerous demagoguery. It leads to wastes in the allocation of scarce resources that may impede not only economic development but even, in the longer view, the diffusion of education itself. It leads to faulty diagnoses of reasons for failures and erroneous prescriptions for their cure. Irresponsibility and organized violence among youth is aggravated by frustrations that follow upon exaggerated notions of what schools can do. Paradoxically, perhaps, the over-selling of education as an investment can aggravate the problem of discrepancies between private and social economic returns to schooling, supporting the persistence and even the expansion of socially diseconomic sinecures. Equally serious, in my judgment, is the fact that the other things education can do for individuals and societies tend to recede almost into invisibility, no matter how much we may pay them lip service.

Private Cost-Benefit Comparisons

A great cloud of smoke has been generated by the arguments over one versus another approach to planning and the associated attacks on "marginalism," "opportunity costs" and "the rate-of-return approach." There is a little real fire, to be sure, but it is not at all commensurate with the smoke. Moreover, with all this smoke in our eyes, we no longer see the important potentials in use of private cost-benefit comparisons as instruments of behavioral analysis and hypothesis-testing, quite aside from their potentials as social-accounting first approximations.

The main arguments are not Russian versus American. In fact the earliest application of this family of analytical models was probably Strumilin's 1924 studies in Leningrad—which he revised and republished in 1960. The first comparable approach was that of Ray Walsh in the United States in the early 1930's, and recent refinements of the method and extensions of its theory and applications have been in the United States.

All of these studies, old and new, have in common the use of earned income differences associated with differences in schooling as a basis for deriving estimates of both private and societal returns or benefits. All take into account the entire life-income stream and compare alternative life-income streams. All include forgone student incomes as a cost, though in some cases this is made explicit whereas in others it slips in under other labels.

The most important Russian-American difference is in treatment of the age-experience component of incomes, and this is where the "rate-of-return approach" gets it label and its Western coloration. Strumilin handled age and experience by a statistical standardization procedure and then compared age standardized differentials in life-income totals without discounting. The American work incorporates the interest concept as the means by which income streams with different time sequence patterns may be compared. Recent studies compute the "internal rate of return" that would equate the costs and returns associated with a given increment (and type) of education. These rates provide a simple way of comparing alternative investments.

The value of rate-of-return models for behavioral analysis of economic processes depends upon the extent to which markets are the mechanism through which an economy is coordinated. But their usefulness in such economies does *not* depend upon the existence of pure competition or upon allocative neutrality in government monetary and fiscal policies, or upon the extent of participation by government in direct production, or even on the non-existence of materials and manpower drafting.

So long as large market-coordinated sectors remain, the investment theory and rate-of-return studies of education and their kin can serve many purposes. They help explain income distribution patterns, they contribute to a much sharper analysis of the various economic versus other elements in demands for schooling and the incidence of drop-outs, they point to inefficiencies and distortions in the allocations of resources to schooling and in the functioning of markets for utilization of human skills. And, they open up important routes into the study of the economics of on-the-job training and learning and the roles of enterprise (both private and public) in human resource development.

In itself any particular empirical rate-of-return estimate is of course derived from a cross-section of education-income-age associations in a particular time and place. As such, these are not econometric analyses of growth. However, multiplication of such studies in time sequence in a particular country and in different countries can begin to give them growth dimensions. Demonstrations of their feasibility and some of what they can reveal for less developed countries have begun—notably for Mexico and India. Others will certainly follow.

One of the most evident and important of the contributions of rate-of-return study in a growth context is in the tracing and interpretation of various sequences in distributions of incomes and of private cost-benefit relationships as these may both condition and reflect self-investments and investments by enterprises in human resource development.

Dropping the precision, real or illusory, of rate-of-return computations and yet retaining the basic investment theory that underlies them, it is possible to extend cost-benefit assessments to incorporate a wide range of past and potential future work on opportunity perceptions and incentives as they shape and are shaped by development. Such work can be of vital importance in the advance of our understanding of the roles of education in growth. With a few important exceptions, the work in this area has suffered from interdisciplinary myopia.

Equally important is the freeing of research from the blinders too often imposed by unquestioned acceptance of particular institutional constraints. A cost-benefit approach to analysis of the history of apprenticeship in England and its metamorphosis, or to the roles of government and private enterprise in human resource development in Meiji (and modern) Japan could provide most illuminating insights. So could an incentive and response analysis of the history of development and utilization of qualified manpower in Soviet Russia, though the structuring and components of the incentive systems are different in many ways.

Complementarities and Substitutabilities

Notions about substitutabilities and complementarities permeate much of the work of both academic researchers and planning practitioners dealing with education and manpower. This is inevitable, for whether the assumptions are explicit or merely implicit they are often of key importance to understanding what and how educational endeavor, of what kinds, may contribute to growth. It is helpful to distinguish two sets of production functions:

1. Those that define the ranges of substitution and complementarity in the formation of human competencies.
2. Those that characterize actual and potential combinations of human resources with each other and with other factors in production.

Economists and many upper echelon educators would do well to pay greater heed to sociological research as it is contributing evidence concerning technical substitutabilities and complementarities in human resource development. For example:

1. The products of schools are in fact products of joint inputs of digging sticks or tractors, sanitation or hookworm, radios, advertisers, books and black magic. Strategies developed in disregard of what exists and might be done outside school doors are disregarding important complementarities and are not likely to be the most efficient. This is not just a matter of curriculum adaptation. Our ignorance is great here, but there is also much unused knowledge.

2. Substitutabilities between vocational training on the job and in school are not as extensive as is often assumed. This is the source of many fallacious educational recommendations. Schools are well adapted to prepare men to be able to learn on the job, but these two kinds and loci of learning are more often complements than substitutes.

3. Motivations and opportunity perceptions are important parameters of learning in addition to their significance with respect to school continuation rates and choices among types of schooling. Moreover, these perceptions are usually more rational than the pronouncements of so-called experts might suggest.

4. Development of innovative behavior is a function of entire systems of opportunity and career patterns and of participation in innovative endeavor. This goes beyond the usual conception of input-output relations to other dimensions of complementarities and to negative as well as positive inputs into human development. Schools that demonstrate innovative behavior are rare indeed.

5. As Kenneth Arrow argued in his "Learning by Doing," human resource development is a function of the stimulus of continuously changing technologies, and these are associated in turn with gross rates of investment in physical capital.

Whereas planners tend to ignore significant complementarities among inputs into human resource development and to see others upside down, the biases in manpower planning all tend toward disregard of potential substitutabilities in the utilization of skills and other factors in production. This can be amply documented from manpower planning experience. It has a number of unfortunate consequences. Briefly:

1. There is circularity in identification of manpower requirements to start with. John Vaizey developed this theme in one of his papers for an ILO conference of experts last year, and it has been often recognized, but as generally ignored in practice. Empirical evidence amply demonstrates the wide range of alternatives in resource combinations among societies and over a period of time.

2. When manpower assessments are attempted in any detail, and are taken seriously, they are very likely to lead to waste in over-training and in

training that is in fact inappropriate in the light of limited resources and forgone opportunities.

3. Manpower planning creates and aggravates dysfunctional inflexibilities associated with the diploma mentality and certification for entry to various kinds of job and career channels. Here, again, a perverted conception of "standards" is involved. The idea of standards is relative and of standard raising as a process in socio-economic progress dies at birth.

4. Detailed manpower plans, if taken seriously, ramify into detailed controls that discourage innovative and adaptive behavior.

5. The fixed factor proportion approach in manpower planning is part of the rigidifying view of school systems and certifications that blocks experimentation and innovation in institutional arrangements for human resource development and in efforts within existing agencies and institutions. Partly this problem is associated with the pre-occupation with schools as *the* agencies for human resource development. But it is a matter also of arrangements that encourage or discourage creative endeavors in which students and faculty participate to overcome obstacles and solve problems. The early history of American land-grant institutions demonstrates some advantages of poverty.

6. These same rigidifying assumptions (if acted upon in practice) will mean a failure to mobilize available human and other resources for education itself. Fortunately, in practice the planning models (and the "standards") break down when pressures are too great; what makes a "teacher," for example, takes on relative dimensions in the dynamics of development through time and the bottlenecks are thereby broken in some degree. But the compromises reached in this way are considerably less than second-best solutions.

7. The large-scale errors that accompany rigidified large-scale planning tend to lead to wasteful cover-up actions to conceal the errors. This is politically almost inevitable.

Some Concluding Remarks

Having aired a number of judgments and prejudices with rather unaccustomed restraint, I shall conclude in the same vein, with two propositions that I would urge upon you. The first is a special, limited one— the case for public encouragement of what I have elsewhere termed "infant training industries." The second is more general, concerning search processes and the assessment of alternatives in a more analytical and creative approach to human resource development planning.

The most significant truth in the "technological dualism" thesis concerns gaps in development complementarities with respect to skills that are best acquired on the job. There can be a vicious circle problem in this. The costs of training an entire group discourage the establishment of the kinds of enterprise that would provide the learning opportunities to develop the labor force to attract the enterprise, and so forth. One alternative has been the international package transfer of entire operations, with their physical capital, directors, engineers, skilled and even semi-skilled operatives. The extent to which this has occurred historically is sometimes forgotten. Even England was helped at an early stage by importation of weavers from Flanders. Entire industries came into the United States with European migrants. Russia imported men along with equipment in the early iron works. Japan's package importations were dramatic and deliberate strategy for investment in the development of native know-how, initially at government expense. The case for one or another public program to protect and encourage training programs in industrial enterprises—and to foster establishment of such enterprises in developing countries—is a strong one provided the subsidized undertakings form the seed-bed for diffusion and multiplication of skills.

If "planning" means anything at all, it must entail some sort of selection among alternatives and logically this means some sort of social cost-benefit assessment. Otherwise what is called "planning" degenerates into mechanistic displays of technical virtuosity, at the one extreme, or of humdrum, automatic and very erroneous bookkeeping, at the other, along with "projections" that are neither accurate predictions nor plans. Attacks by some on rate-of-return estimates and opportunity costing as criteria of use in social decision making are perfectionist, on the one hand—defeatist, on the other. The tests by which these tools are pronounced inadequate could not be met by the methods used instead. Moreover, most of these criticisms take far too narrow a view of the opportunity cost concept and then throw out the whole apparatus of evaluation of alternatives just because simplistic reification is not justified.

Instead of attempting to measure what can be measured and then going on to weigh the other considerations, even the partial measures are discarded. Too often, the straight-jackets of technocratic manpower planning are donned instead. The very inelasticities that were called up to battle marginal analysis as inapplicable are argued as necessitating manpower planning in utter disregard of the fact that inelasticities virtually guarantee that unless the economy is stagnant such planning will promulgate large-scale error.

Rarely are decisions deliberately decentralized to hedge against such error. Neither are flexibility protections built into the planning of education and training to minimize lead times in specialization, to maximize readiness for training, or to locate specialized training close to the job and the employer. Moreover, having both discarded deliberative assessment of alternatives forgone and by-passed the whole problem of the continuous obsolescing of skills, technocratic planners are embarrassed by job mobility. A natural response has been costly cover-up expedients to force fits.

As I see the planner's task, it should be almost the opposite of this. The core of it is in search and comparison—in both the large and the small. The planner must search for strategic and instrumental variables and for openings in the institutional constraints—not only for direct public action but to induce development-supportive behavior over a wide range. Researchers have not yet begun to take on their share of the task and communication is hampered by theologies. Practitioner-technicians have multiplied to fill the gap. The result tends to be increased competence in the avoidance of minor mistakes—and in the repetition of big ones. The result is also bias toward more and more centralization of decisions with a concomitant routinizing of decision processes, which become automatically imitative rather than analytical, deliberate and creative.

31

Long-Term Requirements
for Qualified Manpower
in Relation to Economic Growth

Integration of the demand requirements for manpower and educational
planning constitutes one of the more
difficult tasks facing developed and
less-developed countries alike. Gottfried Bombach, visiting professor at
Stanford University, describes some
of his manpower forecasting experiences while he was with OECD.
A three-stage linkage is needed in
that national output growth must

GOTTFRIED BOMBACH

be translated into future manpower
requirements followed by identification of output of the educational
system. Needless to say, the requisite
analyses are encumbered by a variety
of analytical problems in manpower
forecasting in a developed country—
the emphasis of Bombach's article.

Introduction

The author of this paper is no expert in the field of economics of education.
In particular he has not been able to study carefully the extensive literature
published in this area during recent years. For this reason the paper will have
some shortcomings but . . . perhaps some of the advantages of a contribution from an outsider.

In the discussion on the applicability of econometric methods in economic

Reprinted from Gottfried Bombach, "Long-Term Requirements for Qualified Manpower
in Relation to Economic Growth," *Economic Aspects of Higher Education* (Paris: Organisation
for Economic Co-Operation and Development, 1964), pp. 201–21, with the permission
of the author and publisher.

forecasting, the author has been mainly on the side of the pessimists. Nevertheless an attempt is made here to consider whether some of the methods developed for economic forecasting may be successfully applied to forecasting manpower requirements.

In the field of educational policy, a distinction is made between the *manpower-requirements approach* and the "cultural" *approach*. This paper deals largely with the manpower-requirements approach: its main concern is the translation of the growth of real product into requirements for manpower, mainly highly skilled labor, regardless of whether the starting point is a certain growth target or a mere projection.

It is impossible, however, to leave the "cultural" approach aside. As stated in another paper, education has both vocational and cultural significance to the individual. In the Svennilson report[1] the term "education as consumption *per se*" has been used, and we have to take into account this component of total demand when the problem of income-elasticity of demand for education is discussed later in this study. In addition to this, society may have certain cultural targets besides the growth target. Here again we are confronted with the problem of a conversion of targets into requirements.

It is useless to stress the enormous difficulties of any scientifically based medium or long-term forecast of manpower requirements by type of skill. Because of the obvious obstacles and unfortunate experience of the past, it is advisable to refrain entirely from such projections.

The first argument is that we do not really need such projections because there is no danger of what is usually called "over-education." Educational policy should simply follow the principle of promoting education to the extent the available resources of society allow. There is no danger of "over-production."

Briefly, the argument seems sound as far as the *general level of education* is concerned. It is in fact hard to believe that there could be *a general* over-supply of highly skilled labor in the next ten or twenty years. One has only to think of the export of skilled labor to developing countries, a demand which is practically unlimited. Furthermore, it should be borne in mind that in a modern society, with its ever-increasing productivity, working time becomes shorter and shorter, so that higher educational standards on a broad basis are required to enable men to spend increasing leisure time in a useful way.

However, it is not that one thinks so much in terms of total requirements (in the sense of a rather meaningless aggregate) but rather in terms of the *right balance*, i.e., the structure of manpower requirements by type of profession or skill. Even though one cannot imagine a general over-education, serious structural disequilibria may arise as experienced in the

[1] See *Targets for Education in Europe in 1970*, OECD Washington Conference, 16–20 Oct. 1961, Para 24 *et seq.*

past. When the danger of "intellectual unemployment" or even the development of an "academical proletariat" is described, this is, to the author's
mind, not so much the risk of a general over-supply of highly educated men
but rather a partial over-production.

The very sense of long-term manpower-requirement projections, therefore, is to avoid structural disequilibria, i.e., serious bottlenecks in one field
and over-supply in another. Financial resources for education are limited;
expenditure on education has to compete with other important public
expenditure such as defense and infra-structure. There must be some
guarantee that the available funds are used in an optimum way, and this
can be done only by keeping the right proportions. We have to avoid as far
as possible what in the Svennilson report is called *unbalanced educational
investment.*

It might be argued that in our society the mobility between sectors,
professions and functions is so great that there is no need to watch this
structural aspect; certain structural disequilibria are unavoidable, but will
soon be overcome by the high degree of flexibility. In a state of complete
flexibility this might be so. We are, however, very far from that and it is
unnecessary to quote the many examples. Policies are recommended in order
to achieve a higher degree of mobility, but one has to be careful in case higher
flexibility does not in turn lower quality.

Education is a life-long asset. As is typical for other such assets, one can
observe a clear tendency toward the *formation of various types of cycles.*

First there is the problem of replacement. At present one can find in
almost all branches a rather irregular age structure. The consequence of
these irregularities is the famous *replacement cycle*, known as the echo principle
in the business cycle theory.

There is also the *cob-web cycle.* If in a certain profession demand exceeds
supply, salaries will go up. This will induce young men to take up this
particular career. If the education period is long, supply will not be affected
at an early stage; salaries will remain high, and an increasing number of
people might decide in favor of this career, even though dynamically,
potential supply is already above demand. Finally, the situation will be
just the contrary, i.e., supply exceeding demand and consequent low
salaries.

One of the main purposes of the manpower requirements projections
is to avoid just this type of fluctuation which necessarily has an adverse effect
on economic development and gives rise to serious personal hardships.

The individual has only a very limited insight into the dynamic position
of supply and demand. He is inclined to make his decisions on the immediate
market structure which is intransparent to a large extent. The additional
information to be provided by the projections is the transparency of the
market situation over time.

The Impact of Economic Growth
on Manpower Requirements

The following is a summary of a longer study which the author is under-taking for OECD, except that all technical details have been omitted. The major part of the methods described apply to *developed countries* only.

PROJECTIONS OR TARGETS FOR GNP

Our main concern is the translation of a certain growth of real product into manpower requirements. The first question: from where the estimate of the future rate of growth should be taken, is a crucial one. This is easy if there exists a certain *growth target* as adopted by OECD member countries (50 per cent growth of real product for the decade ending 1970). In such a case the type of model used is a *decision model* rather than a projection model. It is a decision model in that it contains a *target variable* (a certain rate of growth of GNP), a certain number of *instrument variables* and some *autonomous variables*. A variable has to be considered as an instrument variable if the authority interested in the projection is *able to influence that particular variable and at the same time is willing to do so*. Both are necessary, i.e., the intention and the ability to exercise an influence.

A variable may be autonomous *per se*, or must be treated as autonomous because of a given legal and institutional order. The major part of demo-graphic factors might be considered as autonomous *per se* variables in the field of education. A certain distribution of natural human abilities, if this exists, would also belong here. A given legal and institutional order, how-ever, may be changed, and it is just the projection with a target in the background which may lead to the conclusion that such a change is neces-sary in order to reach the target.

A clear separation between autonomous and instrument variables is essential. Instrument variables are entirely within the scope of the authority which requires projections as a basis for some sort of optimum policy. Let us assume that the government has asked for a projection. It is obvious that such a projection can be carried out only if the intentions of the government as regards the use of instrument variables are already known, or, alter-natively, the government wants to know the results of the projections in order to make its decisions. This again means the use of instrument variables on the results of the projections. It demonstrates the well-known "vicious circle" of projection.

There are a number of examples of this. Following the fashion of the time, a given country desires a certain economic growth policy. In order to have some criteria it requests a private institute to forecast the probable average rate of growth of real product during the next decade. However, it is the government itself which determines, consciously or not, this rate of growth in a number of ways by fiscal policy, monetary policy and so forth. What really takes place is that the government requires the projection of its decisions on the result of this forecast. Logically, of course, this is a fundamental contradiction.

Analogies in the field of education are obvious: a government wants to know to what extent the number of students will increase in order to adopt a certain policy and to make financial arrangements to meet the requirements shown. But it is obvious that the government itself mainly determines the increase of numbers of students by its educational policy, and in particular by its method of financing the universities and by its scholarship system.

When projecting, assumptions must always be made concerning the development of autonomous factors. This is sometimes done in connection with the projection itself, sometimes with information drawn from external sources.

If there is uncertainty about the development of the autonomous components, *alternative projections* are recommendable. This is usually done by giving expected minimum and maximum estimates and one in between, which is the most probable one.

What we have in mind for the present purpose is a rather simple type of decision model which does not produce an unequivocal solution, but allows a rather wide range for political decision making. It is then up to the politician to choose the solution he considers the best.

Contrary to this, even in the field of the economics of education, an attempt may be made to apply decision models in the sense of modern, decision-making theory. By application of linear or nonlinear programming, an optimum solution is sought showing types of policy necessary to attain a maximum of education with given resources, or, adversely how certain educational targets may be achieved with a minimum of requirements. Such models are based on certain objective-functions rather than on definite targets.

This very ambitious attempt is certainly worthy of attention. It was Ragnar Frisch's conviction that a decision-making model is the reason itself of a forecast.[2]

This is certainly true, but for some years to come we shall have to be content with the much more simple type of model outlined above, which is not able to produce an optimum solution and which leaves it to the politician to choose the combination of measures he thinks best. The reason

[2] R. Frisch, *A Survey of Types of Economic Forecasting and Programming and a Brief Description of the Oslo Channel Model.* Memorandum of the Institute of Economics, University of Oslo, 1961.

for this is that the proper decision-making model requires very detailed statistical information; in addition, the formulation of a reasonable objective function is not easy.

We are left with the case where no such growth target has been agreed upon. What type of projection method should be recommended? A large variety of methods are in use at present which cannot be discussed in detail here. They include very crude trend-extrapolations and the use of complicated production functions.

One method frequently applied but, in our opinion, rather doubtful, is the extrapolation of productivity trends. It is based on an anticipation of the increase in the total labor force and the historical trend of labor productivity. The assumption is made that the future average productivity increase will be the same as in the past, and on this basis the rate of growth of real product is then derived.

A problem then arises, since, if the growth rate of GNP is estimated by this method—whatever the refinements used—manpower requirements are derived afterward. We then have a vicious circle of trying to get something out which has already been put in.[3]

This brings us up against the important problem of the interplay of growth and manpower-requirement forecasts. We have two points to consider: (1) should we make the growth forecast first, and use the results as a basis for assessing manpower requirements by the productivity trend method, or (2) should we begin by using the anticipated development of manpower and then deduce economic growth by productivity trends? There is a possibility of approaching the problem from both sides and finding a solution by applying an iterative method.

The problem is more substantial than technical, and may be demonstrated by the following example: is the high growth rate in Germany over recent years due to the inflow of foreign labor, or, on the contrary, was the inflow of labor attracted by the "pull" of growth?

Traditional business-cycle forecasts were "demand" directed, whereas growth forecasts are determined by the potential supply, the capacity of production. Growth forecasts, as trend forecasts, indicate the development the real product might achieve if an adequate economic policy provided for a continuously sufficient demand. It is questionable, however, whether this is the right way. Is it primarily the development of the production factors and their efficiency, as well as the way in which they are employed, which determine the growth of the real product, or does demand play a decisive role in the form of a *pull*?

---

[3] Another objection against the use of historical productivity trends is that the very reason of educational policy is to increase productivity more than in the past. If such a policy is successful there is no reason to believe that productivity will grow only at the same rate as before.

Current discussion shows that basically very little is known as to what factors really determine economic growth.

If no target has been adopted one should start with a certain minimum rate of growth, perhaps justified simply by political arguments. Then one has to consider what the maximum could be. Between these pessimistic and optimistic estimates can be situated the rate of growth which is most likely to occur.

This procedure for three alternative estimates might appear rather unsatisfactory. It must be borne in mind, however, that the interest is not so much in aggregate manpower requirements as in the structure.

THE OPTIMUM DEGREE OF AGGREGATION

In economics a large number of projection methods and techniques have been developed which are to some extent in competition with each other. For the purpose of estimating manpower requirements some of them may be excluded from the beginning—for example, the well-known barometer-methods used to forecast business cycles. The number of those which remain, however, is large enough for us to ask which is the most efficient and most reliable technique. The answer is that it *is useless to search for an ideal method*, even though in practice certain techniques receive considerable support. There is *no ideal method; an optimum combination of practicable methods* needs to be found.

The combination of methods we have in mind does not mean that projections of the same thing are carried out by different institutions and by applying different techniques so that they can be controlled by cross-checking. Sometimes such a procedure is recommended, and in certain cases is useful. We are thinking rather of a combination of different methods used *simultaneously*, and taking into account the fact that they are to a large degree complementary. In this way techniques which are quite different may be usefully put together without excluding each other. In particular, there may be a combination of methods built up on highly aggregative statistics on the one side, and, on the other, methods making use of direct inquiries, sampling surveys and field studies undertaken by experts.

An appropriate breakdown of the manpower requirements to be estimated is a precondition of using a combination of the techniques recommended above. Experience shows that a skillful breakdown materially determines success. If this has been done adequately, the choice between conflicting methods is limited, and often only a single method for a specific aggregate remains.

The breakdown may be made in various ways, e.g., according to:

1. *Economic sectors;* e.g. agriculture, manufacturing (with further subdivision), distribution, public sector, etc.

2. *Educational level;* for purposes of forecasting the best way of measurement appears to be according to duration of education; a rough subdivision would be primary education, secondary education, higher education.
3. *"Function";* i.e., requirements due to a growing population, to increasing wealth, or for replacements.

The type of breakdown set out above refers to manpower, i.e., the variable to be predicted. The breakdown is necessary both to apply reasonable projection methods rather than purely mechanistic devices and to obtain significant results.

In addition to this, a breakdown of the variables "explaining" manpower requirements is needed, such as the output of the different sectors, private income, etc. Sometimes this type of breakdown is avoided and an attempt made to link qualified manpower to certain high order aggregates such as industrial production or even total national product by way of regression analysis. Two assumptions may be behind such a simplified procedure, either implicitly or explicitly: i.e., that no structural changes will take place or that a larger number of structural changes offset each other resulting in constant parameters.

REPLACEMENT REQUIREMENTS

It is appropriate to start with the problem of forecasting *replacement requirements,* since careful attention must be paid to this component of the total requirements regardless of the type of breakdown used. In a stagnant economy, replacement would be the only requirement and the methods described here would be sufficient to predict manpower requirements year by year for a future period with a sub-division into various professions.

Irregularities in the age structure of the various professions are quite normal and are the consequence of "erratic shocks" such as trade fluctuations, sudden changes in the birth rate or even wars. Irregularities in the age pyramid become obvious as a factor determining replacement only when certain age groups reach pensionable age. If, for example, there is an unusually large group in the pensionable age, there will be a sudden increase in replacement requirements which, in the field of real capital, is called an "echo" and which may return several times. One refers to such a phenomenon as the so-called *"echo-principle."*

In education, replacement requirements are comparatively easy to estimate if reliable statistics on the age structure of the various professions are available. Specific mortality rates must also be taken into account, and estimates made concerning any future reduction in the working age.

Cross-section analyses are to be recommended here, particularly a comparison of European countries with the United States. If necessary, past trends of the lowering of the retirement age may be extrapolated.

It is astonishing to see how little attention professional associations are paying to the irregular age structure in that part of the labor force which they represent. Although this may be due to lack of statistical information, it is in part deliberate, the intention being to reduce supply by continuously warning against a "surplus supply," thereby keeping wages high. In the field of higher education certain professional associations are continuously warning against surpluses in view of the large number of students, even though age pyramids in the post-war period show a definite bias in favor of the age groups just before pensionable age.

Replacement, though very important, is only *one* component of total requirements. As the result of an era in which arguments were mainly in terms of short-run analysis and the thinking on which classical economics concentrated was in static terms rather than in terms of economic growth, the mere maintenance of the *status quo* may have been exaggerated.

In a dynamic society and a growing economy, however, we are confronted with quite a different picture. In particular, it should be borne in mind that replacement forecasts on the basis of age structure statistics indicate only those requirements which may arise in the future if there is . . . an actual need for replacement. With growing wealth and technical changes, however, the structure is changing continuously, and a number of professions are liable to become extinct. In other words, there is no definite compulsion toward replacement.

FINAL AND INTERMEDIATE DEMAND

If in economic forecasting one needs to estimate the future demand for a certain raw material or intermediate product, an endeavor is made to link this demand to the final product (or group of final products) and to its production. "Final product" in this context means a product leaving the industrial sector and entering private households or into public use, or being exported. A direct link, or the application of a refined technique such as input-output analysis, comes to mind.

In any case the procedure of following the detour described here may be upheld; it is much easier to make reliable statements on future demand for final than for intermediate products, e.g., by linking final demand to increasing income or by the introduction of certain saturation levels. Of course, well-known short cut methods are often applied which do not follow this detour but project the demand for intermediate products and basic materials directly. During recent years these direct methods have been applied, mainly because they are more easily carried out. Consequently, results have very often been unsatisfactory.

It is advisable to adapt the input-output concept we have in mind to the educational sector. Our educational input-output system, however, should not be confused with the well-known Leontief-type system for the production sector, the applicability of which for forecasting manpower will be discussed later. We are thinking rather of a hypothetical system, which refers only to the field of education. Its *output is educated manpower*. Part flows back to the system in the form of school teachers, university professors, research workers, administrators in the educational sector, etc., who are necessary to educate people at all stages, from primary school to university. This is the type of inter-relationship that has been described as "it takes talent to develop talent." The part of total output not used within the educational system itself may be referred to as the "final output."

It is obvious that there is a close connection between the final output of the educational system—the final output, of course, being its ultimate purpose—and the system itself. It is a network of rather complicated inter-relationships very similar to those described by a regular input-output table from which we can derive certain *multipliers* telling us how the system must be fed in order to obtain the desired "final bill of goods."

Obviously it is very important to know something about the size and behaviour of these multipliers for the purpose of forecasting. In regular input-output analysis the assumption is that in the short run these "technical coefficients" are constant. The question is how far the same assumption would be justified with a view to our educational matrix.

The conversion multipliers are dependent on the production period of an educated man, on the pupil/teacher ratio, and on the structure of the whole system. A shift in the direction of better education by lowering the pupil/teacher ratio, increasing the production period, and changing the general structural change in favor of more highly educated professions would tend to increase these multipliers. Some of these parameters are clearly instrument variables of the government, particularly the pupil/teacher ratio. The government's future intentions have to be known concerning these parameters before any forecast can be made.

If one accepts the type of distinction between the "final output" of the educational system and the output needed to feed the system, the first step in the establishment of a forecast would logically be a *projection of final output*. The requirements of the educational system are then considered as *derived demand*, and it is for the conversion of final demand into derived demand that we need the multipliers referred to above.

There is an enormous expansion of the educational sector due to the heavily increased demand for educated manpower. Since the educational sector may be conceived as a long-lived stock of human capital, the inter-relations between final demand for educated manpower and the development of the educational system are very similar to those described by the *acceleration principle*. In some countries the problem today is that the educational sector, in finding enough talent for the expansion needed has to compete with the business sector. The business sector needs increasingly highly educated manpower which cannot be produced because of the impossibility of the further expansion of the educational system. We are confronted with exactly the same problem as capital formation in a poor country.

It is not easy to draw a sharp line between the educational sector and the sector outside the educational system. A large number of people are active in both sectors; a university teacher, for example, may be engaged as a business consultant in addition to his lecturing work, or a doctor may do both educational work at a university and hospital service. Furthermore, an important part of even higher educational work is now done by industry itself. This, however, is sometimes difficult to locate.

Because of all the difficulties in educational forecasting, an attempt has been made to use short-cut methods as described for economic forecasting, i.e. to avoid the detour via a projection of final demand, a direct trend projection was used or the requirements of the educational system were linked to national income, etc. As usual, all these types of correlations fit excellently for a period which is past, but are dangerous if used as the only basis for a look into the future. They will act as a check, but one should try to do more than play with figures in this hazardous way. The borderline may be found by adopting certain rules for agreement. Even though this line might seem to be arbitrary, it would not affect the result of the forecast so long as the structure between the two sectors does not change suddenly, and this is very unlikely to happen.

PROJECTION OF FINAL DEMAND FOR EDUCATED MANPOWER

As described above, the estimating of the future requirements of the educational system is a problem of transforming final demand for education into teachers, other staff, school rooms, material, etc., rather than projecting in the real sense of the word.

There are, of course, several typical forecasting devices indispensable to the carrying out of this conversion. If, for example, we know nothing about the behavior of a certain transformation coefficient over time we may have recourse to some sort of trend extrapolation. But it should always be borne in mind that to use any type of trend curve means an admission that we actually do not know the laws governing a certain kind of development.

On the whole, the conversion of final demand into the requirements of the educational system in its narrow sense may be done in a much less hazardous way and thus avoid serious criticism. In this field fruitful work can be accomplished by research institutes and international organizations.

We have now to discuss the methods of projecting the type of educational requirement called *final demand*. This means, to some extent, projections or forecasts in their proper sense comparable with economic forecasts, and in part simply a transformation of certain educational targets into requirements.

Final demand for educational services is a very *unhomogeneous aggregate*, not amenable to any type of straight-forward extrapolation or linking to another comprehensive aggregate. It must be split up, and as stated above, success very much depends on how this splitting is done.

MAIN COMPONENTS OF DEMAND

The following breakdown is suggested as a minimum requirement to obtain sufficiently homogeneous aggregates to establish projections by the application of methods which are other than purely mechanistic—mechanistic in the sense that they do not reveal the forces governing the development of the variables to be projected.

The components of the final demand may be listed as:

1. Education as input to industry, i.e., qualified manpower needed by the *economic sector* of society (production and distribution).
2. Education as *private consumption*.
3. Education as *public consumption*, i.e., qualified manpower needed by the public sector (the educational system excluded).

THE PUBLIC SECTOR

In this context comparatively little is to be said with regard to the *requirements of the public sector* referred to as "collective consumption" in national accounting. It is obvious that for our present purpose the educational system, including that part of public administration concerned with education, has to be excluded.

There have been long discussions among national accounting experts about how to distinguish between that part of the public sector whose activity is to be taken as input to industry (i.e., as some sort of intermediate output) and that part which is directly linked with needs of private households (final demand). Were it possible to draw a distinction, there would be no need to have a separate category (3): the requirements of the public sector would have to be distributed between (1) and (2) according to the particular type of government activity. Though the discussions are still continuing there does not seem to be an acceptable, practical method of making such distinctions.

A minimum breakdown to facilitate projections would be to separate national defense from public administration. In addition, national defense is very important in connection with forecasting labor requirements for the economic sector. An extension of the military service period means a strain on the labor market and vice versa (problem of opportunity costs).

A serious estimate requires more than minimum breakdown. Central and local government programs in the various branches of public administration have to be taken into account. If this entails too much work, use must be made of some sort of regular expansion analogous to A. Wagner's "Law of

Increasing Public Expenditure." But caution is recommended with this type of structural trend: there always has to be a ceiling, i.e., there has to be a *break in the structural trends*, otherwise there would come a time when 100 per cent of the labor force is occupied in public administration.

EDUCATION AS CONSUMPTION PER SE

Our next step is to predict education as *private consumption*. Here, two different types of "consumption" have to be distinguished. Primarily there is a large and ever-increasing number of educated personnel such as doctors, legal advisers, artists and others who offer their services directly to households and who are products of the educational system.

The entire health service might be included here, regardless of the specific system a country may have adopted.

Besides these requirements, one has to consider what has been called *education as consumption per se.* . . . in a community with continuously increasing material wealth, people desire a better education.

There is, of course, a close inter-relationship between education as vocational training and education as consumption *per se*, or, more precisely, a one-way relation: higher vocational training also means attainment of a higher standard of general education, or should do. In contrast to this, however, there is a desire for improved education quite independent of future professional activity. A secondary education is desired regardless of whether one has the intention of entering university or not; or one attends university without later taking up a job related to the university training received. This applies particularly to the education of women.

An estimate of this education as consumption *per se* gives rise to difficulties, since demand is determined largely by government decisions, i.e., rules of selection when entering secondary school or university, paying or not paying of school fees, scholarships to students, etc. If a government were to want a forecast of its educational requirements without specifying the use of the important "instrument variables," it would provide us with a very clear example of its desire to have its future educational policy based on externals.

As a basis for any forecast of this type, therefore, certain *educational targets* are needed. When translating these targets into requirements much statistical and analytical work has to be done.

First a forecast of the *development of population and its age-structure* are needed. In this context the structural aspect has very often been overlooked. The problem of longevity, for example, raises new questions which are still under discussion. Another example is that of the modern satellite towns which normally have a population with a fairly low average age and which therefore make quite different demands on the educational system from those of the average town. The consequence of this is a serious social imbalance.

It seems difficult to quantify the income elasticity referred to here and to use it as a forecasting tool. Moreover, there is some doubt as to whether it is sufficiently constant over time. Possibly more attention should also be given to the other main determinants such as the growth and structure of population and government targets. These targets are also very closely linked to the growth of material wealth, and they should not be conceived as fixed once and for all. What is needed is a continuous adjustment between educational targets and available resources.

Age structure and educational targets considered together present the following picture: in most OECD countries complete primary education is a self-evident target. Requirements are easy to derive, the main instrument variable of the government being the pupil/teacher ratio which determines the number of teachers and class rooms.

The proportion of the population passing through secondary education still differs substantially among Member countries. An estimate has to be made of how much this proportion will increase during the coming year. *International cross section analysis* is an important aid here. Whether *an upper* limit for this proportion ought to be envisaged raises an important problem here, that is, of the fixing of a ceiling.

A start should always be made with the *total number of potential pupils* according to the age pyramid, then consideration given to the number who will probably enter secondary school. A careful statistical analysis of the past will reveal some clear *structural* trends. Such a procedure appears to be more promising than a direct extrapolation of past trends of the number of pupils, or a linking of the development of the number of pupils to a certain indicator for increasing wealth by way of regression analysis. The latter methods should be used only for checking purposes.

The problem of how to predict the demand for university education remains. Where university training is directly linked to a particular profession—and, of course, the major part of university training is of this type—the methods of forecasting are discussed later on. Our present concern is the type of higher education considered as some kind of a "luxury", i.e., where the student has no intention of following an academic career. In wealthier countries, the number of students belonging to this category is not negligible. The community must decide whether this phenomenon is a waste of public facilities, very similar to the famous social cost problem, or whether any type of higher education should be promoted as an objective in itself.

INDIRECT HOUSEHOLD DEMAND

Demand for the services of doctors, lawyers, and so forth, may be regarded as a form of indirect household demand for educational services, as opposed to education consumption *per se*, mentioned above.

If an attempt is to be made at using more than short-cut methods such as trend extrapolations and simple regression analysis, a projection of future requirements needs careful studies for the various professions in close contact with experts. This applies particularly to the medical service. We shall confine ourselves to listing the main components of demand which have to be taken into account in any branch and which, separately, need specific methods of extrapolation. They are

1. Replacement requirements.
2. Requirements due to increasing population and/or changing age-structure.
3. Requirements due to increasing general welfare.
4. Requirements due to scientific progress.

Requirements in (3) and (4) are, of course, closely inter-related. Here again government has a decisive influence. To take doctors as an example, under the social security system the number of persons or hospital beds per doctor are generally fixed. These *density figures* are the *key parameters* for any type of projection.

REQUIREMENTS OF THE ECONOMIC SECTOR

Among the components of final demand listed above the requirement of the economic sector of the economy is the most important item by order of magnitude. In addition, this item requires different treatment. Government targets and government action have determined to some degree the type of demand dealt with so far. This applies particularly to the first type of requirement, i.e., qualified manpower for the public sector. It is also true for education as final consumption, though increasing wealth has certainly more influence here. It appears to be difficult, however, to establish a rigid relationship between the growth of the national product and the demand for education for "final consumption" purposes.

We are faced with quite a different position in the economic sector, which for our specific purposes should comprise: agriculture; manufacturing, including basic industries and construction; transportation, distribution, banks and insurance companies; and professions which do not offer their services directly to households. In the economic sector, as defined here, there is a close relationship between labor input and output, stable enough to serve as a basis for requirement projections as soon as there exists a definite target for the increase of that output.

Thus there are three sectors: the *public sector*, the manpower requirements of which are almost entirely dependent on central and local government programs and intentions, and which offer very little chance to use econometric methods of projection, apart from hazardous trend extrapolations; the *household sector* with a direct demand for education (education as consumption *per se*) and an indirect demand (health service, lawyers, etc.). Both these categories depend on government programs and national wealth. Finally, there is the *economic sector* with manpower requirements almost entirely determined by economic forces, i.e., the increase of real income and the changing structure of the economy.

Our present concern is the transformation of a certain future average rate of growth of GNP into labor input. This involves a discussion of the *technique* suitable for this purpose.

In addition there is another question of fundamental importance. The purpose of this study is the prediction of qualified or even highly qualified manpower, not total manpower. The problem we have in mind is whether there are promising methods which would allow a *direct forecast* of this type of manpower by way of trend extrapolation and regression analysis respectively, or whether at the beginning there should be an estimate of the total manpower required with a supplementary analysis of structural change of employment, i.e., the process of substitution of unskilled or less-skilled labor by skilled manpower and highly qualified personnel. This will be referred to as the *structural approach or indirect method*.

DIRECT METHOD OR SUBSTITUTION ANALYSIS

It might be useful to start with the question of superiority as between the direct and indirect methods. This offers, at the same time, a chance of reviewing the various projection techniques.

At first glance, the direct method seems to be recommendable because of its simplicity. It avoids a forecast of total manpower requirements in which we might not be interested at all in this context, and by doing so we avoid the necessity of projecting labor productivity trends. Nevertheless, there are strong objections to be raised against this type of direct forecast, mainly because it offers very little chance for a scientifically based judgement as to whether the results obtained are reasonable or not. Such judgement is possible only insofar as one knows enough about total labor force in a certain sector for qualified manpower to be seen as a fraction of this total. There is, in fact, a complete analogy to economic forecasting, where a projection should always be comprehensive enough to comprise the whole market, i.e., not only for that product whose future development has to be estimated but also for those products which would be a substitute for it. If one wants to estimate demand for coal one should start with a projection of total energy consumption, the second step being an analysis of substitution, i.e., of changing shares of the various types of energy in total demand. If this procedure is not adopted, there is the danger of estimating a demand for coal which is far beyond the capacity of the market as a whole. The European coal mining industry has had this experience.

There is, of course, no objection to using methods of direct projection for the purpose of checking the more complicated two-stage technique recommended here.

Perhaps the most popular way of direct projection has so far been the *extrapolation of historical trends.* Objections to this method are well-known, so there is no need to list them in detail. It should be noted that there is no truth in the statement that the results it provides are not ambiguous.

In predicting a certain variable (the "dependent" variable) the regular procedure in econometrics is to look out for other variables ("independent" variables) which have a quantifiable influence on the development to be projected. Normally one will succeed in estimating one or more such "explaining" variables, but very often a group of determinants is left which has an influence that cannot be identified in detail. There is only one possibility for this group, namely to assume that there is a certain regular development over time. Time becomes the explaining variable. There is no objection against such an inclusion of catch-all groups covering those factors which may not be estimated in detail, such as the well-known "technical progress" or "human factor" in the production function. The simple trend projection, however, means that one expects that historical time entirely governs the development, which means that we know nothing about the actual laws determining the development to be predicted.

Regression analysis is almost as popular as trend projection. It consists of linking the development of the variable to be predicted to a certain higher order variable, generally to aggregates such as total production or the national product. Sometimes even multi-stage regression analysis is used, e.g., when linking a variable—let us say qualified manpower—to the output of the branch concerned. and correlating this output in its turn with the index of industrial production. Multi-stage regression analysis is useful only insofar as future structural changes of the economy can be foreseen. Otherwise, it is of no more use than simple regression, though it might be impressive to laymen.

Regression analysis as a means of forecasting is based on the assumption that certain parameters, obtained by the observation of a sufficiently long period in the past by the least square method, will change only very slowly. In this field one has to be much more cautious.

An example may be used to illustrate this. In economics, the relation between the explaining variable and the variable to be explained is normally expressed by an elasticity coefficient. Let us assume that the number of engineers is linked to total employment and that the analysis of a reference period would result in a coefficient above unity, as would certainly happen in most branches. An elasticity > 1 means simply that the number of engineers expands at a higher rate than total employment. Assuming this elasticity persists over a long enough period, we should get a result showing that at some future date total employment would be entirely of engineers.

This is obviously nonsense. Trend extrapolations give a similar nonsensical result, and for this reason methods of direct forecasting in the field of long-term projection are somewhat doubtful.

Finally it should be kept in mind that the linking of qualified manpower to a certain higher order aggregate only is a useful detour *as long as it is easier to forecast that particular aggregate than manpower itself*. Sometimes one will discover that, due to the lack of reliable information for the "explaining" aggregate, a simple trend extrapolation is established, with a linking of manpower requirements by way of regression analysis as a consequence. This, however, amounts to exactly the same as a straightforward trend extrapolation for manpower. Again regression analysis is used only to give a more scientific appeal to the projections.

AGGREGATION PROBLEMS

The problem of the *optimum breakdown of the economic sector* into a number of sub-sectors deserves careful consideration. The reason for making any sort of breakdown of comprehensive aggregates is to obtain a higher degree of homogeneity. But there is no homogeneity *per se*. One has rather to specify in what respect the aggregates have to be homogeneous. In national accounting, for example, it may be the behavior of private households concerning the spending of their income. In input-output analysis it is the production technique. For our present purpose we are interested in the composition of manpower. This means that in principle any type of analysis requires its own specific type of aggregation which rather complicates matters.

Let us start with two opposite positions concerning the degree of aggregation. The first would take the *economic sector as a whole* without any distinction between branches. In this case forecasting would be fairly simple. The expected productivity trend, together with our growth target, would produce total manpower requirements. In a second stage forecast of the structural trends would have to follow, carried out by means of one of the methods described later.

There is no need to discuss whether or not this procedure would give reliable results; they might be satisfactory. Our main objection is that such results are not precise enough to be taken as a basis for an educational policy. The indication of the approximate numbers of qualified manpower with university training needed would not help very much. Even if the total number were right, there is still the serious risk of a *structural disequilibrium*.

The other extreme is *input-output analysis* with its very far-reaching breakdown of economic activity, some tables showing 50 industries or even more.

At first glance, input-output analysis might appear as an ideal instrument for the forecasting of labor requirements, an advantage which has always been stressed by experts in this field. In our opinion, however, the possibilities for the application of this technique are very limited, and vary as among the various Member countries.

Input-output analysis has been developed as an instrument for short-term forecasting. Recently, efforts have been made to extend its applicability beyond these limits, partly by the substitution of static systems by dynamic ones. Though theoretical investigation has made rapid progress there is still very little empirical experience, and much support from this side cannot be expected during the next few years.

Furthermore, the input-output type of breakdown appears much too refined for our purpose. A good number of sectors using different production techniques, but the same type of manpower with a similar composition, may be put together.

An ideal type of aggregation seems to lie somewhere between the two extremes outlined above. Sometimes the well-known three-sectors breakdown introduced by Colin Clark is quoted in this respect, with the observation that the tertiary sector's share in total employment is steadily increasing. Even though this statement is correct, it does not get us much further. Qualified manpower in the tertiary sector is much of the same type and passes through the same educational career as in the secondary sector. There is a high degree of mobility between engineers in manufacturing and in transportation, or between highly qualified management personnel in manufacturing and in the tertiary sector—the public sector is excluded here. In other words, the three-sector model adds very little in homogeneity.

It is, of course, impossible to indicate an exact number of sectors to be considered as the optimum degree of aggregation. This figure would certainly be considerably above three, and much below the number of industries listed in a large input-output table, so would be somewhere between 10 to 20. The number varies with the size of the country, its structure, the specific problem in mind, and, in particular, with the statistical information available.

As stated in another context, any type of breakdown by sector is helpful in improving our projections only insofar as there is some idea of the *future structural development* of the economy. If one simply assumes a constant structure over time because of lack of information, a straight-forward method of forecasting would result in precisely the same trend.

It is unnecessary to say that we must have some idea about the structural development of an economy, quite apart from the need for educational policy and the planning of infra-structural investment, otherwise our target for aggregate economic growth would be somewhat meaningless.

The first task, therefore, is a *translation of the target for aggregate growth into structural trends*. One has to start with the various categories of the final bill of goods, taking into consideration respective income elasticities and saturation levels. In consequence, final demand is to be converted into the demand for intermediate and basic products, thus arriving at growth rates by sector.

A certain input-output concept is indispensable for the conversion of final demand into sectoral growth rates. In our opinion a fairly good estimate can be obtained without using formal input-output techniques involving an enormous effort.

LABOR PRODUCTIVITY AND TECHNICAL PROGRESS

Once the sectoral growth rates have been obtained the next operation is logically to estimate *labor productivity development* in order *to derive the total manpower* increase necessary to meet this growth in the real output of the different sectors.

The traditional method of estimating labor productivity is to use *productivity trends*. Reference is made to past exerience, which showed that for long periods statistical labor productivity increased on the average comparatively steadily, at a constant rate per annum, i.e., along a logarithmic trend line.

The same objections apply to the procedure set out above, the only difference being that the trend extrapolation method is applied to a *ratio* (namely statistical labor productivity) rather than to a certain variable. There is neither *a priori* reason nor statistical evidence that productivity ratios behave more regularly over time than the aggregates themselves. Either method of projection is equally questionable.

Nevertheless, the application of productivity trends for industrial sectors would have at least one definite advantage in that the *influence of structural changes on productivity* would be taken into account more or less automatically.

Increasing labor productivity is a consequence both of a growth of productivity within the various branches and of a shift of labor from the branches with low output per worker to those with high output per worker. Statistical investigation reveals that a considerable part of the total productivity increase is attributable to this movement of labor from less productive to higher productive sectors, referred to as the *structural component of* labor productivity.

The importance of the structural component of labor productivity has obvious implications for both the problem of forecasting and educational policy. At present, an important factor in increasing productivity through the improvement of structure is the international migration of labor.

THE THIRD FACTOR

Today, intensive investigations are being made in various countries on a theoretical as well as an empirical basis, with regard to the *determinants of labor productivity*. What we have in mind is the development of macro-economic production functions and their statistical testing. The traditional approach was to consider labor productivity as mainly determined by the amount of real capital employed per working place: the more capital the higher productivity.

More recent investigations have shown quite a different result. Regardless of the specific type of method used, or the country to which it was applied the outcome always proved that there are *other factors besides real capital that determine the rate of productivity increase.* Up to now it has not been possible to estimate these factors in detail, and they have therefore been left together as some sort of catch-all group (the trend component in the production function); the name generally used, though not quite correctly, is *technical progress.* Other terms are the *human factor* or the *organizational factor.* These latter seem to be more appropriate.

For example, one investigation has shown that *more than two-thirds of the total labor productivity increase* in the United States during half a century (productivity doubled in this period) may be attributed to this "human factor" rather than simply to more capital.[4] In general it may be said that an increase of more than one per cent, and sometimes even a little less than two per cent, in real income can be attained through the "human factor," i.e., *without any additional labor or real capital.*

A striking fact is that the existence of the "human factor" is of decisive importance for both the forecasting problem and educational policy, since this is the component which most obviously reveals the impact of education on growth.

The existence of the "human factor" and its quantitative importance makes clear why expenditure on education has to be treated as *investment expenditure.* Like expenditure on real capital, it is a key factor in endeavor to increase an economy's productivity and real income per head.

Thus an economy is always confronted with an optimization problem. Assuming that it has been decided to spend a certain proportion of national income on investment, a further decision becomes necessary on *how best to allocate investment expenditure on education and real capital in order to obtain the maximum productivity increase.* It appears that formerly the effect of real asset investment was fundamentally over-estimated as compared to educational investment. There is no doubt that the marginal return of a dollar spent on education is at present considerably higher than that of a dollar spent on real capital.

As soon as due attention is paid to the human factor in its dependency on education expenditure, our forecasting model moves further in the direction of a decision or policy model. From the point of view of a traditional type of anticipation model, this would have been considered to be a definite weakness, since a projection with a minimum number of conditions and restrictions was the aim. Today, when thinking in terms of a translation of targets

---

[4] Cf. the paper by W. G. Bowen.

into requirements and policies, the contrary is true. At present we have only some very rough ideas on the inter-relationship between educational expenditure and technical progress. This relationship is obviously very complex mainly because of the fact that the "human factor" in practice is a large group of very different factors, and because of the long time lag between educational expenditure and its return in increased productivity. In reality we are confronted with a complicated network of "distributed lags."

Furthermore, investment in real capital and investment in human capital cannot be treated as independent processes. The verification of technical progress, called *innovation* by Schumpeter, is generally linked to real asset formation.

This opens a wide field to further investigation if more light is to be shed on this complexity. Any progress achieved will provide a more solid basis for an optimum educational policy and will facilitate our task of transforming output trends into labor requirements. International organizations could undertake some useful work of comparison in this field.

CHANGING STRUCTURE OF EMPLOYMENT

This is the last step of our multi-stage projection process. An analysis of the substitution process now remains to be done, i.e., an evaluation of the manpower trends within the sectors shown. One main advantage of the breakdown immediately becomes clear. This not very simple projection of structural trends can be carried out sector by sector, always by using the most appropriate method in each case. It is obvious that there are *marked differences* both in the initial structural position and in *future structural trends* as between sectors.

This is made clear by two very different opinions on possible structural trends. The first is that, because of automation and the use of more and more complicated machinery, the requirements as regards skill continue to increase, giving rise to some type of linear growth of skill. The opposite opinion is that, on the one hand, skill requirements will decrease, since in the age of automation it becomes increasingly simple to operate a machine and a short period of job training is all that is needed. On the other hand, however, an automated factory needs a large staff of highly qualified engineers and management personnel for programming, planning and administration. Shown in a diagram, where on the horizontal axis the degree of skill is measured, and on the vertical axis the number of persons required in a certain skill is shown, this second version would produce a typically *U-shaped curve*.

Both versions may be right, depending on the sector one has in mind.

It is this analysis of structure for which one needs a synthesis of macro-economic techniques and field studies or sampling surveys. An *international cross-section analysis* is indispensable. For European countries, the skill structure in corresponding industries in the United States, gives a good indication of the direction development is taking.

Another approach would be a *cross-section analysis of the various firms* of a certain sector, ranking from the least to the most advanced. Finally, correlations between productivity trends and changes in employment structure may be attempted.

An extrapolation of structural trends—a method sometimes tried—is dangerous, because sooner or later it produces the nonsensical result of an industry with 100 per cent engineers.

An upper limit must always be drawn concerning the proportions of any type of qualified manpower. It is for this all-important problem of how to find the proper *ceiling* (ceiling in this context not to be regarded as an absolute figure but rather as a proportion of the total sectoral manpower) that one needs cross-section studies, international comparisons, sampling surveys and expert advice.

Once the ceiling has been established, consideration must be given to the way in which it might be attained. In economic forecasting, logistic or Gompertz-type curves show such development quite well. More practical experience is needed to say whether the same is true of forecasts of structural changes in manpower skills.

Concluding Remarks

This paper deals with problems of long-run projections of manpower requirements. The term "long run" may be misleading in that one thinks of a forecast which is established for a period of ten years and then holds good for that time. What one really needs is a system of rolling adjustment.

Continuous adjustment is indispensable because of the development of the exogenous variables which may not be as expected, and of a changing internal structure of the forecasting model. In addition, a revision of certain economic growth or educational targets may prove necessary.

International cross-section analysis has been shown as an important analytical tool for improving projections in several fields. The precondition for this type of analysis is a high degree of comparability of employment statistics, otherwise the results would be misleading rather than clarifying. Much work still remains to be done for the achievement of a common classification.

32

Optimum Levels of Investment in Education and Economic Development

Manpower forecasting and educational development of human resources are important to developing nations, as is observed by Professor Anthony Bottomley, Chairman of the School of Social Sciences, University of Bradford, United Kingdom. Using an aggregative model which combines concepts from standard economic theory and the more

ANTHONY BOTTOMLEY

recent rate-of-return approach to human capital formation, an exploration of some of the theoretical and practical aspects of investment in education in poor countries, Bottomley concludes that vocational training is probably preferable to general education.

A new kind of economic adviser to the governments of poor countries now exists; he is the expert in manpower assessment and utilization. He has the task of giving advice on the training of manpower from a purely economic point of view. He must be prepared to recommend that education or training in distinct categories be increased or diminished; ideally he would be able to give directions on the general nature of this training as well as the numbers who should undergo it. In practice, however, his advice will most often fall short of this ideal; that is to say that it will frequently be of a qualitative nature as opposed to detailed quantitative recommendations. In these circumstances it is useful for the manpower expert to have a

Reprinted from Anthony Bottomley, "Optimum Levels of Investment in Education and Economic Development," *Zeitschrift für die Gesamte Staatswissenschaft* 122 (April 1966), pp. 237–46, with the permission of the author and publisher.

theoretical model which, although amenable to quantitative application, will also illustrate the qualitative issues which the expert must bear in mind when he undertakes his investigations or makes his recommendations. Such a model could be as follows.

The object of the model would be to show the optimum number of persons who should be trained within all fields of specialization, as well as the optimum length and nature of their training. It would treat education and training only in terms of their ability to increase the flow of goods and services within the economy. It would not take account of their possible cultural value. The merits and demerits of treating education in this way have been discussed elsewhere,[1] and we need not go into them again. Suffice it to say that we are here concerned with the problems of economic growth in poor countries where the consequences of ignorance, in terms of malnutrition, shanty-living, and ill-health, are evident on every hand, and that in such conditions the economist is entitled to discuss education solely in terms of its ability to put an end to these evils.

Our model must, then, take account of several factors. Broadly speaking it is important to know the cost to society of the particular type of training which may be under review, as well as to form some idea of the advantages which will accrue to society as a result of it. These considerations are best discussed initially in terms of annual monetary charges and annual monetary returns.

Suppose, for example, we are considering the training of a particular type of technician. Each technician completes six years of primary school, six years of secondary school, and two years of training college in the field of his specialization. He may therefore begin his working life in his twentieth year, and, shall we say, on average he concludes it in his sixtieth year; although, of course, this latter will vary with normal retirement ages in the country concerned, as well as with the life expectancy within the class or income group to which the technician belongs. Over the forty years of his working life, the technician must earn enough on net as a result of his training to amortize and pay interest on the cost of his education.[2] Moreover, under equilibrium conditions (to be defined later), it seems likely that initially the annual marginal revenue productivity of the worker's training will not cover its annual cost. That is to say that to begin with he will not earn

[1] See, for example, T. W. Schultz, "Investment in Human Capital," *American Economic Review*, Vol. LI (1962), pp. 2 and 3.

[2] Equal to the summated annual cost of his training plus interest on these costs annually prior to graduation, plus earnings foregone by the student himself as a result of the fact that he does not work while he is in training. These considerations governing the cost of education have already been discussed in considerable detail elsewhere. See for example: Investment in Human Resources, five articles in *Journal of Political Economy*, Vol. LXX (Supplement: Oct., 1962); W. Lee Hansen, "Total and Private Rates of Return to Investment in Schooling," *Journal of Political Economy*, Vol. LXXXI (1963), pp. 128–140; and T. W. Schultz, a.a.O., pp. 1–17.

enough over and above what he would have earned without training (his net MRP) to cover the annual interest and amortization charges on the cost of his training. However, as he gains experience his net MRP will rise to equal and then surpass the annual cost of his education. But in the meantime there will be a continued expense associated with his training beyond the date of graduation. This expense will equal the sum of the annual interest and amortization payments on the cost of his formal education, minus the MRP accruing to it up until the time at which the latter rises to equal the former—shall we say after the twentieth year of his working life. From the twentieth year on, therefore, the annual interest and amortization costs of his education must include charges for the losses on it during the first nineteen years, in addition to those on its whole original cost.[3] Beyond the nineteenth year, however, the net MRP of his training rises above its annual costs, which by now are themselves declining insofar as their interest component is concerned as the unamortized balance grows less with the passage of the years. All this can, perhaps, be clearly illustrated with the use of a diagram.

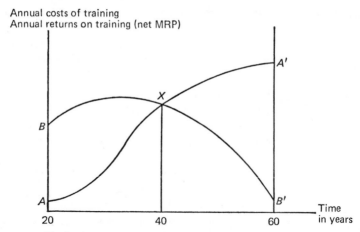

The horizontal axis represents annual MRP of a worker who has not undergone the training considered here.

Figure 1

The curve AA' shows the net MRP accruing to the worker's efforts over time as a result of the investment in his training. It is assumed to be logistic because initially the annual value of the worker's output may not rise so rapidly as it probably will after he has gained experience on the job; while

[3] Employers may also undertake to give some additional formal training to an employee, and this cost must be computed as well. See, Jacob Mincer, "On-the-Job Training: Costs, Returns and some Implications," *Journal of Political Economy* (Supplement: Oct., 1962), a.a.O., pp. 50–79.

toward the end of his working life the rate of increase is assumed to decline due to the effects of aging.[4]

The BB' curve represents the annual interest and amortization payments on the original cost of his training as well as on the net losses associated with that training for the first nineteen years (the area BXA). It first rises as the cost of amortizing and paying interest on the investment prior to graduation is augmented by the interest and amortization charges on the net losses on the education up to the twentieth year. Somewhat before the twentieth year is reached, the annual cost curve begins to fall as the interest payments on the progressively smaller unamortized balance decline.

As more capital is expended on training greater numbers in a particular profession or trade, the value of the output of the marginal recruits may be assumed to fall due to the forces of diminishing marginal productivity on identical individuals, as well as an assumed enlistment of progressively weaker intellects into the professions as recruitment is increased.[5] This process will manifest itself in a movement of the AA' curve to the right. It is also likely that there will be an upward shift of the BB' curve as facilities for training added recruits to the profession are created; the salaries of lecturers in the training colleges may rise as the demand for their services grows, new sites for buildings may cost more than previously, etc.

Ideally this process should go on until the area BXA = the area A'XB'. Only when this has happened will the demand for, and the supply of, these particular technicians be in equilibrium, because it is only here that the marginal cost of the training equals the marginal revenue derived from it over time. Training in all lines of economic endeavor should go on until this state of affairs exists in each one of them. Prior to the achievement of this general equilibrium, the ratio $\frac{A'XB'}{BXA}$ should be kept equal in each trade or profession as education and training advances along all fronts, since it seems likely that almost all types of training in poor countries will initially more than cover their costs over time. Given perfect competition, a policy along these lines will theoretically maximize the monetary return on capital invested in education. The maximum benefit to society at large will accrue under the application of these same principles if the AA' curve is used to represent the annual social return on the marginally recruited individual's education, and the BB' curve its annual social cost. But, since the concepts involved here are

---

[4] Some evidence in support of this shape for the AA' curve as far as workers in the United States are concerned may be found in: U.S. Department of Labour, "Office Jobs: Comparative Job Performances by Age," Bulletin No. 1273, 1960, and U.S. Department of Labour, "Plant Jobs: Job Performance and Age," Bulletin No. 1203, 1956 (both cited by Héctor Correa, *The Economics of Human Resources* [Den Haag: Drukerij Pasmans, 1962], pp. 104–105); and Gary S. Becker, "Investment in Human Capital: A Theoretical Analysis," *Journal of Political Economy* (Supplement: Oct., 1962), a.a.O., pp. 9–49.

[5] See Correa, a.a.O., Chap. III and pp. 62–67.

not easy to grasp, it is better to continue the discussion in purely monetary terms. We can introduce social considerations as we go along.

The question now arises as to how this model can be used to focus the attention of the adviser in the manpower field on the issues with which he must deal.[6] Broadly speaking he can employ one of three kinds of approach to his task, or a combination thereof. These three approaches may be designated: (1) a strict statistical application of the model, (2) a rough quantitative estimate of the equilibrium levels of investment in education, and (3) a qualitative application of the model. We shall deal with each in turn.

A STRICT STATISTICAL APPLICATION OF THE MODEL

With this approach a survey of the earnings of persons with a particular type of training would be undertaken and classified according to the year of their working life. The results of this survey would then be posted on a scatter diagram and an AA' curve fitted to them. The annual cost of training people in this particular line of endeavor would then be imposed upon the diagram and the relative sizes of the areas BXA and A'XB' would be computed. The result would supposedly show whether more or less people should be trained in the trade or profession under review (i.e., if A'XB' is larger than BXA, then society should train more of these people, if it is smaller then fewer persons should be encouraged to enter the field). AA' and BB' cover net sums only.

This application involves many problems. It assumes the wages of the individuals involved equal their MRP (i.e., perfect competition), and that the technician's marginal revenue productivity equals his marginal social productivity. It is clearly not applicable with any degree of accuracy to the salaries of employees of the state for example, and even in private industries the assumption of perfect competition (i.e., MRP = wage) is a hazardous one, particularly in underdeveloped countries. Nevertheless, in some instances this strict statistical application of the model may have its uses.

A ROUGH QUANTITATIVE ESTIMATE OF EQUILIBRIUM LEVELS OF INVESTMENT IN EDUCATION

With this line of approach the equilibrium condition which the model describes is the one which is sought after, but the model itself plays little or no part in determining how it should be reached. The technique is rather one of estimating by means of census returns, industry work-force sample surveys, and the like, the number of people already in each economic activity

---

[6] This same question of equilibrium levels in educational investment has already been dealt with by other writers in terms of present values, or internal rates of return. See: Becker, a.a.O., passim, and A. Weisbrod, "The Valuation of Human Capital," *Journal of Political Economy*, Vol. LXIX (1961), p. 427.

or profession, and calculating how far this number varies from an estimate of existing or future requirements. These requirements are calculated on the basis of some notion of ideal output/employment ratios in each specialized field.[7]

Insofar as the data available are accurate and can be used for this purpose, the required figures in terms of how many people should be trained in various trades and professions can be obtained. In other words, this technique should give the answer which the model would demand, but not as a result of a rigorous application of the methods outlined in it.

Such a purely quantitative approach to manpower assessment has the virtue of probably being more practical of application in terms of available data, particularly in underdeveloped countries, than the technique described under (1) above. Nevertheless, the objective remains the same, namely to calculate the equilibrium which the strict use of the model would give.

A QUALITATIVE APPLICATION OF THE MODEL

This is the approach which will frequently be of greatest use to the manpower adviser. Often he will not have the time or the resources to derive his advice from the techniques outlined in sections one and two. Even where data of the kind which he needs are readily available in an underdeveloped country, there may be strong grounds for suspecting their accuracy. In these circumstances the adviser must either supplement or substitute statistical analysis with, or by, qualitative argument along the lines which the model suggests.

Economic theory falls into two categories. First, and most impressive, it can provide insight into the economic process which is not apparent on largely common sense grounds. Second, it can be used to provide an orderly framework for the discussion of problems in a more or less common sense way. The model here outlined cannot be included in the first category;

[7] For detailed descriptions of this technique, see: S. L. Wolfbein, "Manpower Projections and Techniques," and J. I. Saks and E. C. McVoy, "Techniques of Manpower Assessment," both included in *Human Resources: Training of Scientific and Technical Personnel*, Washington: U.S. Government Printing Office, 1963, pp. 20–44; F. H. Harbison, *Evaluación de Recursos Humanos*, Santiago de Chile: Economic Commission for Latin America, 1963 (Mimeographed); F. W. Mahler, "Manpower Surveys," Geneva: International Labor Office, 1963, Chaps. 4–7 A, and 22 (Mimeographed); W. H. Mason, *Programación de los Servicios de Mano de Obra* (PMAL/6(c)/1), Santiago, ILO Liason Center with ECLA, 1963 (Mimeographed); ILO Liason Center, ECLA, *Conceptos de la Fuerza Trabajadora y de las Necesidades de Mano de Obra*, Santiago, 1963 (Mimeographed); ILO Liason Center, ECLA, *Diagnostico de la Situación de Mano de Obra*, Santiago, 1963 (Mimeographed).

Examples of work carried out along the lines suggested in the above papers are to be found in: ILO, *Report to the Government of Trinidad and Tobago on the Establishment of a Manpower Information Programme* (ILO/TAP/West Indies/R. 1), Geneva, 1960; ILO, *Informe al Gobierno del Perú sobre el programa de informacion acerca de la mano de obra* (ILO/TAP/Peru/R. 7), Geneva, 1961; and, ILO, *Informe dirigido al Gobierno de la República Argentina con motivo de una encuesta parcial sobre la mano de obra* (ILO/TAP/Argentina/R. 3), Geneva, 1957.

it is, however, potentially useful in the second. It illustrates quite clearly that if the net return from training in a particular field is to be maximized, then certain steps must be taken. They are

1. To minimize the cost of education over time.
2. To maximize the returns on education over time.
3. To lengthen the working life of the trained individual.

These considerations are worth further discussion.

1. Minimizing the cost of education over time.—By this we mean minimizing the cost in such a way as not to reduce net returns. This can probably be done in most poor countries by concentrating on vocational training, and by letting the largely cultural aspects of education fall by the way (remember we are here concerned with economic arguments only). It can also be done by providing training with low-cost plant, such as wooden huts, as opposed to stately buildings; a philosophy which comes hard in many underdeveloped countries. Moreover, where social as opposed to purely monetary costs are concerned, the use of plant and equipment which can be created by a hitherto underemployed labor force is an important consideration. Students who need training with concentrations of expensive machinery, etc. are probably best sent abroad—depending upon the wastage among those who fail to return that is. But all this is really quite obvious with or without the use of the model.[8]

Less obvious perhaps is the question of the importance of the rate of interest paid on the unamortized balance of the cost of a person's training. Over time this can form the greater part of the total cost. It is therefore the prime target for economy. In most underdeveloped countries interest rates are higher than in their developed counterparts. The lowest rates of all are to be found with the national or international aid institutions. It therefore becomes almost axiomatic to state that time spent on attempting to negotiate a (substantial) loan from abroad for educational purposes will seldom be wasted. This is again only common sense, but the model does make it immediately and abundantly clear.

2. Maximizing the returns on education over time.—The application of the model in this sense consists of making judgements as to the position and angle of ascent of the curve showing the returns on the particular type of

[8] The initial cost of even a modest educational system can be a tremendous burden in a poor country. Hector Correa (a.a.O., pp. 104–105) has listed the "Relative Importance of the Supply Cost of Education in Countries Having Different Incomes and Different Age Structures of the Population." He has prepared an index in these terms, and from it he shows that providing a per capita education of the order now existing in the United States, would, for example, be almost forty times as burdensome as a proportion of income per active person in, say, Korea. Clearly, then, the costs of education in poor countries must be kept down well below those obtaining in rich countries. The use of expensive plant and equipment is just not permissible to any marked degree.

training under discussion (the AA' curve). Qualitative judgement in this respect takes the adviser into the realm of the dictates of the economy at large, as well as into a discussion of the nutritional and health conditions of the trained personnel themselves.[9] If the country with which he is concerned has a potentially large market for industrial goods, even in spite of low per capita incomes (e.g., India or Brazil), or if it has had a fortuitous increase in capital, entrepreneurs, or low-cost competent workers (e.g., Hong Kong), then perhaps he would conclude that the most highly-placed and most rapidly rising AA' curves will be in industrial training. If, on the other hand, it has a small potential industrial market, but is rich in land and other natural resources (e.g., Ecuador, Thailand, or Liberia), then to begin with the most advantageous AA' curves will probably be found in vocational training in agricultural techniques, land settlement, road building and the like.[10] The adviser reaches his conclusions in this respect by a general consideration of the economy in which he is working, by reading, and by talking to other experts. For example, if he is told that seed selection, grading crops, or whatever can triple the value of output per hectare or per man hour, then he has strong grounds for supposing that the training of vocational workers along these lines will have a high marginal revenue productivity (i.e., the AA' curve will be well to the left).[11] Nor should the adviser neglect social considerations. The training of land settlement experts and road

[9] Hector Correa had estimated (a.a.O., p. 44) that in terms of "Bed-disability Days" alone the typical worker in Egypt, for example, only works at 83 per cent of his capacity as compared with 97 per cent in the United States. He goes on to show (p. 47) in his table "Modifications in Working Capacity Due to the Simultaneous Effects of [Mal-] Nutrition and Health," that working capacity drops to 69 per cent in Egypt as opposed to 93 per cent in the U.S.

[10] For example, Correa (a.a.O.) claims that in Ecuador the combined effects of malnutrition and ill-health reduce the typical worker's output to 48 per cent of full capacity, and this in a country where only 4.5 per cent of an estimated 84 per cent of the total land surface which is potentially cultivable is actually tilled (see, La Secretaria de la Comisión Económica para América Latina, *El Desarrollo Económico del Ecuador* (E/CN. 12/295), Mexico: United Nations, Jan., 1954, p. 43), and where even those areas which are cultivated are not always used with much intensity (Junta Nacional de Planificación y Coordinación Económica, *Bases y Directivas para Programar el Desarrollo del Ecuador*, Tomo I, Quito 1958, p. 127). Quite clearly, then, investment in the training of experts in land settlement, road building, and the like, will yield high marginal returns, particularly in terms of much needed additional food production, in a country such as this.

The general argument in favor of investment in training farmers in better techniques as a prerequisite to industrial growth is developed at some length by Harry T. Oshima in his "A Strategy for Asian Development," and his "Non-Investment Inputs in Asian Agriculture and the 'Leavening Effect': A Rejoinder," *Economic Development and Cultural Change*, Vols. X (1962), pp. 294–316; and XI (1963), pp. 311–314 respectively.

[11] All this abstracts from the question of worsening rural terms of trade as a result of concentrating development in agriculture, and of the question of prospective common market arrangements which might make an industrial advance more feasible. An adviser must also give due regard to these considerations. A most interesting recent discussion of many of the issues involved here can be found in: R. E. Baldwin, "Export Technology and Development from a Subsistence Level," *Economic Journal*, Vol. LXXIII (1963), pp. 80–92.

engineers may, for instance, encourage the most rapid creation of employment opportunities in countries with a good deal of unused land,[12] and this may be a superior educational investment from the social point of view to one which concentrates on the production of technicians for factories where the employment/capital ratio is low.[13] In other words, the AA' curve in social terms will be even further to the left than its monetary counterpart.

3. Lengthening the working life of the trained individual.—From the model it can readily be seen that if the working life of a trained person can be lengthened, then the whole of the additional annual MRPS accruing to his training will be a net gain. The question then arises as to how to lengthen the working lives of trained personnel. Improved health and nutritional conditions will do this in many poor countries,[14] and although it may offend one's sense of social justice, society is probably best served by concentrating medical and nutritional resources on its most productive (i.e., most highly trained) classes whenever these resources are really scarce.[15] Fortunately, if one may use such a term in this way, the operation of the pricing system can generally be expected to yield the required result in this respect.

Then too, purely arbitrary limitations may exist on the working life of highly trained personel in underdeveloped countries. Many civil services, educational institutions, and the like maintain the artificially low retirement ages which were appropriate when the expatriate administrator or teacher bore his burden up to the age of fifty-five, but could not be expected to stay away from his native land much longer. The replacement of these people by local personnel who may work in air-conditioned offices with every sort of anti-biotic at their beck and call has created a situation in which low retirement ages are no longer appropriate. The manpower expert should point this out whenever it occurs.

CONCLUSIONS

Finally let it be said that the writer is aware that events may prove his emphasis in error. An educational system which lays the foundation for a rational, cultivated society, as opposed to one which concentrates very

---

[12] The theoretical value of education as an aid to migration is discussed by: T. W. Schultz, a.a.O., p. 4, and Larry a Sjaastad, "The Costs and Returns on Human Migration," *Journal of Political Economy* (Supplement: Oct., 1962), a.a.O., pp. 80–93.

[13] The writer is aware of the debate which rages around the supposed conflict between the dictates of comparative advantage in a static sense and the requirements of economic growth, or what has been called comparative advantage over time. For a recent balanced discussion of this issue see: H. B. Chenery, "Comparative Advantage and Development Policy," *American Economic Review*, Vol. LI (1962), pp. 18–51.

[14] While the average working life in the United States has been estimated to last for fifty years, in underdeveloped countries it is generally much less. In Guinea, for example, it is calculated at only 18.15 years. Correa, a.a.O., pp. 40–41.

[15] For a discussion of the economics of investment in improved health facilities, see, S. J. Mushkin, "Health as an Investment," *Journal of Political Economy* (Supplement: Oct., 1962), a.a.O., pp. 129–157.

largely on strictly vocational training, may eventually yield the highest economic and social returns. Indeed, vocational training or any other method of altering the status quo may not be permitted in many societies until the existing ruling classes are educated along liberal, rational lines; not permitted this side of a revolution that is. It may also be true that concentration of the kind of training which will encourage the immediate maximization of the employment/capital ratio may prove to be an error when it is at the expense of the creation of a technology which will ultimately yield the highest net investment and growth (although the two are not necessarily in conflict).[16] However, the kind of educational system advocated in this paper will generally yield the most rapid results, and we might therefore recall that the only contribution to economic theory which has proved really unassailable, at least up to now, is that "in the long run we will all be dead."

---

[16] The technology chosen in a developing country really needs to be a compromise between one which minimises costs over a reasonable period in the future and one which maximizes domestic demand. In many cases this is likely to be a labor-intensive technology.

33

Approaches to Educational Planning

Techniques used in educational planning and forecasting manpower requirements into the future vary widely. The consequence is the appearance of contradictory results and the inference of achievement of precision to a greater extent than is warranted. Mark Blaug, currently head of the Research Unit in the

MARK BLAUG

Economics of Education at the University of London, presents a definitive comparison of alternative approaches and the way in which they relate to planned and market economies.

Educational planning is as old as state education, that is, much older than economic planning. Until comparatively recent times, however, educational planning was haphazard rather than deliberate, a matter for local rather than central government, concerned with individual educational institutions rather than entire educational systems, and no effort was ever made to state the objectives that planning was supposed to satisfy. The Second World War changed all that: the post-war explosion in the demand for education, the new interest in central economic planning, the obsession with growth rates in both developed and developing countries combined to promote a new attitude to the administration of education. Educational planning by the State with the purpose of promoting economic objectives is now as universally approved as economic planning itself. However, just as

Reprinted from Mark Blaug, "Approaches to Educational Planning," *Economic Journal* 77 (June 1967), pp. 262–87, with the permission of the author and publisher.

there is a world of difference between central investment planning in the Soviet Union and "indicative planning" in France and Britain, so enthusiasm about educational planning has not yet produced any consensus about the methods and techniques of planning education.

Consider the curious predicament of an educational planner who consults the fast-growing literature on the economics of education for guidance in making policy decisions. On the one hand, he is told to gear the expansion of the educational system to quantitative forecasts of the demand for highly qualified man-power. On the other hand, he is urged to project what is quaintly called "the social demand" for education, that is, the private consumer's demand, and to provide facilities accordingly. Finally, he is furnished with calculations of the rate of return on investment on education and advised to supply just enough schooling to equalize the yield of investment in human capital with the yield of investment in physical capital. Obviously, the three approaches may give different answers, and, strangely enough, the literature offers little assistance in reconciling different methods of educational planning. To add insult to injury, however, the advocates of man-power forecasting scoff at the assumptions underlying rate-of-return calculations, while the proponents of rate-of-return analysis are equally scornful of the idea that man-power requirements can be predicted accurately. In the meantime, higher education is being expanded in many countries simply to accommodate the rising numbers of academically qualified applicants, apparently on the notion that something like Say's Law operates in markets for professional man-power, supply creating its own demand. All this is very confusing, and in the circumstances we can hardly blame some educational planners who are beginning to doubt the value of the contribution of economists to educational decision-making.

This paper is an attempt to resolve the issue, or at least to present it in such a way that it can be resolved. The basic thesis is that the three approaches rightly understood are complementary, not competitive. At one point the argument will involve a comparison between the United States and the United Kingdom, but this is purely illustrative and designed to clarify the problem by discussing it in a concrete setting; the thesis itself is applicable with appropriate modifications to both developed and developing countries.

I An Outline of the Three Approaches

The O.E.C.D. Mediterranean Regional Project provides a sophisticated example of the man-power-forecasting approach to educational planning. The method used was that of proceeding in stages from an initial projection of a desirable G.D.P. in a future year, as given by a prior economic plan, to a supply of educated man-power in some sense "required" to reach it in the target year.[1] The steps are as follows: (1) the target G.D.P. in, say, 1975 is broken down by major sectors, such as agriculture, manufacturing, transport, distribution and the like; (2) these sectoral G.D.P.s are then broken down by industries (this level of disaggregation was not attempted in the M.R.P. studies); (3) an average labor-output coefficient, the reciprocal of the familiar concept of the average productivity of labor, is applied to the sectoral or industrial G.D.P. targets, yielding a forecast of labor require-ments by sector or industry; (4) the labor force is distributed among a number of mutually exclusive occupational categories; (5) the occupational structure of the labor force is converted into an educational structure by applying a standard measure of the level of formal education required to perform "adequately" in each occupation.[2] Allowances are then made for deaths, retirements and emigration, that is, for replacements as well as additions to the stock of educated man-power. The final result is a con-ditional forecast of the demand for educated people in 1975, conditional, that is, on the achievement of the G.D.P. target.

The difficulties in this method center largely on steps (3) and (5), although step (4) also raises controversial questions. The standard pro-cedure for forecasting labor-output coefficients, step (3), is to extrapolate past trends, either as a function of output or as a function of time. An alternative device is that of adopting the coefficient observed in more ad-vanced countries, on the notion that there are definite man-power growth paths that all economies follow in the course of development; a variant is to take the labor-output coefficient ruling in the most advanced sector of the economy on the ground that the best-practice technique of that sector will eventually become the average-practice technique of all sectors. Lastly, there is the technique employed in drawing up *The National Plan* of asking employers to estimate their own future labor requirements, given a stated rate of expansion in the market for their products. We shall return to these estimating procedures later; for the moment, we simply take note that the problems involved in forecasting the productivity of labor are familiar to

---

[1] The M.R.P. Country Reports for Spain, Italy, Greece, Yugoslavia, Turkey and Portugal are now available from O.E.C.D. The method is explained and defended by H. S. Parnes, *Forecasting Educational Needs for Economic and Social Development* (Paris: O.E.C.D., 1962).

[2] The method is summed up in the equation:

$$\left(G.D.P.\right)\left(\frac{G.D.P._{\cdot s}}{G.D.P.}\right)\left(\frac{G.D.P._{\cdot i}}{G.D.P._{\cdot s}}\right)\left(\frac{L_i}{G.D.P._{\cdot i}}\right)\left(\frac{L_j}{L_i}\right)\left(\frac{L_e}{L_j}\right)$$

= Workers of education e in occupation j in industry i in sector s.

where $G.D.P._{\cdot s} = G.D.P.$ originating in each sector;
$G.D.P._{\cdot i} = G.D.P.$ originating in each industry;
L_i = the labor force in each industry;
L_j = the labor force in each occupation;
L_e = the labor force with each level of education; and $L \geqslant \sum\limits^{n} L_{sije}$.

economists. This is not so with the difficulties encountered in step (5) of the exercise, namely, the translation of labor requirements by occupation into labor requirements by educational qualification (*The National Plan* omitted this last step, thus producing a man-power forecast without implications for educational planning). The simplest method of converting occupation into education is to apply the mean number of years of schooling currently observed in each occupation or job-cluster. Unfortunately, the concept of educational attainment is not adequately expressed by a scalar such as years of schooling. In any case, this is not what the educational planner wants to know: his decisions have to be made in terms of different types of education. The problem, therefore, is that of specifying a vector that measures the combination of varying amounts and kinds of formal education required in different occupations. So far, despite many attempts to develop such educational vectors, it cannot be said that this difficulty has been resolved satisfactorily. The difficulty is not merely technical; as we shall see, it is at the root of the inadequacy of the man-power-forecasting approach as now conceived.

We turn now to social-demand projections. Little need be said here. It is all in the Robbins Report, so to speak.[3] At this point, we need to distinguish between "forecasts" and "projections." As these terms are employed in the present paper, a "forecast" will always mean a prediction subject to the achievement of a certain economic growth target, that is, a statement of what would happen if economic growth were deliberately manipulated. In other words, man-power forecasts simply spell out the implications of an economic plan with respect to the characteristics of the labor force. "Projections," on the other hand, predict the outcome of purely spontaneous forces, that is, what will happen in the normal course of events in an unplanned economy (the "normal course of events" includes the information made available by the projection). We can therefore talk about man-power projections, say, in the American economy or the British economy. Similarly, projections of the private demand for non-compulsory education, social-demand projections, attempt to predict student enrollments on the assumption that the "price" of education remains the same, whether the economy is planned or not. This "price" consists of the direct and indirect costs of secondary and higher education, subject to the constraint of meeting entry-qualifications. Thus, social-demand projections of the Robbins type are contingent upon: (1) a given level of provision of secondary education, particularly of fifth and sixth forms; (2) a given standard of admission into higher education; (3) a given level of the direct costs of secondary and higher education, in particular, a given level of student grants; and (4) a given level of earnings of educated people not only because these

[3] See also O.E.C.D., *Policy Conference on Economic Growth and Investment in Education. II. Targets for Education in Europe in 1970* (Paris: O.E.C.D., 1962).

earnings represent an important aspect of the vocational opportunities opened up by additional education but also because they constitute the indirect costs of staying on at school in the form of earnings forgone. Extrapolation of existing enrollment trends is the heart of the matter and, of course, the better the knowledge of the socio-economic determinants of "staying on at school," the more accurate the projection. In principle it is perfectly possible to measure the price-elasticity of the demand for education, that is, to specify the effect of changes in some of the factors that are being held equal, such as the level of student grants, but so far little effort along these lines has been attempted. All this implies that social-demand projections represent something like a minimum effort at foresight, telling the educational planner not what to do but rather what will happen if he does exactly what he has been doing in the past.

This brings us to rate-of-return analysis. Here we start with a cross-tabulation of the labor force by age, education and earnings before and after tax. From these, we construct age-earnings profiles by years of schooling, that is, we use cross-section data to project lifetime earnings associated with additional education. It is convenient to treat the costs of education as merely negative earnings, with the result that we can proceed immediately to calculate the present value of the net earnings differentials associated with extra education at different discount rates. The internal rate of return on investment in education is simply the discount rate that sums the present value of the net lifetime earnings to nought, or that equates the discounted value of the costs of a certain amount of education with the discounted value of the future earnings anticipated from it.[4] However, an allowance must be made for the difficulty that the earnings associated with additional education cannot be entirely attributed to education alone; needless to say, individual earnings are determined partly by native ability, family background, social class origins and so forth, and to that extent take on the character of a rental payment to a non-reproducible factor of production. On the basis of somewhat less than adequate empirical evidence, some American authorities have agreed that about two-thirds of the observable earnings differentials associated with years of schooling are statistically attributable to differences in educational attainment. One can see why the figure of two-thirds might be an overestimate in Great Britain, given our highly selective educational system; on the other hand, higher-educated individuals are relatively scarcer here than in the United States, which argues that two-thirds is an underestimate. Furthermore, no one has yet

---

[4] That is,

$$\sum_{t=15}^{t=65} \frac{E_t - C_t}{(1+r)^t} = 0$$

where r is the internal rate of return, E is earnings before or after tax, C is the costs of education, $t=15$ is the legal school leaving age and $t=65$ is the year of retirement.

succeeded in giving a satisfactory quantitative expression to the considerable uncertainty and illiquidity of investment in human capital. Nevertheless, the common-sense interpretation of the rates of return that have been calculated is that they represent something close to maximum-likelihood estimates of the average yields of additional expenditures on education. In one sense they are merely a summary statistic expressing the prevailing relationship between the costs of more schooling and the earnings that may be more or less confidently expected to result from it.

There are many objections to this approach, some of which are worth re-emphasizing in the present context. First, it assumes that existing earnings differentials in favor of educated people reflect their superior productivity; obviously, if there is no relationship whatever between relative earnings and relative productivities rate-of-return figures are economically meaningless. Secondly, if the demand for and supply of educated people increase at different rates in the future than in the past rates of return will differ from those that have been calculated, or, to put it into jargon, the average rate of return may not be a good guide to the marginal rate of return. Thirdly, the approach ignores the non-monetary consumption benefits of education, and, more seriously, it ignores all the monetary benefits other than those that accrue directly to the educated individual. This is not the place to discuss these objections,[5] although the first and second points will be taken up below. Notice, however, that the man-power-forecasting approach is vulnerable to some of the same objections: for example, it, too, ignores the consumption as well as the spillover benefits of education. Nevertheless, waiving all technical objections, the fact remains that the assumptions underlying rate-of-return analysis are rather different from those of man-power-forecasting and social-demand projections. Can we somehow combine all these approaches, or must we choose one in preference to the two others?

II   A Preliminary Contrast between the Three Approaches

The first thing that strikes us about these three approaches to educational planning is that they are not on the same footing. The man-power-forecasting approach tells the educational planner how many scientists, engineers, technicians and so forth he should supply by, say, 1975 without regard either to their prospective earnings or to the relative costs of producing them. In short, it provides the planner with a forecast of one point of the

---

[5] For a detailed discussion of all the technical objections, see M. Blaug, "The Rate of Return on Investment in Education in Great Britain," *Manchester School*, September 1965, pp. 205–61, and Reprint Series, No. 5, Unit for Economic and Statistical Studies on Higher Education, London School of Economics.

1975 demand schedule for a particular skill. If, for any reason, the supply target stipulated in the man-power forecast is not met, so that relative earnings change, the educational planner will have no way of knowing whether the error was due to an inaccurate forecast of the shift in the demand curve between 1966 and 1975 or simply to the mistaken assumption that students choose to study particular subjects with no regard for earnings prospects.[6] Similarly, a projection of the private demand for education tells the educational planner how many students with different types of professional preparation may be expected to be forthcoming by 1975. He has no way of knowing whether these students can be absorbed in the labor market without a change in the pattern of relative earnings. If relative earnings alter it is very likely that this will affect the structure of the private demand for education by fields of specialization. At this point he may be tempted to combine the social-demand projection with a man-power forecast by providing just enough places in higher education to meet the demands of students qualified for entry, while allowing the distribution of places among faculties and subjects to be governed by a forecast of man-power requirements. Indeed, this is more or less the approach that was adopted by the Robbins Committee.[7] But a moment's reflection will show that this really combines the worst of both worlds: it assumes that economic growth is affected by the relative supply of skilled professionals but not by their absolute supply; it treats the fraction of the labor force that has received higher education as

[6] Take the case of the labor market for scientists. A man-power-forecast states that the demand for scientists in 1975 will be q; as this forecast ignores the earnings of scientists, apparently the notion is that the supply of scientists is entirely a matter of the facilities made available for the study of science (hence, the supply curve is perfectly inelastic). In 1975, however, instead of q scientists at salaries s, q' scientists are forthcoming at salaries s', that is, we observe intersection B instead of C. Are we on the 1975 demand curve, the error being due to the failure to meet our educational supply target, or are we on a different demand curve?

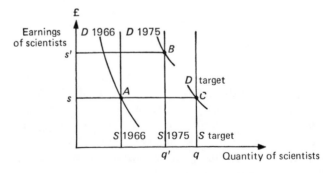

[7] See C. A. Moser and P. R. G. Layard, "Planning the Scale of Higher Education in Great Britain: Some Statistical Problems," *Journal of the Royal Statistical Society*, Series A, Vol. 27, Pt. 4, 1964, pp. 488–9, and Reprints Series, No. 1, Unit for Economic and Statistical Studies on Higher Education, London School of Economics.

a consumption-decision best left in the hands of parents and students, whereas the ratio of scientists to engineers or engineers to technicians is regarded as an investment-decision that must be the responsibility of the State. Furthermore, it is precisely in forecasting the demand for particular skills rather than in forecasting total labor requirements that man-power forecasting is weakest. Thus, this combination of the two approaches makes poor use of the advantages of man-power forecasting, such as they are. The outcome is a policy that is neither *laissez-faire* nor intervention, but a curious mixture of the two. To be sure, it is not difficult to find an ideological justification for the social-demand approach in a private-enterprise economy. But consistency demands that the policy of accommodating the private demand should be applied to the choice of subject as much as to the choice of further schooling.

A logical way of combining man-power forecasting with social-demand projections would be to start with the growth of G.D.P. as a basis for the assessment of man-power requirements via estimated productivity trends, and then to reverse the procedure by forecasting the likely output of the educational system and deriving G.D.P. via labor productivity trends. If there were a discrepancy in the two results one could then decide whether to revise the G.D.P. target or to attempt to alter the future supply of educated people; since it costs something to do either, one would probably do both in the effort to minimize the loss in resources. As the two approaches are concerned with different sides of the labor market, however, it is difficult to see how they could be combined without some reference to relative earnings or at least hiring practices, elements conspicuously absent in the leading examples of man-power forecasting and social-demand projections.[8] What these two approaches do have in common is that they provide the educational planner with exact magnitudes to aim at. Rate-of-return analysis, on the other hand, merely provides a signal of direction: invest more or invest less. But how much more or less? A little more or less is the answer, and then recalculate the rate of return.

So far, rates of return have been calculated only for entire levels of the educational system, or, at best, for years of additional schooling. But in the United States and Canada some evidence is now beginning to emerge on rates of return to different types of professional training,[9] and for the present

---

[8] For an attempt to combine the two approaches via the earnings of educated people, see the diagram in M. Blaug, "An Economic Interpretation of the Private Demand for Education," *Economica*, May 1966, pp. 171–8, and Reprints Series No. 7, Unit for Economic and Statistical Studies on Higher Education, London School of Economics.

[9] See W. Lee Hansen, "The 'Shortage' of Engineers," *Review of Economics and Statistics*, August 1961, pp. 251–6; "Professional Engineers: Salary Structure Problems," *Industrial Relations*, May 1963, pp. 33–44; " 'Shortages' and Investment in Health Manpower," *The Economics of Health and Medical Care* (Ann Arbor, Michigan: The University of Michigan, 1965), pp. 75–92; and B. W. Wilkinson, "Present Values of Lifetime Earnings in Different Occupations," *Journal of Political Economy*, December 1966.

discussion I shall assume that such figures are available. Furthermore, present data limitations have confined rate-of-return analysis to calculations of the average rate of return on investment in education. However, with better data on the career prospects of recent graduates there is no reason why we cannot estimate marginal rates of return, which is what we really need for educational planning. At any rate, whether average or marginal yields are calculated, it is clear that rate-of-return analysis is the method of marginalism, or what Professor Popper has called "piecemeal social engineering."[10] This has long been regarded as the principal weakness of rate-of-return calculations as an instrument of planning, but in practice, it may be the source of its peculiar strength: it forces the educational planner to face the severe limitations in his capacity to foresee the consequences of present action, particularly when action involves, as it often does, the unprecedented expansion of educational facilities or changes in the entire structure of the educational system. Rate-of-return analysis as such does not forecast the demand or the supply of educated man-power. It indicates how the two are matched at present. Curiously enough, however, if man-power forecasts and social-demand projections are reliable the consequence is necessarily an implicit prediction of rates of return. Therefore, either all three methods are valid when used in conjunction with one another or there is something wrong with man-power forecasting, or social-demand projections, or both.

To argue against this conclusion, one must assert both that: (1) the costs of different types and amounts of education, and (2) the relative earnings of highly qualified man-power never vary over time. In some countries and for some periods the first assertion may be correct. The second, however, is palpably false and, indeed, can only be substantiated on theoretical grounds if: (1) Say's Law operates in all labor markets so that demand and supply shift to the right as if hooked together; or (2) relative earnings are entirely supply-determined because the supply curve of every type of scientific man-power is perfectly elastic; or (3) relative earnings are entirely demand-determined because the demand curve for every type of scientific manpower is perfectly elastic. It is easy to see that (2) and (3) are absurd assumptions. The same cannot be said of (1), which is probably the conception in the back of the minds of man-power forecasters. Unlike most assumptions in economics, however, this one is easy to falsify. All we need to observe is fluctuations in the relative earnings of highly qualified man-power and Say's Law is invalidated.

Nevertheless, most educational planners react instinctively to rate-of-return analysis in the conviction that marginalism is not the appropriate technique for educational planning. It is the length of time required to produce skilled professional people that is always cited as the rationale for

[10] K. R. Popper, *The Open Society and Its Enemies*, II (London: Routledge & Kegan Paul, 4th ed., 1962), p. 222.

long-term man-power forecasting. Training a scientist or an engineer takes about fifteen years and the effective production-period may be even longer because the educational system is a hierarchical input-output structure: it is usually necessary first to feed back an intermediate output of teachers if we want a higher final output of scientists and engineers.[11] In consequence, it is likely that labor markets for highly qualified man-power are subject to cobweb effects without a tendency to converge toward equilibrium. When excess demand for a specialized skill raises its relative earnings, the increase in the supply of that skill, assuming students are made aware of and respond to the rise in prospective earnings, takes five or ten years to materialize. Because of this lag in the adjustment of supply, there is every chance that market forces will overshoot the equilibrium, so that what was a shortage turns suddenly into a glut. As earnings fall, the reverse effect takes place. This dynamic adjustment process may never produce market-clearance in any one period, but rather continuous fluctuations in earnings associated with successive phases of labor shortages in one field and labor surpluses in another. Given the strong probability that there will be structural disequilibria in the distribution of educated man-power among occupations, and the high cost of such disequilibria when they occur, it is imperative that some central agency try to forecast the demand for scientific or technical man-power at least ten or fifteen years ahead, in the same way that the Central Electricity Board forecasts the demand for electric power before it commits itself to building a hydro-electric dam that takes almost a decade to complete. Even if we could predict relative earnings fifteen years ahead, these would be of no help to rational investment decisions in the field of education, because these earnings simply reflect disequilibrium situations. So runs the central argument of the proponents of man-power forecasting.[12]

[11] For an excellent illustration of this feedback problem, see V. Stoikov, "The Allocation of Scientific Effort: Some Important Aspects," *Quarterly Journal of Economics*, May 1964, pp. 307–24.

[12] For a powerful defence of the man-power forecasting approach along these lines, see G. Bombach, "Long-term Requirements for Qualified Manpower in Relation to Economic Growth," *Economic Aspects of Higher Education*, ed. S. E. Harris (Paris: O.E.C.D., 1964), pp. 201–23, as revised in "Manpower Forecasting and Educational Policy," *Sociology of Education*, Fall, 1965, pp. 343–74. The fact that the lead-time for the production of scientific man-power is fairly long and, hence, that markets for this type of man-power are characterized by cobweb effect does not itself prove that market forces never converge on equilibrium. K. J. Arrow and W. M. Capron have argued that the "shortage" of engineers and scientists in the United States in recent years is gradually being eliminated by a dynamic adjustment process: "Dynamic Shortages and Price Rises: The Engineer-Scientist Case," *Quarterly Journal of Economics*, May 1959, pp. 292–309. But Arrow and Capron consider only lags on the demand side—such as the time it takes firms to realize that they can only obtain more qualified man-power by offering higher salaries (pp. 297–9)—and refer only briefly (p. 303) to those lags on the supply side that have been emphasized by man-power forecasters. Even so, what is true for the United States may not apply elsewhere. For a brilliant catalogue of all the factors that inhibit market clearance for specialized skills in both developed and underdeveloped countries—such as rigid technologies, conventions in

III Two Views of the State of the World

We can now sharpen the contrast between the three approaches to educational planning by asking what the world would have to be like to make
it unnecessary to forecast the demand for highly specialized man-power,
despite its long production-period. Suppose we had an educational system
that did not permit students to specialize until their second or third year of
higher education, that provided a perfectly general education for everyone
until the ages of nineteen or twenty, that made full use of team teaching and
new educational media in the interest of keeping staff/student ratios as
flexible as possible and capable of ranging from $\frac{1}{10}$ to $\frac{1}{300}$. Suppose also that
vocational counselling was so efficient that students were extremely well informed of career opportunities. Suppose further that the demand for different skills was highly elastic, that capital was an almost perfect substitute for
labor and that, in addition, workers with different skill characteristics were
good substitutes for one another. In short, there were always many people
who could perform a given job, and the job could almost always be displaced
by a machine. Lastly, suppose that most specialized skills were acquired on
the job, not learned in schools, and that technical change demanding new
and hitherto unfamiliar skills proceeded gradually without fits and starts.
In these circumstances would it really matter that education is a durable
asset and that the gestation-period of that asset is ten or twenty years? To
forecast man-power requirements under these conditions would be almost
meaningless for the simple reason that, in this sort of world, educated man-
power could never be a bottleneck to economic growth. Projections of the
private demand for education and calculations of the rate of return, however, would be perfectly meaningful in such a world, and, indeed, the only
guides available to decision-making in education.

We can go to the other extreme and imagine a world created in the image
of man-power forecasting: students and parents would be poorly informed of
career prospects and more interested in acquiring education for consumption
than for investment reasons; specialization by subjects would start very early;
student/staff ratios would be fixed and unalterable, and all school buildings
and school equipment would be indivisible and highly specific in each use;
the demand schedules for separate skills would be highly inelastic, and the
elasticity of substitution between labor and capital, as well as the elasticity

---

hiring practices, ignorance of skill-substitution potentials, the high cost of spreading information both among the buyers and the sellers of skills, skill labelling by paper qualifications in response to imperfect knowledge, etc.—see H. Leibenstein, "Shortages and
Surpluses in Education in Underdeveloped Countries: A Theoretical Foray," *Education
and Economic Development*, eds. C. A. Anderson and M. J. Bowman (Chicago: Aldine
Publishing Company, 1965), pp. 51–62.

of substitution between men with different skills, would be well below unity; industry would provide virtually no training, and the pace of technical change would be so rapid that the demand curves for people with different educational backgrounds would shift through time unevenly and irregularly. Obviously, in this sort of world the private demand for education would be so unstable as to make it impossible to extrapolate existing trends, and all marginal calculations would be irrelevant. Labor-output coefficients would be technologically determined, and earnings associated with education and even the costs of supplying various skills would be ignored.

Enough has been said to suggest that the quarrel really is about the view one takes of the real world. What we have is a picture of a continuum: to the right is a neo-classical universe, characterized by substitutabilities in both the educational system and the productive system; to the left is a Leontief-type universe of fixed-input coefficients, characterized by extreme complementarities in both education and industry. Needless to say, the real world lies somewhere in between. To resolve the conflict that we are examining, we need to decide whether the world lies nearer to the right end or the left end of the continuum (right and left, of course, carry no political connotation).

IV A Wider Conception of Educational Planning

There is much research going on both here and abroad designed to throw light on the ease of substitution among people with different educational backgrounds in particular occupational categories, on the substitutability between formal education and labor training, on hiring practices with respect to educated personnel, on the relationship between choice of technique and the skill mix of the labor force, on occupational mobility and the pattern of career opportunities and so forth.[13] In time to come these inquiries may allow us to give an unequivocal answer to the question whether the productive system is in fact characterized by variable or by fixed educational-input coefficients. But when it is realized that the answer ideally requires specification of the aggregate production function of an economy, not for output as a function of homogeneous labor and capital but as a function of labor classified by levels of education and capital classified by types of machine-operating skills, it seems obvious that educational planning will have to make do for a long time to come with very imperfect knowledge of the precise connection between education and economic growth. In these

[13] The author is participating in a major study of this kind, carried out by the Unit for Economic and Statistical Studies on Higher Education of the London School of Economics, under the direction of M. Hall: for some preliminary results, see M. Blaug, M. H. Peston and A. Ziderman, *The Utilisation of Educated Manpower in Industry* (London: Oliver & Boyd, 1967).

circumstances what is the planner to do? Should he act on a man-power forecast? But what if the forecast were to prompt action exactly opposite to that suggested by a projection of private demand or a calculation of the social rate of return on investment in education? We are back to the problem with which we started. Are we any nearer a resolution?

Planning has been defined as the process of preparing a set of decisions for action to be taken in the future.[14] Since it is oriented to the future, planning partakes of all the difficulties analyzed in the theory of sequential decision-making under uncertainty. Educational planning is, as we have argued, particularly prone to uncertainty about the future, since even the present relationship between the supply of qualified students and the demand for educated people from industry and government is little understood. In the circumstances we are always better off if we can build into the system the kind of flexibility that allows it to adjust automatically to bottlenecks and surpluses. In short, educational planning should largely consist of action designed to move the real world closer to the right end of the continuum, characterized by a multiplicity of alternatives in producing and utilizing educated man-power. For whatever is the state of the world, such action ensures a smoother adjustment of educational output to educational inputs and improves the chances of market clearance.

V Higher Education in Great Britain and the United States

To clarify the argument, let us contrast the man-power situation in Great Britain and the United States. First of all, specialization in schools starts much earlier in Britain than in America: British students begin to concentrate on their major fields (arts or science) by the age of 15, and sometimes as early as 14; by the age of 15 or 16 the science students have largely ceased to study arts subjects, and vice versa, and by the sixth form extreme specialization even between pure and applied science is almost universal.[15] Recently, there have been some changes in the opposite direction, but these do not affect the striking contrast between the British and American situation. Two years ago, Lord Bowden told the House of Lords: "It is almost true to say that the destiny of our universities, their whole expansion program, and, with this, the whole destiny of this country, is at the moment

[14] For an illuminating discussion of concepts of planning as applied to educational planning, see C. A. Anderson and M. J. Bowman, "Theoretical Considerations of Educational Planning," *Educational Planning*, ed. D. Adams (Syracuse, N.Y.: Syracuse University Press, 1964), pp. 4–8.

[15] The evidence is reviewed by J. A. Lauwerys, "United Kingdom," *Access to Higher Education*. II. *National Studies* (Paris: U.N.E.S.C.O., 1965), pp. 362–70.

in the hands of 14-year-old schoolboys,"[16] a remark which might now be amended to read "15-year-old schoolboys." Early specialization is said to be caused by university entrance requirements and excessive competition in sixth forms for a limited number of places in universities. But whatever the reason, the undisputed fact that British students specialize at an earlier age than almost any other developed country means that the supply of, say, scientists and engineers in 1972 is already determined in Britain, whereas in the United States it will be possible to make a substantial impact on the 1972 supply by policies adopted in 1968 or 1969. Thus, the lead-time required to produce skilled man-power in Great Britain is at least twice as long as in the United States, in consequence of which there is much stronger probability in Britain of periodic shortages and surpluses of scientists and engineers.

Added to the first consideration, and directly related to it, is the chronic excess demand for higher education in Great Britain ever since the war, defined simply as an excess of secondary school leavers qualified for entry over the number of student places available. Higher education has been rationed in this country for twenty years, and even under the Robbins targets this situation will continue until well into the 1970s. In the United States, on the other hand, state universities are required by law to admit all applicants with a high-school diploma, and private American universities have generally expanded facilities to keep pace with the rising number of qualified applicants. Standards of admission vary more widely than in Great Britain and, in general, nearly all high-school graduates in America who want to go to college manage to find some institution of higher learning willing to accept them. Paradoxically enough, British students in higher education are generously subsidized by the State, more generously than in any other developed country and certainly more generously than in the United States. In consequence, the costs of higher education to students are much less in Britain than in the United States, and this serves further to raise the demand for places in this country.[17]

Furthermore, not only is the overall supply of places in higher education rationed in Britain but so is the allocation of places between faculties. As we noted earlier, the policy on the balance of faculties in universities appears to have been based on the man-power forecasts of the Barlow Committee in 1946 and those of the Committee on Scientific Man-power of 1956 and 1961.[18]

[16] Debate on Technological Development in House of Lords, December 2, 1964: *Hansard* (House of Lords), Vol. 261, para. 1163.

[17] Blaug, "The Rate of Return on Investment in Education in Great Britain," *op. cit.*, p. 245.

[18] Moser, Layard, *op. cit.*, pp. 510–11, and P. R. G. Layard, "Manpower Needs and the Planning of Higher Education," *Manpower Policy and Employment Trends*, eds. B. C. Roberts and J. H. Smith (London: L.S.E., 1966), pp. 86–7; see also W. G. Bowen, "University Finance in Britain and the United States: Implications of Financing Arrangements for Educational Issues," *Public Finance*, 1963, reprinted in W. G. Bowen, *Economic Aspects of Education. Three Essays* (Princeton, N.J.: Princeton University Press, 1964), pp. 58–65.

In consequence, there have been years when applicants for arts places have been denied entry while at the same time there were vacant places in science and technology. Although the University Grants Committee took the view in 1958 that "student choices have shown themselves to be remarkably sensitive to prospective demand,"[19] this was not allowed to affect the policy on faculty balances. But, clearly, either students are poorly informed of career prospects, in which case they can be better informed, or they are well informed, in which case the argument must be that the labor market fails to produce signals of impending man-power shortages. If the latter, one would think that the State would adopt a differential student-grant policy so as to encourage students to take up those professions in which there is known to be a prospective shortage. This view implies considerable confidence in man-power forecasts; and no doubt a lack of conviction about forecasting accounts for the present inconsistent policy.

In the United States, on the other hand, students are allowed freely to choose their own subject once they have gained admission to university. They are kept informed of trends in the labor market by means of vocational counselling, and full use is made of special scholarship programs and student loans restricted to particular subjects or fields of study that require encouragement.

It seems obvious that the supply of highly qualified man-power is more rigidly predetermined in Britain than in the United States, that students' educational choices are less firmly linked to job opportunities, and that, in general, the demands of the labor market have less influence on the structure of higher education in Britain than in the United States. If we add to this the contrast between the British tripartite secondary education, with a university stream separated from the rest by the age of 12, and the comprehensive high schools of America that allow almost 50% of the age group 16–18 to pass on to college, as well as the rigid paths of British technical education in which professional qualifications are only obtainable by passing the examination of a particular professional institution, albeit by part-time as well as full-time means, and the extraordinary variety of trade and vocational high schools, technical institutes, two-year junior colleges, four-year technical colleges and the like in the United States, we are forced to conclude that there is much less scope for short-run adjustments in the demand and supply of man-power in this country, and therefore the stronger probability of imbalances in the labor market.[20] It may be that all this is

---

[19] U.G.C., *University Development, 1952–1957* (London: H.M.S.O., 1958), p. 75.

[20] It is not easy to provide a definitive reference here because few students of comparative education have examined national systems from this point of view. For some material, however, see The Conference of Engineering Societies of Western Europe and the U.S.A. (E.U.S.E.C.), *Report on Education and Training of Professional Engineers. A Comparative Study of Engineering Education and Training in the E.U.S.E.C. and O.E.E.C. countries* (Brussels: E.U.S.E.C., 1962), I, pp. 70–6; II, pp. 11–12, 36, 39, 67–9, 79–81.

offset by differences in on-the-job training provisions in the two countries, but even here casual impression runs against Britain.[21]

These differences between the two educational systems go a long way to explain the American interest in rate-of-return analysis and their sceptical attitude to man-power forecasting, and exactly the reverse attitude in this country. Faced with a rigid and highly structured educational system, and aware that as much as two-thirds of university graduates and probably a similar fraction of those with G.C.E. "O" and "A" levels are employed by the public sector—the State in respect of education combining monopoly with monopsony—educational planners in Britain have seen no alternative to man-power forecasting with all its admitted shortcomings. But the price of rigidity is that errors are more disastrous. This is the great paradox of the man-power-forecasting approach: because of alleged rigidities in the educational system and imperfections in the labor market, one must forecast the demand for educated people so as to avoid structural disequilibria; but if there is indeed little synchronization between the educational system and the labor market errors in forecasting lead to an irremediable waste of resources, not to mention the disappointment of students who cannot find employment on satisfactory terms. In short, in a Leontief-type economy there is a premium on the accuracy of forecasts, and an inaccurate forecast can aggravate instead of improve the situation. In contrast, if the economic system is sufficiently flexible to adjust to erroneous forecasts, even crude estimates of man-power requirements can serve as useful guides, but at the same time there is less reason to forecast at all, and hence the costs of making forecasts must be scrutinized more closely.

VI Educational Reforms
and an Active Man-power Policy

The way to cut through this Gordian knot is to create a safety-valve against forecasting errors by strengthening the automatic adjustment mechanism of the market-place. In the British context this means attacking the problem of early specialization and, since this is in turn related to the

---

[21] To sum up our argument in terms of the ordinal continuum mentioned above:

Leontief-type universe	U.K.	U.S.A.	Neo-classical universe
‖————— ↑ ————— ↑ ————‖

I am, of course, ignoring all the sociological differences that underlie the two systems; I am describing, not explaining. For a suggestive sociological explanation, see R. H. Turner, "Modes of Social Ascent Through Education: Sponsored and Contest Mobility," *American Sociological Review*, 1960, reprinted in *Education, Economy, and Society*, eds. A. H. Halsey, J. Floud and C. A. Anderson (Glencoe, Ill.: The Free Press, 1962), pp. 121–40.

keen competition for a limited number of university places, further expansion of University facilities to accommodate the unsatisfied demand. The root of the problem is the whole G.C.E. system. Although the nine G.C.E. examining boards are, strictly speaking, autonomous bodies, almost half of their members are drawn from the Universities and, hence, the remedy lies in closer cooperation between the universities and the Secondary School Examination Council. So long as places in universities are rationed, however, no long-term solution is possible. Hitherto, early specialization has been attacked on purely educational grounds. What has not always been realized is that early specialization is also one of the major causes of man-power difficulties in Britain. Obviously, it may be expensive to redesign the educational system so as to minimize the time taken to learn professional skills, and this extra cost must enter into the decision to postpone the age of specialization. What I contend is that the benefits of late specialization for the elimination of man-power bottlenecks have not previously been given their proper due. Likewise, the debate on comprehensive schools, the issue of grants to secondary school students, the question of loans to students in higher education and even the Friedman-Peacock-Wiseman idea of "educational vouchers" all look somewhat different seen through man-power spectacles.

Further, every effort should be made to allow students freely to choose their faculties, concomitant with heavy investment in vocational counselling in schools. Indeed, the provision of career information both in schools and in labor exchanges ought to be a principal activity of the educational authorities. Unfortunately, in most countries this function is divided between the Ministry of Education and the Ministry of Labor, and hence there is little communication between schools and employers. For example, in Britain the Youth Employment Service is still in part under the umbrella of the Ministry of Labor, and this division of control may help to explain why facilities for vocational guidance are poorly co-ordinated and why the level of provision is well behind the United States and most other European countries.[22]

More broadly, any policy action that increases the flexibility with which resources are combined within the educational system must improve the capacity of schools to adjust to shortages and surpluses of various types of man-power. That is, any action that encourages educational innovation in schools, such as constructing school buildings easily adaptable to various class sizes, training teachers to use new educational media, such as closed-circuit television and programmed instruction, must ease the man-power situation, whatever it is. Of course, the case for new educational media is not one to be decided solely or even largely on man-power grounds, but the

---

[22] See R. A. Lester, *Manpower Planning in a Free Society* (Princeton, N.J.: Princeton University Press, 1966), pp. 59–75, for comparative evidence.

fact remains that the more teachers are replaced by mechanical aids, the easier it is to expand enrollment or to adjust faculty balances.

Turning to the labor market, we note that shortages of particular skills, that is, the existence of unfilled vacancies at current salary levels, are overcome in the short run either by raising salaries, by lowering minimal hiring standards or by providing more on-the-job and off-the-job training. There is much less scope here for public policy than in the formal educational system. Nevertheless, in the absence of specific knowledge of the extent of a shortage, it is always possible for the State to ease the situation by altering pay scales in the public sector, by furnishing better information about the future output of the educational system to personnel officers in business enterprises in the hope of encouraging an adjustment of hiring standards and by offering financial incentives to industry to expand its training programs. Recent attempts to experiment with public provision for training and retraining of adult workers, as in the Industrial Training Act in this country and the Man-power Training and Development Act in the United States, are, of course, precisely along these lines. The more we avoid placing all responsibility for man-power development on the schools alone, the less we need to pay the consequences of unemployable school leavers or economic growth held back by shortages of various skills.

What I am proposing is that educational planning should consist in part of reforms of the educational system, and, for the rest, what has been described in America as "an active man-power policy."[23] Educational planning, and particularly educational planning in developing countries, should concern itself more widely with the reciprocal impact of the educational system and the labor market. It is a fallacy to think that there can be no man-power planning without man-power forecasting, and that, in the absence of forecasting, educational planning must consist of a passive attitude toward the economic returns from education.[24] Rather than accepting existing educational patterns and prevailing hiring policies as data in the planning process, much of the effort of educational planning should be directed at altering them so as to give full scope to the process by which industry adapts its demand to the supply of educated man-power, and the supply of students adjusts itself to the changing demands from industry.

[23] See, for example, E. W. Bakke, "An Active and Positive Manpower Policy," *Active Manpower Policy. International Management Seminar. Final Report* (Paris: O.E.C.D., 1965), pp. 127–45.

[24] In a valuable new book, *Education and Social Change in Ghana* (London: Routledge & Kegan Paul, 1965), P. J. Foster shows that educational planners in Ghana have for decades insisted on providing secondary technical schools despite the fact that it proved difficult to fill all the available places and that their graduates failed to obtain employment. Students were, in practice, better informed of the poor returns from technical education than the planners themselves.

VII Man-power Forecasting with a Difference

None of the three conflicting approaches to educational planning has any logical priority over the others. Faced with an uncertain future, educational planning must diversify its portfolio of methods and techniques. Clearly, there are upper limits to the elasticity of substitution for certain critical skills, that is, skills involving long formal preparation and training. And no matter how late we postpone specialization, the effective lead-time of scientific man-power is sufficiently long to create the possibility of unstable cobweb effects. It takes years to put up a complex of school buildings and, obviously, foresight is indispensable to the decision to begin building. In addition, students base their career decisions on today's market forces, and only a forecast can reveal the situation that they will confront when they eventually enter the labor market. There can be no question, therefore, about the necessity of trying to take a forward look at man-power requirements and, in principle, one should look forward as far as possible. However, the period over which we can usefully forecast the demand for man-power in the present state of knowledge is much more limited than is usually admitted. All the evidence shows that we do not yet know how to forecast beyond three or four years with anything remotely resembling the 10% margins of errors that are regarded as just tolerable in general economic forecasting. Some post-mortems on five-year and ten-year man-power forecasts in the Soviet Union, in Sweden and in Iran suggest that such forecasts invariably go wide of the mark.[25] Unfortunately, none of these forecasts were of the type that furnished a range of estimates on various assumptions about the magnitude of the critical variables and coefficients, and single-value conditional forecasts can rarely be falsified by a simple comparison of forecast with outcome.[26] The point is that unless the G.D.P. target itself is

---

[25] On the Soviet Union, N. DeWitt, *Educational and Professional Employment in the U.S.S.R.* (Washington, D.C.: National Science Foundation, 1961), and "Educational and Man-power Planning in the Soviet Union," *The World Yearbook of Education 1967. Educational Planning*, eds. G. Z. F. Bereday, M. Blaug and V. A. Lauwerys (London: Evans Bros., 1967). On Sweden, *Educational Policy and Planning in Sweden* (Paris: O.E.C.D., mimeographed, 1964), pp. 24–5; Appendix XI, pp. 1–25. On Iran, G. B. Baldwin, "Iran's Experience With Manpower Planning: Concept, Techniques, and Lessons," *Manpower and Education. Country Studies in Economic Development* (New York: McGraw-Hill, 1965), pp. 140–73. See also R. G. Hollister, *A Technical Evaluation of the First Stage of the Mediterranean Regional Project* (Paris: O.E.C.D., 1966, that demonstrates that the 1980 man-power forecasts of the M.R.P. are highly sensitive to small changes in the labor-output and in the occupation–education coefficients. No one has yet taken a retrospective look at the many man-power forecasts that have been made in France in the last decade, but see J. Fourastié, "Employment Forecasting in France," *Employment Forecasting* (Paris: O.E.C.D., 1963), particularly pp. 71–2; and J. and A.-M. Hackett, *Economic Planning in France* (London: George Allen & Unwin, 1964), pp. 145–9, 186–8, 303–4.

[26] There are other grounds for objecting to single-value forecasts. In the words of the *Technical Evaluation of the M.R.P.*: "educational strategy should be formulated with the

achieved exactly, we cannot be sure where the fault lies. That is, there are four possibilities:

The Man-power-forecasting Hypothesis

Man-power target \ G.D.P. target	Hit	Miss
Hit	Confirmed	A bottleneck other than man-power?
Miss	Falsified	?

In the vast number of cases where single-valued man-power forecasts were made, the realized economic growth rate fell, for one reason or another, below the target growth rate, with the result that even with hindsight it proves impossible to say whether the forecast was accurate or not. Worse than this, in some instances, such as that of teacher supply, forecasts merely provided a framework for particular policy recommendations, and so were deliberately designed to be self-falsifying. Hence, repeated failures to forecast reliably in cases where G.D.P. growth targets were achieved have taught us little, and despite twenty years of experience we are not much wiser today about the nature of the changing demand for educated man-power. Indeed, so notorious is the unreliability of such forecasts that there is not a single country on record that has made a serious effort to implement comprehensive targets for man-power requirements.

We have spoken so far exclusively of man-power *forecasts* in the sense defined earlier. Some additional insight is gained from experience with man-power *projections* in countries such as the United Kingdom and the United States that have no commitment, or have had no commitment until recently, to a national economic plan. Suffice it to say that the British record of man-power projections is abysmal, possibly because the task was assigned

---

uncertainties engendered by technological change clearly in mind. In the light of such uncertainties, objectives of labor force flexibility may receive more stress in the formulation of the structure and content of education. Manpower requirement estimates which conceal these uncertainties, by presenting single value estimates of requirements rather than ranges of alternatives, may do a great disservice to formulators of educational policy" (*op. cit.*, p. 62).

to physical scientists rather than to economists.[27] The American record is more difficult to judge, as the methodology of American man-power projectors is highly eclectic,[28] and errors in prediction have been as common on the side of enrollments as on the side of employment.[29] Nevertheless, little comfort is derived from the various American efforts at predicting the demand for scientists, engineers and technicians, not to mention teachers, doctors and dentists.

The reasons for this dismal picture are several. First of all, as Kendrick has shown for the United States, the advance of both total-factor productivity and labor productivity in various sectors is quite irregular over time, and seems to exhibit no simple regular pattern that could be used by a man-power forecaster or projector.[30] Furthermore, it is doubtful, simply on theoretical grounds, whether all countries move along the same man-power growth path, that is, arrive at similar occupational distributions of the labor force for identical levels of output per head. At any rate, there is no evidence that man-power forecasting can be based on mere imitation of a richer country.[31] Similarly, we know too little about the rate of diffusion of best-practice techniques within and between industries to make practical use of the method of "catching up" with the most advanced firm or sector of the economy. And, finally, the notion of asking business firms to forecast their labor requirements at income growth rates that they may never have experienced assumes that they can predict their market shares independently of the activities of rival firms.

Even if we could somehow predict productivity changes, we still have to cross the hurdle of occupational classifications and of converting these into educational equivalents. And here the real problem is not simply the failure to observe any unique relationship between educational background

[27] See A. T. Peacock, "Economic Growth and the Demand for Qualified Manpower," *District Bank Review*, June 1963, pp. 3–19; Moser, Layard, *op. cit.*; and the revealing evidence of Sir Solly Zuckerman to the Robbins Committee, *Higher Education. Evidence*, Pt. I, Vol. B, Cmnd. 2154–VII (London: H.M.S.O., 1963), pp. 423–52.

[28] A leading American projection simply extrapolated the ratio of employment of scientists and engineers in a given industry to total employment in that industry on the basis of evidence of a linear trend between 1954 and 1959 (*The Long-range Demand for Scientific and Engineering Personnel*. Washington, D.C.: National Science Foundation, 1961). But in two cases, the chemical industry and the electrical equipment industry, further detailed investigation threw doubt on the assumption of a stable employment fraction for scientific man-power (*ibid.*, pp. 16–17, 21–4). See also *Scientists, Engineers, and Technicians in the 1960's: Requirements and Supply* (Washington, D.C.: National Science Foundation, 1963).

[29] For a thorough review, see J. K. Folger, "Scientific Manpower Planning in the United States," *The World Yearbook of Education 1967, op. cit.*

[30] J. W. Kendrick, *Productivity Trends in the United States* (Princeton: Princeton University Press, 1961), Ch. 6, pp. 133–89.

[31] The case for the existence of man-power-growth paths is thoroughly canvassed with sceptical conclusions by R. G. Hollister, "The Economics of Manpower Forecasting," *International Labour Review*, 1964, reprinted in *The Economics of Manpower Planning*, ed. M. R. Sinha (Bombay: Asian Studies Press, 1965), pp. 73–103.

and occupational affiliation in today's labor force, except for those professions such as medicine and teaching where custom imposes a minimum entrance qualification,[32] but the difficulty of separating the forces of supply from the forces of demand. What we have here is the old "identification problem." After all, the schooling currently associated with each occupation is as much the outcome of the supply of educated people in the past as of the history of the demand for qualified man-power. In any economy with a high level of aggregate demand qualified man-power, however irrationally produced, will somehow be absorbed into employment: what we observe today may simply represent the misallocations of the past.[33] If we want to forecast the demand for educated people we cannot simply read off the existing fit of occupation and education. The task we face is to find an independent method of estimating the optimum amount and type of education for each job-cluster. But satisfactory performance in an occupation is a complicated function of native ability, psycho-motor skills, work experience, on-the-job training and formal educational preparation, and we are far from understanding just how much the latter contributes to this mix. Furthermore, it is doubtful whether one can define the optimum education for an occupation without introducing earnings, a variable that so far has been ignored by man-power forecasters.[34]

[32] The variance about the mean in the number of years of schooling observed in different occupations appears to be considerable: see Parnes, op. cit., pp. 112–13; U.S. Bureau of the Census, U.S. Census of Population: 1960. Subject Reports. Occupation by Earnings and Education. Final Report PC(2)–7B (Washington, D.C.: G.P.O., 1963), pp. 244 ff; and C. A. Anderson, "Patterns and Variability in Distribution and Diffusion of Schooling," Education and Economic Development, op. cit., pp. 321–4.

[33] The whole point of man-power forecasting is precisely the notion that the present situation represents a malutilization of educated people; if it does not, ordinary market forces may be trusted to give results as satisfactory in the future as in the past. By implication, man-power forecasters must assume that the market has everywhere failed to allocate man-power resources optimally. For that reason, attempts to estimate the educational structure of the labor force as a given function of national income or output per head with the aid of cross-section data for different countries falls short of solving the problem of forecasting man-power requirements (Netherlands Economic Institute, "Financial Aspects of Educational Expansion in Developing Regions," Financing of Education for Economic Growth (Paris: O.E.C.D., 1966); E. R. Rado and A. R. Jolly, "The Demand for Manpower: An East African Case Study," The Journal of Development Studies, April 1965, pp. 226–51; and P. R. G. Layard and J. C. Saigal, "Educational and Occupational Characteristics of Manpower: An International Comparison," British Journal of Industrial Relations, July 1966). Educational planning based on these regression equations runs the danger of reproducing the past misallocations of man-power in the more advanced countries.

[34] There appear to be three possible relationships between education and occupation: (1) there is a minimum educational qualification for each occupation and additional qualifications have no economic value; (2) the productivity of a worker in an occupation increases with his educational qualifications, very gradually at first, then at a sharply increasing rate beyond a certain threshold level, after which it levels off again; (3) the productivity of a worker in a specific occupation increases monotonically with his educational qualifications, first at an increasing rate and then at a decreasing rate, and it never levels off. These three cases relating to a specific occupation are illustrated in the following diagram, with educational qualification measured as a scalar on the horizontal axis and productivity or per-

All this has been said before, even by those who advocate long-term man-power forecasting.[35] The point is: do we brush these criticisms aside and forecast as best we can, or do we revise our basic ideas about man-power forecasting? The leading man-power forecasters insist that long-term forecasts, even of the crudest kind, distinguishing merely between occupations requiring general academic education and those requiring scientific and technical preparation, are useful in guiding the allocation of educational expenditures among levels and branches of the educational system. That would be true if one could rely on them. Unfortunately, even the forecasters themselves warn against educational expansion closely tied to forecasts of man-power requirements.[36] The question is not whether to

---

formance-rating in the occupation measured on the vertical axis. The three possibilities mentioned below correspond to the three numbered curves. If the real world is correctly depicted by (1) or (2) there is no serious problem of optimization. But if case (3) is representative of the real world the optimum amount of education is entirely a matter of the

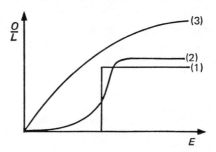

earnings associated with additional education, and cannot be defined independently of them: a man with 16 years of schooling may be twice as productive as one with 12 years, but if he costs three times as much, the optimum amount of education is nevertheless 12 years (see Blaug, Peston and Ziderman, *op. cit.*, pp. 3–4).

[35] See Parnes, *op. cit.*, pp. 19, 20, 33, 36, 38, 41, 44. But after mentioning almost every objection to long-term man-power forecasting, he nevertheless insists that the essence of his own approach is "the rather rigorous link that has been assumed between productivity levels and occupational structure on the one hand, and between occupation and educational qualification on the other" (*ibid.*, p. 51). See, in a similar vein, F. H. Harbison and C. A. Myers, *Education, Manpower, and Economic Growth* (New York: McGraw-Hill, 1965), ch. 9, pp. 189–208.

[36] Parnes' principal line of defense is simplicity itself: "The sceptics call attention to the large margins of error that are likely at virtually every stage of the forecasting process: the estimate of G.N.P. fifteen years in advance; the distribution thereof among the various sectors and branches of the economy; the estimation of future manpower structure within each of the branches; and the equation of occupations with required educational qualification." But "so long as one grants that manpower considerations are one of the elements that *ought* to influence educational decisions, then all such decisions, if they purport to be rational, involve manpower forecast, whether or not they are explicitly made," *Planning Education for Social and Economic Development*, ed. H. S. Parnes (Paris: O.E.C.D., 1963), pp. 74–5. This misses the point. If long-term forecasts of the purely technological kind are really as subject to error as he himself admits (*op. cit.*, pp. 13, 30), it is difficult to see how they can be justified; the fact that all educational decisions have man-power implications makes errors more serious, not less.

forecast or not to forecast, but rather whether to forecast inaccurately as much as ten or fifteen years ahead or to forecast three or four years ahead with a much better chance of being accurate. The case for long-term forecasting is usually made on the basis of the lengthy production-period of scientific man-power. But, as we saw earlier, the fact that it takes fifteen years to educate an engineer does not imply that we must predict the demand for engineers in 1981, not unless there is one, and only one, occupation that an engineer can fill or, at any rate, one and only one set of tasks that an engineer can perform. We need to know much more about these questions, but all the evidence so far suggests that there are many substitutes for professional man-power. Human capital may take a longer time to produce than most physical capital, but it is also less specific in use than most machines.

The need to guide students' career choices is sometimes given as the reason that man-power forecasts must look at least six or seven years ahead. To be sure, students, at least British students, must think about career opportunities six or seven years hence in choosing their major fields of study. Suppose they were furnished with a completely accurate forecast of the demand for a particular profession by 1972. Would this improve their educational choices? Not necessarily, as they would still have to calculate how many other students would react to the forecast in the same way. This is true, of course, of every student in turn. Students are in the same position as oligopolists who cannot decide what price to charge without knowledge of the prices that rivals will be charging. It is not enough, therefore, to be told what will be the demand for engineers in 1972. One also needs to know the probable supply of engineering students by 1972. Provided the student is given the latter as well as the former, he is indeed better off: if a shortage is forecast he need not worry much about his aptitude for engineering, as he is likely to find employment in any case; if, on the other hand, the forecast suggests that there will be a buyers' market he must pay stricter attention to his own occupational aptitudes. This argument shows that even completely accurate medium-term man-power forecasts are not by themselves sufficient for purposes of vocational counselling. But, in practice, even these are rarely accurate.[37] Furthermore, they say nothing about prospective

[37] An interesting test-case is the demand for teachers. Here there is no problem about forecasting labor productivity, as staff/student ratios are invariably an administrative decision, nor any difficulty about specifying the minimum educational qualification for the job, as there is usually a legal minimum requirement for entry into the profession. Nevertheless, the record of teacher forecasts is as poor as all other man-power forecasts: see W. Lee Hansen, "Human Capital Requirements for Educational Expansion: Teacher Shortages and Teacher Supply," *Education and Economic Development, op. cit.*; M. J. Bowman, "Educational Shortage and Excess," *Canadian Journal of Economics and Political Science*, November 1963, pp. 446–61; and A. M. Cartter, "A New Look at the Supply of College Teachers," *The Educational Record*, Summer 1965, pp. 267–77. Another depressing example is the case of doctors: see W. Lee Hansen, " 'Shortages' and Investment in Health Manpower," *op. cit.*; and J. Seale, "Medical Emigration: A Study in the Inadequacy of Official Statistics," *Lessons from Central Forecasting* (London: Institute of Economic Affairs, 1965), pp. 25–41.

professional earnings, which is precisely what interests students. There is a world of difference between stipulating the minimum educational requirements for realizing a G.D.P. target, as in the typical man-power forecast, and predicting the employment opportunities that will most probably materialize in various fields of specialization so as to help students to plan their careers. The confusion between the two may perhaps account for the poor quality of vocational guidance in so many countries.

Despite everything we have said, advocates of man-power forecasting will nevertheless insist that some knowledge of the future ten or fifteen years hence, however hazy, is better than nothing. Put like this, one can only agree. However, the implication of this view is that we ought to build the admitted haziness of long-term forecasts directly into the forecast itself. For instance, one plausible hypothesis is that the variance around the estimated mean of the forecast increases with the square of the length of time over which we are forecasting, producing a margin of error that steadily widens as we look farther into the future. Thus, the margin of error in predicting the demand for man-power might be $\pm 2\%$ of the 1966 figures by 1967, $\pm (0.02)^2$ of 1966 figures by 1968 and so forth, amounting to an error of $\pm 22\%$ in 10 years and $\pm 35\%$ in 15 years; the same argument, possibly with a different margin of error, applies to the supply of man-power. The growth paths for a particular type of educated man-power might then look as follows:

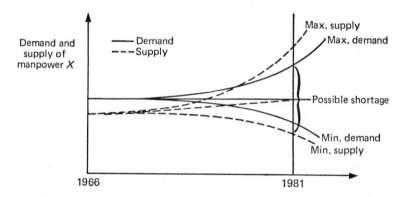

In this case we would have to be satisfied by the undramatic conclusion that there will be a "shortage" of X by 1981 if we have underestimated the demand for X and overestimated its supply, and not otherwise. The diagram is, of course, purely illustrative. I do not know whether the future supply is more uncertain than the future demand or whether the errors are symmetrical around the forecast, as in the above diagram, nor whether the compounding error-term should be 1, 2 or 3%. However, until some such conception of discounting the uncertain future enters explicitly into manpower forecasting, the case for long-term man-power forecasting, particularly of the single-valued type, lacks intellectual foundation. Surely, there is some point at which the penumbra of doubt associated with a forecast becomes so large that the forecast itself misleads rather than informs?

VIII In Conclusion

There is little point in continuing to waste resources on long-term pinpoint forecasts whose results are suspect even by the forecasters themselves. These resources could be much more profitably invested in improving our knowledge of the current stock of qualified man-power and disseminating this knowledge to students and employers. It is no accident that after two decades of considerable activity in man-power forecasting only one country, namely the United States, has anything like adequate data on the distribution of the labor force by sectors, occupations, earnings and years of schooling.[38] Such data are not even expensive to collect, since they can be gathered by sample surveys. The truth is that the mystique of forecasting has discouraged investigations of the current stock of man-power on the grounds that bygones are forever bygones.[39] But the stock of man-power is so large relative to the annual flow that most of the current stock will be with us for decades to come.

Faced with the difficulties of man-power forecasting, difficulties that seem to increase at a progressive rate the longer the time-period over which we are forecasting, the remedy is to begin modestly with short-term forecasts, extrapolated with a compounding margin of error as outlined above. As we accumulate more experience, we can begin to adjust the margin of error, gradually producing more and more reliable medium-term, and eventually long-term, forecasts. As a check on such forecasts of demand, we ought to make continuous rolling projections of the future supply of educated people. Indeed, the forecasts of demand ought to be of the type that provides a range of alternative values for different estimates of the projected supply. If the demand for educational inputs depends in any way on its price, and this will necessarily be so if there is any substitutability between educational

[38] The United States is also the only country that now has an almost complete register of professionally qualified man-power in the labor force.

[39] The almost universal neglect of earnings as a vital piece of information about trends in the use and production of man-power illustrates the effect of this mystique on data collection. For example, the *Review of the Scope and Problems of Scientific and Technological Manpower Policy*, presented last year to the British Parliament by the Committee on Manpower Resources for Science and Technology (Cmnd. 2800), listed a number of investigations now under way that are designed to supplement knowledge of the demand for and supply of scientific man-power in Great Britain, but said not a word about relative earnings. Figures on earnings by level or type of education are not collected by any official agency in Great Britain.

inputs, changes in supply are just as capable of altering that price as changes in demand, and therefore the quantity demanded of educational inputs is not independent of its supply. It follows that man-power forecasts must always be combined with social-demand projections. Similarly, social-demand projections by themselves are not a safe basis for educational planning. The tendency to upgrade skill-requirements when the labor market becomes favorable is a well-attested phenomenon.[40] It seems to have definite limits, however, as witness the incidence of "intellectual unemployment" in many countries. As we combine forecasts of demand with projections of supply, we start thinking quite naturally of earnings associated with education as indicators of impending shortages and surpluses. And since the costs of training various types of specialized man-power differ considerably, we will be led to consider variations in earnings in relation to variations in the costs of education. This is rate-of-return analysis, whether we call it that or not. By making such calculations on a year-to-year basis, we keep a continual check on labor markets for highly qualified man-power and gradually develop insights into the ways in which education interacts with economic growth.

Recent work on mathematical and computable models of the educational system may point the way to a joining of all the approaches.[41] Models of this kind are perfectly neutral instruments of planning and indispensable whatever approach is taken. They become somewhat more tendentious if specific assumptions are made about what education ought to be optimizing. In a recent linear programming model of education in Northern Nigeria, for example, man-power demands were treated as exogenously determined constraints and lifetime net earnings differentials associated with education as the objective function to be maximized.[42] The solutions took the form of an

[40] J. K. Folger and C. B. Nam, "Trends in Education in Relation to Occupational Structure," *Sociology of Education*, Fall 1964, pp. 19–34, demonstrate a moderate but declining association between education and occupation in the United States between 1940 and 1960. Moreover, they show that most of the change that occurred in those twenty years was attributable to a rise in educational attainments within occupations, that is, to upgrading, rather than a shift from jobs requiring little to those requiring more education.

[41] The groundwork was laid by Correa, Tinbergen and Bos with a balanced-growth golden-age model, using fixed linear coefficients to relate the stock of labor with second- and third-level education to national income and the output of the third level of the educational system to the teacher requirements of the second and third level: see J. Tinbergen and H. C. Bos, "A Planning Model for the Educational Requirements of Economic Development," *Econometric Models of Education* (Paris: O.E.C.D., 1965), pp. 9–31. For a somewhat different type of model, see C. A. Moser and P. Redfern, "A Computable Model of the Educational System of England and Wales," *Proceedings of the International Statistical Institute. Bi-Annual Conference* (London: I.S.I., 1966); and P. Armytage and C. Smith, "The Development of Computable Models of the British Educational System and Their Possible Uses," *Meeting of the Ad Hoc Groups on Mathematical Models of the Educational System* (Paris: O.E.C.D., 1967).

[42] S. S. Bowles, *The Efficient Allocation of Resources in Education: A Planning Model with Applications to Northern Nigeria* (Dissertation submitted to Harvard University, 1965).

optimum sequence of decisions about various parts of the educational system over an eight-year period, given different assumptions about staff/student ratios. The interesting conclusion that emerged was that the optimum pattern of resource allocation between primary, secondary and higher education was almost exactly the opposite of that advocated by previous man-power forecasts in Nigeria, not so surprising perhaps if one realizes that these forecasts ignored the problem of the transition path to the target dates.[43]

We have come to the end of our story. The message has been that social-demand projections, man-power forecasting and rate-of-return analysis are reconcilable and in fact complementary techniques of educational planning, but not as these approaches are presently conceived in the literature. Above all, they must be combined with specific educational reforms and an active man-power policy designed to minimize the burden of administrative planning decisions. Economists do have a contribution to make to educational planning, but not by pressing the claims of one particular panacea, not by pretending to foresee the future accurately ten or fifteen years ahead, not by presuming to know how to promote exactly so much economic growth by just so much education. There is no reason to be apologetic about the fact that in most cases all that we can safely recommend is movement in a particular direction for a limited period of time.

[43] For similar evidence, see J. R. Smyth, "Rates of Return on Investment in Education: A Tool for Short Term Educational Planning, Illustrated with Ugandan Data," and E. Rado, "Manpower Planning in East Africa," both in *World Year Book of Education 1967, op. cit.*

Index